Business Research Methods

**The Irwin Series in Information
and
Decision Sciences**

Consulting Editors

ROBERT B. FETTER
Yale University

CLAUDE MCMILLAN
University of Colorado

BUSINESS RESEARCH METHODS

C. William Emory

Washington University

St. Louis

1980

Revised Edition

RICHARD D. IRWIN, INC.   Homewood, Illinois 60430

To Jean

© RICHARD D. IRWIN, INC., 1976 and 1980

ISBN 0-256-02260-7
Library of Congress Catalog Card No. 79–88781

Printed in the United States of America

5 6 7 8 9 0 MP 7 6 5 4 3 2

Preface

ALL MANAGERS FACE a "make or buy" research situation from time to time. They often face this dilemma inadequately equipped either to (1) perform the data gathering and analysis job themselves, or to (2) judge whether they are getting good value when others do the research for them. For either situation, a manager needs an understanding of the processes of research design and implementation.

The study of research methodology among business schools is often restricted to the area of marketing research. Students may develop research competence in their other functional area courses, but usually the focus there is on the subject content of accounting, finance, management, or whatever. Some schools are recognizing that knowledge of research methods and skill in their use are competencies of high value to managers and future managers, regardless of their functional area of concentration.

This book is a response to the perceived need for a cross-discipline text on research methods in business schools as well as a reference manual for managers. Its content, organization and coverage has been guided by the following objectives:

1. Students and managers should be exposed to the set of conceptual tools and techniques that will enable them to:
   a. Understand the nature of scientific method as it applies in a business setting.

   b. Evaluate the worth of research proposals and studies from a design
       and execution point of view.
   c. Do a good amateur job of planning and executing a research project.
2. Professors should be provided with a book that will:
   a. Qualify as the basic text for a challenging course in business research
       methods.
   b. Cover the subject of research methods in sufficient breadth and
       depth to free them from methodological detail to concentrate on the
       more creative aspects of their teaching.

Every book is a compromise between conflicting objectives and this one is
no exception. One such compromise has been between length and coverage.
The length was set as an initial constraint to assure that reading assignments
would be short enough to leave students time for *doing* research. The length
restriction also disciplined the author in balancing detail against breadth of
coverage. The aim has been to "cover the territory" of the fundamentals, but
seldom to venture beyond the minimum needed to plan and execute relatively simple designs.

A second compromise was between what one might call traditional and
modern orientations. The latter is identified with the development of sophisticated multivariate analysis tools. The author has opted for the more traditional emphasis for three reasons. In the first place, good research is a generic
reasoning approach that is more or less divorced from specific tools and
techniques. Secondly, only a limited number of students will master the more
sophisticated analysis techniques, but a much larger number should have a
grounding in research thinking. Finally, sophisticated techniques and complex
research designs can be more effectively learned if the student has first mas-
tered the fundamentals. It is this author's opinion that the fundamentals alone
are a sufficient challenge for one course.

The book is organized into four sections. Section One presents the foundations of scientific thinking. It discusses the nature of business research and the
notions of concepts, hypotheses, theories, and the reasoning process. Section
Two includes four chapters on research design. Much of this section is relatively abstract, considering such topics as the research design process, the
concepts of measurement, the development of indices, and finally, the question of sampling design.

Section Three consists of five chapters concerned largely with data collection procedures. Included are discussions on effective library searching, the
development of questionnaires, scaling, observation research, and experimental design. Section Four is composed of three chapters, the first two being
on data analysis, while the last concerns the reporting of research. In addition,
Appendix A consists of an extensive reference on library research sources,
while Appendix B provides the necessary tables for the various statistical tests
cited in the book.

It is impossible here to acknowledge the many scholars, clients, and students who, in one way or another, have helped me in the development of this book. I owe an incalculable debt to the many pioneers of research methodology in the social sciences. Many of their specific contributions are noted throughout the text. I would like also to express a special thanks to the hundreds of students who, over the years, have struggled along with the author as this manuscript was developed and tested.

For the first edition, my colleagues at Washington University, Walter Nord and Francis Connelly, were especially helpful and supportive. I am also indebted to Robert Fetter of Yale, Claude McMillan of the University of Colorado, and Alexander Voloatta of Montclair State College, all of whom read the original manuscript and suggested improvements.

In this revised edition, my colleague, J. Paul Peter, assisted with parts of Chapter 13, helping me to correct some of its flaws. Phillip Beukema of Whittier College and Stewart E. Fleige of Pepperdine University also provided insightful critiques which have guided me in my efforts at revision.

Finally, I would like to express my deep appreciation to Ruth Scheetz who has typed all of the versions of both editions with great skill and good humor.

December 1979   C. WILLIAM EMORY

Contents

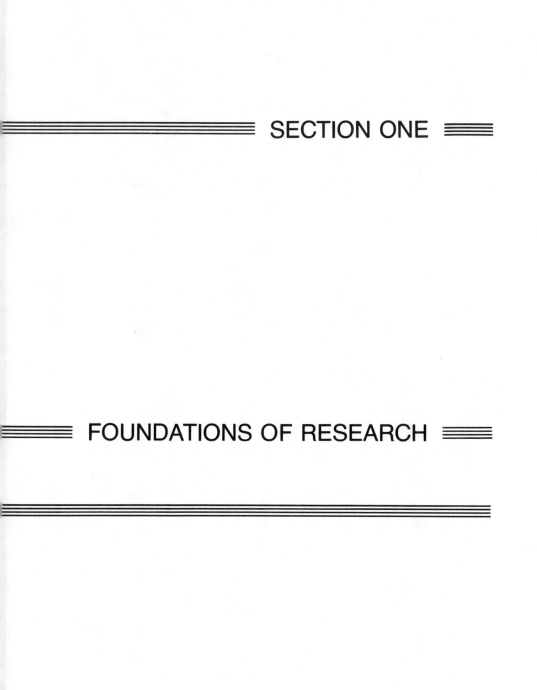

SECTION ONE

FOUNDATIONS OF RESEARCH

Chapter 1

Research and Management

THE INDUSTRIAL REVOLUTION began with the introduction of steam power in the late 18th century. It brought about the emancipation of labor by using mechanical power to magnify human muscle power. In recent years many have observed that a second industrial revolution is underway with the application of scientific knowledge to management. It offers the potential to emancipate the manager by magnifying his decision power.

The manifestations of this second revolution are seen on every hand. The explosive growth in the use of computers and the growing awareness of management information needs are obvious indicators of this trend. Less apparent indicators are the widening application of basic social science findings to management problems, and an expansion of the use of research methods to solve these problems.

Today's managers have a growing need to understand scientific findings and incorporate them into decision making. They also need to understand better how research is conducted and how good research can be identified. Finally, they should be prepared to carry out research in a more scientific manner. This book is addressed to these needs.

Chapter 1 introduces the subject of management-related research. In the first section the nature of research in business is explored. The second section concerns the research role of managers and their emergence as staff specialists. The final section deals with the general "state of the art" in business research, a subject that managers do not always appreciate.

3

WHAT IS RESEARCH?

Writers have supplied many different definitions of "research." Our first step should be to deal with the question, "What is research in a management setting?" A quick answer would be for the author to supply his favorite definition. Students are thus provided with a neat response for the question, should it be included in the course examination, but they are given little of the flavor of research or of the feel for the range of its applications. Rather, why not begin with a few examples of business inquiries? From these we may abstract some of the essence of research, how it is carried out, what it can do, and what it should not be expected to do.

Case 1. The management of your company is preparing for labor negotiations. The vice president of industrial relations asks you to provide some estimates of living costs in Chicago, where the company has its headquarters and major plant. Other plants are located in Atlanta, Los Angeles, and New York, and the vice president would like similar data for these cities. You consult different sources and eventually find that the U.S. Bureau of Labor Statistics publishes periodic statistics on the costs of living in various major metropolitan areas. You find the latest of these reports in the documents section of the local university library, write a memorandum showing the requested figures, and submit the report to the vice president. Is this research?

Case 2. You work in the treasurer's department of a corporation and have been asked to investigate six companies which are potential acquisition candidates. You are to gather pertinent data and make a comparative study of the merger attractiveness of the six. Because of the delicate nature of such an inquiry, you confine your search to published sources. You gather copies of each company's annual reports for a number of years, analyze what financial analysts have said about them, and read everything you can find about each company. After an extensive analysis you submit a report which emphasizes the potential problems and opportunities that an acquisition of each company would present. Is this research?

Case 3. A paint manufacturer is having trouble keeping profits up. The executive vice president feels that inventory management is one of the weak areas of the company's operations. In this industry the many colors, types of paint, and container sizes make it easy for a firm to accumulate large inventories and yet be unable to fill customer orders. You are asked to make recommendations.

You look into the present warehousing and shipping operations and find what appear to be excessive sales losses and delivery delays because of out-of-stock conditions. An informal survey among customers confirms your impression. You conclude that the present inventory reporting system does not provide the prompt, usable information needed for appropriate production decisions.

Your experience and reading of the literature on the latest inventory management techniques indicate to you what a new system should provide. You collect some specific data on one major product class and attempt to simulate how various reporting and replenishment practices might affect sales and costs. You take an inventory and monitor incoming orders to secure information about the ordering patterns for this classification, the average order size, and other pertinent data. You consider several designs for information reporting systems and the types of replenishment and production cycles which might be employed. After developing estimates of costs, you build and operate a simulation model of the inventory process. From this simulation you choose the most profitable model and extrapolate its results to all product classes. You recommend to the executive vice president that the company adopt the procedure chosen in the simulation and cite the expected dollars profits and savings that should accrue. Is this research?

Case 4. The Michigan Bell Telephone Company desires to increase the use of its long distance service by its household consumers. The company has used reduced rates during off hours to stimulate traffic, but still the growth has not absorbed equipment capacities. The company engages the Survey Research Center of the University of Michigan to study why people make long distance calls. The research project is to answer the following three questions.

1. What social and economic factors influence the number of social long distance calls a person will make?
2. What feelings and attitudes about the telephone influence social long distance calls?
3. What personality characteristics influence social long distance calling?

The project leaders devise a working theory to guide the research. This theory may be illustrated as in the accompanying diagram:

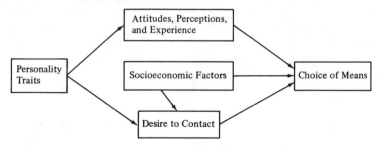

[The] diagram, obviously oversimplified, can be translated into language. Whether a person habitually phones depends on the presence of some factors which make him desire to contact others frequently. How often this desire is present depends on his personality characteristics and upon socioeconomic factors. . . . The desire to contact is undoubtedly influenced by external conditions, such as emergencies or the sudden need for more information. The emphasis in this study, however, is upon those more or less permanent personality characteristics which might influence the strength of the desire to be in contact with friends and relatives. . . . Once the desire to contact is present, whether he uses the telephone or not depends on other socioeconomic factors, as well as certain of his attitudes, his perceptions, and his previous experience with phoning.[1]

With this theoretical model in mind, the investigators conduct 400 interviews, divided equally among households that make a large number of long distance calls and households that make almost no calls. They write a report of their findings, which generally confirm the specifics of their theory. Is this research?

Similar case examples and other business research studies can be found by the hundreds in the various journals in business and in the files of major corporations. These cases will suffice for our illustration purposes here, but Table 1–1 lists a brief selection of journals in which results of business research studies are published.

Table 1–1: Selected List of Journals in Business and Allied Social Science Areas of Interest to Business Research Students

A. Accounting
Accounting Review
Journal of Accounting Research

B. Economics
American Economic Review
Applied Economics
Business Economics
Journal of Industrial Economics
Journal of Political Economy

C. Finance
Financial Management
Journal of Bank Research
Journal of Finance
Journal of Money, Credit, and Banking

D. Management
Administrative Science Quarterly
Journal of Academy of Management
Journal of Business
Management Science
Operations Research
Operations Research Quarterly

E. Marketing
Journal of Advertising Research
Journal of Consumer Research
Journal of Marketing
Journal of Marketing Research
Journal of Retailing

F. Operations Management
International Journal of Production Research
Transactions of the American Institute of Industrial Engineers (AIIE)

G. Organizational Behavior
Journal of Applied Behavioral Science
Journal of Applied Psychology
Organization Behavior and Human Performance

What Is Research in Business?

In these four cases the studies are inquiries made in direct response to decision problems that need solving. This practical problem-solving emphasis

---

[1] *Motives, Attitudes and Long Distance Calls* (Ann Arbor, Mich.: Survey Research Center, University of Michigan, April 1956), p. 10.

is a critical feature of *applied* research, and we should expect such studies to be closely related to action or policy needs. In this respect all four examples appear to qualify as applied research. *Pure* research is also problem solving, but in a different sense. It is aimed at solving perplexing questions (that is, problems) of a theoretical nature that have little direct impact on action or policy decisions. Thus, both applied and pure research are problem-directed, but applied research is much more decision-directed.

Some authorities equate research with pure, or "scientific," investigations and would reject all four examples. History shows, however, that "science" typically had its beginnings in pragmatic problems of real life. Interest in pure research comes much later, after knowledge in the field has been developed. It would appear that research is too narrowly defined if restricted to the "pure" variety.

One respected author offers the definition of scientific research as a "systematic, controlled, empirical, and critical investigation of hypothetical propositions about the presumed relations among natural phenomena."[2] Terms in this definition, such as "systematic, controlled, empirical, and critical . . ." describe characteristics that distinguish good from bad research of all types. These qualities are apparently much of what he means by "scientific." Whether research needs to be an "investigation of hypothetical propositions about presumed relationships" is debatable.

The classical concept of pure research does call for a hypothesis, but in applied research such a narrow definition omits at least two types of investigations that are highly valued. First is the exploration study in which the investigators know so little about the area of study that hypotheses have not yet emerged. An equally if not more important area of study is that which the purists may call "merely descriptive." It deals with the discovery of answers to the "who, what, when, where, how" questions rather than the "why" questions. The defense of descriptive research as a legitimate enterprise is well made by Dubin:

> There is no more devastating condemnation that the self-designated theorist makes of the researcher than to label his work *purely descriptive.* There is an implication that associates "purely descriptive" research with empty-headedness; the label also implies that as a bare minimum every healthy researcher has at least an hypothesis to test, and preferably a whole model. This is nonsense.
>
> In every discipline, but particularly in its early stages of development, purely descriptive research is indispensable. Descriptive research is the stuff out of which the mind of man, the theorist, develops the units that compose his theories. The very essence of description is to name the properties of things: you may do more, but you cannot do less and still have description. The more

---

[2] Fred W. Kerlinger, *Foundations of Behavioral Research,* 2d ed. (New York: Holt, Rinehart, and Winston, Inc., 1973), p. 11.

adequate the description, the greater is the likelihood that the units derived from the description will be useful in subsequent theory building.[3]

Rather than exploring this definition question further, we might conclude that there are differences on this question which largely reflect the subjective and personal concepts of "quality" held by the definers. As a bare minimum let's tentatively define research as an *inquiry carried out to secure information for solving problems.* Whether a given research is simple or complex, sophisticated or primitive, scientific or unscientific, useful or useless depends on its objectives, its design, and the skill and integrity with which it is conducted. Even bad research is still research. The objective of this book is to contribute to the development of better research (that is, more useful, more scientific, and more sophisticated research).

Research Objectives

The four cases presented earlier may be classified according to their immediate objectives. Case 1 calls for the reporting of some data—in this instance statistics. Reporting is a common task, yet the information may be difficult to find, and the assignment may call for knowledge of and skill with information sources. Purists might hold that mere reporting does not deserve to be called "research," but a good report based on carefully gathered data can have great decision value. True, the research design is not complex and does not demand high scientific expertise, but these are not requirements in our definition of research.[4]

Case 2 represents a higher order of investigation objective. As a *descriptive study* of the companies, it goes beyond reporting. The researcher seeks a wide range of information, which is used in a correlative analysis of relationships to discover similarities and differences among the various companies. In business research, descriptive studies are used more than any other type.

Case 3 also involves some descriptive elements during the early stages but goes beyond them. Certain facts and assumptions are assembled into a basis for *prediction* of the outcomes of various courses of action. This type of study is substantially more sophisticated than the first two. The simulation—employing models—represents one of the major current advances underway in business research.

Case 4 is similar to Case 2 in some ways but exemplifies a more sophisticated effort to approach the problem via the classical scientific method. The

[3] Reprinted with permission of Macmillan Publishing Co., Inc. from *Theory Building,* rev. ed. 1978, by Robert Dubin. Copyright © 1969 by The Free Press, a Division of The Macmillan Co.

[4] For a different view, see Paul H. Rigby, *Conceptual Foundations of Business Research* (New York: John Wiley and Sons, Inc., 1965), p. 75.

objective here is to explain the forces that account for a phenomenon (social long distance telephoning). The research directors present a "working theory" to account for long distance calling and then establish a research design to test the theory. While not labeled as such, the model of the inventory system developed in Case 3 is also a working theory as to how customer demands, inventory holding and handling requirements, and production processes can be most profitably combined.

All four of these types of research objectives are legitimate in terms of our definition of research, but they suggest different stages of scientific development. A rough measure of the development of science in any field is the degree to which prediction and explanation have replaced reporting and description as the major research objectives. By this standard, business research is in a relatively primitive state of scientific development.

Research in Functional Areas of Business

The four cases also illustrate that research in business covers a wide range of subject areas. Case 1 involves statistical information about the external environment of the business as well as the internal management of industrial relations. A substantial amount of research has been done in the fields of industrial and employee relations. Studies of morale, employee opinions and attitudes, absenteeism, internal communications, the management of people, and interpersonal transaction processes are all examples of research into human relations management.

Case 2 is oriented toward financial management and is concerned with matters external to the company. Recent years have seen a substantial increase in the amount of financial research being carried on, especially in operational and capital budgeting and investment analysis. Less widespread but also growing is research in accounting. Particularly noteworthy in accounting has been the growing interest in management information systems. While they are not the exclusive preserve of the accountant, interest in such systems has been concentrated more in the accounting sector than in others. The problems of valuation and measurement are also major subjects of accounting research.

Case 3 concerns production and distribution problems. Frequently these two activities are subsumed under the term "operations management." Both accounting and mathematics also play an important role in this case. The use of mathematical models for the analysis of business problems has developed on a large scale only since about 1950. Typically called "operations research" or "management science," this approach has found its widest use to date in the operations management area, although a growing number of applications have been found for it in both marketing and finance.

Case 4 is essentially a marketing study concerned with buyer motivations in relation to the company's service offering. While research is widely used for studies of markets and their opportunities, research is also used to study company marketing operations.

We have now mentioned several times how companies study their external environments. The wide range of these studies includes investigations of potential and actual political actions, public opinion, and competitive and economic conditions as well as the market studies already discussed.

Finally, perhaps the largest single outlay for research in business is for research and development (R&D), dealing largely with engineering and technical problems. While R&D is an area of major managerial concern, it is largely technological research and is outside the scope of this book.

In summary, research opportunities are found in all functional areas of business. The classification used here does not do full justice to the range of research opportunities that exist. It fails to account for the large number of studies that cut across functional lines. Management audits, studies for mergers and acquisitions, and research for long-range planning and major reorganizations are examples of transfunctional studies.

Research as a Specialty

The above subject research areas have achieved varying degrees of recognition as organizational functions with separate identities and budgets. Clearly R&D is the most prevalent and attracts the largest resources. Research in marketing is the second most widely recognized area with separate organizational status. In recent years operations research has grown rapidly and now is the next most widely encountered separate organizational research unit. Operations research (OR) has moved beyond its original concern with production and goods-handling; now the concepts and tools of the OR specialist are being utilized in marketing, finance, and other areas. In due time the organizational dichotomy of the marketing research department and the operations research department will either disappear or be restructured because much of the present separation rests on traditional views of the tools and techniques of investigation.

External environment research is probably fourth in importance. This type of investigation has not usually been recognized organizationally except in the position of the company economist and possibly in the public relations office. Much of the external environment research is carried out in the marketing research department or is performed by outside consulting firms.

Recent years have seen the emergence of research concerned with the human relations aspects of business. Morale and attitude studies have been conducted for many years, but it is now no longer unusual for a company to employ a psychologist or sociologist to study the organization and its functioning.

THE MANAGER–RESEARCHER RELATIONSHIP

Who Does the Research?

Since information gathering is an integral part of the manager's task, it is not surprising that most managers do their own research, at least part of the time. There may be no one else available, or the investigation may be a simple brief study of an ad hoc nature. Alternatively, the investigator may be a staff assistant who is given an occasional research task in addition to his or her normal work. Finally, a research specialist, either on the staff or from elsewhere, may be called in. When this happens, the research function is more clearly delegated, specified, and budgeted. Such delegation tends to occur for major problems that take more time, resources, and special skills than are available from the decision makers and their immediate staff.

Contribution of Research to Decision Making. Applied research has value to the extent that it assists management to make better decisions. "Interesting information" about consumers, employees, competitors, and so forth, is pleasant and comforting to have, but its real value is severely limited if it does not contribute to better problem solving. If a study does not promise to help management to identify more efficient, less risky, or more profitable alternatives than otherwise, its execution should be questioned. More will be said about placing explicit values on a research study in Chapter 3. The important point is: *Applied research in a business environment finds its justification in the contribution it makes to the decision maker's task.* The essence of rationality in management is that the manager knows and can specify what information is needed to make effective decisions.

The Manager's Task. Information gathering is only a part of the manager's job. Managers must also analyze the research findings, interpret their meaning, and add them to the information which they already possess. Finally, good managers will introduce value considerations that are much less amenable to research than are factual considerations. Among such value matters are ethical concerns or questions of company social posture toward the consumer, the employees, government, competition, the public, and others.

Faced with a number of demands on their time and talents, decision makers seek assistance in acquiring the needed information. Since the managers are also often ill equipped for the task, they may delegate the job to research specialists. They must then determine how much of the decision is delegatable and how much remains clearly their own preserve.

The Researcher's Task. Opinions differ about how far researchers' roles should extend into the decision-making function. Should researchers merely collect the data and present them to the managers? Should they go further and interpret meanings and significances for the problem which the managers face? Should they go even further and recommend a course of action based on their findings?

While few would defend the extreme position on either side, this issue is nevertheless more complex than it might first appear. Research usefulness hinges on the ability of researchers to understand the full details of the decision situation. However, managers may withhold key data, often for reasons of security. Researchers may then be forced to adopt a distorted problem definition. Alternatively, managers may specify the research problem and design but lack the necessary skills to do it effectively. In either case the research results are likely to be less useful than they might have been if communication had been more complete. The value of research for decision making is substantially enhanced if managers recognize their obligation to provide the researchers with as much information about the problem and its background as possible.

Researchers also have obligations. They are expected to utilize the insight provided about the problem to develop a creative research design which can provide unambiguous answers of value to decision making. Not only should they provide the data, analyzed in terms of the problem, but they should also point out the implications that appear to flow from the results. When they do so, conflict may arise between the roles of the decision makers and the researchers. The decision makers want certainty, while the researchers provide probability. The decision makers want a simple, explicit recommendation, while the researchers tend to offer complex, hedged interpretations. To this conflict, inherent in the roles of the two parties, there is no simple resolution. However, a workable balance can usually be found if each party is sensitive to the demands and restrictions imposed on the other.

In some cases researchers make specific recommendations. Case 3 is such a situation. The researcher recommended an inventory management system for a problem that could be analyzed in a specific structured manner. When dealing with such problems, researchers can move quickly and easily from research roles to that of consulting advisors. They must not, however, overlook the implications of this switch. They stop merely *interpreting results* of a study and begin *recommending actions*.

Whether researchers can be successful in such a role depends on (1) the relative importance of the research information to the decision, (2) the rapport between researchers and managers, and (3) the competence, experience, and confidence of researchers and managers in the area of concern. When the information is the main basis for the decision, researchers' advice has greater value. When the information is only a small part of the informational input or when there are major questions of values, researchers are in a poor position to recommend. When rapport is good, there is more likelihood that recommendations from researchers will be acceptable. Finally, the relative competence, experience, and confidence of researchers and decision makers in the area study are important in determining how much credence the researchers' recommendations will have. If researchers make recommendations, it is important that they take special care to point out the assumptions and informational limitations on which any recommendations are based.

Why Study Research?

Since the 1920s many universities have offered courses in marketing research. "Business research" courses are of more recent origin and reflect a growing belief that students in all management areas can profit from research training. The broadening of interest in more scientific decision making has been fostered by two factors: (1) the manager's increased need for more and better information, and (2) the availability of improved techniques to meet this need.

The need has come with the trend toward increased size and complexity in business organizations. This trend has also drastically raised the levels of risk associated with business decision making, and this makes it more important that each decision have a sound information base. Along with the increased complexity of business operations have come more variables to consider and many of these are external to the business. Competition is more vigorous, expansion adds new and unfamiliar markets, the public is better informed and more sensitive to its power and self-interest, and government continues to widen its concern with all aspects of our society. All of these factors militate against solo decision making and informal analysis.

At the same time there has been an increase in the number and power of the tools that one can use for business research. After a slow beginning the scientific method is now taking hold in all social sciences, including management. Management scholars have begun to build more impressive theories. The computer has made possible a revolutionary jump in our ability to deal with problems faster and with more power. New techniques of quantitative analysis have taken advantage of this increased calculational power. In addition, communication and measurement techniques have also made great strides. These trends have reinforced each other and are having a massive impact on business management.

Research and the Executives.   Executives who once functioned effectively by relying on their own experience and informal analysis need to be better equipped to manage in the future. Even though their major interests lie elsewhere, they must be able to do research for themselves and others, since they may have neither staff nor funds with which to buy assistance. They may be called upon to make studies at the request of some higher executive, particularly during their early career years.

Executives also need some research competence when they are called upon to "buy" research from outsiders. Many executives have difficulty in properly defining their own information needs and translating these into researchable questions for the specialists. Managers need also to be better equipped to judge proposals made by the research specialists. When the line executives cannot adequately judge the appropriateness of various research methods and techniques, they are forced to abdicate part of their vital decision-making role to the research specialists. Obviously, at some point most executives find that they must depend on the judgment of the researchers. Even then, however, managers need not abdicate their total responsibility if they are grounded in research basics. One can judge the logic of a research approach even with limited technical knowledge of the procedures used.

The trend toward more scientific decision making also presents an attractive career opportunity to the student who wishes to become a research specialist. As has been pointed out earlier, research functions are emerging in all areas of business operations. Systems research, financial analysis, operations research, and marketing research offer especially attractive career opportunities to the well prepared young person.

State of Scientific Development

Business research is an area of applied social science. The social sciences are widely viewed as being relatively backward in scientific development when contrasted with such disciplines as physics and biology. This evaluation is generally fair as far as it goes. While great strides have been made in recent years, there is little doubt that scientific development in social science research still lags behind that in the physical disciplines. The body of developed and tested knowledge is much smaller. The development of generalized principles and laws is much less advanced. Our society pours much more of its resources into physical research than into the social area. In addition, the techniques and tools of the researcher in social science are much less sophisticated than in, say, chemistry.

Why the Slow Development in Business Research?[5]   Science in business research has developed slowly for the same reasons that all social science research has developed slowly. One argument goes that the business environment cannot be sufficiently controlled for scientific research. Those who hold this opinion probably would be reluctant to call any social science research "scientific." This narrow and parochial view is dismissed out of hand as an unwarranted effort to define science in terms of the methods used in a few disciplines.

It is also said that social research is more difficult than natural science because of social relations. No doubt such a complexity does exist, but it is too easy to dismiss the complexities found in the physical sciences. A review of the history of physics, for example, suggests that the problems have been no

---

[5] This section draws heavily upon the critique of social science research found in Gordon Tullock, *The Organization of Inquiry* (Durham, N.C.: Duke University Press, 1966).

more clear or easy in that field in the past than they are today in the social sciences. Complexity appears to be overrated as a justification for the tardy development of scientific social research.

Another explanation is that the techniques of natural scientists cannot be used in the social sciences. This argument is suspect because it is the researchers' task to develop techniques suited to the problems which they face. There is no reason for assuming that natural science techniques should be appropriate in any other field. A fourth argument is that the need to deal with people in research introduces special problems of subjectivity on the part of all persons involved. Clearly this argument is valid to a degree, but in essence this says only that social sciences involve rather special problems for the researcher. The physicist could rightly argue that the study of the nuclear decay of a palladium isotope also presents a serious set of problems. Every branch of study has some special class of problems which constitute the major challenges of the field.

Yet another argument is that the social scientist cannot experiment with the same facility as can the natural scientist, and experimentation is the most powerful tool of scientific research. There is also some truth to this position, though it is often overdrawn. Anyone familiar with the literature in business and social research recognizes that we do experiment and that the experimental method is now being recognized as a fruitful technique too long ignored. The growing use of the experimental method in the social sciences suggests that its tardy application is more likely to be a symptom than a cause of backwardness in the field.

A final argument grows out of the belief that natural scientists simply go to their laboratories, set up the devices to test any hypotheses in which they are interested, run the experiment, and obtain the answers. This is just not true. While the natural scientists may have advanced further in the study of their disciplines, they face essentially the same problem as the social scientists—that of always being at the outer limits of their knowledge, grappling with problems in the unknown.

The Real Sources of Tardiness.   There are more fundamental reasons why scientific social and business research has been slow to develop. In many ways the nature of social relations presents an unfavorable research atmosphere. Natural scientists have an advantage in that they can demonstrate their findings more clearly. They can also replicate research easily, and this enables them to coerce a doubting majority into accepting their views. Persuasion can be much more difficult for social scientists because the findings are less demonstrable and replicable. Conclusions are more tentative and often based on less powerful measurement techniques.

Another important advantage held by physical scientists is the obscurity of their field of study. Social and business research studies involve everyone's immediate concerns—about which there are often strong opinions. The questions studied are often quite familiar to many people who also feel competent to judge them without research.[6]

A third feature of the social environment which makes research more difficult is the motivation leading to research. In business the motivation is almost exclusively that of using results in decision making. Organizations are reluctant to spend money to develop any new technique which they feel a competitor could use. There is no patent system for social inventions, so executives are prone simply to reason out the problem as best they can without research. When research is carried out, there is usually secrecy and an unwillingness for the results to be published.

In the physical sciences there is public support of research and wide publication of the results. In business and management there is no comparable level of public spending for research to supply the basic findings from which practitioners can draw. However, it is now realized that many of our society's great unsolved problems are social in nature, and public funding of social science research is increasing.

Some businesses, too, are becoming more interested in directly supporting basic research. A number of corporations now contribute to the Marketing Science Institute, an organization dedicated to the advancement of the scientific study of marketing processes. Bills have been introduced in Congress to provide research funds for studies in business, particularly with regard to the effects of advertising. In addition, a growing number of companies are making grants to universities for research in business topics.

The Need for Better Research

The current is running toward more sophisticated research applications in the entire field of business and administration, but the developments to date are mixed. New techniques have been advanced with such speed that the journals are becoming increasingly difficult for many to read and understand. This sophistication is expected to accelerate in the future and is already making it possible to answer research questions that could not be answered only a few years ago. However, this progress is too often associated with infatuation with some specific technique at the expense of the methods of science that must underlie any objective investigation. No amount of quantification or speed of data processing can overcome fundamental deficiencies of conceptualization and inference.

Business research will improve when both managers and practitioners learn:

1.   To recognize that inquiry is a major part of management decision making and is too often neglected or undertaken poorly.

---

[6] For example, representatives and senators seem to enjoy exposing "useless" research projects that "waste" the taxpayer's money.

2. To understand and conform to the requirements of the scientific method in applied research.
3. To understand and use the methods and techniques of research which are most appropriate to the posed problem.

SUMMARY

Research is defined as any organized inquiry carried out to provide information for the solution of a problem. It includes reporting as well as descriptive, predictive, and explanatory studies, but only the last three types will be treated in this book. Emphasis is placed on applied rather than pure research.

Research contributes to more effective decisions in all functional areas of business and has emerged as a specialty in marketing and operations research. Even so, managers still must provide most of their own information, although time, skill, and other constraints have encouraged them to seek specialized assistance.

When research specialists are used, there is a potential for role conflict. Managers alone may define the research when they should at least share this task with the researchers. The researchers too often cannot even secure full access to background data. When managers alone set the research question and withhold information, they increase their chances of securing research answers to the wrong questions.

When the study is complete there are other potentials for conflict. First, the manager wants simple, explicit, and certain recommendations, while the researcher offers complex, hedged, probabilistic interpretations. A second conflict point is whether the researcher should gather and report the data, analyze and interpret the findings, or recommend specific action courses. When researchers move beyond interpretation, they become decision consultants rather than researchers.

Business research is behind the physical sciences in development because of the special problems found in all social research. It is difficult for even a correct minority to make its views felt, partly because business research concerns topics about which many have strong opinions, and because the research findings are not easy to demonstrate. Finally, most business research support comes from commercial organizations that are reluctant to make findings and techniques public.

In spite of these barriers the growing body of knowledge derived from business research is stimulating the use of scientific methodology in the field. This move toward the more scientific is expected to continue and will be the subject of the remainder of this book.

SUPPLEMENTAL READINGS

1. Churchill, Gilbert A. *Marketing Research.* 2d ed. Hinsdale, Ill.: The Dryden Press, 1979. Chap. 1 discusses the marketing manager's role and the role of

marketing research. It also covers the place of marketing research in the company organization.

2. Freeman, Howard E., and Sherwood, Clarence C. *Social Research and Social Policy.* Englewood Cliffs, N.J.: Prentice-Hall, Inc., 1970. Chap. 2 discusses the contribution of research to social policy.

3. Nadler, David A. *Feedback and Organization Development: Using Data-Based Methods.* Reading, Mass.: Addison-Wesley Publishing Company, 1977. A book about the use of data as a tool for organization change. The author argues that "the collection, interpretation, and feedback of data are very basic core activities that are present in almost all organization development (OD) interventions."

4. Random, Matthew. *The Social Scientist in American Industry.* New Brunswick, N.J.: Rutgers University Press, 1970. A research report of experiences of social scientists employed in industry. Chap. 9 presents a summary of findings.

5. Rigby, Paul H. *Conceptual Foundations of Business Research.* New York: John Wiley and Sons, Inc., 1965. Chapters 1 and 4 present an excellent discussion of the nature of modern business research and its relation to science.

DISCUSSION QUESTIONS

1. What is research? How can you tell good research from bad research?

2. Is there any real problem if the researcher is not involved in the development and specification of the information needs that the research is expected to meet?

3. Some argue that researchers should make specific action recommendations; others argue that they should not make such recommendations. What do you think?

4. Managers who wish to have information on which to base a decision face a "make or buy" situation. What are the problems they face in selecting either of these alternatives?

5. You are manager of the midwestern division of a major corporation, supervising five animal feed plants scattered over four states. Corporate headquarters asks you to conduct an investigation to determine whether any of these plants should be closed, expanded, moved, or reduced in importance. Is there a possible conflict between your roles as a investigator and manager? Explain.

6. It is widely admitted that research in the social sciences is relatively primitive compared to research in some of the physical sciences. How do you account for this disparity? What are the prospects for the social sciences to overcome these deficiencies?

7. Advise each of the following persons on the specific research studies which he or she might find useful in carrying out the job. Classify each proposed study as either reporting, description, explanation, or prediction.
   a. Manager of the men's furnishings department at a Sears store.
   b. Plant manager at a Ford auto assembly plant.
   c. Director of Admissions at a large state university.

    d. Investment analyst at Merrill Lynch, Pierce, Fenner, and Smith.

    e. Director of Personnel at a large metropolitan hospital.

    f. Product manager for Crest toothpaste at Procter & Gamble.

8. The new president of an old, established company is facing a problem. The company is currently unprofitable and is, in the president's opinion, operating inefficiently. The company sells a wide line of equipment and supplies to the dairy industry. Some items it manufactures, and many it wholesales to dairies, creameries, and similar plants. Because the industry is changing in several ways, survival will be more difficult in the future than it has been in the past. More particularly, many equipment companies are now bypassing the wholesalers and selling directly to dairies. In addition, many of the independent dairies are being taken over by large food chains. How might research help the new president to make the right decisions? In answering this question consider the areas of marketing and finance as well as the whole company.

9. The president of the Bleu Jeans Manufacturing Co. has assigned you the task of collecting data for use in making the long range strategic plan for the company. In particular, you are to investigate the critical environment areas involving technological changes, sociocultural changes, and legal/political factors. What kinds of data would you seek? Where and how might you gather such data?

10. Suppose you were invited to give a talk on "What is needed to make business research more scientific." What specific points would you talk about?

Chapter 2

Scientific Thinking

WHILE THERE MAY BE MANY WAYS to improve the quality of business research, one of the more fruitful is to use a basic approach that maximizes our chances for securing valid results. Such an approach, often called the "scientific method," is the subject of this chapter.

A discussion of the scientific method logically begins with the foundations of rational thought processes. These include conceptualization, definition, and inference. Concepts, clearly defined, are used in the inference process for building propositions, hypotheses, models, theories, principles, laws, and so forth (these terms overlap somewhat and mean different things to different people). The use of concepts and definitions for the development of propositions involves a building and testing process that Dewey has referred to as "the double movement of reflective thinking."[1] While these ideas are associated with all types of reflective thought, they are more narrowly considered here as the critical building blocks in the methods of science.

NATURE OF SCIENTIFIC METHOD

Science has been described in many ways. One writer suggests that there are two basic views: the static and the dynamic.[2] According to the static view, science is a body of systematized information that includes connected princi-

---

[1] John Dewey, *How We Think* (Boston: D. C. Health & Co., 1910), p. 79.

[2] James B. Conant, *Science and Common Sense* (New Haven, Conn.: Yale University Press, 1951), pp. 24–25.

ples, theories, and laws. This view emphasizes the cumulated results of legions of investigations; it defines our present body of knowledge. Under this definition a scientist adds blocks of knowledge to the scientific stockpile.

The dynamic view presents science as a *process*. Those holding the dynamic view claim that theories and principles would soon become dogma if not subjected to constant investigation and development. In the dynamic view, science is a body of generally accepted rules by which one deals with knowledge; that is, it is the *scientific method*.

Both the static and the dynamic concept contribute to the full meaning of science. While we emphasize here the dynamic aspects (the process), clearly our objective is also to test and expand our knowledge of reality. Physicists test their knowledge of the properties of matter in order to explain them further. Finance researchers test their knowledge of financial values in order to determine how these values develop. The specific techniques employed are different, but the general approach and the objectives should be the same. Both seek to (1) describe, explain, and/or predict the form and size of phenomena, and (2) accomplish these aims with an approach that is widely accepted as rational and replicable.

Some go further and argue that the basic aim of science is to develop theory. This view stresses the static concept of science and leads to increased emphasis on pure rather than applied research. The distinction between pure and applied research is useful if one remembers that these terms merely represent two points on a continuum. That is, research studies have differing degrees of "purity" and "applicability," depending on whether their purpose is solely to advance knowledge in a field or to solve some functional problem.

In management we have a modest collection of research-confirmed knowledge to support some tentative theories. In terms of the static concept of science the field of management has not progressed very far. Viewed from the dynamic perspective, however, research in management can be as scientific as research in any other discipline.

While much business research may be "unscientific" it need not be the result of inherent barriers to the use of scientific methods. Management researchers can use tools, techniques, and methods analogous to those found in other fields of study. Some unique approaches have been developed that are especially suited to business problems. When management researchers also adopt the attitudes and ethics associated with "science," they are using the approach of science. To explore the details of this approach we begin by drawing a clear distinction between research activity that is scientific (in the dynamic sense) and that which is unscientific, regardless of the field of study.

Criteria of Good Research

When one wishes to evaluate a research project, one is concerned with two aspects: the contents (findings and conclusions) and the degree of confidence that one can place in the study and its results (in short, the quality of the research). One may employ a number of criteria to evaluate studies. One writer suggests the following seven requirements:

1. *The purpose of the research, or the problem involved, should be clearly defined and sharply delineated in terms as unambiguous as possible.*

    The statement of the research problem should include analysis into its simplest elements, its scope and limitations, and precise specifications of the meanings of all words significant to the research. Failure of the researcher to do this adequately may raise legitimate doubts in the minds of readers as to whether the researcher has sufficient understanding of the problem to make a sound attack upon it.

2. *The research procedures used should be described in sufficient detail to permit another researcher to repeat the research.*

    Excepting when secrecy is imposed in the national interest, research reports should reveal with candor the sources of data and the means by which they were obtained. Omission of significant procedural details makes it difficult or impossible to estimate the validity and reliability of the data and justifiably weakens the confidence of the reader in research.

3. *The procedural design of the research should be carefully planned to yield results that are as objective as possible.*

    When a sampling of a population is involved, the report should include evidence concerning the degree of representativeness of the sample. A questionnaire ought not to be used when more reliable evidence is available from documentary sources or by direct observation. Bibliographic searches should be as thorough and complete as possible. Experiments should have satisfactory controls. Direct observations should be recorded in writing as soon as possible after the event. Efforts should be made to minimize the influence of personal bias in selecting and recording data.

4. *The researcher should report, with complete frankness, flaws in procedural design and estimate their effect upon the findings.*

    There are very few perfect research designs. Some of the imperfections may have little effect upon the validity and reliability of the data; others may invalidate them entirely. A competent researcher should be sensitive to the effects of imperfect design and his experience in analyzing the data should give him a basis for estimating their influence.

5. *Analysis of the data should be sufficiently adequate to reveal its significance; and the methods of analysis used should be appropriate.*

    The extent to which this criterion is met is frequently a good measure of the competence of the researcher. Twenty years of experience in guiding the research of graduate students leads the writer to conclude that adequate analysis of the data is the most difficult phase of research for the novice.

    The validity and reliability of data should be checked carefully. The data should be classified in ways that assist the researcher to reach pertinent conclusions. When statistical methods are used, the probability of error should be estimated and the criteria of statistical significance applied.

6. *Conclusions should be confined to those justified by the data of the research and limited to those for which the data provide an adequate basis.*

Researchers are often tempted to broaden the basis of inductions by including personal experiences not subject to the controls under which the research data were gathered. This tends to decrease the objectivity of the research and weakens confidence in the findings.

Equally undesirable is the all-too-frequent practice of drawing conclusions from study of a limited population and applying them universally. Good researchers specify the conditions under which their conclusions seem to be valid. Failure to do so justifiably weakens confidence in the research.

7. *Greater confidence in the research is warranted if the researcher is experienced, has a good reputation in research, and is a person of integrity.*

Were it possible for the reader of a research report to obtain sufficient information about the researcher, this criterion perhaps would be one of the best bases for judging the degree of confidence a piece of research warrants. For this reason, the research report should be accompanied by more information about the qualification of the researcher than is the usual practice.

Some evidence pertinent to estimates of the competence and integrity of the researcher may be found in the report itself. Language that is restrained, clear, and precise; assertions that are carefully drawn and hedged with appropriate reservations; and an apparent effort to achieve maximum objectivity tend to leave a favorable impression of the researcher. On the other hand, generalizations that outrun the evidence upon which they are based, exaggerations, and unnecessary verbiage tend to leave an unfavorable impression.[3]

This is an excellent set of criteria for evaluating research studies, especially scholarly work. However, any such list is likely to be inadequate in its details; this one is no exception. For example, the call for a clear definition of research problems, criterion 1, ignores one major research approach—that of the exploratory study. This approach is particularly useful in investigations where problems are not clear and methods not yet developed. Then, too, the restriction of secrecy to cases in the national interest (criterion 2) is unrealistically narrow for applied research projects where commercial secrecy may be important.

Perhaps the greatest weakness of these criteria is their vagueness. For example, how much detail is "sufficient detail?" How unambiguous is "unambiguous as possible?" Clearly a large judgmental element exists in these phrases; so it must always be for any general statement of criteria. While many practices are clearly unscientific and therefore unacceptable, others are subject to interpretation. We must add our experience and good sense into the balance.

One important problem not adequately covered by the above criteria is that of bias. The research sponsor may personally contribute to poor research

---

[3] James Harold Fox, "Criteria of Good Research," *Phi Delta Kappan,* vol. 39 (March 1958), pp. 285–86.

through the pressures of vested interests. The researcher's knowledge of the outcome that the sponsor would like to see can influence the findings. One must deal with this problem effectively and quickly. The best approach is for the researcher to secure, before the study is begun, the sponsor's acceptance that the function of research is to uncover reality—wherever it may lead.

Such an understanding about research objectivity is necessary, but an equally important concern is that the researcher must fully comprehend the fundamentals of the scientific method and use them at every step. The remainder of this chapter is concerned with some of these fundamentals.

FOUNDATIONS OF SCIENTIFIC METHOD

When we do research we seek to know "what is" (or reality) in order to predict, explain, or understand phenomena. For example, we might want to answer the question, "What will be the employee reaction to the new pension plan proposal?" Or, "Why did the stock market price surge higher when all normal indicators suggested that the market would go down?" We try to identify and characterize this reality and measure and evaluate it according to certain definitions and classifications of ideas. We also try to develop theories about how these ideas should relate to each other according to certain rules of logic. Before we can design such research efforts in a scientific way we must be able to deal comfortably with ideas such as concepts, constructs, abstraction levels, operational definitions, propositions, hypotheses, models, and theories.

Concepts

If we are to perceive objects and events, think about them, understand them, and communicate about them we must have some means of doing so. For these purposes we use concepts expressed in language. A concept is *an abstraction of meanings from reality to which we assign some word or words in order to be able to communicate about it.*[4] The number of concepts is infinite, and we use them constantly. In fact, this paragraph is filled with them.

Importance to Research.   Concepts are basic to all thought and communication, yet we normally pay too little attention to what they are, how they come about, and the problems in their use. These considerations alone would not justify considering the subject here if it were not that there are special problems in research that grow out of the need for conceptual precision and inventiveness. We design hypothesis statements using concepts. We

---

[4] Kerlinger defines it this way, "A *concept* expresses an abstraction formed by generalization from particulars." See F. Kerlinger *Foundations of Behavioral Research,* 2d. ed. (New York, N.Y.: Holt, Reinhart and Wilson, 1973), p. 28. Another definition, "*Concepts* are terms that refer to the characteristics of events, situations, groups and individuals that we are studying in the social sciences," is from Claire Selltiz, Lawrence S. Wrightsman, and Stuart W. Cook, *Research Methods in Social Relations,* 3d ed. (New York: Holt, Rinehart and Winston, 1976), p. 16.

devise measurement concepts by which to test these hypothesis statements. We gather data using these measurement concepts. We may even invent new concepts to express our ideas. The success of our research hinges on (1) how clearly we conceptualize and (2) how well others understand the concepts we use. For example, when we survey people on the question of tax equity the questions we use need to faithfully tap the attitudes of the respondents. Attitudes are abstract, yet we must attempt to measure them using a few carefully selected concrete concepts.

The second challenge is to develop concepts that others will clearly understand. We might, for example, ask respondents for an estimate of their family's total income. This may seem to be a simple, unambiguous concept, but we will receive varying and confusing answers unless we restrict or narrow the concept by specifying (1) time period, such as weekly, monthly, or annually; (2) before or after income taxes; (3) for head of family only or for all family members; and (4) for salary and wages only, or also for dividends, interest, and capital gains. (How about income in kind such as free rent, employee discounts, food stamps?)

Sources of Concepts. Concepts which are in frequent and general use have been developed over time through shared usage, and we have acquired them through personal experience. If we lived in another society we would hold many of the same concepts (although often in a different language). Some concepts, however, are unique to a particular culture and are not readily translatable into another language.[5]

Ordinary concepts make up the bulk of our communication even in research, but we can often run into difficulty trying to deal with an uncommon concept or a newly advanced idea. One way to handle this problem is to borrow from other languages (for example, gestalt) or borrow from other subject areas to express an analogous phenomenon. For example, the concept of "gravitation" is borrowed from physics and used in marketing in an attempt to explain why people shop where they do. The concept of "distance" is used in attitude measurement to describe varying degrees of difference between the attitudes of two or more persons. "Threshold" is used effectively to describe a concept in perception studies, while "velocity" is a term borrowed by the economist from the physicist.

Borrowing is not always practical, so we may need to (1) adopt new meanings for words (make a word cover a different concept) or (2) develop new labels (words) for concepts. The recent broadening of the meaning of "model" is an example of the first instance, while the development of concepts such as "metatheory" and "status stress" are examples of the second. When we adopt new meanings or develop new labels we begin to develop a

---

[5] "In Lithuanian there is a word for gray when you speak of eyes, another when you speak of hair, a third when you speak of ducks and geese, several others for other purposes, but no word for gray in general." See Rudolph Flesch, *The Art of Clear Thinking* (New York: Crowell-Collier Publishing Company, 1962), p. 59.

specialized jargon or terminology. Researchers in medicine, the physical sciences, and related fields frequently use terms which are unintelligible to outsiders. Jargon no doubt contributes to efficiency of communication among specialists but excludes everyone else.

Concept Characteristics.   The concept of "concept" has three characteristics of interest to us. First, the concept of an object includes only some of the elements or features of that object. Thus, we see an animal which we identify as "our dog" by abstracting out concepts such as its size, shape, color, and the way it acts toward us. For making this identification we pay no attention to the animal's age, temperature, geneology, or whether it is hungry. We make only those abstractions which are pertinent to our situational need.

A second important characteristic of a concept is that people often use the same word label to describe different bundles of meanings and different labels to describe the same meaning. This is so prevalent that it is a core problem in research as well as in all communications. There are also many simple and widely used concepts about which there is little difficulty. We all can agree on the meaning of such concepts as "animal," "table," "electric light," "money," "employee," and "wife." Somewhat more of a problem is encountered when we try to make research use of such widely understood concepts as "household," "retail transaction," "dwelling unit," "regular user," or "wash sale." Still more challenging are concepts that are widely recognized but are not well understood, such as "leadership," motivation," "IQ," "social class," and "fiscal policy."

A third characteristic of concepts is that they reflect varying degrees of abstraction. The concept of "abstract" itself is frequently used in at least two ways. In the first sense it concerns the degree of specificity-generality.[6] The more specific concepts typically include time and spatial designations. For example, "the senior machinist employed currently at Company X" is such a concept. It is also part of a more general class of "machinists employed at Company X," which is a member of a more general class of "Company X employees." This last class, in turn, is a member of the more general class of "employed persons." In research we theorize in terms of the more general concepts but test hypotheses inferred from the theory in terms of the more specific concepts.

In a second sense "abstractness" is used to express the degree to which a concept does or does not have objective referents. This idea is best explained in terms of constructs.

Constructs.   As used in research in the social sciences, *construct* is an image or idea specifically invented for a given research and/or theory-building purpose. We build constructs, which are more complex, by combining the simpler concepts, especially when the idea or image we intend to

---

[6] This is sometimes referred to as the "ladder of abstraction." See S. I. Hayakawa, *Language in Thought and Action* (New York: Harcourt, Brace & World, Inc., 1949), pp. 165–70.

convey is not directly subject to observation. For example, such terms as "intelligence," "achievement motivation," "relative deprivation," "conservatism," "cognitive dissonance," and "purchase predisposition" are constructs.

There is no sharp demarcation between concepts and constructs. For example, the concept of "employee" can be defined rather clearly in terms of empirical fact. This common concept is widely understood, although there may be nuances presenting research problems. Suppose, however, that we are interested in a study of employee opinion. This is clearly a more complex concept and one which is more difficult to observe (unlike employees, opinions cannot be seen, directly observed, or unambiguously defined). Then again, the company management may have a special interest in key employees, an even more abstract concept constructed out of the concepts of (1) employee and (2) "keyness" ("key" here being used to describe persons whose roles in the organization are considered critical). Further, the investigator may be asked to measure "key employee commitment." This construct is even more abstract than the others and is designed to reflect the degree to which persons (1) are employees, (2) hold significant roles in the organization, and (3) have opinions, loyalties, and motivations congruent with the company's objectives.

Researchers may develop new concepts or constructs to represent those ideas, but they must do so in a restrained and responsible manner if they want to communicate with others. The casual advancement of ill-conceived concepts can only create confusion. Concern with the content of concepts and constructs introduces the process of definition and the need for care in specifying concept content.

Definition

The effective conduct of research, as well as all communication, is complicated by the lack of agreement on concept meanings and the use of different abstraction levels. The problems of communication become even more difficult when a researcher decides to advance new concepts. For all of these reasons it is critical to the success of any research study that all persons involved have a common understanding of concept meanings. We do this by using definitions.

Ostensive Definitions. An *ostensive definition* is "any process by which a person is taught to understand a word other than by the use of other words."[7] We might ostensively define a beautiful home by pointing out homes that we believe qualify. We can ostensively define good and bad worker morale by asking persons to point out departments which exemplify such conditions.

---

[7] Bertrand Russell, *Human Knowledge—Its Scope and Limits* (New York: Simon and Schuster, 1948), p. 63.

Ostensive definitions are useful under two types of research conditions. First, they are valuable in the exploratory stages of projects when we are still trying to develop the concepts we need. At such a time we are searching for ideas, and ostensive examples are fertile sources for such ideas. Even at the later and more formal stages of study it may still be productive if we supplement word-defined concepts with ostensive examples for abstractions such as management style, leadership, and modern styling; it can help to have examples pointed out either by the researcher (to help the respondent) or by the respondent (to illustrate his/her meaning).

Verbal Definitions. In a verbal definition we use words to explain a concept in terms of other concepts. Such definitions often involve words at about the same level of abstraction. For example, a customer is defined as "a patron"; a patron, in turn, is defined as "a customer or a client of an establishment"; a client is defined as "one who employs the services of any professional man. . . , also, loosely, a patron of any shop."[8] Such circularity is common when the same abstraction levels are used. Only if we clearly understand the meaning of one of the synonyms will such a definition help us understand the original concept. When a word is defined in terms of concepts higher on the abstraction ladder we learn even less. For example, if we define a customer as a "source of company revenue" (a higher level abstraction), we learn little about the nature of "customerness." It is only when we define in terms of lower abstraction levels that we secure the needed meaning insight. If we define a customer as "one who buys merchandise from store K" (more specific abstraction level) we learn something of the essence of "customerness."

Fortunately we can expect that the normal and accepted word usage is precise enough for most of the concepts used in a research study. When further precision is needed we can often depend upon verbal definitions to provide the common understanding sought. However, there remains a more important meaning problem which concerns a limited number of concepts that are critical to the research study. This problem calls for operational definitions.

Operational Definitions. *An operational definition is stated in terms of specific testing criteria or operations.* These terms must have empirical referents (that is, we must be able to count, measure, or in some other way gather the information through our senses). Whether the object to be defined is physical (for example, a lathe) or highly abstract (for example, achievement motivation) the definition should specify the characteristics to be observed and how they are to be observed. The criteria or operations should be so objective that any competent observer should be able to define a person,

---

[8] *Webster's New Collegiate Dictionary* (Springfield, Mass.: G. &. C. Merriam Company, 1961), pp. 205, 617, 154, respectively.

action, condition, or attitude in a specific situation and secure the same results.

By now the reader should be convinced of the need for precision and specificity in research, and it is for just these reasons that operational definitions are needed. Assume that we are interested in comparing the customers of store K to its noncustomers. A critical step would be to establish whether a given person is a customer or noncustomer. Toward this end we might propose the following three operational definitions for consideration.

1. A customer of store K is any adult who answers "yes" to the question "Are you a customer of store K?" (Adult is defined as anyone who appears to the interviewer to be at least 18 years of age.)
2. A customer of store K is any adult who answers "yes" to the question "Have you purchased anything from store K during the last month?"
3. A customer of store K is any adult who reports buying more from store K than from either store L or store M when asked "From which store do you do most of your shopping, store K, store L, or store M?"

These operational definitions all adequately specify the empirical information needed and how it is to be collected; yet they are not adequate definitions unless they have the proper scope or fit for the research problem. This is largely a judgment matter and can be illustrated by assuming that store K is one of the three major department stores in the city. Further, let's assume that our task is to determine how persons who shop most often at store K differ in attitudes and shopping practices from those who shop more at the other stores. Definition 1 is inadequate because it provides no information about relative store usage. In addition, it would class most people as store K customers, even those who seldom shop there. Definition 2 may give a better balance of customers-noncustomers but still fails to get at the relative usage comparison. Definition 3 is the best of the three because it more accurately identifies customers with their major shopping store.

These examples have dealt with relatively concrete concepts, but operational definitions are even more critical for treating abstract ideas. Consider again the study of long distance telephone use mentioned in Chapter 1. In that study the researchers believed that high callers and low callers might exhibit different personality characteristics.[9] Personality is a highly abstract concept and cannot be measured directly. The researchers needed to trans-

---

[9] The operational definitions for low caller and high caller were:

Low caller—Respondents for whom the company records indicate no long distance calls to places 50 miles or more away for a three-month period.

High caller—Respondents for whom the records show six or more calls in three months to places 50 miles or more away.

See *Motives, Attitudes, and Long Distance Calls* (Ann Arbor, Mich.: Survey Research Center, University of Michigan, April 1956), p. 2.

late this construct of personality into more specific terms before they could gather empirical data.

One widely recognized dimension of personality is that of security-insecurity.[10] In the long distance telephone study the researchers developed a scale consisting of seven statements such as: "You have often lost sleep over your worries."[11] All seven items could be answered by "yes" or "no" responses. Previous research using similar scales indicated that the greatest difference among people occurred between those who answered "no" to all seven statements (secure people) and those who answered "yes" to one or more (insecure people). Therefore, the operational definitions were:

Secure person—One who answers "no" to all seven scale items.
Insecure person—One who answers "yes" to one or more items on the scale.

While operational definitions are needed in the conduct of research, their use presents some problems. There is the ever-present danger of confusing the definition with the concept it represents. We tend to forget that definitions provide only limited insight into the meanings of the concepts and constructs they represent. In fact, operational definitions may be so narrow in meaning that more than one is required to express a concept fully. This narrowness is the price we pay for precision, and it complicates our measurement. By using several definitions we can tap more than one dimension of a concept, but how do we combine them? When, say, two definitions correlate well it supports the view that we are measuring the same concept. If there is little or no correlation it may mean we are tapping separate partial meanings of a construct, but it may also mean one or both of the operational definitions are not measuring our concept. If the definitions correlate negatively then we should reassess the nature of the concept and its proposed operational definitions.

Whatever the form of definition, its purpose in research is basically the same—to provide an understanding and measurement of concepts. We may need to provide operational definitions for only a few critical concepts, but these will almost always be the ones which we use to develop the concept relationships found in hypotheses and theories.

Hypotheses

In the literature of research and inference there are disagreements about the meanings of the terms "proposition" and "hypothesis." Here we define a proposition as a statement about concepts which may be judged as true or false if it refers to observable phenomena. When a proposition is formulated

---

[10] Additional dimensions of personality were included in the study but are not important to our discussion here.

[11] Ibid., p. 42.

for empirical testing we call it a hypothesis. These declarative statements are of a tentative and conjectural nature. They represent inductions if they are suggested by conditions we observe, and deductions if they are implications developed from premises. More on these inference processes later in the chapter.

Hypotheses have also been described as statements in which we assign variables to cases.[12] A "case" is defined in this sense as the "entity or thing the hypothesis talks about. The 'variable' is the characteristic, trait, or attribute which, in the hypothesis, is imputed to the case."[13] For example, we might form the hypothesis "Executive Jones (case) has a higher than average achievement motivation (variable)." If our hypothesis was based on more than one case it would be a *generalization*. For example, "Executives in Company Z (cases) have higher than average achievement motivation (variable)." Both of these hypotheses are examples of *descriptive hypotheses*.

Descriptive Hypotheses. These are propositions that typically state the existence, size, form, or distribution of some variable. For example, "The current unemployment rate in Detroit exceeds 6 percent of the labor force." In this example the case is Detroit and the variable is unemployment. Examples of other simple descriptive hypotheses are: "American cities are experiencing budget difficulties," and "Eighty percent of Company Z stockholders favor increasing the company's cash dividend." In the former illustration "city" is the case and "budget problem" is the variable. In the latter example "Company Z" is the case and "stockholder attitude toward increased dividends" is the variable.

Researchers will often use a research question rather than a descriptive hypothesis. Thus, in place of the above hypotheses we might use the following questions: "What is the unemployment rate in Detroit?" "Are American cities experiencing budget difficulties?" "Do stockholders of Company Z favor an increased cash dividend?" Either format is usually acceptable, but the hypothesis has several advantages. It encourages researchers to crystallize their thinking about the likely relationships to be found; it further encourages them to think beyond the mere quantity or to form expectations to their implications if the hypothesis is supported or rejected. Finally, the hypothesis form is especially useful for testing statistical significance (to be discussed in Chapter 13). The question form is less used with the second type of situation—the one calling for *relational hypotheses*.

Relational Hypotheses. These are statements which describe a relationship between two variables with respect to some case. For example, "Foreign-made cars are perceived by American consumers to be of better quality than domestic-made cars." In this instance the case is "consumer"

---

[12] A variable is a concept which may take on two or more values.

[13] William N. Stephens, *Hypotheses and Evidence* (New York: Thomas Y. Crowell Company, 1968), p. 5.

and the variables are "country of origin" and "perceived quality." The nature of the relationship between the two variables is not specified. Is there only an implication that the variables occur in some predictable relationship, or is one variable somehow responsible for the other? The former interpretation indicates a *correlational* relationship while the latter indicates an *explanatory,* or *causal,* relationship.

Correlational relationships state merely that the variables occur together in some specified manner without an implication that one causes the other. Such weak claims are often made when we believe that there are more basic causal forces that affect both variables, or when we have not developed enough evidence to claim a stronger linkage. Sample correlational hypotheses are: (1) young machinists (under 35 years of age) are less productive than those who are 35 years or older; (2) the height of women's hemlines varies directly with the level of the business cycle; or (3) people in Atlanta give the President a more favorable rating than do people in St. Louis.

By labeling these as correlational hypotheses we make no claim that one variable causes the other to change or take on different values. Other persons, however, may view one or more of these hypotheses as reflecting cause and effect relationships.

With explanatory or causal hypotheses there is an implication that the existence of, or a change in, one variable causes or leads to an effect on the other variable. The causal variable is typically called the *independent variable* (IV) and the other the *dependent variable* (DV). "Cause" as used here means roughly to "help make happen." That is, the IV need not be the sole reason for the existence of, or change in, the DV. Examples of explanatory hypotheses are:

1. An increase in family income leads to an increase in the percent of income saved.
2. Exposure to the company's messages concerning industry problems leads to more favorable attitudes expressed toward the company by production workers.
3. Loyalty to a particular grocery store increases the probability of purchasing the private brands sponsored by that store.

In proposing or interpreting causal hypotheses the researcher must consider the direction of influence. In many cases the direction is obvious from the nature of the variables. Thus, in example 1 one would assume that family income influences savings rate rather than the reverse case. In example 2 our ability to identify the direction of influence depends on the research design. If the message clearly precedes the attitude measurement then the direction of message exposure to attitude seems clear; if information about both exposure and attitude were collected at the same time there may be justification for saying different attitudes led to selective message exposure or nonexposure. Loyalty to a store may increase the probability of buying the store's private brands, but the use of private brands may also lead to greater store loyalty. In this hypothesis the variables would appear to be interdependent.

More discussion of variable linkages is deferred to Chapter 4. We abbreviate the discussion here to continue with a more general discussion of hypotheses and other matters important to the methods of science.

The Role of the Hypothesis. In the research context a hypothesis serves several important functions. Perhaps the most important is that it guides the direction of the study. A frequent problem in research is the proliferation of "interesting information." Unless the urge to include additional elements is curbed, a study can be diluted by trivial concerns which do not answer the basic questions posed. The virtue of the hypothesis is that, if taken seriously, it defines what shall be studied and what shall not. It defines which facts are relevant and which are not; in so doing, it suggests which form of research design is likely to be most appropriate. A final important role of the hypothesis is to provide a framework for organizing the conclusions that result from the study.

To consider specifically the role of the hypothesis in determining the direction of the research, suppose we have the hypothesis "Husbands and wives agree in their perceptions of their respective roles in purchase decisions." The hypothesis specifies who shall be studied, in what context they shall be studied (their consumer decision making), and what shall be studied (their individual perceptions of their roles).

The nature of this hypothesis and the implications of the statement suggest that the best research design is probably a survey. We have at this time no other practical means to ascertain perceptions of people except to ask them in one way or another about their perceptions. In addition, we are interested only in the roles that are assumed in the purchase or consumer decision-making situation. The study should clearly, therefore, not involve itself in seeking information about other types of roles which husband and wife might play. A third suggestion that might flow from a reflection upon this hypothesis is that we might find that husbands and wives do disagree on their perceptions of roles but that these differences may be explained in terms of additional variables, such as age, social class, background, personality differences, and other factors not associated with their differences of sex.

What Is a Good Hypothesis? A good hypothesis should fulfil three conditions. The most elementary requirement is that it be *adequate for its purpose*. For a descriptive hypothesis this means that it clearly states the condition, size, or distribution of some variable in terms of values meaningful to the research task. If it is an explanatory hypothesis it must explain the facts that gave rise to the need for explanation. Using the hypothesis, plus other known and accepted generalizations, one should be able to deduce the original problem condition.

A second major condition is that the hypothesis must be *testable*. A hypothesis is untestable if it calls for techniques which are unavailable with the present state of the art. It is also untestable if it calls for an explanation which defies known physical or psychological laws. Explanatory hypotheses are also untestable if there are no consequences or derivatives that can be deduced for testing purposes.

For explanatory hypotheses there is a third major condition: It must be *better than its rivals.* Generally speaking, the better hypothesis has a greater range; it explains more facts and a greater variety of facts than do its rivals. The better hypothesis is also the one which informed judges accept as being the most likely. Their opinions can be highly subjective but depend chiefly on their judgment of which fits best with other information. Finally, the better hypothesis is the simple one requiring fewer conditions or assumptions.

Hypotheses play an important role in the development of theory. While theory development has not to date been an important aspect of business research, it is likely to become more so in the future.

Theory

The term "theory" is often used by the layman to mean the opposite of "fact." In this sense theory is viewed as being speculative or ivory-tower. One hears that professor X is too theoretical, that managers need to be practical, or that some idea will not work because it is too theoretical. This is an incorrect picture of the relationship between fact and theory.

When you are too theoretical it means that your basis of explanation or decision is not sufficiently attuned to specific empirical conditions. This may be so, but it does not prove that theory and fact are opposites. The truth is that fact and theory are each necessary for the other to be of value. Our ability to make rational decisions, as well as to develop scientific knowledge, is measured by the degree to which we combine fact and theory.

We all operate on the basis of theories we hold. In one sense theories are the generalizations we make about variables and the relationships among them. We use these generalizations to make decisions and predict outcomes. For example, it is midday and you note that the outside natural light is dimming, dark clouds are moving rapidly in from the west, the breeze is freshening, and the air temperature is cooling. Would your understanding of the relationship among these variables (your weather theory) lead you to a prediction of what else will probably occur in a short time?

Consider another situation where you are called upon to interview two persons for possible promotion to the position of department manager. Do you have a theory about what characteristics such a person should have? Suppose you interview Ms. A and observe that she answers your questions well, openly, and apparently sincerely. She also expresses thoughtful ideas about how to improve departmental functioning and is articulate in stating her views. Ms. B, on the other hand, is guarded in her comments and reluctant to advance ideas for improvements. She answers questions by saying what "Mr.

General Manager wants." She is also less articulate and seems less sincere than Ms. A. You would probably choose A, based upon the way you combine the concepts, definitions, and propositions mentioned into a theory of managerial effectiveness. It may not be a good theory because of the variables we have ignored, but it illustrates the point that we all use theory to guide our decisions, predictions, and explanations.

We define theory here as *a set of systematically interrelated concepts, definitions, and propositions that are advanced to explain and predict phenomena (facts)*. In this sense we have many theories and use them continually to explain or predict what goes on around us. To the degree that our theories are sound, and fit the situation, we are successful in our explanations and predictions. Thus, while a given theory and a set of facts may not fit, they are not opposites. Our challenge is to build better theory and to be more skillful in fitting theory and fact together.

A point which may also cause some confusion is that of how theory differs from hypothesis. One person may advance an explanation and call it a theory while another may call it a hypothesis. It may be difficult to distinguish one from the other since both involve concepts, definitions, and relationships among variables. The basic differences are in the level of complexity and abstraction. Theories tend to be abstract and involve multiple variables, while hypotheses tend to be simple, two-variable propositions involving concrete instances.

Hypotheses are derived in two ways. One way already mentioned is the induction of the hypothesis from some observed facts. The second way is by deduction from a theory. As an example of this latter relationship, one author points out that one of the propositions in the theory of group functioning is: "The more uniform the attitudes of group members, the more cohesive the group."[14] From this abstract proposition he deduces a hypothesis that is specific in time and space by which he hopes to test the theoretical proposition: "During the fall term of 1965, couples dating at XYZ University who had the same political orientations, both liberal or both conservative, dated more frequently than couples with unlike political orientations, one liberal and one conservative."[15]

In this book we will follow the general distinction that the difference between theory and hypothesis is one of degree of complexity and abstraction. At times these may be confused, but it should not make much practical research difference.

Theory and Research. It is important that researchers recognize the pervasiveness and value of theory. Theory serves us in many useful ways. First, as orientation it narrows the range of facts that we need to study. Any problem may be studied in a number of different ways, and theory suggests

---

[14] Paul Davidson Reynolds, *A Primer in Theory Construction* (Indianapolis; Ind.: The Bobbs-Merrill Company, Inc., 1971), p. 117.

[15] Ibid.

which ways are likely to yield the greatest meaning. Theory may also suggest a system for the researcher to impose on data in order to classify them in the most meaningful way. Theory also summarizes what is known about an object of study and states the uniformities that lie beyond the immediate observation; when it does so, it can also be used to predict further facts which should be found. The contribution of theory to research may become more apparent if an example of its application in a specific study is illustrated.

Michigan Telephone Study.   Case 4 in Chapter 1 discussed briefly the research study of social long distance telephone calling. The basic purpose of the study was to determine why some people made a large number of long distance calls for social purposes while others did not.

The researchers developed a theory by which they proposed to explain variations in the amount of long distance social calling by different people. It was their theory that some people habitually choose telephones to communicate with people far away. Their theory to explain these variations is elaborated in some detail in Figure 2–1. A discussion of various terms in this theory also illustrates the use of concepts, constructs, hypotheses, and operational definitions.

In sector A of Figure 2–1 the theoretical relationships underlying the research study are shown. The lines between the various construct labels represent proposed relationships that may be summarized in the following three propositions.[16]

1. The desire to contact distant friends and relatives is influenced by one's socioeconomic and personality characteristics.
2. Attitudes and perceptions concerning the means of communication are influenced by one's personality traits.
3. The choice of means used to contact distant friends and relatives is influenced by one's socioeconomic characteristics; the desire to contact those friends and relatives; and one's attitudes, perceptions, and experiences concerning communications.

In order to test this theory the researchers deduced specific hypotheses from these propositions, using operationally defined concepts. Thus, socioeconomic factors were defined in terms of five empirical measures: family income, education of family head, stage in family life cycle, perception of family member roles in placing long distance calls, and the number of family friends and relatives who live at a distance. Roughly, the hypotheses regarding socioeconomic measures were that the higher the income, the higher the education, and the more distant friends and relatives, the more long distance calls. Another hypothesis was that those families in the young and old stages were more frequent callers than those in the middle years of the life cycle.

---

[16] *Motives, Attitudes, and Long Distance Calls* (Ann Arbor, Mich.: Survey Research Center, University of Michigan, April 1956), p. 10.

Figure 2–1: Relating a Theory of Social Long Distance Telephone Calling to Empirical Reality

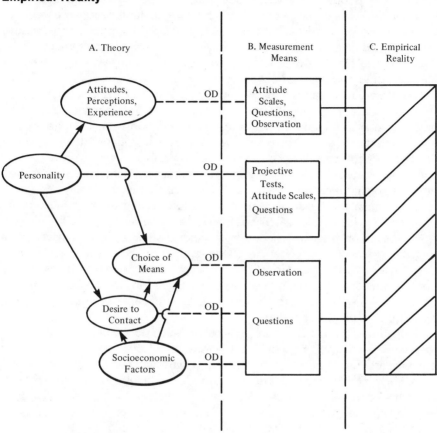

OD = Operational definition.
Source: Adapted from *Motives, Attitudes, and Long Distance Calls* (Ann Arbor, Mich.: Survey Research Center, University of Michigan, 1956).

Finally, it was hypothesized that those families in which the placing of long distance calls was viewed as "man's work" would make fewer calls.

Personality factors were operationally defined in terms of three measures: security-insecurity, need for affiliation, and the underlying attitudes toward money. The hypothesis concerning the relation of security to call rate was not clear. It was hypothesized that those with high need for affiliation and those classed as free spenders would also tend to be high callers.

Testing of the proposition concerning attitudes, perceptions, and experiences involved operationally defined ideas such as frequency of communication (regardless of medium), local phone usage practices as a measure of perception of the phone and its uses, experience in using phones at work, and feelings when using the phone. There was also an exploratory question about an imaginary phone user. It was hypothesized that people who made frequent local calls, who used the phone for visiting and chatting, who were frequent communicators regardless of the medium, who used the phone at work, and who reported pleasant feelings when making long distance calls, would all be frequent long distance callers. The projective question was for probing attitudes further and was not the source of a hypothesis.

The theory as it stands may be persuasive, but is it true? Is it possible that some parts are true and others false? The researchers needed to develop means (sector B in Figure 2–1) for testing the relationships. They developed and used attitude scales, projective techniques, and a detailed survey questionnaire. They also observed persons making calls and inspected telephone company records. By developing specific operational definitions they related empirical reality (sector C, Figure 2–1) to their theory (sector A).

To summarize, the development of the underlying theory provided the blueprint by which the research was planned and carried out. The theory itself drew heavily on prior knowledge from other disciplines (chiefly psychology and economics), the experiences of the company, and the research experiences of the investigators. Constructs, concepts, descriptive definitions, operational definitions, and hypotheses were combined in the development of a theory, which was then tested by the application of various research tools and techniques to empirical reality.

Models. The term "model" has gained such popularity that it threatens to become an all-purpose word for relationships among concepts. Many writers have attempted to define the term more narrowly but with little success to date. For example, one writer defines a model as "anything used to represent something else—a map used to represent a section of countryside is a model, and so is a chart used to represent concurrent changes in fuel oil sales and temperature."[17] Another view is: "Since the purpose of the model is the representation of relationships between or among concepts, the prerequisite for any model is a conceptual scheme. . . . Principle sources of conceptual schemes for model building will be theories, laws, hypotheses, and principles. . . . Models are not substitutes for conceptual schemes, principles, hypotheses, or theories but rather are devices to depict their concepts and the relationships which are involved. . . ."[18] Still another writer holds that models are equated to simulations, and a fourth source says that "Models are created by speculating about processes that could have produced the observed facts."[19]

---

[17] Robert D. Buzzell, *Mathematical Models and Marketing Management* (Boston: Graduate School of Business Administration, Harvard University, 1964), p. 9.

[18] Paul H. Rigby, *Conceptual Foundations of Business Research* (New York: John Wiley and Sons, Inc., 1965), p. 112.

[19] See, respectively, Paul Davidson Reynolds, *A Primer in Theory Construction* (Indianapolis, Ind.: The Bobbs-Merrill Company, Inc., 1971), p. 111, and Charles A. Lave and James G. March, *An Introduction to Models in the Social Sciences* (New York: Harper & Row, Publishers, 1975), p. 19.

In view of this confusion we will continue here to use such traditional terms as "proposition," "hypothesis," "theory," "law," and so forth. However, the popularity of "model" assures that it will creep into the discussion at times; when it does it will be used as a general synonym for any of the above-mentioned terms.

THE INFERENCE PROCESS

We use the inference process to develop understanding and beliefs about relationships among concepts. We build propositions and theories that agree with what we know and believe about the world. We develop our beliefs from a number of sources, not all of which can be defended as logical.

Sources of Belief

One important source is simply ungrounded suggestion. We are all suggestible to a degree, and many of our ideas are held because society takes them for granted or because we are so bombarded with a point of view that we grow to accept it. These ideas are often among our basic beliefs and present us with a particularly difficult handicap because we may hold them in spite of contradictory evidence.

Another source of beliefs is authority. We accept the testimony of someone else whom we judge to be expert in some way, especially if this person has provided reliable information in the past. However, too often the degree of authority depends on status or position rather than expertise. History shows that many "authorities" are later proved to be wrong.

A third major source of evidence is experience. We see, hear, feel, and are otherwise made aware of situations. This is a good source, but it is limited by our narrow range of exposure and distorted by our biases. Difficulties occur, especially when we interpret that experience. However, unless we attempt this interpretation, our knowledge remains meager.

None of these sources is infallible, but the critical analysis and testing of experience constitute our most reliable method. They are the essence of the scientific method. To rationalize our learning from experience, we need to understand the reasoning process.

Argument Analysis

A useful approach to the inference process is through the subject of communication. We normally communicate meanings either in everyday language or in some special-purpose language; we *discourse* on the subject of concern. "Discourse" is defined as a meaningful connection of a few sets of words, such as several sentences or more. One type of sentence commonly used is the declarative sentence, or *statement*. Statements can be opinions, denials, affirmations, or of many other forms, but they have one thing in common; each of them is either true or false.

When we communicate through statements we are engaging in one of two types of discourse. The first, *exposition,* consists of descriptive statements that merely state and do not give reasons. The second type, *argument,* is discourse that contains at least two statements, one of which is presented as a reason for the other. By the use of argument we explain, interpret, defend, challenge, and explore meanings. In essence we are using supposed truths as evidence in support of conclusions which are suppose also to be true. To believe a statement because we think that it logically follows from another statement is to make an *inference* or to *reason.* The two basic inference forms, both of great importance in research, are induction and deduction.

Induction.   This argument form consists of one or more reasons known as *evidence* plus a conclusion or inference drawn from this evidence. The reasons are alleged to be factual, and *the conclusion explains them.* The connection between the evidence and the conclusion is such that the former supports the latter, but there is no necessary logic connection between them in the same way that we will find with deduction.

Inductive conclusions are tentative inferential jumps beyond the evidence presented. That is, the conclusion is suggested by the evidence plus some other insight that occurs to us. For example, consider the situation of John Lacey, a salesman for the Square Box Company. He has one of the poorest sales records in the company. His unsatisfactory performance prompts us to ask the question "Why is he doing so badly?" From our knowledge of John's sales practices, the nature of box selling, and so forth we might conclude (hypothesize) that John's problem is that he makes too few sales calls per day to build a good sales record. There are other hypotheses which might also occur to us on the basis of available evidence. Among them are the following:

1. John's territory does not have the market potential of other territories.
2. John's sales-making skills are so poorly developed that he is not able to close sales effectively.
3. John's territory has been the scene of intense price cutting by local manufacturers, and this has caused him to lose many sales.
4. Some types of people just cannot sell boxes, and John is one of these people.

All of the above hypotheses are inductions which we might base on the evidence of John's poor sales record, plus some assumptions or beliefs which we hold about John and the selling of boxes. All of them have some chance of being true, but we would probably have more confidence in some than in others. All must be subject to further confirmation before we should hold any of them with much confidence. Confirmation comes with more evidence. The task of research is largely to determine the nature of the evidence needed and to design methods by which to discover and measure this other evidence. To help us do this we turn to the process of deduction.

Deduction. Deduction is a form of inference which purports to be conclusive—the conclusion must necessarily follow from the reasons given. These reasons are said *to imply the conclusion and to represent a proof.* This is a much stronger and different bond between reasons and conclusions than is found with induction.

For a deduction to be correct it must be *both true and valid.* That is, the premises (reasons) given for the conclusion must agree with the real world (be true). In addition, the premises must be arranged in a form such that the *conclusion must necessarily follow from the premises.* A deduction is valid if it is impossible for the conclusion to be false if the premises are true. Logicians have established rules by which one can judge whether a deduction is valid. Conclusions are not logically justified if (1) one or more premises is untrue or (2) the argument form is invalid. Yet, the conclusion may still be a true statement, but for reasons other than those given. For example, consider the following simple deduction:

(Premise 1)—All regular employees can be trusted not to steal.
(Premise 2)—John is a regular employee.
(Conclusion)—John can be trusted not to steal.

If we believe that John can be trusted we might feel that this is a sound deduction. But this conclusion cannot be accepted as a sound deduction unless the argument form is valid and the premises true. In this case the form is valid, and premise 2 can be easily confirmed. However, many may challenge the sweeping premise that "all regular employees can be trusted not to steal." While we may believe that John will not steal, such a conclusion is a sound deduction only if both premises are accepted as true. If one premise fails the acceptance test then the conclusion is not a sound deduction. This is so even if we still have great confidence in John's honesty. Our conclusion, in this case, must be based on our confidence in John as an individual rather than on a general premise that all regular employees are honest.

We may not recognize how much we use deduction to reason out the implications of various acts and conditions. For example, in planning a survey we might reason as follows:

(Premise 1)—Inner city household interviewing is especially difficult and expensive.
(Premise 2)—This survey involves substantial inner city household interviewing.
(Conclusion)—The interviewing in this survey will be especially difficult and expensive.

On reflection, it should be apparent to the reader that a conclusion which results from deduction is, in a sense, already "contained in" its premises.[20]

---

[20] Howard Kahane, *Logic and Philosophy,* 2d ed. (Belmont, Calif.: Wadsworth Publishing Company, Inc., 1973), p. 3.

There is no such strength of relationship between reasons and conclusion in induction.

In summary, deduction and induction are alike in one respect; both are inference processes with conclusions that are based on one or more reasons. They differ, however, in the nature of the relationship between reasons and conclusions. The inductive conclusion is a conjectural explanation of facts and observations that involves an inference leap. Such a conclusion may be strongly supported by many other facts, but it can never be proved. A deductive conclusion is a logical outcome of the reasons (premises) and is said to be "contained in" the premises. The conclusion is proved if the premises are true and the relationships between reasons and conclusion are in valid form.

The Induction-Deduction Sequence

There is a relationship between induction and deduction that has been described by John Dewey as the "double movement of reflective thought" (illustrated in Figure 2–2).[21] Induction occurs when one observes a fact and

Figure 2–2: The Double Movement of Reflective Thought

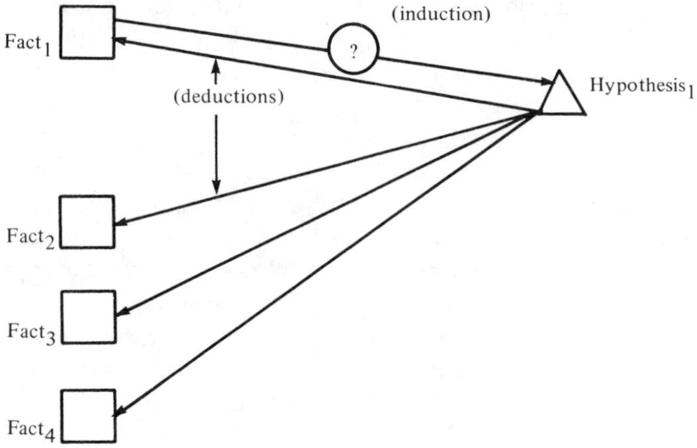

Fact₁—Some families have higher long distance call rates.
Fact₂—These families also have more friends and relatives who live at a distance.
Fact₃—High desire callers also have higher need affiliations.
Fact₄—High desire callers also make more local calls.

asks, "Why is this?" In answer to this question one advances a tentative explanation (hypothesis). The hypothesis is plausible if it explains the fact that prompted it.

A good hypothesis will explain (is a reason for) the fact or facts that lead to

---

[21] John Dewey, *How We Think* (Boston: D. C. Heath & Co., 1910), p. 79.

its being advanced. If it does not explain them, it is not a reasonable inductive conclusion. An inductive conclusion (hypothesis) can be taken as a premise and inserted in a deductive argument, and the observed fact should be the logical conclusion. Graphically speaking, these relationships are as follows:

Induction		*Deduction*	
Assumption (If A is B, then C is D)		Assumption (If A is B, then C is D)	
Fact	C is D	Explanation	A is B
Explanation	A is B	Fact	C is D

An example of the double movement process is shown in Figure 2–2. Consider again the study of long distance telephone users. How might the research designers have reasoned about the situation? A review of data from company call records indicated that some families did more long distance calling than did others. This fact (call it fact$_1$) led to the question of "Why should some families call much more frequently than other families?" One hypothesis advanced as an explanation was "Some families have a greater desire to contact friends and relatives than do others." The reasoning went as illustrated in the accompanying diagram.

Assumption—If there are people with a higher desire to contact others, these people will have a higher long distance telephone call rate.
Fact$_1$—We find that there are certain families with higher call rates.

Hypothesis—These are families with a higher desire to call others by long distance telephone.

If you compare this argument with the induction and deduction models in the preceding paragraph it should be apparent that this is an induction.

To test this hypothesis the researchers had to deduce facts from it (given certain assumptions). The first test was to deduce fact$_1$. That is, given assumption$_1$ and hypothesis$_1$, they must be able to deduce fact$_1$. This is the same as saying that any hypothesis must be a reasonable explanation for the fact that gives rise to it.

To put the hypothesis to a stronger test they had to deduce additional facts that should exist (again including assumptions). They then had to design a study to search for the existence of these facts. For example, they deduced that if there were families with a strong desire to contact friends and relatives by long distance telephone, these families would also have a higher than average number of friends and relatives who lived at a distance (fact$_2$). In like fashion they deduced that fact$_3$ and fact$_4$ should also be found.

This illustration suggests only one hypothesis, but in the actual telephone study there were other hypotheses advanced to explain some of the high call rates. These explanations were in terms both of socioeconomic factors and attitude factors. While this discussion of the long distance calling study is only partial and conjectural, it does illustrate the reasoning process which underlies research thinking. Recall, however, that *hypotheses are never proved.* They can be disproved (or falsified) by cases in which the hypothesis does not hold, but another supporting fact can be accepted only as an additional piece of information which is not contrary to the hypothesis. More will be presented on the problem of hypothesis confirmation in Chapter 4.

SUMMARY

The methods of science may be viewed in either a static or dynamic sense. In the latter case, emphasized here, science is seen as a process by which knowledge is tested. Whether an investigation is considered to be scientific or not depends on the subjective judgment of the evaluator. Generally speaking, one expects scientific research to be purposive, its goals to be clearly defined, the procedure to be replicable, and objectivity to be clearly evident. The reporting of procedures, their strengths and flaws, should be complete and honest; appropriate analytic techniques should be used; and the conclusions drawn should be limited to those clearly justified by the facts. If the researcher has an established reputation, so much the better.

Scientific methods and thinking are based on concepts, the symbols that we attach to bundles of meanings we hold and share with others. We invent concepts in order to be able to think about and communicate abstract meanings. We also use constructs—more highly abstract concepts which are invented for specific scientific explanatory purposes. Concepts and constructs may be defined descriptively or operationally. Operational definitions, which are especially significant in research, are stated in terms of specific testing criteria or operations. Good operational definitions must adequately specify the empirical information needed, how it will be collected, and have the proper scope or fit for the research problem at hand.

Of great interest in research are bivariate and multivariate propositions, describing relationships between or among variables. When we advance a proposition to explain tentatively some phenomenon, we are hypothesizing. A good hypothesis is one which can explain what it claims to explain, is testable, and has greater range, probability, and simplicity than its rivals. Sets of interrelated concepts, definitions, and propositions advanced to explain phenomena are theories.

The inference process is used in the development and testing of various propositions largely through the double movement of reflective thinking. This is a sequencing of induction-deduction processes by which one seeks inductively to explain (by a hypothesis) a puzzling condition. In turn the hypothesis is used in the deduction of further facts, which can be sought to confirm or deny the truth of the hypothesis.

SUPPLEMENTAL READINGS

1. Agnew, Neil Mck., and Pyke, Sandra W. *The Science Game.* Englewood Cliffs, N.J.: Prentice-Hall, Inc., 1969. A brief treatise on the rules of the "sciencing" game. The writers' aim is to help nonscientists to "develop a good feel for the science game." Entire book is recommended.
2. Beardsley, Monroe. *Practical Logic.* Englewood Cliffs, N.J.: Prentice-Hall, Inc., 1961, chaps. 7 and 15. A lucid discussion of deduction and induction as well as excellent coverage of argument analysis.
3. Helmstadter, G. C. *Research Concepts in Human Behavior.* New York: Appleton-Century-Crofts, 1970. Chap. 1 is useful, especially the section on the illogic of scientific practice.
4. Kerlinger, Fred N. *Foundations of Behavioral Research.* 2d ed. New York: Holt, Rinehart and Winston, 1973. An excellent and comprehensive book on most aspects of research methodology. Chaps. 2 and 3 are on hypotheses, definitions, and constructs.
5. Lave, Charles A., and March, James G. *An Introduction to Models in the Social Sciences.* New York: Harper & Row, Publishers, 1975. The first three chapters are especially recommended. They concern "model-building," which roughly equates here to hypothesis formation. Some interesting examples.
6. Phillips, Bernard S. *Social Research.* 2d ed. New York: The Macmillan Company, 1971. Chap. 2 is a good summary of the elements of inquiry.
7. Reynolds, Paul Davidson. *A Primer on Theory Construction.* Indianapolis, Ind.: The Bobbs-Merrill Company, Inc., 1971. This book presents a short but lucid discussion of the evaluation and construction of theories. A number of substantive theories are used to illustrate problems and clarify issues.
8. Selltiz, Claire; Wrightsman, Lawrence S.; and Cook, Stuart W. *Research Methods in Social Relations.* 3d ed. New York: Holt, Rinehart and Winston, 1976. See chap. 2 entitled "The Logic of Analysis."

DISCUSSION QUESTIONS

1. Distinguish among the following sets of terms and suggest the significance of each in a research context:
    a. Concept and construct.
    b. Deduction and induction.
    c. Operational definition and descriptive definition.
    d. Validity and truth in deduction.
    e. Fact and theory.
2. You have been given a research report written by a consulting firm for your organization. You are asked to judge the quality of the study. What would you look for?
3. Here are some terms commonly found in a management setting. Is each a concept or construct? When possible, provide an ostensive definition as well as descriptive and operational definitions for each.

first line supervisor
employee morale
assembly line
overdue account
line management

leadership
price-earnings ratio
union democracy
ethical standards

4. In your company's management development program recently there was a heated discussion between some people who claimed that "theory is impractical and thus no good" and others who claimed that "good theory is the most practical approach to problems." What position would you take and why?

5. You wish to study a condition which you have observed to the effect that "Some workers seem to be much more diligent than others."
   a. Propose at least three concepts and three constructs which you might use in such a study.
   b. How might any of these concepts and/or constructs be related in explanatory hypotheses?

6. Recently some interesting phenomena have been reported in the news. In each case propose two or more hypotheses which might account for the phenomena mentioned.
   a. Short men live significantly longer, on the average, than do taller men.
   b. A prominent professional football offensive lineman has decreased in height by a half inch over the past few years.
   c. College admissions test scores for engineering students average higher than scores for either liberal arts or business students.

7. Research reported by the U.S. Department of Health, Education, and Welfare indicates that from 1968 to 1974 the incidence of smoking stayed at about 15 percent for male teenagers. During this period the percentage of teenage female smokers grew from a little over 8 percent to 15 percent. Propose a theory that will explain why there was such a differential in 1968, but that it had disappeared by 1974.

8. Are the following deductions, inductions, or what? If there are gaps in them, add what is needed to make them complete arguments:
   a. Repeated studies indicate that economic conditions vary with—and lag 6 to 12 months behind—the changes in the national money supply. Therefore, we may conclude that the money supply is the basic economic variable.
   b. If worker morale is high, then worker output is high. We expect our new program to improve worker morale substantially. Therefore, we expect that output will rise.
   c. Research surveys show that heavy smokers have a higher rate of lung cancer than do nonsmokers; therefore, heavy smoking causes lung cancer.
   d. Show me a person who goes to church regularly, and I will show you a person who is a reliable worker.

9. Employ the double movement of reflective thought in each of the following examples to indicate one or more plausible hypotheses to explain the condi-

tion given. In addition deduce the conditions you would need for such a hypothesis to be tested.

a. Sales of Professor E's research book began to decline about a year after publication.

b. Imports from Taiwan under the textile import quota has grown faster in dollar values than in units.

c. Sales and profits for Company X were each expected to be up 10 percent this year. Sales are up 10 percent, but profits are down 3 percent.

SECTION TWO

RESEARCH DESIGN

Chapter 3

The Research Process

ROGER RESEARCHER has just returned to his office from a lunch meeting with Arley W. Banks, Executive Vice President of the First National Bank of Center City. Arley is relatively new at his job, having transferred to it from out of state only a few weeks ago. He soon observed that the bank was standing still compared to the other two major banks in this city of 50,000. The growth in First National's deposits and profits has stagnated and he is worried about getting the bank turned around. At lunch he put the question to Roger directly, "We need to get back on a growth track. Can you help me get a handle on this situation?" Roger asks for a day or so to think about it and look over some materials Arley has provided.

Roger begins to read some of the bank financial statements when the phone rings. It is Ed Bildor, a local contractor whom Roger met several weeks ago at a party. Ed has been very active in the development of subdivisions in Northridge, an old suburban town now becoming a high growth area. He has purchased substantial acreage for future expansion of his developments, but now the local planning board threatens to rezone his land in a way that will virtually eliminate any chance for profitable development. He is marshalling his arguments for a showdown with the planning board and feels a need for some quick research to support his position. He says, "What can you do for me?" Roger makes an appointment to meet him the next day and then leans back in his chair to think. How can he help these men with their problems?

We shall return to the problems of Arley and Ed soon, but first we need to lay some process groundwork. In Chapters 1 and 2 we have suggested that research is an orderly process, but we have deferred most of the process specifics to this point. In this chapter we will consider four topics: (1) the origin of the research need, (2) the decision value of research, (3) a generalized approach to guide the research process, and (4) the development of a research proposal.

THE ORIGIN OF A RESEARCH NEED

Academic Research. In an academic setting a particular study may grow out of no more than a student's need to select some research topic for a class assignment. More serious academic research tends to be developed within the bounds of some theoretical framework. In a classical sense it may be aimed at testing an aspect of some theory or expanding the domain of a theory. For example, much research in marketing is concerned with the development and testing of various aspects of consumer behavior theory. Likewise, in finance there is substantial research concentration on capital market theory, while in organizational behavior there is much research interest in the expectancy theory of motivation.

Applied Management Research. In an applied business context the research topic originates in the decision needs of the manager. While this presents almost infinite research possibilities, we will mention only a few major categories here. One group of problems grows out of questions about purposes and objectives. The general question is "What do we want to achieve?" At a companywide level this might be "What shall be our company purpose in the light of growing public criticism of the social role of business and the maturity of our industry?" A more specific objective may prompt a question such as "What aims shall we try to achieve in our next labor negotiations?"

A specific question can lead to many studies. Concern for the company's image in society might lead to a study among various publics or client groups as to their attitudes toward the company, or it might suggest research into what other industries or companies are doing in this area, or it might call for a forecast of the direction and degree of expected changes in social attitudes. The influence of industry maturity upon the company's purpose might lead to research to evaluate the possibilities for revitalization of the industry, to investigations of other opportunities for the company, or to a search for merger partners.

Another set of management decisions involves the generation and evaluation of solutions. The general question is "How can we achieve the ends we seek?" Research projects in this class usually deal with concrete problems which managers quickly recognize as being useful. Such projects may involve strategic questions such as "How shall we achieve our five-year goal of doubled sales and net profits?" At a more tactical level the questions may be as specific as "Which of three approaches is the most effective way to organize the shipping department?"

A third class of management problems concerns the troubleshooting or control situation. It usually involves monitoring or diagnosing which ways an organization may appear to be failing to achieve its established goals. It includes such questions as "Why is department A the high cost department?" and "How well is our program meeting its goals?"

The business researcher also finds substantial opportunity in the environment in which an organization functions. These external concerns cut across the objectives-strategy-control classification just presented and may include such topics as the study of prospective acquisition candidates, the nature and trend of government regulation, cultural changes, technology developments, and many other topics.

Two Problem Origins.   Although it is desirable for research to be thoroughly grounded in management decision priorities, there is too often a tendency for studies to wander off target or be less effective than they should. Two major causes of this deviation are researcher obsession with certain techniques and an attractive data bank.

Availability of technique is an important factor in determining how research shall be done and even whether a given study can be done. Persons skilled in given techniques are too often blinded by their special competencies. Their concern for technique dominates the decisions concerning what will be studied and how. In recent years operations researchers have frequently been accused of approaching problems with the attitude of "How can I use OR techniques here?" rather than "What is the nature of the problem, and how can it best be approached?" This criticism has often been justified, but the same judgment can be made of many others. Some researchers think chiefly of conducting surveys. Some emphasize the case study, while others seldom consider it. The past reluctance of most social scientists to use experimental designs has been an important factor in retarding the development of scientific research in their fields.

The existence of a pool of information seems to distract one from the need for other research. Modern management information systems can provide massive volumes of data. Too often the feeling is "We should use all of this information before we do anything else." But the provision and use of management information extends beyond what is normally called research. The emphasis here is on information projects that tend to be nonroutine, nonrecurring, and complex in nature. They are separate and discrete decision-oriented activities that managers may cause to be undertaken if they judge them to be worthwhile. This judgment process is the subject of the next section.

THE VALUE OF RESEARCH INFORMATION

Managers' motivations for seeking research help vary, and may not always be fully evident. They may feel a real need for specific information by which to guide a decision. At other times the study may be authorized chiefly because its presence may promote approval for a decision the managers are quite willing to make without research. At other times research may be authorized as a measure of personal protection for the decision makers in case the decision is criticized later.

An appropriate research study can help managers avoid losses and increase profits, or it can be a waste. The decision makers usually must face this evaluation question. Typically they want a firm cost estimate for a project and an equally precise assurance that useful information will result from the study. Even if the researcher can give good cost and information estimates, the managers still must judge whether the benefits outweigh the costs. This evaluation is usually a subjective one, although two other approaches have been tried; they are ex post facto evaluation and the decision theory approach.

The Problems of Information Valuation

Conceptually the value of applied research is not difficult to determine. In a business situation the research should produce added revenues or reduce expenses in much the same way as any other investment of resources. One source suggests that the value of research information may be judged in terms of "the difference between the results of decisions made with the information and the results that would be made without it."[1] While such a criterion is simple to state, its actual use presents some difficult measurement problems.

Ex Post Facto Evaluation.   If there is any measurement of the value of research, it is usually an after-the-fact event. Twedt reported on one such effort, an evaluation of marketing research done at a major corporation.[2] He secured "an objective estimate of the contribution of each project to corporate profitability." He reports that most studies were intended to help management determine which of two (or more) alternatives was preferable. He guessed that in 60 percent of the decision situations the correct decision would have been made *without* the benefit of the research information. In the remaining 40 percent of the cases the research led to the correct decision. Using these data, he estimated that the return on investment in marketing research in this company was 351 percent for the year studied. However, he acknowledges that the "return on investment" figure was inflated because only the direct research costs had been included.

---

[1] Robert D. Buzzell, Donald F. Cox, and Rex V. Brown, *Marketing Research and Information Systems* (New York: McGraw-Hill Book Company, 1969), p. 595.

[2] Dik Warren Twedt, "What Is the 'Return on Investment' in Marketing Research?" *Journal of Marketing*, vol. 30 (January 1966), pp. 62–63.

This effort at cost-benefit analysis is commendable, even though it is only a tentative first step. One may be able to judge after the fact whether the research study was justified, given certain assumptions. While the results come too late to guide the current research decision, such analysis may sharpen the manager's ability to make judgments about future research proposals. However, the critical problem remains, that of project evaluation *before the study is done*.

Prior Evaluation.   The challenge to effective research evaluation is the inability of the evaluator to measure or forecast the benefits and costs of the project. For example, a proposal to conduct a thorough management audit of operations in a company may be a very worthy one, but neither its costs nor its benefits are easily estimated in advance. Such projects are sufficiently unique that managerial experience seldom provides much aid in evaluating such a proposal either.

Even in these complex situations, however, managers often can make some useful judgments. They may be able to determine that a management audit is needed because the company is in dire straits and management does not understand the scope of its problems. The management information need may be so great as to assure that the research is approved. In such cases they may decide to control the research expenditure risk by requesting a stepwise study. They can then review costs and benefits at the end of each step and give or withhold further authorization. Typical of this approach is the two-stage study discussed later in this chapter.

Option Analysis.   Some progress has been made in the development of methods for assessing the value of research input when the management problem is a choice between well-defined options. Each alternative can be judged in terms of estimated costs and benefits associated with it and a formal analysis can be conducted, but managerial judgment still plays a major role.

While both costs and benefits present major estimating problems, the development of the cost side of the equation is normally the easiest. If the research design can be stated clearly, one can estimate an approximate cost. The critical task is to quantify the benefits from the research. At best, estimates of benefits are crude and largely reflect a more orderly way to estimate outcomes under uncertain conditions. To illustrate how the contribution of research is evaluated in such a decision situation, we must digress briefly into the rudiments of decision theory.

Decision Theory Approach

To compare two or more alternatives, a manager must estimate the expected outcome of each alternative. The case of two choices will be discussed here, although the same approach can be used with more than two choices. Two possible actions (A_1 and A_2) may represent two different ways to organize a company, to provide financing, to produce a product, and so forth.

We need not specify the nature of the alternatives in order to describe the approach.

When there are alternatives from which to choose, a rational way to approach the decision is to try to assess the outcomes of each course of action; then one can choose the outcome which best meets the criterion established for judging alternatives. This criterion is a combination of a *decision rule* and a *decision variable.* For example, the decision variable might be "direct dollar savings," "contribution to overhead and profits," "time required for completion of the project," and so forth.

Usually the decision variable is expressed in dollars, representing sales, costs, or some form of profits or contribution. The decision rule may be "choose the course of action with the lowest loss possibility" or perhaps "choose the alternative which provides the greatest annual net profit." The alternative selected depends on the decision variable chosen and the decision rule used. The evaluation of alternatives requires that (1) they be explicitly stated, (2) a decision variable be defined by which the outcome may be measured, and (3) a decision rule be determined by which outcomes may be compared.

For example, Mr. White, the manager, may be trying to decide whether to make a major equipment change in a production department. The new equipment can be leased for five years and will replace several old machines, the operation of which requires constant attention. The problem facing him is "Shall I lease the new machine, with its attendant efficiencies, reduced labor input, and high lease charges, or shall I continue to use the older equipment?"

The decision situation has been precipitated by information that the firm may secure several very large orders from companies which have not previously been customers. With this added volume he expects that his departmental profit contribution will go up substantially if he has the new equipment. For this decision, he adopts as the decision variable "average annual departmental profit contribution."[3] He adopts as a decision rule, "Choose that course of action which will provide the highest average annual contribution to departmental profits."

Table 3–1 indicates the results of the evaluation of the two available courses of action. Under the conditions cited, it is obvious that course A_1 is to be preferred.

Conditions of Certainty. Table 3–1 presents the case with the assumption that the anticipated new business will materialize. It therefore represents, in decision theory terminology, *decision making under conditions of certainty.* It has been assumed that the payoffs are certain to occur if the particular course of action is chosen and that the probability of the additional

---

[3] Recall that the decision variable is the unit of measurement used in the analysis. At this point we need not be concerned with how this measure is calculated or whether it is the appropriate decision variable. Assume for purposes of this illustration that it is appropriate.

Table 3–1: Payoff under Conditions of Certainty

Course of Action	Average Annual Department Profit Contribution
A_1—Lease new equipment	$20,000
A_2—Retain old equipment	12,000

business being secured is 1.0.[4] The decision to choose course of action A_1 is obvious under these conditions with the given payoff data and decision rule.

Conditions of Uncertainty. In a more realistic situation the outcome is recognized to be less than certain. The new business may not materialize, and then the department might be left with costly excess capacity. The union may resist the introduction of the new equipment which replaces a worker. The new equipment may not perform as anticipated. For these or other reasons, the decision maker may be uncertain about the consequences (for instance, that course A_1 will result in a $20,000 contribution).

Suppose that Mr. White gives these other possible outcomes some consideration and concludes that the one serious uncertainty is that the new business may not be forthcoming. For purposes of simplicity of analysis, he concludes that one of two conditions will exist in the future—either the new business will be secured as expected (O_1) or the new business will not materialize (O_2). In the first case the expected payoffs would be the same as in Table 3–1; but if the new business is not secured, then the addition of the new equipment would give the department costly excess capacity with fixed lease changes. The payoff table may now be revised as in Table 3–2.

Table 3–2: Payoff under Conditions of Uncertainty

	Average Annual Departmental Profit Contribution		Expected Monetary Value
	New Business (O_1)	No New Business (O_2)	
A_1—Lease new equipment	$20,000	$5,000	$14,000
A_2—Retain old equipment	12,000	9,000	10,800

---

[4] A probability is a measure between 1.0 and 0.0 which expresses the likelihood of an event occurring. For example, the probability of a "head" on a toss of a coin is 0.5. Under conditions of certainty the forecasted outcome is assumed to have a probability of 1.0 even though we might agree that we normally cannot know the future with certainty. In most forecasting where a specific amount is named, there is an implicit assumption of certainty.

Under these conditions the original decision rule does not apply. That rule said, "Choose that course of action which will provide the highest average annual departmental profit contribution." Under the conditions in Table 3–2, action A_1 would be better if the new business is secured, but A_2 would be the better choice if the new business is not secured. If Mr. White can delay his decision until the new order question is resolved, he can escape this dilemma. On the other hand, because of lead times he may have to make the equipment decision first.

When faced with two or more possible outcomes for each alternative, Mr. White can adopt one of two approaches. He may conclude that he cannot judge the likelihood that the company will receive the new business. Even so, he may still make a rational decision by adopting an appropriate decision rule. For example, he may use the rule "Choose that course of action for which the minimum payoff is the highest." This is known as the *maximin criterion* because it calls for maximizing the minimum payoff. In Table 3–2 the minimum payoff for alternative A_1 is shown as $5,000, and the minimum payoff for A_2 is $9,000. According to the *maximin* rule the choice would be A_2 because it is the best of the worst outcomes. This decision strategy is a "cut your losses" strategy.

The second approach is for Mr. White to use subjective judgment to estimate the probability that either O_1 or O_2 will take place.[5] When the assumption was decision under certainty, he tacitly assumed that only one event was possible (had a probability of 1.0). Now, however, he uses his experience and information from other sources to conclude that there is a less-than-certain chance of the new business materializing and that he should incorporate this doubt into the decision.

He might estimate that there is a 0.6 chance that the new business will be secured and a 0.4 chance that it will not. With this or any other set of similar probabilities, Mr. White can now arrive at an overall evaluation of the two

---

[5] There are three types of situation into which concepts of probability enter. In the classical situation each possible outcome has a known chance of occurrence. For example, a fair coin tossed in the air has a 0.5 chance of landing heads up; a spade card has a 0.25 chance of being drawn from a well-mixed deck.

In the same type of situation, probabilities are thought of in terms of "relative frequency." Even if the probability is not known from the structure of the problem (as it is in the classical case), it can still be estimated if there is a body of empirical evidence. For example, experience may show that about 1 in 50 products produced is defective. From this statistic one can estimate that there is a 0.02 chance that any given product will be defective.

If there is no direct empirical evidence, one can still assess probability on the basis of opinion, intuitions, and/or general experience. In such cases uncertainty is expressed in terms of a subjectively felt "degree of confidence" or "degree of belief" that a given event will occur. The discussions in this chapter are cases in point. For more information on probability concepts, see any modern statistics text.

courses of action. One approach is to calculate an *expected monetary value* (*EMV*) for each alternative.[6]

The Decision Flow Diagram.   The decision problem already has been summarized in a payoff table, but further illustration in the form of a decision flow diagram (or decision "tree") may be helpful. The decision tree for the equipment problem is shown in Figure 3–1. The diagram may be seen as a

Figure 3–1: Decision Tree for Equipment Problem

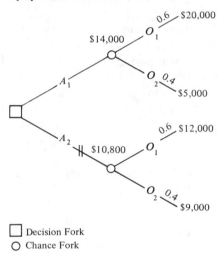

☐ Decision Fork
○ Chance Fork

sequential decision flow. At the square node on the left Mr. White must choose between A_1 and A_2. After he chooses one of these courses of action, a chance event will take place—either the new business will be received by the company (O_1) or it will not be received (O_2). At the right extremity of the branches are listed the conditional payoffs that will occur for each combination of decision and chance event. On each chance branch is placed the expected probability of that chance event occurring. Keep in mind that these are subjective probability estimates by Mr. White, expressing his degree of belief that such a chance event will occur.

---

[6] One caiculates an *EMV* for an alternative by weighting each conditional value (for example, $20,000 and $5,000 for A₁) by the estimated probability of the occurrence of the associated event (for example, 0.6 probability of the $20,000 being made).

$$EMV = P_1 (\$20,000) + P_2 (\$5,000)$$
$$= 0.6 (\$20,000) + 0.4 (\$5,000)$$
$$= \$14,000$$

Having set up this series of relationships, he calculates back from right to left on the diagram by an *averaging out* and *folding back* process. At each decision juncture he selects the path which yields the best alternative to the decision rule. In this case the *EMV* for A_1 averages out to $14,000, while the *EMV* for A_2 is $10,800. The double slash line on the A_2 branch indicates that it is the inferior alternative and should be dropped in favor of A_1.

The Contribution of Research. At this point the contribution of research can be assessed. Recall that the value of research may be judged as "the difference between the results of decisions made with the information and the results that would be made without it." In this example the important research need is to determine whether the new business will be secured. This is the major uncertainty which, if known, would make a perfect forecast possible. Just how much is a perfect forecast worth in this case?

Consider Figure 3–1 once again. What would happen if Mr. White had information by which he could accurately predict whether the new business orders would be secured? He would choose A_1 if the research indicated that the orders would be received, and A_2 if research indicated that the orders

Figure 3–2: The Value of Perfect Information

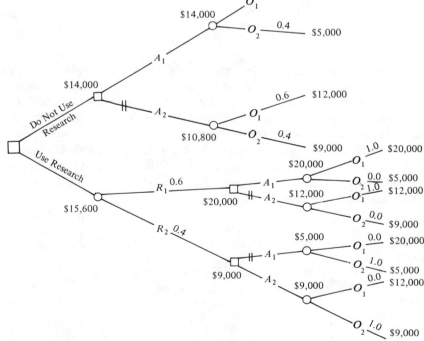

would not be received. However, at the decision point (before the research is undertaken) the best estimate is that there is a 0.6 chance that the research will indicate the O_1 condition and 0.4 that the condition will be O_2. The decision flow implications of the use of research are illustrated in Figure 3–2.

The decision sequence begins with the decision fork at the left. If Mr. White chooses to do research (R), he comes to the first chance fork, where one of two things will occur. Research indicates either that the orders will be received (R_1), or the orders will not be received (R_2). Before he does the research, the best estimate of the probability of R_1 taking place is the same as the estimate that O_1 will occur (This is, 0.6). In like manner the best estimate that R_2 will occur is 0.4.

After Mr. White learns R_1 or R_2, he moves on to a second decision fork; shall he take A_1 or A_2? After the A_1–A_2 decision there is a second chance fork $(O_1$ or $O_2)$, which indicates whether or not the actual orders were received. Note, however, that the probabilities at O_1 and O_2 have now changed from 0.6 and 0.4, respectively, to 1.0 and 0.0, or to 0.0 and 1.0, depending upon what was learned at the research stage. This change occurs because we have evaluated the effect of the research information on our original O_1 and O_2 probability estimates by calculating *posterior probabilities.* These are revisions of our prior probabilities that result from the assumed research findings. The posterior probabilities (for example, $P(O_1|R_i)$ and $P(O_2|R_i)$ are calculated by using Bayes theorem.[7]

Research Outcomes	States of Nature		Marginal Probabilities	Posterior Probabilities	
	O_1	O_2		$P(O_1|R_i)$	$P(O_2|R_i)$
R_1	0.6	0.0	0.6	1.0	0.0
R_2	0.0	0.4	0.4	0.0	1.0
Marginal probabilities	0.6	0.4			

Mr. White is now ready to average out and fold back the analysis from right to left in order to evaluate the research alternative. Clearly, if R_1 is found, he will choose A_1 with its *EMV* of $20,000 over the A_2 alternative of $12,000. In like fashion, if R_2 is reported, then A_2 is more attractive. However, prior to the research, the probabilities of R_1 and R_2 being secured must be incorporated by a second averaging out. The result is an *EMV* of $15,600 for the research alternative versus an *EMV* of $14,000 for the no-research path. The conclu-

---

[7] Bayes theorem with two states of nature is:

$$P(O_1|R_i) = \frac{P(R_i|O_1) \times P(O_1)}{P(R_i|O_1) \times P(O_1) + P(R_i|O_2) \times P(O_2)}$$

$$= \frac{1.0 \times 0.6}{(1.0 \times 0.6) + (0.0 \times 0.4)}$$

$$= 1.0$$

sion then is this: Research which would enable Mr. White to make a perfect forecast regarding the potential new orders would be worth up to $1,600. If the research costs more than $1,600, he would decline to buy it because the net *EMV* of the research alternative would be less than the *EMV* of $14,000 of the no-research alternative.

Imperfect Information. The analysis to this point assumes that research on decision options will give a perfect prediction of the future states of nature O_1 and O_2. Perfect prediction seldom occurs in actual practice. Sometimes research indicates one condition when later evidence shows something else to be the case. Thus, we need to consider that the research in the machinery decision example will provide less than perfect information and is, therefore, worth less than the $1,600 calculated in Figure 3–2.

Suppose that the research in that example involves interviews with the customers' key personnel as well as some of the customers' executives. They might all answer our questions to the best of their ability but still predict imperfectly what will happen. Consequently, we might judge that the chances of their predictions being correct are no better than 3 to 1, or 0.75. If we accept that our research results may provide imperfect information in this manner we need to factor this into our research evaluation decision. We do this by averaging out and folding back again. The results are shown in Figure 3–3. The revised *EMV,* given research judged to be 75 percent reliable, is $14,010. This revised *EMV* is only $10 higher than the $14,000 *EMV* using no research and would seem to be hardly worth consideration.

Pragmatic Complications. This discussion, while simplified, contains the basic concepts for a determination of the value of research. However, practical difficulties complicate the use of these concepts. First, the situation

Figure 3–3: The Value of Imperfect Information

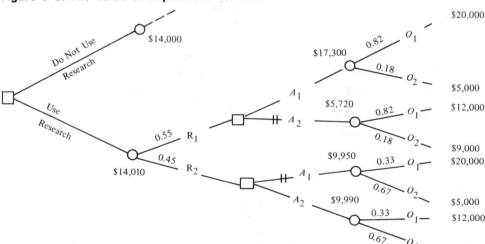

with two events and two alternatives is artificial. Problems with more choices and events are common, and the chief complication is the increased number of calculations.

Research Outcomes	States of Nature		Marginal Probabilities	Posterior Probabilities	
	O_1	O_2		$P(O_1|R_i)$	$P(O_2|R_i)$
R_1	0.45	0.1	0.55	0.82	0.18
R_2	0.15	0.3	0.45	0.33	0.67
Marginal probabilities	0.60	0.40			

A more serious problem is posed by the measurement of outcomes. In the example we assumed that we could assess the various courses of action in terms of an unambiguous dollar value, but often we cannot. It is very difficult to place a dollar value on outcomes related to morale or public image, for example.

An allied problem lies in the exclusive use of *EMV* as the criterion for decision. This approach is correct in an actuarial sense and implies that each decision maker has a linear system of evaluation. In truth we often use another evaluation system. For example, the person who accepts *EMV* as a criterion sees that an even bet of $20 between two people on the toss of a fair coin is a fair bet. Many people, however, may not be willing to make such a bet because they fear the loss of $20 more than they value the gain of $20. They may need to be offered a chance, say, to win $20 but to lose only $10 before they would be willing to bet. These persons have a nonlinear decision scale. The "utility" concept is more relevant in this case.

The development of more precise methods of evaluating the contribution of research is now only at the pioneer stage. In the meantime continued emphasis on improvement of our understanding of the researcher's task and the research process will make research more valuable when it is conducted.

THE DELINEATION OF THE RESEARCH TASK

Researchers can contribute more in some decision areas than in others. How effective they can be is influenced by how well they meet two sets of challenges. The first, which they will encounter in the relationship with others in the organization, is client-oriented. The other set is related to the technical skills they bring to bear. We treat the client-oriented problems first.

Problems of Client Relations

If a management problem dominates the research, then good rapport should exist between researcher and the manager-client. Researchers should have full access to managers, their thinking on the problems, and their priorities regarding them. The specification of the management problem is properly a client responsibility, but the researcher needs to know the problem background in order to function well.

An effective working relationship between researcher and manager is not easily achieved unless several critical barriers can be overcome.[8] Some of these barriers can be traced to the managers' limited exposures to research. They seldom have either formal training in research methodology or research expertise gained through experience.

In addition, managers often see research people as threats to their personal status. They still view management as the domain of the "intuitive artist" who is the master in this area. They may feel that a request for research assistance will imply that they are inadequate to the task. These fears may often be justified. The researcher's function is to test old ideas as well as new ones. The insecure manager may see the researcher as a potential competitor.

The researcher will also inevitably have to consider the political situations that develop in an organization. Members strive to maintain their niches and may seek ascendency over their colleagues. Coalitions tend to form, and people engage in various suboptimizing activities, both overt and covert. As a result, often research is blocked or the findings or objectives of the research are distorted for an individual's self-serving purposes. To allow one's operations to be probed with a critical eye may be to invite trouble from others competing for promotion, resources, or other forms of organizational power.

A fourth organizational problem originates in the explosive growth of research technology in recent years. A knowledge gap has developed between manager and research specialist as model building and more sophisticated investigative techniques have come into use. The manager must now put faith in the research specialist and hope for the best.

A fifth source of client-related stress for the researcher is the frequent isolation from managers. Researchers tend to draw back into their specialty and communicate only among themselves. This problem is compounded by the manager's lack of understanding. The research department thus becomes an isolated, technical job shop. These problems have caused some people to advocate the use of a "research generalist." Such a person would head the research activity, help managers detail their research needs, and translate these needs into research problems. He or she would also facilitate the flow of information between manager and research specialist which is so important for briefing the researcher into the decision-making process. While this is an attractive idea it does not appear to be taking place in many companies.

Research Question Development

Is It Researchable?   Not all questions are researchable, and not all research questions are answerable. To be researchable a question must be

---

[8] Joseph W. Newman, "Put Research into Marketing Decisions," *Harvard Business Review*, vol. 60 (March–April 1962), pp. 105–12.

one for which observation or other data collection in the real world can provide the answer. Many questions cannot be answered on the basis of information alone.

Important value elements that must be weighed are often a part of management decisions. For example, management may be asking, "Should we hold out for a liberalization of the seniority rules in our new labor negotiations?" While factual information can be brought to bear on this question, such additional considerations as "fairness to the workers" or "management's right to manage" may be important in the decision. It may be possible for much in these questions of value to be transformed into questions of fact. For example, concerning "fairness to the workers," one might first gather information from which to estimate the extent and degree to which workers will be affected by a rules change; second, one could gather opinion statements of the workers about the fairness of seniority rules. Even so, substantial value elements still remain. Left unanswered are such questions as "Should we argue for a policy which will adversely affect the security and well-being of older workers who are least well-equipped to cope with this adversity?"

Even if a question appears to be answerable by facts alone, it may not be researchable because our procedures or techniques are inadequate. For example, we may pose such questions as "How will a new policy affect profitability?" or "Which new employees have potential for top management?" Certain facts might suggest answers to these questions, but our present research techniques may be inadequate to the task of gathering the facts. Thus, while the arts of forecasting have advanced markedly, we still cannot predict many things accurately; there is no convincing evidence that a reliable test of employee promotability has been devised.

The Question Hierarchy in Research. A useful way to approach the research process is to view it as a four-level hierarchy of questions. The process begins at the most general level with the *management problem or question,* which initiates the research interest. The management question is the decision problem facing the executive. Since its definition sets the research direction, an incorrect management question leads to misdirected, often useless, research.

Information needs grow out of the management question and lead to the second level, the *research question,* which reflects the general purposes of the research. Often it is only one question, although it may be more. Its successful answering provides the manager with the desired research information.

Once the general research question has been defined, the research moves to the third level—*investigative questions.* These are specific questions which the researcher must answer in order satisfactorily to answer the broad research question. These subquestions, limited in number, are fractionated out of the major research question. They guide the details of the research effort, including the development of concepts, operational definitions, and measurement devices. There may be several sublevels of investigative questions, each being progressively narrower in scope.

Measurement questions constitute the fourth level. In surveys the measurement questions are those which are actually asked of respondents. They make up the questionnaire or interview guide. In an observation study measurement questions are those which each observer must answer about each subject studied. In an experiment the researcher asks and records answers to measurement questions about each subject studied.

In Chapter 2 it was pointed out that research tasks may be specified in either hypothesis or question format. Questions are more typical in applied and descriptive studies; hypotheses are more common in causal and pure research. Within the four-level hierarchy proposed here, the management problem usually is—and the measurement level almost always is—in question form. The ideas expressed at the research and investigative levels may be in either hypothesis or question format.

The four question levels are interrelated, and fractionation is suggested as a useful way of conceptualizing their development. The specific nature of each level and its relationship with other levels may be clearer if illustrated.

Question Hierarchy Example. Let's now return to the problems of Arley Banks which were introduced at the chapter's introduction. Recall that his bank, the First National Bank of Center City, is the dominant and oldest bank in this city of 50,000 people. At present its competitive position is slipping. Deposits and profits have stagnated. How might the research question hierarchy look when Roger Researcher analyzes this situation? His analysis looked like this:

1. Management Question: *"How can we recover the momentum of our deposit and profit growth?"*

    The bank management faces the task of developing some strategies for increasing deposits and profits. A number of directions might be taken. First, the managers might attempt a diagnostic study to determine the major causes of the decline. They might further consider various actions which might improve the situation. They decide to consider the diagnostic situation first.

2. Research Question: *"What are the major factors contributing to the bank's failure to maintain its growth in deposits?"*

    Since this bank has done no research in the past and has little specific information about competitors, a first study is proposed for defining more clearly the sources of the problem. A decision is made that two lines of investigation should be carried out at the same time. One is a study of the bank market structure and competitive situation in this city. This study, which might be called the "external study," is the one discussed further here. The second study is a detailed internal analysis of operating procedures, personalities, cost structures, personnel morale, and so forth. The objective of these internal studies is the improvement of profit margins, while the external study addresses the problem of deposit growth.

3. Investigative Questions: Two major investigative questions, each with subquestions, are posed.
    A. *What is the public's position with regard to financial services and their use?*
        1. What specific financial services are used?
        2. How attractive are various services?
        3. What factors influence a person's use of a particular service?
    B. *What is the bank's competitive position?*
        1. What are the geographic patterns of our customers and of our competitors' customers?
        2. What is indicated by demographic differences among our customers and those of our competitors?
        3. How aware is the public of bank promotional efforts?
        4. What general opinions does the public hold of us and our competitors?
        5. How does growth in service classes compare among competing institutions?
4. Measurement Questions: A survey is conducted among local residents. The questionnaire, which takes about 30 minutes to administer, contains a wide variety of questions concerning specific facts and opinions.

Successive fractionation of questions from (1) the management question to (2) research question to (3) investigative questions to (4) measurement questions is a useful way to move into the details of the research process. This survey was conducted with more than 200 respondents, and the results were used to guide a reorientation of the bank management's strategies.

THE RESEARCH PROCESS

Writers usually treat the research task as a sequential process involving a number of clearly delineated steps. Variations may be suggested for different situations, but there is much similarity among the sequences proposed. No one, however, claims that the research process is truly linear, moving through each clearly defined step in order. Recyclings, circumventions, and skips tend to occur. Some steps are begun out of sequence, some are carried on simultaneously, and some may be omitted. In spite of these variations, a concept of sequence is useful when we try to develop a project and keep it orderly as it unfolds.

The investigation usually begins with a stimulus that provokes interest in a particular subject area. Perhaps some controversy arises, a major commitment of resources is called for, or certain environmental conditions signal the need for a decision. Such events cause managers to reconsider their purposes or objectives, define a problem for solution, or develop strategies for the solution of problems that they have identified. For example, a company may be interested in enhancing its position in a given technology that appears to hold potential for future growth. This interest, or need, might quickly elicit a number of research ideas.

The manager's need for information stimulates a search for a clearer definition of the problem and a determination of the feasibility of specific types of research. How quickly this determination is made is a function of the concreteness of the problem and the experience of the researcher in dealing with it. In general, the research sequence consists of four major stages:

1. Exploration of the situation.
2. Development of the research design.
3. Data collection.
4. Analysis and interpretation of the results.

Each of these will be discussed in some detail.

Exploration

The managers' interests in the particular technology and what they need to know to make decisions about it will lead to certain subsidiary questions, such as:

1. How fast might this technology develop?
2. What are the likely applications of this technology?
3. What companies now possess it, and which ones are likely to make a major effort to get it?
4. What actions will be required for us to acquire it?
5. How much will it take in resources?
6. What are the payoffs likely to be?

These questions are only suggestive of the many angles of interest that managers might have in such a situation.

A problem like this is not easy for the researchers to define, and often they have had little specific prior experience. Nevertheless, the client-managers are anxious to have a definitive research proposal, including time and budget estimates, as well as some predictions of the type of information which may be secured. The clarity with which the research problem and the investigative approach can be defined will suggest one of two research strategies.

If the problem is in an area in which the investigators have previously conducted research, they may move quickly to the development of the basic research proposal with its specific plans and budget. However, the problem posed above is not likely to be so easy to solve. In this ill-defined, complex situation the researchers might propose a different approach.

Two-Stage Approach.   Using this format, the researchers break away the exploration stage as a separate study for the clearer definition of the problem and the appropriate type and scope of research. This first, exploratory, stage is usually proposed as a preliminary, definitional study of limited scope and budget.

In arguing for a two-stage approach, the researchers admit that there is much about the problem which they do not know and which should be known before a major commitment of effort and resources is made. In such circumstances the researchers are operating in unknown areas, where it is difficult to predict the problems and costs of the study. The two-stage proposal is particularly useful when the research is to be done on a fixed-cost basis and the complications and problems that will be encountered are difficult to anticipate. A limited exploration for a specific, modest cost carries less risk for both parties and often uncovers information that reduces the total research cost. Sometimes the evidence uncovered in the exploration indicates that the major study is unnecessary. The amount of exploration should depend on the researchers' general level of knowledge of the subject under study.

Exploratory Steps.   An exploration typically begins with a search of published data. In addition, the researchers often seek out well-informed people on the topic, especially those who have clearly stated positions on controversial aspects of the problem and those who might have been exposed to potentially important variables.

In the above investigation of opportunities in a new area of technology, the researchers would probably begin with specific books and periodicals. They would be looking for only certain aspects in this literature, such as (1) recent developments, (2) predictions by informed figures about the prospects of the technology, (3) identification of those involved in the area, and (4) accounts of successful ventures and failures by others in the field.

After familiarization with the literature, they might seek interviews with scientists and engineers who are well known in the field. They would give special attention to those who stand at the extremes of opinion about the prospects of the technology. If possible, they would talk with persons having knowledge about successes and failures in the area. Of course, much of the information will be confidential and competitive. However, skillful investigation can uncover many useful indicators.

After this relatively unstructured exploration the researchers are in a position to (1) define the research problem more specifically and (2) determine what they have to do to secure the answers to the posed research questions. The problem chosen should be "do-able" within the constraints that have been imposed. Before making the final statement of the problem there should be some additional "scouting" to assure that the information can be secured. This may involve securing permissions of some sort and assuring that certain critical information will be available.

Development of Design

At this point the development of the formal research design begins. The research questions are set, and the general-level investigative questions have been derived. These may be stated in the form of hypotheses to be tested or questions to be answered. The classical form, of course, is the hypothesis.

The steps involved in the designing of a study depend to some extent on the nature of the specific project. As a general procedure, however, the following steps are common:

1. The major concepts or constructs to be used in the study are defined. Further operational definitions emerge as the design process continues.
2. The investigative questions are reviewed and typically need to be further broken down into more specific secondary and tertiary-level questions. In effect this is the process of determining what evidence must be collected to test the major hypotheses or answer the questions.
3. At this point the general direction of the research has probably made clear which of the various research or design types is most appropriate. For example, it may be decided that a survey, or an experiment, or some other design should be used.
4. A fourth task is the construction of the specific measurement instruments. For a survey the interview guide or questionnaire is written, and the way in which the survey is to be carried out is specified. For an observational study the specific form and conditions of the observation and the types of recording processes to be used must be determined.
5. When both the design and the measurement specifics have been determined, a test is needed to assure that they are feasible for the purposes intended. Almost certainly deficiencies requiring revisions and additional testing will be found at this stage.
6. At this point, a plan for the analysis of the data is advisable. Planning may go as far as the development of a set of dummy tables for the expected statistical data. Such detailed planning is not always found in business research projects, but it does help assure that data relevant to the hypotheses or questions will be secured.
7. The final stage of project development is preparation of specific instructions and other arrangements (such as training sessions) to assure that the data will be collected efficiently.

At the end of this series of design steps the researchers can compile the *formal research plan*. [9] In many commercial projects no formal document is prepared, especially when the projects are relatively routine, carried out under severe time pressures, or limited by a very modest budget. If the study is relatively small, the formal plan is often eliminated in the interest of cost saving.

---

[9] See page 76 for suggested content of the formal research plan as well as a discussion on the development of a research proposal.

Data Collection

This stage, the actual gathering of data, may range from relatively simple observation at one location to a grandiose national survey. For example, in a study conducted for *Life* magazine the data-collection stage lasted for 15 months and involved 13 successive waves of nationwide interviews and reinterviews.[10]

Data collection requires substantial resources but perhaps not as big a part of the budget as clients would expect. Employees must be paid, and travel and other expenses are incurred, but this phase of the project often takes no more than one third of the total research budget. The geographic scope and the number of observations required affect the cost allocation, but much of a project's cost is relatively independent of the size of the data-gathering effort. Thus, a rough rule of thumb would be that (1) project planning, (2) data gathering, and (3) analysis, interpretation, and reporting each share about equally in the budget.

Specific details on data-gathering methods and problems are reserved for Chapters 7 through 11.

Analysis and Interpretation

After the field work we still need to analyze the data, derive the various measures called for, and investigate the relationships that are found. Further, we must then interpret these findings in the light of the client's specific problem. Finally, we develop the report and transmit our findings to the client in such a way that they will assist him/her substantially in decision making. Chapters 12 through 14 treat these matters.

An Example of the Process

The research process can be illustrated by returning to the problem which Ed Bildor presented to Roger Researcher in the chapter introduction. Recall that the client (Ed) is threatened by a rezoning action in Northridge, a suburban town that is growing rapidly. Latest counts place the population at 40,000, and the rapid growth is expected to continue for the next decade.

Most of the homes being built in the area are tract homes designed to appeal to a wide range of white-collar and blue-collar families. Home construction over several recent years has showed an upgrading in size and cost with the typical price of a new three-bedroom home in the moderate range. Lot sizes are around 7,500 square feet.

At the lunch meeting between Ed and Roger it is agreed that a project should be launched immediately because the planning commission hearings were scheduled to begin soon. Over the next two weeks two other meetings

---

[10] *Life* magazine, *Life Study of Consumer Expenditures* (New York: Time Inc., 1957).

are held for discussions of the general research problem and how it should be approached. Ed has some ideas about research which are unrealistic in both concept and cost, but discussions clarify the nature of the problem and the type of contribution which various research approaches might make.

The Problem as the Client Sees It.   Ed and his associates have purchased a substantial quantity of land for future development. He now faces a possible rezoning of this land that will virtually eliminate any of his existing plans for profitable development. In cooperation with several other builders he is beginning to mount a broad campaign against the zoning commission's position. The commission has proposed that current zoning, which calls for residential development on lots of 7,500 to 10,000 square feet, be changed to require a minimum of one acre and sometimes two acres for each building site.

The first task that Ed suggests is the development of an economic argument showing how much more municipal revenue the greater building density will bring, how many more stores and shopping centers will be developed, and how many jobs will be generated with the increased population. In addition, Ed feels the need to show that the people who are living in his developments like the area and want to stay there.

After some exploration, Researcher determines that the economic argument can be developed with the use of published studies and data available from the local government. This argument, although useful, will not meet the major contentions of the zoning commission.

The Problem Studied.   The general nature of the commission's argument suggests a need for some research among the people of the area to test the major points which the planning commission is making. None of the commission's five members is considered an expert in planning. A majority of them believe that the present development of the city is inadequate. They are backed in this view by a few long-time residents living on large estates directly in the path of the population movement. Further analysis of the commission majority's argument indicates that an entirely different research direction is called for.

The argument presented by the planning commission and its backers is that existing development of the area is leading to three deficiencies:

1. Aesthetic—Residential development is creating a definite problem of "unsightly urban sprawl." Commercial development is being accomplished by area strip zoning, which brings about further urban unsightliness.
2. Social—The area is primarily working class. The city must attract more affluent people to provide future civic leadership. One way of doing so would be the provision of acre-or-more land plots on which more expensive homes could be built.
3. Economic—The school system, although growing rapidly, is chronically

overcrowded. Further dense housing development would continue to put pressures on the school system. A decrease in the density of residential development would lessen school population pressures.

An analysis of these arguments suggests that a study of residents should provide useful information concerning the first two arguments (the third is answered by an economic analysis). The investigative questions are stated in terms of the following descriptive hypotheses.

1. The population in the city represents a broad cross section that includes many college-educated, concerned citizens who are potential civic leaders.
2. A large share of the population is composed of young families who have been attracted by the life styles and environment in this city and who find them generally satisfactory.
3. These satisfied residents see the city as their permanent home and do not expect to leave the area, even if they buy larger homes.
4. While the residents desire environmental improvements, they do not want any drastic changes in present plans for residential land use.

Research Procedure.   The project begins with an investigation of the literature on the economics of suburban housing development and land use. Contact with the research department of the National Association of Home Builders produces some valuable information about the economics of various types of land use in residential areas. From these and locally collected data it is not difficult for the researcher to develop the necessary estimates to compare the probable economic impacts (municipal costs, tax revenues) of various housing densities.

At the same time the research hypotheses are translated into specific research requirements. For example, hypothesis 2 concerns attitudes of the people toward their area as a place to live and raise a family. To test this, the researcher has to learn the basis for the residents' original attraction to the area; their opinions about schools, churches, shopping, and convenience to work; their satisfaction with their specific neighborhood and neighbors; and their views on the adequacy of their homes and lot size.

Some exploratory in-depth interviews with residents give the researcher a better feel for the types of people and their responses. Out of these interviews a questionnaire is developed; Roger tests it, revises it, and tests it again. Dummy tables are drawn up to suggest the ways in which the final data will be analyzed. These tables and their potential comments are then compared against the specific research requirements for a determination of whether the objectives will be met.

Sampling reliability is determined to be a critical matter. At the same time the research budget suggests that the sample size must be limited. These restrictions, plus the fact that the area of study is clearly defined and geographically limited, lead to the use of probability sampling methods. All addresses in the study areas are listed and a random sample drawn.

After the successful pilot test the project is released to a field interviewing organization, which places a substantial number of interviewers in the field. They complete their study in a few days. The results are then tabulated and analyzed and the final report presented to the client. The schedule for this project is approximately as follows:

July 15—Initiate contact with the client.
July 24—Decide to go ahead with the study.
July 26–Aug. 10—Seek background data on economic aspects and conduct some exploratory interviews.
Aug. 11—Begin the development of specific research design and questionnaire.
Aug. 24—Meet client and set final go-ahead.
Aug. 30—Begin field interviewing.
Sept. 3—Begin coding and tabulation.
Sept. 13—Begin analysis of results.
Sept. 21—Complete report.

This study is not a large project but still involves six people other than the field interviewers and their supervisor. Total man-hours for the study are divided as shown in the accompanying table. As can be seen from the tabulation, the major time demands on the research director are in the planning of the study, analysis of data, and writing of the report. These activities are difficult to delegate. Substantial use of lower-cost personnel comes in the data-gathering and the coding-tabulation stages. The data are hand tabulated from a structured questionnaire. In this particular study data collection takes only about 20 percent of the total budget because of the small sample size and the concentrated population from which the sample is drawn.

	Project Director	Research Assistant	Inter-viewers	Other
Preliminary negotiations	7			
Development and testing of research plan	40	51	15	6
Data collection	5		87	
Coding and tabulating	4			45
Analysis	32			
Report writing	30	—	—	16
	118	51	102	67

This example is not advanced as typical of the allocation of time and funds for a survey. Rather it is suggestive of the problems that one might face and gives some indication of how the various stages of one study are scheduled and the man-hours are allocated. However, one portion of the process that was passed over concerns the formal research plan and proposal writing.

THE RESEARCH PROPOSAL

A written proposal statement is often required when a study is being suggested. It assures that the parties understand the project's purpose and proposed methods of investigation. Cost and time budgets are often spelled out, as are other responsibilities and obligations. Depending upon the needs and desires of the client, there may also be substantial background detail and elaboration of proposed techniques.

The length and complexity of research proposals ranges widely. A graduate student may present a doctoral dissertation proposal that runs 50 pages or more. Applicants for foundation or government research grants typically file a proposal request of a few pages, often in a standardized format specified by the granting agency. Business research proposals normally range from perhaps one to five pages.

Proposal Contents.   Every proposal, regardless of length, should include two basic sections. First is the problem statement. In the brief memo type of proposal the problem statement may be only a paragraph setting out the situation and stating the specific task that the research is going to undertake.

Examples of such problem statements are:

A. The First National Bank of Center City is currently the leading bank in the city but recently has not been growing as fast as its major competitors. Before developing a long-range plan to enhance the bank's competitive position, it is important to determine the bank's present competitive status, its major advantages and opportunities, and its major deficiencies. The major objective of this proposed research is to develop a body of benchmark information about the First National Bank of Center City, its major competitors, and the Center City metropolitan area as a market for banking services.
B. Management is faced with a problem of locating a new plant to serve eastern markets. Before this location decision is made it is proposed that a feasibility study be conducted to determine, for each of five sites, the estimated:
   1. Costs of serving existing customers.
   2. Building, relocation, tax, and operating costs.
   3. Availability of local labor in the six major crafts used in production.
   4. Attractiveness as a living environment for professional and management personnel.

The above statements give the problem facing the respective managements and point out, in a general way, the nature of the research that will be undertaken. Other problem statements might begin with issues raised by behavioral or other theories and state a number of hypotheses for testing. Such statements would usually be more detailed than the examples cited.

A second necessary section of the proposal includes a statement of what will be done. In the bank example cited, the researcher might propose:

Personal interviews will be conducted with a minimum of 200 residents of the area to determine their knowledge of, use of, and attitudes toward local banks. In addition, information will be gathered about their banking and financing practices and preferences. Other information of an economic or demographic nature will also be gathered from published sources and public agencies.

Often proposals will be much more detailed and may include specific measurement devices that will be used, time and cost budgets, sampling plans, and many other operation details.

The Formal Research Plan. Another format, still essentially a proposal, is the formal research plan. It is found both in student and business research situations, especially when a two-stage project is needed. Exploration is undertaken to determine the dimensions of the problem before the proposal is made for the major study. Under these circumstances it is reasonable to expect a written proposal that is more detailed than proposals suggested to this point. Formats will vary, but one set of sample instructions used for student research projects includes the following:

Research Plan Outline

1. Statement of research objective. A clearly stated sentence or two which tells exactly what you expect to do. If the objective is specifically to test a given hypothesis then so state. In many cases, the objective will be a more general statement than that of a hypothesis alone.
2. Statement of problem questions or hypotheses to be answered or tested by the research. Where research is exploratory and where hypotheses will be the result rather than the beginning of your research you should make a statement to this effect.
3. Each major concept or construct which you expect to measure should be defined in operational terms pertinent to this project.
4. State the investigative questions for which you expect to find the answers. Investigative quesions are the specific topical questions that you must resolve in order to test your hypothesis or achieve your research objective. For example, if your hypothesis is that "Our sales are low because our retailers do not carry an adequate range of sizes and styles," some investigative questions might be:
    a. Do our retailers carry significantly fewer sizes and styles than do other outlets?
    b. Do people seek sizes and styles which are not available?
    c. Do people choose retail outlets where there are more sizes and styles available?
5. Specify the research techniques which you expect to use. For example, you might use the following:
    a. Inspect a cross section of the retailers, both ours and those selling other brands, to determine the sizes and styles sold; this is to be done by a shopping study.
    b. Interview a sample of shoppers, in retail outlets as to their size and style preferences, attitudes, and opinions about what they like and dislike.

6. Describe the sampling plan, if any. For example, "I expect to choose eight retail outlets and to interview ten shoppers in each store. These shoppers will be chosen in ten-minute time clusters, selected randomly from the total time periods in which the store is open. Five time clusters will be chosen per store studied. The two shoppers from each time cluster will be the first shopper to enter the store after the time period begins and the first customer to enter the store after the first interview is completed."

7. Report results of pilot test. For example, "I interviewed ten persons with the questionnaire on March 26, and after each interview reviewed the questionnaire with the respondent. In the light of this pilot study I have revised the questionnaire and retested it on another ten persons. I attach a copy of the revised form to this report."

8. Prepare time and cost budgets for the project. A time budget should include an estimate of the man-hours required from the various major types of personnel such as project director, supervisors, field workers, analysts, and so forth. A PERT analysis should be included. Include also an estimate of the expected costs of the project, classified by major expenditure type.[11]

It is not uncommon for the elements of the proposal or research plan to become sections of the final research report.

SUMMARY

In business the research need originates in the decision process. A manager needs specific information to assist in setting objectives, defining tasks, finding the best strategy by which to carry out the tasks, or judging how well the strategy is being implemented.

The value of research to management can, in theory, be measured in terms of the difference between the results of decisions made with the information and the results that would be made without it. To date little progress has been made in developing this approach to valuation, although decision theory can be used under certain circumstances.

Researchers must think of the task as an orderly process. They may, for instance, view project development as a hierarchical sequence of questions. At the initial and most general level is posed the *management question*. This is translated into a *research question*—the major objective of the study. In turn, the research question is factionated into one or more *investigative questions*. These questions may be posed in several levels of generality, but the researcher must answer all of them. At the most specific level are *measurement questions,* those answered by respondents in surveys or answered for each subject in an observational study.

If the research direction is not clear, the investigator often follows a two-stage procedure. The first stage is largely exploratory, aimed at the formula-

---

[11] PERT (program evaluation and review technique) is a technique for planning projects where the timing and sequencing of various activities is critical to the project's success.

tion of hypotheses and development of the specific research design. The general research process contains four major stages:

1. Exploration of the situation.
2. Development of research design.
3. Collection of data.
4. Analysis and interpretation of results.

Written research proposals are often required for either a business study or an academic project. Regardless of size, every proposal should include, at a minimum, two things: (1) a clear statement of the objective of the study and (2) a clear statement of what will be done.

SUPPLEMENTAL READINGS

1. Fox, David J. *The Research Process in Education.* New York: Holt, Rinehart, and Winston, 1969. Chap. 2 includes a research process model somewhat different from the one in this chapter. Chap. 1 presents a case study in research design.
2. Green, Paul, and Tull, Donald. *Research for Marketing Decisions.* 4th ed. Englewood Cliffs, N.J.: Prentice-Hall, Inc., 1978. Chaps. 1 and 2 are recommended. Chap. 2 presents an excellent discussion on the use of Bayesian analysis in the problem of research valuation.
3. Phillips, Bernard. *Social Research, Strategy and Tactics.* 2d ed. New York: The Macmillan Company, 1971. Chap. 1 presents a good research study illustration.
4. Raiffa, Howard. *Decision Analysis.* Reading, Mass.: Addison-Wesley Publishing Company, 1970. An excellent elementary presentation of decision theory from a Bayesian point of view.
5. Selltiz, Claire; Wrightsman, Lawrence S.; and Cook, Stuart W. *Research Methods in Social Relations.* 3d ed. New York: Holt, Rinehart, and Winston, Inc., 1976. Chaps. 1 and 2 present a good research process example and a discussion on formulating a research problem.

DISCUSSION QUESTIONS

1. Distinguish between:
   a. Decision rule and decision variable.
   b. Decision making under certainty and uncertainty.
   c. Expected monetary value and utility.
   d. Classical, relative frequency, and subjective probabilities.
   e. Management and research questions.
2. What are some management and accompanying research questions which might be useful to the following executives:
   a. The production manager of a shoe factory.
   b. The president of First National Bank.
   c. The vice president of labor relations for an auto manufacturer.
   d. The chief of police in a major city.

3. What are the major problems in the valuation of a business research study?

4. Using such concepts as maximin and expected monetary value, suggest appropriate decision rules and variables in each of the following cases:
   a. Whether to switch to a new supplier of raw materials.
   b. Whether to invest in project A or B.
   c. Whether to make a product or buy it from another company.

5. What are some of the important reasons why a research project will fail to make an adequate contribution to the solution of management problems?

6. Some questions are answerable by research, while others are not. Distinguish between them, using some management problem of your choosing.

7. You are considering whether to produce and market a new product. Your choices are:
   a. A_1—Produce and market the new product.
   b. A_2—Do not produce and market it.
   c. A_3—Market test the product to determine whether it should be marketed.

   You are uncertain about what to do, but the research department has proposed a market test. They estimate that it will cost $75,000 but will predict the product's chances for success. On the basis of your experience, you estimate that the product could be very profitable; if it receives strong market acceptance the company should make about $500,000 in incremental profits over the product's life. However, if the acceptance is poor, there would be an incremental loss of perhaps $300,000. Your best judgment now is that there is a 40 percent chance that acceptance will be poor, and 60 percent that it will be strong.
   a. Assuming you use the *EMV* criterion, should you launch this product even if you do not market test?
   b. You are confident of your conditional profit and loss estimates but question your outcome probability estimates. How low could your success probability estimate be and still produce a positive *EMV?*
   c. Would research be a worthwhile action, assuming that it gives a perfect success-failure prediction?
   d. Suppose research of this type is accurate in its prediction only 80 percent of the time. Would it then be worth doing?
   e. How might your answers to the above questions be affected by the fact that your company's net worth is $1 million?

8. Assume that you are the president of a large bank and are considering whether to form a consortium of banks to introduce electronic funds transfer (*EFT*). To do this your bank will have to invest a substantial amount of resources in developing the project but will gain a substantial profit if the project succeeds. The technological problems have been solved, consumer acceptance does not seem to be overly difficult, but there are regulatory problems. Some smaller banks are attempting to block *EFT* through the bank regulatory agencies; if that fails they will go to the courts. It is considered certain that *EFT* will come eventually, but it may be delayed by legal problems for as long as five years.

You and your executives, in trying to assess the project, conclude that one of three conditions will occur: (1) the project will go forward as scheduled, (2) regulatory problems will delay the project by a year if you launch it now, and (3) legal and regulatory problems will stop the project for five years if you launch it now. You estimate that the probabilities of each of these is 0.30, 0.40, and 0.30, respectively. Two alternatives are open to your bank—either take the lead now in forming the consortium, or withdraw and allow a competing bank to become the leader. In either case it will be launched very soon. If you withdraw, your bank can still participate in the project but with much less profit opportunity and less risk. You ask your staff to develop conditional profit estimates for various combinations of action and states of nature, and to convert these estimates to present-value terms. These results are shown in the accompanying table.

	States of Nature		
	EFT Goes Ahead	EFT Delay 1 Year (millions of dollars)	EFT Delay 5 Years
Our bank leads	9.0	4.5	−12.0
Our bank follows	2.0	2.1	− 1.5

a. Draw a decision tree for this decision.
b. Assume the maximin decision criterion. Which course of action would you recommend?
c. Based on an *EMV* criterion which course of action would you take?
d. Assume that someone comes to you with a proposal to do research which will enable you to predict correctly which state of nature will occur. How much would such research be worth?
e. Even if the *EMV* suggests one course of action, what other considerations might cause you to decide against this course?

9. The vice president of administration calls you into her office and states that the computer programming department is not functioning well because there is excessive turnover among the programmers. She suggests that you conduct a survey among other major companies in the region to learn how they handle the problem of high programmer turnover.
a. What do you think of this problem assessment and research suggestion?
b. How, if at all, could you improve on the vice president's formulation of the research problem?

10. You have been approached by the editor of *Gentlemen's Magazine* to carry out a research study. They have been unsuccessful in attracting shoe manufacturers as advertisers. When they have tried to secure advertising from shoe manufacturers, they have been told that men's clothing stores are a small and dying segment of the men's shoe business. Since

Gentlemen's Magazine goes chiefly to men's clothing stores, the manufacturers reason that it is therefore not a good vehicle for their advertising.

The editor believes that a survey (via mail questionnaire) of the man's
clothing stores in the United States will probably show that these stores are
important outlets for men's shoes and that they are not declining in importance as shoe outlets. He asks you to develop a proposal for the study and
submit it to him. Develop research questions or hypotheses of various
levels that will enable you to develop a specific proposal.

Chapter 4

Research Design

TO THIS POINT we have mentioned a number of different research studies without seriously considering the nature of their design. It has been assumed that a certain type of study was called for and that the researcher has gone ahead with it. Now we should consider the many different types of research approaches and the one or ones that can be used for a given problem. In this chapter we will first consider what is meant by "research design," then discuss briefly a crude classification of designs. Finally, we will discuss several designs in greater detail.

WHAT IS RESEARCH DESIGN?

Many definitions of "research design" have been advanced, but no one definition imparts the full range of important aspects. Several examples from leading authors can be cited:

> A research design is the arrangement of conditions for collection and analysis of data in a manner that aims to combine relevance to the research purpose with economy in procedure.[1]

> The research design constitutes the blueprint for the collection, measurement, and analysis of data. It aids the scientist in the allocation of his limited resources

---

[1] Claire Selltiz, Lawrence S. Wrightsman, and Stuart W. Cook, *Research Methods in Social Relations,* 3d ed. (New York: Holt, Rinehart and Winston, Inc., 1976), p. 90.

by posing crucial choices: Is the blueprint to include experiments, interviews, observation, the analysis of records, simulation, or some combination of these? Are the methods of data collection and the research situation to be highly structured? Is an intensive study of a small sample more effective than a less intensive study of a large sample? Should the analysis be primarily quantitative or qualitative?[2]

Research design is the plan, structure, and strategy of investigation conceived so as to obtain answers to research questions and to control variance. The plan is the overall scheme or program of research. It includes an outline of what the investigator will do from writing the hypotheses and their operational implications to the final analysis of the data. The *structure* of the research is . . . the outline, the scheme, and paradigm of the operation of the variables. . . . *Strategy* . . . includes the methods to be used to gather and analyze the data. In other words, strategy implies *how* the research objectives will be reached and *how* the problems encountered in the research will be tackled.[3]

While these definitions differ in detail, together they give the essentials of a good research design. First, it is a *plan* that specifies the sources and types of information relevant to the research question. Second, it is a *strategy* or blueprint specifying which approach will be used for gathering and analyzing the data. Finally, since most business research studies have time and economic constraints, both time and cost budgets are typically included.

CLASSIFICATION OF DESIGNS

One of the above definitions suggests that the researcher faces a number of crucial design choices. These can be summarized in a categorization of research design types, but unfortunately there is no satisfactory single classification system. Various writers on research advance different classification schemes, some of which are:

Exploratory, descriptive, and designs which permit inferences about causality (Selltiz, Wrightsman, and Cook).

Experimental and ex post facto (Kerlinger).

The historical method, descriptive method, and case and clinical studies (Good and Scates).

Sample surveys, field studies, experiments in field settings, and laboratory experiments (Festinger and Katz).

Exploratory, descriptive, and causal (Green and Tull).

Exploratory and conclusive research. Conclusive research, in turn, consists of descriptive studies (case and statistical studies) and experimental studies (Boyd and Westfall).

---

[2] Reprinted with permission of Macmillan Publishing Co., Inc. from *Social Research Strategy and Tactics,* 2d ed., by Bernard S. Phillips, p. 93. Copyright © 1971 by Bernard S. Phillips.

[3] Fred N. Kerlinger, *Foundations of Behavioral Research,* 2d ed. (New York: Holt, Rinehart and Winston, Inc., 1973), p. 300.

This confusing array exists because "research design" is a complex concept which cannot be described in a simple manner. In fact, there appear to be at least seven different perspectives from which any given study can be viewed. They are:

1. The degree to which the research problem has been crystallized (the study may be either *exploratory* or *formalized*).
2. The topical scope—breadth and depth—of the study (it may be a *case* or a *statistical* study).
3. The research environment (most business research is conducted in a *field* setting, although *laboratory* research is not unusual; *simulation* is a third category, somewhat similar to laboratory research).
4. The time dimension (research may be *crosssectional* or *longitudinal*).
5. The communication mode of data collection (studies may be *observational* or *survey*).
6. The power of the researcher to affect the variables under study (the two major types of research along this dimension are the *experimental* and the *ex post facto*).
7. The nature of the relationships among the variables (research studies may be *descriptive* or *causal*).

A brief discussion of these perspectives will illustrate their nature and contribution to research. Several of these approaches are considered in more detail later in the chapter; the remainder are reserved for later chapters.

Degree of Problem Crystallization

A study may be viewed as *exploratory* or *formalized*. "Formalized" is not a particularly apt description, but no better term comes to mind. The essence of the distinction between these two types is the degree of structure and the immediate objective of the study. The exploratory study is ill-structured and much less focused on predetermined objectives. In fact, the immediate purpose of the exploratory study is usually to develop some hypotheses for testing or some investigative questions for further research. The formalized study has much more structure. It begins with a hypothesis or investigative question, and the precise procedures, sources, and so forth are clearly specified.

The exploratory-formalized dichotomy is less precise than some of the other classifications. All studies have elements of exploration in them, and few studies are completely uncharted. Recall that the general project sequence, discussed in Chapter 3, suggests that more formalized studies contain at least an element of exploration prior to the final choice of design. More detailed consideration of exploratory research is found in a later section of this chapter.

The Topical Scope

The *statistical* study differs from the *case* study in several ways, although the line between these two may not always be clear. The first is a study in breadth rather than depth. One attempts to capture adequately the characteristics of a population by analyzing a sample of items. One is concerned with the relative frequency with which certain characteristics or instances are observed. The case study places more emphasis on the full analysis of a limited number of events or conditions and their interrelations. The case study deals with the processes that take place and their interrelationships. The statistical study, on the other hand, is more concerned with the conditions at one point, and ongoing processes and interrelations must be inferred from the statistical findings.

A study of attitudes toward labor-management problems furnishes a good example of the approaches. A survey of the workers and managers in a large plant might provide responses which could be tabulated and reported. These reports would give us typical attitudes, by department, type of worker, and so forth. If the plant is a large one, we might take only a sample of attitudes and estimate total results from this sample. We might cross-tabulate answers to one question with those to another to infer relationships between pairs of such variables as working conditions, worker attitudes, management styles, and so on.

If the research were being done as a case study, we might examine several departments in depth. The study would focus on labor-management attitudes from a variety of perspectives. Systematic interviewing would be used to elicit the reciprocal perceptions and attitudes of workers, supervisors, shop stewards, department managers, and so forth. Stress would be placed on these interrelations and how they might affect attitudes of the various parties.

The Research Environment

This means of classifying research designs distinguishes between those studies that take place under actual environmental conditions and those that take place under artificial or simulated conditions. These might be called *field* and *laboratory* studies, but such terminology might not always be correct. For some studies the natural environment may be a laboratory. The main distinction hinges on whether the study is of actual subjects under environmental conditions which are normal for the problem being studied. Thus, a study of buyer behavior in a store would have a natural setting. On the other hand, consumer participation in a shopping game, devised to simulate certain decision conditions, would be closer to a laboratory study, regardless of whether the event takes place in a central research facility or in the consumers' homes.

To simulate is to duplicate the essence of a system or process. Simulations are being used more and more in research, especially in the operations research area. The major characteristics of various conditions and relationships in actual situations are often represented in mathematical models. Role playing and other behavioral activities may also be viewed as simulation.

The Time Dimension

Some research studies are carried out once; others are repeated over a period of time. The later have come to be known as *longitudinal* studies. The obvious advantage of a longitudinal study is that the investigation can follow changes over time. Indeed, many research questions may be answerable only after an extended period of time. For example, a study of worker attitudes toward the four-day work week revealed gradual changes in attitudes; in many instances attitudes became pronounced only after a year.[4]

In longitudinal studies the researcher may study the same people over a period of time or may use different subjects for each sequenced measurement. The nature of the research problem dictates which alternative is used. Obviously, some types of information, once collected, cannot be collected a second time from the same person without grave risk of bias. For example, a study of public awareness of an advertising campaign over a six-month period would require different samples for each measurement.

The panel method, widely used in marketing, is a type of longitudinal study. Panels are set up to report consumption data on a variety of products. These data, collected from national samples, provide a major data bank on relative market shares, consumer response to new products, new promotional methods, and the like.

While longitudinal research is important, more often one needs to examine a situation in a crosssectional study. Even with this design some of the benefits of a longitudinal study can be secured by adroit questioning about past attitudes, history, and future expectations. Responses to questions should be interpreted with care, however. Most respondents have difficulty accurately reporting events from their past unless the events were either outstanding or recent. It is easy to ask recall questions and to get an answer, but the answer may be incorrect. Examples of this and other questioning difficulties will be discussed in Chapter 8.

The Communication Mode

This classification distinguishes between monitoring and interrogation processes. The former includes *observational* studies, in which the researcher inspects the activities of a subject or the nature of some material without

---

[4] Walter R. Nord and Robert Costigan, "Worker Adjustment to the Four-Day Week," *Journal of Applied Psychology,* vol. 58, no. 1, pp. 60–66.

attempting to elicit responses from anyone. A traffic count at an intersection, a search of the library collection, observation of the actions of a group of decision makers—all are examples of monitoring. In each case the researcher notes and records the information available from observations.

These observational studies may be classed further as either *participatory* or *nonparticipatory*. In the former the researcher engages with the subjects in their activities while simultaneously playing the role of a researcher. In a nonparticipatory study the researcher remains an outsider. In either case, he or she may or may not be known to the subjects as a researcher.

When using the *survey* or interrogation method, the researcher questions the subjects and collects their responses by some means. Studies of this type may also be further classified by the communication medium used—mail survey, telephone survey, or personal interview. What is called a "survey" in common parlance is an ex post facto study (without manipulation of variables) in the interrogation format.

Researcher Control of Variables

The idealized research concept is often thought to be the *experiment* in which the researchers attempt to control and/or manipulate the variables in the study. They need not personally become involved in the situation. It is enough that they cause variables to be changed or held steady in keeping with specified research objectives. Experimental design is most appropriate when proof is sought that certain variables affect other variables in some way. Evidence gathered through experiments is considered to be the most powerful support possible for a hypothesis.

The ex post facto design is more common in social science and business research. With it the investigator has no control over the variables, either because they have already occurred or because they cannot be controlled or manipulated. One can only report what has happened or what is happening. In fact, important to this design is the requirement that the researcher *not influence* the variables, because to do so is to introduce bias. The researcher is limited to "holding factors constant" by judicious selection of subjects according to strict sampling procedures and by statistical manipulation of findings.

Nature of Relationships among Variables

This classification of *descriptive* versus *causal* studies is often confused with the above classification of experimental versus ex post facto research. Indeed, there is a similarity. Most ex post facto designs are used for descriptive studies in which the researcher seeks to measure such items as frequency of shopping, sociological characteristics, or attitudes of people. However, ex post facto studies also include attempts by the researcher to discover causes *even* when the variables cannot be controlled.

The essential difference between descriptive and causal studies is in their objectives. If the research is concerned with finding out who, what, where, when, or how much, then the study is descriptive. If it is concerned with asking why, then it is causal. For example, research into city crime is descriptive when it measures what types of crime are committed, how frequently, when, where, and by whom.

Researchers use causal studies to try to explain relationships among variables—for instance, *why* the murder rate is higher in Detroit than in other major cities. However, what are we to do when experimentation, the preferred causal design, cannot be used? It is difficult to imagine conducting an experimental study on the causes of the high murder rate in Detroit. Our only feasible alternative is a carefully conducted ex post facto study. We must attempt to show causation by statistical association comparisons through cross-tabulation and/or correlation, rather than by control and manipulation of variables.

Exploratory research and formalized research will be discussed at further length in the following sections. Discussion of some of the other designs will be deferred to later chapters.

EXPLORATORY RESEARCH

The value and importance of exploration have already been commented on. It is particularly useful when the researchers lack a clear idea of the problems that they will meet in the course of the study. Through exploration the researchers develop the concepts more clearly, establish priorities, and in many other ways improve the final research design. Exploration may also save time and money if they decide, after study, that the problem is not as important as first thought.

In some cases an area of study is so new or vague that the researcher may propose an exploratory study to learn what problems are considered to be urgent by those who are knowledgeable in the field. In another case the researcher may want to determine whether it is practical to attempt a study in a given area. For example, one U.S. government agency proposed that research be conducted on how executives in a given industry make decisions about raw material purchases. Specifically involved were questions about how and at what price differences companies began substituting one raw material for a more costly one in their manufactured products. A critical prerequisite to this study was knowledge of whether industry executives would divulge adequate information about their decision making in this topic area. An exploration determined that they would not.

In spite of its obvious values, however, many researchers and managers alike give exploration too little attention. There is often strong pressure for quick answers to the problems that need researching. Too often it is "obvious" that exploration is a "stalling around" when urgent projects could be done. However, some time and effort given to exploration often saves research time and money.

Methods of Exploration

Literature Survey.   The obvious first step in an exploration is a survey of the literature. One gains little from discovering anew what is already known. A literature study usually turns up a number of leads for further investigation that will advance the research, especially if we do not confine the investigation to obvious topics. For example, suppose we are interested in estimating the outlook for the copper industry over the next ten years. The obvious first step would be to search the literature for information on copper production and consumption. However, a search restricted to literature under these topics would miss more than it finds. When a study of the copper industry was undertaken, useful information was turned up in literature found under the following reference headings: mines and minerals; nonferrous metals; forecasting; planning; econometrics; such consuming industries as automotive, communications; particular countries where copper is produced, such as Chile; and companies prominent in the industry, such as Anaconda, Kennecott, and others.

Experience Survey.   Seldom is more than a fraction of the existing knowledge in any field put into writing. Thus, we will profit by seeking information from persons experienced in the area of study. Such persons can help us secure an insight into relationships between variables. To get an accurate picture of the current situation we need to solicit the views of those believed to know what is going on. The amount of exploration needed depends on what is being learned. If the last interviews taken turn up some new information of value, then we have not gone far enough. We should keep going until our findings duplicate what we know.

When we interview persons in an experience survey we should seek their ideas on which are the important issues or aspects of the subject. The investigative format we use should be flexible enough that we can explore various avenues that emerge during the interview. We seek to learn what is being done. What has been tried in the past without success? What are the change-producing elements of the situation? How have things changed over time? What problem areas and barriers can be seen? Who is involved in decisions, and what roles do they play? What are the costs of various aspects of the processes under study? Who can we count on to assist and/or participate in the research? What are the priority areas? Many other similar questions might be posed, but these suffice to give the general drift of the process.

The product of such questioning may be a new hypothesis, a discarding of old hypotheses, or information about the practicality of doing the study.

Probing may indicate whether certain facilities are available for study, what factors need to be controlled, which can be controlled and how, and who will cooperate in the study.

Discovery is more easily carried out if the researcher can analyze some cases that provide special insight. Typically in exploration we are less interested in getting a representative crosssection view than in getting information from those sources that might prove especially "insight-stimulating." Assume that we are called on to study an automobile assembly plant which has a recent history of declining productivity, increasing costs, and growing numbers of quality defects. People who might provide such "insight-stimulating" information could include the following:

1. Newcomers to the scene—new employees or personnel who may have recently been transferred to this plant from other similar plants.
2. Marginal or peripheral individuals—persons whose jobs place them on the margin between contending groups. For example, first-line supervisors and lead workers are often neither "management" nor "workers" but something in between.
3. Individuals in transition—recently promoted employees who have been transferred between departments.
4. Deviants and isolates—those in a given group who hold a different position from the majority—workers who are happy with the present situation, highly productive departments and workers, loners of one sort or another.
5. "Pure" cases or cases that show extreme examples of the conditions under study—the most unproductive departments, the most antagonistic workers, and so forth.
6. Those who fit well and those who do not—the workers who are well established in their organizations versus those who are not, those executives who fully reflect "management" views and those who do not.
7. Those who represent different positions in the system—unskilled workers, assemblers, superintendents, and so forth.[5]

The End of Exploration

The end of an exploratory study comes when the researchers are convinced that they have found the major dimensions of the research task. They may have defined a set of subsidiary investigative questions which can be used as specific guides to a detailed research design. Or they may have developed a number of potential hypotheses about possible causes of a specific problem situation. They may also have determined that certain other hypotheses are such remote possibilities that they can be safely ignored in any

---

[5] This classification is suggested in Selltiz, Wrightsman, and Cook, *Research Methods,* pp. 99–101.

further study. Finally, the researchers may end exploration because they feel that further research is not needed or is not presently possible. Where further research is proposed, however, the next step is a consideration of some aspects of the formal research design.

FORMALIZED STUDIES

We have already pointed out that formalized research studies are typically well structured and have unambiguously stated hypotheses or investigative questions. These studies serve a variety of research objectives, among which are (1) descriptions of phenomena or characteristics associated with a subject population, (2) estimates of the proportions of a population that have these characteristics, (3) discovery of associations among different variables, and finally (4) discovery and measurement of cause-and-effect relationships among variables. The first three of these objectives are normally associated with descriptive studies, while the fourth calls for studies of causal relationships.

Descriptive Studies

The objective in a descriptive study is to learn the who, what, when, where, and how of a topic. The study may be simple or complex; it may be done in a laboratory or in the field. It can also be described in terms of the other dimensions we have discussed. Whatever the form, however, a descriptive study can be just as demanding of research skills as the more idealized causal study, and we should insist upon the same high standards for design and execution.

The simplest descriptive study concerns a univariate question or hypothesis in which we ask about, or state something about, the size, form, distribution, or existence of a variable. For example, in an account analysis at a savings and loan association, we might be interested in developing a profile of savers. We may want first to locate them in relation to the association office. In this case the question might be "What percent of the savers live within a two-mile radius of the office?" Using the hypothesis format, we might predict that, "Sixty percent or more of the savers live within a two-mile radius of the office."

We may also be interested in securing information about such other variables as:

1. The relative size of accounts.
2. The number of accounts for minors.
3. The number of accounts opened within the last six months.
4. The amount of activity (number of deposits and withdrawals per year) in accounts.

Data on each of these variables, by themselves, may have value for management decisions. Bivariate relationships among these or other variables may be of even greater interest. Cross-tabulations between distance from the branch and account activity, for example, may suggest that differential rates of activity are related to location of account. A cross-tabulation of account size and sex of account owner may also show interrelation. Such correlative relationships as these may not necessarily imply a causal relationship in a strict sense.

Descriptive studies are often much more complex than this example. One study of savers began as described and then went into much greater depth. Part of the study included an observation of account records, which indicated a concentration of nearby savers. Their accounts were typically larger and more active than those whose owners lived at a distance. A sample survey of savers provided information on stage in the family life cycle, attitudes toward savings, family income levels, and other matters. Correlation of this information with known savings data indicated that accounts in women's names tended to be larger. Further investigation suggested that women with larger accounts were often widowed or working single women and were older than the average account holder. Information about their attitudes and savings practices led to some revised business strategies at the savings and loan association.

Some of the evidence collected suggested causal relationships. For example, the correlation between nearness to the office and the probability of having an account at the office suggested the question, "Why would people who live at some distance from the office have an account there?" It is this type of question situation where hypothesizing makes its greatest contribution by pointing out directions that the research might follow. In this example it might be hypothesized that:

1.   Distant savers (operationally defined as those with addresses more than two miles from the office) have accounts at the office because they once lived near the office; they were "near" when the account decision was made.
2.   Distant savers actually live near the office, but the address on the account is, for some unknown reason, located at a place outside the two-mile radius; they are "near," but the records do not show this.
3.   Distant savers work near the office; they are "near" by virtue of their work location.
4.   Distant savers are not normally near to the office but responded to a promotion that encouraged savers to use the mail system; this is another form of "nearness" in which this concept is transformed into one of "convenience."

When these hypotheses were tested it was determined that a substantial portion of the distant savers could be accounted for by hypotheses 1 and 3. It was concluded that nearby location was closely related to saving at a given association. The determination of cause is not so simple, however.

Causal Studies

The correlation found between location and probability of account holding at a savings and loan association looks like strong evidence to many, but the researcher with a more scientific disposition will argue that this correlation is not causation. Who is right? The essence of the disagreement seems to lie in the concept of "cause."

One writer asserts that, *"there appears to be an inherent gap between the languages of theory and research* which can never be bridged in a completely satisfactory way. One *thinks* in terms of theoretical language that contains notions such as causes, forces, systems, and properties. But one's tests are made in terms of covariations, operations, and pointer readings."[6] The essential element in the theoretical concept of cause is that A "produces" B or A "forces" B to occur. Empirically, however, we can never demonstrate such unambiguous precision in relationships. To show the theoretical ideal of causation would require that we deal with only a finite number of variables, clearly eliminating all others. In addition, we would have to use a model of variable interactions which is highly simplified. Imagine the difficulty of doing this in a human relations situation when even the physicist cannot achieve the perfect study conditions needed to test "laws."

The experiment is the idealized form of causal analysis, but even in this format we cannot be certain that we are controlling all other possible variables. To determine causal relationships in a nonexperimental situation is even more difficult. However, causal inferences are going to be made, and we must make them if we are to have more scientific decision making. Thus, we agree to simplify our designs, make untestable assumptions, and accept the fact that our designs are not as strong as theory demands. Recognizing, therefore, that causal laws can never be proven empirically, let's look further at the problems of causal inference.

CAUSAL INFERENCE

The design of causal research is an exercise in reasoning along complex but well tested lines. First, effective valuation of evidence calls for an appreciation of the practical problems of inductive logic; the first part of the section will deal with this topic. Linkages between factors which are advanced as being causal may take many forms, and a second major part of this section will be concerned with these linkage relationships. The relative positions of factors in a proposed scheme of interrelations must also be analyzed. A third part of this section will discuss these positional relationships among variables. Finally, the unique problems of causal inference found in experimental and ex post facto research designs will be discussed.

---

[6] Hubert M. Blalock, Jr., *Causal Inferences in Nonexperimental Research* (Chapel Hill: The University of North Carolina Press, 1964), p. 5.

Inductive Logic

Induction is a critical part of the research process. Inductive conclusions are hypotheses that we advance to explain factual evidence. We test these hypotheses by gathering further evidence that confirms or disconfirms our inductions. But how do we judge the persuasiveness of this evidence?

Method of Agreement. John Stuart Mill, writing in the mid-19th century, formulated a set of canons that describe the logic basis for empirical causal research. His first canon was called the *method of agreement* and may be summarized as follows: "When two or more cases of a given phenomenon have one and only one condition in common, then that condition may be regarded as the cause (or effect) of the phenomenon."[7] Thus, if we can find Z and only Z in every case where we find C, and no others (for example, A, B, D, or E) are always found with Z, then we can conclude that C and Z are causally related. Figure 4–1 illustrates this method.

Figure 4–1: Mill's Method of Agreement

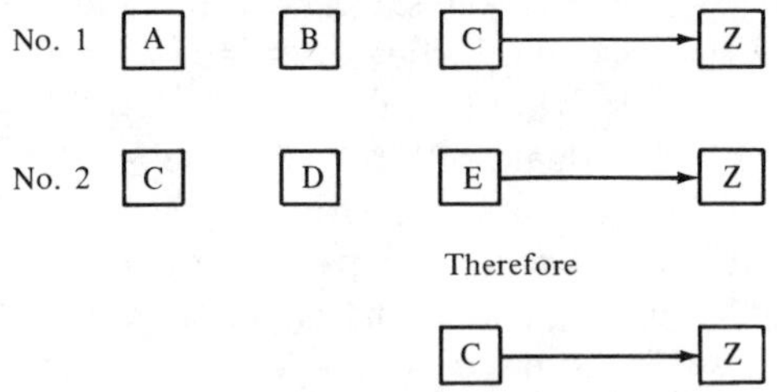

An example of the application of the method of agreement might be a problem involving occasional high absenteeism on Mondays in a factory. Study of two groups of those with high absenteeism (No. 1 and No. 2 in Figure 4–1) indicates that there are no unique job, department, demographic or personal characteristics (A, B, D, and E), but they are all members of a camping club (C). The conclusion is that membership in the club (C) is associated with the high absenteeism.

The method of agreement helps rule out some factors as irrelevant. Thus, Figure 4–1 indicates that A, B, D, and E are unlikely to be causes of Z. In addition, this method points out those factors that occur together and which may, therefore, be related. The weaknesses of this method are many, however. Implicit is the assumption that there are no variables to consider other than A, B, C, D, and E. One can never accept this supposition with certainty because the number of potential variables is infinite. In addition, while C may be the cause, it may function only in the presence of some other factor not

---

[7] As stated in William J. Goode and Paul K. Hatt, *Methods in Social Research* (New York: McGraw-Hill Book Co., Inc., 1952), p. 75.

included. Perhaps also C and Z are both caused by an unknown third factor, or it may be that Z causes C. Because of these weaknesses the method of agreement can be no more than a part of a procedure for evaluating evidence.

Mill's second canon is the *negative canon of agreement*. It states that when condition non-C is found to be associated with observation non-Z, we have evidence that there is a causal relationship between C and Z. For example, lack of membership in the camping club is associated with lack of absenteeism on Mondays. This logical process is similar to that for the method of agreement, and it has the same deficiencies.

Method of Difference. The method of agreement and the negative canon of agreement form the basis for a third method, called the *method of difference*. In its elemental form it states, "If there are two or more cases, and in one of them observation Z can be made, while in the other it cannot; and if factor C occurs when observation Z is made, and does not occur when observation Z is not made; then it can be asserted that there is a causal relationship between C and Z."[8] This method is illustrated in Figure 4–2.

Figure 4–2: Mill's Method of Difference

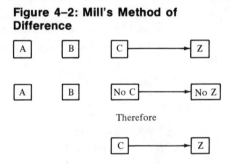

This design is the "classical" experimental form so often found in physical science research. However, Mill recognized that such categorical relationships between factors are rarely found. That is, these methods allow no variations in C or Z. Either C exists or it does not; Z occurs or it does not. To deal with this problem, he introduced another method.

Method of Concomitant Variation. Many, perhaps most, factors vary in amount or degree, and Mill suggested the *method of concomitant variation* for this situation. This method holds that "If a change in the *amount* of one variable is accompanied by a comparable change in the *amount* of another variable in two or more cases, and the latter change does not occur in the absence of the first change, one change is the cause (or effect) of the other."[9] This concept underlies the process of correlation. Such concomitant variation

[8] From *Methods in Social Research* by William J. Goode and Paul K. Hatt. Copyright 1952, McGraw-Hill Book Company. Used with permission of McGraw-Hill Book Company.

[9] Ibid., pp. 86– 87.

can result in positive or negative correlations, either of which can be linear or nonlinear. The causal requirement is that variations in C result in predictable variations in Z.

Value of Mill's Canons. Philosophers and other scholars have stressed the many deficiencies of Mill's canons. Cohen and Nagel, for example, point out that Mill's methods cannot either assure the discovery of relevant variables or provide a certain proof of causation.[10] Blalock states, "At best, they [Mill's proposed methods] can be used only to enable one to eliminate inadequate causal arguments . . . there seems to be no systematic way of knowing for sure whether or not one has located all of the relevant variables. Nor do we have any foolproof procedures for deciding which variables to use."[11]

It is true that Mill's canons offer no "foolproof methods," but then we have no alternatives which do offer such power. The research problems we face call for conclusions about causal relationships; if there are no "foolproof methods," then we must use the imperfect methods we have as best we can. We should recognize the weaknesses of our methods, minimize their effects, and improve our understanding of the relationships among variables. We do this by looking at such relationships from two perspectives. First, while there are many possible factors which might influence a given variable, they may be classified into a small number of *positional relationships*. Second, the connection between any two variables may be described in terms of *linkage* types. We discuss both of these perspectives now.

Positional Relationships

When developing a causal hypothesis one must state the expected positions of the variables relative to each other. In this sense one variable relates to another in either an *explanatory* or *extraneous* way.[12] Among explanatory relationships a given variable is positioned as *independent, dependent,* or *moderating.* Among the extraneous variables we may further distinguish between two classes—*controlled* and *uncontrolled.* Among the uncontrolled variables are those that are *confounding* and those that are *random.* These classifications may be outlined as follows:

I. Explanatory variables.
    A. Independent variables.
    B. Dependent variables.
    C. Moderating variables.

---

[10] Morris R. Cohen and Ernest Nagel, *An Introduction to Logic and Scientific Method* (New York: Harcourt, Brace, Inc., 1934), chap. 13.

[11] Blalock, *Causal Inferences,* p. 14.

[12] This classification is patterned after that of Leslie Kish, "Some Statistical Problems in Research Design," *American Sociological Review,* vol. 24 (1959), pp. 328–38.

II.   Extraneous variables.
   A.   Controlled variables.
   B.   Uncontrolled variables.
      1.   Confounding variables.
      2.   Random variables.

Explanatory Variables.   These are the factors of direct interest to us as researchers and about which we wish to measure hypothesized causal connections. They consist of at least one *independent* variable (*IV*) and a *dependent* variable (*DV*). It is hypothesized that in some way *IV* "causes" *DV*. For simple studies all other variables are extraneous to the relationship between these two factors. Thus, we might be interested in testing the following hypotheses:

A.   A promotion campaign (*IV*) brings increased savings (*DV*).
B.   The advent of a four-day work week (*IV*) leads to increased productivity per man-hour (*DV*).
C.   The adoption of unit pricing (*IV*) is followed by an increase in the purchasing of lower-priced products (*DV*).
D.   A reduction in reported profits brought about by accounting changes (*IV*) results in lower stock prices (*DV*).
E.   Change to self-inspection (*IV*) reduces the number of defective products being passed (*DV*).

A third type of explanatory variable found in many research designs is the moderating variable (*MV*). It is a secondary independent variable which is chosen because it is believed to have a strong contingent or contributory effect on the original *IV-DV* relationship. Thus:

A.   A promotion campaign (*IV*) brings increased savings (*DV*), *but the effect is more pronounced among small-account savers* (*MV*).
B.   The advent of a four-day week (*IV*) leads to increased productivity (*DV*), *especially among younger workers* (*MV*).
C.   Unit pricing (*IV*) is followed by an increase in the purchase of lower-priced products (*DV*) *but only among better educated shoppers* (*MV*).
D.   Inventory accounting changes which reduce reported profits (*IV*) result in lower company stock prices (*DV*) *but only in the short run* (*MV*).
E.   Change to self-inspection (*IV*) reduces the number of defective products being passed (*DV*) *when the assembled product can be identified with its assembler* (*MV*).

The designations of *IV, DV,* and *MV* have been illustrated above in a simple fashion, but in reality the relationships are much more complex. Whether a variable is independent or moderating depends often on the way that we pose the hypothesis. For example, if we are studying the impact of size of account on various saver actions we might well treat "small-account savers" as the major independent variable rather than as a moderator. When we position a given variable in our hypothesis as a moderator we (1) recognize it as an important impactor (2) which we are interested in treating as a subsidiary independent variable, or (3) as one upon which the functioning of our major *IV* is contingent.

The above examples also suggest single *IV-DV* relationships while in truth we often are interested in multiple independent variables. Multiple correlation and multiple regression are techniques which deal with multiple independent variables. Canonical analysis is a type of multiple correlation technique for dealing with both multiple *IV*s and multiple *DV*s.[13]

Controlled Extraneous Variables. An almost infinite number of factors might affect a given causal relationship. We could consider some of them to be independent or moderating variables, but the design problem quickly becomes so complex that we must use other steps to reduce the confounding of the *IV-DV* relationship. These other variables, which we believe may affect our *IV-DV* relationship, are candidates for control (*CV*). For example, consider the following hypotheses:

A. A promotion campaign (*IV*) *among distant account holders* (*CV*) brings increased savings (*DV*), but the effect is more pronounced among small-account holders (*MV*).

B. *In job-shop work situations* (*CV*) the advent of a four-day work week (*IV*) leads to increased productivity per man-hour (*DV*), especially among younger workers (*MV*).

C. *Among buyers of canned vegetables and fruits* (*CV*) the introduction of unit pricing (*IV*) is followed by a purchase shift to lower-priced products (*DV*), especially among better educated shoppers (*MV*).

D. *Under stable economic conditions* (*CV*) inventory accounting changes which reduce reported profits (*IV*) result in lower company stock prices (*DV*) but only in the short run (*MV*).

E. Change to self inspection (*IV*) *of assembled electronic parts* (*CV*) reduces the number of defective parts produced (*DV*) when the assembled product can be identified with the assembler (*MV*).

Thus, in the above examples we choose to study separately the impacts of promotion and small-account holding on saving among distant account holders. In like fashion our investigation of the effect of self-inspection on the number of defective parts is studied separately for assemblers of electronic parts. In this way we "hold constant" this particular extraneous variable.

"Control" is also widely used to designate the group which does not receive the independent variable (or treatment). Thus we have two study groups: the *experimental* group (which receives the promotional message) and the *control group* (which does not receive the message). The savings rate of the control group is used as the standard against which the savings-rate effects of the experimental variable are compared.

---

[13] For more on these techniques see Chapter 13.

The reader might ask, "How does one differentiate between a moderator variable and a control variable?" The decision is judgmental to some degree, but typically we recognize a moderating variable as one which actively affects the IV-DV relationship. It is also one whose impact we often wish to study in an interactive sense; for example, we wish to see the effect of promotion among account holders of differing size. If we wish to control a given variable's effect we are recognizing that it might contaminate the relationship we are studying and we wish only to eliminate this possibility.

Uncontrolled Extraneous Variables.   This final category is the largest and includes all other variables. The assumption is that these factors have little impact on the level of the explanatory variables. In truth, most of them are of little consequence; others may be important but their impact occurs in such a random fashion as to have little effect. The danger is that some of these factors may vary in a systematic way that has a confounding effect on the relationships we are studying.

In the savings example such factors as the imposition of a local sales tax, the election of a new school board, an extended period of stormy weather, and marital changes within families who are savers are all among these uncontrolled extraneous factors. It is not likely that the election of a new school board will affect savings, but the imposition of a new sales tax might have some modest effect. Changes in marital status within families (divorces, death, marriages) could have a substantial effect, but it may be assumed that these will occur randomly among the study groups. On the other hand, an extended period of storms might have a pronounced short-term effect on savings that would confound any results from the promotion program.

Intervening Variables.   Most if not all of the variables discussed in the examples of positional relationships are concrete. They are clearly measurable factors that can be seen, counted, or observed in some way. Sometimes, however, we may not be completely satisfied by the explanations they give. Thus, while we may accept that "promotion leads to increased savings," we may feel that this is not the full explanation. We may hypothesize that there is an *intervening* mechanism or variable (IVV) that connects promotion and savings. Such an intervening variable might be a construct such as "motivation to save." *An intervening variable is a conceptual mechanism through which the IV, MV, and CV all affect the DV.* Tuckman defines the intervening variables "that factor which theoretically affects the observed phenomenon but cannot be seen, measured, or manipulated; its effect must be inferred from the effects of the independent and moderator variables on the observed phenomenon."[14] Examples of hypotheses with intervening variables (IVV) are:

A.   A promotion campaign (IV) brings increased savings (DV) *by increasing motivation to save* (IVV).

---

[14] Bruce Tuckman, *Conducting Educational Research* (New York: Harcourt Brace Jovanovich, Inc., 1972), p. 45.

B. The advent of a four-day week (*IV*) leads to increased productivity (*DV*) *by improving worker job satisfaction* (*IVV*).

C. The introduction of unit pricing is followed by a purchase shift to lower-priced products (*DV*) *by providing the buyer with a rational decision rule* (*IVV*).

D. Change to self-inspection (*IV*) reduces the number of defective parts produced (*DV*) *by increasing worker pride of performance* (*IVV*).

Linkage Relationships

Once the positional relations among explanatory variables have been stated there is a further need to consider the type(s) of linkage that is involved. Zetterberg has suggested seven different linkage forms to describe the nature and degree of causal connection between variables.[15] To explore these linkages let's consider a study of savings activity as a savings and loan association in which the following variables are of interest:

U = Variety of accounts offered by the association.
V = Distance of saver's home from association office.
W = Motivation of account holder to save.
X = Promotional efforts by association to encourage saving.
Y = Income of saver.
Z = Savings activity.

The first question of linkage should be "Are the variables causally connected or not?" The relationship may be *real* or it may be *illusory,* caused by an accidental parallelism. The management of a savings and loan association may observe that an offering of several new account varieties (U) correlates with an increase in savings activity (Z); they conclude that the increase in U has caused the increase in Z—a real linkage. On the other hand the relationship between U and Z may be illusory. The account ideas may have been launched at the same time that a substantial number of the savers received increases in income (Y), so this latter factor may be the cause of the increased savings activity. The concurrence of U and Z is accidental. We might also ask whether introducing a four-day workweek "caused" improved productivity per man-hour or whether this apparent connection is accidental. In similar fashion we should challenge other hypothesized explanatory relationships on the grounds that they may be illusory.

Dependency Nature.   The linkage among explanatory variables may also be characterized by the nature and strength of the dependency relationship between the variables. For example, is the *IV-DV* connection a *necessary* one, or is one *IV substitutable* for another? To claim a necessary relationship between two variables is to claim that a change in W (savings motivation)

---
[15] Hans L. Zetterberg, *On Theory and Verification in Sociology,* 3d ed. (Totowa, N.J., The Bedminister Press, 1953), pp. 69–74.

must accompany any change in *Z* (savings activity). Note that we do not say that increased *W* will always lead to increased *Z*, but only that an increase in *Z* requires an increase in *W*. On the other hand, we might agree that more *U* could lead to more *W* but that more *X*, less *V*, or more *Y* might be substituted for more *U* in this linkage with *W*.

The nature of linkage dependency also hinges on the concepts of *sufficiency* and *contingency*. A sufficient condition exists when the *IV* alone is enough to cause a *DV*. In the savings example we would be assuming sufficiency if we hypothesized that promotional efforts (*X*) alone would cause a change in one's savings activity (*Z*). On the other hand, it would be a contingent relationship if we hypothesized that the promotional efforts (*X*) would have a greater effect on savings activity (*Z*) among those savers with recent changes in income (*Y*).

Linkage dependencies may also be expressed as *deterministic* (*X* and *Z* are always connected in a fixed pattern) or *stochastic* (there is a probability that *X* and *Z* will occur together). Deterministic relationships are infrequent in business and human affairs. None probably exists among the variables in the savings example. Stochastic relationships may be expressed in terms of varying degrees of probability. For example, there may be a low probability that a change in income (*Y*) will affect a given person's savings activity (*Z*), while the combination of *Y* with *X* may increase substantially the probability of *Z*.

Linkage Direction.   Three linkages are essentially directional in nature. First, a relationship may be *reversible* (if *X*, then *Z*; and if *Z*, then *X*) or it may be *irreversible* (if *X*, then *Z*; or if *Z*, then *X*; but not both). A linkage between the distance to association office (*Y*) and savings activity (*Z*) would normally be viewed as irreversible. Seldom would the decline of savings activity lead to a move away from the office. However, consider the relationship between association promotion efforts and savings activity. Management would normally expect intensified promotion (*X*) to result in increased savings (*Z*). However, it is also likely that a change in savings activity (*Z*) might result in changes in promotion activity (*X*).

A relation between two variables may also be either *sequential* or *coextensive*. In the former (if *X*, then later *Z*), there is a clear time order of events. A clear sequence implies an irreversible relationship. On the other hand, if the two variables are coextensive (*X* and *Z* at the same time), the question of direction of causality is less clear. The variable linkages in the savings example are all normally viewed as sequential in nature, but whether they are or not depends on the conceptualization of the problem. It is clearly sequential if one is tracing the immediate impact of a promotional mailing on savings activity. On the other hand a study among families which relates level of income (*Y*) with savings motivation (*W*) requires no assumption of sequence.

Finally, a relation between variables may or may not be viewed as being *interdependent*. In an interdependent relationship an increment of *W* leads to an increment of *Z*, which in turn stimulates further increase in *W*. This complexity is often recognizable in research studies where the normal independent variables are reinforced by changes in dependent variables. In the savings example, an increase in W (motivation) may lead to an increase in savings (Z), which in turn may reinforce the W (motivation) to increase Z (savings) even more.

Each hypothesized relationship should be analyzed for these seven linkage conditions. Whether the relationship is reversible or irreversible may be academic *if* the researchers are confident that they know the direction of possible causation in the design. Usually the independent variables will be substitutable rather than necessary to the dependent effect. Likewise, variables are often contingent on other conditions. Most hypotheses are probably stochastic, but they may be either sequential or coextensive. There is often the possibility that the two variables are interdependent. All of these linkages, however, are predicted on the assumption that there is a *real linkage* between variables.

All seven of these linkage relationships are relevant when proposing hypotheses. We tend, however, to ignore or assume too many of them away. We can illustrate this point with a hypothesis example already used, "A change to self-inspection (IV) of assembled electronic parts (CV) reduces the number of defective parts produced (DV) when the assembled product can be identified with the assembler (MV)." The mere proposing of such a hypothesis should prompt a question as to whether this relationship may not be illusory. The emphasis in the hypothesis statement is placed on whether self-inspection reduces defective parts, not whether self-inspection is the only IV that will do so. Thus, whether self-inspection is necessary or whether some other variable IV could be substituted is not considered.

The sufficiency-contingency question is addressed when it is stated that the operation of the IV on the DV is contingent upon the moderating factor of "product can be identified with the assembler." In business research studies most IV-DV bonds are sufficiently tenuous that researchers do not claim deterministic relationships. In this case the deterministic-stochastic question is not addressed explicitly. The sequential IV-DV relationship is implied (reduction in defective parts follows change in inspection procedures); it is also probably assumed to be an irreversible and noninterdependent relationship.

The need for adequate concern for position and linkage relationships is obvious in drafting hypotheses. They are also important, along with other considerations, when we test causal hypotheses.

Testing Causal Hypotheses

On an operational level the researcher has three aims in testing causal hypotheses. These are:

A. To measure the covariation among the explanatory variables.
B. To determine whether any time order of events is in the hypothesized direction.

C. To assure that other factors do not confound relationships among the explanatory variables.

A good research design is one which achieves these three goals efficiently. Two approaches by which we may improve the testing power of a research design are *strong inference* and *statistical inference*.

Strong Inference.   This approach, so named by Platt, consists of two important concepts.[16] First, he suggests that Chamberlin's "method of multiple working hypotheses" be adopted. The application of this method calls for the researcher to develop multiple hypotheses by which to explain a phenomenon. In developing the multiple hypotheses, "the effort is to bring up into view every rational explanation of the phenomenon in hand and to develop every tenable hypothesis relative to its nature, cause, or origin, and to give to all of these as impartially as possible a working form and a due place in the investigation."[17] The use of multiple hypotheses not only reduces the attachment (and potential bias) of the researcher for a given hypothesis but also encourages the development of efficient research designs that can test several hypotheses in a single study.

The second major feature of strong inference consists of "devising a crucial experiment (or several of them), with alternative possible outcomes, each of which will, as nearly as possible, exclude one or more of the hypotheses."[18] The need to disprove hypotheses is emphasized because a hypothesis can never be proved, only disproved or excluded. This is true even though the evidence we collect appears to be so clear that we are quite confident about our conclusion. How does the method of strong inference work? As an example, let's consider a case in which a plant management is plagued with rising costs and high loss of skilled personnel. Management may wish to identify the cause of these problems. We might advance several hypotheses:

A. Ineffective plant management (*IV*) has led to low morale and high discontent among the workers (*IVV*). As a result productivity has declined and many good workers have quit (*DV*).
B. Our pay scales are not competitive with those of other companies (*IV*), and this low pay has led to worker discontent (*IVV*). The result is lower productivity and worker resignations (*DV*).
C. The physical layout and working conditions in our plant are so bad (*IV*), that they cause low productivity (*DV*).
D. The living environment near our plant, the area where most of the workers live, has deteriorated so badly (*IV*) that it is adversely affecting our employee productivity and worker retention (*DV*).

---

[16] John R. Platt, "Strong Inference," *Science,* October 16, 1964, pp. 346–52.

[17] T. C. Chamberlin, "The Method of Multiple Working Hypotheses," *Journal of Geology,* vol. 5, pp. 837–48.

[18] Platt, "Strong Inference."

To these multiple working hypotheses we might add other rational causes. Then we would design a research study in which we would try to eliminate each of these as a possible source of the problem. The assumption is that those which we cannot eliminate are our best explanations of the causes.

The method of exclusion is popular in the physical sciences and has been acclaimed as the paramount tool for making advances in such fields as molecular biology.[19] In business research, on the other hand, its use is not so widespread. Here there has been more emphasis on finding correlations, indicating that there are associations between variables. The method of statistical inference is particularly helpful in these cases.

Statistical Inference. Statistics serves several major purposes. One is the reduction of large quantities of data to manageable and intelligible form; this is the role of descriptive statistics. Statistics can also aid in drawing inferences from data. This second purpose is important for testing hypotheses and estimating population measures from sample data. Consider again the problem of high Monday absenteeism in a factory; the hypothesis is that absenteeism is associated with membership in a camping club. Normally we would not expect all club members to be absent from work after every camping weekend, nor would we expect all nonmembers to be present every Monday. By using statistical inference we can estimate the probability of a connection between membership in the club and absenteeism even though we study only a portion of the total workers and club members.

If we were to calculate the Monday attendance record for a random sample of employees, it might be higher or lower than daily average attendance at the factory, just because of the "luck of the draw" (called random variation). This sample might also just happen to include many camping club members who are seldom absent. A second sample drawn from the work force might also show this "random" pattern of being higher or lower than the average, again only because of the luck of the draw. With the aid of probability theory we can estimate how likely it is that a given deviation will occur randomly (by chance). In general the greater the deviation from average the smaller the likelihood that it is a true random or chance deviation. Thus, if the deviation we find is so great that it would happen by chance only one time in a large number of samples, we conclude that something more than just chance is the cause of the deviation.

Assume that we reviewed the records of 400 persons in the work force and found that 50 people were members of the camping club. A tabulation of all those who have "high absences" on Mondays (operationally defined here as two or more Monday absences in the last eight weeks) might look like the data in Table 4–1.

The data suggest that club members are much more likely to be in the high absence group than are other members of the work force. A Chi-square

---
[19] Ibid.

Table 4–1: Data on Employee Absenteeism

	Camping Club Member?	
Absences	Yes	No
High	40	70
Low	10	280

analysis indicates that such a departure from the average attendance pattern would occur by chance less than 1 time in 1,000 with such a sample.[20] Thus, we can be very confident that members of the club have an unusually high absence pattern even though we have studied only a portion of the work force. Whether we can conclude that membership in the club causes higher absenteeism on Mondays is not clear. Certainly the evidence is consistent with this conclusion, but what other evidence would be useful?

Time Order of Events. It is logical to expect that, if club membership causes higher absenteeism, there will be a temporal relationship between these two facts. For example, if high Monday absenteeism among club members followed a weekend camping outing, this fact would be good support for the hypothesis. If this time order did not appear, one might reason that the two might not be connected in a causal way.

Time order relationships are not always so clearcut. If the camping trip took place on Monday, it would occur at the same time as the absenteeism, but such an event would also be strong support for the hypothesis that club membership causes absenteeism. It is even possible that the "effect" might precede the "cause." Club members might be absent on a Friday prior to a weekend camping trip in order to prepare for the outing. Thus, while time order of events is an important factor in determination of causal linkages, no simple before-after relationship is adequate explanation for all cases. We must analyze each situation to determine what temporal relationships are implied by the hypothesis.

Elimination of Other Factors. The researcher must predict which of the infinite number of possible variables are major threats to the study and then try to incorporate safeguards into the study design to assure that these factors do not confound the hypothesized relationships. The many forms in which these factors are found suggest that a variety of approaches are required.

One type of extraneous factor is the past event or rather enduring variable that has existed prior to the study. One's family background affects many

---

[20] Chi-square analysis is one of a number of statistical tests which may be used to determine how confident we can be about a statistical conclusion. Specifics about the assumptions underlying the test and the methods of calculation will be presented in Chapter 13.

attitudes; any research that touches these attitudes either must determine what these background-based attitudes are or must arrange to see that, with regard to them, there is no systematic difference between or among study groups. A second type of extraneous factor occurs contemporaneously with the experiment—at the same time that the IV is introduced. An example would be a series of widespread industrial strikes at nearby firms which occurs just as we introduce a new type of savings account.

Another type of confounding variable, maturation or developmental change, can occur when the study is carried out over a period of time. People age and mature, learning more about all sorts of topics; fashions mature and disappear. Even in studies covering as short a period as several hours, persons can become hungry, tired, and so forth. Finally, the act of measurement itself can be a confounding factor; a "before" measurement may sensitize the subject to the problem of research interest. Suppose we use a "before" measurement to determine the level of information prior to an advertising campaign. If the same persons are measured again after the campaign (IV), awareness of the product (DV) might be higher than before because their attention has been drawn to the product by the "before" measurement. There are a number of other problems, but these four suffice to point out the importance of dealing with potentially confounding factors. The approaches the researcher uses to meet these and other problems depend on whether the study is experimental or ex post facto.

Causal Inference and Experimental Design

Covariation. Experimental evidence on covariation is collected in a straightforward way. The investigator determines who or what (the experimental group) is to be exposed to the assumed causal variable (IV) and who or what (the control group) is not to be exposed. The opportunity for manipulation and control in a selective manner is the great strength of experimentation. After the manipulation and selective exposure of the IV, the subjects are measured in terms of the relationships between the IV and the DV.

Time Order. The time order between variables is also dealt with relatively easily. The researcher can often determine a priori which variable, independent or dependent, occurs first. If there is any question of time order, she employs one or both of two methods to assure that the proper time order is determined. She may measure the subjects on the DV prior to the manipulation. Alternatively, she may set up the experimental and control groups so that they do not differ in terms of the DV before the manipulation takes place.

Other Variables. The potential confounding factors are dealt with by several approaches, some of which were alluded to earlier in this chapter. First, when the investigator is aware of potential confounding extraneous factors, she may control for them. One form of control is exclusion from the study of those subjects who do not hold certain characteristics. For example, if a planned study might be confounded by differences in age and social status, we might include only those persons in the age groups and social classes of greatest interest. This procedure limits our ability to generalize the results to all people, but it also eliminates much of the extraneous variation due to age and social class.

A second approach utilizes a *matching* process. We measure selected extraneous variables by subject. Subjects with similar patterns of variables are then apportioned to the experimental and control groups. Two general types of matching are used. One, *precision control,* calls for individual-by-individual matching according to a set of characteristics. Matched subjects are then alloted to experimental and control groups. These can be tedious and difficult tasks especially if the individuals must have an uncommon combination of characteristics.

The other form of control, *frequency control,* is less demanding. Individual matching is not attempted. Rather, averages and dispersions are used. For example, each study group is constituted of 50 percent males, 25 percent in each undergraduate class, 10 percent in engineering, and 60 percent middle-class. This method, while much easier, obviously offers less assurance of group equality than does precision control. However, both matching methods are secondary to randomization.

Randomization is the basic method by which equivalence between experimental and control groups is determined. At the heart of experimental design is the assumption that experimental and control groups can be established in such a way that they are equivalent. Matching and controlling are useful, but they still leave an infinite number of unknowns unaccounted for. The best procedure is to assign subjects either to experimental or control groups randomly (this is not to say haphazardly—randomness must be secured in a carefully controlled fashion according to strict rules of assignment). If the assignments are made randomly, each group should receive its fair share of different factors. The only deviation from this fair share would be that which results from random variation (luck of the draw). The possible impact of these unknown extraneous variables on the dependent variables should also vary randomly. The researcher, using tests of statistical significance, can estimate the probable effect of these chance variations on the *DV* and can then compare this estimated effect of extraneous variation to the actual differences found in the *DV* in the experimental and control groups.

It is important to emphasize again that random assignment to experimental and control groups is the *basic technique* by which the two groups can be made equivalent. Matching and other control forms are supplemental ways of improving the quality of measurement. In a sense, matching and controls reduce the extraneous "noise" in the measurement system and in this way improve the sensitivity of measurement of the hypothesized relationship.

Causal Inference and Ex Post Facto Design

Covariation.   Many studies cannot be carried out with experimental designs, so the theoretically inferior ex post facto design is used. Instead of manipulating exposure to the IV, the researcher must uncover comparative groups which have and have not been exposed to the "causal" factor under study. Correlations are found through cross-classification of these contrasting groups with the DV. The data on the camping club (Table 4–1) illustrate such a comparison. Fifty people had been "exposed" to the IV, (were members of the club), while the other 350 had not.

The major weakness in this type of analysis is that it offers no assurance that the club members (experimental group) are equivalent to the other employees (control group). Members of these two groups are self-selected—that is, for specific age, personality, or other reasons some people find membership in the club appealing and so have joined. Others have selected themselves out of the club by not joining. Thus, the two groups may not be as equivalent as they would have been if we had randomly assigned workers to club membership. Other factors may be causing certain persons to (1) join the club and (2) also be absence-prone, but the extent of these self-selecting factors cannot be estimated statistically.

Tests of statistical significance can be used with both experimental and ex post facto designs. However, consider the differences in the power of our interpretation of the data in Table 4–1, even if we assume that different research designs would produce the same numeric results.

Design	Interpretation
Ex post facto	Less than 1 time in 1,000 would we expect the absenteeism rates to differ so much between the two groups because of chance factors. Therefore, we can conclude that there is a very high probability that members of the camping club are also the persons with the high absenteeism rates. However, both absenteeism and club membership may be due to one or more other factors.
Experimental	Less than 1 time in 1,000 would we expect the absenteeism rates to differ so much between the two groups because of chance factors. Since the subjects were randomly assigned to the two groups, we can say that there is a very high probability that membership in the camping club leads to higher absenteeism.

Time Order.   By its nature ex post facto research precludes any "before" measurement. There is no way actually to observe that IV precedes DV, but there are several substitute techniques which the ex post facto designer can use. First, the researcher may ask subjects about the time order of events.

They are often able to reconstruct event sequences or report when certain events, changes in attitudes, and so forth, took place. This method is the most frequently used.

A second technique is that of the longitudinal study referred to earlier in the chapter. While we may not be able to manipulate the variables in a longitudinal study, we may, over a period of time, collect data about the relationship of the *IV* and *DV*. Many studies using this approach are called "quasiexperiments," which are discussed in Chapter 11.

Other Variables. Random assignment, the best technique for neutralizing the confounding of other factors, is unavailable to the designer of the ex post facto study. Control and matching techniques, however, are possible. First, the collection of data and the use of subjects who possess certain control characteristics will help to reduce extraneous variation. For example, in the camping club study the researcher may take only a part of the work force, those who are of a certain age group, work tenure, job classification, and so on. Comparison of club membership with absenteeism in these limited groups yields "purer" measurement.

While assignment by matching, as described in the experimental section, is not used in ex post facto designs, the researcher does gather information about potentially confounding factors and uses these data to establish crossbreaks, which illustrate how the *IV-DV* relationship is affected when other factors are introduced. For example, assume that age data were introduced into the absenteeism example; the results might look like those in Table 4–2. These data indicate that age is also a factor. Younger people are more

Table 4–2: Data on Employee Absenteeism

Age	Club Member		Nonclub Member	
	High Absentee	Low Absentee	High Absentee	Low Absentee
Under 30 years	36	6	30	48
30 to 45	4	4	35	117
45 and over	0	0	5	115

likely to be among the high absentees. A part of the high absenteeism rate among club members seems to be associated with the fact that most club members are under 30 years of age. On the other hand, within age groups, it is also apparent that club members have substantially higher incidence of excessive absenteeism than nonclub members of the same age. By such comparisons as these we can employ the strong inference approach of testing to eliminate multiple factors as potential "causes." More will be said about the analysis of crossbreak data and the interpretation of relationships in later chapters.

Research Design Example

Some economists at the U.S. Department of Agriculture (USDA) felt a need to do more research about the effect of their policy actions on industry decisions. They chose the vegetable fats and oil industry for a study since government policy had clearly affected the prices of cottonseed and soybean oils. Cottonseed oil was the major oil used in margarine and shortening; soybean oil was cheaper but also unstable and therefore a risk in many product applications. Technological developments, however, suggested that it might be the major oil of the future. Liquid oils, such as corn and safflower oils, were not yet well developed.

The people at USDA felt that an outsider could probably study this problem better, so they invited bids from universities. Ira Fenner, a professor at the Business School of Midwest University submitted a bid and was eventually awarded a modest grant to study industry substitution practices between cottonseed and soybean oils.

Fenner immediately began an exploratory search since he had little knowledge of the specifics of the industry. In particular he needed to learn about the chemistry and technology of vegetable oils, as well as shortening and margarine manufacturing. A second direction for immediate study was the economics of the growing, crushing, refining, and oil-based manufacturing industries.[21] Fortunately the USDA had a massive bank of current and past statistical data plus access to other relevant government information.

After exploring secondary data sources for awhile, Fenner visited USDA to learn more about their specific interests as well as more about the makeup of the industry. USDA people also provided him with some contacts for the upcoming industry meeting which he was to attend. At the industry meeting Fenner talked with industry economists and industry executives, chiefly bean and seed crushers and oil refiners. His strategy at this early point was to learn as much as he could and defer any detailed talk of his study until later.

He returned home, reviewed his notes, did some more secondary source searching, and then wanted to talk with some people in the business. Because of his restricted budget and the fact that 12 major companies owned more than one half of the approximately 130 shortening and margarine plants in the United States, he decided to approach only small independent firms at this stage. After lengthy interviews with executives at two independent firms he settled on his design and drafted up his survey instrument.

Design Characteristics. He had concluded from the start that the study would be a two-stage ex post facto, crosssectional field study with a major exploration first stage. At the original negotiations all parties agreed that

---

[21] Crushers processed the beans or seeds to extract meal and crude oil, both valuable commercial products. Refiners processed the crude oil to a more pure state, while manufacturers further processed the oil and/or combined it with other materials to make finished products. As might be expected, there was frequent vertical integration of these stages.

the study would be largely description, but with certain important causal questions addressed. While the major research effort would be a survey, there was much searching of secondary and statistical sources. Finally, because of the complexity of the study, the limited number of companies in the industry, and budget limitations, it was concluded that he should produce a number of composite case studies of typical operations and practices. It was agreed in the contract that surveys would be conducted with 5 cottonseed oil refiners, and 5 soybean oil refiners, and 25 oil-based product manufacturers.

Further design details were worked out and agreed to. Among them were the following excerpts:

Research Question: What are the important factors that bear on the choice between cottonseed and soybean oil for processing into shortening and margarine?

Investigative Questions: Descriptive Examples.
1.   What are the general characteristics of the firms in the vegetable fats and oil industry, the products they produce, the raw materials they use, and the markets they serve, by plant location?
2.   What are the management practices in buying raw materials as they concern what, where, when, and how they buy for a particular plant?
3.   What are the management practices in selling and how do different factors affect company selling activities?
4.   What are the attitudes and practices of managements regarding the substitution and interchangeability of oils and fats in their products, and the reasons for changes in oil usage rates in recent years?
5.   How does multiple ownership of plants and local environmental factors affect the substitution of oils?

Investigative Questions: Causal Hypothesis Examples.
1.   Changes in the price spread between cottonseed and soybean oil lead to prompt substitution of one for the other, but only at certain identifiable threshold levels.
2.   Over the past ten years the spread threshold has narrowed because of technological developments in oil chemistry and shifts in the industry geography.
3.   The size of the price spread threshold varies by the type of product, and by price-quality level within product type.
4.   Experience with a substitution of cheaper oils typically leads to reluctance to shift back to the more expensive oil when the price spread returns to its original threshold point.
5.   In the short run the decision to use soybean or cottonseed oil is affected by plant location. In the long run plant location is affected by the decision to substitute soybean oil for cottonseed oil.

From the data gathered to this point Fenner developed an interview guide of more than 50 major questions, each usually with several parts to it. Most of the questions were open-ended. It was believed that it would take six hours or more of interviewing in each company to complete the schedule.

Fenner reviewed this first draft with the section chief who was supervising the project and then revised the interview guide. He then took it to a local refiner and food manufacturer and tested it. The interview went well but took longer than planned; there were also some difficulties with some questions. After another revision he repeated this test-revise cycle with two other companies. By this time the interviews were going well and most of the problems seemed to be solved.

Finner then developed the final interview guide, plus a detailed rationale for each question on the guide. He submitted these to the USDA for review. The review went through several levels of the department successfully and was sent on to the U.S. Bureau of the Budget for final approval. At that time the Budget Bureau was charged with final approval of all questionnaires sent to the public under federal auspices.

At the Budget Bureau there was an industry advisory committee whose members review such questionnaires. Severl prominent members of the committee flatly stated that their companies would not cooperate with the study and recommended that it be disapproved on the grounds that it called for disclosure of confidential company information. At this time, also, the major advocate of the study in the USDA left the organization for an academic position; the original study was never approved. The contract was revised and a study was completed using the information already collected plus some further collection of secondary data.

SUMMARY

A research design is the strategy for a study as well as the plans by which the strategy is to be carried out. It specifies the methods and procedures for the collection, measurement, and analysis of data. Research designs can be classified in a variety of ways. Some of the major ones are:

Exploratory versus formalized.
Case versus statistical.
Field versus laboratory versus simulation.
Crosssectional versus longitudinal.
Observational versus survey.
Experimental versus ex post facto.
Descriptive versus causal.

Exploratory research is appropriate for the total study in subject areas where the developed data are limited. In most other studies it is the first stage of a project and is used to orient the researcher and the study. The objective of exploration is the development of hypotheses rather than their testing. Formalized studies are those with substantial structure and with specific hypotheses to be tested or research questions to be answered.

Descriptive studies are those used to describe phenomena associated with a subject population or to estimate the proportions of the population that have certain characteristics. Causal studies seek to determine what effect one variable has on others or why certain conditions obtain.

The theoretical ideal of causation can never be demonstrated because of the need for many simplifying assumptions. We can never prove beyond doubt, because the techniques of inductive inference are tools of limited power. Mill's canons illustrate the strengths and weaknesses of these tools. Two other major sets of problems make the task of causal research difficult.

To identify causal connections between variables, the researcher must also recognize and deal effectively with the positional relationships among variables. These relationships may be classified as:

I. Explanatory variables.
    a. Independent variable.
    b. Dependent variable.
    c. Moderating variables.
II. Extraneous variables.
    a. Controlled variables.
    b. Uncontrolled variables.
        1. Confounding variables.
        2. Random variables.
III. Intervening variables.

There are also a variety of possible linkage relationships between two variables. Seven can be readily identified. Is the relationship:

1. Real or illusory?
2. Necessary or substitutable?
3. Sufficient to cause the effect or contingent on other factors?
4. Deterministic or stochastic?
5. Reversible or irreversible?
6. Sequential or coextensive?
7. Interdependent or not?

We test causal hypotheses by seeking to do three things. These are:

1. Measure the covariation among variables.
2. Determine the time order relationships among variables.
3. Assure that other factors do not confound the explanatory relationships.

The problems of achieving these aims differ somewhat in experimental and ex post facto studies. Using the methods of strong inference and statistical inference, we gather and evaluate evidence for and against the causal hypothesis. Where possible, we try to achieve the ideal of the experimental design with its random assignment of subjects, matching of subject characteristics, and manipulation and control of variables. Using these methods and techniques, we measure relationships as accurately and objectively as possible.

SUPPLEMENTAL READINGS

1. Blalock, Hubert M., Jr. *Causal Inference in Nonexperimental Research.* Chapel Hill, N.C.: The University of North Carolina Press, 1964. A good but somewhat theoretical discussion of causal inference under nonexperimental conditions.
2. Helmstader, G. C. *Research Concepts in Human Behavior.* New York: Appleton-Century-Crofts, 1970. Chaps. 2–4 cover the historical and case approaches, the descriptive approach, and experimentation.
3. Kerlinger, Fred N. *Foundations of Behavioral Research.* 2d ed. New York: Holt, Rinehart and Winston, Inc., 1973. Chaps. 22–24 discuss various types of research.
4. Rosen, Lawrence, and West, Robert. *A Reader for Research Methods.* New York: Random House, 1973. Presents a wide range of complete and integrated examples of the application of research methods in social research areas.
5. Selltiz, Claire; Wrightsman, Lawrence S.; and Cook, Stuart M. *Research Methods in Social Relations.* 3d ed. New York: Holt, Rinehart and Winston, 1976. Chaps. 4 and 5 discuss various various types of research design.
6. Tuckman, Bruce W. *Conducting Educational Research.* New York: Harcourt Brace Jovanovich, Inc., 1972. An excellent discussion of the relationships among variables.

DISCUSSION QUESTIONS

1. Distinguish between:
    a. Case and observation studies.
    b. Ex post facto and statistical studies.
    c. Causal and experimental studies.
    d. Independent and moderating variables.
    e. Necessary and sufficient linkages.
    f. Contingent and deterministic linkages.
    g. Dependent and random variables.
2. Suggest how you would carry out research studies that are specified as:
    a. An exploratory, crosssectional, observational, descriptive, ex post facto, case study of professorial teaching effectiveness.
    b. A formalized, longitudinal, descriptive, ex post facto, statistical survey of professiorial teaching effectiveness.
    c. A crosssectional, causal, field survey, case study, experiment of consumer reactions to food-store advertising.
3. From a business research point of view:
    a. What are the two most useful of Mill's canons?
    b. Of what significance are they?

    c.   Philosophers of science have criticized Mill's canons as providing in-
adequate proof of causation. What is the basis for their argument? How
would you defend the canons?

4.   You are the administrative assistant to a division chief in a large manufacturing organization. You and the division chief have just come from the
general manager's office, where you were informed that your division's
worker morale was unsatisfactory. You had sensed the tension among the
workers but had not considered it unusual. The division chief calls you into
the office after the meeting and instructs you to investigate this morale
situation.

    a.   What would you do first? How would you go about it?

    b.   Illustrate how Mill's canons might be applied to different variables in
this situation.

5.   During the 1970s the stock brokerage industry went through many changes.
Under government pressure the industry abandoned fixed commission
rates. Many firms had financial difficulties because of these rate changes
as well as other factors, such as undercapitalization, sometimes heavy
volumes which overwhelmed backroom processing operations, and at
other times slumps in volume that led to revenue losses. As a result, many
firms ceased operations or were absorbed by others. Even some of the
larger firms on Wall Street met this fate.

    a.   Suppose you wished to study this industry situation and its problems in
the 1970s for a semester term report; suggest the research design
types which would probably be most appropriate for you to use.

    b.   Suppose you were given a $100,000 grant, three assistants, and six
months in which to study this industry situation and its problems in the
1970s. What research design types can you suggest as possibilities?

6.   You have been asked to determine how large corporations go about preparing for labor contract negotiations with unions. Since you know relatively
little about this subject, how would you go about conducting the study? Be
as specific as possible.

7.   *a.*   How can you tell which variable should be the independent variable
and which should be the moderating variable?

    b.   Why not use more control variables rather than depend on randomiza-
tion as the means of controlling extraneous variables?

8.   One useful concept in dealing with causation is the linkage idea. How many
of the seven linkage pairs can you illustrate using as the dependent
variable:

    a.   The purchase of a new auto.

    b.   A change in the national inflation rate.

    c.   The decline in price of common stock of the IBM Corp.

9.   Propose one or more hypotheses for each of the following variable pairs,
specifying which is the *IV* and which the *DV*. Then elaborate the basic
hypothesis to include at least one moderating variable, an intervening variable, and one or more extraneous variables.

    a.   The Index of Consumer Confidence and the business cycle.

    b.   Level of worker output and closeness of supervision of the worker.

    c.   Degree of personal friendship between customer and salesperson and the frequency of sales calls on the customer.

10. Researchers seek causal relationships by either experimental or ex post facto research designs.

    a.   In what ways are these two approaches similar?

    b.   In what ways are they different?

Chapter 5

Measurement

THE GENERAL CONCEPT OF MEASUREMENT is fairly clear. In everyday usage we "measure" when we use some established yardstick to determine the height, weight, or some other feature of a physical object. We also measure when we judge how well we like a song, a painting, or the personalities of our friends. In a dictionary sense to measure is "to ascertain the extent, dimensions, quantity, capacity, etc., of, esp. by comparison with a standard."[1]

We may measure in a rather casual way in our daily life, but in research the requirements are more rigorous. As a result, research measurement can be a complex and demanding task. In this chapter we will identify these complexities and suggest how to deal with them. Specifically we shall consider (1) the nature of the measurement process, (2) the fundamental scales of measurement, (3) the special difficulties of assuring that measurement is effective, (4) the characteristics of sound measurement tools, and (5) the procedure for developing such tools.

THE NATURE OF MEASUREMENT

Measurement is the process by which we test hypotheses and theories. We deduce from a hypothesis that certain conditions should exist in the real world; then we measure for these conditions. If found, they lend support to

---

[1] *The Random House Dictionary of the English Language* (New York: Random House, 1966), p. 889.

the hypothesis; if they are not found, we conclude that the hypothesis fails. An important question at this point is "Just what does one measure?"

What Is Measured?

Concepts used in research may be classified into (1) *objects* and (2) *properties*. Objects include the "things" of ordinary experience, such as tables, people, books, and automobiles. Objects also include things which are not so concrete, such as genes, attitudes, neutrons, and peer group pressures. Properties, on the other hand, are the characteristics of the objects. For example, a man's physical properties may be stated in terms of his weight, height, posture; his psychological properties include his attitudes, intelligence; and his social properties include his leadership ability and his class affiliation or status. These and many other properties of that individual can be of measurement interest in a research study. In a more literal sense we do not measure objects or properties. We measure *indicants* of the properties.[2] Thus, we actually measure *indicants* of the *properties* of *objects*.

Some might feel that this distinction is just an effort to make a simple topic more complex. So it might seem when we are dealing with objective and observable properties. It is easy to observe that A is taller than B and that C participates more than D in a group process. The indicants in these cases are so accepted that we consider the properties to be observed directly. The task is different with such properties as motivation, attitude, creativity, and market potential. Since these can not be measured directly, we must infer their presence or absence by observing some indicant or "pointer" measurement.

Suppose we are analyzing members of a sales force of several hundred people to determine what personal properties make for sales success. Properties such as age, years of experience, number of calls made per week, and so forth, can be measured directly. In contrast it is not easy to measure properties like motivation to succeed, ability to stand stress, problem-solving ability, and persuasiveness. Not only is it a challenge to measure such constructs, but the researcher may also find little agreement that these are even the proper ones to study. The quality of a study depends on the adequacy of the research design and the appropriateness of the measuring concepts and procedures.

Measurement Defined

Measurement has been defined as "the matching of an aspect of one domain to an aspect of another."[3] This matching, often called *mapping*, is the

---

[2] Kerlinger views an indicant as "merely a convenient word used to mean something that points to something else." See Fred N. Kerlinger, *Foundations of Behavioral Research,* 2d ed. (New York: Holt, Rinehart and Winston, Inc., 1973), p. 432.

[3] S. S. Stevens, "Measurement, Statistics, and the Schemapiric View," *Science,* vol. 161, no. 3844 (August 30, 1968), p. 855.

operation of establishing correspondence between properties in one area (or *set*) and properties in another set. Mapping from one set onto the members of the other is done according to some rule of correspondence. The terms *domain* and *range* are used to distinguish between the sets. The process is to assign or match each member of a domain with a member of the range.

Assume that we are conducting a study of persons who attend an auto show where all of the year's new models are on display. We are interested in learning who comes to such shows. One point of interest is the male-to-female attendance ratio. We might observe those who enter the show area and tabulate them as to sex. In set theory terms, this process (see Figure 5–1)

Figure 5–1: Mapping Example with Nominal Scale

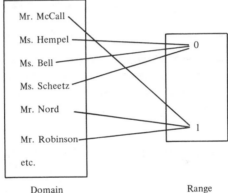

is one of mapping the observed physical properties of attendees (the domain) onto a sex classification (the range). The rule of correspondence is: If the object in the domain appears to be female, assign to "0"; if male, assign to "1." Any other symbols, such as "F" and "M" or "□" and "△" might be used, since the number codes are for identification only.

We might also want to measure the acceptability of the styling of the new Belchfire 8. We interview a sample of visitors and assign one of their psychological properties (attitude on the Belchfire 8) to a scale.[4] Figure 5–2 presents one possibility. In this example the numbers in the range express different degrees or quantities of like and dislike. Some measurement theorists have defined measurement as only those cases in which there is such quantification. For example, one definition of measurement is "the assignment of numbers to objects to represent amounts or degrees of a property possessed by all

---

[4] Actually we secure an indicant of their attitude toward the B-8. By asking the question various ways, we can secure differing measures of attitudes (the property).

Figure 5–2: Mapping Example with Ordinal Scale

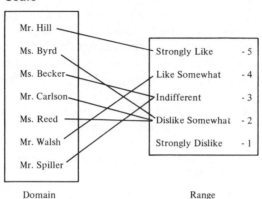

Domain   Range

of the objects."[5] Here we shall accept the more general view that numbers reflect qualitative as well as quantitative concepts. Researchers strive for quantitative measurement, which is more powerful statistically, but there are different types of scales, each of which is appropriate under given circumstances.

MEASUREMENT SCALES

In measuring we devise some form of scale in the range and then transform or map our observation of property indicants from the domain onto this scale. Several types of scales are possible in this situation; the appropriate choice depends on what we assume about the rule of correspondence. Each scale has its own set of underlying assumptions about how the numerals in the range correspond to the real-world observations in the domain.

Scale classifications employ the characteristics of the real numbers system. The most accepted scale conceptualization is based on the following three characteristics:

1. Numbers are ordered. One number is greater than, less than, or equal to another number.
2. Differences between numbers are ordered. The difference between any pair of numbers is greater than, less than, or equal to the difference between any other pair of numbers.
3. The number series has a unique origin indicated by the number zero.

---

[5] W. S. Torgerson, *Theory and Method of Scaling* (New York: John Wiley & Sons, Inc., 1958), p. 19.

Combinations of these characteristics of order, distance, and origin provide the following widely used classification of measurement scales:

Type of Scale	Characteristics of Scale	Basic Empirical Operation
Nominal	No order, distance, or origin.	Determination of equality.
Ordinal	Order but no distance or unique origin.	Determination of greater or lesser values.
Interval	Both order and distance but no unique origin.	Determination of equality of intervals or differences.
Ratio	Order, distance, and unique origin.	Determination of equality of ratios.

Nominal Scales

Some purists would argue that the use of a nominal scale does not qualify as measurement. In the social sciences and business research, however, nominal scales are probably more widely used than any others. When we use a nominal scale we partition a set into subsets or categories that are mutually exclusive and collectively exhaustive. For example, in the camping club illustration used in Table 4–1 persons were classified into four unique categories through cross-classification of club membership and degree of absenteeism. Each employee could be placed in one and only one of the four cells.

The counting of members in each group is the only possible arithmetic operation when a nominal scale is employed. If numbers are used (if club membership is classified as "1" and nonmembership as "0"), the numerals are recognized as labels only and have no quantitative value. Nominal classifications may consist of any number of separate groups so long as the groups are mutually exclusive and collectively exhaustive. Thus, one might class the residents of a city according to their expressed religious preferences in many ways. Classification set "A" given in the accompanying table is not a sound nominal scale because it is neither mutually exclusive nor collectively exhaustive. Set "B" meets these minimum requirements, although the classification may not be the most useful for a given research purpose.

Religious Preferences

A	B
Baptist	Catholic
Catholic	Jewish
Jewish	Protestant
Lutheran	Other
Methodist	None
Presbyterian	
Protestant	

Nominal scales are the least powerful of the four types. They indicate no order or distance relationship and have no arithmetic origin. The scale wastes any information that we may have about varying degrees of attitude, skills, understandings, and so on.

Since the only quantification is the number count of cases in each subset, we are restricted to the use of the mode as the measure of central tendency.[6] We can conclude which class has the most members, but that is all. There is no generally used measure of dispersion for nominal scales. Several tests for statistical significance may be utilized, the most common being the chi-square test. For measures of correlation the contingency coefficient C or one of several other measures may be appropriate. These and other significance tests and measures of association are presented in Chapter 13.

While nominal scales are weak, they are still very useful. If we cannot use any other scale, we can almost always map one set of properties onto a set of equivalent classes in the range. This scale is especially valuable in exploratory work, the objective of which is to uncover relationships rather than secure precise measurements. These scales are also widely used in survey and other ex post facto research when data are being classified by major subgroups of the population. Responses may vary with respondents' age, sex, political persuasion, exposure to a certain experience, and so on. Cross-partitions of these and other factors can provide insight into important data patterns.

Ordinal Scales

These scales include the uniqueness characteristics of the nominal scale plus an indicator of order. Ordinal measurement is possible when the transitivity postulate is justified. This postulate states: If a is greater than b and b is greater than c, then a is greater than c.[7] The use of an ordinal scale implies a statement of "greater than" or "less than" (an equality statement is also acceptable) without our being able to state how much greater or less. It is like a rubber yardstick that can stretch varying amounts at different places along its length. Thus, the real difference between ranks "1" and "2" may be more or less than the difference between ranks "2" and "3."

An ordinal concept can be generalized beyond the simple illustration of $a > b > c$. For example, any number of cases can be ranked. While ordinal

---

[6] We assume that the reader has had an introductory statistics course in which measures of central tendency such as the arithmetic mean, median, and mode have been treated. Similarly, we assume that the student is familiar with measures of dispersion such as the standard deviation, range, and interquartile range. For a review of these concepts please refer to almost any introductory statistics text.

[7] While this might intuitively seem always to be the case, consider that one might prefer a over b, b over c, yet prefer c over a. These results cannot be ordinally scaled because there is apparently more than one dimension involved.

measurement speaks of "greater than" and "less than" measurements, other relationships may be used—for example, "superior to," "happier than," or "above." A third extension of the simple ordinal concept occurs when more than one property is of interest. For example, tasters may be asked to rank varieties of carbonated soft drink by flavor, color, and carbonation as well as a combination of these characteristics. We can secure the combined ranking either by asking the respondent to make such a ranking or by doing our own combining of the individual rankings. The simplest approach is to ask the respondent to make the overall judgment. To develop an overall index, the researcher typically has to add and average ranks for each of the three dimensions. This procedure is technically incorrect and, especially for a given respondent, may yield misleading results. When the number of respondents is large, however, these errors tend to "average out." A more sophisticated way to combine a number of dimensions into a total index is to use a multidimensional scale, which will be discussed in Chapter 9.

The researcher faces another difficulty when combining the rankings of a number of respondents. Here again, it is not uncommon for weighted sums of rank values to be used to provide a combined index. If we have a number of observations this approach will probably give adequate results, though it is not theoretically correct. A more sophisticated approach is to convert the ordinal scale into an interval scale, the values of which can then be added and averaged. One well-known example is Thurstone's *Law of Comparative Judgment*.[8] The simplest conceptualization of Thurstone's procedure is that the distance between scale positions of two objects A and B depends on the percentage of judgments in which A is preferred to B. This would seem to be a reasonable assumption to make.

Examples of regularly used ordinal scales include opinion and preference scales. The widely used paired-comparison technique also uses an ordinal scale. Because the numbers of this scale have only a rank meaning, the appropriate measure of central tendency is the median. A percentile or quartile measure is used for measuring dispersion. Correlations are restricted to various rank-order methods. Measures of statistical significance are technically restricted to that body of methods known as nonparametric methods.[9]

Researchers in the behavioral sciences differ as to whether the more powerful parametric significance tests are appropriate with ordinal measures. One position is that this use of parametric tests is incorrect on both theoretical and practical grounds. This view was strongly argued by Siegel,

---

[8] L. L. Thurstone, *The Measurement of Values* (Chicago: University of Chicago Press, 1959).

[9] Parametric tests are appropriate when the measurement is interval or ratio, and when we can accept certain assumptions about the underlying distribution of the data with which we are working. Nonparametric tests usually involve much weaker assumptions about measurement scales (nominal or ordinal), and the assumptions about the underlying distribution of the population are fewer and less restrictive. More on these tests is found in Chapter 13.

If the measurement is weaker than that of an interval scale, by using parametric methods tests the researcher would "add information" and thereby create distortions. . . . Moreover, the assumptions which must be made to justify the use of parametric tests usually rest on conjecture and hope. . . .[10]

At the other extreme some behavioral scientists argue that parametric tests are usually acceptable for ordinal scales on both practical and theoretical grounds. On this point Anderson has written,

Regarding practical problems, it was noted that the difference between parametric and rank-order tests were not great insofar as significance level and power were concerned. However, only the versatility of parametric statistics meets the everyday needs of psychological research. It was concluded that parametric procedures are the standard tools of psychological statistics although nonparametric procedures are useful minor techniques.

Under this heading of measurement theoretical considerations . . . It was thus concluded that the type of measuring scale used had little relevance to the question of whether to use parametric or nonparametric tests.[11]

Another view, somewhat between these extremes, recognizes that there are risks in using parametric procedures on ordinal type data but these risks are usually not great. Kerlinger expresses this view,

The best procedure would seem to be to treat ordinal measurements as though they were interval measurements but to be constantly on the alert to the possibility of gross inequality of measurement.[12]

The approach in this book on this controversy is one of neutrality with a tilt toward conservatism. Nonparametric tests are confusingly abundant, but most are simple to calculate, have good power efficiencies, and do not force the researcher to accept the assumptions of parametric testing. On the other hand, parametric tests (for example, analysis of variance) are so versatile, accepted, and understood that they will continue to be used with ordinal data when they seem to approach interval scales in nature.

Ordinal Scale with Origin.   Some properties or dimensions, especially when measuring attitudes and preferences, appear to have natural origins on an ordinal scale. On the scale in Figure 5–2 the values in the range could have been:

+2	Strongly like
+1	Like somewhat
0	Indifferent
−1	Dislike somewhat
−2	Strongly dislike

---

[10] Sidney Siegel, *Nonparametric Statistics for the Behavioral Sciences* (New York: McGraw-Hill Publishing Co., Inc., 1956), p. 32.

[11] Norman A. Anderson, "Scales and Statistics: Parametric and Nonparametric," *Psychological Bulletin,* vol. 58, no. 4., pp. 315–16.

[12] Kerlinger, *Foundations,* p. 441.

In this case the center of the scale represents a natural origin of zero preference. This form of ordinal scale is treated statistically in the same way as other ordinal scales.

Interval Scales

The interval scale has the powers of nominal and ordinal scales plus one additional strength: It incorporates the concept of equality of interval (the distance between 1 and 2 equals the distance between 2 and 3). Calendar time is such a scale. For example, the elapsed time between 3 and 6 A.M. equals the time between 4 and 7 A.M. On the other hand, one can not say that 6 A.M. is twice as late as 3 A.M. because "zero time" is an arbitrary origin. Centigrade and fahrenheit temperature scales are other examples of classical interval scales. With both there is an arbitrarily determined zero point.

Many attitude scales are presumed to be interval, although such claims are often challenged. Thurstone's differential scale was an early effort to develop such a scale.[13] Users also often treat intelligence scores, semantic differential scales, and many other multipoint scales as being interval in nature. When contentions arise about this practice it is that the critics believe that the scales should be treated as ordinal. Obviously the data does not know what scale it is, so whether a particular scale is interval or ordinal often is a judgment matter. The question of scale type affects both the interpretation of results and the form of statistical analysis which may be used. As has been mentioned in the discussion on ordinal scales, there often appears to be little difficulty if one uses parametric statistics on ordinal data.

When we can assume that a scale is interval we can use the arithmetic mean as the measure of central tendency. For example, we can compute the average time of first arrival of trucks at a warehouse in the morning, or the average attitude value of union workers versus nonunion workers on certain questions. In like fashion we use the standard deviation as the measure of dispersion for arrival times or worker opinions. Product moment correlation, analysis of variance, and the use of the parametric t-tests and F-tests are the statistical procedures of choice.[14]

Ratio Scales

These scales incorporate all of the powers of the previous ones plus the concept of absolute zero or origin. The ratio scale represents the actual amounts of a variable. Measures of physical dimensions such as weight, height, distance, and area are examples. In the behavioral sciences few situations satisfy the requirements of the ratio scale—the area of psychophysics

---

[13] See Chapter 9 for a discussion of the differential scale.

[14] See Chapter 13 for a discussion of these procedures.

offering some exceptions. In business research we do find ratio scales in a number of areas. For example, we find money values, population counts, distances, return rates, and amounts of time in a time-period sense.

All statistical techniques mentioned to this point are usable with ratio scales. In addition, all other manipulations that one can carry out with real numbers can also be carried out with ratio-scale values. Thus, multiplication and division can be used with this scale but not with the others mentioned. Geometric and harmonic means can be used as measures of central tendency, and coefficients of variation may also be calculated.

SOURCES OF MEASUREMENT DIFFERENCES

The ideal study should be designed and controlled for precise and unambiguous measurement of the variables of interest. Since attainment of this ideal is unlikely, we must recognize the sources of potential error and try to eliminate, neutralize, or otherwise deal with them. Much potential error is systematic (results from a bias) while the remainder is random (occurs in an erratic fashion). One authority has pointed out a number of major sources from which measured differences can come.[15]

Assume that we are conducting an ex post facto survey of the residents of a major city. The study concerns the Prince Corporation, a large manufacturer with headquarters and several major plants located in the city. The objective of the study is to determine the public's opinions about the company and the origin of any generally held adverse opinions.

Ideally, any variation of scores among the respondents would reflect true differences in their opinions about the company. Attitudes toward the firm as an employer, as an ecologically sensitive organization, or as a progressive corporate citizen would be accurately expressed. However, four major error sources may contaminate the results. These sources are the respondent, the situation, the measurer, and the instrument.

The Respondent as an Error Source. Opinion differences will come from relatively stable characteristics of the respondent which affect the scores. Typical of these are employee status, ethnic group membership, social class, and nearness to plants. Many of these dimensions will be anticipated in the design, but others of a less obvious nature will not be. Typical of these latter are specific traumatic experiences which a given respondent may have had with the Prince Corporation or its personnel. The respondent may be reluctant to express strong negative feelings or may have little knowledge about Prince but be reluctant to admit ignorance. This reluctance can lead to an interview of "guesses."

[15] Claire Selltiz, Lawrence S. Wrightsman, and Stuart W. Cook, *Research Methods in Social Relations* 3d ed. (New York: Holt, Rinehart and Winston, Inc., 1976), pp. 164–69.

Respondents may also suffer from transient factors like fatigue, boredom, or anxiety about some other matter; these limit the ability to respond accurately and fully. Hunger, impatience at having been interrupted, or general variations in mood may also have an impact.

Situational Factors. These potential problem areas are legion. Any condition which places a strain on the interview can have serious effects on the interviewer-respondent rapport. If another person is present, that person can distort responses by joining in, by distracting, or merely by being present. If the respondents feel that anonymity is not assured, they may be reluctant to express certain feelings. Curbside interviews are unlikely to elicit elaborate responses, while in-home interviews more often do.

The Measurer as an Error Source. The interviewer can distort responses by rewording, paraphrasing, or reordering questions. Stereotypes in appearance and action introduce bias. Inflections of voice and conscious or unconscious prompting with smiles, nods, and so forth, may encourage or discourage certain replies. Careless mechanical processing—checking of the wrong response or failure to record full replies—will obviously distort findings. In the data-analysis stage, further errors may be introduced by incorrect coding, careless tabulation, and faulty statistical calculation.

The Measurement Instrument as an Error Source. A defective instrument can distort in two major ways. First, it can be too confusing and ambiguous. The use of complex words and syntax beyond respondent comprehension is typical. Leading questions, ambiguous meanings, mechanical defects such as inadequate space for replies, response choice omissions, and poor printing suggest the range of problems.

A second and more elusive type of instrument deficiency is poor sampling of the universe of items of concern. Seldom does the instrument explore all of the potentially important issues. The Prince study might treat company image in areas of employment and ecology but omit the company management's civic leadership posture, its support of local education programs, or its position on various minority assistance issues. Even if the general issues are studied, the questions may not cover enough aspects of each area of concern. While we might study the Prince Corporation's image as an employer in terms of salary and wage scales, promotion opportunities, and work stability, perhaps such topics as working conditions, company management relations with organized labor, and retirement and other benefit programs should also be included.

Many of the remaining chapters in this book deal with specific measurement problems, but at this point it might be useful to discuss the general requirements for good measurement. While discussion will revolve around the research instrument, it is recognized that successful measurement depends on successfully meeting all of the problems which have just been covered.

THE CHARACTERISTICS OF SOUND MEASUREMENT

What are the characteristics of a good measurement tool? An intuitive answer to this question is that the tool should be an accurate counter or indicator of what we are interested in measuring. In addition, it should be easy and efficient to use. These criteria hold up well when compared to the more scholarly statements of criteria which have been advanced. One view is that there are three major considerations we should use in evaluating a measurement tool. They are *validity, reliability,* and *practicality.* They are described thus:

> Validity refers to the extent to which a test measures what we actually wish to measure. Reliability has to do with the accuracy and precision of a measurement procedure. . . . Practicality is concerned with a wide range of factors of economy, convenience, and interpretability. . . .[16]

In the following sections we will discuss the nature of these qualities and how the researcher may achieve them in his measurement procedures.

Validity

Many concepts of validity are mentioned in the research literature, and the number grows as we expand our concern for more scientific measurement. In this text we deal only with two major forms—external and internal validity.[17] The external validity of research findings refers to their generalizability across persons, settings, and times; more will be said about this form in Chapters 6 and 11.[18] In this chapter we will discuss only internal validity or the ability of a research instrument to measure what it is purported to measure. That is, does the instrument really measure what its designer claims it does? In this discussion internal validity will be referred to merely as "validity."

Validity is the extent to which differences found with a measuring tool reflect true differences among those being tested. The difficulty in meeting this test is that usually we do not know what the true differences are; if we did, we would not do the measuring in the first place. In the absence of direct knowledge of the dimension being studied, we must face the question, "How can one determine validity without direct confirming knowledge?" A quick answer is that we seek other relevant evidence that confirms the answers we have found with our measurement device, but this answer leads to a second ques-

---

[16] Robert L. Thorndike and Elizabeth Hagen, *Measurement and Evaluation in Psychology and Education,* 3d ed. (New York: John Wiley & Sons, Inc., 1969), p. 5.

[17] Examples of some of the other concepts of validity are convergent validity, factorial validity, job-analytic validity, synthetic validity, rational validity, and statistical conclusion validity.

[18] Thomas D. Cook and Donald T. Campbell, "The Design and Conduct of Quasi-Experiments and True Experiments in Field Settings," which is published as chap. 7 of Marvin D. Dunnette (ed.), *Handbook of Industrial and Organizational Psychology* (Chicago: Rand McNally College Publishing Company, 1976), p. 223.

tion, "What constitutes 'relevant evidence' "? There is no quick answer this time. What is relevant depends on the nature of the research problem and the researcher's judgment. One way to approach this question is to organize the answer according to types of internal validity. One widely accepted classification consists of three major forms: *content, criterion-related,* and *construct.* [19]

Content Validity.   The *content validity* of a measuring instrument is the extent to which it provides adequate coverage of the topic under study. If the instrument contains a representative sample of the universe of subject matter of interest, then content validity is good. To evaluate the content validity of an instrument we must first agree on what elements constitute adequate coverage of the problem. In the Prince Corporation study, for example, we must decide what knowledge, attitudes, and opinions are relevant to the measurement of corporate public image. We must then determine what forms of these opinions constitute relevant positions on these topics. If the questionnaire adequately covers the topics which have been defined as the relevant dimensions, we conclude that the instrument has good content validity.

The determination of content validity is judgmental and can be approached in several ways. First, the designer may determine the validity through a careful definition of the topic of concern, the items to be scaled, and the scales to be used. This logical process is somewhat intuitive and is unique to each research designer. In fact, the research question hierarchy discussed in Chapter 3 has as its aim the orderly fractionation of the major research question into specific questions that have content validity. A second way to determine content validity is to use a panel of persons to judge how well the instrument meets the standards.

It is important *not* to define "content" too narrowly. For example, if we secure only superficial expressions of opinion in the Prince Corporation public opinion survey it would probably not have adequate content coverage. The research should also probably delve into the processes by which these opinions came about. How did the respondents come to feel as they did, and what is the intensity of feeling?

Criterion-Related Validity.   This form of validity reflects the success of measures used for some empirical estimating purpose. We may want to predict some outcome or estimate the existence of some current behavior or condition. These cases involve *predictive and concurrent validity,* respectively. They differ only in a time perspective. An opinion questionnaire which correctly forecasts the outcome of a union election has predictive validity. An observational method which correctly categorizes families by current income class has concurrent validity. While these examples appear to have rather simple and unambiguous validity criteria, there are difficulties in estimating validity. Consider the problem of estimating family income. There clearly is a

---

[19] *Standards for Educational and Psychological Tests and Manuals* (Washington, D.C.: American Psychological Association, 1974), p. 26.

knowable true income for every family. However, we may find it difficult to secure this criterion figure. Thus, while the criterion is conceptually clear, it may be unavailable.

In other cases there may be several criteria, none of which is completely satisfactory. Consider again the problem of judging success in a sales force. We may want to develop a preemployment test which will predict sales success. For this there may be a number of possible criteria, none of which tells the full story. For example, total sales per salesperson may not adequately reflect territory market potential, competitive conditions, or the different profitability rates of various products. We might rely on the sales manager's overall evaluation, but how unbiased and accurate are those impressions? We must assure that the validity criterion we use is itself "valid." One source suggests that any criterion measure must be judged in terms of four qualities: relevance, freedom from bias, reliability, and availability.[20]

A criterion is *relevant* if it is defined and scored in the terms we judge to be the proper measure of salesperson success. For example, if we believe that sales success is adequately measured by dollar sales volume achieved per year, then this is the relevant criterion. If we believe that success must also include a high level of penetration of large accounts, then sales volume alone is not fully relevant. In making this relevance decision we are eventually thrown back to our judgment in deciding what partial criteria are appropriate indicants of salesperson success.

Freedom from bias is attained when the criterion gives each salesperson an equal opportunity to score well. The sales criterion would be biased if it did not show adjustments for differences in territory potential and competitive conditions.

A *reliable* criterion is stable or reproducible. An erratic criterion (highly variable sales performances from month to month) can hardly be considered a reliable standard by which we judge performances on a sales employment test.

Finally, the information specified by the criterion must be *available*. If not available, how much will it cost and how difficult will it be to secure? The amount of money and effort that should be spent on development of a criterion depends on the importance of the problem for which the test is used.

Once we have test and criterion scores, the problem becomes one of relating them in some way. The usual approach is to correlate them. For example, we might correlate test scores of 40 salespeople who have newly joined the company with first-year sales achievements adjusted to reflect differences in territorial selling conditions.

Construct Validity.   One may also wish to measure or infer the presence of abstract characteristics for which no empirical validation seems possible. Attitude scales and aptitude and personality tests generally concern con-

---

[20] Thorndike and Hagen, *Measurement*, p. 168.

cepts that fall in this category. Even though this validation situation is much more difficult, we still need to have some assurance that our measurement has an acceptable degree of validity.

In attempting to determine *construct validity* we associate a set of other propositions with the results received from using our measurement tool. If measurements on our devised scale correlate in a predicted way with these other propositions, we then conclude that there is some construct validity.

In the Prince Corporation study we may be interested in securing a judgment of "how good a citizen" the corporation is. Variations in respondent ratings may be drastically affected if the respondents have substantial differences in opinion about what constitutes proper corporate citizenship. Respondent Barbara Schoen, for example, may feel that any company is an economic organization designed to make profits for its stockholders. She sees relatively little role for corporations in the wide-ranging social issues of the day. Respondent John Lapp is at the other end of the continuum. He views the corporation as an organization which must become a leader in solving social problems, even at the cost of profits.

Each of these respondent types might clearly understand Prince's role in the community but judge it quite differently in light of their views about what that role should be. If these different views are held, we would theorize that other information about these respondents would be logically compatible with their judgments. We might expect Mrs. Schoen to oppose high corporate taxes, to be critical of increased involvement of government in family affairs, and to believe that a corporation's major responsibility is to its stockholders. Mr. Lapp would be more likely to favor high corporate income taxes, to opt for more government involvement in daily life, and to believe that a corporation's major responsibility is a social one.

Respondents may not be consistent on all of these questions because our measurements may be crude and our "theory" may be deficient in some way. When these hypothesized tests do not confirm our measurement scale, we are faced with a two-edged question: Is our measurement instrument invalid, or is our theory invalid? Answers to this question call for more information and/or exercise of judgment.

The three forms of validity have been discussed separately, but they are interrelated, both theoretically and operationally. For example, predictive validity is obviously important for a test designed to predict employee success. In developing such a test, however, you would probably first postulate the factors (constructs) which provide the basis for useful prediction. That is, you would advance a theory about the variable in employee success—an area for construct validity. Finally, in developing the specific items for inclusion in the success prediction test you would be concerned with how well the specific items sample the full range of each construct (a matter of content validity).

In the corporate image study for the Prince Corporation both content and construct validity considerations have already been discussed, but how about criterion-related validity? The criteria are less obvious than in the employee success prediction, but there will be judgments made of the quality of evidence about the company's image. The criteria used may be subjective (does the evidence agree with what we believe) as well as objective (does the evidence agree with other research findings).

Reliability

The concept of reliability means many things to many people, but in most formulations the notion of consistency emerges. A measure is "reliable" to the degree that it supplies consistent results. Reliability is a contributor to validity and is a necessary but not sufficient condition for validity. The relationship between reliability and validity can be simply illustrated with the use of a bathroom scale. If the scale measures your weight correctly (using a concurrent criterion such as a scale known to be accurate) then it is both reliable and valid. If it consistently overweighs you by six pounds then the scale is reliable but not valid. If the scale measures erratically from time to time then it is not reliable and therefore cannot be valid.

Reliability is concerned with estimates of the degree to which a measurement is free of random or unstable error. It is not as valuable as validity determination, but it is much easier to assess. It is also often the only one which we can assess. Reliable instruments can at least be used with some confidence that a number of transient and situational factors are not interfering. Reliable instruments are robust; they work well at different times under different conditions. This distinction of time and condition is the basis for two frequently used perspectives on reliability—stability and equivalence.

Stability. A measure is said to be stable if we can secure consistent results with repeated measurements of the same person with the same instrument. For example, an observation procedure would be stable if it gives the same reading on a particular person when repeated one or more times. It is often possible to repeat observations on a subject and to compare for consistency. The major problem with this approach is that when there is much time between measurements there is a chance for situational factors to change, thereby affecting the observations. This would appear incorrectly as a drop in reliability of the measurement process.

Stability measurement in survey situations is more difficult and less attractive than for observation studies. While you can observe a certain action repeatedly, you usually can resurvey only once. This leads to a test-retest arrangement—with comparisons between the two tests to determine how reliable they are. Two difficulties occur, in addition to the time delay mentioned with observation study. First, if the retest is given too quickly the respondent will remember the answers already given and repeat them. This will result in a biased higher reliability indication than is justified. On the other hand, the test-retest process itself may introduce bias. For example, the respondent may become testwise or at least exhibit less anxiety on the retest. Another condition might be that the first test sensitizes the respondent to the subject, who may then go on to learn more or form new and different opinions before the retest. Then, too, it may just happen that the opinions change from situational influence between the test and the retest. In all of these cases the tendency is to produce a downward bias in the stability scores.

A suggested approach for reducing these distortions of test-retest results is to extend the time interval between test and the retest in order to reduce the effect of the initial measurement. In psychological testing the suggested delay is from two weeks to a month. While this may help in one respect it hinders in another. The longer the time span, the more the chance that outside factors will contaminate the measurement and distort the stability score. The result of all of these problems is that stability measurement through the test-retest approach is less well regarded in research circles than it once was. More interest has centered on equivalence.

Equivalence. A second perspective on reliability considers how much error may be introduced by different investigators (in observation) or different samples of items being studied (in questioning or scales). Thus, while stability is concerned with personal and situational fluctuations from one time to another, equivalence is concerned with variations at one point in time among observers and samples of items. A good way to test for the equivalence of measurements by different observers is to compare their scoring of the same event.

The test items to be included in any instrument are limited in number and chosen in a somewhat arbitrary fashion. The major interest typically is not how respondents differ from item to item but how well a given set of items will categorize individuals. That is, there may be many differences in response between two samples of items, but if a person is classified the same way by each test, then our tests have a good equivalency.

We test for item sample equivalence by using alternative or *parallel tests* administered to the same persons at roughly the same time. The results of the two tests are then correlated. A second method, the *split-half* technique can be used when the measuring tool has a number of similar questions or statements to which the subject can respond. The instrument is administered to the subject, and then the results are separated by item into two randomly selected halves. These are then compared. If the results are similar, the instrument is said to have high reliability in an equivalence sense; however, the longer the test length in the split-half test, the higher the reliability. The Spearman-Brown correction formula is used to adjust for the effect of test length and to measure the split-half equivalence.

Another approach to the problem of equivalence holds that random rather than split halves should be used. This view emphasizes internal consistency and *homogeneity*. The two most widely used homogeneity indexes are Cronbach's Coefficient Alpha and the Kuder-Richardson Formula 20. Both give average split-half correlation for all possible ways of dividing the test into two parts.

Improving Reliability.   We can improve reliability if we assure that external sources of variation are minimized. For example, we can standardize the conditions under which the measurement takes place. We can achieve enhanced equivalence through improved investigator consistency by using only well-trained, supervised, and motivated persons to conduct the research. We can also do much to improve equivalence by broadening the sample of items used. We can do this by adding similar questions to the questionnaire or adding more observers or occasions to an observation study.

With measurement instruments such as achievement, attitude, or employment tests, we can often increase equivalence by improving the internal consistency of the test. This approach requires the assumption that a high total score reflects high performance and a low total score low performance. We select the extreme scorers, say the top 20 percent and bottom 20 percent, for individual analysis. By this process we can distinguish those items which differentiate high and low scorers. Items which have little discriminatory power can then be dropped from the test.

We decide whether reliability is or is not adequate in terms of our objectives and the basic variability of the data. In terms of our objectives, are we interested in some rough ordering of subjects? If so, then a relatively crude instrument will probably suffice. For more precise estimation, reliability standards must be more demanding. In a relatively homogeneous population a crude measure appears to be reliable because variations in the data are limited. Hence, any reliable instrument should score higher on reliability than would be the case in a heterogeneous population.

Practicality

The scientific requirements of a project call for the measurement process to be reliable and valid, while the operational requirements call for it to be practical. Thorndike and Hagen define practicality in terms of economy, convenience, and interpretability.[21] While they are referring chiefly to the development of educational and psychological tests, their conclusions hold for other measurement instruments as well.

Economy.   Some tradeoff is usually needed between the "ideal research project" and that which the budget can afford. Instrument length is one area where economic pressures are quickly felt. More items give more reliability, but in the interest of limiting the interview or observation time (therefore costs), we hold the item number down. The choice of data collection method is also often dictated by economic factors. The use of long-distance telephone surveys, for example, has been strongly influenced by the rising costs of

---

[21] Ibid., p. 199.

personal interviewing. In standardized tests the cost of test materials alone can be such a significant expense that it encourages multiple reuse. Add to this the need for fast and economical scoring, and we see why computer scoring on special answer sheets is so attractive.

Convenience. A measuring device passes the *convenience* test if it is easy to administer. For instance, a questionnaire with a set of detailed but clear instructions, with examples, is substantially easier to complete correctly than one which lacks these features. In a well prepared study it is not uncommon for the interviewer instructions to be several times longer than the interview guide. Naturally, the more complex the concepts being dealt with, the greater the need for clear and complete instructions. We can also make the instrument easier to administer by giving close attention to the layout of the measuring instrument. Too numerous are the instrument formats which are the designer's dream and the user's nightmare. Crowding of material, poor reproductions of illustrations, and the carryover of items from one page to the next all make completion of the instrument more difficult.

Interpretability. This consideration is particularly important when persons other than the designers of the test must interpret the results. This situation is usually but not exclusively found with standardized tests. In such cases there is a need for a number of aids such as the following:[22]

1. A statement of the functions which the test was designed to measure and of the general procedures by which it was developed.
2. Detailed instructions for administering the test.
3. Scoring keys and specific instructions for scoring the test.
4. Norms for appropriate reference groups.
5. Evidence about the reliability of the test.
6. Evidence on the intercorrelations of subscores.
7. Evidence on the relationship of the test to other evidence.
8. Guides for using the test and for interpreting results.

THE DEVELOPMENT OF MEASUREMENT TOOLS

The tasks facing the researcher are to arrive at an understanding of the major concepts of the study and to measure their existence in some acceptable way. This task calls first for operational definitions of these concepts and then their translation into effective measurement procedures. One authority suggests that this translation process consists of four steps: (1) concept development, (2) dimension specification, (3) selection of observable indicators, and (4) combination of these indicators into indexes.[23]

---

[22] Ibid., pp. 202–4.

[23] Paul F. Lazarsfeld, "Evidence and Inference in Social Research," in David Lerner, *Evidence and Inference* (Glencoe: The Free Press, 1950), pp. 108–17.

Concept Development. Before we can develop a measurement tool we need to decide what it is we are trying to measure. This step usually consists of advancing one or more concepts or constructs. The concepts may be as familiar as "regular customer," less familiar as in "leading indicator," or abstract as in "corporate image." We might even invent a new construct such as the "intermediate criterion" proposed by one researcher.[24]

Persons who are familiar with economic statistics will generally agree that a leading indicator is a time-series index whose changes precede those of a criterion index in some predictable way. We probably also have some general agreement that the concept of corporate image is an expression of how a company's reputation is viewed. With the invented "intermediate criterion," however, we need to know more before we can undestand it, even in a general way. The idea of an intermediate criterion grows out of research into the ways that various stimuli such as product changes, pricing, and advertising affect consumer buying decisions. There are so many such stimuli that managers seldom can identify those which are responsible for changes in the sales of a brand. The construct of "intermediate criterion" was suggested as "a measure that reflects the immediate effect of a stimulus on a consumer but also predicts subsequent purchase behavior."[25]

Concept Specification. For measurement purposes we should carefully specify all of the above concepts. We may specify the various dimensions of the concepts under study by empirical correlation, or do it through deduction. We can illustrate the former approach by operationally defining a leading indicator as any published economic or social time-series index whose turning points, over the last six business cycles, have preceded the major turning points of industry shipments by at least three months. We might also require that the monthly statistics of the leading indicator and industry sales should correlate well when industry sales are lagged by six months.

In the Prince Corporation study we might use deduction to analyze the concept of corporate image into four major aspects: (1) the good community citizen, (2) the ecologically responsible organization, (3) the employer, and (4) the supplier of consumer needs. In place of this more or less intuitive approach we could also use factor analysis or other statistical techniques to determine concept components. One such study, using cluster analysis, concluded that there are six major dimensions of company image: product reputation, employer role, customer treatment, corporate leadership, defense contribution, and concern for individuals.[26] In the study of purchase behavior no similar set of dimensions was explicitly stated. Axelrod, however, suggested

---

[24] Joel N. Axelrod, "Attitude Measures that Predict Purchase," *Journal of Advertising Research,* vol. 8, no. 1, p. 3.

[25] Axelrod, "Attitude Measures," p. 3.

[26] Rueben Cohen, "The Measurement of Corporate Images," in John W. Riley, Jr., ed., *The Corporation and Its Publics* (New York: John Wiley & Sons, Inc., 1963), pp. 48–63.

that the intermediate criterion might be adequately measured by a variety of single concept specifications. Four which he tested were (1) brand awareness, (2) brand preference, (3) brand advertising recall, and (4) predisposition to buy a brand.

Indicator Selection. Once the dimensions have been settled we must still develop indicators by which to measure each concept element. Since there is seldom a perfect or absolute measure of a concept, we should consider several possibilities. Indicators are particular questions, scales, statistical measures, or other devices by which the study concepts are measured. In choosing leading indicators for industry sales forecasting we might consider a number of items such as data for other industries that move earlier in the business cycle (for example, stock market prices), or factory new orders, average factory overtime worked, and the like. We would gather such data, compare them to our industry sales as previously specified, and choose those series which meet the tests.

With the Prince Corporation problem we would want to select the indicators that would express how the members of the general population view the company, for example, as a community citizen. Such indicators might reflect how respondents view Prince as:

1. A supporter of local civic fund drives.
2. A supporter of higher education.
3. A factor in local political issues.
4. A factor in local redevelopment programs.

The indicator concerning company support of civic fund drives could be expressed in a question which compares Prince to other companies. For example, using the method of triads, we might ask:

Which of the following companies has the best and worst reputation for supporting Big City's civic fund-raising drives like United Fund? Please indicate "B" for best and "W" for worst.

_____Prince Corp.   _____King Corp.   _____Baron, Ltd.

In a second but somewhat different approach we could use a scale to rate Prince's reputation for civic responsiveness with the following:

Which of the following best describes the reputation of Prince Corporation with respect to its activity in civic fund drives such as United Fund?
(Please check one.)

_____ The company is a leader in these activities.
_____ The company is a strong supporter but not a leader in these activities.
_____ The company is an average supporter of these activities.
_____ The company is a below-average supporter of these activities.

In the study of purchase behavior previously cited, the researcher devised a total of ten different questions to measure the Intermediate Criterion. In fact, the purpose of the research was to compare the ability of these ten different measures to predict subsequent buying behavior.[27] Several of the specific questions used were:

(Advertising recall)   What brands have you seen or heard advertised for (product class) in the past three months? Are there any others?

(Buying disposition)   I'm going to name some pairs of (product class). I'd like you to tell me which of the pairs you would be more likely to purchase?

Formation of Indexes.   When we have several dimensions of a concept or different measurements of a dimension, we may need to combine them into a single index. Lazarsfeld points out that each "individual indicator has only a probability relation to what we really want to know."[28] That is, the subject might change position without the indicator changing, or the indicator might change without the subject's position changing. Use of more than one indicator lends stability to the scores and probably improves their validity. Thus, we might combine the results of six or eight individual leading indicators into a single index to predict industry shipments.

Some of the difficulties in developing indexes have already been discussed. One simple way around these problems is to provide scale values to the responses and then tally the responses or sum the scores. For example, we might have questions on Prince Corporation's activity in civic fund drives, the company's support of higher education, and its support of cultural affairs. In each case we might ask the respondents to rate Prince Corporation on a scale from one to five. We might then combine these three scales to get an overall index of Prince as a community citizen.

In the purchase behavior study the objective of the research was to compare individual indicators rather than to determine a combined index. Possibly a statistical model, perhaps a regression or discriminant model, might show that several of these specific indicators combined would provide a purchase predictor superior to any single indicator.

Interchangeability of Indexes.   Typically we select relatively few items from many which might be used to indicate broad concepts. Two alternative sets of such items may correlate well with a third outside measure, yet the two sets will classify many individuals differently. Lazarsfeld calls this characteristic the "interchangeability of indexes."[29] While he is referring to broad social and psychological concepts (for example, "conservatism"), re-

---

[27] Axelrod, "Attitude Measures," p. 4.

[28] Lazarsfeld, "Evidence and Inference," p. 112.

[29] Ibid., p. 113.

search has indicated that interchangeability may often appear. For example, in one corporate image study, the following was asked:

Would you tell me which way you feel about Company X?

Do you like the company more than you dislike it, do you dislike the company more than you like it, or don't you care one way or the other about it?[30]

A second measure of corporate image was developed from ten questions dealing with various aspects of Company X's operations. The responses to these ten questions were combined into a single like-dislike index score. The results of a survey using both indicators (Table 5–1) showed an almost

Table 5–1: Attitude of Respondents toward Company X

Response	Based on Like–Dislike Question	Based on ten Questions on Operations
Like	22%	22%
Dislike	3	4
Don't care or don't know	72	74
No answer	3	—

identical pattern of like and dislike. Nevertheless, a cross-tabulation of these two indexes of attitude showed an overlap of only 40 percent. That is, 60 percent of those who, when asked directly, reported that they liked Company X responded to the ten questions in a way that indicated a dislike of Company X. At the same time, many who reported a dislike in response to the direct question indicated by their other responses that they had favorable attitudes. Thus, while both indexes served well in estimating the total number of likes and dislikes, they had many internal differences. These contradictory findings were attributed by the researcher to the shallow level of interest which most people have in corporations.

A Measurement Example[31]

For years researchers have been assessing the attitudes of people in business organizations. Such information on job satisfaction, job interest, and so on, has been used by managers when they make organization decisions. Many researchers have developed and used questionnaires about which

---

[30] Robert O. Carlson, "The Nature of Corporate Images," in Riley, *The Corporation and Its Publics*, pp. 24–27.

[31] Martin Patchen, *Some Questionnaire Measures of Employee Motivation and Morale*, Monograph No. 41 (Ann Arbor, Mich.: Institute for Social Research, University of Michigan, 1965).

there is little known as to their validity or reliability. Often "face validity" (the subjective conclusion by the researcher that the instrument is probably valid) is the only validity concept used.

In one research project Patchen and colleagues were involved in a study of some of the determinants of employee involvement in their jobs, and more specifically with the measurement of employee motivation and morale. In designing and conducting this study they incorporated some procedures for trying to establish the validity and reliability of their measures. The research was done at various TVA plants in addition to an electronics company.

The specific employee characteristics with which they were concerned were:[32]

1. Job motivation: level of aroused motivation on the job.
2. Interest in work innovation: in finding new ways of doing things on the job.
3. Willingness to express disagreement with supervisors.
4. Attitude toward changes introduced into the job situation.
5. Identification with the work organization.

They prepared eight to ten questionnaire items for each characteristic to be measured. After some pretesting they compared the results of various items with available validating evidence. Those items which did not appear to discriminate individuals on the basis of the validity evidence were dropped and other items added for further testing. Finally they combined the best items into a single index measurement for each characteristic.

They sought to evaluate the items on both a criterion-based validity level and a construct validity level. To explain the validating process in detail let's consider the effort to develop the index to measure the interest in work innovation. They eventually developed a questionnaire with six multiple choice questions (see Figure 5–3). Reliability was measured by a test-retest of individual questions. The retest was made about a month after the first test. The test-retest reliability of the index, based on the six items, was 0.87 for individuals at the electronics company where the test was made.

Criterion-based validity was addressed by comparing worker scores on the six questions to ratings of the workers by their supervisors. In some cases, where active suggestion systems were in operation, the data from these sources were also compared to worker responses. The median correlation between index scores and supervisory ratings were about 0.35.[33] At TVA, where there were formal suggestion programs, the index scores of suggestors were significantly higher than those of nonsuggestors.

Construct validity was evaluated by comparing index scores on the interest in innovation index with indexes of job difficulty, identification with one's

---

[32] Ibid., p. 3.

[33] Ibid., p. 25.

Figure 5–3: Interest in Work Innovation Index*

1. In your kind of work, if a person tries to change his usual way of doing things, how does it generally turn out?

   (1)_____Usually turns out worse; the tried and true methods work best in my work.
   (3)_____Usually doesn't make much difference.
   (5)_____Usually turns out better; our methods need improvement.

2. Some people prefer doing a job in pretty much the same way because this way they can count on always doing a good job. Others like to go out of their way in order to think up new ways of doing things. How is it with you on your job?

   (1)_____I always prefer doing things pretty much in the same way.
   (2)_____I mostly prefer doing things pretty much in the same way.
   (4)_____I mostly prefer doing things in new and different ways.
   (5)_____I always prefer doing things in new and different ways.

3. How often do you try out, on your own, a better or faster way of doing something on the job?

   (5)_____Once a week or more often.
   (4)_____Two or three times a month.
   (3)_____About once a month.
   (2)_____Every few months.
   (1)_____Rarely or never.

4. How often do you get chances to try out your own ideas on your job, either before or after checking with your supervisor?

   (5)_____Several times a week or more.
   (4)_____About once a week.
   (3)_____Several times a month.
   (2)_____About once a month.
   (1)_____Less than once a month.

5. In my kind of job, it's usually better to let your supervisor worry about new or better ways of doing things.

   (1)_____Strongly agree.
   (2)_____Mostly agree.
   (4)_____Mostly disagree.
   (5)_____Strongly disagree.

6. How many times in the past year have you suggested to your supervisor a different or better way of doing something on the job?

   (1)_____Never had occasion to do this during the past year.
   (2)_____Once or twice.
   (3)_____About three times.
   (4)_____About five times.
   (5)_____Six to ten times.
   (6)_____More than ten times had occasion to do this during the past year.

* Numbers in parentheses preceding each response category indicate the score assigned to each response.

Source: Martin Patchen, *Some Questionnaire Measures of Employee Motivation and Morale,* Monograph No. 41 (Ann Arbor, Mich.: Institute for Social Research, The University of Michigan, 1965), pp. 15–16.

occupation, general job motivation, and willingness to disagree with supervisors. It had been hypothesized that such correlations would exist.

All in all, the conclusion of Patchen and his associates was that the index of interest in work innovation has sufficient reliability and appears to be valid enough to make rough distinctions among groups of people.

SUMMARY

In general terms measurement is the determination of the extent, qualities, quantity, or other dimensions of an item. In more scientific terms measurement is a process of mapping aspects of a domain onto other aspects of a range according to some rules of correspondence. In a literal sense we measure *indicants* of the *properties* of *objects*. We devise a scale in the range and then transform or map our observation of property indicants from the domain onto this range scale.

There are four major scale types. In increasing order of power, they are nominal, ordinal, interval, and ratio. Nominal scales merely classify without indicating either order, distance, or unique origin. Ordinal scales indicate magnitude relationships of more than and less than but indicate no distance or unique origin. Interval scales have both order and distance values but no unique origin. Ratio scales have all of these features.

Instruments may yield incorrect readings of an indicant for a number of reasons. These may be classified according to major error sources: (1) the respondent or subject, (2) situational factors, (3) the measurer, and (4) the instrument.

Sound measurement must meet the tests of validity, reliability, and practicality. Validity is the most critical and indicates the degree to which an instrument measures what it is supposed to measure. Three major forms of validity are often mentioned. Content validity exists to the degree that a measure provides an adequate reflection of the topic under study. Its determination is primarily judgmental and intuitive. Criterion-related validity relates to our ability to predict some outcome or estimate the existence of some current condition. Construct validity is the most complex and abstract. A measure has construct validity to the degree that it conforms to predicted correlations with other theoretical propositions.

A measure is reliable if it provides consistent results. It is a partial contributor to validity, but a measurement tool may be reliable without being valid. Two major forms of reliability are stability and equivalence. A measure meets the third criterion, practicality, if it is economical, convenient, and interpretable.

Development of measurement tools can be viewed as a four-stage process of (1) concept development, (2) specification of concept dimensions, (3) selection of observable indicators, and (4) combination of these indicators into indexes.

SUPPLEMENTAL READINGS

1. Dunnette, Marvin D. (ed.) *Handbook of Industrial and Organizational Psychology.* Chicago: Rand McNally College Publishing Company, 1976. Chap. 7, by Thomas D. Cook and Donald T. Campbell, is entitled "The Design and Conduct of Quasi-Experiments and True Experiments in Field Settings." It is especially recommended to the serious student of measurement validity.
2. Kerlinger, Fred N. *Foundations of Behavioral Research,* 2d ed. New York: Holt, Rinehart and Winston, Inc., 1973. Chaps. 25, 26, and 27 cover the nature of measurement as well as reliability and validity.
3. Lazarsfeld, Paul F.; Pasanella, Ann K.; and Rosenberg, Morris. *Continuities in the Language of Social Research.* New York: The Free Press, 1972. Sect. I consists of 14 papers concerned with concepts, indexes, classification, and typologies.
4. Leege, David C., and Francis, Wayne L. *Political Research.* New York: Basic Books, Inc., Publishers, 1974. Chap. 6 has a good discussion on index construction.
5. Phillips, Bernard S. *Social Research.* 2d ed. New York: The Macmillan Company, 1971. Chaps. 10, 11, and 12 cover the nature of scales in some depth.
6. Selltiz, Claire; Wrightsman, Lawrence S.; and Cook, Stuart W. *Research Methods in Social Relations.* 3d ed. New York: Holt, Rinehart and Winston, Inc., 1976. Good discussion of the problems of measurement in chap. 6.
7. Stanley, Julian C., and Hopkins, Kenneth D. *Educational and Psychological Measurement and Evaluation.* Englewood Cliffs, N.J.: Prentice-Hall, Inc., 1972. Chaps. 3, 4, and 5 cover the meaning of norms, test validity, and reliability. Remaining chapters deal chiefly with the development of educational measures.
8. Thorndike, Robert L., and Hagen, Elizabeth. *Measurement and Evaluation in Psychology and Education.* 3d ed. New York: John Wiley & Sons, Inc., 1969. Thorough discussion of measurement as it applies to the development of educational tests.
9. Zeisel, Hans. *Say It with Figures.* 5th ed., rev. New York: Harper & Row, Publishers, 1968. Chap. 6 is a good discussion of index construction.

DISCUSSION QUESTIONS

1. Define or explain:
   a. Mapping.
   b. A scale with order but no distance or unique origin.
   c. Practicality as a characteristic of good measurement.
   d. Predictive versus concurrent validity.
2. What do we measure when we measure? What can we measure about the four objects listed below? Be as specific as possible.
   a. Laundry detergent.
   b. Employees.
   c. Factory output.
   d. Job satisfaction.

3. *a.* What are the essential measurement differences among nominal, ordinal, interval, and ratio scales?
    b. How do these differences affect the statistical analysis techniques we can use?

4. Below are listed some objects of varying degrees of abstractness. Suggest properties of each of these objects which can be measured by each of the four basic types of scales.
    a. Store customers.
    b. Voter attitudes.
    c. Hardness of steel alloys.
    d. Preference for a particular common stock.
    e. Profitability of various divisions in a company.

5. What are the four major sources of measurement error? Illustrate by example how each of these might affect measurement results in a face-to-face interview situation.

6. Suppose we conduct two surveys among homemakers in the same area of the city. One study is a telephone survey and the second consists of in-home interviews. Some of the same questions are asked in both studies. When we tabulate the results for these parallel questions we find that answers between these two groups differ. For example, in one group the respondents tend to be younger, have more new cars, and give more candid opinions than do those in the other group. Which group would this be? Why?

7. Do you agree or disagree with the following statements? Explain.
    a. Validity is more critical to measurement than is reliability.
    b. Content validity is the most difficult type of validity to determine.
    c. A valid measurement is reliable but a reliable measurement may not be valid.
    d. Stability and equivalence are essentially the same thing.

8. You have been asked to design an instrument by which students can evaluate the quality and value of their various courses. How might you try to assure that your instrument has:
    a. Stability.
    b. Equivalence.
    c. Content validity.
    d. Predictive validity.
    e. Construct validity.

9. A baseball player's batting performance is usually measured by batting average.
    a. How is this index operationally defined?
    b. How good is it as a measure of a player's batting performance? That is, how valid is this as a measure of a player's batting worth?
    c. What other concepts or constructs might you employ to provide a better measure of a batter's worth?
    d. Choose one or more of these and operationally define them.
    e. How might you compile these into a single "index of batting?"

10. You have been asked to develop an index of student morale at your school.
    a. What constructs or concepts might you employ?
    b. Choose several of the major concepts and specify their dimensions.
    c. Select observable indicators that you might use to measure these dimensions.
    d. How would you compile these various dimensions into a single index?
    e. How would you judge the reliability and/or validity of these measurements?

Chapter 6

Sampling Design

ANOTHER IMPORTANT RESEARCH DECISION is the selection of subjects to study. We must determine how many people to interview and who they will be; what events to observe and how many there will be; or how many records to inspect and which ones. In research studies we often observe only a sample of the possible cases, but the selection of this sample is not a simple problem.

Researchers, when they undertake sampling studies, are interested in estimating one or more population values, and/or testing one or more statistical hypotheses. Population estimating will be covered in this chapter, while hypothesis testing will be discussed in Chapter 13.

Quality control analysis is an important business application of sampling techniques, but it is typically not a research use and will be omitted here. Nor will this discussion deal with the many important statistical questions which any thorough coverage of sampling requires. The explanations presented in this chapter are largely intuitive and not intended to deal with statistics as the central subject. Our emphasis is on practical sampling procedures for designing one-time samples by which to estimate population values.

This chapter has three major sections. The first covers the nature of sampling, including a brief discussion of the types of samples that can be used. The major second section covers probability sampling and how it can be used, while the third section presents a brief coverage of nonprobability sampling.

THE NATURE OF SAMPLING

Most people intuitively understand the nature of sampling and use it on many occasions. One taste from a drink tells us whether it is sweet or sour. If the people interviewed on a downtown street agree with a certain civic action, we tend to think that most people will agree with that action. If some of our office staff favor a four-day week we infer that others would also. These examples may vary in their representativeness, but they are all samples.

The basic idea in sampling is that the analysis of some of the *elements* in a *population* provides useful information on the entire population. As used here, an *element is the subject on which the measurement is being taken.* It is the unit of study. For example, each office worker questioned about the four-day week is a population element, and each account analyzed is an element of an account population. Population is the total collection of elements about which we wish to make inferences. All staff members in the office might comprise the population of interest, or we might define the population in many other ways. The population takes whatever dimensions the researcher's objective dictates.

Why Sample?

Sampling is based on two premises. One is that there is enough similarity among the elements in a population that a few of these elements will adequately represent the characteristics of the total population. For example, we can estimate the attitudes in a large group by learning the attitudes of a few representative persons in that group. If this can be done there can obviously be a great saving in time and cost. However, improved economy alone is not the only value of sampling.

Deming argues that the quality of a study is often better with sampling than with a census. He suggests that "Sampling possesses the possibility of better interviewing (testing), more thorough investigation of missing, wrong, or suspicious information, better supervision, and better processing than is possible with complete coverage."[1] The U.S. Bureau of the Census demonstrates its confidence in sampling by making sample surveys to check the accuracy of censuses.

Sampling also provides much quicker results than does a census. The speed of execution minimizes the time between the recognition of a need for information and the availability of that information. Then, too, some situations require sampling. For example, when we test the breaking strength of materials we must destroy them; a census would mean complete destruction of the materials. Sampling is also the only procedure possible if the population

---

[1] W. E. Deming, *Sample Design in Business Research* (New York: John Wiley & Sons, Inc., 1960), p. 26.

is infinite. For example, we take a sample of throws of dice since the population of dice throws is infinite.

The members of a sample may not be fully representative of the population, and values calculated from sample data may vary from the population values. This problem of discrepancies between a population value (*parameter*) and its parallel sample value (*statistic*) calls up the second premise of sampling: While some sample items underestimate the parameter, others overestimate its value. When the sample is drawn properly, variations in item values tend to counteract each other; this counteraction tendency results in a statistic (sample value) that is generally close to the parameter (population value). For these offsetting effects to take place, however, it is necessary (1) that there be enough members in the sample and (2) they must be drawn in a way to favor neither the overestimating or the underestimating tendencies.

What Is a Good Sample?

The ultimate test of a sample design is how well it represents the characteristics of the population it purports to represent. In measurement terms the sample must be *valid*. Validity of a sample depends upon two considerations.

Accuracy. First is the matter of *accuracy*—defined as *the degree to which bias is absent from the sample*. An accurate (unbiased) sample is one in which the underestimators and the overestimators are balanced among the members of the sample. There is no *systematic variance* with an accurate sample. Systematic variance has been defined as "the variation in measures due to some known or unknown influences that 'cause' the scores to lean in one direction more than another."[2] For example, it has been said that homes on the corner of the block tend to be larger and more valuable than those within blocks. Thus, a sample in which we select corner homes only will cause us to overestimate home values in the area.

The classic example of a sample with systematic variance was the *Literary Digest* presidential election poll in 1936 in which more than 2 million persons participated. The poll indicated that Alfred Landon would defeat Franklin Roosevelt for the presidency of the United States. Even the very large size of this sample did not counteract its systematic bias. Later evidence indicated that the poll drew its sample from the middle and upper classes, while Roosevelt's appeal was heavily among the much larger working class.

Precision. A second criterion of a good sample design is *precision of estimate*. No sample will fully represent its population in all respects. A sample statistic may be expected to differ from its parameter as a result of random fluctuations inherent in the sampling process. This is often referred to as *error variance* or *sampling error* and reflects the influences of chance in drawing the

---

[2] Fred N. Kerlinger, *Foundations of Behavioral Research,* 2d ed. (New York: Holt, Rinehart and Winston, Inc., 1973), p. 74.

sample members. Error variance is that which is left over after all known sources of systematic variance have been accounted for. In theory, error variance consists of random fluctuations only, although there may be some unknown systematic variance included.

Precision is measured by the *standard error of estimate,* a type of standard deviation measurement. The relationship between the standard error of estimate and the precision of the sample is that the smaller the standard error of estimate, the higher is the precision of the sample. After giving due consideration to problems of overcoming bias, it is desirable that the sample design produce a minimum standard error of estimate. However, not all types of sample designs provide estimates of precision, and samples of the same size can produce different amounts of error variance.

Types of Sample Design

There are a variety of sampling techniques available. Which we select depends on the requirements of the project, its objectives, and funds available. The different approaches may be classified by their representation basis and the element selection techniques as in the accompanying table.

	Representation Basis	
Element Selection	*Probability*	*Nonprobability*
Unrestricted	Simple random	Convenience
Restricted	Complex random	Purposive
	Systematic	Expert choice
	Cluster	Quota
	Stratified	
	Double	

Representation. The members of a sample are selected either on a probability basis or by some other means. Probability sampling is based on the concept of *random selection—a controlled procedure that assures that each population element is given a known nonzero chance of selection.*

In contrast, *nonprobability selection* is "nonrandom." That is, each member does not have a known nonzero chance of being included. Allowing interviewers to choose sample members "at random" (meaning as they wish or wherever they find them) is *not random sampling.* Only probability samples provide estimates of precision.

Element Selection. Samples may also be classified by whether the elements are selected individually and directly from the population viewed as a single pool, or whether additional controls are placed on the process of element selection. When each sample element is drawn individually from the population at large, it is an *unrestricted sample. Restricted sampling* covers all other forms of sampling.

PROBABILITY SAMPLING

The unrestricted or simple random sample is conceptually the simplest form of probability sampling. Recall that all probability samples must provide a known nonzero chance of selection for each population element. A simple random sample is the *special case in which each population element has an equal chance of being selected into the sample;* this type will be used here to explore the procedures for choosing probability samples.

Sampling Procedure

There are a number of design decisions that must be made. Assume that we are interested in starting a dining establishment near the campus of Cranial University. Our idea is to make its facilities available on a membership basis. To launch such a venture we will need to make a substantial investment. In addition, the project has a number of risks which we would like to minimize through research. One important research question might be "Who would patronize such a club and on what basis?" More specifically, we might be interested in the following investigative questions:

1. How many would join the club under various membership and fee arrangements?
2. How much would the average member spend per month?
3. What meals and days would be the most popular?
4. What menu and service formats would be the most popular?
5. What other services should be provided?

To find answers to these and other questions we decide to conduct a sample survey. What are the steps to take?

Steps in Sampling Design

Six steps must be taken in designing a sample. While they are presented here sequentially, their order is not fixed, and an answer to one question often forces a revision in an answer given earlier. The critical sampling questions are:

1. What is the relevant population?
2. What type of sample shall we draw?
3. What sampling frame shall we use?
4. What are the parameters of interest?
5. What size sample is needed?
6. How much will the sample cost?

What Is the Relevant Population?   The population of interest is normally apparent from the management problem and the research objectives. In the dining club example the population might be one or a combination of the following: students, faculty, nonacademic personnel, area residents and/or workers, or the general public. Assume that the major need is for student facilities. Therefore, the relevant population might be "all currently enrolled students at Cranial University."

What Type of Sample?   What method should we use? Because the total student body is geographically concentrated, because there is a reasonably accurate list of this population, and because a major investment is planned, we conclude we would like to use a probability design of the simple random type. In a later section we will consider the application of other sampling techniques to this problem.

Choosing the simple random sampling technique has several consequences for us. With this sample design we can make probability-based confidence estimates of various parameters. In using this method we must also give careful attention to the execution of the sampling process. The selection must follow an appropriate procedure in which there is no chance for interviewers or others to modify the selections made. No one other than those selected can be included in the study; strong efforts must be made to include all of the elements in the original sampling frame. We must exclude substitutions except as clearly specified and controlled according to predetermined decision rules.

In spite of all of this care the actual sample achieved will not match perfectly the sample that is originally drawn. Some persons will refuse to participate and others will be difficult to find. The latter represent the well-known "not-at-home" problem and require that a number of callbacks be made to assure that they are adequately represented in the sample.

What Sampling Frame?   The concept of *sampling frame* is closely related to the population. It is defined as the *list of elements from which the sample is actually drawn.* Ideally it is a complete and correct list of population members only. As a practical matter, however, the sampling frame often differs from the theoretical population.

Consider the dining club survey problem. The population is defined in terms of "currently enrolled students at Cranial University." However, the university has a branch campus located ten miles away and the students that attend class there are not logical clients for the club. Thus, we might redefine the population to be "all students currently enrolled at the Cranial University main campus."

The university student directory would be a logical first choice as a list of population elements. This source may represent a sampling frame which is too narrow. Directories are normally published in the fall semester, and the study is being done in the spring. The list is out of date to the extent that students have left school or have come to the university since the directory went to press.

We might redefine the population to include only those in the directory, but this would be a sampling frame that does not fully reflect our desired population. Therefore we would try other solutions first. One way to improve the sampling frame would be to secure a supplemental list of students who have come to Cranial and another list of those who are no longer in residence. We will probably find that there is a supplemental list of new students, but no list of those who have left school. In addition, the lists available may include students at both the main and branch campuses.

These problems do not present great difficulties. The original population concept can be retained by using the directory plus the supplemental list of new students even though this also includes all students from the branch plus those who are no longer enrolled. One procedure in this case is to number consecutively all of the names on the original and supplementary lists. Then use a table of random numbers to draw a sample of the desired size plus an additional list of replacement numbers, recorded in their order of selection. Names are selected for the sample from the list to correspond to the random numbers chosen. If a chosen student has left school or has classes only at the branch campus that student is dropped from the study and replaced by the name chosen with the first unused number on the supplemental list. This process continues until the desired sample is secured. This procedure is often called sampling from a "too inclusive frame."

What Parameters to Estimate?   In determining the nature of the sample design it is important that we determine what specific population parameters are of interest. Some of these will correspond to the investigative questions already asked. For example:

1. The proportion of persons who express an interest in joining the club.
2. The average expected expenditures per month per member.
3. Average number of weekday lunches that will be demanded.

There may also be important subgroups in the population about whom we would like to make estimates. For example, we might want to draw conclusions about the extent of club use that could be expected from married students versus single students, residential students versus in-town students, and so forth. Such questions have a strong impact upon the nature of the sampling frame we accept, the design of the sample, and its size.

Parameters of interest may also be classified as *variables* or *attributes* data. Variables, as used in this special statistical sense, are normally computed from ratio or interval scale data such as dollars, age, length, scores, and so on, and may be *continuous* or *discrete*. Continuous variables such as age and length, can take all possible values within the relevant ranges; discrete variables, such as family size and number of visits per month, can take only selected values. The most common measures of variable data are the arithmetic mean and the standard deviation.

Attribute measures are necessary for nominal data and are widely used for other measures as well. Examples of attribute measurements are the proportion of a sample who express an interest in joining the club, or the proportion of married students who report they now eat in restaurants five times a month or more. The most frequent concentration measure of attributes is the percentage; the variance measure is the *pq* ratio.

How Large a Sample? Much folklore surrounds this question. One false belief is that a sample must be large or it is not representative. This is much less true than most people believe. In recent years there has been controversy in congressional hearings about the representativeness of a national sample of TV listeners. Samples of 1,000 or more have been branded as totally inadequate by many critics but seldom if ever by a statistician. Sample size is only one aspect of representativeness. A sample of more than 2 million can be misleading while a sample of 1,000, drawn in the proper manner, can be more than adequate.

Casual observers generally feel that the size of sample must bear some proportional relationship to the size of the population from which it is drawn. One hears that a sample should represent 10 percent or more of the total population. This is a myth. *The absolute number of people in a random sample is more significant than is the sample's size relative to the population size.* A sample of 400 drawn from a population of 4,000 may be quite appropriate, but for many purposes the size sample may need to be no more than, say, 60 members. Again, a sample of 400 is, for most practical purposes, just as appropriate for a population of 200 million as it is for a population of 4,000. If drawn correctly it will give almost the same precision in either case.

In simple random sampling there are a number of important factors which affect the size of sample. Recall that a sample is only a partial reflection of the population from which it is drawn. It must be an acceptable representation of the population, but what is "acceptable?" Ultimately this is determined by the researcher, who must determine (1) *the desired size of the interval range around the estimated parameter and* (2) *an acceptable confidence level for the estimate.* More will be said about these later in this chapter.

Two other factors which affect size of sample concern the population. First is the size of the population variance. *The greater this dispersion, the greater is the sample size needed to provide a given quality of representation.* For example, if all members of a population hold the same view on a question then a sample of one will perfectly reflect the population on this question. On the other hand, if every member of the population were different on some characteristic it would take a complete census to capture the full variety. A second population aspect which can affect sample size is the population size itself. Elementary sampling typically assumes an infinite population, but populations are often finite. Thus, a population of 46 obviously limits any sample size to no more than this amount.

Other considerations often weigh heavily upon the sample size decision. The conditions under which the sample is being conducted may indicate that only certain designs are feasible. For example, one type of sample may be the appropriate design because we have no lists of population elements and must therefore sample geographic units. Since various designs have differing statistical and economic efficiencies, the choice of design coupled with the other requirements mentioned above will also affect the size of sample.

The researcher may also be interested in making estimates concerning various subgroups of the population; then the sample must be large enough for each of these subgroups to meet the desired quality level. We achieve this in simple random sampling by making the total sample large enough to assure that each critical subgroup meets the minimum size criterion. In more complex sampling procedures we sample the smaller subgroups more heavily and then weight their effect on the total parameter estimates.

How Much Will It Cost?   Cost considerations have a major impact upon decisions about the size and type of sample as well as the data collection methods. Almost all studies have some budgetary constraint, and this can even dictate that a nonprobability sample must be used. Probability sample surveys incur callback costs, listing costs, and a variety of other costs which are not as important when more haphazard methods are used.

Costs also dictate the size of sample that we can draw. For example, if there is a $2,000 budget for interviewing, and it costs an estimated $15 to complete a personal interview using a simple random sample, it is obvious that the sample cannot exceed 133 respondents. By changing the design to a geographic cluster sample we might be able to reduce this to, say, $12 per interview, allowing a sample size of 167. A shift to a self-administered questionnaire might reduce costs to $8 per interview, giving a sample of 250.

Cost factors may also dictate that we abandon personal interviewing in favor of either telephone or mail surveys. Thus, telephone interviews might cost $4 each, allowing a sample of 500.[3] In changing the type of data collection method, of course, we must recognize that the amount and type of data which can be secured also changes. These questions will be discussed in Chapter 10. At this point we wish to continue with the question of developing a simple random sample for the campus dining club project.

Sampling Concepts

To foster understanding of the process of probability sampling we must introduce a limited amount of statistical nomenclature. There are three different statistical distributions. Each of these is illustrated in Figure 6–1. Definitions of key terms are:

Population Distribution.   The distribution that will be found if we take a census of all students concerning how many meals they would eat at the new club during a month. This distribution is illustrated in Part A of Figure 6–1.

---

[3] All estimates of costs given here are hypothetical.

Figure 6–1

Part A

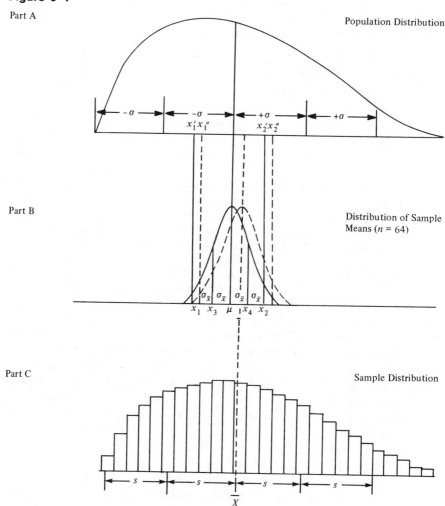

Note: The distributions in these figures are not to scale, but this fact is not critical to an understanding of the dispersion relationships depicted.

Sample Distribution.   If we take a sample of 64 students, we will have a distribution of 64 frequencies of expected meals ranging from 0 meals to some number of meals reflecting very high patronage. This distribution is illustrated in Part C of Figure 6–1. It should approximate the same form as the population distribution.

Distribution of Sample Means.   Assume we draw a random sample of 64 students, calculate their expected average usage, then return their names to the pool. We then draw a second and other repeated samples in the same manner, calculating a mean for each sample we draw. After calculating a number of these sample means they can be plotted in a distribution which will approach the form of that shown in Part B of Figure 6–1.

μ = Mu, the arithmetic mean of the population member responses as to the number of meals per month that they expect to eat at the new club.

σ = The standard deviation of the population and a measure of the dispersion of individual responses about the mean.

$\overline{X}$ = The arithmetic mean of a particular sample drawn from the population.

s = The standard deviation of the particular sample drawn from the population.

$\sigma_{\overline{x}}$ = The standard error of the mean. It is a measure of dispersion of the distribution of sample means and is the standard deviation of this distribution.

Point and Interval Estimating. The researcher makes two types of estimates in using a sample to estimate a population parameter. First is a *point estimate*. That is, after collecting a sample of responses and calculating a sample arithmetic mean of 8.4, the researcher uses this statistic as the estimate of the mean of the population. If we were asked for a best estimate of the population mean, we would choose 8.4, the sample mean.

We state just how close to the parameter a point estimate is in terms of some *interval range*. We can never estimate with certainty the exact value of a population mean by use of a sample. We can give our best point estimate; beyond that we must speak in terms of intervals and probabilities. The only way we can be absolutely certain that we know the population mean is to take a census. Any sample runs some risk of being atypical.

To continue with the example, assume for the moment that we have super insight that tells us that the expected visits to the club are normally distributed about a population mean of 8.0 with a standard deviation of 3.0. The "normal" distribution—the distribution which many chance events take—has certain properties which are important to us. For instance, about 68 percent of the cases in a normal distribution fall within one standard deviation (plus or minus) of the mean. Two standard deviations on either side of the mean encompass just over 95 percent of the population. That is, slightly more than 95 percent (95.45 percent) of the students in our population might visit the club between 2 and 14 times per month $(8.0 \pm 2 \times 3.0)$.

Unfortunately we do not have super insight; we do not know if we are dealing with a normal distribution, and we do not know the population mean or its standard deviation. We can, however, estimate the population mean and even judge how accurate the estimate is. Assume that we take a sample of 64 students and find that the sample yields an arithmetic mean of 8.4. We replace these student names on the population list and draw another sample of 64 randomly, this time securing a sample mean of 7.7; a third sample yields 8.8, while a fourth sample yields another mean value. We go on drawing such samples until we have accumulated a large number of means of samples of 64. *Each one of these is a separate point estimate of the population mean.*

Distribution Relationships. All of these sample means may be presented in a distribution like that shown in Part B of Figure 6–1. Notice that this distribution (B) differs from the population distribution (A) in two ways: The dispersion in distribution B is much smaller and it is also much more "normal" than the population. This is characteristic of a distribution of sample means and other sample statistics. Even if the population is not normal, *the sample means drawn from that population are dispersed around the parameter in a distribution that is generally close to normal;* the mean of the distribution of sample means is equal to the population mean.

One might guess that there is some functional relationship between a population distribution and a distribution of sample means drawn from that population. There is, and the relationship between these two distributions is critical for drawing inferences about parameters. Without going into the theory, the relationship between the dispersion of a population distribution and that of the sample mean can be stated in the following form:

$$\sigma_{\bar{x}} = \frac{\sigma}{\sqrt{n}}$$

$\sigma_{\bar{x}}$ = Standard error of the mean of a given sample size.
σ = Standard deviation of the population.
n = Sample size

The standard error of the mean varies directly with the standard deviation of the population from which it is drawn. If the population standard deviation were smaller, say 2.0 rather than 4.0, the standard error of the mean would be only one half as large. *The standard error of the mean also varies inversely with the square root of the size of the sample.* If the square root of the sample size is doubled, the standard error is cut by one half if the standard deviation is constant. These relationships are:

A

$$\sigma_{\bar{x}} = \frac{\sigma}{\sqrt{n}}$$

C

$$\sigma_{\bar{x}} = \frac{2}{\sqrt{64}} = 0.25$$

B

$$\sigma_{\bar{x}} = \frac{4}{\sqrt{64}} = 0.5$$

D

$$\sigma_{\bar{x}} = \frac{4}{\sqrt{256}} = 0.25$$

The distribution of one sample is shown in Part C of Figure 6–1.

Several characteristics about it are worthy of mention. First, the sample distribution is shown as a histogram, representing a frequency distribution of empirical data, while the smooth curves in Parts A and B are theoretical distributions of continuous data. Second, the sample distribution is much like the population distribution in appearance but not a perfect duplication. We would expect that it would not be; no sample is a perfect replication of its population. Third, the mean of the sample also differs from the mean of the population. Again, this is expected because the mean of this sample is only one of the means used to build the distribution shown in Part B of Figure 6–1. The sample distribution in Part C also has its own standard deviation (here identified by s).

The mean of any sample of a given size will probably fall within the range as indicated by the extremes of the distribution shown in Part B of Figure 6–1. This distribution represents the means of 64 persons.[4] Further, we know that about 68 percent of the means of samples will fall within plus or minus one standard error of the true mean. That is, in the distribution in Part B of Figure 6–1, about two thirds of the means will fall between x_3 and x_4. In addition, about 95 percent of the means of the samples will fall within the interval ranging from x_1 to x_2.

If we project points x_1 and x_2 on the population distribution (Part A of Figure 6–1) at points x_1' and x_2' we see the interval within which any given mean of a random sample of 64 is likely to fall about 95 times out of 100 samples drawn. There is about a 5 percent chance that any particular sample of 64 drawn would have a mean that falls outside the interval x_1' to x_2'.

Estimating the Population Mean.   The only problem with using this reasoning to estimate the population mean is that it literally says the sample mean has a 95 percent chance of falling within two standard errors of the population mean. However, we do not know the population mean from which to measure the standard errors. We get around this problem by inferring that if there is a 95 percent chance that a sample mean is within two standard errors of the population mean, then there is also a 95 percent chance that the population mean is within two standard errors of a sample mean. This inference enables us to find a sample mean, mark off an interval of estimate around it, and state a confidence likelihood that the population mean is within this bracket.

In practice we take only one sample and calculate a mean ($\overline{X}$) of, say, 8.4, and an s of 4.1. We then infer that 8.4 is our best point estimate of the population mean and that there would be a distribution of sample means around this estimate. The dashed-line distribution in Part B of Figure 6–1 illustrates this distribution. The dashed-line projections from the distribution of sample means (B) to the population distribution (A) show the interval range of

---

[4] A distribution of samples of any other size will be similarly shaped but will have a different dispersion depending upon the size of the sample and the dispersion in the population.

estimate about the sample mean. By this process we estimate an interval range (x_1'' to x_2'') within which we believe that the population mean falls.

The best point estimate of the population mean is the sample value of 8.4 times per month. Anything more about the parameter must be stated in probabilistic terms as an interval estimate. Because we plan to invest heavily in this project we want some assurance that the population mean is close to the figure reported in any sample we take. To find out how close the population mean is to the sample mean we must calculate the standard error of the mean ($\sigma_{\bar{x}}$) and estimate an interval range within which the population mean is likely to be. The basic relationship to use is:

$$\sigma_{\bar{x}} = \frac{\sigma}{\sqrt{n}}$$

We know the size of sample to be 64, but we still need a value for σ in order to compute $\sigma_{\bar{x}}$. Almost never will we have the value for the standard deviation of the population (σ), so we must use some proxy figure. Our best estimate of σ is the standard deviation of the sample (s), in this case 4.1. Thus the computation of the standard error of the mean is:[5]

$$\sigma_{\bar{x}} = \frac{s}{\sqrt{n - 1}} = \frac{4.1}{\sqrt{63}} = \frac{4.1}{7.937} = 0.52$$

If one standard error of the mean is equal to 0.52 visits, then 1.96 standard errors is equal to 1.02 visits. That is, we can estimate with 95 percent confidence that the population mean of student visit expectations is within 8.4 $\pm$ 1.02 visits, or from 7.38 to 9.42 visits per month. (Technically, if we were to take a large number of samples of 64 and compute intervals, such as 7.38 to 9.42, we would find that 95 percent of them would include the population mean.)

Changing Interval Estimates. This estimation may not be satisfactory in two ways. First, it may not represent the degree of confidence that we want in the interval estimate. For example, we might want a higher degree of confidence than the 95 percent level used here. This presents no problem. We can refer to a table of areas under the normal curve and determine various combinations of standard deviation and probabilities. The accompanying table summarizes some of those more commonly used. Thus, if we want a greater confidence in the probability of including the population mean in the interval range we can move to a higher standard error, say, a $\bar{x} \pm 3\sigma$. In this case we would estimate that the population mean lies somewhere in the range of 8.4 $\pm$ 3(0.52) or from 6.84 to 9.96. Then 997 out of 1,000 times we would expect this interval to include the population mean.

---

[5] To make the sample standard deviation an unbiased estimate of the population it is necessary to divide the sample standard deviation by $\sqrt{n - 1}$ rather than $\sqrt{n}$.

Standard Error	Percent of Area*	Approximate Degree of Confidence	Interval Range
1.00	68.27	2 to 1	μ is between 7.88 and 8.92
1.65	90.10	9 to 1	μ is between 7.54 and 9.26
1.96	95.00	19 to 1	μ is between 7.38 and 9.42
2.00	95.45	21 to 1	μ is between 7.36 and 9.44
2.33	98.02	50 to 1	μ is between 7.19 and 9.61
3.00	99.73	270 to 1	μ is between 6.84 and 9.96

* Includes both tails in a normal distribution.

We might wish to have an estimate that will hold for a much smaller range, for example, 8.4 ± 0.2. To secure this smaller interval range of estimate we must either (1) accept a smaller degree of confidence in the results or (2) take a sample large enough to provide this smaller interval with adequate confidence levels.

We can calculate that if one standard error is equal to 0.52 visits, then 0.2 visits would be equal to 0.38 standard errors (0.2/0.52). If we refer to a table of area under the normal curve we find that there is a 29.6 percent chance that the true population mean lies within a ± 0.38 standard errors of 8.4.[6] That is, with a sample of 64 we should find the sample mean to be subject to so much error variance that only 30 percent of the time could we expect to find the population mean between 8.2 and 8.6. This is such a small degree of confidence that we would normally move to the second alternative; we would increase the sample size until we can secure the desired interval estimate and degree of confidence.

The Sample Size Decision

We can determine sample size in a number of ways. One way is to choose some sample size on a judgmental basis and then determine how much precision we secure. A second approach is to determine the acceptable degree of precision and from that determine the necessary size of sample. This latter approach is the subject of this section.

Decision Factors. Two subjective decisions affect the size of the random sample that we draw. One is how much confidence we want to place in our population interval estimate; the other is how large we want this estimating interval to be. While we may think in terms of 95 percent confidence levels, this is not required. The 95 percent level is often used, but we may want more or less confidence in our estimate. The researcher must set the level to express the degree of confidence wanted in the resulting interval estimate.

---

[6] See Appendix B, Table B–1.

Second, we must decide on the size of the interval estimate in light of our particular needs. That is, we take a sample to estimate a parameter for some purpose. Depending upon that purpose, we choose a narrower or a wider interval. Both the degree of confidence and the desired interval of estimate are important determinants of the size of sample. They are important because *they determine the standard error of the sample mean that is required to meet our needs.*

Dispersion Factor.   The third factor that affects the size of sample for a given precision is the dispersion of the population. *The smaller the population dispersion, the smaller the sample needed to give a representative picture of population members.* Suppose we are interested in determining the average age of a certain population. If the age ranges from 10 to 15 years a small sample will give us a close estimate of the population's average age. If the population consists of persons ranging from less than 1 to 100 years of age we will need a larger sample for the same degree of confidence in our estimates.

Finite Population Factor.   A final factor that affects the size of a random sample is the size of the population. To this point we have assumed that the population is infinite. Where the size of the sample exceeds about 5 percent of the population it is proper to recognize that the finite limits of the population put a constraint on the size of sample needed.

Sample Size Calculation.   Suppose that we want to be 95 percent confident that the expected average monthly number of meals taken at the proposed campus dinner club will be within an interval of ± 0.1 meals. This means that if we take a sample of students and find the average number of expected meals to be 8.4 then we can be 95 percent confident that the entire student body average is within the range of 8.3 to 8.5 meals. This is a high degree of precision. The interval estimate of ± 0.1 meals must encompass a dispersion of ± 1.96 standard errors of the mean. Hence one standard error of the mean equals $0.051(0.1/1.96)$. Assume further that we have reason to believe that we will find the sample standard deviation to equal about 4.1 meals. With these data we can solve the sample size problem.

$$\sigma_{\bar{x}} = \frac{s}{\sqrt{n-1}} = 0.051 = \frac{4.1}{\sqrt{n-1}}$$
$$n = 6,464$$

if

$\pm 0.1 =$ Desired interval within which the parameter is expected (subjective decision).

$1.96\ \sigma_{\bar{x}} = 0.95$ confidence level for estimating interval within which to expect population mean (subjective decision).

$\sigma_{\bar{x}} = 0.051 =$ Standard error of the mean $(0.1/1.96)$.

$s =$ Standard deviation of sample (used here as estimate of population dispersion) $= 4.1$.

This is the appropriate sample size no matter how large the student body is. But what if the student body is only 6,000 students? It does not make sense to talk of a sample of 6,464 in a population of 6,000. We correct by making an adjustment for the finite population. This adjustment corrects the estimate as follows:

$$\sigma_{\bar{x}} = \frac{s}{\sqrt{n-1}} \times \sqrt{\frac{N-n}{N-1}} = 0.051 = \frac{4.1}{\sqrt{n-1}} \times \sqrt{\frac{6,000-n}{6,000-1}}$$
$$n = 3,112$$

where

N = Size of population.
n = Size of sample.

If the population is 6,000, then the revised sample is 3,112 persons rather than 6,464. Use of the finite adjustment factor reduces the size of the sample required to give a certain precision, but this reduction is insignificant unless the sample is 5 percent or more of the population.

Suppose that in the illustration just given our precision requirements were less demanding. For example, we might be quite satisfied with an interval range that is ±0.6 rather than ±0.1, with all other variables remaining the same. What sample size would we need to be 95 percent confident that the population mean is within a ±0.5 meals of the sample mean? Assuming that there is an infinite population, we find that we would need a sample of 259 persons. If there is a finite population of 6,000, then $n = 249$.

These four factors: (1) desired interval estimate, (2) degree of confidence, (3) population variance, and (4) relative size of population are the major noncost determinants of the size of random sample needed to provide a given precision level of interval estimate. The first two of these factors may be subjectively set by the researcher, while the third and fourth are secured or estimated from knowledge about the population.

Sampling of Attributes

To this point we have talked of sample size needs in terms of variables—measured in terms of arithmetic means and standard errors of the mean. Suppose, however, that an important question involves percentage data such as "What percent of the students will join the club and pay $5 dues per month?" The answer to this question may be critical to determining whether the club is feasible and what the rates and services may be.

Solution Procedure. We choose a sample to answer the above questions using the same general procedure as before. With variables data the measure of concern is the arithmetic mean $(\bar{X})$, while with attributes it is p (the proportion of the population that has a given attribute).[7] When the data involve variables, the population variance is measured by the standard deviation squared (σ^2), while with attributes, the variance is measured in terms of p × q (in which q is the proportion of the population not having the attribute, and $q = 1 - p$). The measure of dispersion of the sample statistic also changes from the standard error of the mean ($\sigma_{\bar{x}}$) to the standard error of the proportion (σ_p). The relationships compare as shown in the accompanying table.

	Variables Data	Attributes Data
Variance	$\sigma_{\bar{x}}^2 = \dfrac{\sigma^2}{n}$	$\sigma_p^2 = \dfrac{pq}{n}$
Standard error	$\sigma_{\bar{x}} = \dfrac{\sigma}{\sqrt{n}}$	$\sigma_p = \sqrt{\dfrac{pq}{n}}$

We calculate a sample size based on attributes data by making the subjective decisions concerning the acceptable interval estimate and the degree of confidence. Assume that exploratory questioning indicates that perhaps 30 percent of the students say they will join the club. We decide that we want to estimate the true proportion in the population within 10 percentage points of this figure ($p = 0.30 \pm 0.10$). Assume further that we want to be 95 percent confident that the population parameter is within ± 0.10 of the sample proportion. The calculation of the sample size proceeds in the same manner as before:

$$\sigma_p = \sqrt{\frac{pq}{n-1}} = 0.051 = \sqrt{\frac{0.3 \times 0.7}{n-1}}$$
$$n = 82$$

± 0.10 = Desired interval range within which population proportion is expected (subjective decision).

$1.96\sigma_p$ = 0.95 confidence level for estimating interval within which to expect the population proportion (subjective decision).

σ_p = 0.051 = Standard error of the proportion (0.10/1.96)

pq = Measure of sample dispersion (used here as an estimate of population dispersion).

The sample size of 82 persons is based upon an infinite population assumption. If the sample size is less than 5 percent of the population there is little to be gained by using the finite population adjustment.

---

[7] A proportion is the mean of a dichotomous variable when members of a class receive the value of 1, and nonmembers receive a value of 0.

In the examples used to this point we have assumed that prior information or preliminary questioning provided us with the variance estimate. Suppose this information is not available. Then what? With attributes data there is a feature concerning the variance that is not found with variables data. The pq ratio can never exceed 0.25. For example, if $p = 0.5$ then $q = 0.5$, and their product is 0.25. If either p or q is greater than 0.5 then their product is smaller than 0.25 (for example, $0.4 \times 0.6 = 0.24$, and so on). When we have no information regarding the probable p value, we can assume that $p = 0.5$ and solve for the sample size.

If we use the maximum variance estimate we find the sample needs to be 97.

$$\sigma_p = \sqrt{\frac{pq}{n-1}} = 0.051 = \sqrt{\frac{0.5 \times 0.5}{n-1}}$$
$$n = 97$$

The interpretation of data found with a sample of 97 chosen randomly from the student population would be: If it is found that 50 percent of the respondents say they will join the club with dues at \$5 a month, then we can be 95 percent confident that, in a census, from 40 to 60 percent of all students would say they would join the club.

Actual Sample Precision.   Suppose we take a sample of 97 students and find that only 20 percent say they will join if the dues are \$5 per month. Do we still estimate that the true population percentage is 0.50 ± 0.10, or do we estimate that the true percentage in the population is 0.20 ± 0.10? We do neither. We recognize that our original variance estimate (pq) was too large; we recalculate the standard error of the percentage, using the actual sample size of 97 and the actual sample variance found. The result is:

$$\sigma_p = \sqrt{\frac{0.2 \times 0.8}{97-1}} = \sqrt{\frac{0.16}{96}} = \sqrt{0.001666}$$
$$\sigma_p = 0.041$$

We estimate, with a 95 percent confidence, that the population proportion falls within the range of 0.20 ± 0.08, or 12 to 28 percent.

Asymmetrical Confidence Regions   To this point we have assumed that confidence levels and interval ranges fall equally on both sides of a mean or proportion. Thus, we talk of a 95 percent confidence that the population proportion falls within 0.20 ± 0.08. With symmetrical confidence levels, as shown in A of Figure 6–2, we accept that there is a 0.025 chance that the population proportion is outside our estimated interval range on each tail of the distribution. However, what if we are chiefly concerned about the *minimum level* of club acceptance? We can also put all of this 0.05 area in the lower tail of the distribution and ask the question "What is the estimate of the

Figure 6–2: Example of Symmetrical and Asymmetrical Confidence Regions

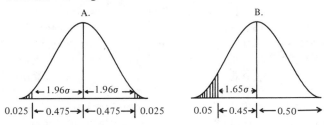

minimum population proportion, with 95 percent confidence? This situation is illustrated in B of Figure 6–2.

Reference to Appendix B, Table B–1 indicates that such an interval range would include 1.65 standard errors below 0.20 and all of the distribution above 0.20. Thus, we estimate, with a 95 percent confidence, that the population proportion is 0.132 or greater.[8] In this case the use of an asymmetrical confidence region enables us to estimate that the probable lower limit for p is 0.132 rather than 0.12.

COMPLEX PROBABILITY SAMPLING

Simple random sampling is often impractical. For example, it requires a population list which is often not available. The use of this design may also be wasteful because we fail to use all of the information which we have about a population; in addition the implementation of a simple random design may be expensive in time and money. These problems have led to the development of alternative designs which are superior to the simple random design in terms of statistical and/or economic efficiency.

A more efficient sample in a statistical sense is one which provides a given precision (standard error of the mean) with a smaller sample size. We achieve this largely by utilizing our knowledge to stratify the population. A sample which is economically more efficient is one which provides a desired precision at a lower dollar cost. We achieve this with designs that enable us to lower the costs of data collecting, usually through reduced travel expense and interviewer time.

In the discussion that follows we consider four alternative probability sampling approaches: systematic, stratified, cluster, and double sampling.

Systematic Sampling

The most widely used version of probability sampling is probably *systematic sampling*. In this approach every kth element in the population is sam-

---

[8] $0.132 = 0.20 - 1.65 \ (0.041)$.

pled, beginning a random start with an element from 1 to k. The major advantage of systematic sampling is its simplicity and flexibility. It is easier to instruct field workers to choose the dwelling unit listed on every kth line of a listing sheet than it is to use random sampling numbers tables. With systematic sampling there is no need to number the cards in a large personnel file prior to drawing a sample. We merely determine (1) the total number of cards in the file, (2) the sampling ratio to use, (3) the random start, and then begin drawing a sample by choosing every kth card. Invoices or customer accounts can be sampled by using the last digit or a combination of digits of an invoice or customer account number. Time sampling is also easier.

While systematic sampling has some theoretical problems from a practical point of view, it is usually treated as a simple random sample. In fact, this design is statistically more efficient than a simple random sample when similar population elements are grouped on the list. This might occur if the list elements are ordered chronologically, by size, class, and so on. Under these conditions the sample approaches a proportional stratified sample. The effect of this ordering is more pronounced on the results of cluster samples than for element samples and may call for using the proportional stratified sampling formula.[9]

A major problem with systematic sampling is the possible periodicity in the population that parallels the sampling ratio. For example, in sampling days of the week, a one in seven sampling ratio would give biased results. A less obvious case might involve a survey in an area of apartment houses where the typical pattern is eight apartments per building. Many systematic sampling fractions, such as one in eight, could easily oversample some types of apartments and undersample others. The only protection against this is constant vigilance by the researcher.

Another type of problem may occur when there is a monotonic trend in the population elements. That is, the population list varies from the smallest to the largest element or vice versa. Even a chronological list may have this effect if a measure has trended in one direction over time. Whether a systematic sample drawn under these conditions provides a biased estimate of the population mean depends upon the initial random draw. Assume that we have a list of 2,000 commercial banks, arrayed from largest to smallest, from which we wish to draw a sample of 50 for analysis. We use a sampling ratio of 1 : 20 and begin with a random start at 16, drawing every 20th bank after that. This sampling pattern would exclude the 15 largest banks and would give a downward size bias to our findings. There are ways to deal with this. One might randomize the population before sampling, change the random start several times in the sampling proces, or replicate a selection of different samples.

---

[9] Leslie Kish, *Survey Sampling* (New York: John Wiley & Sons, Inc., 1965), p. 118.

Stratified Sampling

Most populations can be segregated into a number of mutually exclusive subpopulations, or *strata*. For example, university students can be divided by their class level, school, sex, and so forth. After a population is divided into the appropriate strata a simple random sample can be taken within each stratum. The sampling results can then be weighted and combined into appropriate population estimates.

Why Stratify? There are three reasons why a researcher may choose a stratified random sample. They are to (1) increase a sample's statistical efficiency, (2) provide adequate data for analyzing the various subpopulations, and (3) enable different research methods and procedures to be used in different strata.[10]

Stratification is almost always more efficient statistically than simple random sampling and at worst is equal to it. With the ideal stratification each stratum is homogeneous internally and heterogeneous with other strata. This might occur in a sample which includes members of several distinct ethnic groups. In such a case stratification makes a pronounced improvement in statistical efficiency.

Stratification is also useful when the researcher wants to study the characteristics of certain population subgroups. Thus, if we wish to draw some conclusions about activities in the different classes of a student body it would be useful to sample on a stratified basis.

Stratification is also useful when different methods of observation, sampling, or data collection are called for in different parts of the population. This might occur when we survey company employees at the home office with one method but must use a different approach with employees scattered over the country.

How to Stratify? Assuming that data are available upon which to base a stratification decision, how shall we go about it?[11] There are three major decisions that must be made:

1. What stratification base or bases to use?
2. How many strata to use?
3. What strata sample sizes to draw?

The ideal stratification would be based on the principal variable under study. For example, if our major concern is to learn how many times per month students would use the dining club then we would like to stratify on this expected number of use occasions. The only difficulty with this idea is that if we had this information we would not need to do the study. We must,

---

[10] Ibid., pp. 76–77.

[11] Typically stratification is carried out prior to the actual sampling but when this is not possible, it is still possible to "post-stratify." See ibid., p. 90.

therefore, pick a variable for stratifying which we believe will correlate with the frequency of club use per month.

However, we often have several principal variables about which we want to draw conclusions. A reasonable approach to this problem is to seek some basis for stratification that correlates well with the major variables. It might be a single variable (class level) or it might be compound (class, by sex). In any event, we will have done a good stratifying job if the stratification base maximizes the difference among strata means and minimizes the within-stratum variances for the variables of major concern.

How Many Strata to Use? We have no precise answer to this question, but theoretically the more strata, the closer we are likely to come to maximizing interstrata differences and minimizing intrastratum variances. We must base the decision partially on the number of subpopulation groups about which we wish to draw separate conclusions. Costs of stratification also enter into the decision. Cochran suggests that there is little to be gained in estimating overall population values when the number of strata exceeds six.[12]

What Strata Sample Sizes to Draw? The answer to this question falls in two areas. First is the matter of how large the total sample should be; the second question is how the total sample shall be allocated among strata. Answers to each of these questions depends upon the answer to the other. For example, in deciding how to allocate a total sample among various strata there are several alternatives—use either a proportionate or a disproportionate sample; if disproportionate, then is it based upon some optimization scheme, or is it primarily reflecting the need to have adequate coverage of various strata? We will consider several of these variations.

Proportionate Sampling. Common sense suggests that each stratum is properly represented if the sample drawn from it is in proportion to the stratum's share of the total population. This approach is more popular than any other stratified sampling procedure. Proportionate sampling will generally have higher statistical efficiency than will a simple random sample. The method is also much easier to carry out than other stratifying methods. A third advantage is that such a sampling procedure provides a self-weighting sample; the population mean can be estimated simply by calculating the mean of all sample cases.

On the other hand proportionate stratified samples will often gain little in statistical efficiency if the strata means and variances are somewhat similar for the major variables under study.

Disproportionate Sampling. Any stratification that departs from the proportionate relationships is obviously disproportionate. There may be a large number of disproportionate allocation schemes. One type might be a judgmentally determined disproportion based upon each stratum being large

---

[12] W. G. Cochran, *Sampling Techniques,* 2d ed. (New York: John Wiley & Sons, Inc., 1963), p. 134.

enough to secure adequate confidence levels and interval range estimates for individual strata.

The logic of disproportionate sampling, however, usually is determined by three factors which affect how a sample will be allocated among strata. Cochran points out that

> In a given stratum, take a larger sample if
> 1. The stratum is larger.
> 2. The stratum is more variable internally.
> 3. Sampling is cheaper in the stratum.[13]

If we use these suggestions as a guide it is possible to develop an optimal stratification scheme. When there is no difference in within-stratum variances and when the costs of sampling among strata are equal, this optimal design is a proportionate sample.

While disproportionate sampling is theoretically superior, there is some question as to whether it has wide applicability in a practical sense. If the differences in sampling costs or variances among strata are large then disproportionate sampling is desirable. Kish suggests that "differences of several-fold are required to make disproportionate sampling worth-while."[14]

The Allocation Problem. We can illustrate the differences in allocation between proportionate and disproportionate samples by assuming that we take a sample of 226 students in the dining club study. Assume further that we take an exploratory sample and from this have estimated the means and standard deviations for the five strata as shown in Table 6–1. These figures

Table 6–1: Average Expected Club Usage per Month

	Population N	Mean $\bar{X}$	Standard Deviation s
Freshman	2,000	4	1.6
Sophomore	2,000	5	2.0
Junior	1,800	9	4.4
Senior	1,700	10	4.8
Graduate	2,500	12	6.0

show substantial differences among classes, and suggest that disproportionate sampling might be more efficient. We shall determine the allocation scheme to be used under assumptions both of proportionate and disproportionate sampling.

---

[13] Ibid., p. 96.
[14] Kish, *Survey Sampling,* p. 94.

In proportionate sampling the allocation among the five strata should satisfy the following equalities:[15]

$$\frac{n_1}{N_1} = \frac{n_2}{N_2} = \cdots = \frac{n_s}{N_s}$$

where n_1 = Sample size in stratum 1.
N_1 = Population size in stratum 1.

In disproportionate sampling the sample size for each stratum should be weighted by the stratum variance to satisfy the following equalities:

$$\frac{n_1}{N_1\sigma_1} = \frac{n_2}{N_2\sigma_2} = \cdots = \frac{n_s}{N_s\sigma_s}$$

where σ_1 = Standard deviation of stratum 1.

In cost optimal disproportionate allocation, the size of the sample from each stratum should be weighted by the stratum variance as well as the cost of sampling and data gathering in that stratum to satisfy the following equalities:

$$\frac{n_1}{N_1\sigma_1\sqrt{C_1}} = \frac{n_2}{N_2\sigma_2\sqrt{C_2}} = \cdots = \frac{n_s}{N_s\sigma_s\sqrt{C_s}}$$

where C_1 = Cost associated with data gathering in stratum 1.

Given the assumed data in Table 6–1, the above relationships, and an expected survey cost in the freshman and sophomore strata of $4 per interview and a $6 cost in the other strata, the sample of 226 would be allocated as shown in Table 6–2.

The results from Table 6–2 indicate that the differences in strata variance are indeed large enough to affect allocations. Samples of the freshman and sophomore classes are reduced by one half or more by disproportionate sampling. The introduction of cost differences do not have much effect in this case. At first glance it might appear that the disproportionate samples are sometimes too small to draw class conclusions. However, calculation will show that the various stratum standard errors of the mean are more equal with the disproportionate than with the proportionate sample.

Total Sample Size. In the above example the sample size was set at 226, but how was this obtained? Following the procedures described earlier the researcher makes subjective decisions about the interval estimate and the level of confidence desired. Assume a 0.95 level of confidence with a total sample interval estimate of 0.5 visits per month. Given these requirements, and the calculations in Table 6–3, the sample size is determined as shown. With the disproportionate approach a sample of 226 is needed, while to

---

[15] Robert Ferber, *Statistical Methods in Market Research* (New York: McGraw-Hill Book Company, Inc., 1949), p. 75.

Table 6–2: Stratified Sampling Allocation for Dining Club Study

	(1) Population Relative W_i	(2) S_i	(3) $W_i s_i$	(4) $\sqrt{C_1}$	(5) $W_i s_i/\sqrt{C_i}$	(6) Proportionate	(7) Disproportionate	(8) Cost Optimal
						Sample Allocation		
Freshman	0.20	1.6	0.320	2.0	0.16	45	19	22
Sophomore	0.20	2.0	0.400	2.0	0.20	45	23	28
Junior	0.18	4.4	0.792	2.449	0.3234	41	47	45
Senior	0.17	4.8	0.816	2.449	0.3332	38	48	46
Graduate	0.25	6.0	1.500	2.449	0.6125	57	89	85
Total	1.00		3.828		1.6291	226	226	226

Proportionate:

$n_i = W_i N$

$n_1 = W_1 N = 0.20(226) \doteq 45$

Disproportionate:

$n_i = \dfrac{W_i \sigma_i}{\Sigma(W_i \sigma_i)} N$

$n_i = \dfrac{0.320}{3.828}(226) \doteq 19$

Cost Optimal:

$n_i = \dfrac{W_i \sigma_i/\sqrt{C_i}}{\Sigma(W_i \sigma_i/\sqrt{C_i})} N$

$n_1 = \dfrac{0.16}{1.6291}(226) \doteq 22$

Table 6–3: Stratified Sample Calculation for Dining Club Study

	W_i	s_i^2	$W_i s_i^2$	$\bar{X}_i$	$(\bar{X}_i - \bar{X})^2$	$W_i(\bar{X}_i - \bar{X})^2$
Freshman	0.20	2.56	0.512	4	16.9744	3.39488
Sophomore	0.20	4.00	0.800	5	9.7344	1.94688
Junior	0.18	19.36	3.485	9	0.7744	0.13939
Senior	0.17	23.04	3.917	10	3.5344	0.60085
Graduate	0.25	36.00	9.000	12	15.0544	3.76360
Total	1.00		17.714			9.84560

$\bar{X} = \Sigma(W_i X_i) = .8 + 1.0 + 1.62 + 1.7 + 3.0 = 8.12$

Disproportionate Sample:

$1.96 \sigma_{\bar{x}} = 0.5$

$\sigma_{\bar{x}} = 0.2551$

$\sigma_{\bar{x}}^2 = \dfrac{\Sigma(W_i \sigma_i)^2}{n} \doteq \dfrac{\Sigma(W_i s_i)^2}{n-1}$

$0.2551^2 \doteq \dfrac{(3.828)^2}{n-1}$

$n = 226$

Proportionate Sample:

$\sigma_{\bar{x}}^2 = \dfrac{\Sigma W_i \sigma_i^2}{n} = \dfrac{\Sigma W_i s_i^2}{n-1}$

$0.2551^2 \doteq \dfrac{17.714}{n-1}$

$n \doteq 273$

Simple Random Sample:

$\sigma_{\bar{x}}^2 = \dfrac{\Sigma W_i \sigma_i^2 + \Sigma W_i(\bar{X}_i - \bar{X})^2}{n} \doteq \dfrac{\Sigma W_i s_i^2 + \Sigma W_i(\bar{X}_i - \bar{X})^2}{n-1}$

$0.2551^2 \doteq \dfrac{17.714 + 9.8456}{n-1}$

$n \doteq 424$

secure the same precision calls for a proportionate sample of 273 and a simple random sample of 424.

It is clear in this case that stratification is more efficient than simple random sampling, and disproportionate stratified sampling is 21 percent more efficient than proportionate sampling. These results are secured because both of the means and the variances of the strata are substantially different.

Cluster Sampling

In a simple random sample each population element is selected individually. We can also divide the entire population into groups of elements and randomly choose some of the groups for study. This is *cluster sampling*. An immediate question might be: How does this differ from stratified sampling? They may be compared as follows:

Stratified Sampling	*Cluster Sampling*
1. We divide the population into a few subgroups, each with many elements in it. The subgroups are selected according to some criterion that is related to the variables under study.	1. We divide the population into many subgroups, each with a few elements in it. The subgroups are selected according to some criterion of ease or availability in data collection.
2. We try to secure homogeneity within subgroups and heterogeneity between subgroups.	2. We try to secure heterogeneity within subgroups and homogeneity between subgroups, but we usually get the reverse.
3. We randomly choose elements from within each subgroup.	3. We randomly choose a number of the subgroups which we then typically study in toto.

If properly done, cluster sampling also provides an unbiased estimate of population parameters. Two major problems foster the use of cluster sampling: (1) the need for more economic efficiency than can be provided by simple element sampling, and (2) the frequent unavailability of a practical sampling frame for individual elements.

Cluster Efficiency. Statistical efficiency for cluster samples is usually lower than for simple random samples, chiefly because clusters tend to be homogeneous. Families in the same block (a typical cluster) tend to be similar in social class, income level, ethnic origin, and so forth. Thus, additional interviews in such a cluster provide less information about the population than a cluster that is more heterogeneous.

While statistical efficiency in most cluster sampling may be low, economic efficiency is often great enough to overcome this weakness. The criterion, then, is the *net relative efficiency* resulting from the tradeoff between economic and statistical factors. For example, it may take 690 interviews with a cluster design to give the same precision as 424 simple random interviews. But if it costs only $2 per interview in the cluster situation and $4 in the simple random case, it is obvious that the cluster sample is attractive.

Area Sampling. Much research involves populations which can be identified with some geographic area. When this occurs it is possible to use *area sampling,* the most important form of cluster sampling. This method meets both the problems of high sampling cost and the unavailability of a practical sampling frame for individual elements. Area sampling methods have been applied to national populations, county populations, and even smaller areas where there are well-defined political or natural boundaries.

Suppose that we want to survey the adult residents of a city. We would seldom be able to secure a listing of such individuals. It would be relatively easy, however, to get a detailed city map which shows the blocks of the city. If we take a sample of these blocks we are also taking a sample of the adult residents of the city, because as the saying goes, "Everybody has to be someplace."

Cluster Design. In designing cluster samples, including area samples, there are a number of questions which must be answered. While these questions are interrelated, they are discussed separately:

1. How homogeneous are the clusters?
2. Shall we seek equal or unequal clusters?
3. How large a cluster shall we take?
4. Shall we use single-stage or multistage clusters?
5. How large a sample is needed?

1. Clusters tend to be homogeneous in many internal characteristics and this contributes to low statistical efficiency. We sometimes can improve this efficiency by constructing clusters in a way as to increase intracluster variance. For example, in the dining club study we might construct clusters that would include members from all classes. In area sampling we might combine contiguous blocks that contain different income groups or social classes. Area cluster sections do not have to be contiguous but much of the cost savings are lost if they are not near each other.

2. A cluster sample may be composed of clusters of equal or unequal size. The theory of clustering is that the means of sample clusters are unbiased estimates of the population mean. This is more often true when clusters are equal. It is often possible to construct artificial clusters which are approximately equal, but natural clusters, such as households in city blocks, often vary substantially. While we can deal with clusters of unequal size, it may be desirable to reduce or counteract the effects of unequal size. There are several approaches to this.

One way to overcome the wide variation in cluster size is to combine small clusters and split large clusters until all approximate an average size. A second approach is to stratify clusters by size and choose clusters from each stratum.

A third approach is size-stratified subsampling in which clusters are stratified by size and then subsampled, using varying sampling fractions to secure an overall sampling ratio. For example, we may seek an overall sampling fraction of 1/60 and desire that subsamples be about five elements each. One group of clusters might average about ten elements per cluster. In the "ten elements per cluster" stratum we might choose 1 in 30 of the clusters, and then sub-sample each chosen cluster at 1/2 rate to secure our overall 1/60 sampling fraction. Among clusters of 120 elements we might select clusters as a 1/3 rate and then subsample at a 1/20 rate to secure the 1/60 sampling fraction.[16]

3. The third question concerns the size of cluster. There is no a priori answer to this question. Even with single-stage clusters, say, of 5, 20, or 50, it is not clear which size is superior. Some have found that, in studies using single-stage clusters, the optimal cluster size tends to be no larger than the typical city block.[17] To compare the efficiency of the above three cluster sizes requires that we determine the different costs for each size and estimate the different variances of the cluster means.

4. The fourth question concerns whether to use a single-stage or a multi-stage cluster design. For most area sampling, especially large-scale studies, the tendency is to use multistage methods. Kish expresses the case well when he writes,

> There are four reasons that justify subsampling, in preference to the direct creation of smaller clusters and their selection in one-stage cluster sampling:
>
> (1) *Natural clusters* may exist as convenient sampling units, yet larger than the desired economic size . . . , (2) We can *avoid the cost of creating smaller clusters* in the entire population and confine it to the selected sampling units . . . , (3) The *effect of clustering* . . . is often less in larger clusters. For example, a compact cluster of four dwellings from a city block may bring into the sample similar dwellings, perhaps from one building; but four dwellings selected separately can be spread around the dissimilar sides of the block. (4) The sampling of *compact clusters may present practical difficulties.* For example, independent interviewing of all members of a household may seem impractical.[18]

5. How large a sample is needed? That is, how many subjects must be interviewed or observed? The answer to this question depends heavily upon the specific cluster design and these details can be complicated. Unequal clusters and multistage samples are the chief complications and their statistical treatment is beyond the scope of this book.[19] Here we will treat only single-

---

[16] For detailed treatment of these and other cluster sampling methods and problems see Kish, *Survey Sampling,* pp. 148–247.

[17] J. H. Lorie, and H. V. Roberts, *Basic Methods of Marketing Research* (New York, McGraw-Hill Book Company, Inc., 1951), p. 120.

[18] Kish, *Survey Sampling,* p. 156.

[19] For specifics on these problems and how to solve them the reader is referred to the many good sampling texts. Two that have already been mentioned are Kish, *Survey Sampling,* chaps. 5, 6, and 7, and Cochran, *Sampling Techniques,* chaps. 9, 10, and 11.

stage samples with equal-size clusters (hereafter referred to as *simple cluster sampling*). It is analogous to simple random sampling.

The simple random sample is really a special case of simple cluster sampling. That is, we can think of a population as consisting of $10,000$ clusters of one student each, or $1,0000$ clusters of ten students each, and so on. *The only difference between a simple random and a simple cluster sample is the size of cluster.* Since this is so we should expect that the calculation of a probability sample size would be the same for both types. This is basically true; the only changes that we must make are to take into account that the number of elements in a cluster may vary.

We have calculated that a simple random sample of 424 individual students (that is, clusters of one) provides a 95 percent confidence that an estimate of expected monthly student visits to the club would be within ± 0.5. Our task now is to estimate how many clusters, say of ten elements each, must be studied to give a similar precision. We determine the number of clusters of ten as follows:[20]

$$\sigma_{\bar{x}} = \frac{\sigma_c}{\sqrt{m}}$$

where

σ_c = The standard deviation of cluster means.
m = The number of sample clusters.

We should expect that the population standard deviation will be smaller for clusters of ten than for clusters of one; just how much smaller depends upon the size of the clusters and the degree of homogeneity within the clusters.

An Example.   Consider again the dining club problem. Assume that all students must go through a registration at the beginning of the semester at a specific location. Assume further that we can conveniently sample them there in groups of ten, and that this procedure will cost only $2 per completed questionnaire as compared to $4 for a simple random sample. Would it be better to use cluster sampling or simple random sampling, assuming the same precision requirements?

We must first estimate the standard deviation of the means of clusters of ten in the population. Since all classes register at the same time, these clusters of ten should have more heterogeneity in them—and more homogeneity between clusters than is often the case. A small test sample might indicate that standard deviation of clusters of ten may be about 2.1. With this information, plus our already-determined precision requirements, we can compute that we will need 69 clusters of ten students each.

---

[20] In this discussion we ignore the finite population correction, although it is more often needed in cluster than in simple random sampling.

$$\sigma_{\bar{x}} = \frac{\sigma_c}{\sqrt{m}} = \frac{s_c}{\sqrt{m-1}}$$

$$0.2551 = \frac{2.1}{\sqrt{m-1}}$$

$$m = 69 \text{ clusters}$$

This would mean that a sample of 690 students, taken in clusters of ten, provides the precision of a simple random sample of 424. While the cluster sample requires 266 more interviews, it provides a cost saving of $316. The cluster sample has greater economic efficiency.

Double Sampling

It may be more convenient or economical to collect some information by sample and then use this information as the basis for selecting a subsample for further study. This procedure is called *double sampling,* sequential sampling, or multiphase sampling. It is usually found in conjunction with stratified and/or cluster designs, and the calculation procedures are somewhat complicated and beyond the scope of this chapter. The reader interested in these details is referred to sources such as Kish.[21]

Double sampling can be illustrated by the dining club example. We might use a telephone survey or some other inexpensive survey method to determine (1) the students interested in joining such a club and (2) the degree of their interest. We might then stratify the interested respondents by degree of interest and subsample among them for intensive interviewing on expected consumption patterns, reactions to various service patterns, and so on. Whether it is more desirable to gather such information by one-stage or two-stage sampling depends largely upon the relative costs of the two methods.

THE USE OF NONPROBABILITY SAMPLING

Any discussion of the relative merits of probability and nonprobability sampling clearly shows the technical advantages of the former. Through randomization the danger of unknown sampling bias is minimized, while with nonprobability designs there is always a chance that some sampling-induced element will distort the results. In addition, with nonprobability designs we cannot estimate an interval range in which to expect the population parameter. Why then would anyone want to use nonprobability sampling? There are some very practical reasons for using these "less satisfactory" methods.

---

[21] Kish, *Survey Sampling,* chap. 12.

Conditions of Use

One may use nonprobability sampling because there is no other feasible alternative. The total population may not be available for study. At the scene of a major event some of the participants cannot be interviewed. A study of past correspondence between two companies must use an arbitrary sample because the full correspondence is not available.

In another sense those who are included in a sample may select themselves. In mail surveys those who respond may not represent a true crosssection of those who received the questionnaire. The receivers of the questionnaire decide for themselves whether or not they will participate. There is some of this self-selection in almost all surveys because every respondent chooses whether or not to be interviewed.

Second, while the probability sampling may be superior in theory, there are breakdowns in its application. For example, if interviewers are told to select the sample randomly there is always a question as to how skillfully or diligently they will do it. They may also be subject to unknown biases. These problems can be only partially prevented by establishing clear rules for the guidance of field workers.

Third, a random sample that is a true crosssection of the population may not be the objective of the research. If there is no desire to generalize to a population parameter then there is less concern about whether or not the sample is fully representative. Often, the researcher has more limited objectives; and may be looking only for a feel of the range of conditions, or for examples of dramatic variations, and so on.

Finally, the costs and time required for probability sampling may be so large that the investigator abandons the use of this method. Carefully controlled nonprobability sampling methods seem to give acceptable results, although there is no way to escape the deficiencies mentioned earlier.

Sampling Methods

Convenience. Nonprobability samples that are also unrestricted are called *convenience* samples. This is the least reliable sampling design, although it normally is the cheapest and simplest. A convenience sample has little status, but it may still be useful. Often we take such a sample to test ideas or even to gain ideas about a subject of interest. Such samples may also give us evidence that is so overwhelming as to make more sophisticated sampling unnecessary. As applied to the dining club example, we might ask interviewers to wander around the campus, interviewing people as they meet them.

Purposive. Purposive samples normally involve a more deliberate effort to secure a sample that conforms to some predetermined criteria. Two varieties may be distinguished.

1. *Judgment* (or expert choice) samples are most useful in studying those cases which we believe are in the best position to provide us with information. For example, we may be interested only in those who hold extreme positions, have had certain types of experiences within the last year, and so on. The subjects may be those which are judged by some expert to be the best ones for study. In these cases we seek a particular type of subject and may not even be interested in securing a crosssection of a population.

2. The major type of purposive sample is the *quota sample*. In this type of sampling we are interested in selecting subjects to conform to certain predesignated control measures. For example, we may know that the student body at Cranial University is 65 percent male and 35 percent female. We may require interviewers to interview in this ratio.

In most quota samples we specify more than one control dimension, depending upon our opinions or evidence as to their importance. For example, we may believe that response to a question should vary, depending upon the sex of the respondent. If so, we seek proportional responses from both men and women. We may also feel that undergraduates differ from graduate students, so this would be a dimension. We may also choose dimensions such as the student's academic discipline, ethnic group, religious affiliation, and social group affiliation.

In quota sampling it is desirable to use only a small number of these controls. To use all of the above might, to carry it to the extreme, call for an interviewer to find a white, female, protestant, engineering sophomore who lives in campus housing, comes from a middle-class home, and is a sorority member. While such a person may exist, it would make the sampling task prohibitively expensive if such specifications had to be filled. This form of control, in which a simultaneous set of characteristics is specified for a given person, is called *precision control*. It is not very practical when the number of simultaneous controlling dimensions exceeds three or so.

When we wish to use more than three control dimensions we should depend on *frequency control*. With this control form the overall percentage of those with each characteristic in the sample should match the percentage holding the same characteristic in the population. No attempt is made to find a combination of specific characteristics in a single person. In frequency control we would probably find that the accompanying sample array is an adequate reflection of the population.

	Population	Sample
Male	65%	67%
Married	15	14
Undergraduate	70	72
Campus resident	30	28
Independent	75	73
Protestant	39	42
White	90	89

The logic behind quota sampling is that certain relevant characteristics describe the dimensions of the population. If the sample holds the same proportion of these dimensions as the population, then other information found from the sample members will also reflect the patterns in the population. This reasoning by analogy is obviously dangerous and gives no assurance that the sample is truly representative.

In spite of these and other weaknesses already mentioned, quota sampling is widely used by the opinion pollsters and researchers. Often it is viewed as the only practical method because of cost and time considerations. Its advocates feel that, while there is some danger of systematic bias, the risks are worth taking. They are interested in averages and these tend to be rather stable even if there is some bias involved. Since random sampling's technical requirements are often violated in practice, the reasoning goes "we might as well begin with a good quota sampling design."

APPLIED SAMPLING EXAMPLES

Example 1—Pilot Tests, Exploratory Research[22]

The lowest-quality samples generally consist of 20-50 respondents usually chosen at the convenience of the researcher. If household respondents are used, the interviewer is free to select the household from anywhere in a broad geographic area, although sometimes a block or census tract are specified. Sometimes a church or other voluntary group will be used for either a self-administered questionnaire or a group interview; if the researcher is connected with a university or school, the respondents may be the students in a classroom . . . (Such samples) are appropriate at the earliest stages of a research design, when one is first attempting to develop hypotheses and the procedures for measuring them. Then, along with reading the literature and discussing ideas with colleagues, friends, and relatives, exploratory data gathering is worthwhile. Any sort of sample may be useful when very little is known. Just a few interviews can pinpoint major problems with questions and dimensions of the topic that the researcher may have ignored.

Example 2—Mail Survey[23]

A study was conducted for the U.S. Public Health Service to determine the current smoking habits of physicians after information had been released on the relation between smoking and lung cancer. Face-to-face interviews were considered impractical because of doctors' schedules. Instead, the initial contact was made with a mail questionnaire followed by two additional mailings to doctors who did not cooperate. This resulted in about slightly fewer than

---

[22] Seymour Sudman, *Applied Sampling* (New York, N.Y.: Academic Press, 1976), p. 9.
[23] Ibid., p. 18.

half of the doctors returning a questionnaire. (Because of their tight schedules and the heavy amount of mail they receive, doctors do not respond as well to mail questionnaires as do other professionals.)

A subsample of 40 percent of the noncooperators was selected for long-distance telephone interviewing. Initial calls were made to find a convenient time to call for the interview. From this process, about 80 percent of the doctors in the subsample were interviewed. The final reported results were based on a weighted sample of the two groups, with the doctors in the telephone sample receiving a weight of 2.5 to account for the fact that only 40 percent had been selected.

Example 3—Computing the Sample Interval for a City Directory[24]

Suppose one wishes to select a sample of 1000 completed cases from the city directory for Peoria, Illinois. The directory has 367 pages with three columns per page and 84 lines per column, or a total of 92,484 lines. Note that it is necessary to assume, or is it the case, that each column has the same number of households. Some columns will have more businesses or blank lines. If one of these lines is selected, the line is not used. A systematic sample of ten pages indicates that 63.1 percent of the lines contain a household listing, 9.0 percent contain a business listing, 17.2 percent contain a street name or Zip Code, 7.4 percent are blank, and 3.3 percent contain advertising. Assuming that the cooperation rate is expected to be 80 percent, the sampling interval would be 92,484 (.631)(.80)/1000, or 46.7.

The easiest procedure would be to note that selecting two lines at random from each column would produce a sampling interval of 84/2, or 42, which is smaller than 46.7 and would yield a larger sample. The expected sample based on these estimates is about 1389, although this is only an estimate. An actual sample was selected by using this interval and two random lines per column, numbers 5 and 27. The number of households selected was 1441. Since only 1250 are needed, assuming a cooperation rate of 80 percent, one computes the ratio of 1250/1441 and notes that .867 is approximately equal to the fraction 7/8, which is .875. Thus, randomly deleting every eighth element in the sample of 1441 after a random start yields a sample of 1260. Usually at this stage, the sampling would end: Given the uncertainty about the final cooperation rate, the deletion of 10 additional cases to reach exactly 1250 would not be very important.

Example 4—Optimum Stratified Sampling[25]

Suppose one is interested in the employment practices of hospitals, wage rates, employee benefits, treatment of minority employees, recruitment pro-

---

[24] Ibid., pp. 60–61.
[25] Ibid., pp. 115–16.

cedures, and so on. The complete listing of hospitals is found in the Guide issue of *Hospitals,* published by the American Hospital Association. Table 6–4 gives data on the payroll and the number of employees for hospitals broken into six size groups. (The data are based on a sample of the 1971 list.)

Table 6–4: Characteristics of U.S. Hospitals by Number of Beds

Number of Beds	Number of Hospitals	π_h	Average Payroll	Payroll σ_h	Average Number of Employees	Employees σ_h
Under 50	1614	.246	266	183	54	25
50–99	1566	.238	384	316	123	51
100–199	1419	.216	1484	641	262	95
200–299	683	.104	3110	1347	538	152
300–499	679	.103	5758	2463	912	384
500 and over	609	.093	10964	7227	1548	826
Total	6570	1.000				

Table 6–5 gives the sample allocations under five different procedures for a total sample of 1000 hospitals. Estimates of the total sampling variance are also given for the payroll and the number of employees.

1. The proportional sample allocates the sample based on the number of hospitals per stratum, or by π_h.
2. The optimum payroll sample allocates on the basis of

$$n_h = \frac{\pi_h \sigma_h \,(\text{payroll})}{\Sigma_h \pi_h \sigma_h (\text{payroll})} n.$$

3. The optimum employees sample allocates on the basis of

$$n_h = \frac{\pi_h \sigma_h \,(\text{employees})}{\Sigma_h \pi_h \sigma_h (\text{employees})} n.$$

Table 6–5: U.S. Hospital Study Sample Sizes Using Various Procedures and Total σ^2 for $\nu = 1,000$

Number of Beds	Proportional	Optimum Payroll	Optimum Employees	Using Total Beds as Measure of Size (1)	Using Total Beds as Measure of Size (2)
Under 50.	246	34	36	28	19
50–99.	238	57	71	83	56
100–199	216	104	120	150	103
200–299	104	106	93	120	82
300–499	103	192	231	191	131
500 and over	93	507	449	428	609
Totals	1000	1000	1000	1000	1000
σ^2 employees	71.0	17.1	16.5	17.2	20.6
σ^2 payroll ('000)	4,908	871	908	941	982

4. Estimates (1) and (2) in Table 6–5, using total beds, assume that only the data on the number of hospitals in each stratum are available. It is still possible to estimate size by taking the midpoint of the interval and multiplying by the number of hospitals. Thus, the number of beds in hospitals with under 50 beds is estimated by multiplying the midpoint 25 by 1614 for an estimate of 40,350. Similarly, in the stratum for hospitals with 300–499 beds, the estimated number of beds is 400 × 679, or 271,600. It is often the case, as in Table 6–4, that there is no way of determining the midpoint for the largest stratum. Estimate (1) assumes that the midpoint is twice as large as the lower bound, that is, 1000 beds.

Estimate (2) avoids the issue by taking all the hospitals in the largest stratum and allocating the remaining sample of 391 hospitals among the remaining strata. The allocation is simply on the basis of size and requires no previous estimate of σ. (In many real-world applications, we would have size measures but no estimates of σ.)

$$n_h = \frac{s_h}{\Sigma s_h} n$$

where s_h is the estimated number of beds in the stratum.

The important feature of Table 6–5 is that all the size allocations are similar and all result in variances only one-fourth or one-fifth as large as those from proportional sampling. To put it another way, a proportional sample would need to be four or five times larger to have the same variance as that of the sample using size measures.

Which of the samples using size measures is the optimum? The table indicates that no sample is optimum for all purposes. Obviously, if one were interested only in payroll data for given types of workers, the optimum payroll sample would be best. If one were interested in recruitment procedures, the optimum employee sample would be best. But the differences between these two samples are slight: Using even the number of beds would increase the variance only a little for these variables and number of beds might be optimum for others, such as studies of patient care. If multiple measures of size are available, one should choose the one that is most current and that appears to be most highly correlated with the study's most important variables. As the example illustrates, however, it is not necessary to agonize over the choice or to search for a perfect measure to achieve major improvements in sample efficiency.

SUMMARY

Sampling is based on two premises. One is that there is enough similarity among the elements in a population that a few of these elements will adequately represent the characteristics of the total population. The second premise is that while some elements in a sample underestimate a population value, others overestimate this value. The result of these tendencies is that a sample statistic such as the arithmetic mean is generally a good estimate of a population mean.

A good sample has both accuracy and precision. An accurate sample is one in which there is little or no bias or systematic variance. A sample with adequate precision is one which has an error variance or sampling error that is within acceptable limits for the study's purpose.

There are a variety of sampling techniques available. They may be classified by their representation basis and element selection techniques as shown in the accompanying table.

	Representation Basis	
Element Selection	*Probability*	*Nonprobability*
Unrestricted	Simple random	Convenience
Restricted	Complex random	Purposive
	Systematic	Judgment
	Cluster	Quota
	Stratified	
	Double	

Probability sampling is based on the concept of random selection—a controlled procedure that assures that each population element is given a known nonzero chance of selection. In contrast, nonprobability selection is "not random." When each sample element is drawn individually from the population at large it is unrestricted sampling. Restricted sampling covers those forms of sampling in which the selection process follows more complex rules.

The simplest type of probability approach is simple random sampling. In this design each member of the population has an equal chance of being included in a sample. In developing a probability sample there are six procedural questions that need to be answered:

1. What is the relevant population?
2. What type of sample shall we draw?
3. What sampling frame shall we use?
4. What are the parameters of interest?
5. What size sample is needed?
6. How much will the sample cost?

In probability sampling we make two kinds of estimates of a population parameter. First, we make a point estimate, which is our single best estimate of the population value. In addition, we make an interval estimate which covers the range of values within which we expect the population value to be, with a given degree of confidence. All sample-based estimates of population parameters should be stated in terms of such an interval with its attendant probability value.

The size of a probability sample is determined by the specifications of the researcher and the nature of the population. These requirements are largely expressed in the following four questions:

1.   What is the degree of confidence we want in our parameter estimate?
2.   How large an interval range will we accept?
3.   What is the degree of variance in the population?
4.   Is the population small enough that the sample should be adjusted for finite population?

Cost considerations are also often incorporated into the sample size decision.

Complex probability sampling is used when conditions make simple random sampling impractical, or uneconomical. Four major types of complex sampling are discussed in this chapter: systematic, stratified, cluster, and double sampling. Systematic sampling involves the selection of every kth element in the population, beginning at a random start with an element from 1 to k. Its simplicity in certain cases is its greatest value.

Stratified sampling is based on dividing a population into subpopulations and then randomly sampling from each of these strata. This method almost always results in a smaller total sample size than would a simple random design. Stratified samples may be proportionate or disproportionate.

In a cluster sample we divide the population into convenient groups and then randomly choose a number of these groups for study. It is typically less efficient, statistically, than simple random sampling because of the normally high degree of homogeneity within clusters. Its great advantage is the cost savings if the population is dispersed either geographically or in time. The most widely used form of clustering is area sampling in which geographic areas are the selection elements.

At times it may be more convenient or economical to collect some information by sample and then use it as a basis for selecting a subsample for further study. This procedure is called double sampling.

Nonprobability sampling also has some compelling practical advantages that account for its widespread use. Often probability sampling is not feasible because the population is not available to us. Then too, there are frequent breakdowns in the application of probability sampling that can vitiate its technical advantages. We find also that a true crosssection is often not the aim of the researcher, who may be seeking only some general idea of the range of conditions, and this limited objective does not require probability sampling. Finally, nonprobability sampling tends to be much less expensive to conduct than does probability sampling.

Convenience samples are the simplest and least reliable form of sampling. About their only virtue is their relatively low cost. One type of purposive sample is the judgmental sample in which we are interested in studying only selected types of subjects. The other type of purposive sampling is the quota sample. This can be the most sophisticated type of nonprobability sampling. We select subjects to conform to certain predesignated control measures to secure a representative crosssection of the population.

SUPPLEMENTAL READINGS

1. Deming, W. E. *Sample Design in Business Research.* New York: John Wiley & Sons, Inc., 1960. A classic by an author who has long been one of the major authorities on sampling.
2. Green, Paul, and Tull, Donald. *Research for Marketing Decisions.* 4th ed. Englewood Cliffs, N.J.: Prentice Hall, Inc., 1978. Good discussion of both classical and Bayesian sampling.
3. Kish, Leslie. *Survey Sampling.* New York: John Wiley & Sons, Inc., 1965. A widely read basic reference on survey sampling.
4. Namias, Jean. *Handbook of Selected Sample Surveys in the Federal Government.* New York: St. John's University Press, 1969. A unique collection of illustrative uses of sampling for surveys carried out by various federal agencies. Of interest both for the sampling designs presented and the information on the methodology used to develop various government statistical data.
5. Sudman, Seymour. *Applied Sampling.* New York: Academic Press, 1976. An excellent source for procedures that are practical applications of probability techniques. Especially useful for students and nonexpert samplers.

DISCUSSION QUESTIONS

1. Distinguish between:
   a. Statistic and parameter.
   b. Sample frame and population.
   c. Restricted and unrestricted sampling.
   d. Standard deviation and standard error.
   e. Simple random and complex random sampling.
   f. Convenience and purposive sampling.
   g. Sample precision and sample accuracy.
   h. Systematic and error variance.
   i. Variable and attribute parameters.
   j. Symmetrical and asymmetrical confidence regions.
   k. 0.05 and 0.01 confidence levels.
2. Under what kind of conditions would you recommend:
   a. A probability sample? A nonprobability sample?
   b. A simple random sample? A cluster sample? A stratified sample?
   c. Using the finite population adjustment factor?
   d. A disproportionate stratified probability sample?
3. You plan to conduct a survey using unrestricted sampling. What are the subjective decisions that you must make?
4. You draw a random sample of 300 employee records from the personnel file

and find that the average years of service per employee is 6.3, with a standard deviation of 3.0 years.

   a. What percent of the workers would you expect to have more than 9.3 years service?

   b. What percent would you expect to have more than 5.0 years service?

5. Suppose you needed to interview a representative sample of undergraduate students but had concluded that there was no way to use probability sampling methods. You decide to use nonprobability methods. The university registrar can give you counts of the number of students who are freshmen, sophomores, juniors, or seniors, plus how many male and female students are in each class. How would you conduct a reasonably reliable nonprobability sample?

6. You wish to take an unrestricted random sample of undergraduate students at Cranial University to ascertain their levels of spending per month for food purchased off campus and eaten on the premises where purchased. You ask a test sample of nine students about their food expenditures and find that on the average they report spending $20, with two thirds of them reporting spending from $10 to $30. What size sample do you think you should take? (Assume that your universe is infinite.)

7. You wish to adjust your sample calculations to reflect the fact that there are only 2,500 students in your population. How does this additional information affect your estimated sample size in question 6?

8. Suppose that you are going to take a sample survey and you want to estimate within a probable plus or minus 5 percent the proportion of people who have made a job change within the past year. What size of sample would you take if it was to be an unrestricted sample?

9. One way to visualize the relation of sample size requirements in unrestricted various combinations of four factors which affect sample size. Given the following information calculate the sample sizes needed for the cells of the accompanying table.

		Sample Size			
		Infinite Population Confidence Level		Finite Population (N = 900) Confidence Level	
Standard Deviation s	Desired Interval Range	2σ	3σ	2σ	3σ
$1,000	$300				
	150				
	100				
$2,000	300				
	150				
	100				

10. You are interested in determining the average annual rate of absenteeism among the 10,000 employees in your company. Two thousand of these employees are on the salaried payroll, while 1,000 are in crafts, and 7,000 are assemblers. You have taken a small informal sample, and it appears that the absence statistics will be about as shown in the accompanying table.

	Days	
Employees	$\overline{X}$	s
Salaried	5	2.3
Craftsmen	8	3.9
Assemblers	15	7.0

Because of the differences in means and standard deviations you decide to conduct a stratified probability sample (assume that populations are infinite). Assume further that you wish to be 95 percent confident that your estimate of the average number of employee days of absence will fall within a range of ±0.5 days.

a. How large a sample would you need if you use a proportionate stratified sample? A disproportionate sample? A simple random sample?

b. Supposing that you decide to take a sample of 500 persons, how many salaried persons would you check if a proportionate stratified sample is used? A disproportionate sample?

11. In the absenteeism study the roster of employees does not classify them by compensation or job categories. Rather, it lists them all alphabetically. This suggests to you that it might be feasible to use a cluster sampling technique. You divide the list of 10,000 employees into 1,000 clusters of ten employees each. You again take a few cluster samples and estimate that the standard deviation of cluster means will be 2.1 days. With this information, plus that given in question 10 above, determine the number of clusters you would need to meet the precision requirements stated in question 10.

SECTION THREE

DATA COLLECTION

Chapter 7

Secondary Data Sources

EVERY RESEARCH STUDY is a search for information about some topic. The form and direction that the search takes is strongly affected by what we perceive to be appropriate information sources. If we tap all of the relevant sources we can be more confident of the quality of our findings. Often the most fruitful source of information is the experience of others, especially when this experience is research based.

In this chapter we take up the problems and techniques of gathering published data on the experiences of others. More specifically, we will discuss the nature of these data sources and propose an approach for using them. While some of the major research tools are mentioned here, Appendix A contains a more detailed listing of the important indexes, guides, and other reference tools of value in an investigation that uses secondary data sources.

THE NATURE OF SECONDARY DATA SOURCES

We can classify information sources into *primary* and *secondary* types. Primary data come from the original sources of material and are collected especially for the task at hand. Thus, if we observe certain production operations so as to measure their cost we are collecting primary data. If we get the cost information from others who have collected it for another purpose we have secondary data. Organization files and library holdings are the most frequently used secondary sources, but statistical compendia, movie film, printed literature, audio tapes, and computer files are also widely used sources.

Any argument on the relative merits of primary and secondary data must end inconclusively. Primary data research does have its advantages. We can collect precisely the information we want. We usually have some control over when and how it is collected and the form in which it is gathered. We can use our own operational definitions and can eliminate, or at least monitor and record, the extraneous influences that might be present when the data are gathered. Even so, secondary sources also have many merits.

Advantages of Secondary Data.   Secondary sources can usually be found more quickly and cheaply. Collection of primary data can be so costly and time-consuming as to be impractical for many purposes. In other cases we cannot hope to gather primary information, at any cost, comparable to published data, for example, census reports and industry statistics. These collections are not only voluminous and detailed, their collection is provided for by law. Secondary data sources also extend our time and space range. Most research on past events has to rely on secondary data sources to some degree. In like manner, data gathered about distant places, for example, foreign countries, often can be collected more cheaply through secondary materials.

Disadvantages of Secondary Data.   Secondary data also have their limitations. The most important is that the information often will not meet our specific needs. Secondary source information has been collected by someone else for their purposes rather than ours. Definitions are not the same as ours, units of measure do not match ours, and different time periods may be involved. We often cannot even assess the accuracy of the information because we know little about the conditions under which the research took place or even details of the design used. Finally, the value of secondary information often is partially obsolete before it is available. The study made five years ago may not be relevant in today's environment.

The Search Task.   Research using secondary sources is a special case of the more general information retrieval problem. We must search through a vast information inventory from many sources. This information is stored in books, pamphlets, periodicals, microfilms, computer files, and other media. They are indexed on some basis that should allow us to recover their content for our use. The two most important storage locations for business researchers are organization files and libraries.

Our task is to use the indexing files of information storage systems to find that which is germane to our needs. We do this by searching the files (classifying and cataloging devices) and extracting those index codes (key words or descriptions of the material) that appear to be relevant for our research. In this process we match our information requirements to the indexing statements in the files. Through this matching we choose the data sources to consider further.

A major source of information for research is the many libraries in this country and, more specifically, the research libraries typically found in major cities and universities. Company libraries and general public libraries present the same type of resources as research libraries, but have fewer of the indexing and documents resources required for serious research.

THE USES OF SECONDARY DATA

We may use secondary data for three research purposes. First, we often seek specific reference information on some point. Examples would be the need for the estimated U.S. production of sulfuric acid last year, the population of Atlanta in 1980, or the effective current rate of return on government bonds. We may also seek reference benchmarks against which to test other findings. For example, from a sample survey we may estimate that a certain percentage of the population has various age and income characteristics. We might then check these estimates against census data.

The second major use of secondary data is as an integral part of a larger research study. Typical research procedures call for at least a minimum amount of exploration early in most projects. This exploration is concerned with using what has been learned in the past as a contribution to the present study. In essence, the researcher is trying to keep from "reinventing the wheel." Secondary data sources are also useful guides for deciding what further research needs to be done, as well as being a rich source of hypotheses.

Finally, secondary data may be used as the sole source for a research study. The historical method is the classical example but by no means the only one. Restrospective research typically requires the use of past published data. In many research situations it is impractical for one to conduct primary research because of physical, legal, or cost limitations. The U.S. government, for example, publishes massive amounts of statistical data each year which are the major sources for many research studies.

TYPES OF SECONDARY DATA SOURCES

One way to classify data sources is to label them either as internal organizational or external sources of information. Internal organization sources are so varied that there is little in a general way that can be said about their use. The collection method used is unique to the specific situation, and collection success is greatly affected by how well we know where and how to look. Internal data sources are often the only source of information for many studies. Examples are departmental reports, production summaries, financial and accounting reports, marketing and sales studies, and a host of other types.

External Sources. These are more varied than internal sources and have better defined methods for guiding the search. Even so, there is no fully satisfactory system for classifying external data sources. One useful way is to classify them by the medium through which the data are presented. This discussion is restricted to printed sources although it is recognized that for specific cases other sources of information may be useful.

Published sources of data can be classified into four categories. One of the most obvious categories is that of books. It is estimated that more than 35,000 books were published in the United States in 1977, of which about 90 percent were nonfiction.[1] A second major source of secondary data is periodicals. The 17th edition of *Ulrich's International Periodicals Directory* lists approximately 68,000 in-print periodicals published throughout the world. A third major source of materials for secondary research is government documents. The *Monthly Catalog* of U.S. government publications had almost 17,000 listings in 1977 and this represented only a fraction of the total government output.

The fourth major source of published information consists of a variety of miscellaneous materials. First, there are many reference books, each a compendium of a wide range of information. A second group includes university publications, of which the major categories are master's theses, doctoral dissertations, and research reports. A third important category includes company publications, the most important of which are periodic financial reports. In addition, there are company policy statements, speeches by prominent executives, sales literature, product specifications, and many others. A fourth category of miscellaneous information sources consists of the publications of trade, professional, and other associations. These organizations often publish statistical compilations, research reports, and proceedings of meetings. A final miscellaneous source of information consists of personal documents. These often are used in historical and social science research but less frequently in business studies.

Data may also be classified as being either statistical or nonstatistical in nature. Government documents and company and association publications are often statistical in nature, while periodicals and books tend more to deal with nonstatistical information. Before going on to the general problem of library search procedures we shall outline some of the statistical sources of importance to the business researcher.

STATISTICAL SOURCES

A common reason for researching published sources is to secure statistical information. There is a wide variety of statistical sources with a wealth of data, yet it is often difficult to find the specific information needed. There are guides, however, that can help locate the major statistical sources or provide descriptions of the various statistical publications. Two such sources, from

---

[1] *The Bowker Annual of Library and Book Trade Information,* 23d ed. (New York: R. R. Bowker Co., 1978), p. 308.

among many, are mentioned here. Additional sources may be found in Appendix A.

> *Statistics Sources.* 5th ed. Detroit: Gale Research Co., 1977.

This volume identifies primary sources of statistical data on a wide variety of subjects. Most of the titles listed are issued by the government, but some are published by private agencies such as commercial and trade associations. The sources are arranged alphabetically by subject.

> U.S. Bureau of the Budget. *Statistical Services of the United States Government.* Rev. ed. Washington: U.S. Government Printing Office, 1975.

This handbook describes (1) the relation of the federal statistical programs to those of other governmental and private organizations, (2) the methods of collection and presentation, and (3) the principal series collected by government agencies. There are two appendixes; one describes each agency's area of responsibility and the other gives an annotated bibliography of its principal statistical publications.

The guides mentioned above are directories to the location of the various types of statistics and do not themselves present statistical data. There are, however, several widely available statistical reference books. Perhaps the most important of these is:

> U.S. Bureau of the Census. *Statistical Abstract of the United States.* Washington: U.S. Government Printing Office, 1879 to date.

This is an annual compendium of summary statistics on the political, social, industrial, and economic life of the United States. It should be the starting point in gathering statistical data on most topics. The *Statistical Abstract* has particular value to the business researcher for two reasons. First, it is the most comprehensive and up-to-date compilation of statistics covering wide areas of our national life. Second, even if the specific figures or detail needed are not presented, the source notes for the tables and the appended bibliography of sources of statistics are useful guides for further research.

There are three major supplements to the *Statistical Abstract of the United States.* The *County and City Data Book* provides recent figures for county, city, standard metropolitan area, and urbanized area data on population, vital statistics, industry, voting records, and many other items. The *Congressional District Data Book* presents a similar variety of information by congressional district. Finally, the *Historical Statistics of the United States* brings together historical series of wide general interest from colonial times to 1962.

There are four major monthly governmental periodicals that provide the majority of the current statistics available on our economy and its operation. The *Survey of Current Business* contains about 2,500 statistical series on income, expenditures, production and prices of commodities, and many other aspects of the economy. Historical figures for the statistical data published in the *Survey of Current Business* are available in a supplement entitled *Business Statistics,* published in odd-numbered years. A second major statistical source is the *Federal Reserve Bulletin.* It publishes a large volume of national economic data with emphasis upon financial statistics. The third major governmental publication is the *Monthly Labor Review* which publishes data on work and labor conditions, wage rates, consumer price indexes, and the like. The fourth is the *Business Conditions Digest* which contains about 600 economic time series in a form convenient for forecasters and business analysts.

Many other government periodicals contain regular statistical information about transportation, agriculture, health, education and welfare, and other areas. Hundreds of privately published periodicals alsó provide statistical information. Trade journals, for example, publish estimates of important statistics in their particular industries.

Census Data. One of the major basic statistical data sources in the United States is the periodic cenuses that are conducted by the U.S. government. The oldest of these censuses is the *Census of Population,* first taken for the year 1790; it has been taken at ten-year intervals since then. Over the years there have been substantial additions to the type of information collected in this census so that today it is possible to secure detailed breakdowns of the population by ethnic, economic, social, and occupational characteristics. Many of these data are available by state, county, metropolitan area, city, and census tract (a relatively small homogeneous urban area that consists of a few hundred to a few thousand people). In addition, special enumerations of data may be purchased for smaller areas or for special combinations of variables selected for a specific project.

In recent decades a *Census of Housing* has been conducted in conjunction with the population census. It provides information about the cost of housing, rental values, quality of housing, size of homes, occupancy rates, and other information. In some metropolitan areas housing data are available down to as small a geographic unit as a single city block.

A number of business and industrial censuses have been taken at varying intervals. One is the *Census of Manufactures,* which was first taken for the year 1809, but has been published at frequent intervals only since 1929. Another major census is the *Census of Business.* It was first published for 1929 and has been published since then at intervals of four or five years. The *Census of Business* is divided into three units, the "Census of Retail Trade," the "Census of Wholesale Trade," and the "Census of Selected Services." There are also major censuses taken in agriculture, transportation, government, construction industries, and mining and mineral industries.

Several of the most useful statistical compilations of economic data for small geographic areas in our economy are provided by private sources. One of these is *Sales Management* magazine which publishes annually (usually in July) a "Survey of Consumer Buying Power." It provides current estimates of population, income, retail sales, and a variety of other statistics for every county and standard statistical metropolitan area in the United States, and for most cities of about 10,000 population or more. A similar set of estimates is provided by *The Editor and Publisher Market Guide*. Data from these publications are probably the most widely used indicators of small area economic estimates.

In this brief cataloging of statistical publications we have attempted only to point out some of the major sources of the most readily available statistical data. In each case only those which specialize in statistics are given, and there are many other specialized statistical publications which have been omitted. In addition, many statistics of value will be found in publications which are primarily nonstatistical in nature. It is to these more general data sources and the problems of their use that we now turn.

DATA SEARCH PROCEDURE

Joan Marsh, the investigator conducting library research, has a problem that breaks down into two parts. First, she must search out the appropriate information sources. For this she matches a specification of information needs against the library's indexing systems. When she has completed this matching and has cataloged the sources she is ready for the second task. This is to extract the specific information from these sources and reorganize it into an appropriate pattern for study. This collection can be carried out more efficiently if she first does a thorough search job.

Library Search Procedure

If Joan is unfamiliar with her topic she should first acquire some background in the subject. One approach is to look into general sources such as appropriate encyclopedias. Elementary textbooks in the field are also useful sources, and their perusal will help her evaluate the more technical references.

Good search technique calls for a sequence which moves from the general to the specific, and from a wide-screening search for sources to a narrow in-depth study of specific topics. The exact sequence and importance of specific sources will vary depending upon the subject and Joan's knowledge. One general approach might follow the flow diagram in Figure 7–1.

Search for Bibliography.   Assuming that she has some knowledge in the field, she will usually begin by developing a bibliography. Bibliography development at the first stage makes the entire research project more efficient because the investigator quickly acquires an inventory of the materials on the subject. Merely by inspection of titles, authors, dates, and other indexing information she can often select the priority sources for further study. She sees the development of the subject over time, often discovers who are the

Figure 7–1: Library Search Flow Diagram

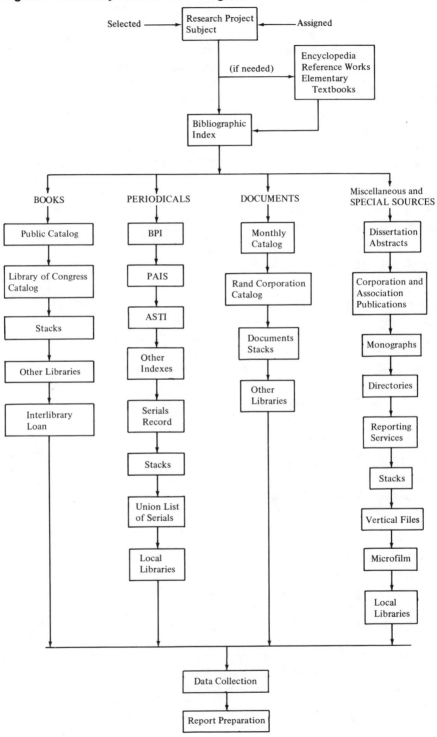

authoritative sources, and can be more assured that she has covered the full range of material on the subject. Every search turns up only a sampling of the available information, but it is important that Joan secure an adequate sample.

The logical first step is for her to determine whether someone else may have already prepared a bibliography on the subject. Bibliographies frequently accompany articles and books, and it is a waste to duplicate such effort. Hence, the first step may be to go to the:

> *Bibliographic Index: A Cumulative Bibliography of Bibliographies.* New York: H. W. Wilson Co., 1937 to date.

This publication, organized by subject, is an index to books, magazine articles, and other printed materials which include a bibliography. Thus, Joan may find publications in which the authors have listed their own reference sources on the subject.

Searching the public catalog may also turn up books which are primarily bibliographies although the subjects treated tend to be rather general. For example, there are bibliographies on business topics such as accounting, marketing, operations research, and many others. Many of these bibliographies have subsections that cover more specific topics.

Books as a Source. Joan may continue the search along one of the major investigative channels indicated in Figure 7–1. The first of these may be to seek information about books on the topic. The obvious first place to look is the public catalog of the library. This is the general bibliography of books in the library. Cards for these books are filed under author, title, and subject. An example of a title card is shown in Figure 7–2.

Figure 7–2: Typical Title Card

```
Bus
HD 58      Life in organizations : workplaces as
.7             people experience them / Rosabeth
L 53           Moss Kanter and Barry A. Stein,
               editors. New York : Basic Books,
               c1979.
               xvi, 444 p. ; 24 cm.
               Bibliography: p. [429]-431.
               Includes index.


               1. Organizational behavior--Case
           studies.  2. Industrial sociology--Case
           studies.  3. Occupations--Social
           aspects--Case studies.  I. Kanter,
           Rosabeth Moss.  II. Stein, Barry A.


MoSW                          WTUNdc        77-20413
```

Joan will save time and effort if she can recognize the information found on this typical catalog card. It gives the title of the book; authors' names; publisher; date of publication; notes on special features, such as illustrations, maps, or bibliographies; and sometimes notes listing contents. In addition, the card shows that the same publication is cataloged under three subject headings (those mentioned with arabic numerals near the bottom of the card) and under both authors' names. In the left upper corner is the call number and a notation that the book is in the Business School branch library.[2]

Subject headings in card catalogs are often a source of frequent trouble. If she is uncertain of the proper subject headings to use in her search of the public catalog there is a special list to which she can refer:

U.S. Library of Congress. Subject Cataloging Division. *Subject Headings Used in the Dictionary Catalog of the Library of Congress.* 8th ed. Washington: U.S. Government Printing Office, 1975.

This reference indicates the headings used in any public catalog following the Library of Congress system. In addition, it suggests related subjects which she might consult. If the subject matter is specialized or narrow in scope, very new, or if relatively little has been published on it, there may not be a reference in the catalog.

It is often a shock to the tyro researchers when they find no references to *their subjects* in the library's public catalog. This may result from one of three circumstances: (1) any library can have only a small sample of the publications that are produced; (2) the topic may be so narrow that it is not the subject of a full book or pamphlet in the library collection; (3) the material on the subject may be in the library in one of the collections not listed in the public catalog.

The holdings of a particular library are always restricted by the limited resources available with which to purchase materials, and by the interests of those people who decide what is to be included in the library's holdings. In a university library the holdings tend to reflect the importance of various fields of study in the university and the more specific interests of the faculty members who place book orders.

There is still a good possibility that there may be books published on the topic even though they are not available in that library. One can track down these references by going to one of a number of guides to published books. Perhaps the best guide to use is:

Cumulative Book Index: World List of Books in the English Language. New York: H. W. Wilson, 1928—

---

[2] This book is cataloged according to the Library of Congress system. In some libraries the Dewey decimal call number system is used.

This guide includes books published in the English language in the United States and, since 1930, in other parts of the world. Books are recorded by author, title, and subject. Other guides are listed in Appendix A.

The second type of failure to find a reference in the public catalog occurs when the topic is not the subject of a separate publication. However, it may be included in some work that covers a more general topic. For example, information on sales bonus systems may not be found in a card catalog. A search under the broader subject of sales management will show many publications which include coverage of sales bonus arrangements.

A third possibility is that the library has holdings on the subject that are not listed in the card catalog. This is the case with most U.S. government publications. The U.S. government is one of the largest publishers in the world. Each month it produces a vast array of materials on a wide variety of subjects. These publications range from a single mimeographed page to sets of books running into the thousands of pages. The volume of this output is so great that the task and cost of cataloging them is prohibitive. As a result most research libraries have large collections of "documents" which are not listed in the public catalog.

Many state and local government publications are not cataloged. The same is true for publications of such organizations as the Rand Corporation. In addition, libraries have vertical files with a wide variety of pamphlets, speeches, bulletins, annual reports of companies, bank reports, and similar items which may be of current interest to the business researcher. Usually these are not recorded in the public catalog.

Documents as a Source.   The topics covered in documentary publications range widely. The best technique for searching U.S. government publications is to use:

U.S. Superintendent of Documents. *United States Government Publications: Monthly Catalog.* Washington: U.S. Government Printing Office, 1893 to date.

Materials issued by all branches of the U.S. government are listed by name of the issuing office. There are monthly and annual subject indexes which are valuable to the investigator.

On looking through the listings in the *Monthly Catalog* one will often notice a heavy black dot placed next to an entry. The dot identifies that item as a publication that is available to depository libraries. Depository libraries have been designated by the U.S. government to hold a collection of major government documents. This program is designed to assure widespread dissemination of governmental literature. A list of depository libraries is given in the September issue of the *Monthly Catalog.* Even the largest depository library will not have *every* depository marked item. In fact, a library usually selects only that part of the designated publications that fits with the interests of its patrons. A metropolitan library, for example, may choose very few of the agriculture depository items. With each entry in the *Monthly Catalog* is a special Superintendent of Documents classification number. Library holdings of documents are often shelved by this number.

Government publications are good sources of information in many topic areas. Obviously, the entire area of economic statistics is one of these areas. There are also important documents concerning many scientific fields, government relations to business, and business operations. The various congressional committee reports frequently have testimony about business operations which is seldom available any place else. The documents literature of agricultural marketing contains many pioneering field experiment research studies.

Periodicals as a Source. Periodicals are often the best single source of information for the business researcher. There are thousands of publications covering almost any subject imaginable. Many of them are relatively useless for research purposes, but one is often amazed at the richness of the periodical lode when some way is found to tap it. Periodicals are especially useful in securing the most current information.

Libraries have indexes by which the investigator may review the contents of many periodicals quickly, and without actually going to the publications themselves. The most widely known of these indexes is the *Reader's Guide to Periodical Literature.* This is a subject guide of about 160 general-interest magazines such as *Time, Newsweek, Business Week, Fortune, Scientific American, Vogue,* and others. It is useful for topics of general interest but also includes many articles on business and technological matters.

Four other widely available indexes are germane to business topics. They are:

1. *Business Periodicals Index.* New York: H. W. Wilson Co., 1958 to date.
2. *Applied Science and Technology Index.* New York: H. W. Wilson Co., 1958—
3. Public Affairs Information Service, *Bulletin.* New York: 1915 to date.
4. *F. & S. Index of Corporations and Industries.* Detroit: Funk & Scott, 1960—

The *Business Periodicals Index* (*BPI*) is a subject index of articles from approximately 165 business and economics periodicals. It is particularly useful as a guide to materials concerning the practical aspects of business operations and for specific industries and businesses.

A companion index is the *Applied Science and Technology Index* (*ASTI*). This index and the *BPI* are the outgrowth of the former *Industrial Arts Index* which was published until 1958. The *ASTI* catalogs those periodicals which concentrate on scientific and technological subjects, but many articles on nontechnical subjects are also included. It is organized by subject and indexes approximately 200 publications.

The third major index of value to the business researcher is the Public

Affairs Information Service *Bulletin* (PAIS). Its coverage overlaps the *BPI* to some extent, but it includes a more wide-ranging list of English-language publications from around the world. In addition, many books, government publications, and pamphlets are also indexed by subject. It covers many nonperiodical publications that become available from time to time.

The *F. & S. Index of Corporations and Industries* indexes articles in periodicals as well as other references on U.S. corporations and industries. Currently this index covers about 750 publications. Through 1966 coverage also included the same topics for Canada, Great Britain, and Japan. Since 1966 there has been a companion volume called the *F. & S. Index International* which covers companies, industries, and countries outside the United States.

The *New York Times, The Wall Street Journal,* and *Fortune* are also indexed and will frequently provide excellent information. *The Wall Street Journal Index,* for example, is a monthly index divided into two sections, one for corporate news arranged by the name of the firm, and one for general news arranged by subject. There are also many other indexes and bibliographies available. Suggestive of this range are the *Psychological Abstracts,* the *Art Index, Biological & Agriculture Index,* and the *Education Index.*

While periodical indexes are invaluable, they may still prove to be inadequate for a specific research study. This may occur because the indexes cover such a small portion of the periodicals published. There are many publications with valuable information which are not indexed in any of the guides mentioned. It is more difficult, but by no means impossible, to find material from these other sources. An example will illustrate one approach to this problem.

Assume for the moment that we are interested in conducting some research into the use of paint by the American consumer. We are interested in such information as (1) how frequently families paint their homes, (2) how many rooms they paint at one time, (3) how much paint they use, and similar information. Such information would be useful as a basis for estimating the consumption of paint.

Obviously, we could interview consumers to obtain answers to these questions. On the other hand, it may be more efficient and less expensive to obtain information from other research studies. A review of the *BPI, PAIS,* and *ASTI* provides relatively little concrete information on these questions. There are two possible reasons for the lack of information. One is that there is just no information available on this subject. In this case we will have no choice but to do field research if we want the answers to our questions. The other explanation is that such information is available in publications which are not indexed in the guides.

One way we could check would be to determine whether paint-oriented periodicals are indexed. A look at the coverage of the traditional periodical indexing services indicates that they do not survey most paint-oriented magazines. There are several references to which we can go to identify the magazines associated with the painting industry. One which is available in most libraries is:

Ayer Directory of Publications. Philadelphia: Ayer Press, 1880 to date.

This is an annual list of American newspapers and periodicals, arranged by state and city of publication; it gives detailed information about each title. It also has an alphabetical list of titles and a classified list of trade, technical, and professional journals. Reference to it indicates that there are at least six periodicals published in the United States that are concerned with some aspect of the paint industry. With this information we are in a position to take one of two courses of action.

One course would be to contact the publishers of these magazines and seek help from them. They often know of specific articles in their own publications or may have a file on the subject which they may make available. A second approach is to continue the library search route by locating the nearest library which has copies of the newly discovered magazines. The best source for this is:

Union List of Serials in Libraries of the United States and Canada. 3d ed. 5 vols. New York: H. W. Wilson Co., 1965.

It is the most comprehensive list of periodicals available and indicates which American libraries hold each publication listed. It is updated by:

New Serial Titles. Washington: Library of Congress, 1953 to date.

This paint illustration is from an actual case known to the author in which the researcher used both approaches cited. The direct contact with a publisher turned out to be the most fruitful. The inquiry brought copies of a half-dozen specific articles and research studies which dealt with paint use practices. This information answered the major research questions satisfactorily without the need to go to expensive field research.

Miscellaneous Sources. A final category listed in Figure 7–1 is the miscellaneous sources. Among these are many reference works, some of which have already been mentioned. Others are listed in Appendix A. Data published by business associations may be listed in the public catalog, or the material may be in vertical files kept by the library. Company annual reports and other similar materials are also more likely to be found in uncataloged collections.

One major miscellaneous source is the publications from other colleges and universities. Doctoral dissertations are one such source that is particularly valuable if one is investigating subjects at the frontiers of knowledge. The dissertations of persons receiving their doctorate at a given university will usually be cataloged in that university's library only. To meet the need for information about dissertations from other universities there are:

American Doctoral Dissertations, 1955/56−. Ann Arbor, Mich.: Xerox University Microfilms, 1957 to date.
Dissertation Abstracts International. Ann Arbor, Mich.: Xerox University Microfilms, 1938 to date.

The first publication provides "a complete listing of all doctoral dissertations accepted by American and Canadian universities." The abstracts typically run a few hundred words in length and may be enough for the reader to determine whether to order a copy of the entire dissertation. Another excellent reference for tracking down university research publications is:

Associated University Bureaus of Business and Economic Research. *Index of Publications of Bureaus of Business and Economic Research, 1950−1956.* Eugene, Ore., 1957 to date.

This is an index to the reports, bulletins, and monographs published by university bureaus of business research. Supplements include some articles appearing in periodicals published by these bureaus.

A Sample Search. Let's summarize the process of searching a library for information by describing an actual investigation. Assume that a higher executive in our organization requests that we prepare a report for her on technological forecasting. She wants to know what it is, how it is carried out, who is doing it, and so on. This executive must decide whether or not our organization should engage in this type of effort.

She is uninformed about the topic and we are equally uninformed. We are fotunate, however, in knowing something about proper research methods so that we feel confident we can carry out the assignment. With this thought in mind we begin the search. The path leads to the library of a local university, and the sequence we follow is illustrated in a general way by the flow diagram in Figure 7−1.[3]

Since we are unfamiliar with the term "technological forecasting" we look in the *Encyclopaedia Britannica* and the *International Encyclopedia of the Social Sciences.* These are usually good sources for some quick information about a topic; but in this case there is no mention of technological forecasting. This is likely to happen if a topic or its terminology is rather new.

Next we try two guides to business reference materials. These provide lists of bibliographies, handbooks, textbooks, and manuals which are often helpful. These sources are: Coman, Edwin T., *Sources of Business Information,* and Harvard University, *Selected Business Reference Sources.* In the Coman book we find nine books listed on forecasting but nothing that specifically mentions technological forecasting. In addition it lists a bibliography on business forecasting.

While putting Coman back on the shelf serendipity takes over. One of the

---

[3] This example is based on an actual study done in late 1970.

skills that researchers need to cultivate is that certain sensitivity that enables them to find things by luck. On the shelf about two books away from the Coman book is a 152-page bibliography dated 1965 entitled *Business Trends and Forecasting,* published as *Management Information Guide No. 9* by the Gale Research Company. This turns out to be an excellent annotated bibliography. In fact, the annotations are so complete that a study of the contents convinces us that there was virtually nothing on technological forecasting in business forecasting books up to 1965. While this is negative information, it is useful. We decide to restrict our search to the period since 1965.

With the preliminary steps not paying off, we decide to go directly to the *Bibliographic Index (BI).* In the *Index* for 1966–1968 we find two entries listing bibliographies on technological forecasting. Search of earlier indexes back to 1960 turns up nothing further. The *BI* for 1969 has no mentions, while the April 1970 *Index* has one reference. Moving now to the public catalog, we learn that the library has only one of the two books mentioned in the *BI* but does list two other books on technological forecasting and one published proceedings of a conference on the subject. Three out of four of these items come from European sources. Their cards in the public catalog indicate that the three books have bibliographies ranging from 3 to 40 pages in length.

While finding four books on our subject in the card catalog is encouraging, we search further by going to the *Library of Congress Subject Catalog.* Our search is rewarded by finding four more books listed there. Now we have identified eight English-language books that have been published on technological forecasting from 1967 to 1970. Some of these new discoveries may be in one of the local libraries, or we may choose to order one or more of them.

Periodical Search. Since our topic includes the word "technological" we decide first to investigate the *Applied Science and Technology Index.* We review its entries from 1963 to June 1970 and find one entry on our subject in the 1966 volume. There are three entries in 1967, five in 1968, four in 1969, and one in 1970. From 1966 to mid-1970 we find a total of 14 entries in *ASTI* referencing articles about technological forecasting. A search of *PAIS* for the same time period turns up 11 more references to articles on technological forecasting, while *BPI* produces 19 which do not duplicate any of the ones found in the other two indexes.

Other Sources With an inventory of eight book references and 44 periodical references there is not much incentive to look further, but for sake of completeness we search through the annual subject indexes of the *Monthly Catalog* of the U.S. Superintendent of Documents. From 1968 through mid-1970 there are eight references to published government documents on technological forecasting. All of them concern technological forecasting in the Soviet Union. None of them is on the depository list.

A search of the retrospective and annual subject indexes of *Dissertation Abstracts International* does not indicate any dissertations on technological forecasting. In total, then, after several hours of search we have a set of bibliography cards which include:

Eight books specifically about technological forecasting, at least four of which have extensive bibliographies to check.
Forty-four periodical references.
Eight government document references.

With this list our reference search is well launched. The problem now is to find the references, weed out those which do not hold promise, and extract information that is appropriate to our task from the remainder. This extraction process is the subject of the next section.

Extracting Information

Gathering and recording information from printed sources is often viewed as a simple chore within the competence of almost anyone. This may be true, but it is also a task which is often done poorly. The task has three aspects which are worthy of consideration. First, we are faced with the job of selecting which information to record. That is, which information is useful and which is not, and which is a net addition to our collection and which is mere repetition. These decisions are not easy to make, but in general we must be guided by our research purpose. We should set up an outline of our topic as quickly as we can, even knowing that it will probably change as we gather more information. The idea that "I'll gather all of the material and then decide how to organize it" is inefficient. There is much interesting information that will turn up on many subjects which is diversionary in nature. It takes self-discipline to ignore these interesting sideshows of information in order to concentrate on the main task; an a priori outline is helpful.

Our second task is to determine how to record what we extract from the published material. Should we report it verbatim, paraphrase it, or outline it? More often than not, outlining is the most efficient method. For specific important definitions or statements we will wish to record them verbatim. In a few other instances a paraphrase statement of the author's position is most suitable.

The third task is to set up and operate an orderly recording system. With it we can have the extracted information available when needed, have a ready reference source for checking, and have maximum flexibility in organizing the information.

Note-Taking. The first requirement is to use some orderly system which is comfortable. Most systems use cards upon which to record both bibliographic references and the notes taken from these references. Putting notes on cards allows for more flexible handling and organizing of the data. Some even advocate putting a single fact or idea on each individual card; this obviously promotes maximum flexibility, but it also fragments the information. The single idea per card concept is probably more desirable in those cases where the researcher does not have a fairly clear idea of subject organization.

One recommended method of note-taking uses two sets of cards and an a priori outline of the key elements or questions regarding the topic. While the outline may change as the researcher acquires further insight into the subject, it is a help in deciding which information is needed and how various bits of information should be related.

One set of cards (probably 3 × 5 cards) is used for bibliographic references, and the second set (probably 5 × 8 cards) is used for the actual note-taking. The 3 × 5 cards should be set up in proper bibliographic format, one reference per card so that they can be used later for footnote statements and for the drafting of the bibliography. These cards can be coded by a simple system that may be used to identify specific passages on the note cards. One useful coding system employs a combination letter and number (F1, F2, and so forth) to identify each author whose last name begins with "F."

The 5 × 8 note cards provide more adequate space for writing information. On the note card margins the bibliography reference codes may be entered to provide a ready source reference for each idea. Allied ideas from different sources may be placed on the same card without losing the ability to track each reference back to its source. The use of this note-taking system will enable us to develop a substantial set of notes, readily sortable into new patterns of organization, and with each idea referenced back to its source. Figure 7–3 illustrates such cards.

Having gathered a data set of this type we are ready to prepare our own analysis. One of the first steps of this analysis, one that we have probably been doing unconsciously along the line, is the evaluation of the quality of information which we have found.

Evaluating Secondary Data

While much attention has been given to the importance of secondary data sources and their use, there is still the task of evaluating the data which are found. This evaluation takes two forms: first, how well does the data fit the needs of the researcher; and, second, what confidence can the researcher put in the accuracy and legitimacy of the data?

Data Pertinency. Paramount in any consideration of secondary data is the inescapable fact that the data were collected for some other purpose and not for our own needs. Care must be taken to understand the definitions and classifications employed to assure that their meanings are consistent with our own. Several aspects that are of particular importance are the nature of the measurements used, the degree to which they conform to the requirements of our research, and the coverage of the secondary research in terms of topic and time.

Figure 7–3: A Note Card Example

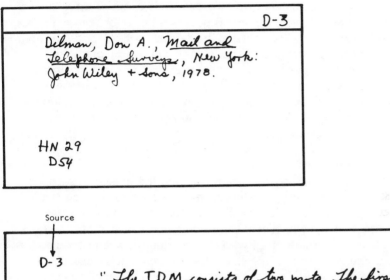

Source

Writer's
Proposed
Chapter

Data Quality.   The question of data quality is essentially a question of data accuracy. In this context it is important to go to the original source of the information rather than to use an immediate source which has quoted from the original. This is good research technique for several reasons: first, it enables us to catch the errors in transcription that exist in secondary sources; second, it enables us to review the cautionary and other attendant comments that went along with the original data; finally, it may uncover revisions that have been made in the data since the secondary source used it.

Another aspect of data accuracy concerns its completeness; that is, how much does the reported material actually cover? Is it based upon an extremely narrow sample, a very large and general population, or what? Answers to these questions may indicate that the data are not appropriate for our problem. Another facet of data quality concerns the capability of the source of the data. In this context there are two concerns: first, the investigators and their competence. Are the persons who conducted the study people in whom we can have confidence? Are they highly regarded? Is their organization well regarded? A second aspect of source capability concerns the original source itself; that is, could the respondent actually answer this question? What are the chances that the respondent will know and be willing to give such information under the study conditions?

A concern that any investigator has in studying the quality of secondary data is to determine the degree to which they accurately reflect reality. A confounding factor here is the question of possible bias. The study was conducted for some purpose which may have dictated a particular orientation or flavor. Here again, the question of who did the study, whether the findings promote their interest, and how the study itself was conducted are all important clues. One must especially be on guard when a study does not report the methodology and sampling design. These and other factors are of prime concern in determining if the secondary data are adequate for the investigator's research purposes.

SUMMARY

The use of secondary data sources for research presents some unique problems. The collection of data from within one's own organization, in particular, defies generalized description. Published data, on the other hand, are cataloged and coded so as to facilitate their use (if we understand library systems and have some facility with search tools).

Literature sources may be classed into three major groups, plus a fourth catch-all group. Books are usually the basic source for general coverage and for established topics of breadth or depth. Periodicals are a second major source and are especially valuable for current information and for topics of limited scope. Documents from governmental organizations are a third major source of literature. Finally, there are miscellaneous materials produced by private organizations, universities, associations, and reference services.

In using secondary data sources researchers have two jobs. First, they must define their research needs so as to be able to use the coding systems that have been developed to make printed information more accessible. This calls for the researchers to have a clear knowledge and understanding of the major reference tools available, as well as some skill in their use. Their second job is to secure adequate usable data from the information storage system. This calls for skill in extracting information efficiently, and the ability to judge how much confidence to place in the data.

Research based on secondary sources may constitute the sole input in some cases but is often significant only in the exploratory phases of a study. Just what role secondary sources play is a function of the study's research design.

SUPPLEMENTAL READINGS

1. Barzun, Jacques, and Graff, Henry F. *The Modern Researcher.* Rev. ed. New York: Harcourt, Brace & World, Inc., 1970, pts. I and II. Chaps. 4 and 5 treat the processes of fact gathering and verification.
2. Harvard University, Graduate School of Business. *Current Periodical Publications in Baker Library.* Boston, Mass. Includes magazines, journals, newspapers, bulletins, statistical annuals, yearbooks, conference proceedings, directories, government agency annual reports, and loose-leaf business services.
3. Helppie, Charles E.; Gibbons, James R.; and Pearson, Donald W. *Research Guide in Economics.* Morristown, N.J.: General Learning Press, 1974. Designed to meet the "need in economics for a practical guide to research for the student."
4. Johnson, H. Webster. *How to Use the Business Library.* 4th ed. Cincinnati: South-Western Publishing Company, 1972. Useful suggestions on the use of a business library.

   For other references see Appendix A.

DISCUSSION QUESTIONS

1. Some researchers find that their sole sources are secondary data. Why might this be? Name some management research situations where secondary data sources are probably the only ones feasible.
2. While public catalogs of libraries are very useful, what problems do you see if a researcher depends only on the catalog for information sources?
3. Many managements gather and analyze statistical data for small geographic areas. For what types of businesses do you think these data might be important? For what purposes might they want such information? What types of data might they use? Where might they secure such information from secondary sources?
4. Assume that you are asked to investigate the use of mathematical programming in accounting applications; you decide to depend upon secondary data sources. What search tools might you use? Which do you think would be the most fruitful? Sketch a flow diagram of your search sequence.
5. What are the problems of secondary data quality that researchers must face? How can they deal with them?
6. Secure a recent copy of the *Statistical Abstract* and determine what information is available on the following topics:

a. Coal mining.
b. Consumer credit.
c. Advertising expenditures.
d. Labor unions.
e. Social welfare expenditures.
f. Hospitals in the United States.
g. Law enforcement.

7. Choose a line of trade and determine what data are available for that line at a state and local level in the *Census of Business.*

8. Choose a two-digit industry classification from the *Census of Manufacturers,* and determine the type of information that is available for it. How much information is available at more detailed (for example, four-digit, and so forth) levels?

9. Below are a number of requests that a young staff assistant might receive. What specific tools or services would you expect to use to find the requisite information? (Appendix A may be helpful.)

a. The president wants a list of perhaps six of the best references that have appeared on executive compensation during the last ten years.

b. Has the FTC published any recent statements (within the last year) concerning their position regarding quality stabilization?

c. A man at a western university is said to have completed his Ph.D. dissertation last year on competition problems in our industry. Can we find out whether or not this is true? How can we get a copy?

d. I need a list of the major companies that are located in Springfield, Missouri.

e. Please get me a list of the directors of General Motors, Dial Finance, and American Investment Company.

f. A new book has recently come out concerning technological forecasting. Can you get the reference for me?

g. We are looking at a man named Franklin T. Pierce who is a senior VP of the Harris Trust Company in Chicago. Can you get some biographical data on him for me?

h. Is there a trade magazine that specializes in the flooring industry?

i. I need a copy of the *Journal of the Oil Chemist's Society,* but our library does not have it. Where is the closest place I could go to look at it?

j. The Fuji Bank of Tokyo, Japan, has issued a special study in their December 1979 *Fuji Bank Bulletin.* Where can I get a copy?

k. I would like to track down a study of small-scale service franchising that was recently published by a Bureau of Business Research at one of the southern universities. Can you help me?

Chapter 8

Survey Instrument Design

WE HAVE ALREADY DISCUSSED concepts, operational definitions, hypotheses, research design, and measurement. We now must draw them together into adequate instruments and procedures for use. In Chapter 4 it was pointed out that data are gathered either by monitoring or by interrogation. The former includes observation studies and will be deferred until Chapter 10. This chapter deals chiefly with survey instruments and consists of four major sections. First we discuss some aspects of the survey approach plus several strategy decisions that dictate instrument design. This is followed by a discussion of the instrument design process itself. We then take up the specifics of question construction, followed by a review of reason analysis.

SURVEY STRATEGY DECISIONS

Why Survey? In interrogation the researcher seeks verbal or written responses to questions or statements. The versatility of this method is its greatest strength. It is the only practical way to learn many types of information and the most economical way in many other situations. For example, we can learn little about what a person knows or believes except by asking. How else can one so easily and efficiently learn a subject's likes and dislikes than through questioning? How one thinks can seldom be demonstrated by overt behavior. Even when other approaches are possible they are often more costly and difficult. For example, we might poll a sample of people on their preferences among various entertainment events much more cheaply than actually setting up test situations to determine which they attend.

Events which have occurred in the past must often be secured through someone's recall. Published documents record major events in history, but most of the past data we seek is recent, personal, and too limited in interest to be published. Questioning is the only way to secure such information. Private behaviors almost never are observable; here again, we must resort to questioning. Finally, expectations data can be secured only by questioning, and this is an area of great management interest. The problem is, therefore, not whether to use questioning, but how to assure that we do a good job of it.

Survey Criticisms. A major criticism of the survey method is that it depends so completely on verbal behavior. The respondent can knowingly give untrue or misleading answers. The interviewer, the situation, and the question under study can help foster this distortion of responses. A survey's success, therefore, depends on a fragile procedure. We can always secure some answer, but can we secure a good one?

Another weakness of surveys is that everyone thinks it is easy to design a questionnaire. The view seems to be, "All we need to do is to write up the questions and then go ask them." With such a cavalier approach to instrument design it is little wonder that survey results are criticized. It is our purpose here to show the type of analytic thinking and construction technique that must go into an adequately designed survey instrument.

How to Survey? Once we have decided to use the survey approach there are three strategy decisions that strongly affect the design of our survey instrument. These concern:

A. The communication mode that we choose by which to conduct the questioning.
B. The degree of structure that is imposed on the questioning and response processes.
C. The degree to which the objectives of the study are to be disguised.

Communication Modes

Communication interactions between researcher and respondent are either personal, impersonal, or mixed in nature. Each of these will be briefly defined, but any evaluation of them will be deferred to Chapter 10.

Personal Mode. This mode typically involves a one-on-one relationship between interviewer and interviewee. The interviewer uses either an *interview schedule* or an *interview guide*. A schedule is a structured set of questions which are usually asked orally and recorded in writing by the interviewer. An interview guide is a list of topic questions or areas which the interviewer uses merely as a prompter during the interview. These responses may be recorded in writing, by tape recorder, or in some other way.

Impersonal Mode. In this communication mode the researcher typically depends upon a printed instrument to carry the two-way communication task. This instrument, a *questionnaire,* carries both the instructions and questions to respondents, and provides space for them to complete their answers. In layman terms "questionnaire" is used to refer to all survey measurement instruments, but it will be used here in the more narrow technical sense defined above. The impersonal mode of questioning makes it possible to use mail or group-administered surveys.

Mixed Mode. While we think of personal and impersonal approaches as alternative methods, there is no reason why they cannot be combined. Examples might be where prior telephone appointments or screenings are made for later personal interviews. There is some question as to whether prior telephoning improves or decreases the chances of securing an interview; there is evidence for both sides of this argument. Telephone screening to qualify respondents has been very effective.

Much more complex research designs call for using all communication modes in a study. One example is the study in which new products to be tested were placed in homes with a personal visit. At that time some information was also collected, and questionnaires were left to be completed and returned by mail. Finally, telephone followups were made to complete the interviews. In this case it was reported that 97 percent of the testing families completed the study.[1]

Process Structure

A second useful perspective on the development of survey instruments is based on the degree of question structure placed on the interviewer and the respondent.

Questioning Structure. With structured questioning the interviewer asks questions in a standardized format and sequence. This helps assure that each question is asked the same way in each interview, promoting measurement reliability. A standardized questioning sequence also makes it easier to develop a standard line of questioning that builds on prior responses. We can also use less skilled interviewers with structured questions.

At the other extreme are the relatively unstructured interview processes. These include the so-called depth interviews, focused, and nondirective methods. A depth interview is a loosely structured effort to question a respondent in detail about opinions, feelings, and attitudes. The researcher usually uses an interview guide to assure coverage of the topics of interest. A focused interview is a special form of depth interview where the researcher attempts to focus the discussion on some particular experience to which the respondent

---

[1] Stanley Payne "Combination of Survey Methods," *Journal of Marketing Research,* vol. 1 (May 1964), p. 61.

has been exposed.[2] A nondirective interview is the least structured of the three. The interviewer's function is to encourage respondents to talk about a given topic with a minimum of prompting or guidance.

Lack of question structure has both advantages and disadvantages. One advantage is that the interviewer can guide the questioning in the direction which insight and the respondent's replies lead. The skilled interviewer recognizes and exploits these opportunities as they arise. Naturally there are also disadvantages to this freedom. The results of one interview are not comparable with others. In addition, there is a risk that the flexibility may become chaos.

Unstructured interviewing is particularly useful in exploratory research where the lines of investigation are not clearly defined. The lack of structure is also useful when investigating many sensitive topical areas in which success depends upon the interviewer's ability to adapt the questioning. In summary, unstructured questioning is more appropriate when the research objective is one of discovery. When the emphasis moves to the testing of hypotheses, or the conduct of large-scale formalized studies, then structured questioning is necessary.

Response Structure.   Forms of response may be classified as open or closed. In the open form respondents are free to reply with their own choice of words and concepts. Open responses are always found with unstructured questions and are particularly useful in studies where discovery is the objective. Response freedom encourages a variety of frames of reference which can provide unanticipated insights to the researcher. The open response form may also be used with structured questioning. In fact, in most surveys there will be at least some open-end questions.

With the closed response form the respondent chooses from two or more predetermined response possibilities. Two varieties are normally distinguished—the dichotomous or two-choice answer, and the multiple choice response. The results in either case are standardized answers, simple to administer, and relatively easy to analyze and compile. The frame of reference is specified for the response and this increases our chances for securing answers which are relevant to our inquiry.

Closed questions also have their disadvantages. They force a statement of opinion that is couched in the researcher's terms rather than the respondent's. Respondents can easily be led to give an opinion which they really do not have, and the limited response alternatives may not adequately represent the respondent's viewpoint. Some alternatives may be omitted, and this can result in bias. While closed alternative questions simplify the frame-of-reference problem, it is still possible that different respondents will interpret the same words and statements differently.

---

[2] For further information see R. K. Merton, M. Fiske, and P. L. Kendall, *The Focused Interview* (Glencoe, Ill.: The Free Press, 1956).

Objective Disguise

A third decision affecting the survey design is whether we should disguise the objectives of the study. Much research on human subjects is disguised because it is believed that if we do otherwise we will introduce too many distortions. Here we are concerned with the narrow form of this problem: Shall we disguise the objectives of our questions? The accepted wisdom is that often we must do this or abandon our research efforts. Our decision as to when to use disguised questioning may be made easier by identifying four types of interview situations relevant to this problem of disguise.

1. We ask for information from respondents who know it at a conscious level and are willing to provide it. For example, we ask whether they have attended a certain movie.
2. We ask for information from respondents who know it at a conscious level but are unwilling to provide it. For example, we ask for an opinion on some topic for which they hold a socially unacceptable view.
3. We ask for information which is knowable at a conscious level but which the respondents do not know. For example, we ask why their actions differ from those of others when the reason lies outside their knowledge and experience.
4. We ask for information which the respondents do not know at a conscious level although they have the information at some deeper level. For example, we seek insight into the basic motivations underlying their consumption practices.

Type 1 situations seldom need disguised questions, but in type 2 situations respondents may not give their true feelings or may give stereotyped answers. The researcher can encourage more accurate answers by phrasing the questions in a hypothetical way, or by asking how "people around here feel about this topic." The assumption is that responses to these questions will indirectly reveal the respondent's opinions.

In another form of a type 2 situation, respondents reply with stereotyped answers because they may not have given the subject much thought. This problem may also be approached in an indirect manner. In one corporate image study the buyers of control instruments were asked for the ". . . five characteristics which a control manufacturer must have if he wants your business." The five highest ranked from a list of more than 20 possible descriptors are given in List A.[3]

The buyers were also asked to choose the descriptors which best characterized each of the six major suppliers in the industry. These latter responses were then analyzed to determine which words best differentiated each buyer's

---

[3] Louis Cohen, "The Differentiation Ratio in Corporate Research," *Journal of Advertising Research,* vol. 4 (September 1967), pp. 34–35.

Rank	List A *"Most Important" Characteristics*	List B *Best Differentiators*
1	Quality products	Diversified line
2	Dependable	Leader
3	Cooperative	Pioneer
4	Quality conscious	Dependable
5	Accurate	Accurate

preferred supplier from the others. This quite different ranking is shown in List B. Further depth interviewing indicated that List B descriptors much more accurately reflected the real decision factors which led to choosing one supplier over another.

Indirect questioning and analysis may often be needed to achieve the research objective in the type 3 decision. A classic example is a study of government bond buying during World War II.[4] A survey was undertaken to determine why some people bought more war bonds than others with equal ability to buy. It was found that heavy buyers tended to be those who had been personally solicited to buy bonds. No direct "why" question to respondents could have answered this question because they did not know that they were receiving a different solicitation approach.

Type 4 situations represent the depth type of study which may or may not be disguised. Projective and other types of tests can be given which thoroughly disguise the study objective, but they are often quite difficult to interpret.

THE INSTRUMENT DEVELOPMENT PROCESS

Researchers-to-be normally want immediately to draft questions which they can ask respondents. They are reluctant to go through the many preliminary phases that take so much time, effort, and thought. The nature of these preliminary phases was pointed out in Chapter 3, but their importance will be reviewed here.

Question Hierarchy

The process of moving from the general management objective or problem to specific measurement questions goes through four major question levels:

1. The management question—that problem which the manager must answer.

---

[4] Dorwin Cartwright, "Some Principles of Mass Persuasion," *Human Relations,* vol. 2 (1948), p. 266.

2. The research question—that basic information question or questions which the researcher must answer in order to contribute to the solution of the management question.
3. The investigative questions—those specific questions which the researcher must ask herself in order to answer her research question. Within this class there may be several levels of questions as the researcher moves from the general to the specific.
4. The measurement questions—those questions which respondents must answer if the researcher is to gather the needed information.

Procedure Example. The process of moving from management question to measurement question is an exercise in analytical reasoning. The example presented in Chapter 3 might be worth review. Here is a second illustration which involves a relatively simple descriptive survey problem.

Gentlemen's Magazine[5]

The editor of Gentlemen's Magazine has asked you to carry out a research study. The magazine has been unsuccessful in attracting advertising revenue from shoe manufacturers. The shoe manufacturers claim that men's clothing stores are a small and declining segment of the men's shoe business. Since Gentlemen's Magazine is sold chiefly to men's clothing store managements, the manufacturers have reasoned that it is therefore not a good advertising medium for their shoes.

The editor disagrees with the manufacturers about the size and importance of shoe marketing through men's clothing stores. Neither side has much direct evidence on the matter, so the editor asks you to carry out a study to determine the facts about these stores as a channel of distribution for men's shoes. You agree to do so and proceed with the first structuring of the problem.

1. *Management Problem.* The problem facing the magazine management is that of trying to expand their advertising revenue. There are a number of ways that this might be done and research might help in many of them. In this case, however, the management has already decided that the management's problem is to secure more advertising from the shoe industry. The researcher accepted the problem definition as stated.
2. *Research Question.* The research question was defined as "Are the actual or potential sales of men's shoes in men's wear stores large enough to represent an advertising opportunity to shoe manufacturers?"
3. *Investigative Question.* Three major investigative questions were proposed:
   a. Are shoe sales important to men's wear stores?
   b. Have shoe sales been growing in importance in men's wear stores and are they expected to grow in the future?

---

[5] Name disguised.

c. Does the situation in men's wear stores present an advertising opportunity for shoe manufacturers?[6]

It was agreed that the only feasible research design which could be carried out within the available budget was a national mail survey. Because of the limited scope of the study and the problems of population estimation from a mail survey it was agreed that the research study would be concerned chiefly with the first two questions. The third question would be approached within the limits of the research design, but a full answer to this question would require information not available to the researcher.

To answer the major investigative questions posed above it was necessary to secure information on a number of much more specific points. These represent investigative subquestions which we must know to answer the three major questions. Parenthetical statements attached to them suggest the rationales for including the questions in the study.

a. Are shoe sales important to men's wear stores?
   1. What percent of men's wear stores carry men's shoes? (One important measure of this channel of distribution and an indicator of the importance of shoes to retailers.)
   2. What percent of men's wear store sales come from shoes? (A measure of the importance of shoes to total store operation.)
   3. How do shoe gross margins compare with total store gross margins? (Another measure of shoe importance to the store and an indicator of whether or not shoes are likely to secure store management attention.)
   4. How do space/sales ratios compare between shoe departments and the total store. (Another measure of the contribution of shoes to the total store health. Also a measure of how secure shoes might be as a part of the store product mix.)
   5. How important are shoes as traffic builders, extra sales, or extra business from those who do not buy other merchandise at the time. (Another measure of the value of shoes to store success and an indicator of the mix security of shoes.)
b. Have shoe sales been growing in importance in men's wear stores and are they expected to grow in the future?
   1. What percent of the stores have added, expanded, dropped, or reduced shoe operations in the last five years? (A measure of the changes in importance of shoes in men's wear stores in recent years.)
   2. Have shoe sales grown or declined in absolute dollars in recent years? As a percent of total store sales? (Measures of the changes that have taken place in men's wear stores concerning shoes.)
   3. What are store managements expecting in the next few years concerning shoes? Add or drop? Reduce or enlarge? (A measure of store operator expectations concerning shoes.)

---

[6] In descriptive surveys the research and investigative questions may be stated either as questions or as hypotheses.

    c. Does the situation in men's wear stores present an advertising opportunity for shoe manufacturers?

       1. What percent of the men's shoe volume is sold through men's wear stores? (A very crude measure of the importance of this channel to the manufacturer. This estimate will be carefully hedged since there is little hope that the survey can provide an unbiased estimate of total sales of men's shoes.)

       2. How important are leased departments in men's shoes operations in men's wear stores? (A measure of the need for shoe manufacturers to contact individual store managements to secure distribution, or whether the approach to a few central buying firms might suffice.)

       3. What price lines are carried, and what are their relative importance? (A measure of the type of demand for men's shoes represented in this channel.)

       4. What is the importance of casual shoe versus dress shoe sales? (Another measure of the type of shoe demand that prevails in this channel.)

       5. What brands are carried and what are their relative importance? (A measure of the penetration by various manufacturers as well as a measure of the product characteristics that are popular in this channel.)

4. *Measurement Questions.* The 13 investigative questions listed above were translated into about 20 specific measurement questions which were finally asked of the respondents. There were six additional classification-type questions. These measurement questions differed from the investigative questions chiefly in wording and format so as to aid the respondent in replying with a minimum of difficulty and a maximum of reliability.

Schedule Design Process

The procedure to follow in developing a survey instrument varies from case to case, but a useful generalized approach consists of five major steps. While this suggests a linear process, there is always a good deal of cycling and recycling as we work through it.

Information Need Determination. The research question hierarchy is a major part of this first step. This fractionation process develops chiefly out of the researcher's perception of the project. In many studies an exploratory investigation is necessary to assure that we understand the full dimensions of the subject. In the *Gentlemen's Magazine* project there was only limited exploration because the concepts were not complicated and the researcher had substantial experience in the industry. In the Prince Corporation image study (Chapter 5) a number of exploratory interviews are needed to assure that the investigative subquestions cover the areas of relevance to the population being studied.

We are concerned both with adequate coverage of the topic and with securing the information in its most usable form. A good way to test how well our study plan meets these needs is to develop "dummy" tables in which to display the data we expect to secure. This step is a good check on whether our plan meets our data needs.

Data Gathering Process Decisions.   At this stage we must choose the manner by which to gather the data. First, which communication process or combination of processes is most appropriate? Personal or impersonal? Telephone or face-to-face? In-home or at other sites? In the *Gentlemen's Magazine* case this decision was easy. The wide dispersion of respondents, nature of the data, and budget limitations all dictated a mail survey. In the Prince Corporation there is a desire to use telephone interviews because of cost savings. However, the study objectives call for data which cannot easily be collected by telephone.

The degree of question and response structure must also be determined. Question structure is affected largely by the communication mode chosen. Response structure decisions depend more on the content and objectives of specific questions. In the mail survey it was necessary to use structured questions. Most of the responses were also structured. In the exploratory stages of the Prince study both questions and responses would be unstructured, but in the final project both would be largely structured.

The degree of disguise is the third decision needed. In the *Gentlemen's Magazine* study the questions were direct and the specific information sought was generally undisguised. However, both the purpose of the study and its sponsorship were disguised. In the Prince Corporation study the questions would concern only a small number of companies, giving the sponsor only a limited disguise. Many of the questions would seek direct answers, but in some cases indirect questioning would be used to (1) seek answers on sensitive topics or to (2) counter the tendency of respondents to give stereotyped answers to general questions.

Instrument Drafting.   We begin actual instrument design by drafting specific measurement questions. In doing this we must consider both the subject content and the wording of each question. As these question formulations are developed we need also to establish some logical question sequences. Often the content in one question assumes that certain questions have already been asked. We must also consider the psychological order of the questions. For example, questions which are more interesting, easier to answer, and less threatening usually are placed early in the sequence to encourage response and promote rapport.

Instrument Testing.   Once a first draft of the instrument has been developed it must be tested. The first testing can usually be done among one's colleagues. The questionnaire which we have so painstakingly put together will almost immediately be found weak in some respects. After this "in-house" testing it should be revised and taken to the field for testing. Usually the respondents should not know that their interrogation is only for testing purposes. Yet, it is very helpful to quiz test survey respondents further about their understanding and interpretation of the questions asked. Such quizzing provides an invaluable guide for instrument revision.

One approach which usually works well is, after completing the questionnaire, for the interviewer to tell the respondent that "we are just beginning the survey study and would appreciate your additional help in evaluating how effective the questions are." This approach will usually elicit cooperation and many useful insights into how well the respondents understood and are able to deal with the questions posed. Such additional discussions about the "questions that were confusing" and the understandings and frames of reference used by the respondents almost always prompt further instrument revision.

It is important in testing that we simulate field conditions as much as possible. One situation where testing differs somewhat is with mail surveys. Test mailings are useful, but it is often quicker to use a substitute procedure. For example, in the *Gentlemen's Magazine* case several stores were visited and the managers were asked to complete the questionnaire. The interviewers left and returned later for it. Upon their return they went over the questions with the manager. It was explained that the study was just beginning and that they wanted the manager's reactions on question clarity and ease of answering. This appeal for advice typically elicits cooperation. After several such interviews, the questionnaire was revised and the testing process repeated with new respondents. On the third trial there appeared to be only minor need for further revision, so the questionnaire was reproduced and mailed.

The importance of the test-revise-retest cycle cannot be overstressed. The failure to take this important step is one of the greatest causes of poor survey results. Testing is the hallmark of the scientific researcher.

Specification of Procedures. After the questioning device has been developed it is important to specify the procedures for its use. This is one way that we can assure that different interviewers will deal with specific questions in a more standardized manner. Such instructions usually should give the rationale behind the question, explain the frame of reference the designer has used, and mention any previous questions to which this one is especially related. Instructions should also mention the types of responses that are adequate and those which are not. Permissible paraphrasing, how the data should be recorded, and how to deal with various interviewing situations are also valuable points to cover in the surveyor instructions. More will be said on these topics in Chapter 10.

QUESTION CONSTRUCTION

Survey instruments normally include three types of information. The most important of these is the *sought data* such as facts, attitudes, preferences, and expectations about the central topic. A second type concerns the respondent characteristics needed for *classification and analysis*. Included are a large variety of items such as sex, age, family life cycle stage, family income, social class, and attitudes toward topics allied to the study's subject. The specific classification (or face-sheet) data sought depends on the particular study and its research objectives. A third type of information is *administrative*. It includes respondent identification, interviewer identification, date, place, and conditions of the interview, and the like.

We are ready to begin question drafting once we have decided on the information needed and the collection processes to use. In developing a survey instrument there are four major decision areas. These are (1) question content, (2) question wording, (3) response form, and (4) question sequence. These will be discussed in order, although in practice the process is not so linear. In the following discussion it is also assumed that the questions are structured.

Question Content

Should This Question Be Asked?   Our initial challenge is to assure that every suggested question is useful enough for us to include it in the instrument. Questions that merely produce "interesting information" cannot be justified on any economic or research grounds. Sometimes they are included because a sponsor insists, but we should challenge each question's function. Does it contribute significant information toward answering one of the investigative questions? Will it hurt if we do not have this information? Is it possible that we can infer the answer from some other source?

Is the Question of Proper Scope?   If a question passes the content relevance test, we should next consider its coverage. Does it cover so much content territory that it should be broken into two or more questions? Brevity is often a virtue, but we can easily fall into the trap of trying to ask two questions in one. An obvious example might be if we were to ask men's wear retailers whether this year's shoe sales and gross profits are higher than last year's. It is better to break this into separate questions. Less obvious doubling up may occur when we ask for a family's TV station preference, when a better question would be to ask the station preference for each family member.

Another test of question coverage is "Does it ask all that needs to be learned?" For example, we ask for the respondent's income when we really want the family's income. We ask "why" when this simple question will not adequately cover the range of causal relationships we want to explore. Perhaps we should ask several additional questions on product use of the heavy consumer, while the questions asked of the light user may be fewer.

Questions are also inadequate if they do not provide the information needed to interpret responses fully. If we ask about the Prince Corporation's image as an employer, does our question imply only one type of employee? Have we recognized that different classes of employees may have different reactions? Do we need to ask the question about other companies so that we can evaluate relative attitudes?

Can the Respondent Answer Adequately? While the question may concern important content, and adequately cover the territory, can the respondent know the answer? Respondents typically want to cooperate in interviews, but they often assume that giving some answer is being more helpful than denying knowledge of a topic. In addition, their desire to impress the interviewer may encourage them to give answers based on no information. A classic illustration of this problem was the pattern of responses secured to the following question:[7]

"Which of the following statements most closely coincides with your opinion of the Metallic Metals Act?"

	Answers	*Responses*
1.	It would be a good move on the part of the U.S.	15%
2.	It would be a good thing but should be left to the individual states	41
3.	It is all right for foreign countries but should not be required here	11
4.	It is of no value at all	3
5.	Have no opinion	30

The response pattern indicates that 70 percent of those interviewed have a fairly clear opinion of the Metallic Metals Act; however, *there is no such act.* The respondents apparently assumed that if a question is asked then they should give it an answer. Give them some reasonable sounding choices and they will select one even if they know nothing about the topic.

We must be on guard against assuming that respondents have prior knowledge or understanding of a subject. If we do otherwise we risk getting many answers which have little basis in fact. The Metallic Metals illustration may be challenged as an unusual case, but Payne cites a Gallup report where 45 percent of the persons surveyed did not know what a "lobbyist in Washington" was, and 88 percent could not give a correct description of "jurisdictional strike."[8] However, we can probably get opinion statements on these topics from most respondents.

There is another side to this problem. In some studies the degree of respondent expertise can be substantial, and simplified explanations are inappropriate. For example, in asking the general public about gross margins in men's wear stores, we must be sure that the respondent understands the nature of gross margin. In a survey of merchants, however, such questions

---

[7] Sam Gill, "How Do You Stand on Sin?" *Tide,* March 14, 1947, p. 72.

[8] Stanley Payne, *The Art of Asking Questions* (Princeton, N.J.: Princeton University Press, 1951), p. 18.

and explanations are not needed. The question designer should consider the respondent information level when determining the content and appropriateness of a question.

The adequacy problem also occurs when we ask questions that overtax the respondent's recall ability. Most of us cannot recall much that has happened in the past, except when it had some dramatic quality. We might well remember the first brand of cigarettes we smoked, and much about the circumstances of the event, yet be unable to recall much about later brand usage changes. If the events surveyed are of incidental interest to respondents, they will probably be unable to recall them correctly even a short time later. Boyd and Westfall report that an unaided recall question, "What radio programs did you listen to last night?" might locate as little as 10 percent of those who actually listened to a program.[9]

The adequacy of answers also depends on our achieving the proper balance between generality and specificity. We often ask questions in terms too general and detached from respondent experiences. Is asking for average annual consumption making an unrealistic demand for generalization on persons who do not think in these terms? Would it be wiser to ask how many times the product was used last week or last month? Too often we ask respondents to recall individual use experiences over an extended period of time and to average them for us. This is asking interviewees to do our work and can only encourage substantial response errors. It may also discourage participation in the study.

We also face the danger of being too specific. We may ask about movie attendance for the last week when this is too short a time span on which to base attendance estimates. It may be better to ask about attendance, say, for the last month. There are no firm rules about this generality-specificity problem. Developing the right level of generality depends upon the situation and the art and experience of the question designer.

The ability of respondents to answer adequately is also often distorted by questions whose content is biased by what is included or omitted. The question may explicitly mention only the positive or negative aspects of the topic, or make unwarranted assumptions about the respondent's position. Consider, for example, an experiment in which the following two forms of a question were asked:

A. What is your favorite brand of ice cream? _____
B. Some people have a favorite brand of ice cream while others do not have a favorite brand. In which group are you? (please check)
_____ I have a favorite brand of ice cream.
_____ I do not have a favorite brand of ice cream.

[9] Unaided recall gives respondents no clues as to possible answers, while aided recall gives them a list of radio programs which played last night and then asks them which they had heard. See Harper W. Boyd, Jr., and Ralph Westfall, *Marketing Research*, 3d ed. (Homewood, Ill.: Richard D. Irwin, Inc., 1972), p. 293.

What is your favorite brand (if you have a favorite)? _____

_____ .

Fifty-seven randomly chosen graduate business students answered version A and 56 answered version B. Their responses are shown in the accompanying table.

Response	Version A	Version B
Gave a favorite brand	77%*	39%*
Gave a favorite flavor rather than a brand	19	18
Have no favorite brand	4	43
Total	100%	100%
	n = 57	56

* Significant difference at the 0.001 level.

The probable cause of the wide difference in brand preference is that A is a leading question. It assumes, and by this assumption suggests, that everyone has a favorite brand of ice cream and should report it. Version B indicates that the respondent need not have a favorite.

A deficiency in both versions is that about one respondent in five misinterpreted the meaning of "brand." This misinterpretation cannot be attributed to low education, low intelligence, or nonexposure to the topic. The subjects were students who had studied at least one course in marketing in which branding was prominently treated. Word confusion difficulties will be considered further in a later section.

Will the Respondents Answer Adequately? Even if respondents have the information, they may be unwilling to give it. Some topics are considered too sensitive to discuss with strangers. These will vary from person to person, but one study suggests that the most sensitive topics concern money matters and family life.[10] More than one fourth of those interviewed mentioned these as the topics about which they would be "least willing to answer questions." Respondents of lower socioeconomic status also included political matters in this "least willing" list. Respondents may also be unwilling to give correct answers for ego reasons. Many tend to exaggerate their incomes, autos owned, social status, and the amount of high-prestige literature they read. They minimize their ages and the amount of low-prestige literature they read. Many respondents are also reluctant to make an effort to give an adequate response. Often this will occur when they see the topic as irrelevant to their own interests or to their perception of the survey's purpose. They participate halfheartedly, often answer with "don't know," give negative replies, refuse to be interviewed, or give stereotyped responses.

---

[10] Gideon Sjoberg, "A Questionnaire on Questionnaires," *Public Opinion Quarterly,* vol. 18 (Winter 1954), p. 425.

The researcher's challenge is to develop approaches to overcome these trouble areas. In general, three approaches can be used to secure more complete and truthful information: (1) Motivate the respondent to provide appropriate information, (2) change the design of the questioning process, and (3) use methods other than questioning to secure the data.

Motivation. The first requirement for increasing motivation is to build good rapport with the respondent. Most information can be secured by direct undisguised questioning if a good rapport has been developed. More will be said about techniques in Chapter 10, but good rapport is particularly useful in building respondent interest in the project, and the more interest respondents have, the more cooperation they will give. We can also overcome respondent unwillingness by providing some material compensation for cooperation. This approach has been especially successful in mail surveys.

We can also increase respondents' motivations by assuring them that answers are confidential. One approach is to give discreet assurances, both by question wording and interviewer comments and actions, that all types of behavior, attitudes, and positions on controversial or sensitive subjects are acceptable and normal. Where it can be said truthfully, we can also assure the respondents that their answers will be used only in combined statistical totals. In addition, if they are convinced that their replies contribute to some important purpose they are more likely to be candid, even with taboo topics.

Redesign. We can also redesign the questioning process to improve the quality of the answers. For example, we might demonstrate that confidentiality is a fact by using a group administration of questionnaires, accompanied by some sort of ballot box collection procedure. Even in face-to-face interviews the respondent may fill in a part of the questionnaire containing the sensitive information, and then seal the entire instrument in an envelope. While this approach does not guarantee confidentiality, it does suggest it. We can also develop appropriate questioning sequences which will more adroitly lead a respondent from "safe" questions gradually to those that are more sensitive.

Indirect questioning is one of the most widely used approaches by which opinions on sensitive topics are secured. The respondents are asked how "other people" or "people around here" feel about a topic. It is assumed that the respondents will reply in terms of their own attitudes and experiences, but this is by no means certain. For example, it may give a good measure of the majority opinion on a topic but fail either to reflect the views of the respondent or of minority segments.

With certain topics it may be possible to secure answers by using a sort of proxy code. For example, when we seek family income classes we can hand the respondent a card with income brackets like:

A . . . . .Under $10,000 per year
B . . . .$10,000 to $19,999 per year
C . . . .$20,000 to $29,999 per year
D . . . .$30,000 and over per year

The respondent is then asked to report the appropriate bracket as either A, B, C, or D. For some reason respondents are more willing to provide such an obvious proxy measure than to give actual dollar values.

Other Approaches. Finally, it may be determined that questioning will not secure the information needed. A classic example in survey literature concerns a survey to determine magazines read by respondents. An unusually high rate was reported for prestige magazines and an unusually low rate was reported for pulp magazines. The study was revised so that, instead of being interviewed, the subjects were asked to contribute their older magazines to a charity drive. This collection gave a much more realistic estimate of readership of both types of magazines.[11] A classic work on the use of similar unobtrusive measures cites many other types of research situations where a variety of techniques have been used to secure more valid information than was possible from a survey.[12]

Question Wording

The difficulties brought about by the problems of question wording exceed most other sources of distortion in surveys. They have led one social scientist to conclude,

> To many who worked in the Research Branch it soon became evident that error or bias attributable to sampling and to methods of questionnaire administration were relatively small as compared with other types of variations—especially variation attributable to different ways of wording questions.[13]

While it is impossible to say which wording of a question is best, we can point out a number of problem areas which cause respondent confusion and measurement error. The diligent question designer will put a given question through many revisions before it satisfies the following six challenges:[14]

1. Is the question stated in terms of a shared vocabulary?
2. Is the question clear?
3. Are there unstated or misleading assumptions?
4. Is there biased wording?
5. Is there the right degree of personalization?
6. Are adequate alternatives presented?

---

[11] Percival White, *Market Analysis* (New York: McGraw-Hill Book Co., Inc., 1921).

[12] Eugene J. Webb, Donald T. Campbell, Richard D. Schwartz, and Lee Sechrest, *Unobtrusive Measures: Nonreactive Research in the Social Sciences* (Chicago: Rand McNally & Company, 1966).

[13] S. A. Stouffer et al., *Measurement and Prediction, Studies in Social Psychology in World War II*, vol. 4 (Princeton, N.J.: Princeton University Press, 1950), p. 709.

[14] An excellent example of the question revision process is presented in Payne, *The Art of Asking Questions*, pp. 214–25. This example illustrates that a relatively simple question can go through as many as 41 different versions before being judged satisfactory.

Shared Vocabulary. A survey is ultimately an exchange in which the objective is a complete and accurate communication of ideas between interviewer and respondent.[15] Each must understand what the other says, and this is possible only if the vocabulary used is common to both parties. Two types of problems arise in this context. First, the words must be simple enough to allow adequate communication with persons of limited education. This is dealt with by reducing the level of word difficulty to basic English; more will be said on this in the section on word clarity.

The second problem is one of technical language. Even highly educated respondents are at a loss to answer questions stated in unfamiliar technical terms. A second facet of the technical language problem concerns possible deficiencies on the part of the interviewer. In one study of how corporation executives handled various financial problems it was necessary that interviewers be able to talk in technical financial terms. This presented the researcher with two alternatives—hire persons knowledgeable in finance and teach them interviewing skills, or teach financial concepts to experienced interviewers.[16]

Question Clarity. It is a frustrating experience when we find that people misunderstand a question which we have painstakingly written. This is partially a problem of the shared vocabularies already mentioned. Beyond this, however, are the problems of understanding long and complex sentences and involved phraseology. The other requirements of question design (need to be explicit, to present alternatives, and to explain meanings) all contribute to longer and more involved sentences.[17]

Payne suggests that one of the great difficulties in question wording is in the choice of words to use. He argues that questions to be asked of the general public should be restricted to the most common 2,000 words in the English language.[18] Even the use of simple words is not enough. Many of these words have vague references or meanings which must be determined from their use context. A question was asked of radio repairmen, "How many radio sets did you repair last month?" This may appear to be an unambiguous question, but respondents interpreted it in two ways. Some viewed it as a question of them alone, while others interpreted it as a more inclusive "you," indicating the total output of the shop. Typical of the many problem words are "any," "could-would-should," "fair," "near," "often," and "average." Payne recommends that, after we have stated a question as precisely as possible, we should test each word with the following six challenges:

1. Does it mean what we intend?
2. Does it have other meanings?

---

[15] Robert L. Kahn and Charles F. Cannell, *The Dynamics of Interviewing* (New York: John Wiley & Sons, Inc., 1957), p. 108.

[16] Ibid., p. 110.

[17] More will be said on the general problems of readability in Chapter 14.

[18] Payne, *The Art of Asking Questions,* p. 140.

3. If so, does the context make the intended meaning clear?
4. Does the word have more than one pronunciation?
5. Is there any word or similar pronunciation that might be confused?
6. Is a simpler word or phrase suggested?[19]

Assumptions. Many problems of question wording can be traced to our making unwarranted assumptions. The difficulties from assuming that the respondents know or understand key words or phrases have already been mentioned. In the Prince Corporation study what percent of the population would understand the term "conglomerate," or "multinational company"? We cause other problems when we use "blab" words—abstract concepts that have many overtones and emotional qualifications.[20] Unless words have concrete referents their meanings are too vague for the researcher's needs. Examples of such words are "business," "government," and "society." Suppose that in the Prince Corporation study we ask the question, "How involved is business in the affairs of our society?" What is meant by "involved?" What parts of "society?" Is there such a thing as "business" per se?

Inherent in word meaning problems is also the matter of frame of reference. Each of us understands concepts, words, and expressions in the light of one's own experience. A classic example of the problems this can bring appeared in research conducted by the U.S. Bureau of Census to determine the number of people in the labor market. To learn whether a person was employed they asked the question "Did you do any work for pay or profit last week?" The researchers erroneously assumed that there would be a common frame of reference between interviewer and respondents on the meaning of "work." Unfortunately many persons viewed themselves primarily as housewives, students, or such. They failed to report that they also worked at a job during the week. This difference in frame of reference resulted in a consistent underestimation of the number of persons working in the United States.

The single question was replaced by two questions, the first of which sought a statement on the respondent's major activity during the week. If the respondent gave a nonwork classification, a second question was asked to determine if he or she had done any work for pay in addition to this major activity. This revision increased the estimate of total employment by more than one million persons, with about one half of them working 35 hours or more per week.[21]

Controlling the frame of reference can be approached in two ways. First, the interviewer may seek to learn the frame of reference used by the respondent. For example, when asking respondents to evaluate their reasons for judging a labor contract offer, it is necessary to learn the frames of reference

---

[19] Ibid., p. 141.

[20] Ibid., p. 149.

[21] Gertrude Bancroft and Emmett H. Welch, "Recent Experiences with Problems of Labor Force Measurement," *Journal of the American Statistical Association,* vol. 41 (1946), pp. 303–12.

they use. Is the labor offer being evaluated in terms of the specific offer being made, the failure of a management to respond to other demands, the personalities involved, or the personal economic pressures that have resulted from a long strike?

We might also specify the frame of reference for the respondent. For example, in asking for an opinion about the new labor contract offer, we might specify that the question concerns the size of the wage offer, the sincerity of management's offer, or whatever other frames of reference are of interest.

Biased Wording. Bias is the distortion of responses in one direction. It can result from many of the other problems already discussed, but word choice is often a major source. Obviously such words as "communist," "American," and the like must be used with great care. Strong adjectives can be particularly distorting. One alleged opinion survey, concerned with the subject of preparation for death, included the following question: "Do you think that decent, low-cost funerals are sensible?" Who could be against anything that is "decent" or "sensible?" There is a question as to whether this was a legitimate survey or a burial service sales compaign, but it shows how suggestive an adjective can be.

We can also strongly bias the respondent by using prestige names in a question. For example, in a survey on whether the War and Navy Departments should be combined into a single Defense Department, one form said, "General Eisenhower says the Army and Navy should be combined . . ." while the other version omitted his name. In the first version (name included) 49 percent of the respondents approved of having one department, while in the second version only 29 percent favored one department.[22]

Other ways that we can bias include the use of superlatives, slang expressions, and fad words. These are best excluded unless they are critical to the objective of the question. Ethnic references should also be stated with care.

Personalization. How personalized should a question be? Should we ask "What would *you* do about . . . ?" or should we ask "What would *people* do about . . . ?" The effect of personalization is shown by an example reported by Cantril.[23] A split test was made of a question concerning people's attitudes about the expansion of our armed forces in 1940.

Should the United States do any of the following at this time?
   (A) Increase our army further, even if it means more taxes.
   (B) Increase our army further, even if you have to pay a special tax.

Eighty-eight percent of those answering question A felt we should increase the army, while only 79 percent of those answering question B were in favor of increasing the army.

---

[22] National Opinion Research Center, *Proceedings of the Central City Conference on Public Opinion Research* (Denver, Colo.: University of Denver, 1946), p. 73.

[23] Hadley Cantril, ed., *Gauging Public Opinion* (Princeton, N.J.: Princeton University Press, 1944), p. 48.

These and other examples show that responses are changed by personalizing questions, but it is not clear whether this is for better or for worse. We often cannot tell which answer is superior. Perhaps the best that can be said is that when either form is acceptable, we should choose that which appears to present the issues more realistically. If there are doubts, then split versions should probably be used.

Adequate Alternatives?   Have we adequately expressed the alternatives with respect to the point of the question? It is usually wise to express each alternative explicitly in order to avoid bias. Payne illustrates this problem well with a pair of questions which were asked of matched samples of respondents.[24] The forms used were:

(A) Do you think most manufacturing companies that lay off workers during slack periods could arrange things to avoid layoffs and give steady work right through the year?

(B) Do you think most manufacturing companies that lay off workers in slack periods could avoid layoffs and provide steady work right through the year, or do you think layoffs are unavoidable?

	A	B
Company could avoid layoffs	63%	35%
Could not avoid layoffs	22	41
No opinion	15	24

Toward Better Questions.   There is no substitute for a thorough understanding of question wording problems. Beyond this, however, there are several things we can do to help improve survey results. At the original question drafting we could try our hand at developing positive, negative, and neutral versions of each question. This practice dramatizes the problems of bias. Sometimes we may even choose to use one of the extreme versions. For example, if we ask people about their children we want our question statement *to encourage* the mention of all children.

Once we have developed a set of questions (including some with the same purpose) we need then to test and revise them. Inexperienced researchers normally underestimate the need for this sequence of design-test-revise. Revising a question three or more times is not unusual. Finally, if there is still some doubt as to which version of a question is the more appropriate, we should use different question versions which go to matched or random selections of the respondents.

Response Structure

A third major decision area in question design is the degree and form of structure imposed on responses. The options range from open (free choice of

---

[24] Payne, *The Art of Asking Questions,* pp. 7–8.

words) to closed (specified alternatives). Free responses, in turn, range from the case in which the respondents express themselves extensively to that in which the freedom is to choose one word in a "fill-in" question. Closed responses typically are categorized as dichotomous or multiple choice.

Situational Determinants. Kahn and Cannell suggest that five situational factors affect the decision whether to use open or closed response questions.[25] They are:

1. Objectives of the interview.
2. Respondent's level of information about the topic.
3. Degree respondent has thought through the topic.
4. Ease of communication and motivation of respondent to talk.
5. Degree to which the above respondent factors are known to the interviewer.

If the objective of the question is only to classify the respondent on some stated point of view then the closed form will serve well. For example, if we are interested only in whether a respondent approves or disapproves of a certain corporate policy, a closed response form will provide this answer. Such a response would ignore the full scope of respondent's opinion and its antecedents. If our objective was to explore this wider territory then an open response form would be more desirable.

As mentioned earlier, open response questions are appropriate when the objective is to discover opinions and degrees of knowledge. They are also appropriate when the interviewer seeks sources of information, dates of events, suggestions, or when probes are used to secure more information.

When the topic of a question is likely to be outside of the respondent's experience the open end question may be the better way to learn his or her level of information. Open end questions also help to determine certainty of feelings and expressions of intensity, although well designed closed questions can do the same.

If a respondent has developed a clear opinion on the topic the closed response question does well. If this process of thinking out an answer has not been done, the open end question may give the respondent a chance to think over a reply, and to elaborate and revise it.

Experience has shown that closed questions typically take less motivation and the process of answering is less threatening to respondents. On the other hand, the response alternatives sometimes suggest which answer is appropriate; in this sense it may be biasing.

Finally, it may be better to use open end questions when the interviewer does not have a clear idea of respondent frame of reference or level of information. Such conditions are likely to occur in exploratory research or the pilot stage of a study. Closed response questions are better when there is a

---

[25] Kahn and Cannell, *Dynamics of Interviewing,* p. 132.

clear frame of reference, the respondent's level of information is predictable, and the researcher believes the respondent understands the topic.

Two-Way Questions. While the open response question has many advantages, closed questions are generally preferable in large surveys. They reduce the variability of response, make fewer demands on interviewer skills, are less costly to administer, and are much easier to code and analyze. In addition, after adequate exploration and testing, we can often develop closed questions which will perform as effectively as open questions in many situations. In fact, experimental studies suggest that closed questions are equal to or superior to open response questions in many more applications than is commonly believed.[26]

Should a closed question call for a two-way or multiple choice response? Often this is a simple decision dictated by the nature of the problem. For example, there may be a clearly dichotomous topic: Something is a fact or it is not, a respondent can either recall or not recall information. In many two-way questions, however, there are potential alternatives beyond the stated two. For example, the respondent may answer "don't know," "no opinion," or even "in-between." In other cases there are two opposing or complementary choices, but there may also be a qualified choice ("yes, if X doesn't occur," or "sometimes yes and sometimes no," or "about the same"). Thus, two-way questions often become multiple choice in fact, and these additional responses should be included.

We may omit the middle ground response if we are interested in which direction the respondent is leaning. We may also omit the middle answer when the topic is one about which people tend to retreat to a safe middle ground if it is available. Dichotomous questions suggest opposing responses, but this is not always the best arrangement. One response may be so unlikely that it would be better to adopt the middle ground alternative as one of the two choices. For example, if we ask respondents whether they are underpaid or overpaid, we are not likely to get many agreements with the latter choice. The choices might better be underpaid and paid about right.

Multiple Choice Questions. Multiple choice questions are clearly appropriate in those cases where there are more than two alternatives, or where we seek gradations of preference, interest, or agreement. Multiple choice questions can be very efficient, but they also present some unique design problems. One vexing problem is that the list of choices may not be exhaustive. Respondents may want to give an answer which is not one of the alternatives. This can occur when the desired response is one which combines two or more of the listed individual alternatives. For example, we might ask whether mine safety rules should be determined by the (1) mine companies, (2) miners, (3) federal government, or (4) state government. Many people

---

[26] Barbara Snell Dohrenwend, "Some Effects of Open and Closed Questions on Respondents' Answers," *Human Organization,* vol. 24 (Summer 1965), pp. 175–84.

may believe that such rules should be set by two or more of these groups acting jointly, but the question does not include this response option.

A second problem occurs when some response category has not been anticipated. For example, the "union" has not been mentioned in the alternatives on mine safety laws. Many respondents would lump this alternative with "miners," but others will view it as a separate category. Some respondents may feel that certain rules should be set by a federal agency, others by industry-national union negotiation, and still others through local management-worker shop committees. When the researcher tries to provide for all possible opinions the list can become exhausting as well as exhaustive. We can guard against this proliferation by determining the major specific choices through pretesting. Then we add the category "other (please specify) _____" to provide for all other options.

Another problem in alternative selection occurs when the choices are not mutually exclusive (the respondent sees two or more responses as overlapping). For example, in a multiple choice question asking students why they went to a certain college the following response alternatives might be listed about the chosen school:

1. Good academic reputation.
2. Specific program of study desired.
3. Enjoyable campus life there.
4. Many friends from home attend.
5. High quality of the faculty.

It is likely that items (1) and (5) will be viewed as overlapping, and some may see items (3) and (4) in the same way.

It is also important to seek a fair balance in choices. One study has shown that an off-balance presentation of alternatives biases results in favor of the more heavily offered side.[27] For example, if there are four gradations of alternatives on one side of a question and two on the other side there will be a tendency to bias responses toward the better represented side.

A third design problem in multiple choice questions is the assuring that all alternatives are reasonable. This is particularly the case when choices are numbers or identifications. For example, if we asked, "Which of the following numbers is closest to the number of students enrolled in American colleges and universities today?" the following choices might be presented:

1.   75,000.
2.   750,000.
3.   7,500,000.
4. 25,000,000.
5. 75,000,000.

---

[27] Cantril, *Gauging Public Opinion,* p. 31.

It should be obvious to most respondents that at least three of these choices are not reasonable in the light of our general knowledge about the population of the United States.

A fourth problem concerns the order of choices. Numbers are normally presented in order of magnitude. This reasonable practice tends to introduce a bias. The respondent assumes that if there is a list of five numbers, the correct answer will lie somewhere in the middle of the group. This is not an unreasonable assumption. Researchers often add a couple of incorrect numbers on each side of the correct one. The obvious way to counteract this bias is to put the correct number at one of the extremes more often.

Order bias with nonnumeric data leads to a tendency to choose first or last alternatives over the middle ones. This bias can be counteracted by using the split ballot technique. A simple way to carry this out, in face-to-face interviews, is to list the alternatives on a card to be handed to the respondent when asking the question. Cards with different choice orders can be alternated to assure positional balance. It is better to leave the choices unnumbered on these cards so that respondents reply by giving the choice itself rather than its identifying number. It is probably a good practice to use cards in this manner any time that question alternatives are four or more. It saves interviewer reading time and assures a more valid answer by keeping the full range of choices in front of the respondent.

In most multiple choice questions there is also a problem of assuring that the choices represent a unidimensional scale. That is, the alternatives all represent different aspects of the same *conceptual dimension.* To illustrate, the foregoing suggested list for choosing a college included features associated with a college which might be attractive to a student. This list, while not exhaustive, illustrated aspects of the concept of "college attractiveness." But it did not mention other concepts which might affect a school attendance decision. Parents and peer advice, local alumni efforts, and school advisor suggestions may influence the decision, but these represent a conceptual dimension different from "school attractiveness."

All types of response styles have their advantages and disadvantages. All forms are often found in the same questionnaire, and the situational factors mentioned earlier are the major decision guides in this matter. There is a tendency, however, to use closed response forms in preference to the more flexible open response type.

Question Sequence

The design of survey questions is also strongly affected by the need to relate each question to the others in the instrument. Question sequencing is particularly important. The basic principle to guide sequence decisions is: *The nature and needs of the respondent must determine the sequence of questions and the organization of the schedule.* Certain guides may be suggested by which to implement this principle of respondent orientation. Some of the major ones are:

1. The question process must quickly awaken interest and motivate the respondent to participate willingly and fully in the interview.
2. The respondent should not be confronted by early requests for information which might be considered personal or ego threatening.
3. The questioning process should begin with simple items and move to the more complex, and from general items to the more specific.
4. Changes in frame of reference should be minimal and should be clearly pointed out.

The interviewer's first challenge is to awaken the respondent's interest in the study and motivate participation. We try to bring this about by choosing early-interview questions that are attention-getting and not controversial in subject or thrust. If the questions have human interest value so much the better. It is possible that the early questions will contribute hard data to the major study objective, but their major task is to overcome the motivational barrier.

The second rule concerns the inappropriate requesting of information too early in the interview. Two forms of this error are common. There is usually a need to ask for personal classification information about respondents. They normally will provide this data, but the request should be made at the end of the interview. If sought immediately it often causes respondents to feel threatened, dampening their interest and motivation to continue. It is also a dangerous practice to ask any question at the start that might appear to be personal or private. For example, respondents in one survey were asked whether they suffered from insomnia problems. When the question was asked immediately after the interviewer's introductory remarks about 12 percent of those interviewed admitted to having insomnia. When a matched sample was asked the same question after two buffer questions (neutral questions designed chiefly to establish rapport with the respondent) 23 percent admitted having insomnia problems.[28]

A third rule is to place simpler questions first and to move progressively to more complex ones. Even simple questions that require much thought should be deferred until later. These recommendations can help reduce the number of "don't know" responses that are so prevalent in the early part of interviews.

The procedure of moving from general to more specific questions is sometimes called the "funnel approach." The objectives of this procedure are to learn the respondent's frame of reference and to extract the full range of desired information while limiting the distortion effect of earlier questions on

---

[28] Frederick J. Thumin, "Watch for These Unseen Variables," *Journal of Marketing*, vol. 26 (July 1962), pp. 58–60.

later ones. Cannell and Kahn illustrate this process with the following series of questions:

1. How do you think this country is getting along in its relations with other countries?
2. How do you think we are doing in our relations with Russia?
3. Do you think we ought to be dealing with Russia differently than we are now?
4. (If yes) what should we be doing differently?
5. Some people say we should get tougher with Russia and others think we are too tough as it is; how do you feel about it?[29]

The first question introduces the general subject and provides some insight into the respondent's frame of reference. The second question narrows the concern to a single country, while the third and fourth seek views on how the United States should deal with Russia. The fifth question illustrates a specific opinion area and would be asked only if this particular point of "toughness" had not been covered in earlier responses.

In addition to the problem of "general-specific sequencing," there is also a risk of interaction whenever two or more questions are related. Cantril reports on a survey which had this problem. The two questions shown in the accompanying table were asked in a national survey at the time of the start of World War II:[30]

| | | Percent Answering Yes | |
	Question	A Asked First	B Asked First
A.	Should the United States permit its citizens to join the French and British Armies?	45%	40%
B.	Should the United States permit its citizens to join the German Army?	31%	22%

Apparently, if respondents first endorsed enlistments with the Allies, some felt obliged to extend this same privilege to joining the Germans. Where the decision was first made against joining the German Army, a percentage of the respondents felt constrained from approving the option to join the Allies.

Finally, questions should be arranged so that there is a minimum of shifting in subject matter and frame of reference. Respondents often interpret questions in the light of earlier questions and will miss shifts of perspective or subject unless they are clearly stated. Respondents fail to listen carefully and

---

[29] Charles F. Cannell and Robert L. Kahn, "The Collection of Data by Interviewing," chap. 8 in Leon Festinger and Daniel Katz, eds., *Research Methods in the Behavioral Sciences* (New York: Holt, Rinehart and Winston, 1953), p. 349.

[30] Cantril, *Gauging Public Opinion*, p. 28.

frequently jump to conclusions about the import of a given question before it is even completely stated. In such cases their answers are strongly influenced by the frame of reference which they have been holding. Any change in subject by the interviewer may not register with them unless made strong and obvious.

REASON ANALYSIS

Questions to determine "reasons for" present a difficult challenge to the question designer. A simple "why?" to determine the causes of an action or opinion is easy to use, but it throws the conceptualization and definition task to the respondent. The resulting answers typically are partial, from various frames of reference, and often not germane to the researcher's objectives. There are more effective approaches by which causal relationships in surveys may be determined. One approach is cross classification and other forms of correlation; these will be discussed in Chapters 12 and 13. A second approach is *reason analysis* which is defined as "a set of procedures used in survey research to construct a causal explanation for the actions, decision, or intentions of individuals."[31] Reason analysis is uniquely appropriate for many research situations. Kadushin suggests that

> If one wants to know how an action came to be—what steps were taken and what the key choices were; what the actor thought he was doing and how he felt about it; what influences were present and what triggered the action; and, finally, what outcomes the actor expected—then no technique other than reason analysis can be used.[32]

Zeisel suggests that the process of reason analysis involves five steps:

1. Formulation of the problem in terms of specific research purposes.
2. Selecting the type of action.
3. Development of the accounting scheme.
4. Interviewing for reasons.
5. Statistical assessment and interpretation.[33]

The discussion which follows draws heavily upon Zeisel's analysis, but only the first three of these steps will be discussed.

Problem Formulation. The first step facing the researcher is to determine the relevant range of factors to include in the study. The major source for this decision is the study's research objective. For example, if we are

---

[31] Reprinted with permission of Macmillan Publishing Co., Inc. from "Reason Analysis" by Charles Kadushin in David L. Sills, ed., *The International Encyclopedia of the Social Sciences,* vol. 13, p. 338. Copyright © 1968 by Crowell Collier and Macmillan, Inc.

[32] Ibid., p. 338.

[33] Hans Zeisel, *Say It with Figures.* Rev. 4th ed. (New York: Harper & Brothers, Publishers, 1957), p. 136.

studying reasons for the purchase of snack foods we may concentrate on certain areas of consumption and conditions of use if our objective is to provide input for an advertising campaign. In this case we will be more interested in the immediate factors that precipitate brand choice. If we were interested in improving nutritional levels the direction of questioning would be quite different. In this latter case, for example, we might be much more interested in biographic or historical determinants that have fostered basic consumption habits.

Selecting the Type of Action. The preliminary analysis of actions, opinions, or intentions often will indicate that there are various types of respondents who need to be dealt with differently. In a study of snack food eaters we may find that there are people who eat snacks selectively as to time, occasion, and product; others may be habitual consumers who eat snacks often, in volume, and with little discrimination to product, time, or occasion. While we may be interested in analyzing the reasons behind actions and decisions in both groups, they may be so different as to require different sets of reason questions. In such a case a filter question or two should be used to identify the classification of snack eater, followed by separate questioning sets for the different classes of respondents.

Developing the Accounting Scheme. To employ reason analysis we must develop an *accounting scheme*—an organized list of factors that are believed to be relevant causes or influences upon some action, opinion, or intention. Zeisel refers to these factors as "dimensions of the action or attitude under study. . . . As long as specific reasons have in common the defining feature of such a single dimension, they are to be treated together, separate from reasons in another dimension."[34] He illustrates a simple accounting concept with a survey designed to find out why women used a particular face cream. From the answers secured he was able to extract three logical dimensions which were relevant for this study. They were:

1. To the respondent—special skin conditions or certain preferences, prejudices, etc.
2. To the product—its qualities, its supposed effects, its prices, etc.
3. To the source through which the respondent learned of the product or its qualities.[35]

From this and similar studies Zeisel generalizes that most simpler purchase propositions can be adequately analyzed with a three-dimension accounting scheme. The dimension of *respondent's condition* he generalizes to embrace all of the respondent's motives prior to the decision to buy. The second major dimension concerns *attributes of the product or object,* while the third reflects *influences* that affect the course of the decision. These influences, in turn,

---

[34] Ibid., p. 138.
[35] Ibid., p. 139.

consist of the *channel* and *content* of *communication* subdimensions.[36] An accounting scheme suggested for a study of the purchase decisions of major appliances included similar elements; they were (1) line of rejection (includes reasons why the product was not selected), (2) lines of acceptance (includes those factors which led to the preference for a given brand), and (3) channels of influence (includes the sources of information which led either to rejection or acceptance).[37]

As an example of how the dimensions chosen must reflect the particular problem under study, four major categories were used in a study of reasons for choosing trial with or without jury. In this study the major dimensions were (1) ultimate advantage aimed at, (2) influences on decisions, (3) expected differences between judge and jury trial, and (4) the case.[38]

Selltiz, Wrightsman, and Cook suggest that accounting schemes often include as many as five broad classes of considerations. They suggest (1) the history of the act or feeling, (2) the characteristics in a given entity that provoke a given reaction, (3) the supports for the beliefs, feelings, and so forth, about a given entity, (4) the personal desires, motives, values, or interests involved in a given reaction, and (5) the specific situations and circumstances in which a given reaction occurs.[39]

Whatever the accounting scheme developed, it must reflect the specific objectives of the study as well as the specific topic of concern. It will also often be necessary to incorporate the time element into the scheme to recognize that individual influences and motives have different impacts at various stages in the decision process. To illustrate the detail that might result from the accounting scheme approach, consider a study reported in the pioneering work on reason analysis.[40] This survey was made of people who attended movies. Preliminary study indicated that there were two types of movie attenders—those who were habitual moviegoers and those who attended because of a desire to see a particular movie. The questionnaire developed to account for these two types and to provide adequate information for the accounting scheme is as follows:

Do you go primarily (I) just to go to a movie, or (II) because of a certain picture?

I_____   II_____   Both_____

If I or both:
1.   When did you decide to go to a movie?
2.   Why and under what circumstances did you decide?

---

[36] Ibid., pp. 141–42.

[37] Ibid., pp. 142–43.

[38] Ibid., p. 143.

[39] Claire Selltiz, Lawrence S. Wrightsman, and Stuart W. Cook, *Research Methods in Social Relations.* 3d ed. (New York: Holt, Rinehart and Winston, 1976), p. 308.

[40] Paul F. Lazarsfeld, "The Art of Asking Why," *National Marketing Review,* vol. 1, no. 1 (Summer 1935), pp. 26–38.

3. (If not yet inserted) When and how was your company chosen?
4. As to the special theater or show: (Check.)
   a. Was it proposed by someone in the company?_____
   b. Did you have it in mind yourself?_____
   c. Did you look for or get special advice or information?_____
      If (b), how did you know about it?_____
      If (c), where did you look for advice or information?_____
5. How many pictures were taken into consideration?
6. Which was more conducive: (Check.)
   a. the theatre_____
   b. the picture_____
   c. do not know_____
   Remarks for Interviewers: If b or c, ask question 7 first. If a, ask question 8 first. But ask both questions in any case.
7. What interested you in the picture? (Please try to remember all the details.)
8. What made the theater suitable to your choice?

If II:
1a. When did you learn about this picture?
2a. How did you learn about it?
3a. What interested you in it when you heard about it? (Please try to remember all the details.)
4a. (If not yet inserted) When and how was your company chosen?

In all cases:
1b. (If not yet inserted) When and under what circumstances was the final decision made? Why did you go at this particular time?
2b. What other uses of the time and money spent in seeing the movie were considered?

THE PRODUCT MANAGER STUDY

One team of students in a business research class decided to do a project on the product manager. They were all interested in the career prospects in product management and felt that the research would give them a better insight into this career path. Their orientation was summarized in the research objective statement: Provide an inventory of companies using product management, descriptive data on the nature and degree of product management, and information on how product managers are recruited, selected, and prepared for product management responsibilities.

The topic was approved as a semester project for the team. After some consideration of different approaches they decided to conduct a mail survey of the major corporations of the United States. As their sampling frame they used the *Fortune* magazine's top 1,000 manufacturing companies.

In order to define the research task further (and to start to limit it) they developed the following set of investigative questions:

1. What is the incidence of use of the product manager system? Included are:
   a. To what degree is it presently being used?
   b. Has it been used in the past and dropped?
   c. Was it considered and not adopted?
   d. What are future expectations regarding its use?
2. How are product managers recruited and selected?
3. What are the qualifications for employment as a product manager?
4. How does the product manager function in your company?
5. Classification information by which to analyze the above questions.

Questionnaire Development. The six team members developed the following procedure for designing the questionnaire. Having agreed upon the investigative questions, each member attempted to write measurement questions aimed at tapping the essence of each investigative question. Each measurement question was written on a 5×8 card in order to facilitate comparisons, revisions, additions, and deletions. At a meeting of the team all questions were reviewed, duplicates eliminated, and a general winnowing took place. After this process the remaining 31 questions were included in questionnaire draft 1, shown in Figure 8–1. In this first questionnaire draft there was no effort to place questions in sequence or to graphically present them as they would eventually be seen by respondents.

Figure 8–1: Preliminary Questionnaire, Product Manager Study—Draft 1

1. What is your position in the company?
2. Is your company engaged primarily in industrial products, consumer products, or both.
3. Does your company use product managers?
4. How many product managers does the company have?
5. How many products are assigned to one PM?
6. Would you please give or include a job description of your company's PM position.
7. How many brands does your company have?
8. Approximately what percentage of your company's brands have product managers?
9. What percentage of sales volume do the brands in question 8 account for as a whole?
10. How long have product managers been used in your company?
11. Has a PM system been used and dropped in your company? If yes, why was it dropped?
12. Has a PM system ever been considered but never adopted in your company? If yes, why was it not adopted?
13. Are there any plans for the adoption of a PM system in the future?
14. What percentage of your product managers come *directly* from each of the following sources? Campuses, within the company, other companies, other (list).

Figure 8–1 (continued)

---

15. If PMs come from within the company, what department or departments do they come from? Sales, marketing, production, advertising, other (list).

16. If PMs come from outside the company (other than campuses), what department or departments do they come from? Product manager, sales, marketing, production, advertising, other (list).

17. If PMs are recruited directly from campuses, what, if any, are typical degrees required?

18. Rank on a scale from 1 to 5 the relative importance of each of the following qualifications for a PM (1 denotes the greatest importance). Education, age, work experience, personality, creativity.

19. If PMs are recruited from within the company, what is the average age, length of work experience (with the company), and educational background?

20. If PMs are recruited from outside the company (not including campuses), what is the average age, length of work experience, and educational background?

21. What functions (e.g., advertising, pricing, etc.) does the PM actually perform in day-to-day activities, and what percentage of time is spent on each?

22. Of those functions listed in 21, which, if any, does the PM have *final* authority over?

23. To whom does the PM report?

24. Does your company have a structured training program for product management? If yes, please explain.

25. On the basis of which of the following is the PM evaluated? Market share, ROI, sales volume, profits, other (list).

26. What were the objectives of the company in instituting the PM concept?

27. How successful has the PM concept been in fulfilling the objectives set for it?

28. What were the characteristics of the PM concept which contributed to the fulfillment of these objectives?

29. What elements, if any, of the PM system did not adequately contribute to the fulfillment of the objectives?

30. What specific actions, if any, have been taken to deal with the inadequacies listed in 29?

31. If your company is currently planning any broad revisions in the present PM program, please describe.

After some discussion the team members concluded that the questionnaire would probably need to be three pages in length. In addition, a covering letter would require a page. They decided to use a printed cover letter and to incorporate it as the first page of the questionnaire. The combination would be printed on both sides of an 11 × 17 inch sheet of paper, folded in booklet form to 8 ½ × 11 size.

Each team member was assigned the individual task of translating draft 1 into a draft 2. In this new draft the questions should be in planned sequence, have response formats chosen, and graphic arrangements selected. These individual drafts were submitted to a subcommittee of three who used them as the basis for developing questionnaire draft 2. This is shown in Figure 8–2.

Figure 8–2: Product Manager Questionnaire—Draft 2

1. Does your company now use product managers? yes _____ no _____ If no, please go to question 17.
2. Would you please send a copy of your job description?
3. How many product managers does your company have? _____
4. What percentage of your total sales are accounted for by product managers? _____%
5. How long have product managers been used by your company? _____ years
6. What percentage of your personnel enter the product management program from the following sources?

   campuses _____%
   within the company _____%
   from elsewhere _____%

7. If product managers come from within the company or elsewhere, what department(s) do they come from?

   sales _____%
   marketing _____%
   production _____%
   advertising _____%
   other product management programs _____%
   advertising agencies _____%
   elsewhere _____%

8. If product managers are recruited directly from campuses, please rank the following degrees from 1 to 6, with 1 being the most desirable, 2 the next most desirable, and so forth?

   BS _____ areas _____
   AB _____ areas _____
   BSBA (BBA) _____ areas _____
   MA _____ areas _____
   MBA _____ areas _____
   PHD _____ areas _____

9. Briefly state what you consider to be an appropriate profile of a product manager recruited directly from the campus.

   age

   work experience (length and type)

   personal traits, i.e., personality, creativity, aggressiveness, etc.

   education

10. What do you consider to be an appropriate profile for a product manager recruited from within or from another company?

    age

    work experience (length and type)

    personal traits, i.e., personality, creativity, aggressiveness, etc.

    education

Figure 8–2 (continued)

---

11. To whom does the product manager report? _____

12. What percentage of his time does the product manager spend in various functionary areas, such as production, advertising, pricing, etc.? Please list.

13. Please rank the following on a scale of 1 to 5 (1 is most important), the criteria used in evaluating a product manager?
    _____ market share
    _____ return on investment
    _____ sales volume
    _____ profits
    _____ other (please explain) _____

14. Does the company have a structured training program? yes_____no_____ If yes, please describe.

15. What prompted your firm to initiate the product manager system?

16. Is your company currently planning any future revisions in the product manager system?
    yes _____ no _____ If yes, please explain.

17. Is your company primarily engaged in:
    industrial goods _____%
    food products _____%
    consumer package goods _____%
    consumer durable goods _____%
    automotive products _____%
    other (list)
    _____ _____%
    _____ _____%

18. What is your company's total sales volume? $_____
    If you answered the first question yes, you have completed the questionnaire. If your answer was no, please answer question 19. Thank you for your cooperation.

19. Please check which of the following best describes your company's use of product managers?
    _____ have never considered product managers
    _____ have considered, but never adopted product management
    _____ have used previously and discontinued
    _____ presently considering adoption of the system in the future

---

Draft 2 was reproduced and submitted to some other members of the research class for critique. In particular, comments and challenges were sought on (1) sources of confusion and vagueness; (2) question value (What useful information does the question provide? Not provide?); (3) appropriateness of the proposed response formats and suggestions for improvement; and (4) gaps in question coverage.

After this critique session a second subcommittee of the team was to revise the questionnaire. This resulted in questionnaire draft 3 which is not presented here. This was again reviewed by the full team and some modest changes made to give draft 4.

By this time the team members were anxious to test the questionnaire with "real respondents." Arrangements were made to have several local corporate executives complete the questionnaire that was left with them. Team members arranged to pick up the completed questionnaires and to interview the executives about their answers as well as any comments they had about the questions or the study. These experiences led to a revised draft 5. This testing process was repeated twice more with other executives, finally ending with draft 7 shown here as Figure 8–3. The limitations of time and money led the team to depend upon local product managers for testing rather than a full-scale dress rehearsal by mail. This decision limited the value of the pretesting but was accepted as a limitation of a student project.

The survey was sent to the top 1,000 manufacturing companies in the form described. Only one mailing was made because of time and money limitations. Usable returns numbered 492 at the cutoff point. Approximately 50 companies sent job descriptions of their product management positions.

SUMMARY

The versatility of the survey method is its greatest strength. It is usually the only practical way to gather opinions, intentions, knowledge, and similar private behaviors. Its dependency upon the respondent's verbal behavior is its greatest weakness. Not only may intentionally false information be given, but verbal behavior can also be dramatically changed by a wide variety of factors.

There are a number of choices to be made in designing a survey instrument. Survey research can be a face-to-face interview or it can be much less personal, using indirect media and self-administered questionnaires. The questioning process can be unstructured as with depth interviewing and similar approaches, or the questions can be clearly structured. Responses may be unstructured with open ended respondent answers or structured with the respondent choosing an answer from a set of listed possibilities. Finally, there is a decision as to the degree to which to disguise the objectives and intent of the question.

The development of a survey instrument is too often slighted by inexperienced researchers who feel that about anyone can do it. Question designing will be easier if the designer follows the research question hierarchy concept in question development. The logical process is usually a fractionation that begins with the management question, then moves on to the research question, the investigative questions, and, finally, to the measurement questions themselves.

Figure 8-3: Product Manager Questionnaire—Final Draft

WASHINGTON UNIVERSITY

ST. LOUIS, MISSOURI 63130

GRADUATE SCHOOL
OF BUSINESS ADMINISTRATION

Inside Address

Dear Sir:

We at the Washington Business School are interested in learning more about the actual recruitment and use of product or brand managers. Our objective is to help expand the body of knowledge about this important area of marketing.

To do this, of course, means going to someone such as yourself who *knows*. Your help with the few questions on the attached pages will take only a few minutes and will make a real contribution to the accuracy and success of this study.

Your reply will be treated in strict confidence and will be available only to my research staff and myself. Any publication will be only of statistical totals for groups of companies.

Your assistance will be greatly appreciated and will help us to know more about product management and to teach about it in a more relevant and effective manner.

Sincerely,

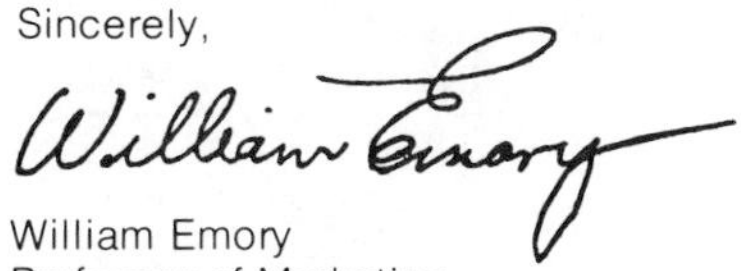

William Emory
Professor of Marketing

We define a *product manager* (also called brand manager, etc.) as one who is responsible for the integration and planning of a broad range of marketing functions (e.g., pricing, distribution, etc.) for a specific product, brand, or homogeneous group of products. The position usually has limited or no line authority, especially over the sales force.

1. Please indicate which of the following best describes your company/division's use of product managers.
    _____ we are currently using product managers
    _____ we have previously used product managers, but discontinued
    _____ we have considered the system, but never implemented it
    _____ presently considering adoption of the system in the future
    _____ we have never considered product managers
    If you are currently using product managers, please continue. If *you are not* currently using product managers you have completed the questionnaire. Thank you for your cooperation.

Figure 8–3 (continued)

2. Will you be answering the following for:
   (please check)
   _____ your company
   _____ your division

3. How many product managers (include all levels such as Group PM, PM, Assoc. PM, and Assistant PM) does your company/division employ? _____

4. How long have product managers been used by your company/division? _____ years

5. What percentage of your company/division total sales are accounted for by products controlled by product managers? _____%

6. From the following, please indicate whether the position exists in your company/division. Then, indicate the source from which the personnel at the various levels were obtained to fill that position. If you have a similar position, but with a different name, please indicate that position in the blank.

(please check)

| | Do You Have? | | | Major Sources | | |
| | | | | | Within Company | | |
	Yes	No	Cam-puses	Other PM Jobs	Other Jobs	Other Com-panies
Group PMs	_____	_____	_____	_____	_____	_____
PMs	_____	_____	_____	_____	_____	_____
Assoc. PMs	_____	_____	_____	_____	_____	_____
Asst. PMs	_____	_____	_____	_____	_____	_____
Other (specify)	_____		_____	_____	_____	_____

7. What is the typical age of your:
   group product managers _____ years
   product managers _____ years
   associate PMs _____ years
   assistant PMs _____ years

8. Of the following personal traits, would you please indicate the degree of importance in the evaluation of a candidate for a product management position.

(please check)

	Not Important	Desirable	Very Desirable	Essential
Leadership	_____	_____	_____	_____
Creativity	_____	_____	_____	_____
Aggressiveness	_____	_____	_____	_____
Analytical Ability	_____	_____	_____	_____
Communications Skill	_____	_____	_____	_____
Ability to work with others	_____	_____	_____	_____
Other _____	_____	_____	_____	_____

Figure 8–3 (continued)

9. (*If you recruit directly from campus*) Please indicate the importance of the following traits of a product manager candidate.

(please check)

	Not Important	Desirable	Very Desirable	Essential
Business Experience	_____	_____	_____	_____
High Grade Point Avg.	_____	_____	_____	_____
Extra Curricular Activities	_____	_____	_____	_____
MBA	_____	_____	_____	_____
Masters, technical	_____	_____	_____	_____
Bachelors, technical	_____	_____	_____	_____
Bachelors, business	_____	_____	_____	_____
Other (specify) _____	_____	_____	_____	_____

10. If you recruit into your PM, group from other jobs (either from your company or other companies) please indicate the importance of the following experiences (please check).

(please check)

Experience:	Not Important	Desirable	Very Desirable	Essential
Sales	_____	_____	_____	_____
Other Product Manager Programs	_____	_____	_____	_____
Other Marketing Positions	_____	_____	_____	_____
Production	_____	_____	_____	_____
Ad Agencies	_____	_____	_____	_____
Undergraduate Degree	_____	_____	_____	_____
Graduate Degree	_____	_____	_____	_____
Other (specify) _____	_____	_____	_____	_____

11. Please indicate the percentage of time a typical product manager spends in the following activities:

```
Advertising ........................ _____%
Pricing ........................... _____
Distribution ....................... _____
Packaging ......................... _____
Product Development ............... _____
Marketing Research ................ _____
Production Liaison ................. _____
Finance and budgeting ............. _____
Other (specify) _____ _____
Other (specify) _____ _____
         Total                    100%
```

Figure 8–3 (concluded)

12. Please indicate which of the following criteria are used in evaluating product managers in your company/division.

    a. _____ market share
          _____ return on investment
          _____ sales volume
          _____ dollar profits
          _____ other (please specify) _____
    b. which one is most important _____

13. Does your company/division have a structured training program for product managers? yes _____ no _____ (If yes, please describe.)

14. Is your company/division currently planning any revision in its product manager system? yes _____ no _____ (If yes, please describe.)

15. Judging from your company's experience, what do you feel is the major problem facing the product management system? _____

16. If would be most valuable to our studies, if you could supply a sample job description of your product manager positions.
    Are such available?
        _____ yes, examples enclosed
        _____ yes, examples sent under separate cover
        _____ not available

    Thank you for your assistance

17. If you would like a summary of the results of this survey please check here. _____

Three general classes of information are normally secured. The most important is the information of major topical concern. A second class is data concerning respondent characteristics and other information used chiefly for classification and analysis purposes. Finally, certain administrative information is needed.

Question construction has four critical decision areas. They are (1) question content, (2) question wording, (3) response form, and (4) question sequence. Question content should pass the following tests:

1. Should the question be asked?
2. Is the question of proper scope?
3. Can the respondent answer adequately?
4. Will respondents answer adequately?

Question wording difficulties exceed most other sources of distortion in surveys. Each question should pass the following six tests on wording:

1. Is the question stated in terms of a shared vocabulary?
2. Is the question clear?
3. Are there unstated or misleading assumptions?
4. Is there biased wording?
5. Is there the right degree of personalization?
6. Are adequate alternatives presented?

In response form the third major decision area, situational determinants are major choice factors. Five such determinants are:

1. Objectives of the interview.
2. Respondent's level of information about the topic.
3. Degree respondent has thought through the topic.
4. Ease of communication and motivation of respondent to talk.
5. Degree to which the above respondent factors are known to the interviewer.

Both two-way and multiple choice questions have their values and their deficiencies, but on balance the latter tend to be preferred if only because few questions have only two possible answers.

Question sequence can drastically affect respondent willingness to cooperate and the quality of responses received. Generally, the sequence should begin with efforts to awaken the respondent's interest in continuing the interview. Early questions should be simple rather than complex, easy rather than difficult, nonthreatening, and obviously germane to the announced objective of the study. Frame of reference changes should be minimal and questions should be sequenced in such a way that earlier questions do not distort the replies of later ones.

A special problem in question design is that of learning the reasons for actions or opinions. A simple "why" question is too often used and almost as often fails to secure the needed information. To measure reasons why, the researcher needs first to analyze the research objectives and the type of actions or opinions under study. In the context of this analysis an accounting scheme should be used. This is an organized list of factors believed to be relevant causes or influences upon the actions, attitudes, or intentions under study. When done in this manner, substantial causal information can be secured.

SUPPLEMENTAL READINGS

1. Berdie, Douglas R., and Anderson, John F. *Questionnaires: Design and Use.* Metuchen, N.J.: The Scarecrow Press, Inc., 1974. Chaps. 3 and 4 are on questionnaire design. Appendixes have four sample questionnaires. Also extensive bibliography.
2. Dillman, Don A. *Mail and Telephone Surveys.* New York: John Wiley & Sons, 1978. Chaps. 3, 4, and 6 are on question construction and questionnaire design. Extensive bibliography.
3. Kahn, Robert L., and Cannell, Charles F. *The Dynamics of Interviewing.* New York: John Wiley & Sons, Inc., 1957. Chaps. 5 and 6 cover questionnaire design.
4. Parten, Mildred. *Surveys, Polls, and Samples.* New York: Harper & Brothers, Publishers, 1950. Chap. 6 is on questionnaire design.
5. Payne, Stanley L. *The Art of Asking Questions.* Princeton, N.J.: Princeton University Press, 1951. An enjoyable book on the many problems found in developing useful survey questions. It is a classic.
6. Selltiz, Claire; Wrightsman, Lawrence S.; and Cook, Stuart W. *Research Methods in Social Relations.* 3d ed. New York: Holt, Rinehart and Winston, 1976. Appendix B is an especially well-organized set of guides for the questionnaire designer.
7. Zeisel, Hans. *Say It with Figures.* Rev. 5th ed. New York: Harper & Brothers, Publishers, 1968, Chap. 6 presents a thorough discussion of the concept of an accounting scheme.

DISCUSSION QUESTIONS

1. Distinguish between:
    a. Interview guide and questionnaire.
    b. Direct and indirect questions.
    c. Open and closed questions.
    d. Research, investigative, and measurement questions.
    e. Questioning structure and response structure.
2. Why is the survey technique so popular? When is it not appropriate?
3. What special problems do open ended questions have? How can these be minimized? In what situations it the open end question most useful?
4. Why might a researcher wish to disguise the questioning objective of a study?
5. One of the major reasons that survey research may be less effective than we would like is that the survey instruments are less useful than they should be.

What would you say are the four major faults of the survey instrument designer?

6. Why is it desirable to pretest survey instruments? What information can you secure from such a pretest?

 How can one go about finding the best wording for a question on a questionnaire?

7. One design problem in the development of survey instruments concerns the sequence of questions. What suggestions would you make on this problem to persons who are designing their first questionnaire?

8. One of the major problems facing the designer of a survey instrument is the assumptions made. What are the major "problem assumptions?"

9. Below are six questions which might be found on questionnaires. Comment on each as to whether or not it is a good question. If not, tell why. (Assume that no lead-in or screening questions are required for these. That is, judge the question on its own merits.)

 a. Do you read the *National Geographic Magazine* regularly?

 b. What percent of your time is spent asking for information from others in your organization?

 c. When did you first start chewing gum?

 d. How much discretionary buying power do you have per year?

 e. Why did you decide to attend Big State University?

 f. Do you think the President is doing a good job now?

10. Develop an accounting scheme to determine why people attend business school. Using this accounting scheme, develop a short questioning instrument by which to interview persons who have gone to business school.

11. One student class project was to develop a brief self-administered questionnaire by which students might quickly evaluate a professor. One student submitted the following instrument. Evaluate the questions asked and the format of the instrument.

Professor Evaluation Form

1. Overall, how would you rate this professor?

 _____good; _____fair; _____poor;

2. Does this professor:

 a. have good class delivery? _____

 b. know the subject? _____

 c. have a positive attitude toward the subject? _____

 d. grade fairly? _____

 e. have a sense of humor? _____

 f. use audiovisuals, case examples, or other classroom aids? _____

 g. return exams promptly? _____

3. What is the professor's strongest point? _____

4. What is the professor's weakest point? _____

5. What kind of class does the professor teach? _____

6. Is this course required? _____

7. Would you take another course from this professor? _____

12. Below is a copy of the letter and mail questionnaire which was received by a professor who is a member of the American Society of Training Directors. Please evaluate the value and tone of the letter and the questions and format of the instrument.

Dear ASTD Member:

In partial fulfillment of Masters Degree work, I have chosen to do a descriptive study of the industrial trainer in our area. Using the roster of the ASTD as a mailing list, your name came to me. I am enclosing a short questionnaire and a return envelope. I hope you will take a few minutes and fill out the questionnaire as soon as possible, as the sooner the information is returned to me, the better.

Sincerely,

QUESTIONNAIRE

DIRECTIONS: Please answer as briefly as possible.

1. With what company did you enter the field of training? _____
2. How long have you been in the field of training? _____
3. How long have you been in the training department of the company with which you are presently employed? _____
4. How long has the training department in your company been in existance? _____
5. Is the training department a subdivision of another department? ___ If so, what department? _____
6. For what functions other than training is your department responsible?
   _____
7. How many people, including yourself, are in the training department of your company? (Local plant or establishment) _____
8. What degrees do you hold, and from what institutions? _____
   Major_____ Minor_____
9. Why were you chosen for training? What special qualifications do you have that prompted your entry into training? _____
   _____
10. What experience would you consider necessary for an individual to enter into the field of training with your company? Include both educational requirements and actual experience. _____
    _____
    _____
    _____

Chapter 9

Scaling

A MAJOR BUSINESS RESEARCH MEASUREMENT PROBLEM is that the available tools are often crude, while the concepts to be measured are complex and abstract. We want a valid measurement, but we often get a difference between the *true score* and the *test score*. If the object is a concrete concept, and the measurement tools well-standardized, the variation between the test and true scores may be small. For example, we should expect high accuracy in measuring a length of pipe with a yardstick. On the other hand, if the concept is abstract (attitudes toward various institutions) and the measurement tools not standardized (questions about attitudes), then we are less confident that the test results reflect true scores.

In this chapter we shall consider procedures which can help us to measure abstract concepts more accurately. We will concentrate upon the problems of measuring attitudes and opinions, but the same problems are found when measuring physical concepts, psychological concepts, such as intelligence, or institutional concepts, such as organizational effectiveness.

THE NATURE OF SCALING

Scaling Defined

In the social sciences the term "scaling" is applied to the procedures for attempting to determine quantitative measures of subjective abstract concepts. Scaling is defined as a "procedure for the assignment of numbers (or other symbols) to a property of objects in order to impart some of the characteristics of numbers to the properties in question."[1] Thus, we assign a number scale to the various levels of heat and cold and call it a thermometer.

What Is Scaled? A more correct statement would be that we assign numbers to *indicants* of the properties of objects. We want to measure the temperature of the air; we know that a property of temperature is that its variation leads to an expansion or contraction of materials such as mercury. We devise a glass tube arrangement with mercury. It provides us with an indicant of the temperature by the rise and fall of the mercury column in the tube as temperatures change.

In another context we might devise a scale by which to measure the durability (property) of paint. We secure a machine with an attached scrub brush that applies a predetermined amount of pressure as it scrubs. We then count the number of brush strokes that it takes to wear through a 10-mil thickness of paint. The scrub count is the indicant of the paint's durability. Or, we may judge a person's supervisory capacity (property) by asking a peer group to rate that person on various questions (indicants) which we devise.

Scales may be easy to construct, but it is difficult to assure that they measure reliably. It is even more of a challenge to determine scale validity, especially with abstract concepts. Where different methods of scaling provide approximately comparable results, especially when each is based upon a different logic of measurement, we tend to accept the measures as valid. More often we accept the type of face validity in which several reasonable persons agree that a particular scale should be a good indicator.

Scale Classification

Scales may be classified in many ways, but the discussion here is restricted to those approaches which are of greatest value for business research purposes.[2] Even with such a limited objective there is no widely accepted system of classification. Six different approaches will be mentioned.

Study Objective. A scale may be designed to (1) measure the characteristics of the respondents who complete it or (2) use these respondents as judges of the objects or stimuli presented to them. For example, we might present people with a series of scale items about government regulatory programs and ask them to express their approval or disapproval of each program. If we are interested in measuring the respondent's attitudes we will combine each person's answers to form an indicator of each's conservatism, political position, and so forth. In this case our emphasis is on measuring

---

[1] Bernard S. Phillips, *Social Research Strategy and Tactics,* 2d ed. (New York: The Macmillan Company, 1971), p. 205.

[2] For a discussion of various scale classifications see W. S. Torgerson, *Theory and Methods of Scaling* (New York: John Wiley & Sons, 1958), chap. 3.

differences among the people, and their responses to specific stimuli (scale items) are of only incidental concern. In the second case we use the same data but are interested in how people view different government programs. Now we have little concern for how respondents vary among themselves in their answers. Our concern is the variation in public attitudes among different programs.

Response Scales. Scales may also be classified as *categorical* and *comparative.* These approaches are also known as *rating* and *ranking,* respectively. Categorical (rating) scales are used when respondents score some object without direct reference to other objects. For example, they may be asked to rate the beauty of styling of new autos on a five-point scale. In the comparative (ranking) scaling the respondents are asked to choose which one of various pairs of cars has more beautiful styling.

Degree of Preference. Scaling approaches may also involve *preference* measurement or *nonpreference* evaluation. In the first case respondents are asked to choose which object each favors or which solution each would prefer. In the second case they are asked to judge which object has the most of some characteristic or which solution takes the most resources, without reflecting any personal preference toward object or solutions. For example, a respondent would judge the first of the following two statements as being more prounion, regardless of personal feeling toward unions.

A. Unions are necessary to protect the workers.
B. Unions are responsible for most of our labor unrest today.

Scale Properties. Scaling approaches may also be viewed in terms of the scale properties possessed by each. The discussion in Chapter 5 pointed out that scales may be classified as nominal, ordinal, interval, or ratio. Their characteristics need not be treated further here, except to note again that the assumptions underlying each scale property type determine how the scale may be used statistically.

Number of Dimensions. Scales are either *unidimensional* or *multidimensional.* With a unidimensional scale we seek to measure only one attribute of the respondent or object. Thus, we measure employees as to promotability, assuming that it is a single dimension. We may use several items by which to measure this dimension, but we will combine them into a single measure and place employees along a linear continuum called "promotability." Multiple dimension scaling recognizes that an object might be better described by the concept of an attribute space of *n* dimensions rather than a single-dimension continuum. For example, we might recognize that employee promotability might be better expressed by two distinct dimensions— managerial performance and technical performance. Most of this chapter will deal with unidimensional scaling.

Scale Construction. Scales may also be classified by the method used to build them. According to one view there are five major scale design techniques.[3] One is the *arbitrary* approach in which the scale is developed on an ad hoc basis. We assume that such scales measure the concepts for which they have been designed, but we have little evidence to support this assumption. Even so, this is probably the most widely used technique.

A second approach is the *consensus* scale. A panel of judges evaluate the items chosen for inclusion in the instrument in terms of whether they are (1) relevant to the topic area and (2) unambiguous in implication. A third technique is the *item analysis* approach. A number of individual items are developed into a test which is given to a group of respondents. After administering the test, total scores are calculated for everyone. Individual items are then analyzed to determine which discriminate between persons or objects with high total scores and those with low scores.

Cumulative scales are chosen on the basis of their conforming to some ranking of items with ascending and descending discriminating power. For example, in such a scale the endorsement of an item representing an extreme position should result also in the endorsement of all items indicating a less extreme position. Finally, *factor* scales may be constructed on the basis of intercorrelations of items that indicate that a common factor accounts for the relationships between items. This relationship is typically measured through factor analysis or another clustering method.

The following sections of this chapter will be organized along the lines of two of these classifications: response methods and scale construction techniques. Other classification bases will be considered when appropriate.

RESPONSE METHODS

In Chapter 8 it was pointed out that the asking of questions is a widely used method for measuring concepts. For example, a manager may be asked to state her views concerning a certain employee. The respondent may give replies such as "good machinist," "a troublemaker," "union activist," "reliable," or a "fast worker with a poor record of attendance." These answers appear to represent different dimensions, or frames of reference, by which the worker is perceived. Such a variety of responses is often of limited research value.

Two approaches are used to improve the usefulness of such replies. First, various properties may be separated out and the respondent asked to judge these specific facets. In this manner we substitute several questions for a single question. The second approach is to establish structured patterns by which to guide responses. In this approach we substitute structuring devices for the free

---

[3] E. A. Suchman and R. G. Francis, "Scaling Techniques in Social Research," in J. T. Doby, ed., *An Introduction to Social Research* (Harrisburg, Pa.: The Stackpole Company, 1954), pp. 126–29.

response reply pattern. When we wish to quantify dimensions that are essentially qualitative we do this structuring by using rating and/or ranking scales.

Rating Scales

We use rating scales to judge properties of objects without reference to other similar objects. These ratings may be in such forms as "like-dislike," "approve-indifferent-disapprove," or other classifications using even more categories. Whether to use a two-point scale, three-point scale, or scales with more points is a subject which is debated; there is little conclusive support for any particular scale length. One argument is that more points on a scale provide an opportunity for greater sensitivity of measurement. However, the most widely used scales range from three to seven points, and it does not seem to make much difference which number is used.[4]

The *graphic rating scale* is a common and simple form to use. The judge checks his responses or evaluation along a continuum. An example of one element of such a scale is the statement found in an employee evaluation form:

"How well does the employee get along with co-workers?"
(Please check)

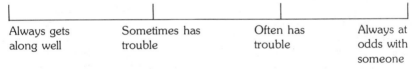

| Always gets along well | Sometimes has trouble | Often has trouble | Always at odds with someone |

This scale illustrates the graphic principle but is not a very good scale for several reasons. One defect is that only three of the four positions are likely to be used. It will be the rare situation when the choice "always at odds with someone" will be used. In effect, then, it is a three-point scale. Another deficiency concerns the vagueness of "sometimes" and "often." The meaning of these terms depends upon each judge's frame of reference so completely that the statement might be challenged in terms of its equivalency, and perhaps its stability. At the other extreme is "always" which implies no exceptions. A final problem is that the graphics are set up at such a way that respondents may check at almost any position along the line. This increases the difficulty of analysis.

Several other rating scale variants are presented next; illustrated also are various lengths of rating scales.

---

[4] A study of research literature in 1940 found that more than three fourths of the attitude scales used were of the five-point type. A cursory examination of more recent literature suggests that the five-point scale is still quite common but there also seems to be a growing use of longer scales. For the 1940 study see Daniel D. Day, "Methods in Attitude Research," *American Sociological Review,* vol. 5 (1940), pp. 395–410.

Variation 1. Boxes replace the line and make it more certain that respondents will choose only one of four points.

☐ | ☐ | ☐ | ☐
Always gets along well | Sometimes has trouble | Often has trouble | Always at odds with someone

Variation 2. Two polar positions shown with a number scale used to show degree of opinion.

Gets along well ☐ ☐ ☐ ☐ ☐ Has trouble
  1   2   3   4   5

Other Variations. Listed below are some of the common phrasing examples which are used to indicate degrees of judgment in surveys.[5]

Three-Point Scales

Greater _____ Equal _____ Less _____
Yes _____ Depends _____ No _____
Above
average _____ Average _____ Below
average _____

Four-Point Scales

Many _____ Some _____ Few _____ None _____
Excellent _____ Good _____ Fair _____ Poor _____
  | Next
highest _____ | Next
lowest _____
Highest _____ | | | Lowest _____

Five-Point Scales

Strongly
approve ____ Approve ____ Undecided ____ Dis-
approve _____ Strongly dis-
approve ____
Much
greater ____ Somewhat
greater ____ Equal ____ Somewhat
less _____ Not at
all _____
Like very
much _____ Like
somewhat ____ Neutral ____ Dislike
somewhat ____ Dislike very
much _____

Longer Scales

(Semantic
differential) | Good | : : : : : : | Bad

Modern | : : : : : : | Old fashioned

(Stapel) ☐ ☐ ☐ ☐ ☐ ■ ■ ■ ■ ■
  + Taste −

---

[5] Mildred Parten, *Surveys, Polls, and Samples: Practical Procedures* (New York: Harper & Borthers, 1950), pp. 190–92.

A second form, the *itemized scale,* presents a series of statements from which respondents select one as best reflecting their evaluation. These judgments are ordered progressively in terms of more or less of some property. It is typical to use five to seven categories, with each being defined or illustrated in words. An example is:

How well does the employee get along with coworkers?

_____Almost always involved in some friction or argument with a coworker.

_____Often at odds with one or more coworkers. The frequency of involvement is clearly above that of the average worker.

_____Sometimes gets involved in friction. The frequency of involvement is about equal to that of the average worker.

_____Infrequently becomes involved in friction with others, definitely less often than most workers.

_____Almost never gets involved in friction situations with other workers.

This form is more difficult to develop, and the statements may not say exactly what the respondent would like to express. On the other hand, it provides more information and meaning to the rater; itemized scales probably increase reliability because the more detailed statements help respondents to develop and hold the same frame of reference as they use the form.

Even with rating scales there must be some criterion that the subject uses to judge that one object is attractive and a second less attractive. This criterion is typically not explicit, allowing for each person's subjective judgment. In the *comparative rating scale* this criterion is made explicit. The subject is asked to compare against some experience standard. Job evaluation rating forms use the concept of a standard job as the basis for rating others. Job interview analysis forms might specify that the rater should compare the interviewee with the typical recruit that the company has hired in the past.

Problems in Using Rating Scales. The value of rating scales for measurement purposes depends upon the assumption that a person can and will make good judgments. Before we accept respondent's ratings we should consider the tendencies to constant error. Three of the most common types are the errors of *leniency, central tendency,* and *halo effect.*[6]

The error of leniency occurs when certain persons are either "easy raters" or "hard raters," the latter being an error of negative leniency. It has been found that raters tend to rate those people higher whom they know well and with whom they are ego-involved. There is also the contrary of this situation—the case where one rates those acquaintances lower because one is aware of the leniency danger and attempts to counteract it. One way to deal with the tendency to positive leniency, the most common form, is to design the rating scale to anticipate it. An example might be an asymmetrical graphic

---

[6] J. P. Guilford, *Psychometric Methods* (New York: McGraw-Hill Book Co., Inc., 1954), pp. 278–79.

scale which has only one unfavorable descriptive term and four favorable terms (poor–fair–good–very good–excellent). In this case the scale designer expects that the mean ratings will be near "good" and that there will be a more or less symmetrical distribution about that point.

Raters are reluctant to give extreme judgments, and this fact accounts for the error of central tendency. This is most often seen where the rater does not know the person being rated. Efforts to counteract this error are to (1) adjust the strength of descriptive adjectives, (2) to space the intermediate descriptive phrases further apart in graphic scales, (3) provide smaller differences in meaning between steps near the ends of the scale than between the steps near the center, and (4) use more points in the scale.

A third major problem concerns the halo effect—the systematic bias that the rater introduces by carrying over a generalized impression of the subject from one rating to another. We tend to expect the student who does well on question 1 of an examination also to do well on question 2. In other cases we conclude that a report is good because we like its form, or we believe someone is intelligent because we agree on something. Halo is one of the most pervasive errors; it is especially difficult to avoid when the property being studied is not clearly defined, not easily observed, not frequently discussed, involves reactions with others, or is a trait of high moral importance.[7] One way to counteract halo is to rate one trait at a time for all subjects or to have one trait per page rather than one subject per page.

Advantages of Rating Scales. Rating scales are now widely used in business research and generally deserve their popularity. While careless use is common, the results obtained with careful use compares favorably with alternative methods. Rating scales typically require less time, are interesting to use, and have a wider range of application than most other methods. In addition, they may be used with a large number of properties or variables.

Ranking Scales

In the ranking methods the subject directly compares two or more objects and makes choices among them. Widely encountered is the situation where the respondent is asked to select one as the "best" or the "preferred." When dealing with only two choices this approach is satisfactory, but it may often result in the "vote splitting" phenomenon when more than two choices are found. This may occur in the situation when the respondent is asked to select the most preferred among three or more models of a product. Assume that 40 percent choose model A, 30 percent choose model B, and 30 percent choose model C. The question is, "Which is the preferred model?" The analyst would be taking a risk to suggest that A is most preferred. Perhaps such an

---

[7] P. M. Synonds, "Notes on Rating," *Journal of Applied Psychology*, vol. 9 (1925), pp. 188–95.

interpretation is correct, but 60 percent of the respondents chose some model other than A. It may be that all B and C voters would place A last, preferring either B or C to it. This ambiguity can be avoided through the use of paired comparisons or rank-ordering techniques.

Method of Paired Comparisons. With this technique the respondent can express attitudes in an unambiguous manner by making a choice between two objects. Typical of such a situation would be a product testing study where a new flavor of soft drink is tested against an established brand. Another example might be to compare two bargaining proposals available to union negotiators. In the general situation there are often many more than two stimuli to judge, resulting in a potentially tedious task for respondents. The number of judgments required in a paired comparison is:

$$N = \frac{n(n - 1)}{2}$$

where
N = Number of judgments and
n = Number of stimuli or objects to be judged.

For example, if there are 15 suggestions for bargaining proposals available to a union, there are 105 paired comparisons that can be made with them.

With paired comparing there is a risk that the respondents will tire to the point that they give ill-considered answers or even refuse to continue. Opinions differ as to what the upper limit is, but five or six stimuli are not unreasonable when the respondent has other questions to answer. If the interview consists only of comparisons, as many as 15 stimuli may be compared.

We can lighten this burden by reducing the number of comparisons per respondent without reducing the number of objects being studied. One approach is to present each respondent with only a sample of the stimuli. If we use this method we must assure that each pair of objects is compared an equal number of times. A second approach is to choose a few objects which are believed to cover the range of attractiveness at about equal intervals. All other stimuli are then compared to these few standard objects. For example, there may be 36 employees to be judged. Four may be selected as standards and the others divided into four groups of eight each. Within each group all eight are compared to each other. Then the 32 are individually compared to each of the 4 standard persons. This reduces the number of comparisons from 630 to 240.

Paired-comparison data may be treated in several ways. If there is substantial consistency we will find that, if A is preferred to B, and B to C, then A will consistently be preferred to C. This condition of transitivity need not always be true but should occur most of the time. When this is so we may take the total number of preferences among the comparisons as the score for that stimulus. For example, assume that there are five major demand proposals which a union bargaining committee is considering. The committee would like to know how the union membership ranks these proposals. One way to determine this would be to ask a sample of the members to pair-compare the proposal suggestions. A sample of 200 members might express the views shown by the hypothetical data found in Table 9–1.

Table 9–1: Response Patterns of 200 Union Members' Paired Comparisons of Five Suggestions for Union Bargaining Proposal Priorities

	Suggestion				
	A	B	C	D	E
A	—	164*	138	50	70
B	36	—	54	14	30
C	62	146	—	32	50
D	150	186	168	—	118
E	130	170	150	82	—
Total	378	666	.510	178	268
Rank order	3	1	2	5	4
M_p	0.478	0.766	0.610	0.278	0.368
Z_j	−0.06	0.73	0.28	−0.59	−0.34
R_j	0.53	1.32	0.87	0.00	0.25

* Read 164 members preferred suggestion B (column) to suggestion A (row).

By a crude comparison of the total number of preferences stated for each option it is apparent that B is the most popular. The rank order for the suggestions is shown.

While a paired comparison provides ordinal data, Thurstone has developed a method by which such data may be converted into an interval scale. Known as the Law of Comparative Judgment, it involves the conversion of frequencies of preferences (such as in Table 9–1) into a table of proportions which are then transformed into a Z matrix by referring to the table of areas under the normal curve.[8] Guilford has presented a procedure which is computationally much easier than Thurstone's and secures essentially the same results. It is called the *composite-standard* method and is illustrated here.[9]

With the composite-standard method we can develop an interval scale from paired comparisons by the following steps. First, using the data in Table 9–1, we calculate the column means using the equation:

$$M_p = \frac{C + 0.5N}{nN} = \frac{378 + 0.5(200)}{5(200)} = 0.478$$

[8] See L. L. Thurstone, "A Law of Comparative Judgment," *Psychological Review,* vol. 34 (1927), pp. 273–86.

[9] From *Psychometric Methods* by J. P. Guilford. Copyright 1954, McGraw-Hill Book Company. Used with permission of McGraw-Hill Book Company.

where

M_p = The mean proportion of the columns, and

C = The total number of choices for a given suggestion.

Guilford points out, "The correction $0.5N$ in the numerator is for the assumed number of choices the stimulus would have received if it had been compared with itself. . . . It is assumed that the standard is the composite of all the stimuli in the series and that M_p is the proportion of times any given stimulus is chosen in preference to that standard."[10] These calculated means are shown in Table 9–1.

The Z values for M_p are secured from the normal curve tables. When the proportion (M_p) is less than 0.5, the Z value is negative, while all proportions over 0.5 are positive.[11] These values are also shown in Table 9–1 as Z_j. Since this scale is an interval scale the zero is an arbitrary value. We can eliminate negative scale values by giving the value of zero to the lowest scale value and then adding the absolute value of this lowest scale value to all other scale items. This scale (R_j) is shown in Figure 9–1.

Figure 9–1: Interval Scale Derived from Paired-Comparison Data Using the Composite-Standard Method

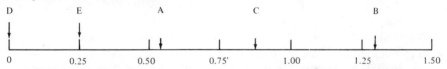

Method of Rank Order. Another comparative scaling approach is to ask respondents to rank their choices. This method is faster than paired comparisons and is usually easier and more motivating to the respondent. For example, with 7 items it takes 21 pair comparisons to complete the task while the simple ranking of 7 is easier. With ranking there is no transitivity problem where A is preferred to B, B to C, but C preferred to A.

On the negative side there is some question as to how many stimuli may be handled by this method. Less than five objects can usually be ranked easily, but respondents may grow careless in ranking, say, ten or more items. In addition, the rank ordering is still an ordinal scale with all of its limitations.

There are several simple ways to combine rankings into an overall index. Means cannot properly be calculated, but it is possible to compute medians.

---

[10] Ibid., p. 170.

[11] The Z values in this transformation are associated with a given proportion of the *total area* under the normal curve, while Appendix Table B–1 gives the area for one side (or one half) of the normal curve. To use Appendix Table B–1 in this calculation we must subtract all M_p values which exceed 0.5 from 1.0 to secure the value with which to enter Table B–1. For example, 1.0 − 0.766 = 0.234. Entering the body of Table B–1 with this number we find the nearest value is 0.2327, which gives a Z_j of approximately 0.73; recall that all M_p values of less than 0.5 will give Z_j values which are negative.

Some suggest that the sum of rank values will probably give the best simple indication of composite ranking of stimuli.[12] If there are a substantial number of respondents it is possible also to translate ordinal rank data into an interval scale. Two general methods are the *normalized-rank* and the *comparative-judgment*.[13] The latter approach is similar to scaling from paired comparisons. Guilford also suggests a *composite-standard* approach similar to that already discussed.[14]

A complete ranking is sometimes not needed or involves too many stimuli. We may secure more cooperation by asking only that the first *k* ranks be selected. For example, respondents may be asked to judge 25 different automobile designs by ranking only their first five choices. To secure a simple ranking of all designs we merely total rank values received by each model. We can also develop an interval scale of these data by using either a pair-comparison or composite-standard solution.[15]

The Method of Successive Intervals. Neither the paired-comparison nor the rank-order method is particularly attractive when there are a large number of items to choose among. Under these circumstances the method of successive intervals is sometimes used. In this method the subject is asked to sort the items (usually one per card) into piles or groups representing a succession of values. From these sortings an interval scale can be developed.[16]

Both rating and ranking scales are used for stimulus-centered scaling, while respondent-centered studies typically use the rating response form. Rating scales are also the response form of choice with all types of scale construction technique.

SCALE CONSTRUCTION TECHNIQUES

Arbitrary Scales

We can design arbitrary scales by collecting a number of items which we believe are unambiguous and appropriate to a given topic. We choose some of these items for inclusion in our instrument. To illustrate, consider the problem of conducting a company image study among the general public. We choose a sample of items which we believe are the components of company image. Some of the items we might choose are:

---

[12] Guilford, *Psychometric Methods,* pp. 179–80.

[13] Ibid., p. 180.

[14] Ibid., p. 186.

[15] For details on these methods see Ibid., pp. 188–90.

[16] See Milton A. Saffir, "A Comparative Study of Scales Constructed by Three Psychophysical Methods," *Psychometrica,* vol. 11, no. 3 (September 1937), pp. 179–98.

How do you regard (*name*) Company's reputation

1. As a place to
   work?   Bad _____ _____ _____ _____ _____ Good
2. As a sponsor of
   civic projects? Bad _____ _____ _____ _____ _____ Good
3. For ecological
   concern?   Bad _____ _____ _____ _____ _____ Good
4. As an employer
   of minorities?   Bad _____ _____ _____ _____ _____ Good

We might score each of these from 0 to 4 depending upon the degree of favorableness reported. The results may be studied in several ways. Totals may be made by individual items, by company, to determine how various companies rate as places to work, for ecological concern, and so on. Or totals for each company, by individual, may be calculated to determine how each company compares to the others in an overall sense. Based on a total for these four items each company would be scored from 0 to 16 by each respondent. While not a company-image orientation, these data may also be analyzed from a respondent-centered point of view. Thus, we might use the attitude scores of each individual as a basis for studying differences among the individuals.

Pros and Cons. Arbitrary scales are easy to develop and can be designed to be highly specific to the case and content of interest. They are developed quickly and inexpensively. They can provide much useful information, and can be quite adequate if developed by one who is skilled in scale design. These are all practical benefits and account for the widespread use of arbitrary scales.

There are also some weaknesses. A major one is that this approach is based solely upon the designer's subjective logic. If this logic is good, then the scale can be good. The only assurance we have that the items chosen are a representative sample of the universe of content (the totality of what constitutes "company image") is the researcher's insight and ability. We have no objective evidence that items will all be viewed by respondents from the same frame of reference.

While arbitrary scales are often used, in the last few decades there has been a great effort, in the behavioral sciences, to develop scale construction techniques which overcome some of the deficiencies cited above. One of the earliest of these was consensus scaling.

Consensus Scaling

In this approach the selection of items is made by a panel of judges who evaluate a proposed scale item as to (1) its relevance to the topic area, (2) its potential for ambiguity, and (3) the level of attitude it represents. A widely known form of this approach is the Thurstone Differential Scale.

Differential Scales. This approach, known also as the Method of Equal Appearing Intervals, was an effort to develop an interval rating scale for attitude measurement. Whether this goal was achieved is still debated. The standard development approach is to ask a large number of judges (often 50 or more) to evaluate a large number of statements. These statements express different degrees of favorableness toward an object and are presented one per card. The judges are asked to sort each card into 1 of 11 piles representing their evaluation of the degree of favorableness that the statement expresses; the judge's agreement or disagreement with the statement is not involved. Three of the 11 piles are identified to the judges by labels of "favorable" and "unfavorable" at the extremes, and "neutral" at the midpoint. The eight intermediate piles are unlabeled to encourage the judges to view them as being at equal-appearing intervals between the three labeled positions.

The scale position for a given statement is determined by calculating its median score when placement in the least favorable pile is scored as "1," in the most favorable pile as "11," and in the other piles according to their place in the order. A measure of dispersion, usually the interquartile range, is calculated for each statement.[17] If a given statement has a large interquartile range it is judged to be too ambiguous to be used in the final scale. The selection of statements to be included in the final attitude scale is made by taking a sample of statements whose median scores are spread evenly from one extreme to the other and whose interquartile ranges are small. Duplicate scales may be constructed and are sometimes used to provide greater score reliability.

The scale is administered to respondents by asking them to read the 20 or so statements and to select those items with which they agree. The mean or median value of the chosen scale items is then calculated as the measure of the respondent's attitude. Below is an example of part of a 50-item scale which was designed to determine the attitude of employees of a company toward their employer. The scale values are shown here but would not be on the instrument when it is used.[18]

Scale Value
10.4   I think this company treats it employees better than any other company does.
 8.9   A man can get ahead in this company if he tries.
 8.5   The company is sincere in wanting to know what its employees think about it.
 5.4   I believe accidents will happen no matter what you do about them.
 5.1   The workers put as much over on the company as the company puts over on them.

---

[17] The interquartile range is a measure of dispersion which includes the middle 50 percent of the items in a distribution.

[18] R. S. Uhrbrock, "Attitudes of 4,430 Employees," *Journal of Social Psychology,* vol. 5 (1934), pp. 367–68.

4.1 Soldiering on the job is on the increase.

2.9 My boss gives all the breaks to his lodge and church friends.

2.5 I think the company goes outside to fill good jobs instead of promoting men who are here.

1.5 In the long run this company will "put it over" on you.

1.0 The pay in this company is terrible.

In the actual instrument the statements are arranged in random order of scale value. If the values are valid, and if the questionnaire deals with only one attitude dimension, the typical respondent will choose one or several contiguous items (in terms of scale values). At times, however, divergences will occur because a statement appears to tap a different attitude dimension. In the example above it is possible that the statement "I think accidents will happen no matter what you do about them" may evoke an entirely different frame of reference than will "company treatment of its employees" which pervades the other items. A person may honestly select the accident statement (with a 5.4 score) and then choose either lower or higher scored items.

Differential scales have been used more widely in sociological studies than in business research. An important deterrent to their use has been the cost and effort required to construct them. This approach has also been criticized on the grounds that the values assigned to various statements by the judges may reflect their own attitudes. Some studies have indicated the statement evaluations are independent of the judges' personal attitudes, but other studies indicate the opposite. The latter case was found with questions on topics about which the judges held extreme positions. Even here, however, the rank order of the various evaluations was the same among judges with different attitudes. A final criticism of the differential method is that some other scale designs give more information about the respondent's attitude.

Using a panel of judges to evaluate scale items is better than relying only on the researcher's opinion; but the method is costly, time consuming, and ultimately involves the same subjective decision process although repeated by 50 or more different individuals. There is a different logic underlying the scale construction techniques yet to be discussed. They rely upon the analysis of actual responses to the items as the basis for determining item acceptability. The first of these is the Item Analysis technique.

Item Analysis

In this procedure a particular item is evaluated on the basis of how well it discriminates between those persons whose total score is high and those whose score is low. The most popular type using this approach is the summated scale.

Summated Scale. This consists of a number of statements which express either a favorable or unfavorable attitude toward the object of interest. The respondent is asked to agree or disagree with each statement. Each response is given a numerical score to reflect its degree of attitude favorableness, and the scores are totaled to measure the respondent's attitude.

The most frequently used form is the Likert scale. With this scale the respondent is asked to respond to each statement in terms of five degrees of agreement (three-point and seven-point scales are also used). An example from a job satisfaction scale is:[19]

I consider my job rather unpleasant.

| Strongly Agree (1) | Agree (2) | Undecided (3) | Disagree (4) | Strongly Disagree (5) |

The numbers indicate the scale value to be assigned to each possible answer with "1" indicating the least favorable degree of job satisfaction and "5" the most favorable. These values are normally not printed on the instrument but are shown here to indicate the scoring system. The full Brayfield and Rothe Index includes 18 statements, making it possible for a respondent to score from 18 to 90, with 54 points being equivalent to a neutral position. If respondents score near 18 it is clear that they hold an unfavorable job attitude; likewise, if the score is quite high we conclude that there is a high degree of job satisfaction. But the interpretation of scores nearer the middle of the scale is less clear if our objective is to describe the respondent in any absolute sense. For example, a score of 60 is slightly over in the "favorable" side, but it may actually represent a relatively poor job attitude score when compared to those of other workers.

Summated scales are most useful when it is possible to compare the person's score with a distribution of scores from some well-defined group. They are also very useful when we expect to conduct an experiment, undertake a program of change or improvement, and the like. We can use the scales to measure attitudes before and after the experiment, or to judge whether our efforts have had the desired effects. Furthermore, if we wish to correlate scores on the scale to other measures it can also be done without concern for the absolute value of what is "favorable" and what is "unfavorable."

Likert-type scales are relatively easy to develop as compared to the differential scales.[20] The first step is to collect a large number of statements that

---

[19] From the Brayfield and Rothe Index of Job Satisfaction. See A. H. Brayfield and H. F. Rothe, "An Index of Job Satisfaction," *Journal of Applied Psychology*, vol. 35 (October 1951), pp. 307–11.

[20] One study reported that the construction of a Likert scale took only half the time required to construct a Thurstone scale. See A. L. Thurstone and K. K. Kenney, "A Comparison of the Thurstone and Likert Techniques of Attitude Scale Construction," *Journal of Applied Psychology*, vol. 30 (1946), pp. 72–83.

meet two criteria: (1) Each statement is believed to be relevant to the attitude being studied, and (2) each is believed to reflect a favorable or unfavorable position on that attitude. A group of persons, similar to those who are going to be studied, are asked to read each statement and to state the level of their agreement with it, using a five-point scale. For example, a scale value of "1" might indicate a strongly unfavorable attitude and "5" a strongly favorable attitude.

Each person's response values are then added to secure a total score per person. The next step is to array these total scores and select some part of the highest and lowest *total scores,* say, the top 25 percent and the bottom 25 percent. These two extreme groups are interpreted to represent the most favorable and least favorable attitudes toward the topic being studied. They are used as criterion groups by which to evaluate individual statements. That is, through a comparative analysis of response patterns to each statement by members of these two criterion groups, we determine which statements consistently correlate with low favorability and which with high favorability attitudes.

One approach to item analysis involves calculating the mean scores for each scale item among the low scorers and high scorers. The item means between the high-score group and the low-score groups are then tested for significance by calculating t values. Finally, the 20 to 25 items which have the greatest t values (significant differences between means) are selected for inclusion in the final scale.[21]

This procedure can be illustrated in the following manner. In evaluating response patterns of the high and low groups to the statement "I consider my job rather unpleasant" we might secure the results shown in Table 9–2.

After finding the t values for each statement we rank order them and select those statements with the highest t values. As a crude indicator of a statement's discrimination power, Edwards suggests using only those statements whose t value is 1.75 or greater, provided there are 25 or more subjects in each group.[22] As an added safeguard against response-set bias we should select approximately one half of the statements to be favorable and the other half unfavorable.

The Likert scale has many advantages which account for its popularity. It is easy and quick to construct. Each item that is included has met an empirical test for discriminating ability. Since respondents answer each item it is probably more reliable than the Thurstone scale, and it provides a greater volume of data than does the Thurstone scale. It is easy to use this scale both in respondent-centered and stimulus-centered studies. That is, we can study

---

[21] Allen L. Edwards, *Techniques of Attitude Scale Construction* (New York: Appleton-Century-Crofts, Inc., 1957), pp. 152–54.

[22] Ibid., p. 153.

Table 9–2: Evaluating a Scale Statement by Item Analysis

Response Categories	Low Total Score Group				High Total Score Group			
	X	f	fX	fX²	X	f	fX	fX²
Strongly agree	5	3	15	75	5	22	110	550
Agree	4	4	16	64	4	30	120	480
Undecided	3	29	87	261	3	15	45	135
Disagree	2	22	44	88	2	4	8	16
Strongly disagree	1	15	15	15	1	2	2	2
Total		73	177	503		73	285	1,183
		n_L	ΣX_L	ΣX_L^2		n_H	ΣX_H	ΣX_H^2

$$\overline{X}_L = \frac{177}{73} = 2.42 \qquad\qquad \overline{X}_H = \frac{285}{73} = 3.90$$

$$\Sigma(X_L - \overline{X}_L)^2 = 503 - \frac{(177)^2}{73} \qquad \Sigma(X_H - \overline{X}_H)^2 = 1,183 - \frac{(285)^2}{73}$$

$$= 73.84 \qquad\qquad\qquad = 70.33$$

$$t = \frac{\overline{X}_H - \overline{X}_L}{\sqrt{\dfrac{\Sigma(X_H - \overline{X}_H)^2 + \Sigma(X_L - \overline{X}_L)^2}{n(n-1)}}}$$

$$= \frac{3.90 - 2.42}{\sqrt{\dfrac{70.33 + 73.84}{73(73-1)}}}$$

$$= 8.92$$

how responses differ between people, and how responses differ between various stimuli.

In our discussions it has been implied that the Thurstone and Likert scales can be developed only by using the consensus and item analysis methods, respectively. This is not the case. We can develop scales of these types in an arbitrary manner; this is common practice, especially with the Likert scale. Such scales have the same validity problems as all arbitrary scales. The classic procedure for developing the Likert and Thurstone scales is as described in this chapter.

The Likert scale is ordinal only while the Thurstone scale designers claim theirs to be an interval scale. With the Likert scale we can report respondents are more or less favorable to a topic, but we cannot tell how much more or less favorable they are. Another potential problem is that a given total score can be secured by a wide variety of answer patterns, bringing the meaning of the total score into question. This particular problem can be addressed by using a cumulative scale.

Cumulative Scales

Total scores on cumulative scales have the same meaning. Given a person's total score it is possible to estimate which items were answered positively and which negatively. The major scale of this type is the Guttman *scalogram.*

Scalogram analysis is a procedure for determining whether a set of items forms a unidimensional scale as defined by Guttman.[23] A scale is said to be unidimensional if the responses fall into a pattern in which endorsement of the item reflecting the extreme position results also in endorsing all items which are less extreme.

Assume that we are surveying opinions regarding a new style of fortesary (a hypothetical product). We have developed a preference scale of 4 items as follows:

1. Style X is a very attractive fortesary.
2. I will insist on a style X fortesary next time because it is so beautiful.
3. The appearance of style X fortesary is acceptable to me.
4. I prefer style X fortesaries to other styles.

Respondents are asked to express themselves on each item by indicating whether they agree or disagree. If these items form a unidimensional scale the response patterns will approach the ideal configuration shown in Table 9–3:

Table 9–3: Ideal Scalogram Response Pattern

Item				Respondent Score
2	4	1	3	
X	X	X	X	4
—	X	X	X	3
—	—	X	X	2
—	—	—	X	1
—	—	—	—	0

X = Agree.
— = Disagree.

A score of "4" indicates that all statements are agreed to, and represents the most favorable attitude. Persons with a score of "3" should disagree with item 2, but agree with all others, and so on. According to scalogram theory this pattern confirms that the universe of content (attitude toward the appearance of this fortesary) is scalable.

In developing a scalogram we first define the universe of content. Assume that we are interested in determining the attitudes of people toward television advertising. We might define the universe of content as "viewer attitudes toward TV advertising." The second step is to develop items which can be used in a pretest to determine whether this topic is scalable. Guttman suggests

---

[23] Louis Guttman, "A Basis for Scaling Qualitative Data," *American Sociological Review,* vol. 9 (1944), pp. 139–50.

that a pretest should include 12 or more items, while the final scale may have only 4 to 6 items. Pretest respondent numbers may be small, say 20 or 30, but final scale use should involve 100 or more respondents.[24]

We take the pretest results and order the respondents from top to bottom—from those with the most favorable total score to the least favorable. We then order the statements from left to right from the most favorable to the least favorable. The next step is to discard those statements that fail to discriminate well between favorable and unfavorable respondents. Finally we calculate a Coefficient of Reproducibility (CR).

$$\text{Reproducibility} = 1 - \frac{e}{n(N)}$$

where e is the number of errors, n is the number of items, and N is the number of cases. It is suggested that reproducibility should be 0.90 or better for a scale to be considered unidimensional.

The scalogram approach was a pioneering attempt to develop a homogeneous scale. While the claim for unidimensionality has been challenged, at worst if a scale fails to meet the CR test it would seem clearly to be too heterogeneous for use. The fact that the scale calls for a small number of items is another of its attractive features.

The major criticism of the method grows out of research which has shown that the CR is too permissive a criterion to assure unidimensionality. In one study it was determined that a six-item Guttman scale could contain as many as three spuriously related items and still be statistically significant.[25] While other and better measures than the CR have been developed, critics still recommend against scalogram use. Typical is Robinson's view that ". . . the Guttman model is simply inappropriate for describing the structure of all but a most limited subset of social research data."[26] He suggests that the most appropriate use for the scalogram is among behaviors that are highly structured—such as social distance, organizational hierarchies, and evolutionary stages.

Factor Scales

The methods discussed to this point are all efforts to define certain concepts or constructs and to devise a small set of variables or items by which to measure these concepts. The term *factor scales* is used here to identify a

---

[24] For details on construction procedure see Louis Guttman, "The Cornell Technique for Scale and Intensity Analysis," *Educational and Psychological Measurement,* vol. 7 (1947), pp. 247–80.

[25] Carmi Schooler, "A Note of Extreme Caution on the Use of Guttman Scales," *American Journal of Sociology,* vol. 29 (June 1966).

[26] John P. Robinson, "Toward a More Appropriate Use of Guttman Scaling," *Public Opinion Quarterly,* vol. 37 (Summer 1973), pp. 260–67.

variety of techniques that have been developed to deal with two problems which have so far been glossed over. They are (1) how to deal more adequately with the universe of content which is multidimensional and (2) how to uncover underlying (latent) dimensions which have not been identified.

These techniques are designed to intercorrelate items in order to determine their degree of interdependence and in this way give meaning to the set of variables. There are many such approaches which the serious student will want to explore, such as latent structure analysis (of which the scalogram is a special case), factor analysis, cluster analysis, and metric and nonmetric multidimensional scaling. We restrict the discussion here to a major scaling technique, the semantic differential, which is based on factor analysis, and a brief discussion of multidimensional scaling.[27]

Semantic Differential (SD). This scaling method, developed by Osgood and his associates, is an attempt to measure the psychological meanings of an object to an individual.[28] It is based on the proposition that an object can have several dimensions of connotative meanings which can be located in multidimensional property space, in this case called *semantic space*. While there is a substantial body of theory concerning this technique, the emphasis here is on its development and use.

The method consists of a set of bipolar rating scales, usually seven-point, by which one or more subjects rate one or more concepts on each scale item. The scale items appears as follows:

Good   ____ : ____ : ____ : ____ : ____ : ____ : ____ Bad
Passive   ____ : ____ : ____ : ____ : ____ : ____ : ____ Active

The technique has been widely used in brand image and other marketing studies of institutional images, political issues and personalities, organizational morale, and others.

Osgood and his associates have produced a long list of adjective pairs useful for attitude research purposes. In a major study they searched *Roget's Thesaurus* for such adjectives, locating 289 pairs. These were screened down to 76 pairs which were then formed into rating scales. They then chose 20 concepts whose psychological meaning they wished to probe. These concepts, which illustrate the wide applicability of the technique, were:

Person concepts—Adlai Stevenson, me, foreigner, my mother.
Abstract concepts—modern art, sin, time, leadership.
Event concepts—debate, birth, dawn, symphony.
Institutions—hospital, America, United Nations, family life.
Physical concepts—knife, boulder, snow, engine.[29]

---

[27] For more on the process of factor analysis see Chapter 13.

[28] Charles E. Osgood, G. J. Suci, and P. H. Tannenbaum, *The Measurement of Meaning* (Urbana, Ill.: The University of Illinois Press, 1957).

[29] Ibid., p. 49.

By factor analyzing the data they concluded that semantic space is multidimensional rather than unidimensional. Repeatedly they found that three factors contributed most to meaningful judgments by respondents. While the precise nature and importance of the factors varied, depending on the concepts being studied, the major factors that emerged were (1) *evaluation,* (2) *potency* or *power,* and (3) *activity.* The evaluation dimension usually accounted for one half to three fourths of the extractable variance. Potency and activity are about equal and accounted for a little over one fourth of the extractable variance. In some cases the potency and activity dimensions combined into one labeled "dynamism." In other studies they also identified lesser dimensions which have been labeled "stability," "tautness," "novelty," and "receptivity."

Some major results of this *Thesaurus* study are shown in Table 9–4.

Table 9–4: Results of *Thesaurus* Study, Unrotated Square Root Factor Analysis

Evaluation	Potency	Activity
good–bad	hard–soft	active–passive
positive–negative	strong–weak	fast–slow
optimistic–pessimistic	heavy–light	hot–cold
complete–incomplete	masculine–feminine	excitable–calm
timely–untimely	severe–lenient	
	tenacious–yielding	

Evaluation Subcategories

Meek Goodness	Dynamic Goodness	Dependable Goodness	Hedonistic Goodness
clean–dirty	successful–unsuccessful	true–false	pleasurable–painful
kind–cruel	high–low	reputable–disreputable	beautiful–ugly
sociable–unsociable	meaningful–meaningless	believing–skeptical	sociable–unsociable
light–dark	important–unimportant	wise–foolish	meaningful–meaningless
altruistic–egotistic	progressive–regressive	healthy–sick	
grateful–ungrateful		clean–dirty	
beautiful–ugly			
harmonious–dissonant			

Source: Adapted from Charles E. Osgood, G. J. Suci, and P. H. Tannenbaum, *The Measurement of Meaning* (Urbana, Ill. The University of Illinois Press, 1957), Table 5, pp. 52–61.

Evidence was found for eight factors but the three already mentioned were again the major ones. In addition, there was evidence that the evaluation factor might also be broken into subgroups based upon subsidiary loadings (correlations) on other factors:

Subfactor:

Meek goodness	Positive loading on evaluation plus a negative loading on the potency factor.
Dynamic goodness	Positive loading on evaluation plus a positive loading on activity factor.
Dependable goodness	Positive loading on evaluation plus a positive loading on a subsidiary factor identified as "stability."
Hedonistic goodness	Positive loading on evaluation plus a positive loading on subsidiary factor which includes "pleasurable" and similar adjectives.

While it is claimed that the *SD* scale is highly generalizable, it should be adapted to each research problem. The first step in scale development is to select the concepts to be studied. While concepts tend to be nouns or noun phrases, nonverbal stimuli such as visual sketches may also be used. The concepts are chosen by personal judgment and reflect the nature of the problem under study.

Once the concepts are chosen we must select specific scale items. Here opinions diverge; some argue that the original bipolar word pairs should be used, while others argue that tailor-made scales are better. If the traditional scale items are used, three criteria should guide their selection. The first criterion for selecting scale items is the factor(s) composition. If we use the traditional three of evaluation, potency, and activity, we should probably use at least three bipolar pairs for each factor. Scores on these individual items should be averaged, by factor, to improve their test reliability. The second selection criterion is the scale's relevance to the concepts being judged. It is important to choose adjectives that permit *connotative* perceptions to be expressed. Irrelevant concept-scale pairings tend to yield neutral midpoint values that have little information value. A third criterion is that scales should be stable across subjects and concepts. For example, a pair such as "large-small" may be interpreted by some to be denotative when judging a physical object such as "automobile" but be used connotatively in judging abstract concepts such as "management by objectives." Such variability would distort the measurement process. Scales should also be linear between polar opposites and pass through the origin. A pair that might fail this test is "rugged-delicate," which are nonlinear relative to evaluation; when used separately both of these adjectives tend to have favorable meanings.[30] Finally, scales of unknown composition may be relevant to a particular problem and might be included.

To illustrate the use of the *SD* assume that we are designing a scale to compare four candidates for the leadership position in an important industry organization. The scale is to be used by a panel of corporate leaders to rate

---

[30] Ibid., p. 79.

candidates. The selection of concepts in this case is relatively simple; there are the four candidates, plus a fifth—the "ideal candidate."

The nature of the problem influences the scale selection. First, shall we develop an instrument which has only evaluative scales, or shall we include scales for potency and activity? Since the person who wins this position must lead business leaders it is decided to use all three factors. This person must deal with many people, often in a social setting; must have high integrity; and take a leadership role in encouraging more progressive policies in his industry. The position will also involve high personal activity. On the basis of these requirements we might choose ten scales by which to score the candidates from +3 to −3. Figure 9−2 illustrates the scale makeup that might be used in

Figure 9–2: *SD* Scale for Analyzing Candidates for an Industry Leadership Position

(E) Sociable	(+3) :	____ :	____ :	____ :	____ :	____ :	(−3)	Unsociable
(P) Weak	(−3) :	____ :	____ :	____ :	____ :	____ :	(+3)	Strong
(A) Active	(+3) :	____ :	____ :	____ :	____ :	____ :	(−3)	Passive
(E) Progressive	(+3) :	____ :	____ :	____ :	____ :	____ :	(−3)	Regressive
(P) Yielding	(−3) :	____ :	____ :	____ :	____ :	____ :	(+3)	Tenacious
(A) Slow	(−3) :	____ :	____ :	____ :	____ :	____ :	(+3)	Fast
(E) True	(+3) :	____ :	____ :	____ :	____ :	____ :	(−3)	False
(P) Heavy	(+3) :	____ :	____ :	____ :	____ :	____ :	(−3)	Light
(A) Hot	(+3) :	____ :	____ :	____ :	____ :	____ :	(−3)	Cold
(E) Unsuccessful	(−3) :	____ :	____ :	____ :	____ :	____ :	(+3)	Successful

this situation. The letters along the left side, which show the relevant factor, would be omitted from the actual scale, as would the numeric values shown. Note also that the evaluation, potency, and activity scales are mixed and that about one half are reversed in order to minimize the halo effect. In analyzing the results of this scaling the set of evaluation values are averaged, as are those for the potency and activity scales.

The perceptions by one judge of these five objects, four candidates (A, B, C, and D), and the "ideal candidate" are shown in two-dimension form in Figure 9−3. This judge rates candidate "D" superior to the others and closer to the concept of the ideal candidate. Candidate "A" rates well on evaluation and potency but falls down on the activity perception. The responses of all judges would be combined to determine a composite scaling similar to that shown in Figure 9−3.

Tailor-made *SD* Scales. Many researchers use ad hoc *SD*-type scales. For example, one such effort explored the problem a retail store image with 35 pairs of words or phrases classified into eight groups. Excerpts from this scale are presented in Figure 9−4.

Figure 9–3: Graphic Representation of *SD* Analysis of Five Concepts by One Judge, Hypothetical Data

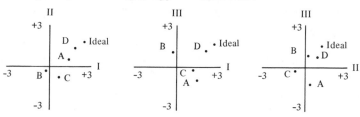

I—Evaluation.
II—Potency.
III—Activity.

Figure 9–4: Excerpts from an Ad Hoc *SD*-Type Scale for Retail Store Image

CONVENIENCE OF REACHING THE STORE FROM YOUR LOCATION

near by	____:	____:	____:	____:	____:	____:	____: distant
short time required to reach store	____:	____:	____:	____:	____:	____:	____: long time required to reach store
difficult drive	____:	____:	____:	____:	____:	____:	____: easy drive
difficult to find parking place	____:	____:	____:	____:	____:	____:	____: easy to find parking place
convenient to other stores I shop	____:	____:	____:	____:	____:	____:	____: inconvenient to other stores I shop

PRODUCTS OFFERED

wide selection of different kinds of products	____:	____:	____:	____:	____:	____:	____: limited selection of different kinds of products
fully stocked	____:	____:	____:	____:	____:	____:	____: understocked
undependable products	____:	____:	____:	____:	____:	____:	____: dependable products
high quality	____:	____:	____:	____:	____:	____:	____: low quality
numerous brands	____:	____:	____:	____:	____:	____:	____: few brands
unknown brands	____:	____:	____:	____:	____:	____:	____: well-known brands

Source: Robert F. Kelly and Ronald Stephenson, "The Semantic Differential: An Information Source for Designing Retail Patronage Appeals," *Journal of Marketing,* vol. 31 (October 1967), p. 45.

Other categories of scale items were:

General characteristics of the company.
Physical characteristics of the store.
Prices charged by the store.
Store personnel.
Advertising by the store.
Your friends and the store.

Since the scale pairs are closely associated with the characteristics of the store and its use, one could develop image profiles of various stores. Such data may be relevant at the manifest level, but in this form represent an arbitrary scale development effort. There is little chance to interpret the results in terms of SD theory, nor can one uncover latent meanings unless the results are factor-analyzed.

On the other hand, recent research aimed at using the Osgood et al. approach in the development of tailor-made SD scales looks promising.[31] There is also some evidence to suggest that the traditional scales do not work well in such research situations,[32] while other studies tend to confirm the value of the original scales.[33] In the light of this conflicting evidence the verdict is still out on which approach is the more useful. Even so, there is evidence of a growing popularity for SD-type scales.

In summary, the SD has a number of specific advantages. It is an efficient and easy way to secure attitudes from a large sample. These attitudes may be measured in both direction and intensity. The total set of responses provides a comprehensive picture of the meaning of an object, as well as a measure of the subject doing the rating. It is a standardized technique that is easily repeated but escapes many of the problems of response distortion found with more direct methods.

Multidimensional Scaling. This term describes a set of techniques that deal with property space in a more general way than does the semantic differential. With multidimensional scaling we can scale objects, individuals, or both with a minimum of information. The method discussed here, nonmetric scaling, requires nothing more than ordinal input data, although the output is essentially metric (interval). Two other forms, fully metric and fully nonmetric, will not be discussed here.

We may think of three types of attribute space, each representing a multidimensional map. First, there is objective space in which an object can be positioned in terms of, say, its flavor, weight, and nutritional value. There is also subjective space in which a person's perceptions of the object's flavor, weight, and nutritional value may be positioned. These objective and subjective attribute measurements may coincide, but often they do not. A comparison of the two allows us to judge how accurately an object is being perceived.

Various individuals may hold different perceptions of an object at the same time, and these may be averaged to present a summary measure of perceptions. In addition, a person's perceptions may vary over time and in different circumstances; such measurements are valuable to indicate the impact of various perception-affecting actions.

---

[31] John Dickson and Gerald Albaum, "A Method for Developing Tailormade Semantic Differentials for Specific Marketing Content Areas," *Journal of Marketing Research,* vol. 14 (February 1977), pp. 87–91.

[32] Louis K. Sharp and W. Thomas Anderson, Jr., "Concept-Scale Interaction in the Semantic Differential," *Journal of Marketing Research,* vol. 9 (November 1972), pp. 432–34.

[33] William S. Peters and Richard Kuhn, "An Exploration in Store Image Measurement," *Decision Sciences,* vol. 1 (1970), pp. 113–28.

With the third map we can describe our preferences in terms of the object's attributes. This represents our "ideal"; all objects close to this ideal point are interpreted as being preferred by us over those that are more distant. Ideal points from a number of persons can all be positioned in this preference space to indicate the pattern and size of preference clusters and how well they correspond to perception clusters.

The use of nonmetric scaling can be illustrated with a study of 11 automobile models.[34] In this study a group of respondents were given 55 cards, each of which bore the name of a pair of the 1968 car models. They were asked to judge the model pairs in terms of the degree of perceived similarity between them. The judging process was somewhat involved, but the eventual outcome was to secure a ranking, with the pair judged most similar being ranked as "1" and the least similar as "55." The average rankings received by the cars are shown in Table 9–5. The criterion used for judging similarity is left to the respondent.

Table 9–5: Rank Order of Dissimilarities between Pairs of Car Models

Stimuli	1	2	3	4	5	6	7	8	9	10	11
1	—	8	50	31	12	48	36	2	5	39	10
2		—	38	9	33	37	22	6	4	14	32
3			—	11	55	1	23	46	41	17	52
4				—	44	13	16	19	25	18	42
5					—	54	53	30	28	45	7
6						—	26	47	40	24	51
7							—	29	35	34	49
8								—	3	27	15
9									—	20	21
10										—	43
11											—

Note: The rank number "1" represents the most similar pair.
Source: Paul E. Green and F. J. Carmone, *Multidimensional Scaling in Marketing Analysis* (Boston, Mass.: Allyn and Bacon, Inc., 1970), p. 33. Reprinted with the permission of the publisher.

When the judging is completed an appropriate computer algorithm is applied to the rank data. The objective of the nonmetric scaling is to find a configuration whose rank order distances, in a certain number of dimensions, best reproduce the original rank order of the data. For example, the most similar pair must be located in this multidimensional space closer together than any other pair. In like manner the least similar pair must be the farthest apart. By means of a computer algorithm we represent these rank relationships as a geometric configuration so that all distances between pairs of points in the configuration closely correspond to their ranks.

---

[34] Paul E. Green and F. J. Carmone, *Multidimensional Scaling in Marketing Analysis* (Boston: Allyn and Bacon, Inc., 1970), pp. 22–37.

A problem occurs in determining how many dimensions to use to position the points. A complete answer to this question is too complex to be presented here, but the concept of the process can be understood intuitively.[35] Given a number of points, the more dimensions of space we have the easier it is to secure a point configuration with the same distance ranks as the input data. Any set of n points can be satisfied by a configuration of $n - 1$ dimensions. Our aim, however, is to secure a configuration which provides a good fit to the data and has the fewest dimensions.

Most nonmetric algorithms include the calculation of a *stress index* which indicates the lack of fit between points and the rank configuration requirements. The more the dimensions the better the fit, the lower the stress value, and also the less the explanatory value of the process. It remains for the researcher to study the calculated stress indexes to determine how few dimensions provide an acceptable fit for the data. Usually two or three dimensions will suffice.

In the car problem it was concluded that two dimensions represented an acceptable geometric configuration. This configuration is shown in Figure 9–5. The distance between Continental and Imperial is the shortest, while

Figure 9–5: Illustration of Similarities-Preference Space of Ideal Points and Objects

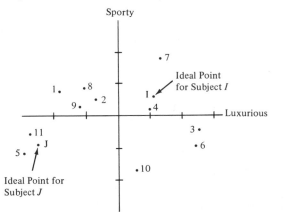

Stimuli—1968 Car Models
1. Ford Mustang 6
2. Mercury Cougar V8
3. Lincoln Continental V8
4. Ford Thunderbird V8
5. Ford Falcon 6
6. Chrysler Imperial V8
7. Jaguar Sedan
8. AMC Javelin V8
9. Plymouth Barracuda V8
10. Buick Le Sabre V8
11. Chevrolet Corvair

Source: Green and Carmone, *Multidimensional Scaling*, p. 23.

that between Falcon and Continental is the longest. By connecting any two points with a line (called a rod) we can measure the degree of similarity between any two cars.

The researcher must also define the nature of the dimensions which have been found. As with factor analysis, there is no statistical solution to this

---

[35] Ibid., p. 36.

problem. The labeling is judgmental and depends upon the insight of the researcher, an analysis of other information collected from subjects, or some other basis. For example, respondents may be asked to state the criteria they used for judging the similarities. In this study it was concluded that the horizontal dimension represented "luxuriousness," while the vertical dimension represented "sportiness."

We can also determine preference judgments for these car models by asking each respondent to rank all 11 cars in order of decreasing preference. Such a ranking may be used to locate a respondent's "ideal" model. For example, respondent "I" gave a rank order of Thunderbird, Jaguar, Cougar . . . Corvair, and Falcon in terms of decreasing preference. The assumption made is that the rank orders by different respondents reflect different preferences for sportiness and luxuriousness, resulting in different ideal points.

The apparent clustering of certain models in the attribute space indicates that they are perceived by the respondents as being similar. If we also plotted all of the ideal points of the respondents we would probably develop clusters indicating concentrations of preference. This particular comparison can be useful in determining how well the perceived values of the models meet the needs of the consumer as expressed by the ideal point clusters. Where there is a car model located in geometric space distant from any cluster of ideal points we may assume that car model is not meeting a market segment need. On the other hand if clusters of ideal points are found relatively distant from any car model it is an indication of an unsatisfied market segment. If this segment is large enough it may justify developing a model to meet the need.

While multidimensional scaling is still not being widely applied to real business problems, it gives promise of being a versatile research tool in attitude and preference mapping. Many development problems still remain, but progress is being made in solving them.

A JOB SATISFACTION SCALE[36]

Brayfield and Rothe have developed a simple scale called An Index of Job Satisfaction which is frequently referenced in the management research literature. They began with the premise that job satisfaction could be inferred from individuals' attitudes toward their work. They formulated the following as desirable attributes for their attitude scale to possess:

1. It should give an index to overall job satisfaction rather than to specific aspects of the job situation.
2. It should be applicable to a wide variety of jobs.
3. It should be sensitive to variations in attitude.
4. The items should be of such a nature (interesting, realistic, and varied)

---

[36] Arthur H. Brayfield and Harold F. Rothe, "An Index of Job Satisfaction," *Journal of Applied Psychology* (October 1951), pp. 307–11.

that the scale would evoke cooperation from both management and employees.
5. It should yield a reliable index.
6. It should yield a valid index.
7. It should be brief and easily scored.

They initially considered both the Thurstone and Likert scale designs. They settled on the Thurstone technique chiefly because they had no readily available group of employed persons who could be used for the item analysis process. They did, however, have a class of 77 mature students in a course in Personnel Psychology, most of whom had several years of work experience.

The authors collected more than 1,000 statements which were edited down to 246. These were mimeographed, compiled into sets, and distributed to the students for judging. Sorting was done under supervision, using the Thurstone approach.[37] Scale values (medians) and Q values (interquartile ranges) for each statement were determined graphically.

Four specific criteria were used to judge which statements to include in the preliminary scale.

1. Select items which cover the entire continuum at approximately 0.5 step intervals, eliminating statements at the ends of the continuum as being too extreme.
2. Choose only those statements which received consistent judgments as measured by Q scores of 2.0 or less. That is, on an 11-point scale, the middle one half of the judgments were within a 2-point range.
3. Items referring to specific aspects of a job were eliminated since an overall attitudinal factor was desired. For example, items regarding pay, working conditions, and so forth, were eliminated because they might be too specific.
4. Acceptability to employees and management was judged. For example, the item "I am tempted to use illness as an excuse to stay home from this job" was rejected as reflecting unfavorably upon the individual worker.

A preliminary scale of 18 items was tested, using a rank correlation of odd and even items. This measure of reliability was low enough to prompt the authors to convert to a Likert-type scale, which evidence has shown typically produces a higher reliability than does a Thurstone scale.

The final scale still consisted of 18 items, each with a five-point agreement-disagreement response category set. From the Thurstone scale value it was known what direction to apply the scoring method to assure that a low total score would represent the dissatisfied end of the scale. The neutral response point was *undecided*. A copy of the final scale is presented in Figure 9–6.

---

[37] For detailed instructions on using the Thurstone approach see Allen L. Edwards, *Techniques of Attitude Scale Construction* (New York: Appleton-Century-Crofts, Inc., 1957).

Figure 9–6: Brayfield-Rothe Index of Job Satisfaction

Some jobs are more interesting and satisfying than others. We want to know how people feel about different jobs. This blank contains 18 statements about jobs. You are to cross out the phrase below each statement which best describes how you feel about your present job. There are no right or wrong answers. We should like your honest opinion on each one of the statements. Work out the sample item numbered (0).

0. There are some conditions concerning my job that could be improved.
   STRONGLY AGREE   AGREE   UNDECIDED   DISAGREE   STRONGLY DISAGREE

1. My job is like a hobby to me.
   STRONGLY AGREE   AGREE   UNDECIDED   DISAGREE   STRONGLY DISAGREE

2. My job is usually interesting enough to keep me from getting bored.
   STRONGLY AGREE   AGREE   UNDECIDED   DISAGREE   STRONGLY DISAGREE

3. It seems that my friends are more interested in their jobs.
   STRONGLY AGREE   AGREE   UNDECIDED   DISAGREE   STRONGLY DISAGREE

4. I consider my job rather unpleasant.
   STRONGLY AGREE   AGREE   UNDECIDED   DISAGREE   STRONGLY DISAGREE

5. I enjoy my work more than my leisure time.
   STRONGLY AGREE   AGREE   UNDECIDED   DISAGREE   STRONGLY DISAGREE

6. I am often bored with my job.
   STRONGLY AGREE   AGREE   UNDECIDED   DISAGREE   STRONGLY DISAGREE

7. I feel fairly well-satisfied with my present job.
   STRONGLY AGREE   AGREE   UNDECIDED   DISAGREE   STRONGLY DISAGREE

8. Most of the time I have to force myself to go to work.
   STRONGLY AGREE   AGREE   UNDECIDED   DISAGREE   STRONGLY DISAGREE

9. I am satisfied with my job for the time being.
   STRONGLY AGREE   AGREE   UNDECIDED   DISAGREE   STRONGLY DISAGREE

10. I feel that my job is no more interesting than others I could get.
    STRONGLY AGREE   AGREE   UNDECIDED   DISAGREE   STRONGLY DISAGREE

11. I definitely dislike my work.
    STRONGLY AGREE   AGREE   UNDECIDED   DISAGREE   STRONGLY DISAGREE

12. I feel that I am happier in my work than most other people.
    STRONGLY AGREE   AGREE   UNDECIDED   DISAGREE   STRONGLY DISAGREE

13. Most days I am enthusiastic about my work.
    STRONGLY AGREE   AGREE   UNDECIDED   DISAGREE   STRONGLY DISAGREE

14. Each day of work seems like it will never end.
    STRONGLY AGREE   AGREE   UNDECIDED   DISAGREE   STRONGLY DISAGREE

15. I like my job better than the average worker does.
    STRONGLY AGREE   AGREE   UNDECIDED   DISAGREE   STRONGLY DISAGREE

16. My job is pretty uninteresting.
    STRONGLY AGREE   AGREE   UNDECIDED   DISAGREE   STRONGLY DISAGREE

17. I find real enjoyment in my work.
    STRONGLY AGREE   AGREE   UNDECIDED   DISAGREE   STRONGLY DISAGREE

18. I am disappointed that I ever took this job.
    STRONGLY AGREE   AGREE   UNDECIDED   DISAGREE   STRONGLY DISAGREE

Source: Arthur H. Brayfield and Harold F. Rothe, "An Index of Job Satisfaction," *Journal of Applied Psychology* (October 1951), p. 309.

The reliability of this scale has been measured by computing an odd-even item correlation which, when corrected by the Spearman-Brown formula, gives a reliability coefficient of 0.87. Validity was evaluated by correlating with the Hoppock job satisfaction scale. The product-moment correlation between these two scales was 0.92. In addition, the form was tested with a group of people who could be separated into two groups—those employed in personnel occupations and those not employed in such occupations. It was hypothesized that those in personnel occupations would be more satisfied with their jobs than those not in personnel jobs. This hypothesis was confirmed by the data. On the basis of these tests it was concluded that the index has adequate reliability and validity.

SUMMARY

"Scaling" describes the procedures by which we assign numbers to various degrees of opinion, attitude, and other concepts. These procedures may be classified in six different ways:

1. Study objective—do we measure the characteristics of the respondent or the stimulus object?
2. Response form—do we measure by using a categorical or comparative scale?
3. Degree of preference—do we measure our preferences or make non-preference judgments?
4. Scale properties—do we measure by using nominal, ordinal, interval, or ratio scales?
5. Number of dimensions—do we measure using a unidimensional or multidimensional scale?
6. Scale construction technique—do we develop scales by arbitrary decision, consensus, item analysis, cumulative scaling, or factor analysis?

In this chapter we have concentrated on two of these classifications—the response form and scale construction techniques.

When we use categorical scales we judge an object in absolute terms against certain specified criteria. We can use either a graphic or an itemized rating scale. When we use comparative or ranking methods we make relative judgments against other similar objects. Three well-known methods are the paired-comparison, the rank order, and successive intervals methods.

Arbitrary scales are designed largely through the researcher's own subjective selection of items. These scales are simple and inexpensive to construct and have a certain face validity for their designer, but it is generally not possible to judge their validity in any other way.

In the consensus method we use a panel to judge the relevancy, ambiguity, and attitude level of scale items. Those items which are judged best are then included in the final instrument. The Thurstone method of equal-appearing intervals is developed by the consensus methods.

With the item analysis approach we develop a number of items believed to express either a favorable or an unfavorable attitude toward some general object. These items are then pretested to determine which discriminate between persons with high total scores and those with low total scores on the test. Those items that best meet this discrimination test are included in the final instrument. Likert scales are often developed through this approach.

With cumulative scales it is possible to estimate how a respondent has answered individual items by knowing the total score. The items are related to each other, on a particular attitude dimension, in such a way that if we agree with a more extreme item, we will also agree with items representing less extreme views. Guttman's scalogram is the classic example of this type of scale development.

Factor scales are developed through factor analysis or similar correlation techniques. They are particularly useful in uncovering latent attitude dimensions and approach scaling through the concept of multiple-dimension attribute space. Semantic differential scales and nonmetric multidimensional scales are two examples discussed.

SUPPLEMENTAL READINGS

1. Edwards, Allen L. *Techniques of Attitude Scale Construction.* New York: Appleton-Century-Crofts, Inc., 1957. Thorough discussion of basic unidimensional scaling techniques.

2. Green, Paul E., and Rao, Vithala R. *Applied Multidimensional Scaling.* Hinsdale, Ill.: Dryden Press, 1972. A lucid discussion on, and comparison of, "various conceptual approaches and scaling algorithms" in multidimensional scaling methodology.

3. Kerlinger, Fred N. *Foundations of Behavioral Research.* 2d ed. New York: Holt, Rinehart and Winston, 1973. Chaps. 29–34 cover various scaling and other data collection techniques, some of which are not discussed in this text.

4. Miller, Delbert C. *Handbook of Research Design and Social Measurement.* 3d ed. New York: David McKay Company, Inc., 1977. Presents a large number of existing sociometric scales and indexes, as well as information on their characteristics, validity, and sources.

5. Osgood, Charles E.; Suci, George J.; and Tannenbaum, Percy H. *The Measurement of Meaning.* Urbana, Ill.: University of Illinois Press, 1957. The basic reference on *SD* scaling.

6. Snider, James G., and Osgood, Charles E., eds. *Semantic Differential Technique.* Chicago: Aldine Publishing Company, 1969. A collection of 52 papers on *SD* technique plus a semantic atlas for 550 concepts.

7. Summers, Gene F., ed. *Attitude Measurement.* Chicago: Rand McNally & Company, 1970. An excellent collection of papers on various aspects of scaling.

DISCUSSION QUESTIONS

1. Discuss the relative merits and demerits of:
   a. Rating versus ranking scales.
   b. Likert versus differential scales.
   c. Unidimensional versus multidimensional scales.

2. Suppose some researcher gives you a scale to complete. It has as its subject the economic system currently found in the United States.
   a. Describe the various measurement objectives that the researcher might have in mind in asking you to complete this questionnaire.
   b. What would the scale be like and how would it be developed if it were a:
   Thurstone differential scale.
   Likert-type summated scale.
   Semantic differential scale.
   Scalogram.
   Multidimensional scale.

3. This chapter has been partially organized on the basis of five methods of scale construction. What are these methods and how do they differ? Is this difference of real importance? Explain.

4. You receive the results of a paired-comparison preference test of four soft drinks from a sample of 200 persons. The results are as follows:

	Koak	Zip	Pabze	Mr. Peepers
Koak	X	50*	115	35
Zip	150	X	160	70
Pabze	85	40	X	45
Mr. Peepers	165	130	155	X

* Read as 50 persons preferred Zip over Koak.

   a. How do these brands rank in overall preference in this sample?
   b. Develop an interval scale for these four brands.

5. One of the problems in developing rating scales is the choice of response terms to use. Below are samples of some widely used scaling codes. Do you see any problems with them?
   A. Yes _____ Depends _____ No _____
   B. Excellent _____ Good _____ Fair _____ Poor _____
   C. Excellent _____ Good _____ Average _____ Fair _____ Poor _____
   D. Strongly   Un-   Dis-   Strongly
      Approve ____Approve ____certain ____approve ____Disapprove ____

6. Assume that you are to judge a set of statements that will be used in developing a differential scale for an employee attitude survey. Score each of the below listed statements from 1 to 10, with "10" being the most positive favorable statement, and "1" the least favorable. After scoring these

statements refer to page 270 to compare your judgment with the average judgments made in the actual study. How do you account for any substantial differences between your scores and the average scores?

Score

_____ The pay in this company is terrible.

_____ I think the company goes outside to fill good jobs instead of promoting people who are here.

_____ The company is sincere in wanting to know what its employees think about it.

_____ I think this company treats its employees better than any other company does.

_____ I believe accidents will happen no matter what you do about them.

_____ One can get ahead in this company if one tries.

_____ The workers put as much over on the company as the company puts over on them.

_____ My boss gives all the breaks to lodge and church friends.

_____ Soldiering on the job is on the increase.

_____ In the long run this company will "put it over" on you.

7. Below is a Likert type of scale which might be used to evaluate your opinion of the educational program you are in. There are five response categories: Strongly Agree through Neutral to Strong Disagree. If "5" represents the most positive attitude, how would the different items be valued?

   a. This program is not very challenging.
   > SA A N D SD

   b. The general level of teaching is good.
   > SA A N D SD

   c. I really think I am learning a lot from this program.
   > SA A N D SD

   d. Students' suggestions are given little attention here.
   > SA A N D SD

   e. This program does a good job of preparing one for a career.
   > SA A N D SD

   f. This program is below my expectations.
   > SA A N D SD

   Record your answers to the above items. In what two different ways could such responses be used? What would be the purpose of each?

8. Using the semantic differential scale below record your impressions of the educational program you are in.

```
      good _____:_____:_____:_____:_____:_____:_____bad
      weak _____:_____:_____:_____:_____:_____:_____strong
    active _____:_____:_____:_____:_____:_____:_____passive
  complete _____:_____:_____:_____:_____:_____:_____incomplete
    severe _____:_____:_____:_____:_____:_____:_____lenient
      fast _____:_____:_____:_____:_____:_____:_____slow
      cold _____:_____:_____:_____:_____:_____:_____hot
meaningful _____:_____:_____:_____:_____:_____:_____meaningless
     heavy _____:_____:_____:_____:_____:_____:_____light
```

a. Assuming "7" is a positive score, how would you score the response alternatives above?

b. Which of these items are evaluative? Activity? Potency?

c. What are your scores on the above three dimensions?

d. How does your answer compare to the answers you gave in question 7?

9. Using the above *SD* scale again, score your "ideal" educational program and calculate your evaluation, activity, and potency scales for this ideal program. How does this one compare with your answer in question 8?

10. What are the critical differences between a classical *SD* scale and an ad hoc *SD* scale? What are the advantages and disadvantages of each?

11. Suppose you wished to use multidimensional scaling to have high school seniors compare five colleges. How would you go about it? How might you use the results of such a study if you were the director of admissions at one of these colleges?

Chapter 10

Data Collection—Field Procedures

IN THE LAST TWO CHAPTERS we have discussed the development of research measurement instruments, but not much was said about actual field data collection procedures. These are the topics in this chapter and will be discussed in terms of both the monitoring and interrogation communication modes. In the former we directly or indirectly observe conditions, activities, and events. In the interrogation mode we seek replies from respondents either through in-person contact, by telephone, or by mail. We shall discuss the interrogation mode first.

PERSONAL INTERVIEWING

Personal interviewing is a two-way purposeful conversation initiated by an interviewer to obtain information that is relevant to some research purpose. The differences in roles between interviewer and respondent are pronounced. These participants are typically strangers; the topics and pattern of discussion are dictated by the interviewer. The consequences of the event are normally minimal in effect on the respondent. The respondent is asked to provide information in the form of facts, attitudes, opinions, and intentions, with little hope of receiving any immediate or direct benefit from this cooperation. Yet, if the interview is carried off successfully, it is an excellent data collection technique.

The Value of Personal Interviewing

There are some real advantages as well as some clear limitations to personal interviewing. The greatest value of this method is the depth and detail of information that can be secured. It far exceeds, in volume and quality, the information we can usually secure from telephone and mail surveys. The interviewer can also do more things to improve the quality of the information received than with other methods. She can note conditions of the interview, probe with additional questions when appropriate, request to see a product that the respondent claims to have, and gather other supplemental information through observation.[1]

The interviewer also has more control over the personal interview than other interrogation types. She can prescreen to assure that the correct respondent is replying; she can influence, and often can set up and control interviewing conditions. She can use special scoring devices, visual materials, and the like. Finally, while not an unalloyed advantage, the interviewer can make adjustments to the language of the interview because she can observe the problems and effects that the interview is having on the respondent.

With such advantages why would anyone want to use any other survey method? Probably the greatest reason is that the method is costly, both in money and time. A personal interview can cost from a few dollars up to $100 or more for an interview with a hard-to-reach person such as a top corporate executive. Costs are particularly high if the study covers a large geographic area or has stringent sampling requirements.

Costs have risen rapidly in recent years because changes in the social climate have made personal interviewing more difficult. Many persons are reluctant to talk with strangers who visit their home. Interviewers are reluctant to visit unfamiliar neighborhoods alone, especially for evening interviewing. Finally, personal interview results are often affected adversely by interviewers who alter the questions asked, and in many other ways bias the respondent's replies. More will be said of this later in the chapter. If we are to overcome these deficiencies and assure that personal interviews are productive, we must appreciate the conditions necessary for interview success.

Requirements for Interview Success

Three broad conditions are needed for a successful personal interview. They are (1) accessibility of the needed information to the respondents, (2) understanding by the respondents of their roles, and (3) motivation of the respondents to accept such a role and to fulfill its requirements.

Accessibility means that the needed information is available to the respondents and that they can express it in terms useful to the study. The researchers

---

[1] Robert L. Kahn, and Charles F. Cannell, "Interviewing," *International Encyclopedia of the Social Sciences,* vol. 8 (New York: The Macmillan Company and Free Press, 1968), p. 152.

should have assured themselves of this point at the research design and testing stage; the interviewer can affect this factor to only a limited degree. Whether the respondents understand their role or not is more controllable by the interviewer. As a minimum the respondents must learn what is relevant as an answer, how complete it should be, and in what terms it should be provided. They can learn much of this from the interviewer's introductory remarks, explanations, and questioning procedures. How much the respondents need to know of the project depends upon their sophistication and perceptions of the study as a personal threat. If the respondents' information needs are met, the chances for a successful interview are enhanced.

Respondent motivation is heavily in the hands of the interviewer. Studies of reactions to a number of surveys indicate that respondents can be motivated to participate in personal interviews and, in fact, enjoy it. Typically, more than 90 percent of respondents said that the experience was interesting and three fourths reported that they were willing to be interviewed again.[2] These high proportions were found for a variety of studies over a wide range of subject matter.

Kahn and Cannell suggest that there are two sets of motivations that foster this willingness of the respondents to participate. First there is *extrinsic* motivation, described as the desire to bring about a change or take an action that they consider desirable.[3] The respondents see the interviewer as an instrument that can help bring about this change. People will often express opinions in public opinion polls because it gives them the feeling that they are being heard by those in positions of influence.

Figure 10-1: Opposing Motivation Levels Affecting a Respondent in an Interview

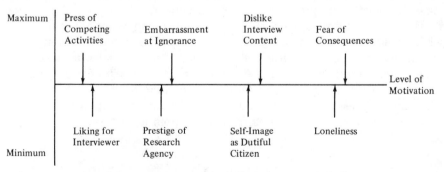

Source: Kahn and Cannell, "Interviewing," p. 153. Reprinted with permission of the publisher from the *International Encyclopedia of the Social Sciences,* David L. Sills, ed., vol. 8, p. 153. Copyright © 1968 by Crowell Collier and Macmillan, Inc.

---

[2] Charles F. Cannell and Morris Axelrod, "The Respondent Reports on the Interview," *American Journal of Sociology,* vol. 62 (1956), pp. 177–81.

[3] Robert L. Kahn and Charles F. Cannell, *The Dynamics of Interviewing* (New York: John Wiley & Sons, Inc., 1957), pp. 45–51.

Motivation of the *intrinsic* type depends much more on the personal relationship between the interviewer and the respondents. The interview is a unique social situation and how the parties perceive each other has much to do with the interaction that takes place. Respondents react to the interviewer's behavior, receive cues from the interviewer's appearance, and are affected by the interviewing situation, their perception of the thrust of the questions, and their personal needs. A graphic way to represent these various forces that tend to affect respondent motivation is presented in Figure 10–1.

Interviewing Technique[4]

It may seem easy to ask another person some questions about various topics, but research interviewing is not so simple. What we do or say as interviewers can make or break a study. Respondents often react more to their relationships with the interviewer than to the content of the questions they are asked. It is also important that the interviewer ask the questions properly, record the responses accurately, and probe meaningfully. To achieve these aims the interviewer must understand and carry out those procedures which foster a good interviewing relationship.

Increasing Respondent's Receptiveness. The first goal in an interview is to establish a friendly relationship with the respondent. There are three major factors which will help bring about respondent receptiveness. The respondent must (1) feel that the experience will be pleasant and satisfying, (2) believe that the survey is important and worthwhile, and (3) have any mental reservations satisfied. Whether the experience will be pleasant and satisfying depends heavily upon the interviewer. Typically respondents will accept an interviewer, even one perceived to be different from themselves, if that interviewer appears to be understanding and accepting.

The respondent must also see the survey as being important and worthwhile. This typically requires some explanation of the study, although the amount will vary by case. It is the interviewer's responsibility to determine what explanation is needed and to supply it. This usually requires that the interviewer state the purpose of the study, tell how the information will be used, and suggest what is expected of the respondent. Respondents should feel that their cooperation will be meaningful both to themselves and to the survey results. When such understanding is achieved most respondents will express their views willingly. Respondents often have reservations about being interviewed which must be overcome. Often they suspect that the interviewer is a disguised salesperson, bill collector, or the like. In addition, they may also feel inadequate, or fear that they will be embarrassed by the questioning.

---

[4] One of the premier survey research organizations in the world is the Survey Research Center of the University of Michigan. The material in this section draws heavily upon the *Interviewer's Manual* (Ann Arbor, Mich.: Survey Research Center, University of Michigan, 1969).

The Introduction. The respondent's first reaction to the request for an interview is at best a mix of guarded curiosity and reserved courtesy. Interviewer appearance and action is critical in forming a good first impression. Interviewers should immediately identify themselves by name and organization, showing any special identification. Introductory letters or other information can demonstrate the study's legitimacy. In this brief period of ambivalent interest the interviewer must demonstrate friendly intentions and stimulate further interest by the respondent.

The interviewer's introductory explanations should be no more detailed than necessary. Too much information can introduce a bias. On the other hand, some respondents will demand more detail. For them the interviewer might explain the objective of the study, its background, how the respondent was selected, the confidential nature of the interview (if it is such), and the beneficial values of the research findings. Be prepared to deal with such questions as:

"How did you happen to pick me?"
"Who gave you our name?"
"I don't know enough about this. Why don't you go next door?"
"Why are you doing this study?"[5]

The home interview typically involves two stages. The first occurs at the door when the introductory remarks are made, but this is not a satisfactory location for many interviews. In trying to secure entrance it is considered more effective to suggest the desired course of action rather than to ask permission. It is argued that "May I come in?" can be easily countered with a respondent's "No," while "I would like to come in and talk with you about 'X'," is more successful.

If the Respondent Is Busy or Away. If it is obvious that the respondent is busy it may be a good idea to give a general introduction and try to stimulate enough interest to arrange an interview at a later date. If the designated respondent is not at home, the interviewer should briefly explain the proposed visit to the person who is contacted. It is desirable to establish good relations with intermediaries since their attitudes can help in contacting the proper respondent.

The Good Interviewing Relationship. The successful interview has the characteristics of any good interpersonal relationship. It can be described by the term "rapport," meaning that a relationship of confidence and understanding exists between interviewer and respondent. Interview situations are often new to the respondents and they need help in defining their roles. The interviewer can help by conveying the fact that the interview is confidential and important, and that the respondent can discuss the topics with freedom

---

[5] Ibid., pp. 3–4.

from censure, coercion, or pressure. Under such conditions the respondent can obtain much satisfaction in "opening up" without pressure being exerted.

Gathering the Data.   To this point we have stressed the communication aspects of the interviewing process. Having completed the introduction and established initial rapport, the interviewer turns to the technical task of gathering information. The interview centers around the interview schedule. The technical task is well-defined in studies with a structured questioning procedure (in contrast to an exploratory interview situation). The interviewer should follow the exact wording of the questions, ask them in the order presented, and ask every question that is specified. When questions are misunderstood or misinterpreted they should be repeated.

One of the most difficult tasks in interviewing is to make certain that the answers adequately satisfy the question objectives. To do this the interviewer must learn the objectives of each question from a study of the survey instructions or by asking the project director. It is important to know this information thoroughly because many first responses are inadequate even in the best-planned studies.

The technique of stimulating respondents to answer more fully and relevantly is termed *probing*. Since it presents a great potential for bias, a probe should be neutral in nature and appear as a natural part of the conversation. There are a number of different probe styles which may be used.

1. A brief assertion of understanding and interest. With comments such as "I see" or "yes" or "uh-huh" the interviewer can tell the respondent that the interviewer is listening and is interested in more.
2. An expectant pause. The simplest way to suggest to the respondent to say more is a pause along with an expectant look or a nod of the head. This approach must be used with caution. Some respondents have nothing more to say and frequent pausing could give them some embarrassing silences.
3. Repeating the question. This is particularly useful when the respondent appears not to understand the question or has strayed from the subject.
4. Repeating the respondent's reply. This can be done while writing it down and often serves as a good probe. Hearing thoughts restated often prompts revisions or further comments.
5. A neutral question or comment. Such comments make a direct bid for more information. Examples are: "How do you mean? Can you tell me more about your thinking on that? Why do you think that is so? Anything else?"[6]

Another valuable technique is to ask for further clarification. This approach is particularly effective when the answer is unclear or is inconsistent with something already said. In this case the interviewers suggest that *they* failed to understand fully. Typical of such probes is, "I'm not *quite* sure I know what you mean by that—could you tell me a little more?" or "I'm sorry, but I'm not

---

[6] Ibid., pp. 5–2.

sure I understand. Did you mention previously . . . ?" It is important in this approach that the interviewer take the blame for failure to understand so as not to appear to cross-examine the respondent.

A specific type of response that requires persistent probing is the "I don't know." This is a satisfactory response if the respondent actually does not know. But, too often, "I don't know" means that the respondent (1) does not understand, (2) says this to get time to think, or (3) is trying to evade the question. The interviewer can best probe this type of reply by using the expectant pause or by some reassuring remark such as "We are interested in your ideas about this." [7]

Recording the Interview. While the methods used in recording will vary, the interviewer usually writes down the answers of the respondent. There are some guidelines which can make this task more efficient. First, it is important to record responses as they take place. If we wait until later we lose much of what is said. If hard pressed for time during the session, the interviewer should use some system of shorthand recording that will preserve the essence of respondent's replies without converting them into an interviewer's paraphrases. Abbreviating words, leaving out articles and prepositions, using only key words, and the like, are good ways to do this.

It is a good technique for the interviewer to repeat the response while writing it down. This helps hold the respondent's interest during the writing and checks the interviewer's understanding of what the respondent said. Normally the interviewer should start the writing as soon as the respondent begins to reply. The interviewer should also record all probes and other comments on the questionnaire in parentheses to set them off from responses.

Personal Interview Problems

In personal interviewing the researcher must deal with two major problems, bias and cost. While we will discuss them separately they are strongly interrelated. Biased results grow out of three major types of error: sampling error, nonresponse error and response error. Sampling error was discussed in Chapter 6.

Nonresponse Error. This type of error can result when we have difficulties in finding the respondent who has been selected into the sample, especially a probability sample. It can cause a strong bias when the nonrespondents vary from the respondents in some systematic way. The data in Figure 10–2 suggest that such distortions can be substantial.

Only 31 percent of all first calls, and 20 percent of the first calls in major metropolitan areas, were completed. The best first-call contact rate of 52 percent was for rural male respondents contacted after 6 P.M. on a weekday.

---

[7] Ibid., pp. 5–3.

Figure 10-2: Completion Rates on First Call

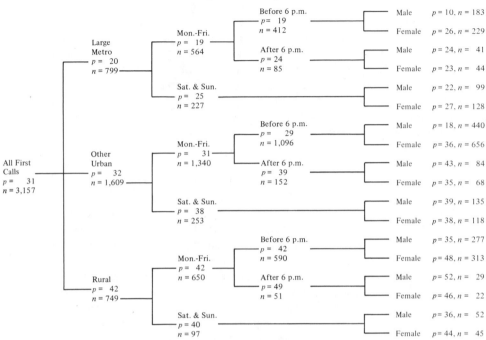

Percentage of Calls Resulting in Completed Interviews

Source: Reprinted from Charles S. Mayer, "The Interviewer and His Environment," *Journal of Marketing Research,* vol. 1 (November 1964), p. 26, published by the American Marketing Association.

Even in this case almost one half of the designated respondents were not contacted. One way to overcome this nonresponse problem is to substitute someone else for the missing respondent, but this is a dangerous practice. "At home" respondents are likely to differ from "not at home" persons in systematic ways. One study indicates that "not at home" persons tend to be younger, better educated, more urban, and have a higher income than the average.[8]

A better substitution is for the interviewer to query others in the household about the designated respondent. This approach has worked reasonably well "when questions are relatively objective, when informants have a high degree of observability with respect to respondents, when the population is homogeneous, and when the setting of the interview provides no clear-cut motivation to distort responses in one direction or another. . . ."[9]

---

[8] W. C. Dunkleberg and G. S. Day, "Nonresponse Bias and Callbacks in Sample Surveys," *Journal of Marketing Research,* vol. 10 (May 1973), pp. 160–68.

[9] Eleanore Singer, "Agreement between Inaccessible Respondents and Informants," *Public Opinion Quarterly,* vol. 36 (Winter 1972–73), pp. 603–11.

Another approach that is sometimes used is to adjust the results secured by weighting.[10] For example, in a survey in which central city residents are underrepresented we can weight the results of the central city interviews that are secured in order to give them full representation in the results. The weakness of this approach is that weighted returns often differ from those that would be secured if callbacks were made. Weighting for nonresponse after only one contact attempt will probably not overcome nonresponse bias, but respondent characteristics do tend to converge on their population values after two to three callbacks.[11]

A more reliable solution to nonresponse problems is to make callbacks if the first call fails. If enough attempts are made it is usually possible to contact most target respondents.[12] But unlimited callbacks are expensive. An original contact plus three callbacks should usually secure about 85 percent of the target respondents. Yet in one study 36 percent of central city residents still were not contacted after three callbacks.[13] One way to improve the productivity of callbacks is to vary them by time of day and day of the week. Sometimes neighbors can also suggest the best time to call.

A method which has been used with success is, after a limited number of callbacks, to treat all remaining nonrespondents as a new subpopulation. A random sample is then drawn from this group and every effort is made to complete this sample with 100 percent response. These findings can then be weighted into the total population estimate.

Response Error. This bias occurs when the data reported differ from the actual data. There are many ways that such errors can appear. One form is errors in processing and tabulating, but discussion of these is reserved to Chapter 12. Another important source of error is the respondent who fails to report fully and accurately. In studies of economic matters it has been found that liquid asset holdings are typically underreported by as much as 25 to 50 percent.[14] Other data, such as income and purchases of consumer durables, are more accurately reported. It has already been pointed out that respondents also have difficulty in reporting fully and accurately on topics that are "sensitive" or involve ego matters. Consistent control or elimination of these types of respondent bias is a constant problem that has not yet been solved. Probably the best simple advice is to use trained interviewers who are knowledgeable about such problems.

The interviewer is another important cause of response bias. A particularly bothersome type of conscious error is interviewer cheating. This is partly a

---

[10] C. H. Fuller, "Weighting to Adjust for Survey Nonresponse," *Public Opinion Quarterly*, vol. 38 (Summer 1974), pp. 239–46.

[11] Dunkleberg and Day, "Nonresponse Bias," Table 3.

[12] In one study 5.5 percent of white respondents and 11 percent of nonwhite respondents remained uncontacted after six calls. See ibid., Table 3.

[13] Ibid.

[14] J. B. Lansing, G. P. Ginsburg, and K. Braaten, *An Investigation of Response Error* (Urbana, Ill.: University of Illinois Bureau of Economic and Business Research, 1961), p. 201.

matter of weak individual morals in a difficult working situation where a short-term casual employee has little supervision. Cheating can also grow out of morale problems that develop because of this lack of supervision, plus difficult interviewing tasks and pressures that reduce interviewer motivation.

It is obvious that an interviewer can distort the results of any survey by inappropriate suggestions, word emphasis, tone of voice, and question re-phrasing. Such activities, whether premeditated or merely due to carelessness are widespread. Schyberger investigated this problem with a relatively simple structured questionnaire and using planted respondents to report on the in-terviewers. His conclusion was "the high frequency of deviations from in-structed behavior are alarming. . . ."[15]

In addition to these factors there are many other ways that interviewers can influence respondents. For example, older interviewers are often seen as authority figures by young respondents who modify their responses accord-ingly. Some research indicates that perceived social distance between inter-viewer and respondent has a distorting effect, although the studies do not fully agree on just what this relationship is.[16]

There have been a large number of studies on the various aspects of interviewer bias, most of which support the conclusion that it is a major problem area. However, many of the findings are at odds on the exact dimensions of this bias and the conditions under which it occurs. In the light of this confusion the safest course for research directors is to recognize that there is a constant potential for response error. They should select carefully and preferably use trained personnel whose age, sex, social status, and ethnic origin conform to that of the population being studied. When the study is a crosssection of the general population this matching is not possible. In such a case the typical interviewer, a middle-aged, middle-class woman, is probably the best choice. Respondents generally perceive such an interviewer as being accepting, understanding, and nonthreatening.

Costs.   While professional interviewers' wage scales are typically not high, interviewing is costly and these costs continue to rise. Much of the cost results from the substantial interviewer time taken up with administrative and travel tasks. Respondents are often geographically scattered and this adds to the cost. In recent years some professional research organizations have at-tempted to gain control of these spiraling costs. Interviewers have typically been paid on an hourly rate, but Sudman suggests that this method rewards the inefficient interviewers and often results in field costs exceeding budgets. The U.S. Bureau of the Census and The National Opinion Research Center have experimented with production standards and a formula pay system that

---

[15] Bo W:son Schyberger, "A Study of Interviewer Behavior," *Journal of Marketing Research,* vol. 4 (February 1967), p. 35.

[16] B. S. Dohrenwend, J. A. Williams Jr., and C. H. Weiss, "Interviewer Biasing Effects: toward a Reconciliation of Findings," *Public Opinion Quarterly,* vol. 33 (Spring 1969), pp. 121–29.

provides an incentive for efficient interviewers. It is reported that this approach has cut field costs by about 10 percent and has improved the accuracy of the forecasts of field work costs.[17]

A second approach to the reduction of field costs has been to use the telephone to schedule personal interviews. Telephone calls to set up appointments for interviews are reported to reduce personal calls by 25 percent without reducing cooperation rates.[18] Telephone screening is also very valuable when a study is concerned with a rare population. In one such case where blind persons were sought it was found that telephone screening of households by telephone was only one third the cost of screening on a face-to-face basis.[19]

A third approach to the problem of high field costs is to use self-administered questionnaires. In one study a personal interview was conducted in the household with a self-administered questionnaire left for one or more other members of the household to complete. In this study the cost per completed case were reduced by about one half as compared to using personal interviews. A comparison between personal interview and self-administered questionnaire results indicated that there was generally sufficient similarity of answers to enable them to be combined.[20]

Another study compared the use of a "drop off" delivery of a self-administered questionnaire to a mail survey.[21] Under the "drop off" system a lightly trained survey taker personally delivered the questionnaires to target households and returned in a couple of days for the completed instrument. Response rates for the "drop off" system were typically above 70 percent—much higher than for comparable mail surveys. At the same time the cost per completed questionnaire was from 18 to 40 percent lower than the mail surveys.

In addition, to a higher rate and lower cost per response, the "drop off" method gives greater control over sample design, permits more complete identification of the respondents' geographic location, and allows the researcher to eliminate those persons who fall outside of a predefined sample frame (persons of the wrong age, income, or other characteristics). Other information can also be gathered by observation on the visits. On the other hand, the cost advantage of this method is probably restricted to those studies where the respondents can be reached with relatively little travel.

---

[17] Seymour Sudman, *Reducing the Costs of Surveys* (Chicago: Aldine Publishing Company, 1967), p. 67.

[18] Ibid., p. 59.

[19] Ibid., p. 63.

[20] Ibid., p. 53.

[21] C. H. Lovelock, Ronald Stiff, David Cullwick, and Ira M. Kaufman, "An Evaluation of the Effectiveness of Drop-Off Questionnaire Delivery," *Journal of Marketing Research,* vol. 13 (November 1976), pp. 358–64.

Interviewer Selection and Training

A limited number of studies have shown that good interviewer selection and training can substantially improve field staff performance. Just how much these findings have resulted in better field personnel is not known, but much survey research is probably carried out by persons poorly equipped for the task they face.

Selection.   One of the early studies between interviewer characteristics and performance reported that women were better interviewers than men, married men were better than single women, and that they all improved with experience.[22] Studies at the U.S. Bureau of the Census indicated that the Census Enumerator Selection Aid Test is useful in selecting more effective interviewers.[23] This test is designed to measure reading comprehension and ability to follow instructions.

A more recent report on the relation between interviewer characteristics and interview quality and costs has been published by the National Opinion Research Center (NORC). This study emphasized nondemographic and personality characteristics. Some of its findings are:

1. Interviewers who are high in intelligence and education are more likely to have better quality-cost performances (high quality and low cost).
2. Interviewers with longer experience with NORC are more likely to be high quality-low cost interviewers. On the other hand interviewers with experience in other organizations tend to be high cost.
3. High need achievement is also positively correlated with high quality interviewing but has no apparent connection with cost.
4. Interviewers with heavy family responsibilities are more likely to resign, but when they work they tend to have a better than average quality-cost performance
5. Efficiency in planning is related to low cost as is a high score on manipulative tests (Machiavellian).[24]

Training.   Field interviewers receive varying degrees of training ranging from brief written instructions to extensive training sessions. Commercial market research studies tend to the former level of training, while governmental, educational, and other similar research organizations tend to the more extensive training.

Written instructions should be provided in all studies. Such instructions should cover at least the general objectives of the study, something on the problems which have been encountered in tests of the interview procedure,

[22] P. B. Sheatsley, "An Analysis of Interviewer Characteristics and Their Relationship to Performance, Part III," *International Journal of Opinion and Attitude Research,* vol. 5 (Summer 1951), pp. 191–220.

[23] R. H. Hansen and E. S. Marks, "Influence of the Interviewer on the Accuracy of Survey Results," *Journal of the American Statistical Association,* vol. 53 (September 1958), pp. 635–55.

[24] Sudman, *Reducing the Costs of Surveys,* pp. 100–153.

and how they were solved. In addition most questions should be discussed separately, giving the interviewer some insight into the purpose of the question, examples of adequate and inadequate responses, and other suggestions such as how to probe for more information. Definitions should be included so that the interviewer can explain and interpret in a standard manner.

Those who believe in the values of training have some evidence to support their views. In one widely cited study, intensive training produced significant improvements in interviewer performance. The training effect was so great that performances of individual interviewers before training were poor predictors of posttraining performance.[25] Cannell and Kahn suggest that a training program for interviewers should include the following:

1. Provide the new interviewers with the principles of measurement, give them an intellectual grasp of the data-collection function and a basis for evaluating interviewing behavior.
2. Teach the techniques of interviewing.
3. Provide the opportunity for practice and evaluation by actually conducting interviews under controlled conditions.
4. Offer careful evaluation of interviews, especially at the beginning of actual data collection. Such evaluation should include review of interview protocols.[26]

TELEPHONE INTERVIEWING

Mention has already been made of the use of telephones to set up personal interviews and to screen for rare respondent types, but they are even more useful as the major or sole data collection method. This popularity is possible because of the widespread acceptance of the telephone as a necessary family communication device. Telephone interviewing has some substantial advantages and disadvantages as compared to alternative methods. Both are summarized here.

Evaluation of the Telephone

Advantages. Of all the advantages of telephone interviewing probably none ranks higher than its low cost. Travel time can be drastically reduced because all calls can be made from a single location. Telephones are especially economical when there are many callbacks to make and respondents are widely scattered. Long-distance telephone interviewing has also grown in importance because of the substantial savings over personal interviews in

---

[25] S. A. Richardson, B. S. Dohrenwend, and D. Klein, *Interviewing: Its Forms and Functions* (New York: Basic Books, 1965), pp. 328–58.

[26] Reprinted by special permission from Cannell–Kahn, "Interviewing," in *The Handbook of Social Psychology,* 2d ed., vol. 2, edited by Lindzey–Aronson (Reading, Mass.: Addison-Wesley, 1968.)

distant cities. Lengthy long distance interviews were completed with 80 percent of a selected sample of medical doctors at a cost estimated to be 25 percent below personal interviewing.[27] Even greater savings have been reported in other telephone studies.

Quality of response is excellent in many cases, depending upon the topic and study conditions. Interviewer bias is normally reduced because of the lack of face-to-face contact between interviewer and respondent. In addition, calls can be made from a central location where supervisors can monitor interviewer actions. This type of interviewing is also less demanding upon the interviewer, especially since a supervisor is on hand. when problems occur. Interviewers with special language or other skills can be used more efficiently. Another advantage is the speed with which studies can be carried out. Using the telephone is about the only method by which a study can be planned and carried out in a few days over a wide geographic area.

Limitations.   There are also limits to the research use of telephone. The obvious first requirement is that the respondent must be reachable by phone. In the past this has been a major drawback, but this deficiency has been receding year by year. It is estimated that in 1977 about 96 percent of households, and almost all businesses, had telephones.[28] The usage rates were not so high in rural areas, among lower-income groups, and among households with younger heads, and these variations can be a source of bias.[29]

Because about 20 percent of the householders move each year, there are always a large number of obsolete numbers and newly located households for which numbers have not yet been published. In addition, it is estimated that about 22 percent of all household phone numbers are unlisted.[30] Another source indicates that the highest incidence of nonlisting is in the West, in large metropolitan areas, among nonwhites, and persons 18 to 34 years of age.[31] Several methods have been developed to overcome this deficiency of directories; among them are techniques for choosing phone numbers by using random digit dialing or combinations of directories and random dialing.[32]

---

[27] Sudman, *Reducing the Costs of Surveys,* p. 66. A major factor in reducing the costs of long-distance telephone surveys has been the offering of Wide Area Telephone Service (WATS) by the Bell System. This provides for fixed monthly charges for the use of long distance lines in place of the normal per-call rates.

[28] *Statistical Abstract of the United States,* 1978, p. 589.

[29] D. A. Leuthold and R. Scheele, "Patterns of Bias in Samples Based on Telephone Directories," *Public Opinion Quarterly,* vol. 35 (Summer 1971), pp. 249–57.

[30] R. W. Graves, "An Empirical Comparison of Two Telephone Sample Designs." *Journal of Marketing Research,* vol. 15 (November 1978), p. 622.

[31] G. J. Glasser and G. D. Metzger, "National Estimates of Nonlisted Telephone Households and Their Characteristics," *Journal of Marketing Research,* vol. 12 (August 1975), p. 360.

[32] G. J. Glasser and G. D. Metzger, "Random Digit Dialing as a Method of Telephone Sampling," *Journal of Marketing Research,* vol. 11 (February 1972), pp. 59–64, and S. Sudman, "The Uses of Telephone Directories for Survey Sampling," *Journal of Marketing Research,* vol. 10 (May 1973), pp. 204–7.

Random dialing procedures normally call for choosing exchanges or exchange blocks and then generating random numbers within these blocks for calling.[33]

Limits on the length of interview is another disadvantage of the telephone, but the degree of this limitation depends on the respondent's interest in the topic. Ten minutes or so has generally been thought of as the practical maximum, but interviews of 20 minutes or more are common. Interviews ran as long as 1½ hours in one long distance survey.[34]

In telephone interviewing it is not possible to use budgets, maps, illustrations, or complex scales. The medium also limits the complexity of the questioning and the use of sorting techniques. One rather ingenious solution to the scale deficiency, however, has been to employ a nine-point scaling approach and to ask the respondent to visualize this by using the telephone dial.[35] Respondents find it easier to terminate an interview by telephone than in the face-to-face situation.

The telephone has become a widely used medium for interviewing, and the trends suggest that it will continue to gain at the expense of personal interviewing.

INTERVIEWING BY MAIL

The self-administered questionnaire has been mentioned as a substitute for the personal interview, but its more frequent use is in mail surveys. In this section we will discuss the merits of the mail questionnaire, its special problems, and techniques for using it more successfully.

Evaluation of Mail Surveys

Advantages. Mail surveys are typically lower in cost than personal interviews. Telephone and mail costs are in the same general range although in specific cases either may be lower. The more dispersed the sample, the more likely it is that mail will be the low-cost method. One reason for the cost advantage of a mail study is that it can largely be a one-person job. Another value in using mail is that we can contact respondents who might otherwise be inaccessible. Persons such as major corporate executives are difficult to reach in any other way. When the researcher has no specific person to contact, say in a study of corporations, the mail survey often will be routed to the appropriate respondent.

---

[33] A block is defined as an exchange group composed of the first four or more digits of a seven-digit number such as 721–0, 721–1, etc.

[34] S. Sudman, *Reducing the Cost of Surveys,* p. 65.

[35] J. J. Wheatley, "Self-Administered Written Questionnaires or Telephone Interviews," *Journal of Marketing Research,* vol. 10 (February 1973), pp. 94–95.

In a mail survey the respondent can more easily take time to collect facts, talk with others, or consider replies at length than is possible with either telephone or personal interview. Finally, mail surveys are typically perceived as being more impersonal, providing more anonymity than the other communication modes.

Disadvantages. The major weakness of the mail survey is that it is usually subject to a strong bias of nonresponse. Many studies have shown that the better educated and those more interested in the topic tend to answer mail surveys. A high percentage of those who reply to a given survey have usually replied to others, while a large share of those who do not respond are "habitual nonrespondents."[36] Unless we can identify the respondents we cannot even tell who answered the study and by this knowledge have some insight into the probable bias.

Mail survey projects with a return of 30 percent or so are often considered quite satisfactory, but there are instances of more than 70 percent response.[37] The response rate achievable is strongly influenced by the subject of a study, the interest in that subject by respondents, and the prestige of the sponsoring organization. The researcher can improve returns by making a diligent effort to stimulate responses by careful design, skillful execution, and follow-up mailings, perhaps even telephone or personal interview follow-ups. When using telephone or personal interview follow-ups it is usually sufficient to take a random sample of the nonrespondents to determine the presence and form of any nonresponse bias. More specific techniques which can stimulate responses will be discussed in the next section.

The second major limitation of mail surveys concerns the type and amount of information which can be secured by this means. We normally do not expect to secure large amounts of information, nor should we expect to probe deeply into questions. It is generally believed that respondents will refuse to cooperate with a long and/or complex mail questionnaire. Returned mail questionnaires with many questions unanswered testify to this problem, but there are also many exceptions. One general rule of thumb is that the respondent should be able to answer the questionnaire in no more than ten minutes. On the other hand, Dillman reports on a study of the general population in which he secured more than a 70 percent response to a questionnaire calling for 158 answers.

Improving Mail Survey Returns

The literature of research is filled with studies addressing the problems of improving mail survey returns. Seemingly every possible variable has been

[36] D. Wallace, "A Case for and against Mail Questionnaires," *Public Opinion Quarterly,* vol. 18 (Spring 1954), pp. 40–52.

[37] D. A. Dillman, "Increasing Mail Questionnaire Response in Large Samples of the General Public," *Public Opinion Quarterly,* vol. 36 (Summer 1972), pp. 254–57.

studied. Dillman reports that well over 200 methodological articles have been published on efforts to improve mail response rates.[38] From such an outpouring one would expect that the methodological problems of improving mail research response rates have largely been solved. Unfortunately this is not true. In 1975 two major review articles appeared in the research literature.[39] Both concluded that there were relatively few variables which consistently show positive response rates. The conclusions of Kanuck and Berenson were:[40]

A number of tentative conclusions can be drawn on the basis of the empirical studies reported here. Unfortunately, there is so little evidence on which to base conclusions that those which follow, though valid, appear to be weak.

Follow-ups

Follow-ups, or reminders, are almost universally successful in increasing response rates. Since each successive follow-up results in added returns, the very persistent (and well-financed) researcher can potentially achieve an extremely high total response rate. However, the value of additional information thus obtained must be weighed against the costs required for successive contacts.

Preliminary Notification

The evidence indicates that advance notification, particularly by telephone, is effective in increasing response rates; it also serves to accelerate the rate of return. However, follow-ups appear to be a better investment than preliminary notification.

Concurrent Techniques

1. *Questionnaire Length.* Despite the fact that common sense suggests that short questionnaires should obtain higher response rates than longer questionnaires, research evidence does not support this view.
2. *Survey Sponsorship.* There is little experimental evidence concerning the influence of survey sponsorship on response rates; however, the sparse evidence that does exist indicates that official or "respected" sponsorship tends to increase response.
3. *Return Envelopes.* The one study which tested the hypothesis that return envelopes increase response rates suggests that the inclusion of a stamped, return envelope does encourage response because it facilitates questionnaire return.
4. *Postage.* Though a number of tests regarding postage are reported in the literature, few studies have tested the same variables. The existing evidence indicates that special delivery is very effective in increasing response rates and that air mail is more effective than first class. Findings do not show a significant advantage for first class over

---

[38] Don A. Dillman, *Mail and Telephone Surveys* (New York, John Wiley & Sons, 1978), p. 6.

[39] Leslie Kanuk and Conrad Berenson, "Mail Surveys and Response Rates: A Literature Review," *Journal of Marketing Research* (November 1975), pp. 440–53; and Arnold S. Linsky, "Stimulating Responses to Mailed Questionnaires: A Review," *Public Opinion Quarterly,* vol. 39 (1975), pp. 82–101.

[40] Kanuk and Berenson, "Mail Surveys," p. 450. Reprinted from the *Journal of Marketing Research,* published by the American Marketing Association.

third class, for commemorative stamps over ordinary postage, for stamped mail over metered mail, or for multiple small denomination stamps over single larger denomination stamps.

5. *Personalization.*   Empirical evidence indicates that personalization of the mailing has no clear-cut advantage in terms of improved response rates. For example, neither personal inside addresses nor individually signed cover letters significantly increased response rates; personally typed cover letters proved to be somewhat effective in most cases cited, but not in all. The one study which tested the use of a titled signature versus one without a title did show a significant advantage in favor of the title.

6. *Cover Letters.*   The influence of the cover letter on response rates has received almost no experimental attention, despite the fact that the cover letter is an integral part of the mail survey. The cover letter appears to be the most logical vehicle for persuading individuals to respond, yet the very few studies which are reported offer no insights as to its formulation.

7. *Anonymity.*   Experimental evidence indicates that the promise of anonymity to respondents—either explicit or implied—has no significant effect on response rates.

8. *Size, Reproduction, and Color.*   The few studies which examined the effects of questionnaire size, method of reproduction, and color found no significant differences in response rates.

9. *Money Incentives.*   A number of studies indicate that a 25¢ incentive sent with the questionnaire is very effective in increasing response rates. Larger sums tend to bring in added response, but at a cost that may exceed the value of the added information.

10. *Deadline Dates.*   The few studies which tested the impact of deadline dates found that they did not increase the response rate; however, they did serve to accelerate the rate of questionnaire return.

Dillman argues that these ambiguous results occur because "the manipulation of one or two techniques independently of all others may do little to stimulate response."[41] He believes that efforts should be directed toward the more important question of maximizing the overall probability of response. He proposes the Total Design Method (TDM) to meet this need. The TDM consist of two parts.[42] First, identify the aspects of the survey process which may affect the response rate, either qualitatively or quantitatively. Each aspect must be shaped to obtain the best response. The second part consists of organizing the survey efforts so that the design intentions are carried out in detail. He reports the results achieved with the TDM in 48 surveys. Response rates ranged from 50 to 94 percent, with the median response rate of 74 percent.[43]

---

[41] Dillman, *Mail,* p. 8.

[42] Ibid., p. 12.

[43] Ibid., pp. 22–24.

Implementing the Mail Survey

In the TDM approach explicit attention is given to each point of the survey process at which the response may break down. For example:[44]

1. The wrong address and a low class postage can result in nondelivery plus nonreturn.
2. The letter may look like junk mail and be discarded without opening.
3. Lack of proper instructions as to who should complete it leads to nonresponse.
4. The wrong person opens letter but fails to call it to attention of the right person.
5. Respondent finds no convincing explanation as to why survey should be completed so discards it.
6. Respondent temporarily lays questionnaire aside and fails to complete it.
7. Return address is lost so questionnaire can not be returned.

The efforts to overcome these problem areas will vary according to the circumstances, but some general suggestions can be made.

The Process. In addition to a questionnaire a cover letter and a return envelope are also sent. Incentives, such as a quarter, are often attached to the letter in commercial studies. Follow-ups are usually needed to get the maximum response. There are differences in opinion as to how many follow-ups are needed and how they should be timed. Some researchers mail the first follow-up only several days after the original mailing. Dilman, in his TDM approach, suggests these follow-ups:

1. One week later—a preprinted postcard to all recipients thanking them for returns and reminding others to complete and mail the questionnaire.
2. Three weeks after the original mailout—A new questionnaire plus a letter telling nonrespondents that questionnaire has not been received and including a repetition of the basic appeals of the original letter.
3. Seven weeks after original mailing. A third cover letter and questionnaire is sent by certified mail to the remaining nonrespondents.

The Appeal. The appeal to make to respondents may be an altruistic one or it may be a more powerful stimulation effort. The former is often found when the questionnaire is short, easy to complete, and does not require much effort from a respondent. Anonymity may or may not be mentioned. A brief letter emphasizes the "Would you do me a favor?" approach. Often some token (for example, a quarter) is sent along as a show of appreciation.

However, in many cases the approach is not powerful enough. What is needed is an appeal that tells how important the problem is to a group with which the respondent can identify. Second the cover letter must convey that

---

[44] Ibid., pp. 160–61.

the respondent's help is needed to solve the problem. The researchers are portrayed as reasonable persons making a reasonable appeal for help. They are identified as intermediaries between the person asked to help and an important problem. Some simple steps are indicated that the respondent can take to help solve the problem.

The TDM approach depends heavily on personalization as the vehicle for conveying to the respondents that they are important to the study. Such personalization requires much more than just putting the respondent's name on the cover letter and using a real signature. The total effect must be one of personalization and should include typing of names and addresses on the envelope rather than labels, signing the researchers' names in a contrasting color and using first class mail. Another strong element of personalization is available on the follow-ups when the respondent can be told, "as of today we have not received your questionnaire." Other techniques such as computer printing enables one to make personalized references within the body of the letter. The standard is to make the appeals comparable in appearance and content to that which one would expect in a business or professional letter.

OBSERVATION

Most of what we know comes from our own observation or that by others. We notice such things as the weather, what is going on about us, how people react to events, and a host of other activities and conditions. While such observation is the basis for most of our knowledge, our collection process is often haphazard. For research purposes we need to improve the quality of our observation, and this begins with understanding the strengths and weaknesses of this method.

The Usefulness of Observation

Strengths.   There is a vast area of information for which observation is the only method available. Obviously the study of records, mechanical processes, and lower animals fall into this category. Most small children cannot be questioned very successfully. Even among studies of human group processes it is extremely difficult to gather useful information by questioning respondents. Their involvement in a group process is usually such that they are unable to report accurately what happened.

Another value of observation is that we can collect the original data ourselves at the time it occurs. We need not depend upon later reports by others. Every respondent filters the information no matter how well-intentioned. Forgetting occurs, and at times there are reasons why the respondent may not want to report fully and fairly. Observation overcomes many of these deficiencies of questioning.

A third strength is that we can secure information which most participants would ignore either because it is so common and expected or because it is not seen as relevant. For example, if we are observing the sales activity in a department of a large store there may be a mass of conditions of great interest to our research but which the normal shopper would consider to be unimportant. Such questions as: What is the weather? the day of the week? the time of day? the number of employees in the department at the time of shopping? customer traffic in the department at the time? existence of special promotions in the department? promotions in other departments of the store? promotional activity in competing stores? and the like. We can expect to learn only a part of the answers to these questions from most respondents.

Another strength of observation is that only with this method can we capture the whole event as it occurs. We may be interested in all of the conditions surrounding a confrontation at a bargaining session between union and management representatives. These sessions may extend over a period of time, and any effort to study the unfolding of the negotiation process is greatly facilitated by the use of observation. Questioning could seldom provide the insight of observation for many of the aspects of the negotiation process.

Finally, subjects usually seem to accept an observational type of intrusion better than questioning. It is less demanding of them and normally has less biasing effect on their conduct than does questioning. In addition, it is also possible to conduct disguised and unobtrusive observation studies much more easily than disguised questioning.

Weaknesses.   There are also some severe research limitations of the observational method. A major problem is that the observer normally must be at the scene of the event when it takes place. Yet it is often impossible to predict where and when the event will occur. One way to guard against missing an event is to observe for prolonged periods until it does occur, but this brings up a second disadvantage. Observation is a slow and expensive process which requires either human observers or some type of surveillance equipment which is often costly.

A third limitation of observation is that its most reliable results are restricted to data which can be determined by overt action or surface indicators. To go "below the surface" the observer must make inferences from surface indicators. Two observers will probably agree on the nature of various surface events, but the inferences they draw from such data are much more varied.

Finally, observation is limited as a way to learn of the past. It is limited in a similar manner as a method by which to learn what is going on at present at some distant place. It is also difficult to gather information on such topics as intentions, attitudes, opinions, or preferences.

Any consideration of the merits of observation indicates that it is a valuable research tool when used with care and understanding. To enhance our appreciation of its applicability, let us consider its useful range of research applications.

The Use of Observation

Some people restrict the concept of observation to "watching," but this is too narrow a view; it also involves listening and reading. Behavioral scientists tend to define observation in terms of animal or human behavior, but this is also too narrow. As used in this text observation includes the full range of monitoring behavioral and nonbehavioral activities and conditions, which can roughly be classified into the following types:

A. Nonbehavioral observation.
   1. Record analysis.
   2. Physical condition analysis.
   3. Physical process analysis.
B. Behavioral observation.
   1. Nonverbal analysis.
   2. Linguistic analysis.
   3. Extra-linguistic analysis.
   4. Spatial analysis.

Nonbehavioral Observation. One of the most prevalent forms of observation research is *record analysis.* Such analysis may involve historical or current records, public or private records; they may be written, printed, sound recorded, photographic, or video recorded. Historical statistical data are often the only source used for a study. Analysis of current financial records and economic data also provides a major data source for studies. Other examples of this type of observation are the content analysis of competitive advertising and the analysis of personnel records.

Physical condition analysis is typified by store audits to determine availability of merchandise, studies of plant safety compliance, analysis of inventory conditions, and the analysis of the financial statements of organizations. *Process or activity* studies include time studies of manufacturing processes, traffic flows in a distribution system, paperwork flow in an office, and the study of financial flows in our banking system.

Behavioral Observation. The observational study of persons can be classified into four major categories.[45] *Nonverbal behavior* is the most prevalent of these and includes body movement, motor expressions, and even exchanged glances. At the gross body movement level we might study how a salesperson travels a territory. At a narrower level we can study the body movements of a worker assembling a product, or time sample the activity of a department's work force to determine the share of time each spends in various ways. At a more abstract level we can study body movement as an

---

[45] K. E. Weick, "Systematic Observational Methods," in G. Lindzey and E. Aronson, *The Handbook of Social Psychology,* vol. 2 (Reading, Mass.: Addison-Wesley Publishing Company, 1968), p. 360.

indicator of interest or boredom, anger or pleasure in a certain environment. Motor expressions such as facial movements can be observed as a sign of emotional states. Eyeblink rates are studied as indicators of interest in advertising messages. Finally, exchanged glances might be of interest in studies of interpersonal behavior.

Linguistic behavior is a second frequently used form of behavior observation. One simple type, familiar to most students, is the tally of "ahs" (or other annoying sounds or words) that a professor emits during a class. More serious applications are to the study of sales presentation content, or the study of what, how, and how much information is conveyed in a training situation. A third form of linguistic behavior involves interaction processes that take place between two persons or in small groups. Bales has proposed one widely used system for classifying such linguistic interactions.[46]

Behavior may also be analyzed on an *extra-linguistic* level. Sometimes this is as important a means of communication as the linguistic. One author has suggested that there are four dimensions to extra-linguistic activity.[47] They are (1) vocal, including pitch, loudness, and timbre, (2) temporal, including rate of speaking duration of utterance and rhythm, (3) interaction, including the tendencies to interrupt, dominate, or inhibit, and (4) verbal stylistic, including vocabulary and pronunciation peculiarities, dialect, and characteristic expressions. These dimensions could add substantial insight to the linguistic content of the interactions between supervisors and subordinates or salespeople and customers.

A fourth type of behavior study involves *spatial relationships,* especially as to how we relate physically to others. One form of this study, "proxemics," concerns how people organize the territory about them as well as how they maintain discrete distances between themselves and others. A study of how salespeople physically approach customers or a study of the effects of crowding in a workplace are examples of this type of observation.

Often in a given study we will be interested in two or more of these types of information. This will normally require more than one observer. In all of these forms of behavior study it is also important to consider the relationship between observers and subjects.

The Observer-Subject Relationship

In interrogation there is a clear opportunity for interviewer bias. The problem is less pronounced with observation but is still very real. The relationship between observer and subject may be viewed from three perspectives: (1) whether the observation is direct or indirect, (2) whether the observer's pres-

---

[46] R. Bales, *Interaction Process Analysis* (Reading, Mass.: Addison-Wesley Publishing Company, 1951).

[47] Weick, "Systematic Observational Methods," p. 381.

ence is known or unknown to the subject, and (3) what role the observer plays.

Directness of Observation. The direct method describes the situation in which the observer is physically present and personally monitors what takes place. This approach is very flexible because it allows the observer to react to and report subtle aspects of events and behavior as they occur. She is also free to shift places, change the focus of the observation, or concentrate on unexpected events if they should occur. A weakness of this approach is that the observer's perception circuits may become overloaded as events move quickly; she is left with the alternative of later trying to reconstruct what she was not able to record. Then, too, observer fatigue, boredom, and distracting events can reduce the accuracy and completeness of such observation.

Indirect observation is the term used to describe studies in which the recording is done by mechanical, photographic, or electronic means. For example, a special motion picture camera which takes one frame every second is mounted in a department of a large store to study customer and employee movement. Such methods are less flexible than direct observation, but they are much less biasing and may be less erratic in their recording accuracy. Another advantage of such indirect systems is the permanent record that can be reanalyzed to record many different aspects of an event. Electronic recording devices, which have improved in quality and declined in cost, are being used more frequently in observation research.

Observer Concealment. A second decision affecting the observer-subject relationship concerns whether the presence of the observer should be known to the subject. When the observer is known there is a risk of atypical activity by the subjects. The famous Hawthorne experiments are the classic example of this effect.[48] The initial entry of an observer into a situation often tends to upset activity patterns of the subjects, but this influence can usually be dissipated rather quickly. This is especially so when subjects are engaged in some absorbing activity and/or the presence of observers offers no potential threat to the subjects' self-interest. The potential bias from subject awareness of observers is always a matter of concern, however.

In some situations observers are concealed by using one-way mirrors, or hidden cameras or microphones. These methods reduce the risk of observer bias but bring up a question of ethics. Hidden observation is a form of spying, and the propriety of this action must be determined by each researcher. However, it is a widely used technique.

A modified approach involves partial concealment. In this case the presence of the observer is not concealed, but her objectives and content of

---

[48] This study concerned the measurement of varying conditions of illumination on factory worker output. No matter how the illumination was varied, an improvement in output was secured. It was concluded that the *fact of being observed* was itself a stronger variable than any degree of illumination. Apparently the workers reacted to the unaccustomed attention they were receiving by working harder. See F. J. Roethlisberger and W. J. Dickson, *Management and the Worker* (Cambridge, Mass.: Harvard University Press, 1939).

interest are. For example, a study of selling methods may be carried out by sending an observer with a salesperson who is making calls on customers. However, the observer's real purpose may be hidden from both the salesperson and the customer. For example, she may pretend that she is analyzing the display and layout characteristics of the stores they are visiting.

Observer Participation. A third decision concerns whether the observer should participate in the situation she is observing. The more involved arrangement, *participant observation,* exists when the observer enters into the social setting and acts both as an observer and a participant. Sometimes she is known as an observer to some or all of the participants, while at other times her true role is concealed. This again raises the ethical problem but reduces the potential for bias.

Another problem of participant observation is the dual demand made on the observer. Recording can interfere with participation, and participation can, in turn, interfere with observation. In addition, there is the problem of the influence that the observer's role has on the way others act. Because of these problems, participant observation is less used in business research than, say, in anthropology or sociology. It is typically restricted to those cases where nonparticipant observation is not practical, for example, a study of the functioning of a traveling auditing team.

Observation Design

The Decision to Observe. Observation is found in almost all research studies, at least in the exploratory stage. Such data collection is often known as *simple observation.* Its practice is not very standardized, as befits the heuristic nature of exploratory research. Participant studies are also usually classed as simple observation because participant roles do not permit systematic observing. *Systematic observation,* on the other hand, employs standardized procedures, training of observers, schedules for recording, and other devices to control the observer and sometimes even the subject. Clearly some systemization is valuable in research observation, but the situation often limits what can be done.

The decision whether to use observation as the major data collection method may be made as early as when the researcher moves from research question to the investigative questions. The latter specify the outcomes of the study—the specific questions that the researcher must answer with the collected data. In a time sampling study of workers in department X the outcome may be a judgment as to how well the department is being supervised. In a study of sales presentations the research outcome may be a judgment of a given salesperson's effectiveness, or the effectiveness of different types of selling messages.

Content Specification. When a specification of outcomes suggests an observational study, we move on to observation content—those specific conditions, events, and/or activities that we want to observe. These content specifics, when incorporated into an observational reporting system, correspond with the measurement questions already discussed. To specify the observation content we should include both the major variables of interest and any other variables that may affect them. From this cataloging we then select those items which we plan specifically to observe. For each variable chosen we must decide whether to define it operationally, or to allow the observers to define it for themselves. Where there is any question of concept agreement or special meanings it is advisable to specify operational definitions.

Even if the definition is left to the observers we must make certain that all agree upon the measurement terms by which to record results. For example, we may agree that variable W will be reported by count, while variable Y will be counted and the effectiveness of its use judged qualitatively.

Observation may be at either a *factual* or an *inferential* level. For example, in the study of a salesperson's presentation we might specify the following data as being of interest:

Factual	*Inferential*
Identification of salesperson and customer.	Salesperson's degree of enthusiasm for the interview.
Day of week and time of day.	Welcoming attitude of customer.
Products presented.	Customer acceptance of selling points per product.
Selling points presented per product.	Effectiveness of salesperson rebuttal attempts.
Customer objections raised per product.	General evaluation of sales presentation skill.
Salesperson rebuttal attempts.	
Salesperson attempt to secure order.	
Customer purchase decision.	
Environmental factors interfering with interview.	
Length of interview.	

This listing is suggestive only; it does not include many other variables which might be of interest. Data on customer purchase history, company, industry, and general economic conditions, the order in which sales arguments are presented, and specific words used to describe certain product characteristics are illustrations of still other items which might be included. The particular content of observation will also be affected by the nature of the observation setting.

The Observation Setting. Variations in the observation environment present another dimension that somewhat parallels the simple-systematic dichotomy. Settings may be viewed as being either *natural* or *contrived*. Field observation tends to be in a natural setting and laboratory study in a contrived setting, but the distinctions are not this simple. A natural setting generally exists when no controls are placed on the subject, the environment is the normal one for the event to occur, and no changes or controls have been introduced into that environment. For example, the observation of workers by time sampling of normal departmental work activities involves a natural setting. On the other hand, a degree of contrivance exists if certain events are introduced into the setting to see how various workers respond. A common form of contrived observation is experimentation, a topic to be discussed in Chapter 11.

The Observer. The selection and training of observers is typically given too little attention. There are a few general rules to guide the selection. First, the observer must have sufficient concentration powers to function in settings full of distractions. In addition, ability to remember details of an experience is an asset. There is also the need to select persons who will be unobtrusive in the situation. For example, an attractive young female observer would introduce an obvious distraction in some settings but be ideal in other cases. The same can be said for persons of other ages, ethnic groups, and the like.

If observation is at the surface level and involves a few relatively simple concepts, then experience is less important. Inexperience may even be an advantage if there is some risk that experienced observers may bring pre-set convictions about the topic. On the other hand, experience is valuable if the observer must work under trying conditions with inferential level content. In any event, it is important that the observer be thoroughly versed in the requirements of the specific study.

Each observer should be informed of the specific outcomes sought and the precise content elements to be studied. Ample opportunity for questions should be provided in training sessions. This should be followed by practice, evaluation, correction, and more practice until all observers show a high degree of reliability in their observations. Included should be substantial practice in a simulated study setting. Where there is interpretative differences between observers they should be discussed and reconciled.

Data Collection Plan. Data collection plans specify the details of the task. In essence they answer the question of who, what, where, when, and how. Who are the targets? What qualifies a subject to be observed? Are they randomly selected—every fifth person who passes, as in a traffic survey? Must each one meet a given criterion—those who initiate a specific action? Who are the contacts to reach if conditions change or trouble develops? Who has the responsibility for various aspects of the study?

What? This has already been mentioned in the discussion on content, but additional specifics are called for. For example, the dimension of the basic observational unit must be set. This may be specified both in terms of a time dimension and in "act" terms. In the former case the observer is instructed to observe for some period of time, say ten minutes out of each hour. Such time sampling can give a good estimate of the total pattern of activities over a period of time if a number of time samples are drawn randomly.

Dimensions of importance often have to be defined in act terms. The concept of an "act" is affected by the needs of the given study. It is the basic unit of observation such as (1) a single expressed thought, (2) a physical movement, (3) a facial expression, (4) a transaction, (5) a type of behavior, or the like. While these must be defined, they will often continue to present difficulties to the observer. For example, in a single statement a salesperson may include several different thoughts, such as product advantages B and C, a rebuttal of objection K, and some remark about competitor X. The observer is hard pressed to sort out each thought, decide whether it represents a separate unit of observation, and then record it quickly enough to be able to follow continued statements.

When?   Is the time of study important or can any time be used? For example, in a study of out-of-stock conditions in a supermarket the exact times of observation may be important. Inventory is shipped to the store on certain days only, and buying peaks occur on other days. The likelihood of a given product being out-of-stock is a function of both of these time-related activities.

How?   Shall the data be directly observed? If there is more than one observer, how shall they divide the task? How shall the results be recorded for later analysis? How shall the observers deal with various situations which may occur—when expected actions do not take place, or when the observer is challenged by someone in the setting?

The number of possible variations of conditions which face an observer is unlimited. Fortunately, most of these problems do not occur at one time. When the plans are carefully laid, and the observers well-trained, observation research can be successful.

Unobtrusive Measures.   To this point we have considered observation as a relatively traditional approach to data collection. Sometimes, however, such straightforward methods are not adequate. Webb and his colleagues have given us an insight into new dimensions of innovative observation called unobtrusive measures.[49] Suggestive of such approaches are natural erosion measures such as measuring the frequency of replacement of vinyl tile in front of various museum exhibits as an indicator of their popularity, and the study of wear and tear on book pages as a measure of library book use. Examples also include natural accretion measures such as determining the advertising listenership of various radio stations by observing car radio settings as autos are brought to service garages. Another type of unobtrusive study includes estimating liquor and magazine consumption by collecting and analyzing family trash. For many other interesting approaches to unobtrusive observation research the reader is urged to consult Webb et al.

---

[49] E. J. Webb, D. T. Campbell, R. D. Schwartz, and L. Sechrest, *Unobtrusive Measures; Nonreactive Research in the Social Sciences* (Chicago: Rand McNally & Company, 1966).

MARKETING CONCEPTS INCORPORATED (MCI)[50]

Early in 1977 the author received the letter shown in Figure 10–3. It was printed on an executive size letterhead (7 × 10 ½ inches) and had the printed signature of R. G. Robertson, president of the organization. It was sent by first class mail and stated that the recipient would be receiving "an invitation to participate in a national survey that is being conducted by mail." The letter stressed the importance of the study, asked for participation, pointed out why each reply was important, and assured the reader that names and replies would be kept confidential.

Several days later a large envelope (8 ¾ × 11 ¼ inches) arrived by first class mail. The envelope carried commemorative stamps rather than being metered and "first class" was printed on the front in large red type. Inside were four items. The cover letter was printed on an 8 ½ × 11 letterhead with the same R. G. Robertson signature (see Figure 10–4). No effort was made to personalize the letter. The text again stressed those items which are believed to motivate respondents to participate. In addition, a small plastic envelope with a new quarter in it was attached to the letter. Enclosed also was a prepaid postcard by which the respondent could request a free summary report. The third enclosure was an 8 ½ × 11 return envelope addressed to R. G. Robertson, President of MCI. It was stamped with a regular first class stamp (not a commemorative).

The final enclosure, of course, was the questionnaire entitled "The Study of American Opinion, 1977." It was a booklet eight pages long and covered a variety of subjects on economic, political, and social topics. A sample of the questions, pages 1 and 3 of the instrument, are shown in Figure 10–5. Note that the respondent could reply merely by checking appropriate boxes. The paper stock of the questionnaire and reply postcard were both cream in color while all other materials were white. At the bottom of the last page of the questionnaire was typed "Study F1382." Since this represented the only nonprinted item in the entire set of materials it probably was the respondent's identification code rather than the project identification.

The author, interested in the process of the study, decided not to reply in order to see if there were follow-ups. Three weeks later he received another large envelope from MCI. It included a second questionnaire, a return post-card, and a reply envelope. There was also a cover letter with a second quarter attached. The letter's writer (again the president) thanked the respon-dent if they had already answered, urged the laggards to reply, and again stressed the need for all respondents to participate in order to make the study reliable. Again the author decided to wait and see what else would occur. This time nothing further happened. We do not know how successful the survey was, whether they sampled the nonrespondents further, or just how effective

---

[50] Used with the kind permission of R. G. Robertson, President of Marketing Concepts Incorporated.

Figure 10-3: First Letter, Study of American Opinion Project

MARKETING CONCEPTS INCORPORATED
1235 N Avenue, Nevada, Iowa 50201

Dear Reader:

In the next several days, you will receive an invitation to participate in a national survey that is being conducted by mail. This "Study of American Opinion" is designed to measure opinions and attitudes of the American people toward business and the government.

This survey is a major undertaking -- one of the most significant studies yet undertaken in these critical public opinion areas.

We hope that you will agree to participate in the study by filling out the questionnaire you will receive in a few days. They are being sent to a mathematically selected cross section of the nation's household heads. As in any study, the reliability of the findings depends heavily on the coopera- tion of each person in the sample.

Your name will not be divulged -- individual answers will be used only in a composite report of American opinion.

We will greatly appreciate your cooperation.

Sincerely,

R. S. Robertson

Figure 10–4: Cover Letter, Study of American Opinion Project

 MARKETING CONCEPTS INCORPORATED
1235 N Avenue, Nevada, Iowa 50201

Is the person to whom this letter was addressed the <u>HEAD OF THE HOUSEHOLD</u> -- that is, the person whose income is the chief source of support of the household? If not, will you please give the letter and questionnaire to the person who is the household head and ask him/her to complete the questionnaire for us?

Dear Household Head:

A few days ago we wrote to you asking for your participation in a major study of American opinions and attitudes. You will find the questionnaire for this "Study of American Opinion" enclosed. We would greatly appreciate your cooperation in providing your answers to the questions asked.

This is one of the most significant studies yet undertaken on the attitudes and opinions of the American people toward business and government. Your answers will make a most important contribution to the project.

It will take you a little time and some thought to answer the questions. However, we have tried to make it as convenient as possible for you to answer, by asking you simply to check your answers to most questions. In a few cases, we hope you will take the time to write in your answers -- and, of course, if you would like to add a comment to <u>any</u> of your answers, we will be very much interested in what you have to say.

Your answers and opinions are extremely important to us, <u>even if you do not have opinions on some of the questions asked</u>. Questionnaires are being mailed only to a representative sample of household heads. The reliability of the findings depends heavily on our receiving a response from each person in the sample. Responses from all participants will be combined to form a composite interpretive report on American opinion.

The attached shiny new quarter is simply to tell you that we appreciate your help. It is not, of course, intended to reimburse you for your time, but merely to say "thank you".

A postage-paid self-addressed envelope is enclosed for your convenience in returning the questionnaire. Thank you very much for your help.

Sincerely,

R. &. Robertson

P.S.: If you would like a FREE Summary report of the study, simply fill in and return the self-addressed, postage-paid card provided. Maybe you would like to compare your opinions and attitudes with those of your fellow Americans.

Figure 10–5: Selected Sample Pages from MCI Questionnaire

Please be sure that this questionnaire is filled out by the <u>HEAD OF THE HOUSEHOLD</u>—that is, the person whose income is the chief source of support of the household.

THE STUDY OF AMERICAN OPINION, 1977

We will greatly appreciate your assistance in this major study. Your answers are of particular importance since you have been selected as part of a "sample" representative of America today. Under no circumstances will your individual answers be divulged —they will be used only in combination with those of other people responding to the study. For most of the questions, your answers can be given simply by checking the appropriate box or boxes. Please disregard the numbers before the boxes—they are for tabulation purposes only. <u>THANK YOU.</u>

If you would like a FREE Summary Report of this study, simply return the business reply card enclosed. A copy will be sent as soon as possible after completion of the survey.

1. **Please check whether you are:** ¹☐ Male ²☐ Female

2. **Please check whether you are:** ¹☐ Married ²☐ Single ³☐ Widowed ⁴☐ Divorced, separated

3. **What is <u>your</u> approximate age?** *(Please check.)*

¹☐ Under 18 ³☐ 25-34 ⁵☐ 45-49 ⁷☐ 55-64
²☐ 18-24 ⁴☐ 35-44 ⁶☐ 50-54 ⁸☐ 65 or older

4. **Please check the <u>highest</u> level of education achieved by you.** *(Please check ONLY one box.)*

¹☐ Post graduate degree ⁶☐ Completed less than 1 year of college
²☐ Post graduate work, no PG degree ⁷☐ High school graduate
³☐ Graduate of 4-year college ⁸☐ Trade or technical school graduate
⁴☐ Graduate of 2-year (junior) college ⁹☐ Did not graduate from high school,
⁵☐ Completed 1-3 years college, not a graduate   or from trade or technical school

5a. **Have you ever taken any courses in economics?** ¹☐ Yes ²☐ No
b. **If yes, were these courses taken in:** ¹☐ College ²☐ High school ³☐ Other

6. **Do you consider <u>yourself</u> a Democrat, a Republican or an Independent?**

¹☐ Democrat ²☐ Independent ³☐ Republican ⁴☐ Other _____ ⁵☐ None
                                                      (Please specify)

7a. **Generally speaking, do you consider yourself a conservative, a liberal, or somewhere between the two?**

¹☐ Conservative ²☐ Liberal ³☐ Somewhere in-between
b. **If "somewhere in-between", would you say you tend to lean more toward the conservative or the liberal point of view?**

¹☐ Conservative ²☐ Liberal ³☐ Neither

8. **Are <u>you personally</u> now registered to vote?** ¹☐ Yes ²☐ No

9. **Did you vote in the LAST presidential election?** ¹☐ Yes ²☐ No

Figure 10–5 (*continued*)

b. About how much of the sales dollar do you think the manufacturer **should** be able to keep as profit? *(Please check.)*

¹☐ 1 or 2 cents	⁴☐ 10-14 cents	⁷☐ 25-29 cents	⁹☐ 40-49 cents
²☐ 3 or 4 cents	⁵☐ 15-19 cents	⁸☐ 30-39 cents	⁰☐ 50 cents or more
³☐ 5-9 cents	⁶☐ 20-24 cents		

13a. During the past year, did you personally return anything you bought **to the place where you bought** it because the item was unsatisfactory?

¹☐ Yes   ²☐ No

b. In general, were you satisfied or dissatisfied with the way your complaint was handled?

¹☐ Satisfied   ²☐ Dissatisfied

14a. During the past year, did you personally complain to a manufacturer about the quality of his product, **either in writing or by telephone?**

¹☐ Yes   ²☐ No

b. In general, were you satisfied or dissatisfied with the way your complaint was handled?

¹☐ Satisfied   ²☐ Dissatisfied

15a. During the past year, did you personally register a complaint with **a local, state or federal government agency** about (governmental) delays, errors, poor service, etc.?

¹☐ Yes   ²☐ No

b. In general, were you satisfied or dissatisfied with the way your complaint was handled?

¹☐ Satisfied   ²☐ Dissatisfied

16. Below is a list of functions of the American business system along with a rating scale. *(The higher the number, the higher the rating—1 is a "poor" rating and 7 is "excellent".)*

For **each** function, please check the rating for business which you feel **best** describes your feeling on the job business is doing for that function.

	RATING OF AMERICAN BUSINESS SYSTEM						
	Poor Job						Excel- lent Job
	1	2	3	4	5	6	7
Providing products and services that meet people's needs	¹☐	²☐	³☐	⁴☐	⁵☐	⁶☐	⁷☐
Producing safe products	¹☐	²☐	³☐	⁴☐	⁵☐	⁶☐	⁷☐
Paying good wages	¹☐	²☐	³☐	⁴☐	⁵☐	⁶☐	⁷☐
Providing value for the money	¹☐	²☐	³☐	⁴☐	⁵☐	⁶☐	⁷☐
Improving the standard of living	¹☐	²☐	³☐	⁴☐	⁵☐	⁶☐	⁷☐
Controlling pollution	¹☐	²☐	³☐	⁴☐	⁵☐	⁶☐	⁷☐
Dealing with shortages	¹☐	²☐	³☐	⁴☐	⁵☐	⁶☐	⁷☐
Maintaining strong competition	¹☐	²☐	³☐	⁴☐	⁵☐	⁶☐	⁷☐
Providing steady work	¹☐	²☐	³☐	⁴☐	⁵☐	⁶☐	⁷☐
Conserving natural resources	¹☐	²☐	³☐	⁴☐	⁵☐	⁶☐	⁷☐
Developing new products	¹☐	²☐	³☐	⁴☐	⁵☐	⁶☐	⁷☐
Hiring members of minority groups	¹☐	²☐	³☐	⁴☐	⁵☐	⁶☐	⁷☐
Being honest in what they say about their products	¹☐	²☐	³☐	⁴☐	⁵☐	⁶☐	⁷☐
Being interested in customers	¹☐	²☐	³☐	⁴☐	⁵☐	⁶☐	⁷☐
Helping solve social problems	¹☐	²☐	³☐	⁴☐	⁵☐	⁶☐	⁷☐
Communicating with: Employees	¹☐	²☐	³☐	⁴☐	⁵☐	⁶☐	⁷☐
Stockholders	¹☐	²☐	³☐	⁴☐	⁵☐	⁶☐	⁷☐
Customers	¹☐	²☐	³☐	⁴☐	⁵☐	⁶☐	⁷☐
General Public	¹☐	²☐	³☐	⁴☐	⁵☐	⁶☐	⁷☐

3

two shiny new quarters were as an incentive. From the evidence at hand one would judge that the project should have received a good response rate.

SUMMARY

The major advantages of personal interviewing are the ability it gives us to explore topics in great depth, to achieve a high degree of interviewer control, and to provide maximum interviewer flexibility for meeting unique situations. On the other hand, this method is costly and time-consuming; and the flexibility we secure often results in excessive interviewer bias.

A successful interview requires that we seek information that the respondent can provide, that the respondent understands the role, and is motivated to play this role. Motivation, in particular, is a task for the interviewer. Good rapport with the respondent should be quickly established and then the technical process of collecting data should be begun. The latter often calls for skillful probing to supplement the answers volunteered by the respondent.

There are two major problems of bias in interviewing. One is the "nonresponse" problem; it is of major concern with all types of surveys. Some studies show that first calls will often secure as few as 20 percent of the designated respondents. Various methods are useful for increasing this representation, the most effective being the making of callbacks until we secure adequate numbers of completed interviews. Another major personal interviewing problem is that of "response error" in which the respondent fails to give a complete answer. The interviewer can make a major contribution to the correction of this problem.

Telephone interviewing has become much more popular in recent years because of the widespread adoption of the telephone in American households, and the low cost of this method compared with personal interviewing. Long distance telephone interviewing is also growing in use. There are also disadvantages to telephone interviewing. Many phones are unlisted, and directory listings become obsolete quickly; there is also a limit on the length and depth of interviews using the telephone.

Mail surveys are another widely used low-cost method, especially when the population is scattered geographically. Replying to a mail survey calls for some overt action by the respondent. As a result, the response rates for mail surveys tend to be low, although there are many techniques by which respondents can be motivated to participate.

Observation is about the only feasible type of research in those cases where we are studying records, mechanical processes, lower animals, small children, or complex interactive processes. We can gather data as the event occurs, and can come closer to capturing the whole event than with interrogation. On the other hand, we have to be present to catch the event or have some recording device there to do the job.

Observation includes a variety of monitoring situations which can be classified as follows:

A. Nonbehavioral observation.
1. Record analysis.
2. Physical condition analysis.
3. Physical process analysis.

B. Behavioral observation.
1. Nonverbal analysis.
2. Linguistic analysis.
3. Extra-linguistic analysis.
4. Spatial analysis.

We can also look at observation in terms of the observer-subject relationship. This relationship may be viewed from three perspectives: (1) Is the observation direct or indirect? (2) Is the observer's presence known or unknown? (3) Is the observer a participant or nonparticipant?

The design of an observation study follows the same general procedure as other research. When the researcher has specified the outcomes desired (the investigation questions), it often becomes apparent that the best way to secure the desired data is by observation. The researcher then must define the content of the study, determine what the observation settings will be, develop and test a specific data collecting plan, secure observers, train them, and launch the study.

SUPPLEMENTAL READINGS

1. Converse, Jean M., and Schuman, Howard. *Conversations at Random: Survey Research as Interviewers See It.* New York: John Wiley and Sons, Inc., 1974. A short but insightful book on survey interviewing as seen by interviewers themselves.

2. Dexter, Louis A. *Elite and Specialized Interviewing.* Evanston, Ill.: Northwestern University Press, 1970. Discusses the techniques and problems of interviewing "people in important or exposed positions."

3. Dillman, Don A. *Mail and Telephone Surveys.* New York: John Wiley & Sons, 1978. An up-to-date practical book on mail and telephone survey projects. Entire book recommended. Extensive bibliography.

4. Erdos, Paul L. *Professional Mail Surveys.* New York: McGraw-Hill Book Co., Inc., 1970. A thorough discussion of commercial mail survey methodology by a leading practitioner.

5. Gorden, Raymond L. *Interviewing: Strategic Techniques and Tactics.* Rev. ed. Homewood, Ill.: The Dorsey Press, 1975. A comprehensive coverage of interviewing for survey planners and supervisors as well as field workers.

6. Richardson, S. A.; Dohrenwend, B. S.; and Klein, D. *Interviewing: Its Forms and Functions.* New York: Basic Books, 1965. An excellent coverage of the interview process including a consideration of the roles of interviewers and respondents.

7. Sudman, Seymour, and Bradburn, Norman M. *Response Effects in Surveys.* Chicago: Aldine Publishing Company, 1974. A National Opinion Research

Center Monograph that surveys the literature on response effects that may distort survey results. The definitive study in this area.

8. Survey Research Center. *Interviewer's Manual.* Rev. ed. Ann Arbor, Mich.: Institute for Social Research, University of Michigan, 1976. An excellent guide for interviewers. Also discusses sampling procedures and survey administrative procedures used by the Survey Research Center.

9. Webb, E. J.; Campbell, D. T.; Schwartz, R. D.; and Sechrest, L. *Unobtrusive Measures; Nonreactive Research in the Social Sciences.* Chicago: Rand McNally & Co., 1966.

DISCUSSION QUESTIONS

1. Distinguish:
   a. Extrinsic and intrinsic response motivation.
   b. Response and nonresponse error.
   c. Relative values of questioning and observation.
   d. Nonverbal, linguistic, and extra-linguistic analysis.
   e. Factual and inferential observation.

2. Assume that you are planning to interview women in a shopping center about their views on increased food prices and what the federal government should do about them. In what different ways might you try to motivate them to cooperate in your survey?

3. In recent years the conduct of in-home personal interviews has grown more costly and more difficult to complete. Suppose, however, that you have a project in which you need to talk with women in the home. What might you do to hold down the costs and increase the response rate?

4. How do environmental factors affect response rates in personal interviews? How can we overcome these environmental problems?

5. In the following situations would you use a personal interview, telephone survey, or mail survey? Give your reasons.
   a. A survey of the residents of a new subdivision on why they happened to select that particular area in which to live. You also wish to secure some information about what they like and do not like about life in the subdivision.
   b. A poll of students at Cranial University on their preferences among three candidates who are running for the presidency of the student government.
   c. A survey of 58 wholesale grocery companies, scattered over the eastern United States, on their personnel management policies for warehouse personnel.
   d. A survey of financial officers of the *Fortune* top 500 corporations to learn their prediction for the economic outlook in their industries for next year.
   e. A survey of pharmacists in the state of Illinois to secure their opinions concerning a proposed state law to permit the advertising of prescription drugs.

6. You decide to take a telephone survey sample of 40 families in the 721-exchange area. You would like this sample to be an excellent representation of all subscribers in the exchange area. Explain how you would draw this sample and how you would carry out the sampling process.

7. You plan to conduct a mail survey of the traffic managers of 1,000 major manufacturing companies over the country. The study concerns their company policies regarding the payment of moving expenses for employees who are transferred. What might you do to improve the response rate of such a survey?

8. The observer-subject relationship is an important consideration in the design of observational studies. What kind of relationship would you recommend in each of the following cases?
   a. Observation of professorial conduct in the classroom by the student author of a course evaluation guide.
   b. Observation of retail shoppers by a researcher who is interested in determining the customer purchase time, by type of good purchased.
   c. Observation of a focus group interview by a client.
   d. Effectiveness of individual farm worker organizers in their efforts to organize employees of grape growers.

9. Assume that you are to set up an observational study in which we will observe five students engaging in a discussion of the question "How should students conduct themselves so as to profit most from college experience?"
   a. What are the varieties of information which might be observed in such a setting?
   b. Select a limited number of content areas for study and operationally define the observation "acts" that should be measured.
   c. Develop a recording form to be used by observers in the study.
   d. Determine how many observers you need and assign each to a specific observation task.

10. You wish to analyze the pedestrian traffic that passes a given store in a major shopping center. You are interested in determining how many shoppers pass by this store, and you would like to classify these shoppers on various relevant dimensions. Any information you secure should be obtainable from observation alone.
    a. What other information might you find useful to observe?
    b. How would you decide what information to collect?
    c. Devise the operational definitions you would need.
    d. What would you say in the way of instructions to the observers you plan to use?
    e. How might you sample this shopper traffic?

Chapter 11

≡ Experimentation and Simulation ====

ONE MAJOR OBJECTIVE OF RESEARCH is to determine why certain events occur and why they happen under some conditions and not others. Methods to answer such questions have been labeled causal research in Chapter 4. Discussions of causal research to this point has been largely of the ex post facto design in which we either interview others about the subject of interest or we observe what is or what has been. A classic example of this approach is the massive study which led to the conclusion that smoking is dangerous to health. The original research consisted of correlations which indicated that heavy smokers suffered more illnesses and had a higher rate of death than did nonsmokers. While we agree that the evidence suggested that smoking is bad for the health, we must also agree with those who argued that these findings did not prove the causal link. What is needed to establish such a causal link is some more powerful research design. In theory, at least, we have such a method in experimental design. This research approach is the major topic of this chapter.

THE NATURE OF EXPERIMENTATION

What Is Experimentation? Experimentation is a special type of investigation used to determine *whether* and *in what manner* variables are related to each other. In the classical concept of an experiment we are concerned with determining *whether* there is a relation between an independent variable

(IV) and a dependent variable (DV). We do this by intervening in the research setting in two ways. First, we manipulate the IV by causing it to be present in some cases and absent in others. We then observe the effect of this manipulation on the presence or absence of the DV. Second, we arrange conditions so that other variables are not allowed to affect the DV, usually through some type of control.

It may be possible to approach this idealized concept under laboratory conditions, but it is not very practical in business research for two reasons. First, full manipulation and control is usually not possible. Second, we are often more interested in the question of concomitant variation, that is, *in what manner* variables are related to each other. In this approach we think of the effect of IV on DV in probabilistic terms and we think of the amount of effect on the DV from various levels of the IV. For example, we study different amounts or forms of training on later job performance.

Techniques and theory have been developed that enable us to use such statistical inference in designing experiments. These developments, chiefly growing out of pioneering efforts in agricultural research, now make it more practical to design experiments for business settings.

An Evaluation of Experimentation. There are some clear advantages and disadvantages to the experimental method as a research design. It is difficult to establish comparable control and experimental groups. Yet, if this is not done there is a good chance that the IV-DV relationship will be contaminated by extraneous variables. In addition, business research is often concerned with the study of people and there are limits to the amount of manipulation and control which is either possible or ethical. Experiments are often difficult to design, tend to be expensive and time-consuming, and may lack realism. All experiments are "artificial" to some degree. In addition, experimentation can be used only in research concerned with the present or perhaps the immediate future. Experimental studies of the past are impossible, and studies about intentions or predictions are difficult. In the light of these weaknesses why has experimentation become so attractive?

The overwhelming advantage of experimentation is that no other method approaches its power to determine causal relationships between variables. Albeit imperfectly, the researcher can control contamination from extraneous variables more effectively than in other designs and can bring together combinations of variables to test rather than having to search for some fortuitous combination of these variables in nature. These advantages are so great as to lead one scholar to write, ". . . I think it is essential that we always keep in mind the model of the controlled experiment, even if in practice we may have to deviate from an ideal model."[1]

---

[1] Samuel A. Stouffer, "Some Observations on Study Design," *American Journal of Sociology,* vol. 4 (January 1950), pp. 355–61.

Validity and Experimentation

Even when the experiment is the ideal research design it is not without its problems. It is easy to carry out an "experiment," but are the results valid? In an earlier chapter validity was roughly defined in terms of whether a measurement does what it claims to do. Recently, some scholars have suggested that there are four types of validity which must be considered when one is conducting experiments. They are roughly defined as follows:

Internal validity—refers to the validity of any conclusions we draw about whether a demonstrated statistical relationship implies cause.
External validity—refers to the validity with which a causal relationship can be generalized across persons, settings, and times.
Statistical conclusion validity—refers to the validity of conclusions we draw on the basis of statistical evidence about whether a presumed cause and effect co-vary.
Construct validity—refers to the validity with which cause and effect operations are labeled in theory-relevant or generalizable terms.[2]

In the discussion which follows we will focus chiefly upon internal and external validity considerations. To illustrate, assume that we wish to conduct an experiment with some employees engaged in assembly work. We might be interested in whether piecework payments would cause them to produce more units per day than would an hourly wage. In this example we would be confident of achieving internal validity to the degree that we had reason to believe that any changes in output were solely the result of the incentive pay. The external validity of the experiment would be judged in terms of our ability to generalize from the findings of this limited test to some larger population.

Internal Validity.   There are many threats to the internal validity of every experiment. For ease of discussion they may be classified as follows:

1. History.   There are events or factors that may have an impact on the IV-DV relationship during the period when the experimental stimulus (IV) is acting. Often a *before* measurement (O_1) is taken, followed by the experimental stimulus (X), and then a second measurement (the *after* measurement or O_2) is taken. The difference between O_2 and O_1 indicates the effect of the independent variable on the dependent variable, but it may do more. For example, the new work incentive plan may be introduced during a period when economic conditions are changing. Both this history factor and the incentive system might affect the O_1-O_2 change in worker output. Personnel problems, supply shortages, and many other contaminants also qualify as history factors that must be countered if we are to have internal validity.

---

[2] Thomas D. Cook and Donald T. Campbell, "The Design and Conduct of Quasi-Experiments and True Experiments in Field Settings," Marvin D. Dunnette (ed.), *Handbook of Industrial and Organizational Psychology* (Chicago; Rand McNally College Publishing Company, 1976), p. 223.

2. Maturation.   Some changes may take place in the dependent variable which are a function of the passage of time and are not specific to any particular events or condition. These are of particular concern when the study covers a long period of time. For example, the worker may grow older, develop new skills or strengths, become bored with the process, or not want to continue the old work style. This problem can occur even in experiments covering a short time period. For example, food tasters may be hungrier at one time than another, or workers may score differently on tests given at various times during the day because of fatigue.

3. Testing.   The testing process can also have a distorting effect on experiment results. One form of this is the learning effect by which people improve on taking a second test even if it is an alternative form of the original. This effect is especially pronounced when the before measurement (O_1) is an achievement, attitude, or intelligence test.

The testing effect may also be felt when the pretest situation involves persons who are not accustomed to testing. For example, a special pretesting of worker output may cause anxiety on the part of those participating. As a result, some may decide to act in atypical ways, producing output changes that confound the experimental effect of incentive pay.

Recognition tests, rating scales, and knowledge tests are often called *reactive measures* because of the ease with which they are the source of testing distortion. *Nonreactive measures* are safer, more passive, and more desirable if they can provide the needed measures. Typical of nonreactive measures are normally collected records of production, participant observer reports, and other disguised measures.

4. Instrumentation.   This threat to internal validity results from changes, between observations, in the measuring instrument or observers. A mechanical device may malfunction or become unreliable, but the greatest threat is the human factor such as observer boredom, fatigue, experience, or anticipation of results. For example, in the study of piecework payment and its effect on production, the observer might change the product quality acceptance standards during the period of the study.

5. Selection.   Another important threat to internal validity is the differential selection of persons to be included in the experimental and control groups. For example, the conclusion from the piecerate study might be invalidated if the workers in the piecerate group were volunteers, newly hired workers, or in any other major way different from those in the control group.

6. Statistical Regression.   This factor operates especially when study groups have been selected on the basis of their extreme scores. Usually there will be a shift of the mean of the extreme scores at O_1 toward the direction of the overall mean at O_2. For example, suppose that we measure the output of all workers in the department for a few days prior to the experiment, and then choose to conduct the experiment only with those who are in the top 25 percent and bottom 25 percent of the productivity groups. No matter what is done between O_1 and O_2 there is a strong tendency for the average of the high scores at O_1 to decline at O_2, and the low scores at O_1 to increase. This tendency results from imperfect measurement which, in effect, records some persons abnormally high and abnormally low at O_1. In the second measurement members of both groups tend to score more closely to their long-run mean scores.

7. *Experiment Mortality.* This operates by changing the composition of the study classes during the test. Attrition is especially likely in the experimental group, and each dropout changes the makeup of the group. Members of the control group, because they are not affected by the testing situation, are less likely to withdraw. In the piecerate incentive study, for example, some employees might not like the change in compensation method and withdraw from the test group; this could distort the comparison with the control group which has continued working under the established system, perhaps without knowing that a test is underway.

In addition to the above, one sometimes finds an interaction effect between selection and, say, different maturation levels among experimental treatment groups. This may result in forces which are mistaken for experimental effects. All of the threats mentioned to this point are generally, but not always, dealt with adequately in experiments by random assignment. In addition, however, there are five added threats to internal validity that are independent of whether one randomizes.[3] Three of these have the effect of equalizing experimental and control groups. They are:

1. *Diffusion or imitation of treatment* — If people in the experimental and control groups communicate, then those in the control group may learn the treatment, eliminating the difference between the groups.
2. *Compensatory equalization* — Where the experimental treatment is much more desirable there may be an administrative reluctance to deprive the control group members. In this case some compensatory actions for the control groups may confound the experiment.
3. *Compensatory rivalry* — This may occur when members of the control group know that they are the control group. This may generate competitive pressures, causing the control group members to try harder.

In addition, there are two other possible forces which may threaten internal validity and whose effects are to create a spurious difference. They are:

4. *Resentful demoralization of the disadvantaged* — When the treatment is desirable and the experiment is obtrusive, the control group may become resentful of their deprivation and lower their cooperation and output.
5. *Local history* — The regular history effect already mentioned impacts both experimental and control groups alike. However, when one assigns all

---

[3] Ibid., pp. 227–28.

experimental persons to one group session and all control people to another session there is a chance for some idiosyncratic event to confound results. This problem can be handled by administering treatments to individuals or small groups which are randomly assigned to experimental or control sessions.

External Validity. Internal validity factors cause confusion about whether the experimental factor (X) or extraneous factors are the source of observation differences. In contrast, external validity is concerned with the interaction of the experimental stimulus (X) with other factors and the resulting impact on our abilities to generalize to (and across) times, settings, or persons. Among the major threats to external validity are the following interactive possibilities.[4]

1. Interaction of Treatments and Treatments. This threat occurs if respondents experience more than one treatment. We cannot validly generalize to situations where subjects received fewer or more treatments. For example, in a store experiment of a price reduction in which the product is displayed in two locations, we cannot safely generalize a finding of increased sales to situations where only one display location is used.

2. Interaction of Testing and Treatment. In an experiment pretest we may sensitize subjects so that they respond to the experimental stimulus in a different way. For example, a before-measurement of the level of knowledge about the ecology programs of a certain company can sensitize the subject to the various experimental communication efforts that might then be made about that company. This before-measurement effect would seriously reduce our ability to generalize from such findings.

3. Interaction of Selection and Treatment. There is also the question of generalizing to other categories of people beyond the groups upon which the original relationship is founded. Much academic research faces special problems of this nature because students are used as subjects. Volunteer subjects also exacerbate this validity problem.

4. Interaction of Setting and Treatment. How well will the findings in a machine shop transfer to an assembly line? The unwillingness of some organizations to participate in a study may also promote the use of settings which are different from the average.

5. Interaction of History and Treatment. How well can a particular causal relationship be generalized to the past or the future? Sometimes major events which occur during the study have the potential to confound treatment effects. Even when no unusual events occur, there is still the question of how confidently one can extrapolate to the future.

Four general strategies are used to improve external validity.[5] Perhaps the best is randomly to select persons, settings, or times for study from the popu-

---

[4] Ibid., pp. 234–35.

[5] Ibid., pp. 236–37.

lations to which you wish to generalize. This is, of course, in addition to the random assignment of treatment and control groups designed to improve internal validity. If random selection is not possible, one may deliberately create heterogeneous groups of persons, settings, or times which are probably more representative of the populations than might otherwise be true. A third approach is to concentrate on those types of persons, settings, and times which are typical of modal groups in the population. Finally, there may be instances when one wishes to generalize only to specific target populations of times, people, or settings. In this case one would choose people, settings, or times to be representative of these target groups.

Problems of internal validity are amenable to solution through the careful design of experiments, but this is not as true for external validity. External validity is largely a matter of generalization, and in a logical sense, this is an inductive process of extrapolating beyond the data collected. It is an inferential leap that is only partially supported by the data. In generalizing we guess which factors can be ignored and which will interact with our experimental variable. We assume that the closer two events are in time, space, and measurement the more likely they are to follow the same laws. As a general approach we typically seek internal validity above all. At the same time, we try to secure as much external validity as is compatible with our internal validity requirements by making experimental conditions as similar as possible to conditions under which we wish to apply our results.

Ethics and Experimentation

There is a growing concern for protecting the rights of the subjects used in research projects. This is a problem in all studies using human beings as subjects, but it is of special concern in experiments because the subject is exposed to manipulation. To carry out the experiment the researcher often deceives the subject as to the purpose, nature, and possible personal repercussions from the study. Such actions can lead to embarrassment or invasion of privacy, and in other ways run counter to a subject's rights and interests as a member of a free society.

A good general rule is *not* to deceive subjects in a research study, but strict adherence to this rule often destroys any chance of conducting a study. For example, one cannot hope to secure valid results in a study of the effect of distasteful situations, malfunctioning products, and stressful interpersonal events on a subject who is fully on guard. Therefore, if there is to be research involving human beings there is a need to weigh the values of the study against the risks to the subjects. Fortunately, business research studies are largely innocuous in their impact, and a relatively harmless cover story can be used to satisfy the subject's curiosity. If there is reason to believe that the rights of the subject may be infringed upon, the researcher can consider several courses of action. If there is substantial risk to the subject the project may be abandoned or drastically revised. Such revision may call for securing the subject's prior consent after a thorough briefing on the project. At a minimum the subject should be debriefed after the experiment is completed.[6]

EXPERIMENTAL RESEARCH DESIGNS

There are many so-called experimental designs that a researcher may use, depending upon study conditions. They vary widely in terms of their power to control contamination of the relationship between the independent and dependent variables. The most widely accepted classification is based on this characteristic of control. In these terms there are three basic types: (1) preexperiments, (2) true experiments, and (3) quasiexperiments.

In addition, more sophisticated designs have been developed to increase the power of the basic designs. These approaches enable the researcher more effectively to control variables which have an unusual potential for contamination; some designs also enable the researcher to study the simultaneous impact and interaction effect of more than one independent variable. While there are many such designs the discussion here will be limited to the randomized block design, Latin square, and factorial designs.

Preexperimental Designs

Before discussing the details of the various designs it may be useful to explain the graphic notation to be employed. An *"X"* represents the introduction of an experimental stimulus to a group. It is the stimulus whose effects are of major interest. *"O"* identifies a measurement or observation event. The Xs and Os in a design diagram are read time-wise from left to right. Xs and Os which are vertical to each other indicate that the stimulus and/or observation take place simultaneously. *"R"* indicates that the group members have been selected randomly. Parallel rows unseparated by dashes indicate comparison groups which have been chosen randomly, while parallel rows separated by a dashed line indicate comparison groups which have not been selected by randomization.

One-Shot Case Study. All of three of the preexperiment designs are presented to illustrate the crudest forms of "experimentation." They are the weakest designs in terms of their scientific value and measurement power. This is especially the case with the one-shot case study. It may be diagrammed as follows:

$$X \qquad\qquad O \qquad\qquad (1)$$

Treatment or independent variable	Observation or measurement of dependent variable

---

[6] For a more detailed discussion of this topic as well as a discussion of debriefing techniques, see E. Aronson and J. M. Carlsmith, "Experimentation in Social Psychology," G. Lindzey and E. Aronson, eds., *The Handbook of Social Psychology* (Reading, Mass.: Addison-Wesley Publishing Company, 1968), pp. 29–36.

An example of such a study would be if we were to place all production workers on a piecework payment system basis and call it an experiment. While this may be good management it is not a good way to conduct experimental research.

This design obviously fails to provide controls over extraneous variables, but it also suffers from a second serious weakness. It omits the process of base-line comparison which is fundamental to evidence gathering. It is not the absolute values of isolated events which have meaning but comparisons with some criterion. In the one-shot design the only comparisons must be based on "common knowledge," our past general experience, or some hypothetical impression of what the conditions would have been if X had not been introduced.

Careful efforts to gather accurate measurements cannot compensate for the fundamental defects of this design. In spite of these deficiencies many of these studies are conducted and interpreted in ways unjustified by the quality of the design. As researchers we are well-advised to reduce the size of such a study and use the released resources to include a before-measurement or another comparison group.

The One-Group Pretest-Posttest Design. While this design has many defects, it does provide a comparison measurement. It is worth doing when nothing else can be done. It is diagrammed as follows:

$$O_1 \qquad\qquad X \qquad\qquad O_2 \qquad\qquad (2)$$
$$\text{Pretest} \qquad \text{Treatment} \qquad \text{Posttest}$$

This design is subject to most of the extraneous confounding factors discussed earlier. History can be a major problem, as many change-producing events can occur undiscovered between O_1 and O_2. Obviously, the shorter the time between observations the less chance of a history problem, but quick distractions such as a passing fire truck, someone entering or leaving the room, or laughter may affect the results. Since there is no way to measure this history effect the only alternatives are to isolate the experiment from the environment or to control environmental conditions as much as possible.

Maturation is also a problem in this design as subjects may grow older, become fatigued, bored or hungrier. The effect of the pretest also introduces the testing factor. Where the subject is identified the testing effect may make her reluctant to give answers which are not socially approved. The testing process may also be a stimulus in itself. For example, the introduction of overt observers into a work situation has been shown to have an effect on the workers regardless of the experimental variables being introduced. Generally, the more obvious or novel the measurement the more one may expect reactive effects from it.

Instrumentation problems are also encountered with the one-group pretest-posttest design. Undetected shifts in scoring standards may occur, or a change in observers may take place. Observers may also become more skilled or bored with their tasks and, in effect, observe differently at these two times. If the subjects under study are chosen for their extreme positions on the subject of study then they will also be susceptible to the regression problem.

Since there is only one study group, there is no problem of differential selection in terms of internal validity. Likewise, since there can be no differential drop-out rate there is no problem of mortality. On balance, however, this design contains inadequate safeguards and should be used only when nothing better is possible.

The Static-Group Comparison. This design provides for two study groups, one of which receives the experimental stimulus while the other serves as a control. The diagram is as follows:

$$X \qquad\qquad O_1 \qquad\qquad\qquad (3)$$
$$\text{------------------}$$
$$O_2$$

Selection risk is the major deficiency of this design because the two groups are chosen by nonrandom means. For example, two departments are studied, or triers and nontriers of a new product are compared, but we have no assurance that the groups are equivalent. This design is also subject to the mortality problem, but it is a substantial improvement over the two previously mentioned designs with regard to history, maturation, testing, and instrumentation effects.

None of these designs has been evaluated for external validity because they are so deficient in internal validity. In general, however, these designs also fall far short in meeting external validity standards.

True Experimental Designs

The major deficiencies of the previous designs is that they fail to provide comparison groups that are truly equivalent. The way to achieve this equivalency has already been discussed in an earlier chapter—random assignment to groups.[7] Matching is also a useful device by which to make improvements in equivalency, but *the basic safeguard is random assignment.* With randomly assigned study groups one can employ tests of statistical significance of the observed differences $(O_2 - O_1)$.

In these and other experimental designs it is common to indicate an X for the test stimulus and a blank for the existence of a control situation. This is an oversimplification of what really occurs. In the more typical case there is

---

[7] See page 107. A distinction should be made between *random selection* and *random assignment.* The former concerns the drawing of a representative sample from a population and is of concern in external validity. Random assignment concerns the equating of experimental and control groups and is chiefly of concern to internal validity. Too often in experimental research there is interest only in random assignment.

actually an X_1 and an X_2, and sometimes more. The X_1 identifies one specific independent variable while X_2 is another independent variable which has been chosen, often arbitrarily, as the control case. Different levels of the same independent variable may also be used with one level serving as the control. Therefore, when the comparison is shown of X versus non-X in the design diagrams, the reader should recognize that this is simply for illustration convenience.

Pretest-Posttest Control Group Design.   This design consists of (1) adding a control group to the design number 2 (one group pretest-posttest) and (2) assigning the subjects to either of the groups by a random procedure. The diagram is:

$$R \qquad O_1 \qquad X \qquad O_2 \qquad\qquad (4)$$
$$R \qquad O_3 \qquad\qquad O_4$$

The effect of the experimental variable is

$$E = (O_2 - O_1) - (O_4 - O_3).$$

In this design we can control for all seven of the internal validity factors, but its adoption does not automatically assure such validity. For example, history is controlled if events which produce a difference between O_2 and O_1 also produce a difference between O_4 and O_3. Yet there may be unique intrasession history effects when randomly assigned subjects are treated in a single session. Some event (a disturbance or diversion) may occur in one group and not in the other. One way to reduce this possibility is to test subjects individually and assign both subjects and experimental sessions randomly to experimental and control conditions.

Maturation, testing, and regression are well-controlled by this design since we should expect any effect to be felt equally in both experimental and control groups. Instrumentation can be handled when conditions for intrasession history are met, although when observers or interviewers are used there is a chance for distortion. To reduce this risk the same observer should be used for both experimental and control groups, if possible. Another instrumentation problem which can develop is a biasing effect from observers knowing who receives the experimental treatment and who does not. To guard against this problem the "double blind" design is recommended. In this approach the observer does not know who is receiving the experimental or control treatments. Mortality can also be a problem, even with true experiments, because members of the experimental group may have a different drop-out rate than do control group members.

Selection is adequately dealt with by random assignment, but it is not total insurance against nonequivalent experimental and control groups. Sampling variance is present and on occasion there will be a significant difference between groups. While randomization is not perfect, it is the only workable method by which to assure compatibility within some known error interval.

Matching can also be used to improve equivalence but should be used *only as a supplement to random assignment.*

The record of this design is not as good on external validity. There is clearly a chance for a reactive effect from testing. This might be a substantial influence in attitude change studies where pretests introduce unusual topics and content. Nor does this design insure against reaction between selection and the experimental variable. Even random selection may be defeated by a high decline rate by subjects. This would result in using a disproportionate share of persons who are essentially volunteers and who may not be typical of the population. If this is the case we will need to replicate the experiment a number of times with other groups under other conditions before we can be confident of the external validity.

Posttest-Only Control Group Design. This design is identical to design number 4 except that the pretest measurements are omitted. These pretests are well-established in classical research design but are not really necessary when it is possible to randomize. The design is:

$$R \quad X \quad O_1$$
$$R \qquad\quad O_2 \tag{5}$$

The experimental effect is measured by the difference between O_1 and O_2. The simplicity of this design makes it more attractive than the pretest-posttest control group design. Internal validity threats from history, maturation, selection, and statistical regression are adequately controlled by random assignment. Since the subjects are measured only once, the threats of testing and instrumentation are reduced, but differential mortality between experimental and control groups continues to be a potential problem. In terms of external validity this design reduces the problem of testing interaction effect, although other problems remain.

Solomon Four-Group Design. This complex design is not widely used, although it enables the researcher to learn more about the factors affecting both internal and external validity. The design is:

$$R \quad O_1 \quad X \quad O_2$$
$$R \quad O_3 \qquad\quad O_4$$
$$R \qquad\quad X \quad O_5 \tag{6}$$
$$R \qquad\qquad\quad O_6$$

This design, basically a combination of designs 4 and 5, provides that both the direct testing effects and the reactive effects of testing on X can be determined. Our ability to generalize is enhanced, and in addition, the experimental effect can be tested in four ways: $O_2 - O_1, O_2 - O_4, O_5 - O_6$, and $O_5 - O_3$. If these four comparisons agree, then the power of our inferences about the effect of X are greatly strengthened. With this design one can also estimate the effect of pretesting (the difference between the row means) and the combined effect of history and maturation by a comparison of O_6 with O_1 and O_3.

Extensions of True Experimental Designs

The three true experimental designs have been discussed in their classical forms, but researchers normally use an operational extension of the basic design. These extensions differ from the classical design forms in terms of (1) the number of different experimental stimuli that are considered simultaneously by the experimenter and (2) the extent to which manipulation and assignment procedures are used to increase precision.

Before considering the types of extensions we introduce some terms which are commonly used in the literature of applied experimentation. *Factor* is widely used to denote an independent variable. Factors are divided into *levels,* which represent various subgroups. A factor may have two or more levels such as (1) male and female, (2) large, medium, and small, or (3) no training, brief training, and extended training. These levels should be operationally defined.

Factors may also be classed as to whether the experimenter can manipulate the levels to be associated with the subject. *Active factors* are those the experimenter can manipulate by causing a given subject to receive one level or another. *Treatment* is used to denote the different levels of active factors. With the second type, the *blocking factor,* the experimenter can only identify and classify the subject on the basis of an existing level. Sex, age group, customer status, and organizational rank are examples of blocking factors because the subject comes to the experiment with a given level of each.

To this point we have implicitly assumed that experimental subjects are persons, but this is often not the case. A better term for subject is *test unit;* it can refer equally well to an individual, organization, geographic market, animal, machine type, mix of materials, and innumerable other entities.

Multigroup Designs. There are several multigroup designs which are direct extensions of the true experiments already discussed. Probably the most widely used of these is the posttest-only design:

$$
\begin{array}{lll}
R & X_1 & O_1 \\
R & X_2 & O_2 \\
R & X_3 & O_3
\end{array}
\tag{7}
$$

This illustrates three treatment groups, but more treatments can be used. Extensions of the pretest-posttest and Solomon four-group designs are also used. Multigroup designs have the obvious advantage of providing for the testing of more variables or more levels of one variable in one experiment. In the discussion that follows the posttest-only design is used exclusively.

The basic forms of the true experiment presented to this point are often called *completely randomized designs* to distinguish them from more complex designs. To compare the application of the completely randomized design with these more complex designs consider a research situation where the president of a retail grocery chain wishes us to conduct some experiments in pricing. Specifically, the company sells their own brand of canned foods and would like to conduct an experiment to determine how these products should be priced relative to competing national brands.

We decide to set up an experiment on price differentials for canned green beans. Eighteen of the company's stores are chosen for study and three price spreads (treatments) of one cent, three cents, and five cents between the company brand and national brands are selected. Six of the stores are assigned randomly to each of the treatment groups.[8] The price differentials are maintained for a period of time and then a tally is made of the sales volumes of each brand in each store. In this case it is assumed that the randomization of stores to treatments has made the members of each treatment group equivalent as far as extraneous variables are concerned. The completely randomized design is usually satisfactory if the test units in the experiment are relatively homogeneous except for the treatment effect. On the other hand, a more complex design will improve the results if there are major extraneous factors.

Randomized Block Design. When there is a single major source of extraneous variation the *randomized block design* is used. Random assignment is still the basic procedure for assuring equivalency among treatment groups, but something more is desired for two reasons. The more critical reason is that the sample being studied may be so small that it is risky to depend upon random assignment alone to assure equivalency. Small samples, such as the 18 stores in the example, are typical in field experiments because of high costs or because few test units are available. For example, departments, stores, companies, territories, and the like are often the test units used, and they are limited in number. Another reason for blocking is to learn whether treatments bring differing results among various groups of subjects.

Consider again the retail pricing experiment with canned green beans. Assume that we have good reason to believe that lower income families are more sensitive to price differentials than are higher income families. Such a factor could seriously distort our results, so we decide to stratify the stores we choose by the average customer average family income. On this basis we assign each of the 18 stores to one of three customer income blocks and then randomly assign them, within blocks, to the various price difference treatments. The design is shown in the accompanying table.

	Blocking Factor–Customer Income		
Active Factor–Price Difference	High	Medium	Low
1 cent .... R	X_1	X_1	X_1
3 cents .... R	X_2	X_2	X_2
5 cents .... R	X_3	X_3	X_3

(8)

---

[8] In this design the emphasis is on the different stores as test units for the green beans experiment. Other designs are possible. For example, we may use only one store and six different varieties of canned vegetables, two each of which are randomly assigned to different price differential treatments.

Note that the "Os" have been omitted from this diagram. The horizontal rows no longer indicate a time sequence but various levels of the blocking factor. However, there is an after-measurement ("O") associated with each of the treatments.

In this design we can measure both *main effect* and *interaction effect*. Main effect is the average direct influence that a particular treatment has independent of other factors. Interaction is the influence of one factor on the effect of another. The main effect of each price differential is secured by calculating the impact of each of the three treatments averaged over the different blocks. An interaction effect occurs if we find that different customer income levels have a pronounced influence on the customer reactions to the price differentials.

Whether this design improves the precision of the experimental measurement depends upon how successfully the design minimizes the variance within blocks and maximizes the variance between blocks. That is, if the response patterns are about the same in each block then there is little value to the more complex design. In fact, blocking may be counterproductive.

Latin Square Design. The Latin square may be used when there are two major extraneous factors. To continue with the pricing example, assume that we decide to block on the size of store as well as on customer income. It is convenient to consider these two blocking factors as forming the rows and columns of a table. Each factor is divided into three levels to provide nine groups of stores, each representing a unique combination of the two blocking variables. Treatments are then randomly assigned to these cells so that a given treatment appears only once in each row and column. Because of this restriction a Latin square must have the same number of rows, columns, and treatments. The design looks like the accompanying table.

	Customer Income			
Store Size	High	Medium	Low	
Large	X_3	X_1	X_2	
Medium	X_2	X_3	X_1	(9)
Small	X_1	X_2	X_3	

Treatments can be assigned by using a table of random numbers to determine the order of treatment in the first row. For example, the pattern may be 3, 1, 2 as shown above. Following this the other two cells of the first column are filled in a similar manner and the remaining treatments are then assigned to meet the restriction that there can be no more than one treatment type in each row and column.

The experiment is carried out, sales results are gathered, and the average treatment effect calculated. From this we can determine the main effect of the various price spreads on the sales of company and national brands. With cost information we can determine which price differential produces the greatest margin.

A major limitation of the Latin square is that we must assume that there is no interaction between treatments and blocking factors. Therefore, we cannot determine how store size, customer income, and price spreads interrelate. This limitation exists because we do not have an exposure of all combinations of treatments, store sizes, and customer income groups. To do so would take a table of 27 cells, while ours has only 9. This can be accomplished by replicating the experiment twice in order to furnish the number needed to provide for every combination of store size, customer income, and treatment. On the other hand, when we are not very interested in interaction the Latin square is much more economical.

Factorial Design.   One misconception that many have about experiments is that we can manipulate only one variable at a time. This is not true; with *factorial designs* we can deal with more than one treatment simultaneously. Consider again the pricing experiment. The president of the chain might also be interested in determining the effect of posting unit prices on the shelf to aid shopper decision making. The accompanying table can be used to design an experiment to include both the price differentials and the unit pricing.

Unit Price Information?	Price Spread			
	1 Cent	3 Cents	5 Cents	
Yes....................	X_1Y_1	X_1Y_2	X_1Y_3	(10)
No	X_2Y_1	X_2Y_2	X_2Y_3	

This is known as a 2 by 3 factorial design in which we use two factors: one with two levels and one with three levels of intensity. The version shown here is completely randomized with the stores being randomly assigned to one of six treatment combinations. With such a design it is possible to estimate the main effects of each of the two independent variables as well as the interactions between them. The results can give us answers to the following questions.

1.   What are the sales effects of the different price spreads between company and national brands?
2.   What are the sales effects of using unit price marking on the shelves?
3.   What are the sales effect interrelations between price spread and the presence of unit price information?

There are practical limits as to how many active factors can be introduced, but five were utilized in one experiment. This study concerned the evaluation of five production and storage factors upon the stability of the flavor of peanuts. The following questions were simultaneously tested:

1. Is it better to pack the peanuts in an air or a carbon-dioxide atmosphere?
2. Is it better to use antioxidants in the fat in which the peanuts are fried or not?
3. Does an increase in storage temperature affect flavor?
4. Is it better to bag the peanuts in aluminum foil or in cellophane?
5. Is it better to pack bagged peanuts in a can?

In addition to the above five main effects there were nine first-order (package × temperature, and so forth) interactions to consider·as well as higher order effects (package × temperature × antioxidant, and so on).[9]

Other Designs. There are many other experimental design variations to meet different research needs. A Latin square can be used to simplify factorial designs, at a substantial cost saving, if only the main effects are of interest. *Double changeover designs* are used to increase precision of experiments by exposing each test unit to each treatment during consecutive periods of time. *Greco-Latin squares, incomplete block designs, incomplete Latin squares,* and *lattice designs* are other variations which may be of value for particular situations. The readings list at the end of the chapter provides sources for more detailed information about these and other designs.

Covariance Analysis. To this point we have discussed direct controlling for extraneous variables through blocking. It is also possible to apply some degree of indirect statistical control on one or more such variables through analysis of covariance. For example, even with randomization we may find that the "before" measurement shows an average knowledge level difference between experimental and control groups. With covariance analysis we can adjust statistically for this "before" difference. Another application might occur if we carry out the canned green beans pricing experiment with a completely randomized design, only to find that there is a contamination effect from differences in average customer income levels. With covariance analysis we can still do some "statistical blocking" on average customer income even after the experiment has been run.

Quasiexperiments[10]

To this point we have discussed two basic types of experimental designs. The preexperiments are carried out only as a last resort because they have virtually no control of the many sources of confounding. At the other extreme, the true experiments provide the most valid information available although

---

[9] Committee on Food Research, *Deterioration of Fats and Oils,* QMC Manual 17-7 (Chicago: Quartermaster Food and Container Institute for the Armed Forces, 1945), pp. 84–88.

[10] For a discussion in depth of many quasiexperiment designs and their internal validity see Cook and Campbell, "Design and Conduct," pp. 246–98.

even these are not perfect. Between these two extremes, however, there are a number of research designs that are called *quasiexperiments*. They are used when we can control some of the variables but not enough to use the true experiment. In the quasiexperiment we usually cannot establish equivalent experimental and control groups through random assignment, nor can we usually determine when or to whom we can expose the experimental variable. On the other hand, we often can determine when and whom we measure.

While a quasiexperiment is inferior to a true experiment it may be superior to other alternative designs. There are many possible quasiexperiments but the discussion here will be limited to a few major types.

Nonequivalent Control Group Design. This is one of the strongest and most widely used quasiexperimental designs. It differs from experimental design (4) because the test and control groups are not equivalent. The design is diagrammed as follows:

$$O_1 \quad X \quad O_2$$
$$\text{-------------------} \tag{11}$$
$$O_3 \qquad O_4$$

There are two varieties of this design. One is the *intact equivalent design* in which the membership of the experimental and control groups are naturally assembled. For example, we may use different classes in a school, membership in similar clubs, customers from similar stores, and the like. Ideally the two groups should be as alike as possible. This design is especially useful when any type of individual selecting process would be reactive.

A second variation, the *self-selected experimental group design,* is weaker because volunteers are recruited to form the experimental group, while non-volunteer subjects are used for control. Such a design is likely when a number of subjects believe that it would be interesting or in their interest to be a subject in an experiment—say, an experimental training program.

Comparison of pretest results $(O_1 - O_3)$ is one indicator of the degree of equivalency between test and control groups. If the pretest results are significantly different there is a real question as to the groups' comparability. On the other hand, if pretest observations are similar between groups there is more reason to believe that internal validity of the experiment is good. Thus, while the internal validity of this design is generally good, it depends somewhat on the circumstances. One potential danger is the regression effect if either the experimental or control groups is selected for its extreme scores. The threats to external validity are essentially the same as those found with design number 4.

Separate Sample Pretest-Posttest Design. This design is most applicable in those situations where we cannot determine when and to whom to introduce the treatment but can determine when and whom to measure. The basic design is:

$$R \quad O \quad (X)$$
$$R \qquad \quad X \quad O_2 \qquad \qquad (12)$$

The bracketed treatment (X) is irrelevant to the purpose of the study but is shown to indicate that the experimenter cannot control the treatment.

This is not a strong design because a number of threats to internal validity are not handled adequately. For example, history can confound the results, and about the only way to overcome this is to repeat the study at other times in other settings. If the same effect is found under these changed conditions it is not likely to be the result of history influences. Mortality can be a problem if there is much time between the before and after observations. Instrumentation is also a possible contaminant, especially if the interviewers know the nature of the experiment. On the other hand, this design is considered to be superior in external validity to true experiments. This strength results from it being a field experiment in which the samples are usually drawn from the population to which we wish to generalize our results.

This design is more appropriate when the population is large, a before-measurement is probably reactive, and there is no way to restrict the application of the treatment. For example, suppose that a large corporation is planning an intense campaign to change its employees' attitudes toward energy conservation. It might draw two random samples of employees, one of which is interviewed regarding energy use attitudes prior to the information campaign. After the campaign the other group is interviewed.

There are several variations of this basic design; one which substantially improves on the internal validity problems is the *separate-sample pretest-posttest control group design*. It is diagrammed as follows:

$$R \quad O_1 \quad (X)$$
$$R \qquad \quad X \quad O_2$$
$$------------------$$
$$R \quad O_3 \qquad \qquad \qquad (13)$$
$$R \qquad \qquad \qquad O_4$$

When it is possible to withhold some members from treatment exposure it is possible to use design 13. This is similar to design 11 except that there is no retesting of subjects which could lead to interaction of the testing and the treatment. Design 13 comes as close as any quasiexperiment to meeting the standards of a true experiment. However, since the added control group is comparable rather than equivalent there is a chance that the treatment effect is confounded with some specific local trend or condition that arises in the experimental group only.

Single Group Time-Series Design. This design introduces repeated observations before and after the treatment. This allows subjects to act as their own controls. Three versions are diagrammed here:

A. Single group with temporary single group treatment
$$O_1 \ O_2 \ O_3 \ O_4 \ XO_5 \ O_6 \ O_7 \ O_8 \qquad (14)$$
B. Single group with continuous single treatment and withdrawal
$$O_1 \ O_2 \ O_3 \ O_4 \ XO_5 \ XO_6 \ O_7 \ O_8$$
C. Single group with continuous single treatment
$$O_1 \ O_2 \ O_3 \ O_4 \ XO_5 \ XO_6 \ XO_7 \ XO_8$$

In design 14A there is a single temporary treatment that is preceded and followed by measurements at specified intervals. The number of these before and after measurements can vary from as few as two each to as many as desired. Versions 14B and 14C illustrate cases in which the treatment continues for several observation periods or as long as observations are made.

To illustrate the application of design 14B, assume that we choose the time-series design for the price experiment involving canned green beans. We might record weekly sales for both the company and the national brands of beans for a period of weeks before introducing, say, a five-cent price differential. After two weeks we return the price spread to its original level. We then continue to observe sales for several more weeks. With design 14C we would continue the price spread of five cents for the entire period of the observation.

The time-series format is especially useful in those institutional settings where regularly kept records are a natural part of the environment. If special measurements must be made there is a good chance that the process will be reactive. The time-series design is also a good way to study unplanned events in an ex post facto manner. For example, the federal government might suddenly institute a policy such as price control; we can still study the effects of this action later if we have the regular collected records for a period of time before and after the imposition of controls.

The time-series design deals adequately with most internal validity problems such as maturation, testing effects, regression, and selection. Mortality effects are handled if the study is made of individuals rather than groups. If the data collection is made only in group totals it is possible that the group composition will change over the period of research. The degree of instrumentation effect depends largely on how certain we are that observer expectations do not play a biasing role in the results.

The major internal validity problem is with history. It is plausible that some simultaneous event might occur to confound the treatment effect. To reduce this risk we can keep a log of nonexperimental stimuli during the period of the experiment and then evaluate which of these might have an effect. The potential for history contamination depends largely upon the degree of *experimental isolation* which we can claim. If our study is isolated from many potential contaminants, and if we are well aware of those that remain, and can discount their effect, then we can be less concerned about the problems of history.

The external validity of this design depends on the nature of the study conditions. Unless natural groups and unobtrusive observation are used there is likely to be a problem of testing and its interaction with the treatment. Selection interaction depends on how well the group chosen is typical of a more general population. One way to secure more external validity is to repeat this design in other places under other conditions.

Multiple Group Time-Series Designs.   This design is similar to the single group design except for the addition of one or more control or comparison groups. There are many variations in these designs, but typical of them is the following:

A. $\underline{O_1 \quad O_2 \quad O_3 \quad O_4} \quad X \quad \underline{O_5 \quad O_6 \quad O_7 \quad O_8}$

B. $\underline{O_9 \quad O_{10} \quad O_{11} \quad O_{12}} \quad Y \quad \underline{O_{13} \quad O_{14} \quad O_{15} \quad O_{16}}$ (15)

C. $O_{17} \quad O_{18} \quad O_{19} \quad O_{20} \qquad O_{21} \quad O_{22} \quad O_{23} \quad O_{24}$

This design illustrates two comparison treatment groups and one control group. Dashed lines indicate that the groups are nonequivalent, but since they are often naturally formed they tend to be similar in many respects. Such a design may be used if we wish to test the impact of two types of training on departmental productivity. Treatment X might be a work simplification training program given to the employees of department A, while treatment Y might be a program in creative problem solving given to employees in department B. Department C workers would receive neither treatment and function as the control group.

This design receives generally excellent marks for internal validity. It has all of the advantages of the single time-series design and, in addition, generally deals effectively with the history problem. In terms of external validity this design suffers from the same weaknesses of the single group time-series design.

Equivalent Time Sample.   Allied to the time-series design is that in which equivalent samples of occasions are used to introduce one or more treatment or control situations. The basic diagram for this design is:

$$XO_1 \quad O_2 \quad XO_3 \quad XO_4 \quad O_5 \quad O_6 \ldots \text{etc.} \qquad (16)$$

The pattern shown above is intended to indicate that treatment and control occasions occur randomly. This design is clearly restricted to those occasions where there is only a transient treatment effect. While most studies using this design have relatively few repetitions, a study of the effect of music on factory production had 56 days with an experimental treatment (music being played in the factory) and 51 control days (no music).[11]

The equivalent time sample design effectively deals with the various major threats to internal validity, but the potential for reactive effects from the frequent testing is a major weakness. It has the same external validity problems as other time-series designs.

---

[11] W. A. Kerr, "Experiments on the Effect of Music on Factory Production," *Applied Psychological Monographs,* 1945, no. 5.

Experimentation Examples

A Marketing Experiment.[12]   A major scarce resource in supermarkets is the amount of shelf space for display. One unanswered question in this regard is how much space should be given to a particular product type or brand. Two decision rules are generally proposed for this problem. One is that a brand should be given more space if the additional revenue generated by the larger shelf facing is greater than the added cost associated with it (contribution to profit concept). Given a positive profit contribution, a second rule is that there should be no other alternative use which provides a better contribution (the opportunity cost concept).

One experimental study has explored the relationship between space and profit, depending on whether (1) a product is a staple or impulse item and whether (2) a product has high or low consumer acceptance. The four products studied were two leading brands of salt and two brands of powdered coffee cream. The hypotheses were:

1. There is no relationship between the amount of shelf space given to a staple product brand and total unit sales of that brand.
2. There is a relationship between the amount of shelf space given to an impulse product brand that has high consumer acceptance and total unit sales of the product brand.
3. There is no relationship between the amount of shelf space given to an impulse brand that has low consumer acceptance and total unit sales of that product brand.

The experiment was conducted over a three-week period in six stores in a supermarket chain. A randomized block design was used, blocking on the individual store. Total shelf space for the two product categories was held constant throughout the experiment, but different relative allocations of space were made between the brands (see Table 11–1).

Table 11–1: Space Allocation Experiment (in proportions of shelf space)

Treatment (week)	Powdered Coffee Cream		Salt	
	Coffeemate	Creamora	Morton	Food Club
1	1/3	2/3	1/3	2/3
2	1/2	1/2	1/2	1/2
3	2/3	1/3	2/3	1/3

---

[12] Keith M. Cox, "The Effect of Shelf Space upon Sales of Branded Products," *Journal of Marketing Research* (February 1970), pp. 55–58.

Product unit sales were collected through an inventory of test products each day, and analysis of variance procedures were used to test the findings. The author's conclusions were that all three hypotheses were supported by the findings.

A Job Enrichment Quasiexperiment.[13]   One theory of job attitudes holds that "hygiene" factors, which include working conditions, pay, security, status, interpersonal relationships, and company policy can be a major source of dissatisfaction among workers but have little positive motivational power. This theory holds that the positive motivator factors are intrinsic to the job; they include achievement, recognition for achievement, the work itself, responsibility, and growth or advancement.[14]

One study of the value of job enrichment as a builder of job satisfaction was carried out with laboratory technicians or "experimental officers" (*EOs*) in a British chemical company. The project was a multiple group time-series quasiexperiment. The project can be diagrammed as:

$$O \quad O \quad O \quad X \quad O \quad O \quad O \quad O \quad O \quad O \quad O \quad O \quad O \quad O \quad O$$

$$O \quad O \quad O \quad O \quad O \quad O \quad O \quad O \quad X \quad O \quad O \quad O \quad O \quad O \quad O$$

$$O \quad O \quad O \quad O \quad O \quad O \quad O \quad O \quad O \quad O \quad O \quad O \quad O \quad O \quad O$$

Two sections of the department acted as experimental groups and two as control groups. It is not clear how these were chosen, but there was no mention of random assignment. One of the experimental groups and one of the control groups worked closely together, while the other two groups were separated geographically and were engaged on quite different research. Hygiene factors were held constant during the period of the research, and the studies were kept confidential in order to avoid the tendency on the part of participants to act in artificial ways.

A before-measurement was made using a job reaction survey instrument. This indicated that the *EOs* typically had low morale and many wrote of their frustrations. All *EOs* were asked to write monthly progress reports, and these were used to assess the quality of their work. The assessment was made against eight specifically defined criteria by a panel of three managers who were not members of the department. These assessors were never told which laboratory technicians were in the experimental group and which were in the control group.

The study extended over a year, with the treatments being introduced in the experimental groups at the start of the 12 months study period. Changes were made to give experimental group *EOs* important chances for achieve-

---

[13] William J. Paul, Jr., Keith B. Robertson, and Frederick Herzberg, "Job Enrichment Pays Off," *Harvard Business Review* (March–April 1969), pp. 61–78.

[14] Frederick J. Herzberg, "One More Time: How Do You Motivate Employees?" *Harvard Business Review* (January–February 1968), pp. 53–62.

ment; these changes also made the work more challenging. Recognition of achievement was given, authority over certain work aspects was increased, new managerial responsibilities were assigned to the senior *EO*s, added advancements were given to others, and the opportunity for self-initiated work was provided. After a period of about six months these same changes were instituted with one of the control groups, while the remaining group continued for the entire period as a control. Several months of *EO* progress reports were available as a prior base line for evaluation. The results of this project are shown in Figure 11–1.

Figure 11–1: Assessment of *EO*s Monthly Reports

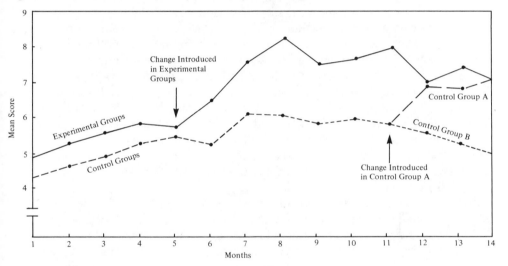

SIMULATION

Simulation is a method with great potential for business research. While some types of simulations have been used for many decades, the great surge of interest in this method dates from the advent of the large-scale computer. A discussion of simulation in any depth is beyond the scope of this book, but for those interested in more detail there are several references at the end of the chapter. The discussion here will be restricted to a discussion of the general nature of simulation, a brief summary of its business applications, and an example of its use.

What Is Simulation?

Simulation has been variously described and defined, but it still suffers from a lack of uniform terminology. There is no generally accepted classification of simulation types. In its most general form simulation may be described as *the process of conducting experiments on a model of a system.* As used in this context a "model" is anything used to represent the system. For example, a physical operating model might be a set of pipes through which liquid moves to simulate the flow of monetary values in our economic system. We can simulate behavioral activity by role-playing, as in various business games. For the most part, however, the literature of simulation is concerned with symbolic or mathematics-based models. The availability of large-scale computers has made it possible for us to experiment with symbolic models in ways which were heretofore unknown. Simulation is particularly useful when there are complex interactions among many variables, especially if some of the variables are random and/or their relationships are nonlinear.

Essentials of Simulation. The essentials of a simulation are (1) a mathematical model of the process or system being studied and (2) a sample of inputs.[15] These inputs may be samples of actual data or synthetic data based on the general characteristics of real input data. When we operate the model we secure a yield of outputs based on the sample of inputs. For example, in an inventory simulation the input may be customer orders received over a number of time periods, and the output is a set of production requirements, based on the nature of the inventory system being simulated. In another simulation model the input may be a set of predictions for various specific economic indicators, and the output a set of gross national product (GNP) projections for the coming year.

Other data may be produced during a simulation; this additional output may include such information as costs of various configurations of production facilities, the timing and amount of idle resources, and estimates of unsatisfied demand that occur with a certain resource allocation. The nature of such additional information, of course, is different for each simulation model.

Conditions Favorable to Simulation. Simulation, using computer-based models, is especially useful in two circumstances. In the first case, we may want to conduct an experiment on some business process, but find that it is not feasible to do it. For example, in Chapter 1 the researcher developed an inventory management system for a paint manufacturer. The researcher considered several approaches, developed a model, and simulated the inventory replenishment and disbursement processes. While an actual experiment would have been more realistic, there were several compelling reasons why simulation was used. Any real-life experiment would disrupt the company operations and run the risk of alienating customers. Trying several different approaches would disrupt operations for an extended period of time. In addition, management would find it very costly to experiment with their operations in this manner.

---

[15] C. William Emory and Powell Niland, *Making Management Decisions* (Boston: Houghton Mifflin Co., 1968), p. 213.

When we build a model to solve a problem we may have the choice between an analytic model and a simulation. With the former we can calculate the optimal solution to the problem. For example, the economic order quantity model can be solved through the use of the calculus. Linear programming and other calculus-based models are further examples of the analytic approach.

In contrast, simulation is more of a trial-and-error procedure, one that does not assure the researcher of finding an optimal solution. We develop the model, operate it with a number of sets of input data, and then use the analysis of these results to determine which seems to be the best course to follow. Since this is the case, why would we use simulation when we can use an analytic approach? The answer, generally speaking, is that we would not use simulation. However, there are many processes for which there is no analytic solution, or at least not one obtainable at a reasonable cost. Often the processes are so complex as to defy analytic solution with the present state of the art. It is in these cases that simulation has the advantage. Even when an analytic approach may be possible, however, a simulation often does well enough and may be much easier to perform.

Business Applications of Simulation

The determination of proper order quantities was one of the first uses for simulation, and it continues to be a major application. A second early use was in production operations, especially job shop scheduling. A job shop is a group of machines, often with different characteristics, which are operated independently in the production of goods. Routings of materials and goods in process among the machines varies with the nature of the products, the work to be performed on each product, and the functions that can be performed on each machine. Even in relatively small job shops the variety and complexity of routing configurations is so great as to defy analytic solution.

Simulation has also found an important application in the design of complex distribution systems. When one considers the large number of potential plant, warehouse, and customer locations, plus the variety of different customer demand patterns, different transportation methods and costs, and different inventory strategies and customer service levels, it is easy to see why simulation might make a substantial contribution to the reduction of distribution costs.

A major class of simulation applications is queuing or waiting line problems. Queuing theory has been characterized as the "study of congestion." It has been suggested that such congestion is a common feature in a modern industrial society. Simple examples of queuing situations are the check-out stand in a supermarket or the problems associated with any service facility which is subject to variations in workload. A more complex example is a factory production line which can be viewed as a "series of stations, each highly specialized in function, through which a product must flow, in sequence, in the process of manufacture."[16]

The simulations discussed to this point generally involve an application of the Monte Carlo technique. This technique is used to incorporate random variables into the models. The exact value that a certain variable has at a given point in the simulation is determined by a chance process described in the form of a probability distribution. The behavior of each variable is defined in the model by describing the values that a random variable can take and the probability associated with each value. Monte Carlo is the technique used for choosing samples of these random variables for use in the simulation.

Not all simulations use the Monte Carlo technique, however, because they may not include random variables. One such approach, which has been identified with large system simulations, is *system dynamics*.[17] This approach focuses on analyzing decision processes in a complex interacting economic environment. Two attributes associated with each variable in the model are the *level of the variable* and its *rate of change*. Typical examples are models incorporating cyclical and/or seasonal fluctuations. Leads and lags in variable interactions are represented by difference equations. The analysis concentrates on the behavior of the system in response to changes in levels, given the leads and lags incorporated in the model.

Other forms of simulation exist and descriptions can be found of them in the literature. One recent cataloging of the variety of applications for which simulation has been used is shown in Table 11–2.

A Simulation Example

The example presented here, a simple inventory problem involving one product, is sufficient to display the basic ideas of a simulation. The problem also demonstrates the use of the Monte Carlo technique.

The Problem. Assume that we are interested in determining how we might better manage the buying, stocking, and disbursing of product X. We want to provide an adequate service level for our customers, but at the same time hold our costs down. We investigate the demand pattern for product X and learn that there is substantial week-to-week variation in orders, but there are no distinctive patterns to make demand forecasting easier.

We would like an immediate delivery of all orders from our customers, but we realize that this would require uneconomic levels of inventory. We accept that we will sometimes be out of stock for a given item, and that the problem is one of a tradeoff between inventory levels and costs versus service levels. A brief analysis of our records suggests that we have sufficient information to simulate the process of ordering, stocking, and shipping product X.

---

[16] Ibid., p. 204.

[17] For a comprehensive treatment of *system dynamics* see Edward B. Roberts (ed), *Managerial Applications of System Dynamics* (Cambridge, Mass: The MIT Press, 1978).

Table 11–2: Areas in Which Simulation Methods Are Currently Being Used

Air traffic control queuing
Aircraft maintenance scheduling
Airport design
Ambulance location and dispatching
Assembly line scheduling
Bank teller scheduling
Bus (city) scheduling
Circuit design
Clerical processing system design
Communication system design
   Computer time sharing
   Telephone traffic routing
   Message system
   Mobile communications
Computer memory-fabrication test-facility
   design
Consumer behavior prediction
   Brand selection
   Promotion decisions
   Advertising allocation
Court system resource allocation
Distribution system design
   Warehouse location
   Mail (post office)
   Soft drink bottling
   Bank courier
   Intrahospital material flow
Enterprise models
   Steel production
   Hospital
   Shipping line
   Railroad operations
   School district
Equipment scheduling
   Aircraft
Facility layout
   Pharmaceutical center
Financial forecasting
   Insurance
   Schools
   Computer leasing
Insurance manpower hiring decisions
Grain terminal operation
Harbor design
Industry models
   Textile
   Petroleum (financial aspects)

Information system design
Intergroup communication (sociological
   studies)
Inventory reorder rule design
   Aerospace
   Manufacturing
   Military logistics
   Hospitals
Job shop scheduling
   Aircraft parts
   Metals forming
   Work in-process control
   Shipyard
Library operations design
Maintenance scheduling
   Airlines
   Glass furnaces
   Steel furnaces
   Computer field service
National manpower adjustment system
Natural resource (mine) scheduling
   Iron ore
   Strip mining
Parking facility design
Numerically controlled production facility
   design
Personnel scheduling
   Inspection department
   Spacecraft trips
Petrochemical process design
   Solvent recovery
Police response system design
Political voting prediction
Rail freight car dispatching
Railroad traffic scheduling
Steel mill scheduling
Taxi dispatching
Traffic light timing
Truck dispatching and loading
University financial and operational
   forecasting
Urban traffic system design
Water resources development

Data Gathering. Our first step is to study the weekly demand patterns for product X. We gather information on orders for the past 50 weeks. An investigation of weekly customer patterns shows that in two of the weeks there were no orders, while in the busiest week there were orders for seven cases. Over the 50-week period there were 154 cases ordered, an average of 3.1 per week. The probability distribution of customer weekly orders is shown in section A of Table 11–3.

Table 11–3: Assumed Distributions of Weekly Demand and Supplier Delivery Times for Product X

A. Demand			B. Delivery Time	
Size (Cases)	No. of Weeks	Relative Frequency	Weeks	Relative Frequency
0	2	4%	1	40%
1	5	10	2	45
2	10	20	3	15
3	14	28		100%
4	10	20		
5	6	12		
6	2	4		
7	1	2		
	50	100%		

C. Method of Assigning Values to Random Variables by Random Numbers

Random Numbers	Demand (Cases)	Random Numbers	Time (Weeks) Delivery
01–04	0	01–40	1
05–14	1	41–85	2
15–34	2	86–00	3
35–62	3		
63–82	4		
83–94	5		
95–98	6		
99–00	7		

D. Cost Assumptions		E. Ordering Strategy
Inventory costs	$8 + $1/week/case	Order quantity—6 cases
Order cost	$5.00 order	Reorder point—5 cases or less at end of week,
Lost profits (out of stock).....................	$3.00/case	either in inventory and/or already on order.

A second important variable is the time it takes to order and receive purchases from our supplier of product X. We study the purchase files and conclude that about 40 percent of the time we receive an order one week after we have placed it. Other times, however, it takes two or three weeks to receive an order. The probability distribution of delivery times is shown in section B of Table 11–3.

Since the Monte Carlo technique is appropriate for this problem we resort to a table of random numbers to secure a sample of customer demand levels for 20 weeks of simulated activity. The same must be done for each ordering occasion. We assign two-digit numbers over the range of 01–00 (assuming "00" equal "100") to each of the eight customer demand levels, and to the three supply time levels. These assignments must be in cumulative probability form and are shown in section C of Table 11–3. For example, in 4 percent of the weeks we received no orders for product X, so we assign random numbers 01 to 04 to the condition of zero weekly demand. In like fashion we assign 05 to 14 to the 10 percent chance of there being a one-case weekly demand, and so on.

Our third step is to determine the costs associated with various decisions and conditions. These are shown in section D of Table 11–3. It is estimated that the costs of holding inventory (storage, investment, insurance, handling, and so forth) of product X amounts to the fixed sum of $8 per week plus $1 for each case in inventory. It costs $5 to place an order for product X. In addition, we expect $3 in lost profits per case undelivered in the week ordered.

We next select an ordering and inventory strategy to test. We decide to order six cases at a time, and to review our stock level at the end of each week, placing an order for product X at that time if the combined ending inventory and "on order" is five cases or less. If the combined ending inventory and purchase orders outstanding are six or more cases we will not reorder.

Operating the Simulation. Finally we set up a model of the inventory replenishment and disbursement process, and enter the inputs of consumer demand, costs, and our decision rules for stock review and order size. We simulate 20 weeks of operations and secure an output of resupply orders, inventory levels, and lost customer orders. The results, and the estimated costs associated with this performance, are shown in Table 11–4.

Column 1 of Table 11–4 is a list of the random numbers which are used, in conjunction with the distribution shown in section C of Table 11–3, to determine the size of customer orders for each week. Column 2 shows a second set of random numbers which are used, when needed, to determine how long it takes a reorder to be received. In both cases a particular random number is transposed into demand or delivery time values by referring to the tables shown in section C of Table 11–3. Columns 3, 4, and 5 show the simulated amount of customer orders received, reorders received, and shipments to customers, respectively. Column 6 shows the end-of-the-week inventory, while column 7 shows the number of orders lost because we were out of stock. Columns 8, 9, and 10 show estimated costs incurred for each week and for the total 20-week period.

Table 11-4: Simulation of Product X Inventory Problem

Week	Random Numbers Demand (1)	Random Numbers Delivery (2)	Activity Orders (3)	Activity Receipts (4)	Activity Shipment (5)	Activity Ending Inventory (6)	Activity Lost Orders (7)	Inventory (8)	Costs Order (9)	Costs Lost Profits (10)
0				0	0	8		$16		
1	04	81	0	0	0	8		13	$5	
2	46	30	3	0	3	5[a]		11		
3	29	76	2	0	2	3		13	5	
4	68	07	4	6[a]	4	5[b]		11		
5	17	06	2	0	2	3		14		
6	50	27	3	6[b]	3	6		11		
7	39	98	3	0	3	3[c]		8	5	
8	75	18	4	0	3	0	1	8		$3
9	01	17	0	0	0	0		8		
10	08	53	1	6[c]	0	2[d]	1	10	5	3
11	76	70	4	0	4	0		8		
12	39	49	3	0	2	0	1	8		3
13	89	88	5	0	0	4[e]	5	12	5	15
14	25	48	2	6[d]	2	0		8		
15	71	77	4	0	4	2[f]		8	5	
16	61	77	3	6[e]	0	0	3	10		9
17	80	69	4	0	4	0		8		
18	45	31	3	0	2	0	1	8	5	3
19	12	23	1	0	0	0	1	11		3
20	62	42	3	6[f]	3	3			5	
			54		41		13	204	35	39

Service level = $\frac{41}{54}$ = 0.76 total cost = $278.

[a] Place order for 6 cases each; receipts available at beginning of week shown. For example, order "a" placed at end of week 2 is received at end of week 3 and is available for sale at beginning of week 4. Points "b," "c," . . . "f" also indicate when orders were placed and when received.

This run of the simulation indicates that the service level for product X customers would be 0.76, and the total of the three processing costs would be $278. If we wished to be very sure of the accuracy of these estimates, we should rerun this simulation for a longer period or one or more times using different sets of random numbers. The results of these various runs should then be averaged.

Are the costs and service level performances we secured good or bad? To answer this question adequately we should repeat the simulation using different ordering strategies but using the same sets of random numbers. To illustrate, if we had used a reorder point of six cases rather than five in the example in Table 11–4 but kept everything else the same, we would have obtained the following results: service level raised from 0.76 to 0.94 and service cost raised from $278 to $299.

Is this the best that we can do? We cannot identify the optimal answer to this problem with a simulation. However, if we rerun the simulation a number of times with different ordering strategies, we can identify the best of the strategies that we test. Therefore, if we identify a good selection of strategies for testing, we can be reasonably confident that the one we identify as the "best" is a good solution to the problem.

SUMMARY

Experimentation is a research method which in the past has not been widely used in business research. Recently it has grown in popularity as researchers recognize its power for uncovering causal relationships. Its distinctive characteristics are that the researcher can manipulate some of the variables of concern while controlling the effects of others.

There are many forms of research designs in which we manipulate variables, but not all of them deserve to be called experiments. We can judge various types of manipulative research designs on how well they meet the tests of internal and external validity. An experiment has high internal validity if we have confidence that the experimental treatment has, in fact, been the source of change in the dependent variable. More specifically, we judge a design's internal validity by how well it meets seven threats. These are history, maturation, testing, instrumentation, selection, statistical regression, and experimental mortality.

External validity is high when the results of an experiment are judged to be generalizable to some larger population. Such an experiment is said to have high external validity with regard to that population. There are three potential threats to external validity. They are testing reactivity, selection interaction, and other reactive factors.

Experimental research designs can be classified into three major groups: (1) preexperiments, (2) true experiments, and (3) quasiexperiments. The main distinction among these types is the degree of control that the researcher can exercise over validity problems.

Three preexperimental designs are presented. These represent the crudest form of experimentation and are only undertaken when nothing else stronger is possible. Their major weakness is the lack of an equivalent comparison group, and as a result, they largely fail to meet internal validity criteria. The three preexperimental designs are:

1. One-shot study.
2. One-group pretest-posttest design.
3. Static-group comparison.

Three forms of the true experiment are also presented. Their central characteristic is that they provide a means by which we can assure equivalence between experimental and control groups through random assignment to the groups. These designs are:

1. Pretest-posttest control group.
2. Posttest-only control group.
3. Solomon four-group design.

The classical two-group experiment can be extended to multigroup designs in which different levels of the test variable are used as controls rather than the classical nontest control. In addition, the true experimental design is extended into more sophisticated forms that make use of "blocking." Two such forms, the randomized block and the Latin square, are discussed. Finally, we discuss the factorial design, in which two or more independent variables can be accommodated.

Between the extremes of preexperiments, with little or no control, and true experiments, with random assignment, there is a gray area in which are found quasiexperiments. These are useful designs when we can control some variables, but we usually cannot establish equivalent experimental and control groups by random assignment. There are many quasiexperimental designs, but only five are discussed in this chapter. They are:

1. Nonequivalent control group design.
2. Separate sample pretest-posttest design.
3. Single-group time-series design.
4. Multigroup times-series design.
5. Equivalent time sample.

Simulation is a way to conduct experiments on a model of a system. The discussion here concerns symbolic models, although there are other type. Simulation as a research approach has grown rapidly since the advent of large-scale computers and is expected to continue to grow in importance. It is especially useful for solving inventory management problems, complex distribution problems, job shop scheduling problems, queuing or waiting-line problems involving large complex interactive systems, and many others.

The essentials of a simulation are a mathematical model of the process or system being studied and a sample of inputs to that system. From the operation of the model we secure outputs in terms of such factors as production, costs, company operating results, estimates of basic economic system aggregates, and the like.

We can solve many decision problems, either by using analytic models or simulation models. When we can calculate an optimal solution to a problem, the analytic solution is generally the better. However, simulation makes its greatest contribution in those situations in which the complexities are so great, or analytic solutions are so expensive, that only a simulation is feasible.

When there are random variables in the simulation model we use the Monte Carlo technique. However, many simulation models included no random variables, and in this case nonprobability techniques are used.

SUPPLEMENTAL READINGS

1. Banks, Seymour. *Experimentation in Marketing.* New York: McGraw-Hill Book Company, 1965. The pioneering book on the application of experimentation to marketing research. Excellent discussion with good examples.

2. Campbell, Donald T., and Stanley, Julian C. *Experimental and Quasi-Experimental Designs for Research.* Chicago: Rand McNally & Co., 1963. The almost universally quoted discussion of experimental designs in the social sciences.

3. Cook, Thomas D., and Campbell, Donald T. "The Design and Conduct of Quasi-Experiments and True Experiments in Field Settings," in Dunnette, Marvin D. (ed). *Handbook of Industrial and Organizational Psychology.* Chicago: Rand McNally College Publishing Company, 1976). A major authoritative work on both true and quasiexperiments and their design. It is already a classic reference.

4. Dayton, C. Mitchell. *The Design of Educational Experiments.* New York: McGraw-Hill Book Company, 1970). This book is "designed to provide a workable compromise between exhaustive coverage of designs and the practical facts of their utility." Each chapter includes summaries of actual experiments in an educational setting.

5. Edwards, Allen L. *Experimental Design in Psychological Research.* 4th ed. New York: Holt, Rinehart and Winston, Inc., 1972. A thorough treatment of experimental design with illustrative examples. Requires only elementary statistical analysis and a working knowledge of algebra.

6. Mize, Joe H., and Cox, J. Grady. *Essentials of Simulation.* Englewood Cliffs, N.J.: Prentice-Hall, Inc., 1968. An introductory presentation of the fundamentals of simulation methodology as they apply to the analysis and design of systems.

7. Roberts, Edward B. (ed.) *Managerial Applications of Systems Dynamics.* Cambridge, Mass: The MIT Press, 1978. A comprehensive volume on systems dynamics, including more than 30 articles on applications in manufacturing, marketing, management control, R&D, and societal problems.

DISCUSSION QUESTIONS

1. Distinguish between:
   a. Internal and external validity.
   b. Preexperiment and quasiexperiment.
   c. Reactive and nonreactive measurement.
   d. Contribution of randomization and matching to experimentation.
   e. Active and blocking factors.
   f. Main and interactive effects.

2. What are the essential characteristics that distinguish a true experiment from other research designs?

3. Why would a noted social science researcher say, "It is essential that we always keep in mind the model of the controlled experiment, even if in practice we have to deviate from an ideal model."?

4. What ethical problems do you see in conducting experiments with human beings? What ethical guidelines should we follow?

5. Suggest at least two specific situations, each, in marketing, finance, and production, in which you think an experiment would be an appropriate research design.

   Which of the various designs would you recommend for each of the above situations? What specific internal and/or external validity threats would you face with your suggested designs?

6. Under what general research conditions would you recommend using the following experimental designs?
   a. Separate-sample pretest-posttest control group design.
   b. Static group comparison design.
   c. Latin square design.
   d. Pretest-posttest control group design.
   e. Solomon four-group design.

7. You are asked to develop an experiment for a study on the effect that compensation has upon the response rates secured from personal interview subjects. This study will involve 300 people who will be assigned to one of the following conditions: (1) no compensation, (2) $1 compensation, and (3) $3 compensation. A number of sensitive issues will be explored concerning various social problems, and the 300 persons will be drawn from the adult population.

   Describe how your design would be set up if it were a completely randomized design, randomized block design, Latin square, factorial (suggest another active variable to use). Which would you use? Why?

8. How is simulation like a laboratory experiment? How is it different from a laboratory experiment?

9. Would you recommend an experimental design or a simulation for each of the following? In each case suggest in some detail how you would design it.
   a. A test of three methods of compensation of factory workers. The methods are hourly wage, incentive pay, and weekly salary. The dependent variable is direct labor cost per unit of output.

    b.   The effects of various levels of advertising effort and price reduction on the sale of specific branded grocery products by a retail grocery chain.

    c.   The values placed upon specific pieces of corporate financial information (cash flow per share, return on assets, and so on) by securities analysts.

10.   Refer to the simulation example reported in Tables 11–3 and 11–4. Assume that you wished to try the following inventory and ordering strategy:

    Order quantity—seven cases

    Reorder point—five cases or less at end of week (either in inventory or on order).

What would be the 20-week results, in costs and service levels, of such a strategy using the random numbers shown in Table 11–4?

SECTION FOUR

ANALYSIS AND REPORTING

Chapter 12

Elements of Analysis

CONCERN FOR DATA ANALYSIS PROBLEMS should begin during the planning of the project. It is at that early stage that we can most effectively incorporate the features needed to meet later analysis requirements. This is a common sense idea, but it is frequently ignored. The result is that we often recognize too late that certain comparisons are needed but we do not have the data to make them.

This chapter is concerned with three major topics. First is *data preparation,* which includes the processes of editing, coding, and tabulation. These are activities to assure (1) the accuracy of data and (2) its conversion from raw form to classified and/or reduced forms more appropriate for the analysis and interpretation stages. Second, *analysis* involves breaking down and rearranging data into more meaningful groups to aid the search for significant relationships. Third, in its narrower sense *interpretation* somewhat overlaps analysis by also being concerned with relationships within the data. The major difference is that interpretation chiefly involves the drawing of inferences from data relationships. In its broader sense interpretation extends beyond the study data to include the comparison of inferences to those of other studies, hypotheses, and theories. We begin with data preparation.

DATA PREPARATION

Editing

The normal first step in analysis, especially in surveys, is the editing of the collected raw data. It is basically a process of examination to detect errors and omissions, and to correct these when possible. The editor is responsible for seeing that the data are (1) as accurate as possible, (2) consistent with other facts secured, (3) uniformly entered, (4) as complete as possible, (5) acceptable for tabulation, and (6) arranged to facilitate coding and tabulation.[1]

Field Editing. During the stress of data collection the interviewer cannot always write out complete and legible responses. Ad hoc abbreviations and individual writing styles can be difficult for others to decipher. Therefore, as soon as possible, the interviewer should review the reporting forms to complete what was abbreviated, translate personal shorthand, and rewrite illegible responses. However, there is a danger here in trying to correct errors of omission by guessing what the respondent would have said if the question had been asked. This is nothing more than "self-interviewing" and should not be done.

In commercial studies it is common practice to have a supervisor do some field editing. In addition, the supervisor checks on the quality of the work performed and the honesty of the interviewers. Many commercial firms promise to confirm 10 percent of the completed interviews to assure that they were conducted properly. This work should be done shortly after the interview, preferably daily.

Central Editing. At this point the complete research form should get a thorough editing. For a small study the use of a single editor will assure maximum consistency of work. In larger studies, the tasks may be broken down so that each editor can deal with all of one section. This approach will miss inconsistencies between answers in different sections, but this problem can be handled by identifying points of possible inconsistency and having one editor check specifically for them.

In some cases it is obvious that an entry is incorrect, is entered in the wrong place, or states time in months when it was requested in weeks. These transposition and arithmetic errors can normally be changed by the editor, although this revision privilege should be used with care. When replies clearly are inappropriate or missing, the editor can sometimes determine the proper answer by reviewing the other information in the schedule. This practice, however, should be limited to those few cases where it is obvious what the correct answer is. It may be better to contact the respondent for correct information if time and budget permit. Another alternative is for the editor to strike out the answer if it is clearly inappropriate and there is no reasonable basis for determining the correct response. Here an editing entry of "no answer" or "unknown" is called for.

Another editing problem concerns "faking." Sometimes on mail surveys one will receive a reply which is obviously wrong. In most cases these replies must be dropped from the final results. Interviewer faking is a bigger problem.

---

[1] Mildred B. Parten, *Surveys, Polls and Samples* (New York: Harper & Brothers, 1950), p. 425.

"Arm-chair interviewing" is not unknown and may be difficult to spot, but the editor is in the best position to do so. One approach is to check responses to open-end questions. These are more difficult to fake. Distinctive response patterns in other questions will often emerge if faking is taking place. To uncover this the editor must analyze the interview schedules by interviewer.

Some useful rules to guide editors in their work are:

1. Be familiar with instructions given to interviewers and coders.
2. Do not destroy, erase, or make illegible the original entry by the interviewer. Original entries should be crossed out with a single line so as to remain legible.
3. Make all entries on a schedule in some distinctive color and in a standardized form.
4. Initial all answers changed or supplied.
5. Place initials and date of editing on each schedule completed.

Coding

The coding process consists of assigning numerals or other symbols to answers so as to enable the responses to be grouped into a limited number of classes or categories. This mapping of data onto a limited number of categories sacrifices some of the data detail but is necessary for efficient analysis. By this method, several thousand replies may be reduced to six or eight carefully chosen categories which contain the critical information needed for analysis. A category is a partition or subpartition of a set; and *categorization* is the process of using a set of rules to partition a body of data. Four major rules should guide the establishment of category sets. Categories should be:

1. Appropriate to the research problem and purpose.
2. Exhaustive.
3. Mutually exclusive.
4. Derived from one classification principle.

Appropriateness. The first rule might appear to be so obvious that nothing further needs to be said about it, but this is not the case. Categories must be set up to provide the information required to test the hypotheses or investigative questions. If the categories do not adequately serve these critical needs, then all else is trivial. Relevancy is the criterion here, but it is often violated. Irrelevancies occur because some topic suggests another interesting bit of information which can be "easily secured while we are at it."

Another problem concerns the definition of category boundaries. Often, it is possible to compare our data with information from other sources if the definitions of categories are the same. This is obviously of great concern when one is defining complex constructs, but even such a simple concept as age can present problems. It is disheartening to find, after the data have been collected and tabulated, that our respondent age categories of "Under 20 years, 20 to 29, 30 to 39, and so on do not match those of the comparison study we wanted to use.

Exhaustiveness. The rule on exhaustiveness states that there must be a category for *every* data item. A simple way to make each category set exhaustive is to include an "other" cell in each set. If we depend on this tactic alone, however, we may avoid the real problem of *properly defining response categories in the research design stage*. If new responses show up later in the study (usually in the form of a large number of "other" responses) it means our design work and pretesting were inadequate. Failure to present an adequate list of alternatives is especially damaging when multiple choice questions are used. Any answer that is not specified in the set presented for choice will surely be underrepresented in the final tally.

While the exhaustiveness requirement in a single category set may be obvious, there is a second aspect which is less apparent. A given body of data may also be analyzed in terms of more than one set of categories. If we fail to do this we may overlook information which can enrich our understanding. For example, responses to an open-ended question about a family's prospects for next year may originally be classified only in terms of whether the expectations are optimistic or pessimistic. It may be more enlightening if we also classify these responses in terms of more specific topics such as (1) income prospects, (2) buying intentions, and (3) other types of family change expectations.

Mutual Exclusivity. A third important rule is that category components should be mutually exclusive. This standard is met when a specific answer can be placed in one and only one cell in a given category set. For example, in an occupation survey the classifications may be (1) professional, (2) managerial, (3) sales, (4) clerical, (5) crafts, (6) operatives, and (7) unemployed. Some respondents will think of themselves as being in more than one of these groups. The man who views selling as a profession and who spends part of his time supervising others may feel that he fits under three of these categories. One of the functions of operational definitions is to provide categories that are composed of mutually exclusive elements. In this case operational definitions of the occupations to be classified under "professional," "managerial," and "sales" should clarify the situation. The problem of how to handle an unemployed salesman brings up the fourth rule of category design.

Single Dimension. The need for a category set to follow a single classificatory principle means, simply, that every class in the category set is defined in terms of one concept. Returning to the occupation survey example, the man in the study might be both a salesman and unemployed. The "salesman" label expresses the concept of an *occupation type,* while the response "unemployed" is another dimension concerned with *current employment status* without regard to the respondent's normal occupation. When a category set employs more than one dimension, there is a strong risk that the classes will not be mutually exclusive unless the cells in the set combine the dimensions (employed manager, unemployed manager, and so on.)

A Classification Example. The problems of classification are especially marked with responses to open-end questions. Suppose, for example, that in a survey the members of a factory work force are asked, "How can management-employee relations be improved?" Among the responses received from the workers might be the following:

1. Management should treat the worker with more respect.
2. They should stop trying to speed up the assembly line.
3. Working conditions in the shop are terrible. They should correct them.
4. Foreman "Z" should be fired. He is unfair in his treatment of workers.
5. They should form management-worker councils in the department to iron out problems and improve relations.
6. Management should stop trying to undermine union leadership.
7. Management should accept the union's latest proposals on new work rules.

In most surveys there would be many more than seven replies, but these are enough to illustrate the problems of forming appropriate categories. First, the type of categories that are developed should reflect the objectives that the data are being collected to serve (be appropriate for the research problem and purpose). For example, the survey might be concerned largely with learning the general perceptions of the workers as to the locus or responsibility for improving company-employee relations. In this case the categories might be as few and as general as in the following:

Who Should Initiate Action?	Mentioned	Not Mentioned
A. Management	_____	_____
B. Union	_____	_____
C. Worker (other than union)	_____	_____
D. Joint management-union	_____	_____
E. Joint management-workers	_____	_____
F. Other	_____	_____

This set of categories would appear to be mutually exclusive and to contain only one concept dimension. The provision of the "other" classification assures that the category set is exhaustive. If many responses suggest actions by the general public, government, or certain regulatory bodies, then to include all of these in "other" ignores much of the richness of the data.

If we used only the above set of categories for analysis we would be ignoring most of the information in the answers. The comments often suggest specific actions, and most researchers would want to collect and analyze these suggestions. For this purpose the replies might be classified in terms of decision areas in which actions may be taken:

1. Human relations.
2. Production processes.
3. Working conditions.
4. Other action areas.
5. No action area mentioned.

How could we classify a response suggesting a combined production process-working condition action? This could be handled by adding combination alternatives or by splitting the combination response into its parts and tallying each separately. In the latter case we lose information about combinations, and the total would be the total items mentioned rather than the total number of respondents.

This decision area set of responses may also be used as subcategories under the first list, giving the accompanying joint set of classification possibilities:

	Mentioned	Not Mentioned
A. Management		
1. Human relations	_____	_____
2. Production processes	_____	_____
3. Working conditions	_____	_____
4. Other action areas	_____	_____
5. No area mentioned	_____	_____
B. . . .		
C. . . .		
D. . . .		
E. . . .		
F. Other		
1. Human relations	_____	_____
2. Production processes	_____	_____
3. Working conditions	_____	_____
4. Other action areas	_____	_____
5. No area mentioned	_____	_____

Even with the 30 category classes the data are not exhausted. Depending upon objectives, the researcher may be interested in even more specific classifications. For example, within the category of management-initiated production process actions we might establish another subset to cover specific suggestions made for improvement. Other classification dimensions are also possible.

The above category sets provide for separate recording of "mentioned" or "not mentioned." Often the "not mentioned" is omitted; then it is assumed that no entry in the "mentioned" column indicates a "not mentioned." While this is easier, it fails to provide the desired positive control. It is easy to overlook some items in hand tabulating or to make errors which remain unnoticed. When positive recording is required for each response and non-response the total for each category should add to the total number of items.

Coding Procedure. Many coding decisions are made in the questionnaire design stage when multiple-choice alternatives are developed. This leaves only the difficult task of coding open-end questions to be done at the analysis stage. When codes are established early in the research process it is possible to precode the questionnaire choices. Precoding, shown in Figure 12–1, is especially valuable for computer tabulation because we can usually key punch directly from the original questionnaires.

Figure 12–1: Excerpts from a Precoded Questionnaire

How would you rate the *growth potential* of the following companies? (Please check only *one* for each company.)

	Avco	Gulf + Western	Leasco	Litton	Textron
Excellent	11–1 ☐	12–1 ☐	13–1 ☐	14–1 ☐	15–1 ☐
Good	–2 ☐	–2 ☐	–2 ☐	–2 ☐	–2 ☐
Fair	–3 ☐	–3 ☐	–3 ☐	–3 ☐	–3 ☐
Poor	–4 ☐	–4 ☐	–4 ☐	–4 ☐	–4 ☐
Don't know	–5 ☐	–5 ☐	–5 ☐	–5 ☐	–5 ☐

Figure 12–2: Coding Sheet for Punch Cards

Project __FSB__   __2/72__   ID __203__

Column	Code		Column	Code
1	0 ① 2 3 4 5 6 7 8 9		41	0 1 2 3 4 5 6 7 8 9
2	0 1 ② 3 4 5 6 7 8 9		42	0 1 2 3 4 5 6 7 8 9
3	0 1 2 3 ④ 5 6 7 8 9		43	0 1 2 3 4 5 6 7 8 9
4	0 1 ② 3 4 5 6 7 8 9		44	0 1 2 3 4 5 6 7 8 9
5	0 1 2 3 ④ 5 6 7 8 9		45	0 1 2 3 4 5 6 7 8 9
36	0 ① 2 3 4 5 6 7 8 9		76	0 1 2 3 4 5 6 7 8 9
37	0 1 2 3 4 5 6 7 8 9		77	0 1 2 3 4 5 6 7 8 9
38	0 1 2 3 4 5 6 7 8 9		78	0 1 ② 3 4 5 6 7 8 9
39	0 1 2 3 4 5 6 7 8 9		79	⓪ 1 2 3 4 5 6 7 8 9
40	0 1 2 3 4 5 6 7 8 9		80	0 1 2 ③ 4 5 6 7 8 9

With hand coding it is wise to use a standard method and code in the margin with a colored pencil. This procedure will reduce key punch and tabulating errors, especially if the data are punched into cards directly from the questionnaire. Sometimes a safer method is to transcribe the data from the questionnaire to a coding sheet. An example of such a sheet to be used for computer tabulating is shown in Figure 12–2.

If the data are to be hand tabulated it may also be desirable to use a transcription sheet or card. The paper used should be of a shape and size that is easy to handle and durable enough to withstand heavy use. If there is a substantial amount of hand coding to do, it is better to code only a few questions at a time in the interest of reducing coding errors.

SPECIAL DATA PROBLEMS

"Don't Know" Responses

No matter how good a research instrument is, there are always some responses that are difficult to handle. Two common types are (1) the incorrect or incomplete answer and (2) the "don't know" (DK) response. The former has already been discussed in the section on editing, but the DK problem remains to be treated.

DK Situations.   When the DK response group is small it is of little significance, but there are times when it is of major concern; and it may even be the most frequent response received. Does this mean that the question which elicited this response is useless? As is often true, the answer is "It all depends." There are two categories into which most DK answers fall.[2] First, there is the legitimate DK response when the respondent actually does not know the answer and this response meets our research objectives (we expect a number of DK responses and consider them to be useful answers).

In the second situation a DK reply illustrates the researcher's failure to get the appropriate information. Consider the following illustrative questions:

1.   Who developed the Managerial Grid concept?
2.   Do you believe the President's new fiscal policy is sound?
3.   Do you like your present job?
4.   Which of the various brands of chewing gum do you believe has the best quality?
5.   How many times a year do you go to the movies?

It is reasonable to expect that some legitimate DK responses will be made to each of these questions. However, in the first question the respondents are asked for a level of information that they often will not have. There would

---

[2] Hans Zeisel, *Say It with Figures,* rev. 4th ed. (New York: Harper & Brothers, Publishers, 1957), p. 42.

seem to be little reason to withhold a correct answer if known, and it is as easy to give the name of the developer of the Managerial Grid concept as it is to evade doing so. Thus, most *DK* answers to this question should be considered as legitimate.

DK response in the second question would also probably be accepted as legitimate, but it is a somewhat different problem. It is not immediately clear whether the respondent is ignorant of the President's fiscal policy or knows the policy but has not made a judgment about it. The researchers should have asked two questions: In the first they would have determined the respondent's level of awareness of fiscal policy; if the interviewee passed the awareness test, then a second question would have secured judgment on fiscal policy.

In the remaining three questions the *DK* response is more likely to be a failure of the questioning process, although some will surely be legitimate. The respondent may be reluctant to give the information. *DK* response to question three may be a way of saying, "I do not want to answer that question because it involves a sensitive subject." Question four might also elicit a *DK* response in which the reply translates to "This is too unimportant to talk about." In question five the respondents are being asked to do some calculation about a topic to which they attach little importance. In this case the *DK* may mean "I do not want to do that work for something that has so little importance."

Dealing with Undesired *DK* Responses.   The way for a researcher to deal with undesired *DK* answers is to design better questions at the beginning. The interviewer, however, must deal with the problem in the field; prior to interviewing she should identify the questions for which a *DK* response is unsatisfactory. Several actions are then possible. First, good interviewer-respondent rapport will motivate respondents to provide more usable answers. When the interviewer recognizes an evasive *DK* response she can repeat the question or probe for a more definite answer. Finally, the interviewer may record verbatim any elaboration by the respondent and buck the problem on to the editor.

If the editor finds a number of undesired responses she can do little unless the verbatim comments can be interpreted. About the only hope for understanding the real meaning rests on securing some clue from the respondent's other questions. One way to do this is to estimate the allocation of *DK* answers from other data in the questionnaire. It may be that the pattern of responses parallels the pattern of responses, say, of certain income, educational, or experience groups. For example, suppose that a question concerning whether the employee likes his present job elicited the answers in the accompanying table. The correlation between years of service and the "don't know" answers and the "no" answers would suggest that most of the "don't knows" are disguised "no" responses.

Do you like your present job?			
Years of Service	*Yes*	*No*	*Don't Know*
Less than 1 year	10%	40%	38%
1–3 years	30	30	32
4 years or more	60	30	30
Total	100%	100%	100%
n = ...	650	150	200

There are several other ways to handle "don't know" responses in the tabulations. If there are only a few it does not make much difference how they are handled, but they will probably be kept as a separate category. If the *DK* response is legitimate it should remain as a separate reply category. If we are not sure how to treat it we should also keep it as a separate category and let the reader make the decision.

Another way to treat *DK* responses is to assume that they occur more or less randomly. Using this approach, we may decide to distribute them among the other answers in the same ratio that the other answers occur. This assumes that those who reply "don't know" are proportionally distributed among all of the groups studied. This can be achieved either by prorating the *DK* responses or by excluding all *DK* replies from the tabulation. The latter approach is better since it does not inflate the actual number of other responses. This proration can be risky in opinion polls, as was learned in the 1948 presidential election. The polls at that time indicated that Dewey was leading Truman but with a large *DK* opinion group. The pollsters assumed that this body of undecided voters would allocate themselves about as the decided voters had, but on election day almost all of the uncommitted voted for Truman.

The Use of Percentages

Percentages serve two purposes in data presentation. They simplify by reducing all numbers to a range of from 0 to 100. Second, the use of percentages translates the data into standard form, with a base of 100, for relative comparisons. For example, in a sampling situation the number of cases that fall into a category is meaningless unless it is related to some base. A count of 314 families with two or more autos has little meaning unless we know that this is from a total sample of 654. Using the latter as the base, we conclude that 48 percent of the families have two or more autos.

While the above calculation is useful, it is even more useful when the research problem calls for a comparison of several distributions of data. For example, assume that a similar study of auto ownership five years ago showed that 551 families out of a sample of 1,450 owned two or more autos.

By using percentages we can see the relative relationships and shifts in these data (see accompanying table).

Family Auto Status	Five Years Ago		Today	
	No.	%	No.	%
No auto	290	20	98	15
One auto	609	42	242	37
Two or more	551	38	314	48
	1,450	100	654	100

Tabular Percentages. When two-dimension tables are used there is a question in which direction the percentages should be calculated. Zeisel advocates the rule that "percentages should be computed in the direction of the causal factor" (use the total number of cases in each category of the independent variable as the base for calculating the percentages).[3] Thus we must decide which of the two factors will be considered to be the cause (independent variable) and which the effect (dependent variable). This is not to say that we think A actually causes B, but only that, for cross-classifying purposes, we consider A to affect the percentage distribution of B. At times either may be considered the causal factor, although usually one is more significant than the other. For example, consider the data in Table 12–1. In which direction should any calculated percentages run?

Table 12–1: 1972 Unemployment in the United States by Age (in thousands)

Age Group	Unemployed	Employed	Total Civilian Labor Force
16–19 years	1,017	6,158	7,175
20 years and over	2,867	66,916	69,783
Total	3,884	73,074	76,958

Source: *Monthly Labor Review* (April 1974), p. 92.

If the percentages run vertically, as in part A of Table 12–2, they imply that employment status has some effect on age. This is an illogical proposition. On the other hand, when the percentages run as shown in part B, the suggestion is that age has some effect on whether a person is employed. It is

[3] Zeisel, *Say It with Figures*, p. 24.

Table 12–2: 1972 Unemployment in the United States, by Age

Age Group	Unemployed	Employed	Total Civilian Labor Force
A.			
16–19 years	26%	8%	9%
20 years and over....................	74	92	91
Total	100%	100%	100%
B.			
16–19 years	14%	86%	100%
20 years and over....................	4	96	100
Total	5%	95%	100%

apparent from part B of Table 12–2 that the unemployment rate among the 16–19 year old group was more than three times as high, in 1972, as that of persons 20 years and older.

Problems in the Use of Percentages. Percentages are used by virtually everyone dealing with numbers, and in too many cases they are used incorrectly. Boyd and Westfall suggest the following rules.[4]

1. *Averaging percentages.* Percentages cannot be averaged unless each is weighted by the size of the group from which it is derived. Thus, in most cases, a simple average will not suffice and it is necessary to use a weighted average.
2. *Use of too large percentages.* This often defeats the purpose of percentages—which is to simplify. A large percentage is difficult to understand and tends to confuse. If a 1,000 percent increase is experienced, it is better to describe this as a tenfold increase.
3. *Using too small a base.* Percentages hide the base from which they have been computed. A figure of 60 percent when contrasted with 30 percent would appear to indicate a sizable difference. Yet if there are only three cases in the one category and six in the other, the differences would not be as significant as they have been made to appear through the use of percentages.
4. *Percentage decreases can never exceed 100 percent.* This is obvious, but this type of mistake occurs frequently. The higher figure should always be used as the base. For example, if a price was reduced from $1.00 to $0.25 the decrease would be 75 percent (75/100).

TABULATION

Tabulation is the process of summarizing raw data and displaying it in compact form for further analysis. It is another stage which should be consid-

---

[4] Harper W. Boyd, Jr. and Ralph Westfall, *Marketing Research,* 3d ed. (Homewood, Ill.: Richard D. Irwin, Inc., 1972), p. 540.

ered early in the research sequence. Dummy tables, to illustrate the tabulations and comparisons that will be needed, should be set up before the final research design details are settled. Data from the pilot study may be entered in these tables to indicate whether the anticipated relationships are likely to be found in the main study.

Tabulation may be by hand, mechanical, or electronic. The choice is made largely on the basis of the size and type of study, alternative costs, time pressures, and the availability of computers and computer programs. If the number of questionnaires is small, and their length short, hand tabulation is quite satisfactory. Electronic or mechanical tabulation is more appropriate when the opposite conditions hold. If computer-based tabulation programs are available it may be desirable to design the questionnaire to fit the program's requirements.

Hand Tabulation

In hand tabulation we may use (1) the direct tally, (2) the list and tally, or (3) the card sort and count methods. When there are simple codes and few cross-tabulations it is feasible to tally directly from the questionnaire. In the listing method the code responses may be transcribed onto a large worksheet, allowing a line for each questionnaire. A large number of questionnaires may be listed on one worksheet. Tallies are then made for each question. There will usually be more than one such worksheet so that intermediate tally tables are useful to record the page totals for each item. Various counting and tallying methods may be used, depending upon personal preferences. One simple approach is to lay a ruler along a row or column and count the number of times each code, for a given question, has been entered on the worksheet.

The listing method is especially convenient if one wishes to begin the tabulation before the field work is over. As soon as a worksheet page is completed it may be tabulated. Listing is also attractive if the tabulation is a rather straightforward count of the responses with only limited cross-tabulation. When there are a variety of cross-tabulation bases, it is usually advisable to shift to a sorting method.

The card sorting method is the most flexible hand tabulation approach. Any grouping can be broken out and tabulated, and a large number of cross-classifications can be made quickly and easily. Hand tabulation can be surprisingly fast if one develops a modest skill in card sorting. Ideally, one should use a relatively small card (a 3″ × 5″ card) in order to increase ease of handling. However, a larger size, say 5″ × 8″, provides more space for entering data and is easier to read.

Figure 12–3 illustrates a simple card developed for tabulating a survey with about 40 variables. In this study the researcher needed many cross-tabulations of about 100 questionnaires. As long as the questionnaires are relatively few, say 200 or less, and as long as the number of items per

Figure 12–3: Sample Hand Sorting Card

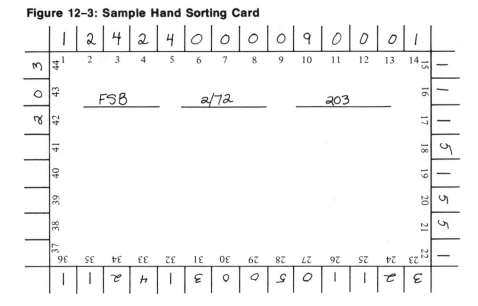

questionnaire is not great, hand tabulation is quite expeditious. Even if a computer is available, it may be quicker and easier to use hand tabulation.

Computer Tabulation

About the only mechanical tabulation which one sees today is that done with a punch card sorting machine. This use survives largely because the machines are in place, are easy to operate, and can provide quick and relatively simple tabulations. Other than for this limited application most mechanical tabulation has been replaced by computers. Computer tabulation is particularly appropriate when there is a large volume of data involving a number of crossbreaks.

One of the barriers to a more general use of computers for research analysis has been the unavailability of appropriate computer programs. The researcher who wishes to use computer analysis is often forced to develop a program, but the costs are usually so great as to make this a last resort.

In recent years some computer programs have been developed to simplify the researcher's tabulation and analysis task; this part of the research process can now be completed easily and quickly. In addition, these programs greatly increase the researcher's analysis repertoire. To avail ourselves of these versatile tools we generally need only to (1) assure ourselves that the data can be used conveniently in the chosen computer program, (2) have a computer with the appropriate program available, and (3) be able to provide to the computer certain simple instruction and control messages, along with the data.

SPSS. One versatile statistical analysis package now available is the *Statistical Package for the Social Sciences* (SPSS).[5] It is an integrated set of computer programs that are invaluable to the business researcher. Included in this package are procedures for various types of regression and correlation analysis, analysis of variance, discriminant analysis, factor analysis, and canonical correlation. In addition, of course, it includes programs for simple descriptive statistics, scatter plots, cross-tabulations, and even a program for Guttman scalogram analysis.

While SPSS and similar programs provide massive power for statistical analysis, the feature of interest here is its contingency table program. When data are classified according to two or more characteristics the resulting matrix is generally known as a *contingency table.* For example, an $r \times c$ contingency table describes a matrix with r rows and c columns. This data analysis form, also called a *cross-tabulation,* is probably the most commonly used analysis method in the social sciences.

The SPSS has a subprogram CROSSTABS which we can use to produce a two-dimensional table in the form shown in Figure 12–4. The data in this table represent the tabulation of responses to a four-point opinion scale which

Figure 12–4: Two-Dimensional Table Produced by Subprogram CROSSTABS of SPSS

* * * * * * * * * * * * * * * * * C R O S S T A B U L A T I O N O F *
VAR001 BY VAR012
* PAGE 1 OF 1

VAR001	VAR012 COUNT ROW PCT COL PCT TOT PCT	DEFINITE YES 1.	GENERAL YES 2.	GENERAL NO 3.	DEFINITE NO 4.	NO ANSWER 5.	ROW TOTAL
GROUP 1	1.	2 6.3 8.7 1.9	16 50.0 34.8 15.2	10 31.3 41.7 9.5	3 9.4 30.0 2.9	1 3.1 50.0 1.0	32 30.5
GROUP 2	2.	7 23.3 30.4 6.7	11 36.7 23.9 10.5	9 30.0 37.5 8.6	3 10.0 30.0 2.9	0 0.0 0.0 0.0	30 28.6
GROUP 3	3.	2 16.7 8.7 1.9	4 33.3 8.7 3.8	4 33.3 16.7 3.8	1 8.3 10.0 1.0	1 8.3 50.0 1.0	12 11.4
GROUP 4	4.	12 38.7 52.2 11.4	15 48.4 32.6 14.3	1 3.2 4.2 1.0	3 9.7 30.0 2.9	0 0.0 0.0 0.0	31 29.5
	COLUMN TOTAL	23 21.9	46 43.8	24 22.9	10 9.5	2 1.9	105 100.0

```
CHI SQUARE =     20.33421 WITH  12 DEGREES OF FREEDOM    SIGNIFICANCE =  0.0610
CRAMER'S V =      0.25407
CONTINGENCY COEFFICIENT =     0.40279
LAMBDA (ASYMMETRIC) =  0.13699 WITH VAR001   DEPENDENT.          =  0.0      WITH VAR012   DEPENDENT.
LAMBDA (SYMMETRIC) =  0.07576
UNCERTAINTY COEFFICIENT (ASYMMETRIC) =  0.08523 WITH VAR001   DEPENDENT.          =  0.08505 WITH VAR012   DEPENDENT.
UNCERTAINTY COEFFICIENT (SYMMETRIC) =  0.08514
KENDALL'S TAU B =    -0.23628  SIGNIFICANCE =  0.0023
KENDALL'S TAU C =    -0.22422  SIGNIFICANCE =  0.0023
GAMMA =    -0.32424
SOMERS'S D (ASYMMETRIC) = -0.24078 WITH VAR001   DEPENDENT.          = -0.23187 WITH VAR012   DEPENDENT.
SOMERS'S D (SYMMETRIC) = -0.23624
ETA =  0.34073 WITH VAR001   DEPENDENT.          =  0.30483 WITH VAR012   DEPENDENT.
```

[5] Norman H. Nie, C. Hadlai Hull, Jean G. Jenkins, Karin Steinbrenner, and Dale H. Bent, *SPSS,* 2d ed. (New York: McGraw-Hill Book Co., 1975), p. 1. Another powerful statistical analysis package is the SAS. In some ways it is more versatile and easier to use than SPSS. For specifics see Anthony J. Barr, James H. Goodnight, John P. Sall, and Jane T. Helwig, *A User's Guide to SAS 76* (Raleigh, N.C.: SAS Institute Inc., 1976).

was administered to the employees of a commercial bank. In this particular table the cross tabulation is between variables 001 and 012 in which:

001 = The department classification of the employees.
012 = The opinion responses to the statement "My supervisor gives me credit and praise for work well done."

In each cell of the table are four values: (1) the actual frequency count of persons in each department who chose each of the four response alternatives to statement 012, (2) row percentages, (3) column percentages, and (4) percent of total responses for these frequencies.

This two-dimensional table allows us to test for a hypothesized relationship between the department in which respondents are employed and their attitude toward their supervisor as measured by variable 012. A glance at the data in Figure 12–4 suggests that those persons in group 4 of department 001 have a more favorable opinion of their supervisor's "credit and praise" practices than do persons in the other three groups.

Another feature of the SPSS is that we can recode variables to make new combinations out of our original data. For example, we can combine the two "yes" and two "no" classes into single "yes" and "no" categories, drop the "no answer" responses, and even combine the members of groups 1, 2, and 3 into one classification and members of group 4 into a second classification.

In addition to this two-way analysis we might also want to analyze the responses classified simultaneously by group and length of service. This requires a three-way tabulation, and CROSSTABS can provide for up to eight-way tabulations. Unless we have a very large data file, however, seldom will we use tables more complex than three-way. Three-way tables are invaluable, as we will soon learn, for analyzing potential causal relationships between variables. This ability to provide three-way tables is one of the outstanding features of the CROSSTABS program. With it we can analyze the relationship between attitude and employee group, while holding length of service constant.

Figure 12–4 also includes a large number of statistical test values. The availability of such statistics can certainly be of great value to researchers, but their automatic inclusion in the printout points up an important danger of "canned" computer programs. The outpouring of test values suggests to the statistically unsophisticated user that such calculations must be appropriate for the data presented. This may clearly not be the case. These measures are merely mechanical computations applied blindly to whatever data are put into the program. The computer will calculate the measures, using proper calculational algorithms, but it is left to the user to determine whether the measures are appropriate to the situation. For example, Chi Square is computed for the contingency table in Figure 12–4, even though these data do not meet one of the basic conditions for the use of this test.

A second danger with a program such as the SPSS grows out of its power to generate output so quickly and easily. For example, merely by introducing a card in the CROSSTABS subprogram that states

CROSSTABS Table = A to Z by A to Z

we can generate every two-way table for all variables from A to Z. The computer can produce these hundreds of tables in a matter of minutes. In addition, we might also ask for three-way tables, four-way tables, and so on. In fact, we can easily be swamped with output far beyond our capacity to use it effectively. This output deluge may also encourage us to engage in a sort of wholesale data-searching for relationships which are "statistically significant." Such searching, unguided by logic, runs counter to generally accepted research thinking. In any 100 contingency tables we would expect to find about five sets of data which are "statistically significant" at the 0.05 level, merely by chance.

A limitation of the SPSS is that it is usable only with a batch processing computer system. This does not restrict our data analysis power, but batch processing does lack certain versatilities. There are many cases where we might be interested in analyzing only a limited amount of data. In addition, we may wish to explore various ways of dealing with the data or perhaps even to analyze step by step, when the findings from step one determine what we do in step two. The ideal way to conduct such analysis is with an interactive terminal facility (ITF) with an on-line computer system. In 1977 the authors of SPSS put out a conversational version called *SPSS—Conversational Statistical System* (SCSS), but it is not as widely available as the batch process SPSS. However, other conversation systems are more widely available: Among them is STAT/BASIC.

STAT/BASIC. This system, written in BASIC programming language, is designed for the interactive computer mode. It includes 40 statistical programs, grouped into eight major application categories:[6]

Data generation	4 programs
Elementary statistics	6 programs
Regression and correlation analysis	5 programs
Multivariate analysis	4 programs
Analysis of variance	2 programs
Nonparametric statistics	11 programs
Time-series analysis	6 programs
Biostatistics	2 programs

One can quickly learn to use these programs with virtually no knowledge of computer operations or programming. One can activate the computer terminal with a few simple instructions and begin analysis. Included among

---

[6] *STAT/BASIC for System/3 Model 6, ITF, and VM/370-CMS Program Reference Manual* (White Plains, N.Y.: International Business Machines Corporation, 1973), p. 2.

the programs is one which will produce two-way cross-tabulations for as many as 15 variables with up to 100 observations for each.

DATA PRESENTATION

Data Reduction

Many research studies result in a large volume of raw statistical information which must be reduced to more manageable dimensions if we are to see the meaningful relationships in it. This process of data reduction is the preserve of descriptive statistics.[7] We can do this reduction task manually, or we can use one of the computer-based statistical packages such as STAT/BASIC, SPSS, or SAS.

We assign the data to groups in order to reduce the number of classes to a more manageable number. If the data are numeric these classifications form a set known as a frequency distribution. Table 12–3 presents two different frequency distributions of the same data. Deciding on the number and width of the frequency class intervals calls for skill and judgment. Our objective, of course, is to display the data in such a way as to make it more meaningful for the analyst. Typically we use from 5 to 15 classes, and they may be of equal or unequal width.

The frequency distribution shown in section A of Table 12–3 has 11 equal-width intervals and 1 open-ended interval.[8] This distribution has one half of the accounts in one class in the distribution, making this class interval too gross for us to understand much about the real distribution of many accounts. The distribution in section B is an improvement in that it shows some of the small accounts detail which might be helpful in our interpretation. It also reduces the number of accounts in the largest class to 32 percent of the total. On the other hand, it introduces frequency classes of different width which are somewhat more difficult to use. In both cases there is a bimodal distribution with a second peak at around $10,000. At the time of this study the maximum insured value of a savings account was $10,000. This appears to have placed a practical ceiling on the size of many accounts.

Summary Statistics. The data in frequency distributions are transformed by the calculation of a number of statistical indexes which summarize the results even further. One major set of indexes are measures of central tendency, of which the three most important are the arithmetic mean, median, and mode. The geometric mean and harmonic mean are also sometimes used. With attributes data the p is the equivalent of the arithmetic mean. A

---

[7] There are two major areas of statistics—descriptive and inferential. Descriptive statistics concern the development of certain indexes from the raw data, while inferential statistics are concerned with the process of generalization from small groups to populations.

[8] Open-ended intervals are generally not desirable, but often cannot be avoided. In the data shown in Table 12–3 this class was largely concentrated in the $10,000 to $14,999 class, but there was a scattering of holdings as high as $40,000.

Table 12–3: Two Frequency Distributions of Savings Accounts by Size of Account, 1968

A			B		
Account Size		No. of Accounts	Account Size		No. of Accounts
$ 1–$ 999		8,200	Under $ 10		1,000
1,000– 1,999		2,000	$ 10– 99		2,000
2,000– 2,999		1,000	100– 999		5,200
3,000– 3,999		800	1,000– 2,999		3,100
4,000– 4,999		600	3,000– 4,999		1,400
5,000– 5,999		800	5,000– 6,999		1,200
6,000– 6,999		400	7,000– 8,999		600
7,000– 7,999		300	9,000– 10,999		1,500
8,000– 8,999		300	11,000+		300
9,000– 9,999		300			16,300
10,000– 10,999		1,200			
11,000+		300			
		16,300			

Source: Files of Suburban City Bank.

second important group of indexes are the measures of dispersion, of which the major ones are the variance and its square root—the standard deviation. Other measures such as the mean deviation, range, and interquartile range are also used. With nominal data the pq ratio is the analogue of the variance. There are other classes of standard indexes to measure the skewness and kurtosis (or height) of distributions, but these will not be explored here. In addition, we often develop special indexes to reflect the constructs and concepts that are unique to our study. This process has already been discussed in Chapter 5.

DATA ANALYSIS

Descriptive Analysis

Descriptive analysis is largely the study of distributions of one variable. This study provides us with profiles of companies, work groups, persons, and other subjects on any of a multitude of characteristics such as size, composition, efficiency, or preferences. These tabulations are especially useful when the approximate distribution of a variable is unknown. For example, in the Suburban City Bank study (see Table 12–3) the management has no precise idea of the size distribution of their savings accounts. Such descriptive data is an important first entry in their bank of data if they are thoroughly to understand their savers.

One-dimensional analysis does more than merely show the size and shape of a distribution. In addition, it provides useful benchmark data for measuring the state or condition at any particular time. For example, it will tell us the average work performance level for new employees. Management decision-making effort is often directed toward changing the shape of the distribution of such variables (for example, raising the average or reducing the variance). In addition, distributions of one dimension facilitate prediction when they tell us, for example, that two thirds of the members of a camping club are usually absent from work on the Monday after a weekend excursion.

While unidimensional analysis is often a prelude to bivariate and multivariate analysis, even some of these more complex forms are chiefly descriptive in nature. For example, we might conduct a study of employees to determine who might be eligible for a proposed early retirement program. We might classify those of a certain age group by position, tenure, department location, skills classification, and other factors. In such an analysis our objective would be to determine where and to what degree this new program would affect operations.

Causal Analysis

Our concern in causal analysis is with the study of how one variable affects, or is "responsible for," changes in another variable. The stricter interpretation of "causation," found in experimentation, is that some external factor "produces" a change in the dependent variable. In much business research, however, we are interested in cases in which the cause-effect relationship is less explicit. In fact, we are more interested in understanding, explaining, predicting, and controlling relationships between variables than we are with determining causes per se.

We can seldom affect anyone's age, sex, club membership, religion, social class, education, and childhood history; yet these and similar factors influence people's attitudes, work, and consumption practices, as well as other dispositions and behaviors. We must deal with associations between these factors if we are to understand how such dispositions and behaviors come about. For example, do age differences explain consumption variations? What indicators predict who are the superior machinists? What factors lead a person to become a consistent saver? While our tools in ex post facto analysis research are less powerful than in experimentation, we can still use the experiment as our logic model; we can also employ the strong inference approach of establishing a number of hypotheses which we can then try to disconfirm.

Correlation. When two variables covary we say they are correlated. Does this covariation mean that there is some connection between them? There are several ways by which we might determine whether such correlations do exist. We might informally observe events in which A occurs to see if B also occurs. In research, however, we usually want a more orderly method.

One way to approach the task is to classify each variable into two or more categories and then cross-classify the variables in these subcategories. This approach is especially useful when the data are in nominal form. If the data are ordinal, interval, or ratio we can use more powerful forms of statistical correlation. In all of these approaches we are applying Mill's Methods of Differences and Concomitant Variation, as discussed in Chapter 4.

Cross-Tabulation

A first stage in the search for relationships between two variables is to cross-classify each variable and present the results in a two-way table. In the examples which follow we will use dichotomous classifications in the interests of simplicity of presentation. Obviously, however, more than two categories can be used for each variable. In an earlier chapter, we used the hypothetical example of a factory with high absenteeism on Mondays. Observation suggested that many of the workers who were frequently absent on Mondays were also members of a camping club. Table 12–4 shows club membership and Monday absentee pattern. Percentages are calculated in the direction which logic suggests is the more likely flow of influence.

Table 12–4: Club Membership and Levels of Monday Absenteeism (percent)*

Absentee Status	Club Member?	
	Yes	No
High	40	20
Low	60	80
Total	100	100
n = ...	(60)	(300)

* Data hypothetical.

While we might conclude from Table 12–4 that club membership is the cause of high absenteeism, let us consider the possible relationships that might be found in such a two-way table. Rosenberg suggests that interactions between two sets of variables may reflect relationships which are symmetrical, reciprocal, or asymmetrical.[9]

A symmetrical relationship is one in which two variables fluctuate together but we assume that neither variable is due to the other. Symmetrical conditions are most often found because two variables are alternative indicators of

[9] Morris Rosenberg, *The Logic of Survey Analysis* (New York: Basic Books, Inc., 1968), p. 3. The discussion in this section draws heavily on the concepts advanced by Rosenberg.

the same common concept, or the effects of some common cause, or because of fortuitous circumstances. We might conclude that a correlation between low work attendance records and high camping activity is symmetrical and that they are alternative indicators of some personal alienation. Or we might find that our data represents experience on a certain weekend when there was also substantial labor unrest in departments which include many camping club members.

A reciprocal relationship exists when the two variables mutually influence or reinforce each other. This could occur if club membership in some way leads to absenteeism, which then leads to more interest in camping club activities. This does not seem very likely. A reciprocal relationship which has been found in marketing is between buying a particular brand of a product and exposure to the advertising for that brand. Exposure to advertising may lead persons to buy that particular brand, but once the purchase has been made the new owners tend to read more of the advertising of the brand they have bought.

Asymmetrical Relationships

The major relationships of interest to the research analyst are those which are *asymmetrical*. With these relationships we postulate that one variable (the independent variable, or *IV*) is responsible for another variable (the dependent variable, or *DV*). The identification of the *IV* and *DV* is often obvious, but there are times when the choice is not clear. In these latter cases we evaluate them on the basis of (1) the fixity or alterability of each variable and (2) the time order between them. For example, since age, social class, climate, world events, present manufacturing technology, and the like are relatively unalterable we normally choose them as independent variables. In addition, when we can determine a time order we usually find that the *IV* precedes the *DV*.

Types of Asymmetrical Relationships. There are different types of asymmetrical relationships of interest to the research analyst. Among the most important are:

1. Stimulus-Response Relationship. This is the most direct causal type of connection. Typical examples are the effect of a price rise on sales, a change in work rules on worker output, or a change in government economic policy on corporate financing decisions. Experiments and quasiexperiments usually involve these relationships.

2. Property-Disposition Relationship. A "property" is a relatively enduring characteristic which does not depend upon circumstances for its activation. Age and ethnic group are examples. It is the *IV* but is not a stimulus in the sense of some external force that impinges on a *DV*. A "disposition" is a tendency to respond in a certain way under designated circumstances. Dispositions include attitudes, abilities, habits, values, drives, and the like. Examples of a property-disposition relationship are the effect of age on social activities, sex on attitude towards certain product types, or social class and opinions regarding "right to work" laws. Dispositions and properties constitute major concepts used in business and social research.

3. *Disposition-Behavior Relationship.* Behavior responses include consumption practices, work performance, aggressive actions, and action decisions of all sorts. Examples of relationships between dispositions and behavior include opinions toward a brand and its purchase, job satisfaction and worker productivity, moral values and tax cheating. Much of ex post facto causal research involves relationships between properties, dispositions, and behavior.

4. *Property-Behavior Relationship.* Examples include such relationships as the stage in the family life cycle and purchases of furniture, worker seniority, and job performance, or social class and family savings patterns.

Elaboration

Our observation that there is an asymmetrical relationship between two variables is only the first step of analysis. Even if we find that there is a substantial covariation and are convinced there is an asymmetrical relationship, we may still want to ask two questions: "why" and "under what conditions?" We advance hypotheses to answer these questions and then use elaboration both to test our reasoning and serve as a tool of discovery.

By the process of *elaboration* we introduce a third or test factor into the association through cross-classifying the three variables. We might introduce the age of the employees as a test factor in the absenteeism study and find the relationships shown in Table 12–5. Here we show the relationship between club membership and absenteeism while "holding age constant." Obviously, age is not literally being held constant, but we are showing how absenteeism and club membership correlate within two different age groups.

In Table 12–5 we stratify on age and through this process examine the

Table 12–5: Club Membership and Levels of Absenteeism by Age of Employee (percent)*

Absentee Status	Young		Old	
	Club Member	Not a Club Member	Club Member	Not a Club Member
High	48	46	14	15
Low	52	54	86	85
Total	100	100	100	100
n = ...	(46)	(50)	(14)	(250)

* Data hypothetical.

contingent relationships between (1) age and club membership, (2) age and absenteeism, and (3) club membership and absenteeism. This elaboration indicates that there are associations between all three. First, persons classified as "young" are much more likely to be club members than are "old" workers. Second, there is clearly a much higher rate of absenteeism among young workers than among older ones. Third, as we have already seen in Table 12–4, club members have higher absenteeism rates than do nonclub members. The elaboration shows, however, that the introduction of age virtually eliminates the effect of club membership on absenteeism. The original club-absenteeism correlation resulted from the high concentration of young workers in the club rather than from the effect of club membership itself.

When we analyze associations through elaboration there are six different ways that we may logically relate the third variable to the two original variables. The third variables can be (1) extraneous or component variables, (2) intervening or antecedent variables, or (3) suppressor or distorter variables.[10]

Extraneous Variables. We may stratify on some third factor and find that the original relationship between two variables disappears. This is evidence that the original IV-DV association is a spurious one. For example, in Table 12–5, we see that club membership turns out *not* to be an important causal factor for explaining absenteeism among the workers. Thus, we find that a highly plausible interpretation is actually misleading.

On the other hand, we might use this same process to provide evidence that dubious interpretations are actually sound. That is, if the introduction of the third variable does not affect the original relationship then we would have some support for the original relationship. This point is illustrated in Table 12–6 in which the new-found relationship between absenteeism and age is

Table 12–6: Levels of Absenteeism and Age of Worker by Worker Skill Level (percent)

Absentee Status	Unskilled		Skilled	
	Young	Old	Young	Old
High	47	16	46	14
Low	53	84	54	86
Total	100	100	100	100
n = ...	(59)	(104)	(37)	(160)

analyzed further by adding a test factor of "job skill." This analysis indicates that the absenteeism-age relationship holds up; the skill variable appears to be largely extraneous. Each time we introduce what appears to be a relevant

---

[10] Ibid., chaps. 2, 3, and 4.

third variable and find our relationship remains, the more confidence we can have in the relationship between age and absenteeism.

Component Variables. In business research there may often be propositions which are true, but the *IV* is so global as to offer little real insight. In this case if we break the *IV* concept down into its components we may be able to understand a great deal more about the relationship. For example, we might find that blue collar and white collar workers react differently to a training exercise. This is less enlightening than to track down that the difference is due more to specific work culture differences between the two groups. Or it is one thing to find that expenditures for wine vary among families at different stages in the family life cycle, but it is something more if we can find the component within family life cycle which is controlling.

To illustrate the nature of the component variable consider that it is often thought that successful salespeople have a certain type of personality. To test this hypothesis, assume that we give personality tests to 200 newly hired salespeople. After a period of time we determine which people have been successful and which have not. Then we cross-classify them by their total scores on the personality tests. We may secure results like those found in Part A of Table 12–7. These hypothetical data indicate that scores on the person-

Table 12–7: Personality and Sales Success (percent)*

| Sales Success | Part A Personality Test Scores | | Part B Empathy Test | | | |
| | | | High | | Low | |
	High	Low	High	Low	High	Low
Yes	60	30	68	55	32	23
No	40	70	32	45	68	77
Total	100	100	100	100	100	100
n = ...	(100)	(100)	(78)	(22)	(22)	(78)

* Data hypothetical.

ality battery are helpful predictors. On the other hand such a global variable tells us little about the specific personality factors that may be operating.

The hypothesis has also been advanced, however, that successful salespeople generally have a high empathy for others. We decide to test this by using the empathy component of the general personality test as the test factor. When we do, we may secure the relationships shown in Part B of Table 12–7. This indicates that the empathy component of the test battery is an important contributor to our ability to predict which salespeople will be successful.

Intervening Variables. When we make a causal analysis, especially of social phenomena, we are "tapping in" on an ongoing stream of events that proceed serially, and in some complexity, from causes to effects. In such a chain of connections there is a chance that our original *IV* affects the *DV* through some intervening factor. Thus B is a consequence of A and a determinant of C. In Chapter 5 we referred to the case where an increase in income leads to a higher savings rate. It was hypothesized that there was an intervening variable of "motivation to save." This argument is:

Change in income → Change in motivation to save → Change in saving.

To illustrate the nature of this intervention, we again consider the case in which younger workers show a much higher absenteeism rate than do older workers. However, it is hard to imagine that age, per se, brings about this absenteeism. There must be something in the relationship that we have yet to see. Much has been made in recent years of the decline of the "work ethic" in our society. It is suggested that many of the younger generation do not accept this ethic. Therefore, we might hypothesize that the higher absenteeism from younger workers results from their greater rejection of the work ethic. We administer a scale to the workers which measures their attitudes toward work; we find the relationships shown in Table 12–8.

Table 12–8: Worker Age and Absenteeism by Work Ethic Attitude (percent)*

Absentee Status	Reject Work Ethic		Accept Work Ethic	
	Young	Old	Young	Old
High	96	71	13	3
Low	4	29	87	97
Total	100	100	100	100
n =	(70)	(35)	(15)	(240)

* Data hypothetical.

Antecedent Variables. While the intervening variable comes between the *IV* and *DV*, the antecedent variable comes before the *IV* in the sequence. The antecedent variable leads to the *IV* and adds depth to our understanding of the *IV-DV* relationship. If a certain factor is considered logically to be an antecedent variable (AV), it can be tested statistically. To pass such a test it must meet three requirements:

1. All three variables must be related.
2. When the AV is controlled, the *IV-DV* relationship does not disappear.
3. When *IV* is controlled the AV-DV relationship disappears.

Consider the following example. There is some claim that better educated people are more skillful shoppers. Suppose that we conduct a study in which a shopping test is devised and administered to 600 women, half of whom are classed as well-educated (at least a high school degree) and the other half as poorly educated (less than a high school degree). Assume that we find that our hypothesis is confirmed—that the better educated women are the better shoppers.

We may wish to trace the causal sequence back a step to learn more about what conditions might have led to the education level differences. To do this we introduce the antecedent variable of the shopper's mother's education. The results of these analysis steps are shown in Table 12–9. It should be

Table 12–9: Shopping Skill and Shopper Education by Shopper's Mother's Education (percent)*

Shopping Skill	Mother Poorly Educated		Mother Well-Educated	
	Shopper Poorly Educated	Shopper Well-Educated	Shopper Poorly Educated	Shopper Well-Educated
High	30	70	30	70
Low	70	30	70	30
Total	100	100	100	100
$n =$	(240)	(60)	(60)	(240)

* Data hypothetical.

apparent from these data that the shopper's mother's education is an antecedent variable. It is related both to the *IV* and *DV*, and its introduction as a test factor does not eliminate the *IV-DV* relationship. However, when the *IV* is controlled, the *AV-DV* relationship disappears.

Suppressor Variables.   When these variables are at work we find no relationship between two variables while logic suggests that there should be one. We may be misled into thinking that an absence of correlation is true when actually the *IV-DV* relationship is blocked out or dampened by the suppressor variable. For example, we might expect that shoppers from lower-income families would be more responsive than middle-class shoppers to the introduction of unit pricing in grocery stores. Suppose, however, that we conduct a study and find little difference between lower-income and middle-income families in their response to unit pricing (see Part A of Table 12–10). We might hypothesize, however, that the expected higher responsiveness of lower-income families has been suppressed in the statistics because the better educated would respond more to unit pricing, but it is the more poorly educated who are concentrated in the lower income group. This revised hypothesis is tested in Part B of Table 12–10. The results show that the lower-income shopper does respond more than the middle-income shopper to unit pricing when education level is held constant.

Table 12–10: Shopper Income Class and Use of Unit Pricing Information by Shopper Education Level (percent)*

| | Part A Income Class | | Part B | | | |
| | | | High Education | | Low Education | |
Use of Unit Price Information	Middle Income	Lower Income	Middle Income	Lower Income	Middle Income	Lower Income
High	30	30	34	50	18	23
Low	70	70	66	50	82	77
Total	100	100	100	100	100	100
$n =$	(200)	(200)	(150)	(50)	(50)	(150)

* Data hypothetical.

Distorter Variables. Distorter variables are those which, when accounted for, reveal that the correct interpretation is the reverse of that suggested by the original data. For example, it is often argued that families typically use the bank closest to their home. Suppose, however, that we conduct a study of 400 households, 200 of which are located within a mile of our client bank while the other 200 are located more than a mile from the bank. The results indicate something unusual. It seems that a higher percentage of the more distant families are customers of the bank than is the case with the nearby families. These results are shown in Part A of Table 12–11. Since this does not seem reasonable we look for further information which might explain this anomaly. We introduce a third variable, the comparison of the distance from the family's home to the nearest competing bank. Then each family is classified as to whether the competing bank is closer or more distant to the family's home than is our bank. The results of this analysis,

Table 12–11: Bank Use and Home-Bank Distance by Distance of Competition (percent)*

| | Part A | | Part B | | | |
| | | | Competition Is Farther | | Competition Is Closer | |
Have Account?	0–1 Miles	1 Mile +	0–1 Miles	1 + Miles	0–1 Miles	1 + Miles
Yes	35	40	60	52	27	22
No	65	60	40	48	73	78
Total	100	100	100	100	100	100
$n =$	(200)	(200)	(50)	(120)	(150)	(80)

* Data hypothetical.

shown in Part B of Table 12–11, indicate that the correct interpretation is the opposite of the original. After adjusting for the nearness of the competing bank we find that the closer a family's home is to our bank, the more likely it is to have an account with us.

In summary there are two contributions which the introduction of test factors can make. In the first instance elaboration may keep us from being misled. There are two such dangers from a two-variable relationship: (1) we may accept a hypothesis which is false and (2) we may reject a hypothesis which is true. When we consider extraneous variables we help avert the acceptance of a false hypothesis. Use of suppressor variable analysis helps avoid the rejection of hypotheses which are true while the use of distorter variable analysis helps us avoid both of these cases.

A second contribution is to provide more precise and specific understanding of a two-variable relationship. For example, by using component variables one can find out what it is in a general variable that is critical to the relationship. The use of an intervening variable may give a more precise understanding of the temporal and logical process of movement from IV to DV; the use of an antecedent variable may allow us to extend the causal sequence.

Conditional Relationships. In the elaboration examples used to this point the introduction of a test factor has generally affected various subgroups in approximately the same way. It may be, however, that the impact of the test factor affects one subgroup more than another. These are *conditional relationships* and represent a situation where we wish to specify the conditions under which the original relationship is strengthened or weakened. For example, assume that in the absenteeism study we used a test variable of worker seniority (rather than age) along with the original club membership-absenteeism relationship. This is illustrated in Table 12–12 and suggests that seniority is an important factor in explaining absenteeism. However, there is an interaction between seniority and club membership and their effects on absenteeism. With low seniority employees, club membership appears to stimulate added absenteeism. Among more senior employees, just the opposite occurs.

Table 12–12: Club Membership and Levels of Absenteeism by Seniority (percent)

Absentee Status	Less than 3 Years Seniority		3 Years or More Seniority	
	Club Member	Not a Club Member	Club Member	Not a Club Member
High	51	35	7	17
Low	49	65	93	83
	100	100	100	100
$n =$	(45)	(150)	(15)	(249)

Conjoint Influence. In the procedures discussed to this point we have used the introduction of a test variable for clarifying the meaning of an original two-variable relationship. We have done this either by using the third variable as a control or as a specifying factor. We have also explored conditional relationships among the variables. In addition, we often wish to see how a third variable and the original *IV* separately and/or jointly affect the *DV*. The third variable is viewed as another *IV* rather than as a test variable. This is called a *conjoint relationship* and represents those cases where each independent variable exercises a separate influence on the *DV*. These influences may be studied as to which *IV* is the stronger, what is the cumulative effect of them both, and what is the effect of new types which emerge from a fusion of the *IV*s.

The example in Table 12–13 illustrates a conjoint relationship concerning

Table 12–13: High Users of Unit Price Information by Education and Family Income Levels (percent)*

	High Education		Low Education	
	Middle Income	Low Income	Middle Income	Low Income
High use of unit price information	34	50	18	23

* Data hypothetical.

the effect of education and income on the use of unit pricing information. We can see from the data that high education and low family income promotes higher usage of unit price information. But the question is which of these two factors is more important. To determine this we compare the high education/middle income group (HE/MI) with the low income/low education (LI/LE) group. We find that 34 percent of the HE/MI group are high users while only 23 percent of the LI/LE group are high users of unit price information. Thus, we conclude that education is a more powerful factor than low income in promoting the use of unit price information.[11]

Computerized Analysis

Cross-classification is a cumbersome and time-consuming process, although the excellent computer-based tabulation programs such as SPSS have made it easier and more useful. In addition, a new multivariate approach gives promise of even more powerful classification analysis. One such program is the Automatic Interaction Detector (AID) program.[12]

---

[11] Ibid., chap. 7.

[12] John A. Sonquist, Elizabeth L. Baker, James N. Morgan, *Searching for Structure* (Ann Arbor, Mich.: Institute for Social Research, The University of Michigan, 1971).

**Figure 12–5: Hours of Home Production Done in 1964 by Heads of
Families and Wives (for 2,214 families)***

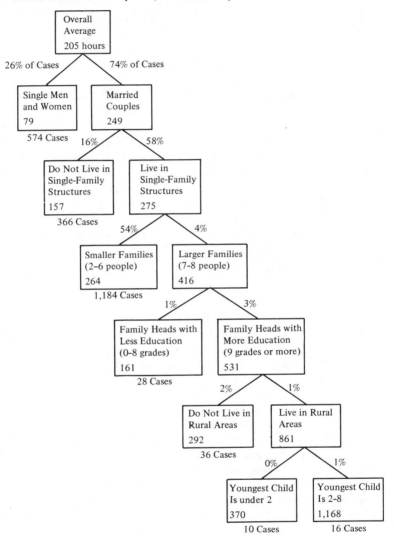

* Home production is defined as unpaid work other than regular housework, minus
volunteer work, and minus courses and lessons.

Source: J. Morgan, I. Sirageldin and N. Baerwaldt, *Productive Americans* (Ann Arbor,
Mich.: Survey Research Center, University of Michigan, 1965), p. 128.

AID is basically a sequential partitioning procedure that begins with a specified dependent variable and a set of predicting characteristics. It searches among up to 300 variables for the best single division according to each predictor variable, chooses one, and splits the sample into two subgroups so as to maximize the reduction in the unexplained sum of squares of the dependent variable. These two subgroups then become two separate samples for further analysis. The search procedure is repeated to find that variable which, when split into two parts, makes the next largest contribution to the reduction of unexplained variation in each subsample, and so on.

Figure 12–5 illustrates the analysis tree that resulted from an AID study of the do-it-yourself activities of families. The initial dependent variable is the annual hours spent in home production by heads of families and wives. The illustration indicates that the best binary split was between married couples and single persons. The latter spent substantially less time in do-it-yourself activities. The married couples sample was then analyzed against the remaining variables and the best binary split for reducing unexplained variance was the type of family dwelling. Further analysis indicated that larger families, with more education, who lived in rural areas and whose youngest child was between two and eight years of age, were the most active do-it-yourselfers, with an average of 1,168 hours per year per family.

While this technique holds promise as an analysis tool it has several limitations. Large samples are generally required, with some suggesting that 1,000 to 2,000 or more are needed. Then too, AID takes no account of intercorrelated predictors. As a result the order of appearance of variables is no indication of their relative importance; exclusion does not necessarily imply insignificance.[13]

SUMMARY

The first step in analysis is to edit the collected raw data to assure that it is accurate, consistent with other data, uniformly entered, as complete as possible, and ready for coding and tabulation. In survey work it is common to use both field and central editing.

Coding is the process of assigning numerals or other symbols to answers so we can group the responses into a limited number of categories. These categories should be appropriate to the research problem, exhaustive of the data, mutually exclusive, and unidimensional. Since coding eliminates much of the information in the raw data, it is important that the researcher design category sets carefully in order to utilize the available data more fully.

"Don't know" replies are evaluated in the light of the nature of the question and the respondent. While many are legitimate *DK* responses, some result from a question that is ambiguous or an interviewing situation that is not

---

[13] Peter Doyle and Ian Fenwick, "The Pitfalls of AID Analysis," *Journal of Marketing Research* (November 1975), pp. 408–13.

motivating. It is generally better to report DK responses as a separate category unless there is some compelling reason to treat them otherwise.

Survey results are usually hand tabulated if the study is small, if there are relatively few cross-tabulations, and if computer facilities are not available. There are three types of hand tabulation—the direct tally, the list and tally, and the card-sort methods. When studies involve large numbers or many cross-tabulations we now find greater use of computers, since software programs have been developed. The SPSS and the STAT/BASIC programs are discussed.

Causal analysis is the term used to describe the study of how one or more variables affect, or are "responsible for" changes in, one or more other variables. In experimental research we interpret "causal" more strictly than we do with ex post facto studies. In the latter case we must usually think in terms of the correlation or association of variables.

A first stage in the search for relationships between two variables often is to cross-classify each variable against one or more others and to look for interactions between them. Such interactions may be symmetrical, reciprocal, or asymmetrical. Only the latter are discussed at length. An asymmetrical relationship between two concepts is generally one of:

1. Stimulus-response.
2. Property-disposition.
3. Disposition-behavior.
4. Property-behavior.

The cross-classification procedure begins with a two-way table which indicates whether there is or is not an interrelationship between the variables. We continue the analysis through *elaboration,* in which we introduce a third variable to form a three-way table. By this process we often find *conditional* relationships in which factor A appears to affect factor B, but only when factor C is held constant. There are six ways that we may logically relate the third variable to the two original variables. The third variable can be:

1. Extraneous or a component.
2. Intervening or antecedent.
3. A suppressor or distorter.

Computer cross-tabulation programs have greatly facilitated the cross-tabulation type of analysis. In addition, special algorithms, such as the Automatic Interaction Detector program (AID), have been developed as a means for extending our powers to analyze data in terms of classifications.

SUPPLEMENTAL READINGS

1. Nie, Norman H.; Hull, C. Hadlai; Jenkins, Jean G.; Steinbrenner, Karin; and Bent, Dale H. *SPSS: Statistical Package for the Social Sciences.* 2d ed. New

York: McGraw-Hill Book Company, 1975. The complete writing on the *SPSS* statistical package. It also contains excellent summaries on various statistical techniques and measurers.

2. Parten, Mildred B. *Surveys, Polls and Samples.* New York: Harper & Brothers, 1950. An old but still valuable reference on the various problems of editing, coding, and hand tabulation.

3. Phillips, Bernard S. *Social Research.* 2d ed. New York: The Macmillan Co., 1971. See chaps. 13–16 for good discussion on analysis of data.

4. Reichard, Robert S. *The Numbers Game.* New York: McGraw-Hill Book Company, 1972. A highly readable text on the use and abuse of managerial statistics. Worthwhile reading for every researcher.

5. Rosenberg, Morris. *The Logic of Survey Analysis.* New York: Basic Books, Inc., Publishers, 1968. An excellent treatment of causal analysis using crossbreaks. Recommend the entire book.

6. Sonquist, John A.; Baker, Elizabeth L.; and Morgan, James N. *Searching for Structure.* Ann Arbor, Mich.: Institute for Social Research, The University of Michigan, 1971. The best single source on the Automatic Interaction Detector program.

7. Zeisel, Hans. *Say It with Figures.* Rev. 5th ed. New York: Harper & Brothers, 1968. Entire book is worth reading for its excellent discussion of numerical presentation and causal analysis.

DISCUSSION QUESTIONS

1. Define or explain:
   a. The purpose of coding.
   b. The rules for establishing category sets.
   c. SPSS.
   d. Elaboration.
   e. Asymmetrical relationship.

2. How should one handle "don't know" responses?

3. Suppose you are planning to conduct a survey of about 60 persons in which you will secure about 40 different items of information which are easily coded. You expect to do a number of cross-tabulations of the results. What type of hand tabulation would you recommend?

4. One of the problems facing the shoe store manager is that many shoes must eventually be sold at markdown prices. Suppose that this prompts us to conduct a mail survey of shoe store managements in which we ask the question: "What methods have you found most successful for reducing the 'high markdowns' problem?" We are interested in extracting as much information as possible from these answers in order better to understand the full range of strategies that store managements use. Establish what you think is a sound group of category sets by which to code, say, 500 responses like the 14 below. Try to develop an integrated set of classifications that reflects your "theory" of markdown management. After developing the set, use it to code the 14 responses.

1. Have not found the answer. As long as we buy style shoes will have markdowns. We use PMs on slow merchandise but it does not eliminate markdowns. (PM is "push-money"—special item bonuses for selling a particular style of shoe.)
2. Using PM before too old. Also reducing price during season. Holding meetings with salespeople indicating which shoes to push.
3. By putting PMs on any slow-selling items and promoting same. More careful check of shoes purchased.
4. Keep a close watch on your stock and markdown when you have to, that is, rather than wait take a small markdown on a shoe that is not moving at the time.
5. Using the PM method.
6. Less advance buying—more dependence on in-stock shoes.
7. Sales—catch bad buys before it's too late and close out.
8. Buy as much good merchandise as you can at special prices to help make up some markdowns.
9. Reducing opening buys and depending on fill-in service. PMs for salespeople.
10. Buy more frequently, better buying, PM on slow-moving merchandise.
11. Careful buying at lowest prices. Cash-on-the-buying-line. Buying closeouts, FDs, overstock, "cancellations." (FD—factory discontinued style.)
12. By buying less "chanceable" shoes. Buy only what you need, watch sizes, don't go overboard on new fads.
13. Buying more staple merchandise. Buying more from fewer lines. Sticking with better nationally advertised merchandise.
14. No successful method with the current style situation. Manufacturers are experimenting, the retailer takes the markdowns—cuts gross profit by about 3 percent—keep your stock at lowest level without losing sales.

5. Using yourself as the subject, give an example of each of the following asymmetrical relationships:
   a. Stimulus-response.
   b. Property-disposition.
   c. Disposition-behavior.
   d. Property-behavior.
6. Classify the relationships between the following variables as probably symmetrical, asymmetrical, or reciprocal.
   a. Education and income.
   b. Opinion about and purchase of brand X.
   c. Job satisfaction and existence of a company suggestion system.
   d. Sales of product y and dollars spent advertising product y.
7. Suppose you were preparing two-way tables of percentages for the following pairs of variables. How would you run the percentages?
   a. Age and consumption of breakfast cereal.
   b. Family income and confidence about the family's future.
   c. Marital status and sports participation.

8. Assume that you conduct a study of food usage practices and find that Catholics seem to spend more for cereal than do Protestants. You elaborate the relationship further by introducing size of family.

Total Amount Spent on Cereal		5 or More		1–4	
Catholic	Protestant	Cath.	Prot.	Cath.	Prot.
$120	$75	$140	$118	$70	$60

How do you interpret this additional information?

9. At a local health agency they are experimenting with two appeal letters, A and B, by which to raise funds. They send out 400 of the A appeal and 400 of the B appeal (divided equally among working class and middle class neighborhoods). They secured the following results:

	Appeal A		Appeal B	
	Middle Class	Working Class	Middle Class	Working Class
Contribution	20	40	15	30
No contribution	80	60	85	70
	100	100	100	100

a. Which appeal is the best?
b. Which class responded better?
c. Is appeal or social class a more powerful independent variable? By how much?

10. Assume that you have collected data on employees of a large corporation in a major metropolitan area. You analyze the data by type of work classification, education level, and whether the workers were reared in a rural or urban setting. The results are as shown below. How would you interpret them?

Annual Employee Turnover per 100 Employees

	Part A		Part B			
			High Education		Low Education	
	Salaried	Wage	Salaried	Wage	Salaried	Wage
Rural	8	16	6	14	18	18
Urban	12	16	10	12	19	20

Chapter 13

Statistical Analysis

IN CHAPTER 12 we discussed the problems and procedures for preparing data for analysis; we also explored some of the logic of analysis, especially as applied to classificatory data. This type of analysis may often be sufficient, but sometimes we may wish to quantify the asymmetrical relationships and submit them to statistical testing.

Statistical inference is one of the two major categories of statistical procedures, the other being descriptive statistics. Within the topic of statistical inference there are two major problems. One of these, the estimation of population values, has been discussed in Chapter 6 and will not be pursued further here. The second, the testing of statistical hypotheses, is the topic of this chapter. The first section includes a general treatment of the process of hypothesis testing, while later sections will cover more specific types of parametric and nonparametric tests for statistical significance. Finally, measures of statistical association and techniques of multivariate analysis will be reviewed briefly.

HYPOTHESIS TESTING

Testing Approaches

There are two approaches to hypothesis testing. The more established is the so-called *classical* or *sampling-theory* approach; the second is known as

405

the *Bayesian* approach. The classical is the traditional approach; it is found in all of the major statistics books and is widely used in research applications. This approach represents an objectivist view of probability in which the analysis and decision making rests totally upon an analysis of sampling data. We establish a testing hypothesis which we then reject or fail to reject, based on the sample data.

The Bayesian approach is an extension of the classical approach in that it also uses sampling data for making decisions. However, it goes beyond this to incorporate all other information that is available to the decision makers. Most of this additional information consists of subjective probability estimates, stated in terms of degrees of belief, about various states of nature. These are expressed as a prior distribution which we may revise after we have gathered sample information. The revised estimate, known as a posterior distribution, may be further revised by additional information, and so on. Various decision rules are established, cost and other estimates can be introduced, and the expected outcomes of combinations of these elements are made by which to judge decision alternatives.

The Bayesian approach, while based on a centuries-old theorem known as the Bayes theorem, has emerged as an alternative hypothesis-testing procedure since the mid-1950s. Many believe that this approach will eventually win a major place in applied statistical inference, but its acceptance in actual research practice to date has been slow. Further discussion of Bayesian procedures is beyond the planned scope of this text, but the reader interested in learning more about Bayesian inference is urged to consult the references at the end of this chapter.

Statistical Significance

Following the sampling-theory approach, we accept or reject a hypothesis on the basis of sampling information alone. Since any sample we draw will almost surely vary somewhat from its population, we must judge whether these differences are *statistically significant* or insignificant. A difference is statistically significant if it actually occurs in the population. For example, the controller of a large retail chain may be concerned about a possible slowdown in payments by the company's customers. He or she measures the rate of payment in terms of the average number of days receivables outstanding. Generally the company has maintained an average age of about 50 days for accounts receivable, with a standard deviation of 10 days. Suppose the controller has all of the customer accounts analyzed and finds that the average is now 51 days. Is this difference statistically significant from 50? Of course it is, because this difference is based on a census of the accounts and there is no sampling involved. It is a fact that the population average has moved from 50 to 51 days. While it is of statistical significance, whether it is of practical significance is another question. If the controller judges that this variation has no decision importance then it is of little practical significance.

Since it would be too expensive to analyze all of a company's receivables frequently, we normally resort to sampling. Assume that we randomly select a sample of 25 accounts and calculate the average days outstanding to be 54. Is this statistically significant? The answer is not obvious. It is a statistically significant difference if we establish that such a difference in the sample mean would seldom happen because of random sampling fluctuations (sampling error).

There are two major significance-testing situations. One is the comparison of a sample statistic to a population parameter just illustrated. In the other case we compare the results from two or more samples to determine if they might be from the same population. For example, a sample drawn from among the accounts in the Chicago division of the retail chain might show an average account age of 49 days, while in Cleveland a similar sample indicates an average age of 55 days. Does this indicate that these two divisions are different in this respect, or could this difference result from sampling variations alone? To answer this question we need to consider further the logic of hypothesis testing.

The Logic of Hypothesis Testing

In the sampling-theory approach to hypothesis testing we develop the *null hypothesis* (H_0) for testing statistical significance. The null hypothesis is a statement that no difference exists between the parameter and the statistic being compared to it. Any observed difference found, according to this hypothesis, is due to random sampling fluctuations only. The null hypothesis is expressly formulated for testing for possible rejection. A companion, the *alternative hypothesis* (H_A), is the logical opposite of the null and is usually the operational statement of the researcher's regular hypothesis.

Let's return to the accounts receivable problem to illustrate these concepts. We might state the null hypothesis (H_0) as: There has been no change from the 50 days average age of account. The alternative hypothesis may take several forms, depending upon the objective of the researcher. The H_A may be of the "not the same" form: The average age of account has changed from 50 days. A second variety may be the "more than" or "less than" type: The average age of receivables has increased (decreased) from 50 days. These types of alternative hypotheses, known as two-tailed and one-tailed hypotheses, respectively, will be discussed again later. The hypotheses may also be expressed in the following form:

Null $H_0: \mu$ (mu) $= 50$ days
Alternative $H_A: \mu$ $\neq 50$ days ("not the same" case)
or $H_A: \mu$ > 50 days ("more than" case)
or $H_A: \mu$ < 50 days ("less than" case)

In testing these hypotheses we adopt the decision rule: Accept the H_0 and take no corrective action if the analysis shows that we cannot reject the null hypothesis. If we reject the null hypothesis (find a statistically significant difference) we accept the alternative hypothesis and take appropriate corrective action. In making such decisions, however, we run the risk of making an incorrect decision. This will occur if we accept the null hypothesis when we should have rejected it, or reject it when we should have accepted it. This decision problem can be illustrated in the following manner:

Decision	State of Nature	
	H_0 Is True (S_1)	H_0 Is False (S_2)
(A_1) Accept H_0 (A_2) Reject H_0	Correct decision Type I error (α)	Type II error (β) Correct decision

One of two conditions (states of nature) exists in the population—either the null hypothesis is true or it is false. There are also two decision alternatives—we either accept or reject the null hypothesis. Two of these four conditional situations result in correct decisions, while the other two lead to decision errors. In the Type I case (α) we reject a true hypothesis. The α value is called the *level of significance* and is the probability of our rejecting a true hypothesis. With the Type II error (β) we accept a null hypothesis that is false. Let's consider each of these errors in more detail.

Type I Error. Assume that we face the controller's problem of deciding whether the average age of accounts receivable has changed. We assume that the population mean is 50 days, the standard deviation of the population is 10 days, and the size of the sample is 25 accounts. With this information we can calculate the standard error of the mean $(\sigma_{\bar{x}})$ (the standard deviation of the distribution of sample means). This hypothetical distribution is pictured in Figure 13–1. The standard error of the mean is calculated to be 2 days.

$$\sigma_{\bar{x}} = \frac{\sigma}{\sqrt{n}} = \frac{10}{\sqrt{25}} = 2$$

If the decision rule is to reject H_0 and take action A_2 when $\bar{X}$ is less than 46 or greater than 54 the probability of a Type I error is shown by the shaded area in part A of Figure 13–1. This area is known as the *region of rejection,* while the area from 46 to 54 is known as the *region of acceptance* of the null hypothesis. The dividing points between the areas of acceptance and rejection (46 and 54) are known as the *critical values.* Since the distribution of

**Figure 13–1: Probability of Making a
Type I Error Given H_0 Is True**

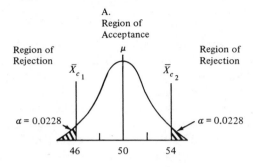

A.
Region of
Acceptance

Region of
Rejection

Region of
Rejection

$\overline{X}_{c_1}$ $\overline{X}_{c_2}$

$\alpha = 0.0228$ $\alpha = 0.0228$

46 50 54

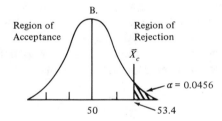

B.
Region of
Acceptance

Region of
Rejection

$\overline{X}_c$

$\alpha = 0.0456$

50 53.4

sample means is normal, the probability of a Type I error can be computed in terms of the standardized random variable.[1]

$$z = \frac{\overline{X} - \mu}{\sigma_X}$$

$$z_1 = \frac{\overline{X}_{c1} - \mu}{\sigma_X} = \frac{46 - 50}{2} = -2$$

$$z_2 = \frac{\overline{X}_{c2} - \mu}{\sigma_X} = \frac{54 - 50}{2} = 2$$

where

$\overline{X}_c$ = The critical value of the sample mean.
μ = The population value stated in H_0.
$\sigma_{\overline{X}}$ = The standard error of a distribution of means of samples of 25.

By referring to the table for the area under the normal curve (Appendix B–1) we find that 0.0228 of the area lies to the left of 46, and a like

---

[1] The standardized random variable, which we denote by z, is a deviation from expectation, and is expressed in terms of standard deviation units. The mean of the distribution of a standardized random variable is 0 and the standard deviation is 1. With this distribution the deviation from the mean by any value of X can be expressed in terms of standard deviation units.

amount to the right of 54. Under these circumstances the probability of a Type I error is:

$$P(A_2 | S_1) = 0.0456, \text{ or } 4.56 \text{ percent}$$

The probability of a correct decision if the null hypothesis is true is 95.44 percent. We may change the probability of a Type I error by moving our critical values either closer to, or farther away from, the assumed parameter of 50. We can do this if we subjectively decide to accept a smaller or larger α error and move the critical values to reflect this. We can also change the size sample, which changes the dispersion of the distribution. For example, if we take a sample of 100 the critical values that provide a total region of rejection of 4.56 percent become 48 and 52.

We have assumed that the alternative hypothesis concerned a change in either direction from 50, but the controller may be interested only in increases in the age of receivables. For this we use a one-tailed (more than) H_A and place the entire region of rejection in the upper tail of the distribution. If we accept a 4.56 percent α risk we compute a new critical value (X_c) by entering Appendix Table B–1 with the value of 0.0456 to find the z value of 1.69. We substitute this in the z equation and solve for $\overline{X}_c$.

$$z = 1.69 = \frac{\overline{X}_c - 50}{2}$$
$$\overline{X}_c = 53.38$$

This new critical value, the boundary between the regions of acceptance and rejection, is pictured in part B of Figure 13–1.

Type II Error. The Type II error is difficult to determine because its size depends on the α error we specify, the size of sample we use, and especially the new population parameter we assume. We secure a different β error if the new μ moves from 50 to 54 than if it moves only to 52. We must compute separate β error estimates for each of a number of assumed new population parameters and $\overline{X}_c$ values. To illustrate, assume that the μ has actually moved to 52 from 50. Under these conditions what is the probability of our making a Type II error if our critical value is set at 54? This may be expressed in the following fashion:

$$P(A_2 | S_1) = \alpha = 0.0228 \text{ (assume a one-tailed alternative hypothesis)}$$
$$P(A_1 | S_2) = \beta = ?$$

If the new μ is 52 then

		β Probability
$z_2 = \dfrac{54 - 52}{10/\sqrt{25}} = 1$	=	0.341
z_1 of lower half of distribution = 3+ =		0.50
Total		0.841

**Figure 13–2: Probability of Making a
Type II Error Given that H_0 Is False**

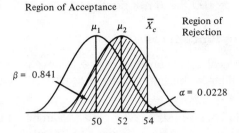

This condition is shown in Figure 13–2. With the specified α and a sample size of 25, there is an 84.1 percent probability of our making a Type II error *if* μ is now 52. If the revised μ is some other value the probability of this Type II error will also be different. Figure 13–3, called an operating characteristic

**Figure 13–3: Operating Characteristic
Curve**

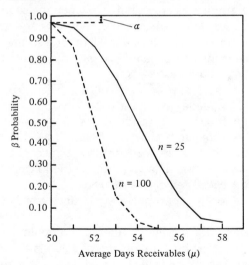

curve, indicates the probabilities of a β error given various assumed μs and a critical value of 54. For example, with $n = 25$, if μ changes from 50 to 51 there is a 94 percent chance that we will still accept the H_0. If μ moves to 56 there is only about a 16 percent chance that we will accept the H_0 under these circumstances.

There are several ways that we can improve our β risk. We can shift our critical value closer to the original μ of 50, but this exposes us to a higher α risk. Whether to take this action depends on our evaluation of the relative importance of the α and β risks. A second, and probably more useful, approach is to increase the size of the sample. For example, if the sample is increased from 25 to 100 the β risk decreases as shown in Figure 13–3.

Statistical Testing Procedures

Testing for statistical significance follows a relatively well defined pattern although authors differ in the number and sequence of steps. One six-stage sequence is as follows:

1. *State the null hypothesis.* While the researcher is usually interested in testing a hypothesis of change or differences, we always use the null hypothesis for statistical testing purposes.

2. *Choose the statistical test.* In order to test a hypothesis we must choose an appropriate statistical test. There are many tests from which to choose, and there are at least four criteria which we can use in choosing a test. One is the power efficiency of the test. A more powerful test provides a given level of significance with a smaller sample than will a less powerful test. In addition, in choosing a test we can consider the manner in which we draw the sample, the nature of the population, and the type of measurement scale used. For instance, some tests are useful only when the sequence of scores is known, or when observations are paired. Other tests are appropriate only if the population has certain characteristics; still other tests are useful only if the measurement scale is interval or ratio. We give more attention to the problems of test selection in the next section.

3. *Select the desired level of significance.* The choice of the level of significance should be made before we collect the data. The most common level is 0.05, although 0.01 is also widely used. Other α levels such as 0.10, 0.025, or 0.001 are sometimes chosen. The exact level to choose is largely determined by how much α risk we are willing to accept and the effect that this choice has on our β risk. The larger the α the lower the β.

4. *Compute the calculated difference value.* After the data are collected we use the formula for the appropriate significance test to obtain the calculated value.

5. *Obtain the critical test value.* After we compute the calculated t, χ^2, or other measure we must look up the critical value in the appropriate table for that distribution. The critical value is the criterion which defines our region of rejection from our region of acceptance of the null hypothesis.

6. *Make the decision.* For most tests if the calculated value is larger than the critical value we reject the null hypothesis and conclude that the alternative hypothesis is supported (although it is by no means proved). If the critical value is the larger we conclude that we have failed to reject the null.[2]

---

[2] While differing in details, this procedure format was suggested by that found in Sidney Siegel, *Nonparametric Statistics for the Behavioral Sciences* (New York: McGraw-Hill Book Co., 1956), chap. 2.

TESTS OF SIGNIFICANCE

Types of Tests

There are two general classes of significance tests—the parametric and nonparametric. The parametric tests are more powerful and are generally the tests of choice if their use assumptions are reasonably met. The use of both the t test and the F test are based on the following assumptions:

1. The observations must be independent. That is, the selection of any one case should not affect the chances for any other case to be included in the sample.
2. The observations should be drawn from normally distributed populations.
3. These populations should have equal variances.
4. The measurement scales should be at least interval so that arithmetic operations can be used with them.

When one uses a parametric test it is assumed that these conditions are met, although typically no special tests are made to assure this conformance. However, the assumptions have been tested empirically with artificial populations, and the indications are that the tests are quite robust. That is, they hold up well even though actual conditions depart substantially from those theoretically required.[3] Therefore, it is common to find such tests being used in circumstances where, under a strict interpretation, only nonparametric tests are appropriate.

Nonparametric tests have fewer and less stringent assumptions. They do not specify normally distributed populations or homogeneity of variance. Some tests require independence of cases while others are expressly designed for situations with related cases. Nonparametric tests are the only ones usable with nominal data; they are the only technically correct tests to use with ordinal data, although parametric tests are sometimes employed in this case. Nonparametric tests may also be used for interval and ratio data although they waste some of the information available. Nonparametric tests are also easy to understand and to use, although this is not a major scientific reason for their use. The parametric tests have greater power efficiency when their use is appropriate, but even in such cases nonparametric tests often achieve a power efficiency as high as 95 percent. This means that the nonparametric test will provide the same statistical testing power with a sample of 100 as a parametric test with a sample of 95.

What Test to Use? Any attempt to choose a particular significance test requires that we consider the following three questions:

---

[3] See Fred N. Kerlinger, *Foundations of Behavioral Research* (New York: Holt, Rinehart, and Winston, Inc., 1973), p. 287, for more on this point plus an extensive referencing of the studies on this question.

1. Does the test involve one sample, two samples, or k samples?
2. If two samples or k samples, are the individual cases independent or related?
3. Is the measurement scale nominal, ordinal, interval, or ratio?

Other factors also affect the choice of test although they are of lesser importance. The discussion which follows is largely organized around the testing situation in which we first consider the number of samples involved and, second, whether the observations are related or independent.

The One-Sample Case

The one-sample case occurs when we have a single sample and wish to test the hypothesis that it comes from a specified population. In this case we encounter questions such as:

1. Is there a difference between observed frequencies and the frequencies we would expect, based on some theory?
2. Is there a difference between observed and expected proportions?
3. Is it reasonable to conclude that a sample is drawn from a population with some specified distribution (normal, Poisson, and so forth)?
4. Is there a significant difference between some measure of central tendency $(\overline{X})$ and its population parameter (μ)?

There are a number of tests which may be appropriate in this situation. We consider the parametric test first.

Parametric Test. The t test is used to determine the statistical significance between a sample distribution mean and a parameter. Typical of the one-sample applications of a t test are:

1. Comparison of the average burn life of a sample of light bulbs to determine if a production lot meets quality specifications.
2. A comparison of the proportion of persons who would join a dining club to an assumed population proportion.
3. Determination of whether the average performance of a sample of employees who have received special training has increased over the average past performance of all employees.

Example. To illustrate the application of the t test to the one-sample case, let's consider again the controller's problem mentioned earlier. Assume we take a sample of 100 accounts and find that the mean of the sample is 52.5 days outstanding receivables, with a sample standard deviation of 14. Do these results indicate that the population mean might still be 50 days?

In this problem we find the more usual situation in which we have only the sample standard deviation (s). We must use this in place of the population standard deviation (σ). When we substitute s for σ we should also use the t distribution, especially when the sample size is less than 30. We define t as

$$t = \frac{\overline{X} - \mu}{s/\sqrt{n}}$$

As t increases past 30 observations the distribution approaches that of the standard normal curve. The distribution of t varies, depending on the degrees of freedom (defined here as $n - 1$).

We conduct this significance test by following the six-step procedure recommended earlier.

1. *Null hypothesis.* H_0: = 50 days
   H_A: > 50 days (one tailed test)

2. *Statistical test.*   We choose the t test because the data are ratio measurements. We assume that the underlying population is normal, and that we have randomly selected the sample from the population of customer accounts.

3. *Significance level.*   Let $\alpha = 0.05$, with $n = 100$.

4. *Calculated value.* $t = \dfrac{52.5 - 50}{14/\sqrt{100}} = \dfrac{2.5}{1.4} = 1.786$; d.f. $= n - 1 = 99$.

5. *Critical test value.*   We obtain this by entering the table of the t distribution (Appendix B–2) with 99 d.f. and a level of significance value of 0.05. We secure a critical value of about 1.66 (interpolated between d.f. $= 60$ and d.f. $= 120$).

6. *Decision.*   In this case the calculated value is greater than the critical value (1.786 > 1.66), so we reject the null hypothesis and conclude that the average accounts receivable outstanding has increased.

Nonparametric Tests.   There are a variety of nonparametric tests which may be used in a one-sample situation, depending upon the measurement scale used and other conditions. If the measurement scale is nominal (classificatory only) it is possible to use either the binomial test or the (χ^2) one-sample test. The binomial test is appropriate when the population is viewed as only two classes, such as male and female, buyer and nonbuyer, and successful and unsuccessful. Thus, all observations fall into one or the other of these categories. This test is particularly useful when the size of sample is so small that the χ^2 test cannot be used.

Chi Square (χ^2) Test.   Probably the most widely used nonparametric test of significance is the χ^2 test. It is particularly useful in tests involving nominal data but can be used for higher scales. Typical are cases where persons, events, or objects are grouped in two or more nominal categories such as "yes-no," "favor-undecided-against," or class "A, B, C, or D."

The technique is of the goodness-of-fit type in which we test for significant differences between the *observed* distribution of data among categories and the *expected* distribution based upon the null hypothesis. Chi square is useful in cases of one-sample analysis, two independent samples, or k independent samples. It must be calculated with actual counts rather than percentages.

In the one-sample case we establish a null hypothesis from which we deduce the expected frequency of objects in each category. We then compare the deviations of the actual frequencies per category with the hypothesized frequencies. The greater the difference between them, the less the probability that these differences can be attributed to chance. The value of χ^2 is the measure that expresses the extent of this difference. The larger the divergence the larger the χ^2 value.

The formula by which the χ^2 test is calculated is:

$$\chi^2 = \sum_{i=1}^{k} \frac{(O_i - E_i)^2}{E_i}$$

in which

O_i = Observed number of cases categorized in the ith category.
E_i = Expected number of cases in the ith category under H_0.
k = The number of categories.

There is a different distribution for χ^2 for each number of degrees of freedom, defined here as $k - 1$. For example, if there are ten categories there are nine d.f., and so on. Depending on the number of d.f., we must be certain that the numbers in each cell are large enough to make the χ^2 test appropriate. When d.f. $= 1$, each expected frequency should be at least 5 in size. If d.f. > 1, then the χ^2 test should not be used if more than 20 percent of the expected frequencies are smaller than 5, or when any expected frequency is less than 1. Expected frequencies can often be increased by combining adjacent categories. For example, four categories of freshmen, sophomores, juniors, and seniors might be classified into upper class and lower class. If there are but two categories, and still there are too few in a given class, it would be better to use the binomial test.

Assume that we have taken the survey of student interest in the dining club that was discussed in Chapter 6. We have interviewed 200 students and learned of their intentions to join such a club if opened. We would like to analyze the results by living arrangement (type and location of student housing and eating arrangements). We classify the 200 responses into the four categories shown in the table on the next page. Do these variations in intention indicate that there is a significant difference among these students or are these sampling variations only? We proceed as follows:

1. *Null hypothesis.* $H_0: O_i = E_i$
   That is, the proportion in the population who intend to join the club is independent of living arrangement: $H_A: O_i \neq E_i$. That is, the proportion in the population who intend to join the club is dependent on living arrangement.
2. *Statistical test.*   We choose the one-sample χ^2 test to compare the observed distribution to a hypothesized distribution. The χ^2 test is used because the responses are classified into nominal categories and there are sufficient observations.
3. *Significance level.*   Let $\alpha = 0.05, n = 60$.
4. *Calculated value.* $\chi^2 = \sum_{i=1}^{k} \dfrac{(O_i - E_i)^2}{E_i}$

   We calculate the expected distribution by determining what proportion of the 200 students interviewed were in each group. We then apply these proportions to the number who intend to join the club. We then calculate the following:

   $$\chi^2 = \frac{(16 - 27)^2}{27} + \frac{(13 - 12)^2}{12} + \frac{(16 - 12)^2}{12} + \frac{(15 - 9)^2}{9}$$
   $$= 4.48 + 0.08 + 1.33 + 4.0$$
   $$= 9.89; \text{ d.f.} = 3$$

5. *Critical test value.*   We enter the table of critical value for χ^2 (Appendix B–3) with 3 d.f. and secure a value of 7.82 for $\alpha = 0.05$.
6. *Decision.*   The calculated value is greater than the critical value, so we reject the null hypothesis and conclude that there is a significant difference among these groups in the student population as to intention to join the dining club.

Living Arrangement	(1) Intend to Join	(2) Number Interviewed	(3) Percent ([2]/200)	(4) Expected Frequencies ([3] × 60)
A. Dorm/fraternity	16	90	0.45	27
B. Apartment/rooming house, nearby	13	40	0.20	12
C. Apartment/rooming house, distant	16	40	0.20	12
D. Live at home	15	30	0.15	9
Total	60	200	1.00	60

Kolmogorov Smirnov (KS) Test.   The *KS* is the test of choice when the data are at least ordinal, and the research situation calls for a comparison of an observed sample distribution with a theoretical distribution. Under these conditions the KS one-sample test is more powerful than the χ^2 test and can be used for very small samples when the χ^2 test cannot. The KS is a test of goodness-of-fit in which we specify the *cumulative* frequency distribution which would occur under the theoretical distribution and compare that with the observed cumulative frequency distribution. The theoretical distribution represents our expectations under H_0. We determine the point of greatest divergence between the observed and theoretical distributions and identify this value as D (maximum deviation). From a table of critical values for D we determine whether such a large divergence is likely on the basis of random sampling variations from the theoretical distribution. The value for D is calculated as follows:

$$D = \text{maximum} \left| F_0(X) - F_T(X) \right|$$

in which

$F_0(X)$ = The observed cumulative frequency distribution of a random sample of n observations. Where X is any possible score, $F_0(X) = k/n$, where k = the number of observations equal to or less than X.

$F_T(X)$ = The theoretical frequency distribution specified under H_0.

We illustrate the KS test, with an analysis of the results of the dining club study in terms of various class levels. We take an equal number of interviews from each class but secure unequal numbers of persons interested in joining. We assume that class levels are ordinal measurements. The testing process is as follows: (See accompanying table.)

1. *Null hypothesis.* H_0: There is no difference among student classes as to their intention of joining the dining club.
   H_A: There is a difference among students in various classes as to their intention of joining the dining club.
2. *Statistical test.* We choose the KS one-sample test because the data are ordinal measured, and we are interested in comparing an observed distribution with a theoretical one.
3. *Significance level.* $\alpha = 0.05$, $n = 60$.
4. *Calculated value.* $D = \text{maximum} \left| F_0(X) - F_T(X) \right|$

	Freshman	Sophomore	Junior	Senior	Graduate
Number in each class	5	9	11	16	19
$F_0(X)$	5/60	14/60	25/60	41/60	60/60
$F_T(X)$	12/60	24/60	36/60	48/60	60/60
$\left\| F_0(X) - F_T(X) \right\|$	7/60	10/60	11/60	7/60	0

$D = 11/60 = 0.183$; $n = 60$

5. *Critical test value.* We enter the table of critical values of D in the KS one-sample test (Appendix B–4) and learn that with $\alpha = 0.05$ the critical value for D is

$$D = \frac{1.36}{\sqrt{60}} = 0.175$$

6. *Decision.* The calculated value is greater than the critical value, indicating that we should reject the null hypothesis.

Two-Sample Case

In this case we have two samples and wish to test whether they might have come from the same population. Our null hypothesis is that any difference in the sample statistics or distributions is due to random sampling fluctuations only. Examples of such situations includes studies of output of two samples of workers, different samples in a public opinion poll, the comparison of test and control groups in an experiment, and the like. We shall briefly discuss two major variations of the two-sample case—one in which the sample members are related and the other in which they are independent.

Two Related Samples.   The two related sample cases concern those situations in which persons are closely matched (such as husband and wife) or where the same person is measured twice. For example, we might compare the output of specific workers before and after vacations, or we might match persons before randomly assigning them to test and control groups in a tasting experiment. We again discuss both parametric and nonparametric tests which are applicable under these conditions.

Parametric Test.   The t test would normally be inappropriate for this situation because one of the t test's basic assumptions is that observations are independent. This problem is solved, however, by finding the difference between each matched pair of observations and thereby collapsing the two samples into a one-sample case. That is, we now have a number of differences, each independent of the other, for which we can compute an arithmetic mean and other statistics. For example, we might secure the average units produced per day for each of 25 workers, both before and after a work rules change. By securing the before-after differences we have reduced this to one sample of 25 independent observations.

McNemar Test.   This nonparametric test may be used with either nominal or ordinal data, and is especially useful with before-after measurement of the same subjects. We test the significance of any observed change by setting up a fourfold table of frequencies to represent the first and second set of responses:

Before	After	
	Do Not Favor	Favor
Favor	A	B
Do not favor	C	D

Since $A + D$ represent the total number of people who changed (B and C are no-change responses), the expectation under a null hypothesis is that $\frac{1}{2}(A + D)$ cases change in one direction and the same proportion in the other direction. The McNemar test uses the following transformation of the χ^2 test:

$$\chi^2 = \frac{(|A - D| - 1)^2}{A + D} \text{ with d.f.} = 1$$

The "minus 1" in the equation is a correction for continuity since the χ^2 is a continuous distribution and the observed frequencies represent a discrete distribution.

We illustrate this test's application with a survey taken in a large corporation whose management decided to tell their employees of the "values of our economic system" in an internal education campaign. Assume that they took a random sample of their employees before the campaign, asking them to complete a questionnaire on their attitudes on this topic. On the basis of their responses we divide the workers into equal groups as to their favorable or unfavorable views of our economic system. After the campaign the same 200 employees are asked again to complete the questionnaire. They are again classified as to favorable or unfavorable attitudes. Our testing process is:

1. *Null hypothesis.* H_0: $P(A) = P(D)$
   H_A: $P(A) \neq P(D)$
2. *Statistical test.* The McNemar test is chosen because nominal data are used, and the study involves before-after measurements of two related samples.
3. *Significance level.* Let $\alpha = 0.05$, with $n = 200$.
4. *Calculated value.* $\chi^2 = \dfrac{(|10 - 40| - 1)^2}{10 + 40} = \dfrac{29^2}{50} = 16.82$; d.f. $= 1$

Before	After	
	Unfavorable	Favorable
Favorable	10	90
Unfavorable	60	40

5. *Critical test value.* We enter the table of the χ^2 distribution and find the critical value to be 3.84 with $\alpha = 0.05$ and d.f. = 1.

6. *Decision.* The calculated value is greater than the critical value (16.82 > 3.84) indicating that we should reject the null hypothesis. In fact, χ^2 is so large that it would have surpassed an α of 0.001.

Sign Test. This test is used with matched pairs when the only information we have is the identification of the pair member that is larger or smaller or has more or less of some characteristic. Under H_0 we would expect that the number of cases in which $X_A > X_B$ to equal the number of pairs in which $X_B > X_A$. All ties are dropped from the analysis and n is adjusted to allow for these eliminated pairs. This test is based on the binomial expansion and has a good power efficiency for small samples.

Wilcoxon Matched-Pairs Test. When we can determine both *direction* and *magnitude* of difference between carefully matched pairs we can use the Wilcoxon matched-pairs test. This test has excellent power efficiency and can be more powerful than the t test in cases where the latter is not particularly appropriate. The mechanics of calculation are also quite simple. We find the difference score (d_i) between each pair of values and rank order the differences from smallest to largest without regard to sign. The actual signs of each difference are then added to the rank values and the test statistic T is calculated. T is the sum of the ranks with the less frequent sign. Typical of such research situations might be a study where husband and wife are matched, where twins are used, where a given subject is used in a before-after study, or where the output of two similar machines is compared.

Two types of ties may occur with this test. When two observations are equal, the d score becomes zero and we drop this pair of observations from the calculation. When two or more pairs have the same d value, we average their rank positions. For example, if two pairs have a rank score of 1 we assign the rank of 1.5 to each and rank the next largest difference as third. When $n < 25$ we can use the table of critical values (Appendix B–5). When $n > 25$ the sampling distribution of T is approximately normal with:

$$\text{Mean} = \mu_T = \frac{n(n + 1)}{4}$$

$$\text{Standard deviation} = \sigma_T = \sqrt{\frac{n(n + 1)(2n + 1)}{24}}$$

$$\text{The formula for the test is } z = \frac{T - \mu_T}{\sigma_T}$$

Suppose that we conduct an experiment on the effect of brand name on quality perception. We recruit ten subjects and ask them to taste and compare two samples of product, one identified as a well-known drink and the other as a similar type of new formulation which is being tested. In truth, however, the samples are identical. The subjects are then asked to rate the two samples on a set of scale items judged to be ordinal. We test these results for significance by the usual procedure.

1. *Null hypothesis.* H_0: There is no difference between the perceived qualities of the two samples.

   H_A: There is a difference in the perceived quality of the two samples.

2. *Statistical test.* The Wilcoxon matched-pairs test is used because the study is of related samples in which the differences can be ranked in magnitude.

3. *Significance level.* $a = 0.05$, with $n = 10$ pairs of comparisons minus any pairs with a d of zero.

4. *Calculated value.* T equals the sum of the ranks with the less frequent sign. Assume that we secure the following results:

Pair		Branded	Unbranded	d_i	Rank of d_i	Rank with Less Frequent Sign
1	....	52	48	4	4	
2	....	37	32	5	5.5*	
3	....	50	52	−2	−2	2
4	....	45	32	13	9	
5	....	56	59	−3	−3	3
6	....	51	50	1	1	
7	....	40	29	11	8	
8	....	59	54	5	5.5*	
9	....	38	38	0	*	
10	....	40	32	8	7	
						$T = 5$

* There are two types of tie situations. We drop out the pair with the type of tie shown by pair 9. Pairs 2 and 8 have a tie in rank of difference. In this case we average the ranks and assign the average value to each.

5. *Critical test value.* We enter the table of critical values of T with $n = 9$ (Appendix B–5) and find that the critical value with $\alpha = 0.05$ is 6. Note that with this test the calculated value must be smaller than the critical value in order to reject the null hypothesis.

6. *Decision.* Since the calculated value is less than the critical value we reject the null hypothesis.

Two Independent Samples. We find this testing situation very often in research studies. For example, we compare the buying attitudes of a sample of subscribers from each of two magazines to determine whether they are from the same population. We test output results from two different production methods or we test price movements of two samples of common stocks to see if they are from the same population.

Parametric Test. The t test is the more frequently used parametric test for two independent samples, although the F test can be used. If we wish to use the t test in this case, however, we must make some adjustments to the calculation procedure. With two independent samples we now have two sets of sample data with two separate estimates of the population mean. We are interested in the differences between means. If we could take a large number of similar pairs of samples we would secure a distribution of *differences between means,* in which μ would be zero if the samples are from the same population. We could also calculate a standard error of the differences between two means. Since we are interested in the differences between two means we should use the difference standard error as the denominator of our t equation:

$$ t = \frac{(\overline{X}_1 - \overline{X}_2)}{\sigma_{\bar{x}_1 - \bar{x}_2}} $$

in which

$$ \sigma_{\bar{x}_1 - \bar{x}_2} = \sqrt{\frac{S_1^2}{n_1} + \frac{S_2^2}{n_2}} $$

To illustrate this application consider a problem which might face a manager who wishes to test the effectiveness of two methods for training new salespeople. The company selects 22 sales trainees who are randomly divided into two experimental groups—one of which receives type A and the other type B training. The salespeople are then assigned and managed without regard to the training they have received. At the year end the manager reviews the performances of salespeople in these groups and find the following results:

	A Group	B Group
Average weekly sales	$\overline{X}_1 = \$1,500$	$\overline{X}_2 = \$1,300$
Standard deviation	$s_1 = \$\ \ 225$	$s_2 = \$\ \ 251$

We use the standard procedure to determine whether one training method may be superior to the other.

1. *Null hypothesis.* H_0: There is no difference in sales results produced by the two training methods.
   H_A: Training method A produces sales results superior to the results of method B.
2. *Statistical test.* The t test is chosen because the data are at least interval in form and the samples are independent.
3. *Significance level.* $\alpha = 0.05$ (one-tailed test)
4. *Calculated value.*

D is calculated in the same manner as before, but the table for critical values for D (two-sample case) is presented in Appendix Table B–5 when $n_1 = n_2$ and is less than 40 observations. When n_1 and/or n_2 are larger than 40, Appendix Table B–7 should be used. With this larger sample it is not necessary that $n_1 = n_2$.

Return again to the smoking-accident study just analyzed. Suppose that we accept that the smoking classifications represent an ordinal scale and test these data with the KS two-sample test. We proceed as follows:

1. *Null hypothesis.* H_0: There is no difference in on-the-job-accident occurrences between smokers and nonsmokers.
   H_A: The more a person smokes, the more likely that person is to have an on-the-job accident.
2. *Statistical test.* The KS two-sample test is used because it is assumed that the data are ordinal.
3. *Significance level.* $\alpha = 0.05$, $n_1 = n_2 = 40$
4. *Calculated value.*

	Heavy Smoker	Medium Smoker	Light Smoker	Nonsmoker
$F_{n_1}(X)$	12/40	21/40	27/40	40/40
$F_{n_2}(X)$	4/40	10/40	17/40	40/40
d_i	8/40	11/40	10/40	0

5. *Critical test value.* We enter Appendix Table B–6 with $n = 40$ to find that $D = 11$ when $p \le 0.05$ for a one-tailed distribution.
6. *Decision.* Since the critical value equals the calculated value, we reject the null hypothesis. Note in this case that the KS test has found the results to be statistically significant while the χ^2 test of the same data did not.

Mann-Whitney U Test. This test is also used with two independent samples if the data are at least ordinal; it is an alternative to the t test without the latter's limiting assumptions. When the larger of the two samples is 20 or less there are special tables for interpreting U; when the larger sample exceeds 20 a normal curve approximation is used.

In calculating the U test we treat all observations in a combined fashion and rank them, algebraically, from smallest to largest. The larger negative score receives the lowest rank. In case of ties we assign the average rank as in other tests. With this test we can also test samples which are unequal. After the ranking, the rank values for each sample are totalled. We then compute the U statistic as follows:

$$U = n_1 n_2 + \frac{n_1(n_1 + 1)}{2} - R_1$$

or

$$U = n_1 n_2 + \frac{n_2(n_2 - 1)}{2} - R_2$$

in which

n_1 = Number in sample 1
n_2 = Number in sample 2
R_1 = Sum of ranks in sample 1

With this equation we can secure two U values, one using R_1 and the second using R_2. For testing purposes we use the smaller U.

An example may help to clarify the U statistic calculation procedure. Let's consider again the sales training example just used with the t distribution discussion. Recall that salespeople with training method A averaged higher sales than salespeople with training method B. While these data are ratio measured, we still might not want to accept the other assumptions which underly the t test. What kind of a result would we secure with the U test? While the U test is designed for ordinal data, it can be used with interval and ratio measurements.

1. *Null hypothesis.* H_0: There is no difference in sales results produced by the two training methods.
             H_A: Training method A produces sales results superior to the results of method B.
2. *Statistical test.*   The Mann-Whitney U test is chosen because the measurement is at least ordinal, and we do not wish to accept the assumptions under the parametric t test.
3. *Significance level.* $\alpha = 0.05$ (one-tailed test)
4. *Calculated value.*

Sales per Week per Salesperson

Training Method A	Rank	Training Method B	Rank
1,500	15	1,340	10
1,540	16	1,300	8.5
1,860	22	1,620	18
1,230	6	1,070	3
1,370	12	1,210	5
1,550	17	1,170	4
1,840	21	1,770	20
1,250	7	950	1
1,300	8.5	1,380	13
1,350	11	1,460	14
1,710	19	1,030	2
	$R_1 = 154.5$		$R_2 = 98.5$

$U = (11)(11) + \dfrac{11(11 + 1)}{2} - 154.5$ $U = (11)(11) + \dfrac{11(11 + 1)}{2} - 98.5$

$= 32.5$ $= 88.5$

5. *Critical test value.* We enter Appendix Table B–8 with $n_1 = n_2 = 11$, and find a critical value of 34 for $\alpha = 0.05$, one-tailed test. Note that with this test the calculated value must be smaller than the critical value in order to reject the null hypothesis.

6. *Decision.* Since the calculated value is smaller than the critical value ($34 > 32.5$) we reject the null hypothesis and conclude that training method A is probably superior.

Thus, we would reject the null hypothesis at $\alpha = 0.05$ in a one-tailed test using either the t or the U test. In this example, the U test has approximately the same power as the parametric test.

When $n > 20$ in one of the samples, the sampling distribution of U approaches the normal distribution with

$$\text{Mean} = \mu_U = \frac{n_1 n_2}{2}$$

$$\text{Standard deviation } \sigma_U = \sqrt{\frac{(n_1)(n_2)(n_1 + n_2 + 1)}{12}}$$

and

$$z = \frac{U - \mu_U}{\sigma_U}$$

Other Nonparametric Tests. Other nonparametric tests are appropriate under certain conditions when we are testing two independent samples. When the measurement is only nominal, the Fisher exact probability test may be used. When the data are at least ordinal we can use the median and Wald-Wolfowitz runs tests. When the data are interval we can use the randomization test for two independent samples.[4]

k Sample Case

We are often faced with the problem of testing for significance when three or more samples are involved. Under these conditions we determine, simultaneously, whether the samples might have been drawn from the same or identical populations. We are interested in testing for an overall difference among the samples. In this section we consider the k independent sample case before the related sample case because parametric testing under independent sampling conditions introduces the simpler problem of variance analysis.

---

[4] For details on these and other nonparametric tests see Siegel, *Nonparametric Statistics;* Linton C. Freeman, *Elementary Applied Statistics* (New York: John Wiley & Sons, Inc., 1965); or Frederick Mosteller and Robert E. K. Rourke, *Sturdy Statistics* (Reading, Mass.: Addison-Wesley Publishing Company, 1973).

k Independent Sample Case. As with the two sample cases, the samples are assumed to be independent of one another. This is the condition that we find when a completely randomized experiment is carried out, or even a factorial design when the subjects are assigned to treatment groups in a simple random manner. We also often wish to compare more than two samples in ex post facto studies.

Parametric Tests. When conditions are appropriate for parametric tests of more than two samples we use *analysis of variance* (ANOVA). As Kerlinger has pointed out, however, analysis of variance is ". . . not just a statistical method. It is an approach and a way of thinking."[5] In this testing procedure we analyze the total variance in a set of data by breaking it down into its component sources which can be attributed to various factors in the research. Theoretically any number of component factors can be extracted, but as a practical matter we seldom go above three, and more usually one or two. We determine statistical significance of each of these factors by expressing the variance attributed to it as a ratio to the estimated sampling variance of the data. We do this by means of the F test which can be stated as:

$$F = \frac{\text{Variance due to factor} X + \text{Sampling variance}}{\text{Sampling variance}}$$

If the variance due to factor X is small then the F ratio will be small. On the other hand, if the F ratio is large, factor X accounts for a large part of the total variance in the data.

The simplest form of ANOVA is the one-way model which we use with simple random samples to compare the impact of a single independent variable on the dependent variable. To simplify the discussion we consider only the case in which samples are of equal size and the fixed-effects model is assumed.[6] To illustrate one-way ANOVA let's consider again the pricing example from the experimentation chapter (see page 343). The objective of that study was to determine the sales impact when the chain's private brand of canned green beans was priced at various discounts below the national brand of beans that the company carried. Assume that the traditional price discount has been one cent per can and that we wish to test this against differentials of three and five cents. The IV is the price differential used, and the DV is the monthly case sales, per store, of the store brands minus the case sales of the national brand.

In one-way analysis of variance we can think of the value of a specific dependent variable measurement as being made up of three parts: the grand mean of all observations, the treatment or IV effect, and random error. This three-part partition can be expressed as:

---

[5] Kerlinger, *Foundations,* p. 216.

[6] With the fixed-effects model we assume that the test treatments are not randomly selected from a larger population of test treatments. Because of this assumption our test results cannot be generalized to other levels of treatment. The alternative is the random-effects model.

$$X_{ij} = \mu + C_j + e_{ij}$$

in which

X_{ij} = The observation in row i, column j
C_j = The column or treatment effect in column j
e_{ij} = Random error or sampling effect

The total variance (SS_T) can be broken into two components representing the last two items of the above equation. These components are usually referred to as "between columns" variance (SS_K) and "within columns" variance (SS_W). The former represents the effect of treatments while the latter represents the remaining variance. While we call the latter "sampling variance," it includes all other unidentified forms of variance.

To illustrate one-way ANOVA assume that we conduct the pricing experiment using a total of 18 stores, randomly assigned to the three treatments (price discounts of one cent, three cents, and five cents per can). We follow the normal procedure:

1. *Null hypothesis.* H_0: There is no difference in sales response among the three price difference groups.
                           H_A: There is a difference between sales response among the three price groups.
2. *Statistical test.*   We use the F test with analysis of variance because there are k independent samples and we accept the assumptions underlying the parametric test.

4. *Calculated value.* $F = \dfrac{\text{Between-groups mean square}}{\text{Within-groups mean square}}$
                           $= 3.62$, d.f. $= (2, 15)$

See calculation details in Table 13–1.
5. *Critical test value.*   We enter Appendix Table B–9 with d.f. $= (2, 15)$, $\alpha = 0.05$, and secure a critical value for $F = 3.68$.
6. *Decision.*   Since calculated F is less than critical value $(3.62 < 3.68)$ we fail to reject the null hypothesis and conclude that the differences in sales volume may be due to sampling variations only. Note, however, that the value is very close. Our failure to reject the null hypothesis grows out of the fact that a large part of the total variance in the data remains unexplained and therefore is assumed to be due to random variation. We will take up this example again in a later section.

Chi Square Test.   When we have k independent samples in which the data are nominal, the χ^2 is the test of choice. While it can also be used for classificatory data of a higher measurement scale it wastes some of the information found in the data. The k sample χ^2 test is merely an extension of the two-independent-samples case treated in an earlier section. It is calculated and interpreted in the same way and will not be elaborated here.

Table 13–1: Calculation of a One-Way Analysis of Variance (data hypothetical)

			Price Differentials				
	One Cent		Three Cents		Five Cents		
	X_A	$X_A{}^2$	X_B	$X_B{}^2$	X_C	$X_C{}^2$	
	6	36	8	64	9	81	$N = 18$
	7	49	9	81	9	81	$n = 6$
	8	64	8	64	11	121	$k = 3$
	7	49	10	100	10	100	
	9	81	11	121	14	196	
	11	121	13	169	13	169	
ΣX	48		59		66		$\Sigma X_T = 173$
$\overline{X}$	8		9.83		11		$\overline{X}_T = 9.61$
ΣX^2		400		599		748	$\Sigma X_T{}^2 = 1,747$

Correction term $= \dfrac{(\Sigma X_T)^2}{N} = \dfrac{(173)^2}{N} = 1,662.72$

Total sum of squares $= SS_T = \Sigma X_T{}^2 - C = 1747 - 1,662.72$
$\qquad = 84.28$

Between columns sum of squares $= SS_K = \dfrac{(\Sigma X_A)^2}{n_A} + \dfrac{(\Sigma X_B)^2}{n_B} + \dfrac{(\Sigma X_C)^2}{n_C} - \dfrac{(\Sigma X_T)^2}{N}$
$\qquad = (384 + 580\ 16 + 726) - 1,662.72$
$\qquad = 1,690.16 - 1,662.72$
$\qquad = 27.44$

Within columns sum of squares $= SS_W = SS_T - SS_K$
$\qquad = 84.28 - 27.44$
$\qquad = 56.85$

Source	Sum of Squares	d.f.	Mean Square	F
Between columns	27.44	2	13.72	3.62
Within columns	56.84	15	3.79	
	84.28	17		

Other Nonparametric Tests. We can use tests more powerful than χ^2 with data which are at least ordinal in nature. One such test is an extension of the median test mentioned earlier. We will illustrate here the application of a second ordinal measurement test known as the Kruskal-Wallis one-way analysis of variance.

The Kruskal-Wallis test is a generalized version of the Mann-Whitney test. With it we rank all scores in the entire pool of observations from smallest to largest. The rank sum of each sample is then calculated, with ties being distributed as in other examples. We then compute the value of H as follows:

$$H = \frac{12}{N(N - 1)} \sum_{j=1}^{k} \frac{T_j^2}{n_j} - 3(N + 1)$$

in which

T_j = Sum of ranks in column j
n_j = Number of cases in jth sample
$N = \Sigma w_j$ = Total number of cases
k = Number of samples

When there are a number of ties it is recommended that a correction factor (C) be calculated and used to correct the H value as follows:

$$C = 1 - \left\{ \frac{\sum_{i}^{G} (t_i{}^3 - t_i)}{N^3 - N} \right\}$$

in which

G = Number of sets of tied observations
t_i = Number tied in any set i
$H' = H/C$

To secure the critical value for H' we use the table for the distribution of χ^2 (Appendix B–3), and enter it with the value of H', and d.f. $= k - 1$.

To illustrate the application of this test we use again the price discount experiment problem. The data and calculations are shown in Table 13–2 and indicate that, by the Kruskal-Wallis test, we again barely fail to reject the null hypothesis with $\alpha = 0.05$.

k Related Samples.   When there are k samples in which observations or subjects are matched, or where the same subject is used more than once, we have a situation calling for a two-way analysis of variance. In the parametric case we again employ the F test but with efforts made to extract additional variance. We again use the price discount experiment to illustrate the procedure.

Recall that in the one-way ANOVA we were unable to reject the null hypothesis even at the $\alpha = 0.05$ level. Yet a look at the data in Table 13–1 suggests that there is some impact from the larger discounts. Another conclusion that we might make from inspecting that data is that there is substantial variation within samples. Could it be that there are other variables operating within columns and that all of this variance is not random variation?

It might be reasonable to conclude, for example, that if the stores varied in size then the sales would also vary substantially because of this store size effect. If we could block on store size we might be able to extract this source of variance. Recall again that this is the object of ANOVA—to break total variance down into its component parts so as account for each and to judge its effect.

Assume that we do block on store size, developing six sets of three stores with approximately equal sales volume. We then randomly assign the stores

Table 13–2: Kruskal-Wallis One-Way Analysis of Variance (price differentials)

One Cent		Three Cents		Five Cents	
X_A	Rank	X_B	Rank	X_C	Rank
6...............	1	8...............	5	9...............	8.5
7...............	2.5	9...............	8.5	9...............	8.5
8...............	5	8...............	5	11...............	14
7...............	2.5	10...............	11.5	10...............	11.5
9...............	8.5	11...............	14	14...............	18
11...............	14	13	16 5	13...............	16.5
	$T_j = 33.5$		60.5		77

$T = 33.5 + 60.5 + 77$
  $= 171$

$H = \dfrac{12}{18(18-1)} \left[\dfrac{33.5^2 + 60.5^2 + 77^2}{6} \right] - 3(18+1)$

$\quad = \dfrac{12}{342} \left[\dfrac{1,122.25 + 3,660.25 + 5,929}{6} \right] - 57$

$\quad = 0.0351 \left[\dfrac{10,711.5}{6} \right] - 57$

$H = 5.66$

$C = 1 - \left(\dfrac{3[(2)^3 - 2] + 2[(3)^3 - 3] + [(4)^3 - 4]}{18^3 + 18} \right)$

$\quad = 1 - \dfrac{18 + 48 + 60}{5814}$

$\quad = 0.978$

$H' = \dfrac{H}{C} = \dfrac{5.66}{0.978} = 5.79$

d.f. $= k - 1 = 2$

$\quad p > 0.05$

in each of the six size sets to each of the three test sample groups. Assume further that when we do this, and run the experiment, we secure exactly the same results as shown in Table 13–1. Now, however, each row of that table represents a stratum of three stores matched for size. With this additional information we can extract the variance that may be in the data because of store size differences. We do this extracting by calculating means for each row (stratum or block) and the "between rows" sum of squares and mean square. These calculations are shown in Table 13–3. The results of this two-way analysis are that we find the effects of store size and price discount both highly significant ($p < 0.01$). We see further that most of the residual unexplained variance found in the one-way case has now been explained by the store size. Seldom in practice do we find a second blocking factor which has such a marked effect in removing additional variance, but it is not uncommon to find that randomized block designs such as this can substantially improve our ability to account for variance and determine statistical significance.

Table 13–3: Two-Way Analysis of Variance

| Size Group | Price Differences | | | | | |
	One Cent X_A	Three Cents X_B	Five Cents X_C	ΣX_R	$\overline{X}$	X^2
X_1	6	8	9	23	7.67	181
X_2	7	9	9	25	8.33	211
X_3	8	8	11	27	9	249
X_4	7	10	10	27	9	249
X_5	9	11	14	34	11.33	398
X_6	11	13	13	37	12.33	459
ΣX	48	59	66	173		1,747

Between-row sum of squares

$$= ss_R = \frac{(\Sigma X_1)^2}{n_1} + \frac{(\Sigma X_2)^2}{n_2} + \frac{(\Sigma X_3)^2}{n_3} + \frac{(\Sigma X_4)^2}{n_4} + \frac{(\Sigma X_5)^2}{n_5} + \frac{(\Sigma X_6)^2}{n_6} - \frac{(\Sigma X_T)^2}{N}$$
$$= [176.33 + 208.33 + 243 + 243 + 385.33 + 456.33] - 1,662.72$$
$$= 1,712.32 - 1,662.72$$
$$ss_R = 49.6$$

Source	SS	dt	MS	F
Between columns	27.44	2	13.72	19.05
Between rows	49.6	5	9.92	13.78
Residual	7.24	10	0.72	
	84.28	17		

Nonparametric Tests.   In the *k* related sample case in which the measurement is only nominal we can use the Cochran *Q* test, an extension of the McNemar test discussed earlier. When the data are at least ordinal we may also use the Friedman two-way analysis of variance test, an extension of the Wilcoxon matched-pairs test discussed earlier. Details on the calculation procedures for these tests are found in many statistics references.[7]

MEASURES OF ASSOCIATION

To this point we have been concerned chiefly with whether there is a statistically significant association between variables, but this is not our only interest. We often would like to use our knowledge of one variable to estimate a second one. The methods by which we do this are commonly known as *regression analysis*. We also want to know the amount or degree of association between variables, and for this we use *correlation analysis*. Regression and correlation are closely related and are generally presented together.

With correlation analysis we calculate a coefficient by which to measure the closeness of association between variables. With regression we develop

---

[7] See Siegel, *Nonparametric Statistics,* or W. L. Hays, *Statistics for the Social Sciences* (New York: Holt, Rinehart and Winston, Inc., 1973).

an estimating equation by which we can use data from one or more independent variables to estimate values for a dependent variable. Both correlation and regression are affected by the assumptions we make about the measurement levels involved and the distributions which underlie the data. For example, when we are associating two nominal variables only certain types of procedures are appropriate. Other procedures apply when ordinal variables are used and still others when higher measurement levels are used. In each case, however, we are interested in calculating a summary statistic or equation which expresses the association of different levels of one variable with different levels of one or more other variables. We discuss correlation for nominal measurement levels first.

Nonparametric Correlation

Nominal Date. There is no fully satisfactory measure of association for categorical data. The most widely known measure is C, the contingency coefficient, but it suffers from the defect that its upper limit may not be 1. It is determined by the number of cells in the category matrix. For example, with a 2×2 table the maximum value for C is $= 0.707$.

The example of an SPSS CROSSTABS printout (see Figure 12–4) lists other nonparametric measures that are available. Two that may be the most useful are *Cramer's statistic* and the *index of predictive association*, or *lamda*.

Cramer's Statistic.[8] This association measure is based on first calculating a Chi square (χ^2). Cramer's statistic (V) is then computed from the equation

$$V = \sqrt{\frac{\chi^2}{mn}}$$

where n is the size of sample and m is the number of rows or columns minus 1.0, whichever is less $(r - 1$ or $c - 1)$. For example, from the hypothetical example on the incidence of smoking and accidents (see page 424) we found a χ^2 of 7.44. Cramer's V for this example is:

$$V = \sqrt{\frac{7.44}{(1)80}} = 0.30$$

This indicates that there is a moderate statistical relationship between workers who smoke and accidents on the job, but there is no suggestion from this statistic that one causes the other, nor is there an indication of direction to this association. The range of this statistic is from zero (no association) to as high as 1.0 (complete association) when the row totals give a frequency distribu-

---

[8] For more details see W. L. Hays and R. L. Winkler, *Statistics: Probability, Inference and Decision,* 2d ed. (New York: Holt, Rinehart and Winston, Inc., 1975) pp. 835–37.

tion identical to the column totals. In other cases, however, the upper limit approaches 1.0.

Lambda. The coefficient *Lambda* (λ) is a second and different approach to measuring the degree of association between two nominal variables. It is based on how well the frequencies of one nominal variable offer predictive evidence about the frequency of the second nominal variable. Thus it is not based on chi square. The lambda coefficient is also asymmetrical; we can calculate the direction of prediction or association.

Lambda is computed in a straightforward way. Assume, for example, that we secure the results shown in Table 13–4 from an opinion survey among a sample of 400 adults.

Table 13–4: What Is Your Opinion about a Proposal to Liberalize the Capital Gains Tax?

Occupation Class	Favor	Do Not Favor	Total
Managerial	90	20	110
White collar	60	80	140
Blue collar	30	120	150
Total	180	220	400

Assume for the moment that we know only that 180 out of the 400 (or 45 percent) favor the tax liberalization, while 220 (or 55 percent) do not favor it. With this information alone, if we were asked to predict the opinions of the individuals in the sample we would achieve the best prediction record by always choosing the model opinion of "do not favor." By so doing, however, we would be wrong 180 times out of 400.

Now suppose we had prior information about respondent occupation status and then were asked to predict opinion. Would it improve our predictions? Of course it would! We would make the predictions in the accompanying table

	Our Prediction Score	
	Correct	Error
If managerial, choose "favorable"	90	20
If white collar, choose "do not favor"	80	60
If blue collar, choose "do not favor"	120	30
Total	290	110

By this tally we can see that the additional information reduced our error prediction from 180 to 110. In terms of the lambda criterion the results are:

$$\lambda = \frac{\text{Number of errors in first case} - \text{Number of errors in second case}}{\text{Number of errors in first case}}$$

$$= \frac{180 - 110}{180} = 0.39$$

Lambda is interpreted as the percent improvement in prediction of opinion as a result of knowing the respondent's occupation category.

The general form for calculating lambda is:

$$\lambda_{D|I} = \frac{\Sigma f_{KI} - F_D}{n - F_D}$$

where

f_{KI} = The maximum frequency found within each subclass of the independent or prior variable.

F_D = The maximum frequency among the marginal totals of the dependent variable.

n = Size of sample

If we wished to estimate occupation categories from opinions on the proposed capital gains liberalization, that is, we start with opinions as the prior or independent variable, we would secure the following:

$$\lambda_{D|I} = \frac{(90 + 120) - 150}{400 - 150} = 0.24$$

This is interpreted as meaning 24 percent of the error in predicting respondent occupation class is eliminated by knowing the person's opinion on the capital gains tax question. Lambda varies between zero (no ability to eliminate errors) and 1.0 (ability to eliminate all errors).

Ordinal Data. When data are at least ordinal measurements we have the choice of two excellent rank order correlations methods, both of which possess a power efficiency of about 0.9 when compared with parametric measures. Neither requires the assumption of a bivariate normal distribution. The most widely used is Spearman's rank-order correlation coefficient (r_s). The second nonparametric correlation method is the Kendall *tau*. It is somewhat more complicated in calculation but is generalizable to partial correlation coefficients while the Spearman is not. Finally, there is the Kendall coefficient of concordance (W), a nonparametric measure of association which may be used when we have k sets of rankings.[9] Here we discuss Spearman's coefficient only.

Spearman's Rank Correlation. Spearman's *rho* (as it is often called) is actually a special form of the Pearsonian correlation coefficient (r) which will be introduced next. It is a relatively easy statistic to compute. The major deficiency of *rho* is said to be its sensitivity to distortion from ties in ranks. When this is a problem one can use a slightly more complicated formula with a tie correction factor. (See Table 13–5.)

[9] See Siegel, *Nonparametric Statistics*, pp. 202–38.

Table 13–5: Spearman Rank Correlation

| | Rank by | | | |
| | Panel | Psychologist | | |
Applicant	x	y	d	d²
A	3.5	6	−2.5	6.25
B	10.	5	5	25.00
C	6.5	8	1.5	2.25
D	2.	1.5	0.5	0.25
E	1	3	−2	4.00
F	9	7	2	4.00
G	3.5	1.5	2	4.00
H	6.5	9	2.5	6.25
I	8	10	2	4.00
J	5	4	1	1.00
				57.0

To illustrate the use of *rho* consider a situation where the Big Corporation is recruiting new management trainees. Assume that the field has been narrowed to ten applicants for the final evaluation. They all come to company headquarters, go through a battery of tests, and are interviewed by a panel of three executives. The test results are evaluated by a psychologist who then ranks the ten in terms of the test evidence. The executive panel also ranks the applicants on the basis of their interviews. In assessing the results of these measurements you decide to compare how well these two sets of rankings agree.

You list the applicants, and beside each applicant's name you enter his/her ranks by each evaluation method. Where scores are tied you assign the average of the ranks that would have been assigned if no ties had occurred. Then you determine the difference (*d*) between the two ranks, square these differences, and total the squared values as follows:
The computation of *rho* is

$$r_s = 1 - \frac{6\Sigma d^2}{n^3 - n} = 1 - \frac{6(57)}{(10)^3 - 10} = 0.654$$

Where n = the number of subjects being ranked. This computation confirms that there is substantial correlation between the two measurements and suggests they are reasonably valid. There may be some question as to the effect of the three pairs of ties in the data. You may choose to guard against this distortion threat by recalculating the results with the tie correction factor.[10] In this case the correction factor reduces r_s from 0.654 to 0.651. It would appear that a few ties have little effect on the value of *rho*.

---

[10] Ibid., pp. 207–10, for computation details.

Parametric Correlation Analysis

When we decide that parametric methods are suitable for determining association between variables we must accept the following assumptions: (1) the data are at least an interval scale, and (2) the variables are from a normally distributed population.

Bivariate Correlation. When we deal with sample information the parametric correlation measure most often used is the Pearson product-moment coefficient r. It is the summary statistic which represents the linear relationship between two sets of variables. Assume that we are considering the simple bivariate case in which we seek to measure the relationship between family food expenditures and family income. We have data for 15 families drawn from the files of a much larger study. We correlate these data and secure a Pearsonian coefficient of correlation (r) of 0.41 (see Table 13–6). What does this mean? The r statistic can range from $+1$ (perfect positive correlation) through 0 (absence of correlation) to -1 (perfect inverse correlation). The precise relationship of the association is given by the regression equation which represents the line of best fit to the data. For linear bivariate regression the line is:

$$Y = a + bX$$

in which

$a =$ A regression coefficient or amount of Y when $X = 0$. It is also known as the Y intercept.

$b =$ A regression coefficient or amount that Y varies, on the average, with an increase of one unit of X.

This regression line is fitted to the data by means of the *least squares* technique and is a statement of the way that the dependent variable changes with variations in the independent variable. The least squares line of best fit is that line about which the squared deviations are at a minimum, and the algebraic sum of the deviations equals zero. It is analogous to calculating an arithmetic mean line of relationship between the two variables. In fact, the line must go through the intersection point of the means of the two variables.

These and other relationships are shown graphically in Figure 13–4. This scatterplot illustrates the relationship between annual family income and family food expenditures. The line is the least squares line of best fit. Also shown is the mean family food expenditure $(\overline{Y})$. From this $\overline{Y}$ we can see that expenditures for many families depart substantially from the average expenditure level. It is apparent also from the scatter of points that knowledge about family income can explain part of the deviations of family food expenditures from the average.[11] It is a characteristic of r that its square (the coefficient of

---

[11] "Explain" as used here is not in terms of causation logic, but rather it means that the regression line statistically accounts for or correlates with, on the average, a certain proportion of the total deviation of observations from the mean of Y.

Table 13–6: Correlations among Annual Family Food Expenditures, Family Income, and Family Size (values in thousands)

Food Expenditures (Y)	Family Income (X_1)	Family Size (X_2)	X_1Y	Y^2	X_1^2	X_2Y	X_2^2	X_1X_2
0.8	5.5	1	4.40	.64	30.25	0.8	1	5.5
1.0	8.9	1	8.90	1.00	79.21	1.0	1	8.9
1.7	21.8	1	37.06	2.89	475.24	1.7	1	21.8
1.4	6.8	2	9.52	1.96	46.24	2.8	4	13.6
1.2	7.5	2	9.00	1.44	56.25	2.4	4	15.0
1.8	17.2	2	30.96	3.24	295.84	3.6	4	34.4
1.9	22.1	2	41.99	3.61	488.41	3.8	4	44.2
2.3	19.0	3	43.70	5.29	361.00	6.9	9	57.0
1.7	12.0	3	20.40	2.89	144.00	5.1	9	36.0
1.5	14.0	4	21.00	2.25	196.00	6.0	16	56.0
1.8	10.9	4	19.62	3.24	118.81	7.2	16	43.6
2.0	7.5	5	15.00	4.00	56.25	10.0	25	37.5
2.2	14.0	5	30.80	4.84	196.00	11.0	25	70.0
2.8	13.7	6	38.36	7.84	187.69	16.8	36	82.2
2.1	6.0	7	12.60	4.41	36.00	14.7	49	42.0
26.2	186.9	48	343.31	49.54	2,767.19	93.8	204	567.7
$\overline{X}$ 1.74	12.46	3.2						

$\Sigma x_1 y = \Sigma X_1 Y - (\Sigma X_1)(\Sigma Y)/n = 343.31 - (186.9)(26.2)/15 = 16.858$

$\Sigma x_1^2 = \Sigma X_1^2 - (\Sigma X_1)^2/n = 2{,}767.19 - (186.9)^2/15 = 438.416$

$\Sigma y^2 = \Sigma Y^2 - (\Sigma Y)^2/n = 49.54 - (26.2)^2/15 = 3.777$

$$r_{x_1}y = \frac{\Sigma x_1 y}{\sqrt{(\Sigma x_1^2)(\Sigma y^2)}} = \frac{16.858}{\sqrt{(438.416)(3.777)}} = \frac{16.858}{40.693} = 0.41$$

$\Sigma x_2 y = \Sigma X_2 Y - (\Sigma X_2)(\Sigma Y)/n = 93.8 - (48)(26.2)/15 = 9.96$
$\Sigma x_2^2 = \Sigma X_2^2 - (\Sigma X_2)^2/n = 204 - (48)^2/15 = 50.4$

$$r_{x_2 y} = \frac{\Sigma x_2 y}{\sqrt{(\Sigma x_2^2)(\Sigma y^2)}} = \frac{9.96}{\sqrt{(50.4)(3.777)}} = \frac{9.96}{13.797} = 0.72$$

$\Sigma x_1 x_2 = \Sigma X_1 X_2 - (\Sigma X_1)(\Sigma X_2)/n = 567.7 - (186.9)(48)/15 = -30.38$

$$r_{x_1 x_2} = \frac{\Sigma x_1 x_2}{\sqrt{(\Sigma x_1^2)(\Sigma y^2)}} = \frac{-30.38}{\sqrt{(438.416)(50.4)}} = \frac{-30.38}{148.65} = -0.20$$

determination) is an estimate of the explained deviation of individual items from $\overline{Y}$. For example, if $r = 0.42$ for the data in Figure 13–4, then 0.42^2 or about 18 percent of the total deviation from $\overline{Y}$ of these 15 paired observations can be explained in terms of family income.

Hypothesis Testing. To this point we have discussed only the descriptive application of correlation and regression, but we also use it for statistical inference. For example, we might test the null hypothesis that $\rho = 0$.[12] We use the t test and the following equation to secure the calculated value:

---

[12] ρ = rho = The population coefficient of correlation for which r is a sample-based estimate.

$$t = \frac{r\sqrt{n-2}}{\sqrt{1-r^2}} = \frac{0.41\sqrt{(13)}}{\sqrt{1-0.41^2}}$$
$$t = 1.62 \qquad \text{d.f.} = 15 - 2 = 13$$

Assume that we establish a critical value based on a one-tailed test of $\alpha = 0.05$. We enter the t table and find that we can reject the null hypothesis only if the calculated t value > 1.771 (one-tailed test) with d.f. $= 13$. Therefore, we fail to reject the hypothesis and conclude that there is a chance that the true correlation is zero. It might seem surprising that such a relatively high correlation coefficient would not be significant, but the failure to reject the null hypothesis results largely from the very small sample size of 15.

Figure 13–4: Scatterplot of Annual Family Income and Family Food Expenditures

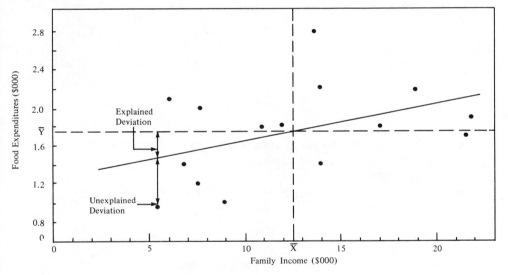

If we wish to test a hypothesis that r is some value other than zero (say, $r = 0.4$) we cannot use the t test because of the skewness of the r sampling distribution whenever the population correlation coefficient differs much from zero. In this case we can use an r to Z transformation.[13]

While it is logical to expect that family income affects food expenditures, it is obvious that one or more other factors must also be influential. For example, the size of family should have an impact on food expenditures. Since data on the size of these 15 families is available we also correlate family size with

---

[13] For more on this see William L. Hays and Robert Winkler, *Statistics: Probability Inference,* 2d ed. (New York: Holt, Rinehart and Winston, Inc., 1975), p. 653, or any of a number of popular statistics texts.

food expenditures and secure an r of 0.72 (see Table 13–6). The coefficient of determination (r^2) is 0.52—indicating that family size is a more important independent variable than is family income. But now another question arises: How much impact might income have if we were able to control for family size (hold family size "constant")? Bivariate correlation is not adequate to this task. We must use partial and/or multiple correlation analysis.

Partial Correlation. The effect of this technique is analogous to the elaboration, using nominal data, which was discussed in Chapter 12. With it we are able to compare the impact of a given IV on a DV, while statistically controlling for one or more other independent variables. To carry out the partial correlation analysis we need first to compute zero order coefficients (the simple bivariate correlations) for various combinations of variables as in the accompanying correlation matrix.

Variable	(1) Food Expenditures	(2) Family Income	(3) Family Size
(1) Food expenditures	1.00	0.41	0.72
(2) Family income		1.00	−0.20
(3) Family size			1.00

We can then calculate the partial correlation between food expenditures and family income, holding family size constant.

$$r_{12.3} = \frac{r_{12} - (r_{13})(r_{23})}{\sqrt{1 - r_{13}^2}\ \sqrt{1 - r_{23}^2}} = \frac{0.41 - (0.72)(-0.20)}{\sqrt{1 - 0.72^2}\ \sqrt{1 - 0.20^2}}$$

$$= \frac{0.554}{0.694 \times 0.98} = 0.81$$

This indicates that family income has a strong influence on family food expenditures, once the influence of family size has been extracted. However, one more question arises. How well can we estimate family food expenditures if we include both independent variables? This is a problem for multiple correlation.

Multiple Correlation. With multiple correlation we can introduce, simultaneously, the effect of two or more independent variables and calculate their net statistical effect on a dependent variable. The coefficient of multiple correlation for a sample is known as R, and its square (R^2) is the coefficient of multiple determination. While R is usually secured as part of multiple regression computations, cases with only two IVs may be calculated directly from bivariate correlation measures.

$$R_{1.23}^2 = r_{13}^2 + (1 - r_{13}^2)(r_{12.3}^2)$$
$$= 0.72^2 + (1 - 0.72^2)(0.81^2)$$
$$= 0.83$$

To summarize, the coefficients used in this example may be interpreted as in the accompanying list.

Interpretation

$r_{12}^2 = (0.41)^2 = 0.18$	About 18 percent of the variation in family food expenditures is explained by variations in family income, with other factors not considered.
$r_{13}^2 = (0.72)^2 = 0.52$	About 52 percent of the variation in family food expenditures is explained by variations in family size, with other factors not considered.
$r_{12.3}^2 = (0.81)^2 = 0.66$	About two thirds of the variation in family food expenditures is explained by variations in family income when the effects of family size are held constant.
$R_{1.23}^2 = (0.91)^2 = 0.83$	About 83 percent of the variation in family food expenditures is explained by a combination of family income and family size.

So far we have discussed parametric and nonparametric tests which are applicable under various conditions. Their use is summarized in Figure 13–5.

Correlation and Computers. Correlation and regression analysis can require many highly precise calculations. For this reason much bivariate correlation and regression, and almost all multiple correlation and regression, is done with computers. There are a large number of programs in existence by which to carry out these complex calculations. For example, SAS, SPSS, and STAT/BASIC software packages have programs to compute multiple, partial, and bivariate regressions and correlations. Because of the widespread availability of these programs, the complexity of calculation, and the limited statistical objectives of this text, the following section on multivariate analysis will omit computational details.

Multivariate Analysis

To this point the emphasis has been on associating two variables in a paired relationship. In recent years, however, there has been a rapid development and application of multivariate statistical tools to business research problems. These developments have been stimulated by the increased availability of large-scale electronic computers. Most of these analysis techniques have been borrowed from psychology and other social sciences.

One author defines multivariate analysis as "those statistical techniques which focus upon, and bring out in bold relief, the structure of *simultaneous* relationships among three or more phenomena."[14] The major point in this definition is that multivariate analysis is a shift away from the pairwise relationships between two variables to the simultaneous relationships among three or more variables.

Since there are many multivariate techniques it may be helpful to classify them in some orderly fashion. One widely used classification is based on the

---

[14] Jagdish N. Sheth (ed.), *Multivariate Methods for Market and Survey Research* (Chicago: American Marketing Association, 1977), p. 3.

Figure 13–5: Recommended Statistical Techniques by Measurement Level and Testing Situation

Measurement Level	One-Sample Case	Two-Sample Case		k-Sample Case		Measures of Association
		Related Samples	Independent Samples	Related Samples	Independent Samples	
Nominal	Binominal χ^2 one-sample	McNemar	Fisher exact probability χ^2 two-sample	Cochran Q	χ^2 for k samples	Contingency Coefficient C Cramer's statistic Lambda
Ordinal	Kolmogorov-Smirnov one-sample test Runs test	Sign test Wilcoxon matched pairs	Median test Mann-Whitney U test Kolmogorov-Smirnov Wald-Wolfowitz	Friedman two-way ANOVA	Median extension Kruskal-Wallis one-way ANOVA	Spearman rank correlation Kendall *tau* Kendall partial rank coefficient Kendall W.
Interval and ratio	t test*	t test of differences*	t test*	Two-way ANOVA*	One-way ANOVA*	Pearson product-moment r* Partial correlation* Multiple correlation*

* Parametric tests; all others are nonparametric.

nature of the relationships among the variables. In this sense the analysis may be based on either dependence or independence assumptions. The dependence condition is found when one or more of the variables are criterion variables (*DVs*) and one or more are predictor variables (*IVs*). Multiple regression and discriminate analysis are popular examples of dependence techniques. With the independence condition the variables are interrelated without the assumption that some are predictors and others are criterion measures. Factor analysis, cluster analysis, and multidimensional scaling are examples of this set of procedures.

A second classification scheme is based on the measurement scale levels of nonmetric (for example, nominal scales) and metric (for example, interval scales). Finally, if criterion and predictor variables are used, the appropriate technique will depend upon the number of each variable type. A combination of these three considerations, with suggestions for the appropriate technique to use for each, is shown in Figure 13–6.

Multiple Regression. This is the best known and most widely used of the multivariate statistical methods. It is an extension of the bivariate least squares model presented earlier in the chapter. It assumes interval level data although there is a frequent use of dummy variables as predictors.[15] The generalized equation for multiple regression is:

$$Y = a + b_1 X_1 + b_2 X_2 + b_3 X_3 \ldots b_n X_n$$

where

a = The value of Y when all X values are zero.

b_i = The regression coefficient associated with each unit of X_i

The b values are stated either in raw score units (the actual X values) or as standardized scores (X values are restated in terms of their standard deviations). In either case the value of the regression coefficient states the amount that Y varies with each unit change of the associated X variable when the effects of all other X variables are being held constant. When the regression coefficients are in standardized terms they are called *beta weights* (β) and their values indicate the relative importance of the associated X values. For example, in an equation where $\beta_1 = 0.60$ and $\beta_2 = 0.20$ we would conclude that X_1 has three times the influence on Y as does X_2.

Multiple regression is used as a descriptive tool in three types of situations. First, it is used often to develop a self-weighting estimating equation by which to predict values for a criterion variable (*DV*) from the values for several predictor variables (*IVs*). Thus, we might try to predict company sales on the basis of new housing starts, new marriage rates, annual disposable income, and a time factor. Another prediction study might be a regression in which we

---

[15] A dummy variable is a binary 0—1 variable and is often used to introduce nominal dichotomies such as sex, race, and so on, as predictor variables.

Figure 13–6: Recommended Multivariate Techniques by Use Situation*

ANALYSIS OF DEPENDENCE

Situation	Variable	Number of Variables	Measurement Level	Technique
1	Dependent	1	Metric	Simple regression or ANOVA
	Independent	1	Metric	
2	Dependent	1	Metric	Multiple regression
	Independent	>1	Metric	
3	Dependent	1	Metric	1. Dummy variable multiple regression
	Independent	>1	Nonmetric	2. Multiple classification analysis (MCA)
				3. Automatic interaction detection (AID)
4	Dependent	1	Nonmetric	Discriminant Analysis
	Independent	>1	Metric	
5	Dependent	1	Nonmetric	MCA with 0-1 *DV*
	Independent	>1	Nonmetric	
6	Dependent	>1	Metric	Canonical analysis
	Independent	>1	Metric	
7	Dependent	>1	Metric	Multivariate ANOVA
	Independent	>1	Nonmetric	
8	Dependent	>1	Nonmetric	Convert to canonical
	Independent	>1	or Metric	analysis

ANALYSIS OF INDEPENDENCE

Situation	Number of Variables	Measurement Level	Grouping	Technique
1	Several	Metric	Variables	R-factor analysis
2	Several	Metric	Objects (e.g., people)	1. Q-factor analysis 2. Cluster analysis 3. Multidimensional scaling
3	Several	Nonmetric	Variables	1. Nonmetric factor analysis 2. Latent structure analysis
4	Several	Nonmetric	Objects	1. Nonmetric MDS 2. Latent class analysis 3. Nonmetric cluster analysis

* Thanks to my colleague J. Paul Peter for suggesting this organization scheme. Partially adapted from T. C. Kinnear and J. R. Taylor "Multivariate Methods in Marketing Research: A Further Attempt at Classification," *Journal of Marketing* (October 1971), p. 57.

estimate a student's academic performance in college from the variables of (1) rank in high school class, (2) SAT verbal scores, (3) SAT quantitative scores, and (4) a rating scale reflecting impressions from an interview.

A second descriptive application is to control for confounding variables so as better to evaluate the contribution of other variables. For example, we might wish to control the brand of a product, and the store in which it is bought, in order to study the effects of price as an indicator of product quality.[16] A third use of multiple regression as a descriptive tool is to test and explicate causal theories. In this approach, often referred to as *path analysis,* regression is used to describe an entire structure of linkages that have been advanced a priori from some causal theory.[17] In addition to being a descriptive tool, multiple regression is also used as an inference tool to test hypotheses and to estimate population values from simple data.

A Multiple Regression Illustration. Parker and Seguro applied multiple regression to a problem of company sales forecasting.[18] They sought to predict annual sales for a home furnishing manufacturer by using the following predictor variables:

X_1 = Marriages during the year
X_2 = Housing starts during the year
X_3 = Annual disposable personal income
X_4 = Time trend (first year = 1, second year = 2, etc.)

Using data for 24 years, they calculated the following estimating equation:

$$Y = 49.85 - 0.068X_1 + 0.036X_2 + 1.22X_3 - 19.54X_4$$

They tested the statistical significance of each regression coefficient, using a t test, and found each one significant. They also calculated an R^2 of 0.92 and a standard error of estimate of 11.9. The R^2 value indicates that the four IVs statistically accounted for 92 percent of the variation in annual company sales during the 24 year period. The standard error of estimate is a measure of the precision of the Y estimates. This value of ± 11.9 million dollars indicates that in two out of three times the equation estimates of company sales (which ranged from $93 million to $254 million) were within a ± 11.9 million of the true sales figure.

The negative regression coefficient for X_1 (number of marriages) indicated that sales varied inversely with the number of marriages—an illogical relationship. In an effort to improve the estimating equation they dropped the marriage variable and replaced it with last year's sales. The assumption was that a key element in predicting sales for this year is the level of sales last year. In addition, they decided to lag the relationship between sales and new housing starts. Their assumption was that there was a delay between housing starts and the resultant home furnishings sales effect and that this could better be reflected by correlating housing starts in year $t - 1$ with company sales in year t.

    [16] Benson Shapiro, "Price Reliance: Existence and Sources," *Journal of Marketing Research,* vol. 10 (August 1973), pp. 286–89.

    [17] For a discussion of path analysis see Fred Kerlinger and E. Pedhazer, *Multiple Regression in Behavioral Research* (New York: Holt Rinehart and Winston, 1973), chap. 11.

    [18] George G. C. Parker and Ediberto Segura, "How to Get a Better Forecast," *Harvard Business Review* (March–April 1971), pp. 99–109.

The new equation was:

$$Y = -33.51 + 0.373X_1 + 0.033X_2 + 0.672X_3 - 11.03X_4$$

where

X_1 = Previous year's company sales
X_2 = Last year's housing starts

The calculation of t test values indicated that all of the regression coefficients were statistically significant. The R^2 increased from 0.92 to 0.95, and the standard error of estimate declined from 11.9 to 9.7 million. Since the predictor variables are in original values rather than standardized scores it is not possible to state the relative importance of the four predictor variables. From the t test results it would appear that annual disposable income is the most important variable.

Regression Problems.   One difficulty with multiple regression is that of multicollinearity—the situation where some or all of the independent variables are very highly correlated. When such a condition exists the estimated regression coefficients can fluctuate widely from sample to sample, making it risky to use the coefficients as an indicator of the relative importance of predictor variables. Just how high can acceptable intercorrelations be between independent variables? There is no definitive answer but correlations at a 0.8 or greater level should be dealt with in one of two ways: (1) Choose one of the variables and delete the other or (2) create a new variable which is a composite of the highly intercorrelated variables and use this new variable in place of its components.

Another problem with regression is that users of this technique too often fail to cross-validate their equation with data beyond that which was used to calculate the equation originally. The most practical approach is for the researcher to set aside a portion of the data (say, one fourth to a third) and use only the remainder to compute the estimating equation. One then uses the equation on the set-aside data to calculate an R^2 for the held out data. This can then be compared to the original R^2 to determine how well the equation predicts beyond its data base.

Multiple Discriminant Analysis.   This technique is similar to multiple regression although there are several key differences. One such difference is that the criterion variable in discriminant analysis is a set of unordered categories (a nominal scale) rather than an interval scale. Hence, our task is to use other information to determine which classification a given case falls into rather than to determine how large it is.

While discriminant analysis often involves a dichotomous criterion variable, the technique can accommodate cases with more than two categories. When there are more than two criterion variables, a different discriminant function is needed for every pair of criterion groups; with regression analysis only one regression equation is needed. A third difference is that the objective in discriminant analysis is to minimize the misclassifications rather than minimizing the sum of the squares of deviations in the estimates of Y. Finally, in place of R^2 the goodness-of-fit of the functional relationship in discriminant analysis is measured by an index known as Mahalanobis' D^2. The larger the D^2, the greater the distance between criterion groups.

Discriminant analysis can be used in two ways. Probably the most frequent use is as a classification method. Thus, we might attempt to classify people into owners versus nonowners, heavy versus light users, different occupational groups, political categories, opinion positions, social class memberships, and many other unordered categories. For example, we might attempt to set up a model by which to predict good and bad credit risks. For discriminator variables we might use family income, marital status, number of credit cards, age of family head, and the like.

Discriminant analysis may also be used to analyze known groups to determine the relative influence of specific factors in determining into which group various cases fall. For example, we might have supervisor ratings which enable us to classify administrators as successful or unsuccessful on administrative performance. We might also be able to secure test results on these people concerning the three measures of Ability to Work with Others (X_1), Motivation for Administrative Work (X_2), and General Professional Skill (X_3). Suppose the discriminant equation is:

$$Y = 0.06X_1 + 0.45X_2 + 0.30X_3$$

Since a feature of discriminant analysis is that it uses standardized values for the discriminant variables, we can conclude from the coefficients that Ability to Work with Others is less important than the other two in classifying administrators as being successful or unsuccessful.[19]

Other Dependence Measures. Multiple classification analysis (MCA) is a form of multiple regression in which the predictor variables are nominally scaled while the criterion variable is metric.[20] Another dependence measure is automatic interaction detection (AID). A discussion and example of this technique is found in Chapter 12. A final dependence technique to be discussed here is canonical analysis. It also is an extension of regression analysis, in this case to predict simultaneously a *set* of criterion variables from their joint covariance with a set of predictor variables.[21]

Factor Analysis. Factor analysis is a general descriptor for a number of specific computational techniques. All of these techniques, however, have the

[19] Fred Kerlinger, *Foundations of Behavioral Research,* 2d ed. (New York: Holt Rinehart and Winston, 1973), p. 651.

[20] For details on MCA see F. M. Andrews, J. N. Morgan, J. A. Sonquist and L. Klein, *Multiple Classification Analysis,* 2d ed. (Ann Arbor, Mich.: Institute for Social Research, 1973).

[21] For details on canonical analysis see P. E. Green, M. H. Halbert, and P. J. Robinson, "Canonical Analysis: An Exposition and Illustrative Application," *Journal of Marketing Research,* vol. 3 (February 1966), pp. 32–39.

objective of reducing a large number of measures or tests to some smaller number by telling us which belong together and which seem to measure the same thing. The predictor-criterion relationship that we found in the dependence situation is replaced by a matrix of intercorrelations between a number of variables, none of which are viewed as being dependent upon the others. For example, we may have data on 100 employees in terms of scores on six attitude scale items. We would begin factor analysis by correlating each pair of scale items (an R type analysis) or each pair of individuals (a Q type analysis).

The second step in factor analysis is to construct a new set of variables on the basis of relationships in the correlation matrix. While this can be done in a number of ways, the most frequently used approach.is *principal component analysis.* By this method a set of variables is transformed into a new set of composite variables or principal components which are uncorrelated with each other. These are *factors.* This is done by finding the best linear combination of variables as far as accounting for the variance in the data as a whole. Such a combination makes up the first principal component and is the first factor. The second principal component is defined as the best linear combination of variables in terms of explaining the variance *not* accounted for by the first factor. In turn, there may be a third, fourth, and so on, components, each being the best linear combination of variables in terms of explaining the variance not accounted for by the previous factors. This process can continue until all of the variance is accounted for, but as a practical matter it is usually stopped after a small number of factors have been extracted. The output of a principal components analysis might look like the hypothetical data shown in the unrotated factors section of Table 13–7. (For the moment ignore the rotated factors section of the table.) The values in the table are correlation coefficients between the factor and the variables (0.7 is the r between variable A and factor I). These correlation coefficients are called *loadings.* Two other

Table 13–7: Factor Matrices

Variable	A Unrotated Factors			B Rotated Factors	
	I	II	h^2	I	II
A	0.7	−0.4	0.65	0.79	0.15
B	0.6	−0.5	0.61	0.75	0.03
C	0.6	−0.35	0.48	0.68	0.10
D	0.5	0.5	0.50	0.06	0.70
E	0.6	0.5	0.61	0.13	0.77
F	0.6	0.6	0.72	0.07	0.85
Eigenvalue	2.18	1.39			
Percent of variance	36.3	23.2			
Cumulative percent	36.3	59.5			

elements in Table 13–7 need explanation. Eigenvalues are the sum of the variances of the factor values (for factor I the eigenvalue is $0.7^2 + 0.6^2 + 0.6^2 + 0.5^2 + 0.6^2 + 0.6^2$). When divided by the number of variables it yields an estimate of the amount of total variance explained by the factor. For example, factor I accounts for 36 percent of the total variance. The column headed h^2 gives the *communalities* or estimates of the variance in each variable which is explained by the two factors. With variable A, for example, the communality is $0.7^2 + (-0.4)^2 = 0.65$, indicating that 65 percent of the variance in variable A is statistically explained in terms of factors I and II.

In this case the unrotated factor loadings are not very enlightening. What we would like to find is some pattern in which factor I would be heavily loaded (have a high r) on some variables and factor II on others. Such a condition would suggest rather "pure" constructs underlying each factor. We attempt to secure this less ambiguous condition between factors and variables by *rotation*. This procedure can be carried out by either orthogonal or oblique methods, but only the former will be illustrated here.

To understand the rotation concept consider that we are dealing only with simple two-dimensional rather than multidimensional space. The variables in Table 13–7 can be plotted in two-dimensional space as shown in Figure 13–7. Two axes cut this space, and we position the points relative to these axes. The location of these axes is arbitrary, and they represent only one of an infinite number of reference frames which could be used to reproduce the matrix. As long as we do not change the intersection point and keep the axes at right angles, when an orthogonal method is used, we can rotate them until we find a better solution or position for the reference axes. "Better" in this case means a matrix which makes the factors as pure as possible (load each variable with as few factors as possible and as many zeros or near zeros as possible). From the rotation shown in Figure 13–7 it can be seen that the solution is improved substantially. Using the rotated solution suggests that the six scales actually reflect only two underlying factors (see the rotated factors section of Table 13–7).

Interpreting Factors. The interpretation of factor loadings is largely subjective. It is at this point that factor analysis stops being sophisticated mathematics and becomes interpretive art. *There is no way to calculate the meanings of factors; they are what we see in them.* For this reason factor analysis is used largely for exploration. We can detect patternings of latent variables with the aim to discover new concepts and/or reduce data. Factor analysis is also used to test hypotheses, although this is a less well-developed use and more controversial than the exploration.

Other Independence Methods. Two other major independence methods are multidimensional scaling (MDS) and cluster analysis. MDS is discussed in Chapter 9. The objective of cluster analysis is "to separate objects into groups such that each object is more like other objects in its group

Figure 13–7: Orthogonal Factor Rotations

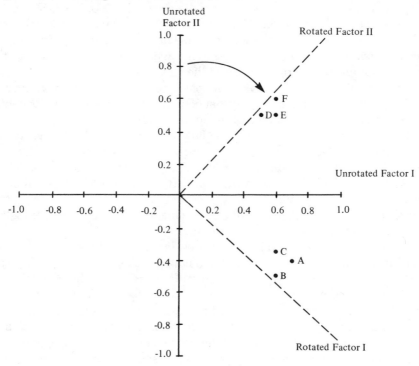

than like objects outside the group . . . its techniques are part of the field of numerical taxonomy."[22]

Multivariate Analysis Use Illustration. Pinches and Mingo provide an interesting example of the combination of factor analysis and multiple discriminant analysis.[23] Their objective was "to develop and test a factor analysis/multiple discriminant model for predicting industrial bond ratings." Organizations such as Moody's rate bonds as to their investment quality and score them in one of nine classifications from Aaa to C. In this study only bonds rated Aa, A, Baa, Ba, and B were used.

They chose as their sample all bonds rated B through Aa which were listed in the new issue section of Moody's *Bond Survey* from January 1, 1967, to December 31, 1968. The sample consisted of 180 firms; 132 were used for developing the model while 48 formed the set-aside cross-validation group.

They collected or calculated data on 35 different variables and factor-

[22] Paul E. Green and Donald S. Tull, *Research for Marketing Decisions,* 4th ed. (Englewood Cliffs, N.J.: Prentice-Hall, Inc., 1978), p. 480.

[23] George E. Pinches and Kent A. Mingo, "A Multivariate Analysis of Industrial Bond Ratings," *The Journal of Finance,* vol. 28 (March 1973), pp. 1–17.

Table 13–8: Factor Patterns for Industrial Firms Issuing Newly Rated Bonds in 1967–1968

	Financial Data			Factor Loading			
		1	2	3	4	5	6	7
	Total assets	-0.95						
	Net working capital	-0.66						
	Sales	-0.87						
(X₃)	Issue size	-0.81						
	Number of shares of common stock	-0.89						
	Total assets: Mean	-0.93						
	Long-term debt/total assets		-0.88					
	Long-term debt/net worth: Mean		-0.78					
(X₅)	Long-term debt/total assets: Mean		-0.77					
	Long-term debt/net worth		-0.91					
	Sales/net worth			-0.90				
	Sales/total assets			-0.95				
	Sales/total assets: Mean			-0.95				
	Net income/sales				0.61			
	Net income/net worth				0.60			
	Net income/total assets: Mean				0.81			
(X₆)	Net income/total assets				0.86			
	Net working capital/sales					0.76		
	Net worth/total assets					-0.71		
(X₂)	Price earnings ratio						0.55	
	Years of consecutive dividends						-0.60	
	Earnings per share						-0.57	
	Net income: Coefficient of variation						0.70	
	Net income/total assets: Coefficient of variation						0.57	
(X₄)	Net income + interest/interest: Mean							-0.58
	Long-term debt/total assets: Coefficient of variation							-0.71
	Net income + interest/interest: Coefficient of variation							-0.78
	Market value of common stock/long-term debt: Mean							-0.82

* Only variables with factor loadings of 0.55 or greater were reported.

analyzed them using the principal components solution with a varimax (orthogonal) rotating technique. Seven factor patterns were identified which accounted for 63 percent of the variation in the data matrix. These seven factors appear to be:

1. Size.
2. Financial leverage.
3. Long-term capital intensiveness.
4. Return on investment.
5. Short-term capital intensiveness.
6. Earnings stability.
7. Debt coverage stability.

The major loadings on these factors are shown in Table 13–8.

After some trials with various combinations the MDA model which performed best incorporated six variables:

X_1—Subordination.
X_2—Years of consecutive dividends.
X_3—Issue size.
X_4—Net income + interest/interest: Five year mean
X_5—Long-term debt/total assets: Five year mean
X_6—Net income/total assets

Using multiple discriminant analysis they were able to correctly predict the ratings of 69 percent of the bonds in the original sample and 60 percent of the bonds in the set-aside sample.

SUMMARY

There are two approaches to hypothesis testing—the *classical* or *sampling theory* and the *Bayesian*. With the sampling theory approach we establish a null hypothesis and then gather sample information with which to test the hypothesis. The Bayesian approach also employs sampling data but as an additional element of information by which to improve the decision maker's prior objective judgment based on other information.

A difference between two or more sets of data is statistically significant if it actually occurs in a population. In sampling, however, we define a result to be statistically significant if sample evidence indicates a difference so great that there is little chance that it could result from random sampling fluctuations.

Hypothesis testing can be viewed as a six-step procedure:

1. Establish a null hypothesis as well as the alternative hypothesis. It is a one-tailed test of significance if the alternative hypothesis states the direction of difference. If no direction of difference is given it is a two-tailed test.

2. Choose the statistical test on the basis of the assumption about the

population distribution and measurement level which underlay the test. The form of the data can also be a factor. In the light of these considerations we typically choose that test which we believe has the greatest power efficiency or ability to reduce decision errors.

    3.   Select the desired level of confidence. While $\alpha = 0.05$ is the most frequently used, many others are also used. The α is the significance level that we desire and is typically set in advance of the study. Alpha is the risk of rejecting a true null hypothesis and represents a decision error. The β or type II error is the decision error that results from our accepting a false null hypothesis. Normally we determine a level of acceptable α error, then seek to reduce the β error by increasing the size sample, shifting from a two-tailed to a one-tailed significance test, or both.

    4.   Compute the actual test value of the data.

    5.   Obtain the critical test value, usually by referring to a table for the appropriate type of distribution.

    6.   Make the decision by comparing the actual test value with the critical test value.

In this chapter we discuss a number of parametric and nonparametric significance tests which are applicable under various conditions. They are summarized in Figure 13–5. Also discussed are a number of multivariate methods; their application conditions are illustrated in Figure 13–6.

SUPPLEMENTAL READINGS

1.   Green, Paul E., and Tull, Donald S. *Research for Marketing Decisions.* 4th ed. Englewood Cliffs, N.J.: Prentice-Hall, Inc., 1978. Especially chaps. 9–14, which present topics such as regression, discriminant analysis, canonical correlation, factor analysis, and cluster analysis.

2.   Hays, William L., and Winkler, Robert L. *Statistics: Probability, Inference, and Decision.* 2d ed. New York, N.Y.: Holt, Rinehart and Winston, Inc., 1975. Chap. 12 is a good summary of nonparametric statistics.

3.   Huck, Schuyler W.; Cormier, William; and Bounds, William G. *Reading Statistics and Research.* New York, N.Y.: Harper and Row, 1974. A unique book which briefly explains the meanings of various statistical inference concepts and tests found in scholarly research journals. A book for the reader of research who is overwhelmed by the statistics in journal articles.

4.   Kerlinger, Fred N. *Foundations of Behavioral Research.* New York: Holt, Rinehart and Winston, Inc., 1973. Especially chaps. 13–16 on analysis of variance and chaps. 35–37 on multiple regression and factor analysis.

5.   Leege, David C., and Francis, Wayne L. *Political Research.* New York: Basic Books, Inc., Publishers, 1974. Lucid discussion of several multivariate techniques.

6.   Mosteller, Frederick, and Rourke, Robert E. K. *Sturdy Statistics.* Reading, Mass: Addison-Wesley Publishing Company, 1973. Excellent discussion on significance testing.

7. Siegel, Sidney. *Nonparametric Statistics for the Behavioral Sciences.* New York: McGraw-Hill Publishing Co., Inc., 1956. The classic book on nonparametric statistics.

DISCUSSION QUESTIONS

1. Distinguish between:
   a. Parametric and nonparametric test.
   b. Type I and Type II error.
   c. Null hypothesis and alternative hypothesis.
   d. Acceptance region and rejection region.
   e. F test and t test.
   f. One-tailed test and two-tailed test.
2. a. How can the probability of a Type I error be reduced? A Type II error?
   b. How does practical significance differ from statistical significance?
   c. Suppose you interview all members of the freshman and senior classes and find that 65 percent of the freshmen and 62 percent of the seniors favor a certain ecological proposal. Is this difference significant?
3. We contact a random sample of 36 graduates of Western University and learn that their starting salaries were $14,000 last year. We contact a random sample of 40 graduates from Eastern University and find that their average starting salary was $14,800. In each case the standard deviation of the sample was $1,000. Test the hypothesis that there is no difference between average salaries received by the graduates of these two schools.
4. A random sample of students are interviewed to determine if there is an association between class and attitude toward corporations. With the following results test the hypothesis that there is no difference among students on this attitude.

	Favorable	Neutral	Unfavorable
Freshmen	100	50	70
Sophomore	80	60	70
Junior	50	50	80
Senior	40	60	90

5. We obtain the following bivariate correlation matrix by correlating three variables X, Y, and Z.

	X	Y	Z
X	1.00	0.7	0.8
Y		1.0	0.7
Z			1.0

    a.   What is the meaning of r_{YZ}^2?
    b.   What is the meaning of $r_{XY.Z}^2$?
    c.   What is the meaning of $R_{X.YZ}^2$?

6.   You are interested in the effect that a public relations motion picture produced by the oil industry might have on people's attitudes. You set up an
experiment in which 16 subjects take an attitude pretest, see the film, and
take a posttest. You calculate the following attitude scores (higher score
indicates a more favorable attitude). Has the film had an effect?

Subject	Pretest	Posttest
1	4.0	4.4
2	2.6	2.5
3	6.9	7.3
4	1.9	1.5
5	3.1	4.2
6	5.1	5.1
7	6.6	7.0
8	5.9	6.3
9	5.5	6.7
10	4.6	4.7
11	6.2	6.9
12	1.7	1.5
13	3.6	5.2
14	4.6	5.7
15	5.6	5.9
16	4.3	4.5

7.   A coffee company is interested in whether there is a pattern of differences in
consumption of decaffeinated coffee. They choose a random sample of 90
families that use coffee, question them, and find the following results. Is
there a significant difference among age groups in the consumption of this
type of coffee?

Age of Family Head	Number of Interviews	Users of Decaffeinated Coffee
65+	20	10
45–64	20	8
30–44	25	7
Under 30	25	6

8.   The management of the One-Koat Paint Company has developed a new
type of porch paint which they hope will be the most durable on the market.
They test their product against the two leading competing products through
the use of a machine that scrubs until it wears through the coating. They run
five trials with each product and secure the following results (in thousands
of scrubs).

Trial	One-Koat	Competitor A	Competitor B
1 37		34	24
2 30		19	25
3 34		22	23
4 28		31	20
5 29		27	20

Test the null hypothesis that there is no difference among the means of these products.

9. In problem 8 assume now that the five trials were made with five different types of primer. Perform a two-way ANOVA.

10. We ask a random sample of 300 persons to rate Corporation A on an 11-point scale as to its contribution to the welfare of the community in which it is headquartered. A second group of 200 persons rated Corporation A on the same scale, with the following results. Assuming $\alpha = 0.05$, is there a significant difference?

Scale Value	Group 1	Group 2
+5	35%	23%
+4	22	17
+3	17	19
+2	9	9
+1	7	11
0	4	7
−1	0	4
−2	1	1
−3	1	3
−4	0	1
−5	4	5
$n =$	300	200

11. What type of multivariate methods do you recommend in each of the following and why?
    a. You want to develop an estimating equation which will be used to predict which applicants will come to your university as students.
    b. You would like to predict family income using such variables as education, stage in family life cycle, and so forth.
    c. You wish to estimate standard labor costs for manufacturing a new dress design.
    d. You have been studying a group of successful salespeople. They have taken a number of psychological tests. You desire to bring meaning out of these test results.
    e. You would like to develop an image analysis of ten graduate schools of business.

Chapter 14

Research Communications

COMMUNICATION is critical throughout the research process. In early chapters we discussed communication problems between the client and the researcher. At that stage of the process the focus was on problem definition and the drafting of a research proposal. Then in Chapter 10 we discussed interviewer-respondent communication. Now at the end of the research process we again consider communication between researcher and clients and other audiences. On this occasion there often are two major tasks. First is the writing of a formal report that sets forth the findings, conclusions, procedures, and other details of the study. A second task may be to make an oral presentation to key persons who wish to be briefed on the research and its results. These two reporting topics are the subject of this chapter.

It may seem unscientific, and even unfair, but the intrinsic value of a study can be easily overshadowed by a poor report or presentation. Research technicians may appreciate the brilliance of a study that is badly reported, but most of us will be heavily influenced by the communication quality of the reporting. This fact should prompt researchers to special efforts to communicate clearly and fully.

THE WRITTEN RESEARCH REPORT

Written reports may be classified as *informational* or *research* reports. The former presents factual information with limited commentary, analysis, conclusions, or recommendations. The research report contains findings, analysis of these findings, interpretations, conclusions, and sometimes recommendations. Research reporting differs from writing management reports in another way. As the researcher you are clearly the expert on the topic. You know the specifics in a way that no one else can. Your report is an authoritative one-way communication. This condition imposes a special obligation for you to maintain objectivity and a nonpersuasive posture. Even if your findings point to a given course of action, for example, show extra restraint in your advocacy of particular actions.

Reports may also be defined in terms of their degree of formality and design. The formal report tends to be long and follows a well-defined format. This contrasts to the more informal report types which may be classed as "short reports."

Short Reports

Short reports are appropriate for studies in which the problem is well-defined, of limited scope, requires only modest effort, and for which methodologies are simple and straightforward. Most information reports and progress and interim reports are of this sort. For example, you may wish to write up an investigation into cost of living changes that is needed for upcoming labor negotiations. Or you might report on a preliminary look into the feasibility of filing dumping charges against a foreign competitor.

Short reports usually are five pages or less but may exceed ten pages. They may or may not have section headings but should have liberal margins and short paragraphs. At the beginning of the report there should be a brief statement on the authorization of the study, the problem examined, and its breadth and depth. Next may be the conclusions and recommendations, followed by the findings that support the conclusions.

The letter report is one form of a short report. It is often used when there is a single point to investigate. Its tone tends to be informal. The format should follow that found in any good business letter and should normally not exceed four pages. A letter report is often written in personal style ("we, you") although this depends on the situation.

Memorandum reports are another variety and follow the *From, To,* and *Subject* format. There is little uniformity in these reports but the following suggestions may be helpful:

1. Tell the readers why you are writing this report; often it is in response to their request.
2. If the memo is in response to a request for information, remind the readers of the exact point raised, answer it, and then follow with any necessary details.

3. Write in news style, emphasizing brevity and directness.
4. If time permits, write it today and leave it for review tomorrow before sending it.
5. Attach detailed materials as an appendix where needed.

Long Reports

Long reports are often divided into two types, the *technical* or *base* report and the *popular* report. Which of these two to use depends chiefly on the audience and the researcher's objectives. While some researchers try to write a single report that incorporates features of both, this complicates the communication task.

The Technical Report. There should be a technical report for most research studies. It is the basic vehicle that includes full study documentation and detail. It will be the record which normally survives the working papers, computer printouts, and original documents. Partly it is a matter of professionalism to provide a complete report of your study. There may also be challenges that occur later when original documents are no longer at hand. This occurs most often when the topic involves controversy or possible litigation.

While completeness is the goal in a technical report, you must guard against including nonessential material. One good guideline is that sufficient information of a procedural nature should be included to enable others to replicate the study. This should include sources of data, research procedures, sampling design, data gathering instruments, index construction, data analysis methods, and other technical matters. Much of this information may be put in an appendix.

A technical report should also include a full presentation and exploration of significant data. Conclusions and recommendations should be presented and clearly related to specific findings. Technical jargon should be minimized but defined when used. There can be brief references to other research, theories, and techniques. While you may expect the reader to be familiar with these references it is useful to include some short explanations, perhaps as footnotes or endnotes.

In some cases the client may not have a technical research background and be almost totally interested in results rather than methodology. The major communication medium in this case will be the popular report. It may still be helpful to have a basic report in case the client may later wish to have a technical appraisal made of the study.

Popular Report. The fact that the popular report is designed for a nontechnical audience presents the researcher with some special communication problems. Readers are less concerned with methodological details but more interested in learning quickly the major findings and conclusions. They are interested in applying the findings to decisions. Sometimes the report is developed for a single manager and needs to be written with that person's individual characteristics and needs in mind.

The style of the popular report should encourage rapid reading, quick comprehension of major findings, and prompt understanding of the implications and conclusions. While the report tone is journalistic it must still be accurate. More headlines and underlining for emphasis will be used; pictures and graphs will often replace tables. Sentences and paragraphs should be short and direct. There should be liberal use of white space and wide margins. It may even be desirable to put a single finding on each page for accent reasons. There may also be a theme running through the report and even graphic or animated characters designed to humanize the presentation. The popular report is usually shorter than the basic report and frequently follows the psychological format.

RESEARCH REPORT FORMAT

There is no one best format for all long reports. Three arrangements are typically found:

1. *Logical.* In this format the introductory information covering the purpose of the study, methodology, and limitations is followed by the findings. The findings are analyzed and then followed by the conclusions and recommendations.
2. *Psychological.* This is largely an inversion of the logical order. The conclusions and recommendations are presented immediately after the introduction, with the findings coming later. This is probably the most widely used format, especially in popular reports. With this arrangement readers are quickly exposed to the most critical information—the conclusions and recommendations. Then if they wish to go further they may read on into the findings which support the conclusions already given.
3. *Chronological.* The organization of a report along the time sequence dimension is usually the least desirable and least used of the three formats. It tends to bury important elements that should be drawn together and directly related. This format is reserved to those situations where the time sequence relationship is clearly the critical factor in the results.

Report Format Details

A long report usually has clearly defined parts. While some may be dropped, others added, and their order varied from one situation to another, the following outline is often used in student research reports. It is in the *logical* format typical of technical reports.

Report Outline

Prefatory
Pages
{
A. Title page
B. Letters of transmittal and authorization
C. Tables of contents, charts, and illustrations
D. Synopsis

Body
of
Report
{
E. Introduction
F. Findings
G. Summary and conclusions
H. Recommendations

Appended
Sections
{
I. Appendix
J. Bibliography

Title Page.   The title page should normally include four items: the title of the report, the date, for whom prepared, and by whom prepared. A satisfactory title for a research report should probably not exceed 15 words and should include the following three elements: (1) the variables included in the study, (2) the type of relationship between the variables, and (3) the population to which the results may be applied.[1]

Redundancies such as, "A Report of . . . , A Discussion of . . . ," merely add length to the titles but little else of value. Single word titles are also generally of little value. Several acceptable ways of stating report titles are:

Descriptive study: The Five Year Demand Outlook for Plastic
                          Pipe in the United States
Correlational study: The Relationship between the Value of the
                          Dollar in World Markets and Relative National
                          Inflation Rates
Causal study: The Effect of Various Motivation Methods
                          on Worker Attitudes among Textile Workers

Table of Contents.   A table of contents is needed if the report is long or is divided into a number of selections. As a rough guide, any report of several sections that total more than ten pages should probably have a table of contents. If there are many tables, charts, or other exhibits they should also be listed after the table of contents in a table of illustrations.

Letters.   For many intraorganizational projects it is not necessary to have a letter of transmittal. Such a letter should be included if the study is for a specific client (the company president or some outside organization) and/or the relationship between the parties is formal. Such a letter should contain some reference to the authorization for the project and any specific instruc-

---

[1] Paul E. Resta, *The Research Report* (New York: American Book Company, 1972), p. 5.

tions or limitations that were placed on the study. The letter should also state the purpose of the study and its general scope.

A letter of authorization is sometimes included just ahead of the transmittal letter. The authorization letter is seldom used for studies which are carried out within an organization. However, for public reports for external organizations (for example, the federal government) it is common to include such a letter to show the authority and the charge that was given.

Synopsis. The synopsis in a research report can serve in one of two ways. It may be a "report in miniature" in which case it may, but need not be, in the same organizational format as the body of the report. The synopsis should be a concise summary of the major findings and conclusions and should probably not exceed one or two pages, depending on the total report length. The second version of a synopsis represents little more than a prose table of contents indicating the major topics in the study or the major actions taken. Such a presentation, often called an *abstract,* is found most often in engineering reports. Abstracts are usually restricted to 150 words or less.

In either case the synopsis should be written after the rest of the report has been finished. It should not mention any new information and normally should have no graphics in it. In writing the synopsis you should expect to have a high density of significant words since the essence of synopses is that they are concise summaries.

Introduction. This section of the report normally contains several major subsections. While patterns may vary, one common model consists of three parts—the *problem* statement, the *methods* statement, and the *limitations* statement.

Problem. The statement of the problem normally comes first and may contain three parts—the background, the problem statement itself, and any hypotheses. When discussing the background of the problem, researchers should introduce the major variables and relate them to previous research and theory when appropriate. In applied research studies the background statements normally relate the study to a management problem and/or organizational situation which has led to the study. If some of the relevant variables will not be studied this fact should also be mentioned.

The background discussion should lead into a statement of the specific problem which the research is addressing. Often this might best be discussed in terms of a research question and its associated investigative questions. Concepts such as "investigative questions" may confuse the reader unless they are defined. In the problem statement it is important to state clearly the variables of concern, the type of relationship between them, and the target group which is being studied. Operational definitions of critical variables should also be included. In correlational or causal studies you might also include hypotheses statements, but these would be omitted in descriptive studies.

Methods. In this section you should cover at least the following five items. First, explicitly define the target population which is being studied and the sampling methods used, if any. If explanations are called for, and they usually are, make them brief. A second part of the methods section should cover the research design used and the presentation of the rationale for using what you have chosen. Then briefly discuss the materials and instruments. Copies of such materials, as well as any detailed discussion of them, should be placed in an appendix to the report. The fourth portion of the methods section should deal with the specific data collection methods. Again, if there are detailed materials, such as field worker instructions, place them in the appendix. Finally, there should be a summary discussion of the data analysis methods. The identification of any statistical tests, canned computer programs, and the like, should be made, but relegate details to the appendix.

Limitations. The topic of study limitations tends often to be handled in an ambivalent fashion. Many wish to ignore the matter, feeling that any pointing out of limitations detracts from the impact of their study. Such an attitude is unprofessional and borders on the unethical. Others seem to adopt a masochistic approach of "putting down" their own study in great detail. Balance is called for; this section should not be an uncontrolled listing of faults but a thoughtful presentation of significant definitional, methodological, or implementational problems. An even-handed treatment is one of the hallmarks of an honest and competent investigator. All research studies have their limitations, and the sincere investigator recognizes that readers need aid in judging the validity of research studies.

Some authorities on research reporting recommend that statements of limitations should be placed along with the discussion of findings and conclusions. In some cases this may be better, but it is not common practice in business research.

Findings. This is normally the longest section of the report. It should be an organized presentation of results and not a clutter of prose, charts, and tables. The objective here is an exposition of the data rather than drawing interpretations or conclusions. When quantitative data can be presented it should be done in as simple a way as possible. This almost always means simple charts and tables, not complex ones.

The data need not include all that you have collected. However, you should show that which is unfavorable to your hypotheses as well as that which supports them. The criterion for inclusion is "Is this material important to the reader's understanding of the problem and the findings?"

It is often useful to present findings in numbered paragraphs or to present one finding per page with the quantitative data supporting the finding presented in a small table or chart on the same page. (See Figure 14–1). While this practice adds to the bulk of the report, it presents data in a convenient way for the reader.

Figure 14-1: Example of a Findings Page in a Commercial Bank Market Study

Findings: 1. In this city *commercial banks are not the preferred savings medium.* Banks are in a weak third place behind Savings and Loans Associations and government bonds.

2. Customers of the First National Bank have a *somewhat more favorable attitude towards bank savings,* and less of a preference for government bonds.

Question: Suppose that you have just received an extra $1,000 and have decided to save it. Which of the savings methods listed would be your preferred way to save it?

Savings Method	Total Replies	First National Customers	Other Bank Customers
Government bonds	24%	20%	29%
Savings and loan	43	45	42
Bank	13	18	8
Credit union	9	7	11
Stock	7	8	5
Other	4	2	5
Total	100%	100%	100%
	n = 216	105	111

Summary and Conclusions. The summary is a brief restatement of the essential findings (facts). Sectional summaries may be used if there are a substantial number of specific findings, especially when they cover a variety of topics. These may then be combined into an overall summary. In simple descriptive research a summary of findings may complete the report, as conclusions and recommendations may not be required.

Findings state facts while conclusions represent inferences (inductions or deductions) drawn from the findings. These inferences, of course, are subject to human frailty and may be wrong; even worse, the writer is sometimes reluctant to make conclusions and leaves the task to the reader. If you do this, it is an abdication of research responsibilities. Readers often make their own inferences and challenge yours, but as the researcher you are the one person best informed on all of the factors of the study which critically influence both findings and conclusions.

Conclusions may be presented in some tabulated format for easy reading and reference. Summary findings may be subordinated under the related conclusion statements. All of these may be numbered and coded in a way to refer the reader to related pages or tables in the findings sections.

Recommendations. These are usually a limited number of the writer's opinions on suggested future actions. The nature of these actions depends on the study. If it is academic research the recommendations are likely to be for further study to test, deepen, or broaden understanding in the subject area. In applied research for decision making the recommendations will usually be for managerial actions rather than research actions. In this instance the writer may offer several alternative actions but probably should express a preference among them. Often the manager-client prefers no recommendations from the researcher. This is likely to occur when the research results are only one of the inputs on which the action decision rests.

Appendix. Here should be included complex tables, statistical tests, supporting documents, copies of the forms used, detailed descriptions of the methodology, instructions to field workers, and any other evidence that may be important as backup detail for the research report. The reader who wishes to learn about the technical details of the study and/or look at the more detailed breakdowns of the statistics will usually want a complete appendix.

Bibliography. There should be a bibliography section if the study makes heavy use of secondary research sources. For specific references use footnotes or endnotes placed at the end of each major section rather than referring to the bibliography listing. Proper bibliographic formats are illustrated by the references at the end of this chapter.

Popular Report Format

A popular report is usually presented in a psychological order, but the differences between it and the technical report are much deeper than mere sequence. As pointed out earlier, the detail, depth, writing style, and communication forms also differ. A typical outline of a popular report might be as follows:

Popular Report Format

1. Title Page. This should indicate the subject, date of the report, for whom prepared, and by whom prepared.

2. Table of Contents. Needed if the report is more than a few pages long.

3. Objectives of the Study. A brief summary that explains the factors that brought about the study, including any hypotheses to be tested or research questions to be answered.

4. Methodology. A brief nontechnical statement of the methods used, the type of sample and its size, the limitations of the study and its methods, and something of the manner in which the study was carried out. In all cases these should be relatively nontechnical in nature. Any supporting data should go into an appendix.

5. Conclusions and Recommendations. Highlights of the major findings are presented here in summary form. If recommendations or implications are called for they should also be placed here.

6. Findings. This should be a simplified presentation of the basic factual data found in the study. Statistical data should be presented in charts or simple tables. Each graph or table should present only one or a few basic points. Commentary on the specific findings and their relationships should also be briefly presented near the graphic. Presentation density (the amount of material per page) should be low. Often it is desirable to allow one page per single graph or table with its attendant commentary.

7. *Appendix.* The size of the appendix should be much smaller than in the technical report but should include a copy of the measuring instrument, technical information on the sampling design, reference materials, detailed statistical tables, and the like.

Other Formats

An organization may have its own special format for reporting research. This is often the case when the results of the research are submitted to a professional journal. It is important to determine in advance whether the publication does have specific format requirements. For example, the *Journal of Applied Psychology* publishes the results of many research studies carried out in businesses and other organizations. From a perusal of some copies of this journal it would appear that the editors encourage a format along the following lines:

1. *Introduction.* A statement of the nature of the problem studied and a brief discussion of previous studies that are pertinent to the development of the specific question or hypothesis to be tested.

2. *Method.* A brief statement of what was done, where it was done, and how it was done. Included is a statement of the specific techniques and tools used.

3. *Results.* A combined tabular or graphic presentation of salient findings with a discussion of these findings. The discussion is both a statement of the relationships found and a comparison of these findings with the hypotheses or questions originally posed.

4. *Conclusion.* A very brief recapitulation of the results and sometimes some comments about broader implications of the findings.

Regardless of the type of report or the format followed, however, the problems of writing tend to be the same.

WRITING THE REPORT

Many investigators give inadequate attention to the reporting of their findings and conclusions. This is unfortunate because a well-presented study often impresses the client more than another study which may have greater scientific quality but a weaker presentation.

Report writing skill is especially valuable to the junior executive or management trainee who aspires to rise in the organization. Reporting skill may be overrated, but the executive who can write a good report may find career prospects enhanced thereby.

Prewriting Considerations

There are a few general considerations useful to us before beginning to write. We should ask again, "What is the purpose of this report?" Writing our reply to this question helps assure that we have the problem clearly in mind.

A second prewriting question is "Who will read the report?" This question suggests that we must give some thought to the needs, temperament, and biases of the audience. We should not distort the facts to meet these needs and biases, but a skillful writer considers these factors in developing the presentation. Knowing who reads the report may also suggest its appropriate length. Generally the higher the report destination in an organization, the shorter it should be; the decision on how much to write is related to how much the client is willing to read.

Another important reader consideration is the "ignorance distance"—the gap in knowledge on the subject between the reader and the writer. The greater the ignorance distance, the more difficult it is to convey the full findings meaningfully and concisely.

A third prewriting question is "What are the circumstances and limitations under which we write?" Is the nature of our subject highly technical? Do we need statistics? Charts? What is the importance of our topic? An important subject justifies more effort than a minor one. What should be the scope of our report? How much time is available? Deadlines often impose limitations upon the type of report that can be written.

A final prewriting question is "How will the report be used?" We must try to visualize the reader using the report. Will it be read by more than one reader? If so, how many copies should be made? How can the report be made more convenient to use? What is the "direction of travel?" How much attention must be given to getting the attention and interest of the reader?

The Outline.   Once the researcher has made the first analysis of the data, drawn tentative conclusions, and performed statistical significance tests, it is time to develop a writing outline. One widely used outlining system employs the following organization structure:

1.   MAJOR TOPIC HEADING
   A.   Major subtopic heading
      1.   Subtopic
         a.   Minor subtopic
            (1)   Further detail
               (a)   Even further detail

Two styles of outlining are widely used—the topic outline and the sentence outline. In the topic form a key word or two is put down; the assumption is that the writer knows and will later remember the nature of the argument represented by that point. It is also used when the outliner knows that a given point should be covered but is not yet sure how to do it.

The sentence outline expresses the essential thoughts that are associated with the specific topic. This approach leaves less development work for later writing, other than elaborations and explanations which may improve report readability. It has the obvious advantages of pushing the writer now to make the decisions on what to include and how to say it. It guards against later forgetting certain specific points that one wanted to make. It is probably the best outlining style for the inexperienced researcher because it breaks the writing job into its two major components—what to say, and how to say it. An example which illustrates the type of detail found with each of these outlining formats is:

Topic Outline	*Sentence Outline*
I. Demand	I. Demand for refrigerators
A. How measured	A. Measured in terms of factory shipments as reported to the U.S. Department of Commerce
1. Voluntary error	1. Error is introduced into year-to-year comparisons because reporting is voluntary.
2. Shipping error	2. A second factor is variations from month to month because of shipping and invoicing patterns.
a. Monthly variance	a. Variations up to 30 percent in 198X depending upon whether shipments were measured by actual shipment date or invoice date.

Presentation Considerations

Well-written reports are not as common as one might think, but help exists for those who wish to improve their writing skills. There are many excellent manuals on report writing, and every serious researcher should have one. The general message in such manuals is that reports should be physically inviting, easy to read, and match the comprehension abilities of the designated audience. Some key elements of these three considerations will be summarized here.

Physical Presentation. One frequent problem is poor report appearance. Duplicated reports may be difficult to read because of poor reproduction. The organization of the report (or lack of it) may suggest a slapdash approach. Student reports, in particular, suffer from dirty typewriter type, typing print that is barely legible (old ribbon), or very smudgy (new ribbon). Students writing team reports often use several typewriters with different type faces, and this contributes to an amateurish appearance.

Incorrect spelling and poor punctuation will also destroy a report's good impression. Indeed, probably no single element detracts more from a report's quality image than spelling errors. It is often apparent to the reader that many of these are simple typographic mistakes, suggesting careless report preparation. *There is no substitute for very careful proofreading,* preferably by several people.

Overcrowding of text represents a third major appearance problem. Readers need the visual relief provided by ample white space. We define "ample" as inch of white space at the top, bottom, and right-hand margins. On the left side the margin should be at least one and one fourth inches to provide room for binding or punched holes. Even greater margins will often improve report appearance and highlight key points or sections. Overcrowding also occurs when the report contains page after page of large blocks of unbroken text. This produces a bad psychological effect on readers through its formidable appearance. The problem of overcrowded text may be overcome if writers will:

1. Use shorter paragraphs. As a rough guide, any paragraph longer than half page should be suspect. Remember that a paragraph should represent a distinct thought. It is usually a group of sentences but may be only a single sentence.
2. Indent parts of text that represent listings, long quotations, or examples.
3. Use headings and subheadings to divide the report and its major sections into homogeneous topical parts.
4. Use vertical listings of points (such as this list).

Inadequate labeling is a fourth physical presentation problem. Each graph or table should contain enough information to be self-explanatory without reference to the text. Text headings and subheadings also help with the labeling problem. They function as signposts for the audience, telling them the organization of the report and indicating the progress of discussion. They also help readers to skim the material and to return easily to particular sections of the report.

Readability. Sensitive and skillful writers must consider the reading ability of report recipients if they expect to secure high readership. We can achieve high readership more easily if the topic interests the readers and is in their field of expertise. In addition, we can show the usefulness of the report by pointing out how it might help the readers. We can also humanize the writing style when appropriate to the topic and occasion. Finally, we can write at a difficulty level which is appropriate to the recipients' reading abilities. To test our writing for difficulty level we use one of the standard readability indexes.

Gunning Fog Index. Research on the readability of prose has led to the development of measuring formulas by which to estimate the reading difficulty of prose material. One such estimating system is the Gunning Fog Index. Gunning maintains that the reading difficulty of a piece of prose can be measured by (1) the average length of sentence and (2) the percent of words of three syllables or more per 100 words of text. He suggests the following procedure for testing readability levels:

The Fog Index

1. Find the average number of words per sentence. Use a sample at least 100 words long. Divide total number of words by number of sentences. This gives you average sentence length.
2. Count the number of words of three syllables or more per 100 words. Don't count (*a*) words that are capitalized; (*b*) combinations of short easy words—like "bookkeeper," "butterfly"; (*c*) verbs that are made three syllables by adding "ed" or "es"—like "created" or "trespasses."
3. Add the two factors above and multiply by 0.4. This will give you the Fog Index. It corresponds roughly with the number of years of schooling a person would require to read a passage with ease and understanding. (The Fog Index of this entire passage is 6.7.)[2]

Advocates of readability measurement do not claim that all written material should be at the simplest level possible. They argue only that the level should be appropriate for the audience. They point out that comic books score about six on the Gunning scale (that is, a person with a sixth-grade education should be able to read that material). *Time* usually scores about the 10 level, while the *Atlantic Monthly* is reported to score at 11 or 12. Material that scores much above 12 becomes difficult for the general public to read comfortably.

Such measures obviously give only a rough approximation of the true readability of a report. We should not try to write by formula alone, nor should we rely only on Fog Index calculations. The use of a readability measurement can help in matching a report to its audience, but good writing calls for a variety of other skills to assure reader comprehension.

Comprehensibility. Writing is more than physical appearance and readability formulas. It is an art whose form varies with the writing objective. Research writing is designed to convey information of a precise nature. It should contain none of the multiple meanings and elegant allusions which are prized in fiction or poetry. As research writers the more carefully we choose our terms and fit them together, the plainer is the discourse and the more effective it is for research communication. This is not to say that the writing should be dull; rather, it should be without frills. With plain discourse it is easier to avoid ambiguity. Care should also be taken to choose the right words—words that convey thoughts accurately, clearly, and efficiently. There is a special problem when concepts and constructs are used and not clearly defined, either operationally or descriptively.

---

[2] Robert Gunning, "How to Improve Your Writing," reprinted with permission from the June 1952 issue of *Factory,* A Morgan-Grampian publication, page 132.

At another level of meaning the problem is in terms of how words and sentences are related. Misplaced modifiers run rampant in carelessly written reports. Subordinate ideas are mixed with major ideas in such a way as to make the mass confusing to readers. In this case they must sort out what is important and what is secondary when this should have been done for them by the writer.

Finally, there is the matter of "pace." Rathbone defines this as:

". . . the rate at which the printed page presents information to the reader. . . . The proper pace in technical writing is one that enables the reader to keep his mind working just a fraction of a second behind his eye as he reads along. It logically would be slow when the information is complex or difficult to understand; fast when the information is straightforward and familiar. If the reader's mind lags behind his eye, the pace is too rapid; if his mind wanders ahead of his eye (or wants to) the pace is too slow.[3]

If the text is overcrowded with concepts there is too much information per sentence. By contrast, sparse writing has too few significant ideas per sentence.

Writers use a variety of methods to adjust the pace of their writings. Many of these have already been mentioned but their importance bears repeating here for emphasis:

1. Use ample white space and wide margins to create a positive psychological effect on the reader.
2. Break large units of text into smaller units with headings to show organization of the topics.
3. Relieve difficult text with visual aids when possible.
4. Emphasize important material and deemphasize secondary material through sentence construction and through judicious use of italicizing, underlining, capitalization, and parentheses.
5. Choose words carefully, opting for the known and the short rather than the unknown and long. Graduate students, in particular, seem to revel in using jargon, pompous constructions, and long or arcane words. Naturally, there are times when technical terms are appropriate. It is also true that scientists can communicate efficiently with jargon, but in most applied business research the audiences are not scientifically trained and need more help than many writers appear to want to supply.
6. Repeat and summarize critical and difficult points and ideas to assure that readers have time to absorb them.
7. Make strategic use of "service words." Rathbone identifies these words as those which "do not represent objects or ideas, but show relationship. Transitional words, such as the conjunctions, are service words. So are

---

[3] Robert R. Rathbone, *Communicating Technical Information* (Reading, Mass.: Addison-Wesley Publishing Company, © 1966), p. 64. Reprinted with permission.

introductory phrases such as 'on the other hand,' 'in summary,' and 'in contrast.' "[4]

Presentation of Statistics.[5]   The presentation of statistics in research reports is a special challenge to writers. Four basic ways to present such data are (1) include them in a text paragraph, (2) pull them out of the paragraph and place in semitabular form, (3) put in tables, or (4) express graphically.

Text Presentation.   This is probably the most common approach, especially when there are only a few statistics used as simple comparisons. In this way the writer can direct the reader's attention to certain numbers or comparisons or can place an emphasis on specific points. On the other hand, statistical data too often are submerged in the body of text, requiring the reader to scan the entire paragraph to get the meaning of the figures. For example, the following material, while including only a few simple comparisons, becomes more complicated when we combine text with statistics.

> A comparison of the three major competing firms in our industry show that Ajax Ltd. has the best sales growth record over the five years 1973–1977. They averaged an annual sales growth, in constant dollars, of 8.3 percent as compared to a 4.7 percent sales increase for the Beta Corp. Cotter Co. was third with a 1.6 percent sales increase. Ajax also turned in the best average return on investment among the three companies for the same time period. The average annual ROI for Ajax was 19.6 percent as compared to 12.1 percent for Beta and 8.5 percent for Cotter Co.

Semitabular Presentation.   When there are only a few simple figures in a discussion they may be taken out of the text and set up in a simple listing. This method makes reading and understanding quantitative comparison much easier than when the statistics are imbedded in the text. An example of semitabular presentation is shown in the accompanying table.

A comparison of the three major competitors over the five year period, 1973 through 1978, indicates that Ajax Ltd. performed better than the other two companies, both on sales growth and ROI. Beta Corp. had the second best performance on both scores.

	Average Annual Sales Growth (constant dollars)	Average Annual Return on Investment
Ajax Ltd.	+9.3%	+19.6%
Beta Corp.	+4.7	+12.1
Cotter Co.	+1.6	+ 8.5

---

[4] Ibid., p. 72.

[5] The material in this section draws heavily on chaps. 3 through 6 of Frederick E. Croxton, Dudley J. Cowden, and Sidney Klein, *Applied General Statistics,* 3d ed. (Englewood Cliffs, N.J., Prentice-Hall, Inc., 1967).

Tabular Presentation. Tables are generally superior to text as a way to present statistics, although they are often accompanied by text comments directing reader attention to important figures. Tables facilitate quantitative comparisons and provide a concise, efficient way to present numerical data.

Tables may be classified as (1) general or reference and (2) summary or text. General tables tend to be large, complex, and detailed. They serve as the general repository for the statistical findings of the study and normally are in the appendix of the report.

Summary tables are usually smaller in size and contain only a few key pieces of data. The data which are included are closely related to a specific finding. To make these tables inviting to the reader (who often tends to skip them) the table designer should omit unimportant details and collapse multiple classifications into only those few which are clearly relevant. Averages, percentages, indexes, and other computed measures should often be substituted for the data in original units.

Any table should contain sufficient information for the reader fully to understand its contents. The *title* should explain the subject of the table, how the data are classified, the time period, and other relevant coverage statements. A *subtitle* is sometimes included under the title to explain something about the table; most often this is a statement of the measurement units in which the data are expressed. The contents of the *columns* should be clearly identified by the *column heads,* and the contents of the *stub* should do the same for the rows. The *body* of the table contains the data, while the *footnotes* contain any needed explanations. Footnotes should be identified by letters or symbols such as asterisks, rather than by numbers, in order to avoid confusion with data values. Finally, there should be a *source note* if the data do not come from your original research. Table 14–1 illustrates the various parts of a table.

Table 14–1: U.S. Production of Shoes and Slippers, by Class, 1965 and 1975 (millions of pairs)* } **Title**

	Class	*1965*	*1975* } **Column Heads**
Stub	Total	626.7	433.7
	Footwear, except slippers	536.0	365.2
	Mens'	118.2	104.8
	Youths' and boys'	25.6	17.7
	Womens'	280.0	173.5
	Misses'	36.5	15.2 (**Body**)
	Childrens'	33.5	17.2
	Infants' and babies	32.5	21.9
	Athletic shoes	7.0	11.4
	Other footwear	2.8	3.5
	Slippers	90.7	68.5

Footnote { * Excludes Alaska and excludes rubber footwear.
Source Note { Source: U.S. Bureau of Census, *Current Industrial Reports,* M31A.

Graphic Presentation. Compared to a table, graphs can show only a few pieces of information. They also show only approximate values, and normally they take more time and effort to construct than do tables. Their great advantage, however, is that they can more easily convey general quantitative values and comparisons than can tables. In addition, readers are more likely to read graphs than tables.

There are many graphic forms, but only curves or line diagrams and bar charts will be discussed here. Others, such as area charts, volume charts, and statistical maps are also used. Curves and bar charts involve one-dimensional comparisons, while area charts make two-dimensional comparisons although one form, the pie chart, can be either in one or two dimensions. Volume charts seem to show three dimensions. Two- and three-dimensional charts easily confuse and should be used only sparingly.

1. Line Diagrams. Curves or line diagrams are used chiefly for time-series and frequency distributions. While there are no agreed upon presentation standards, there are several problems which affect the way readers perceive line diagrams. The first concerns the use of a zero base line. Since the amount of a statistic is indicated by distance on a chart (length of a bar or distance above a base line) it is important that graphs give accurate visual impressions of values. One good way to achieve this is to include a zero base line on the scale on which the curves are plotted. To set the base at some other value is to introduce a visual bias. This can be seen by comparing the visual impressions in parts A and B of Figure 14–2. Both are accurate plots of the Gross National Product of the United States from 1972 through 1977. In part A, however, using the base line of zero places the curve well up on the chart and gives a better perception of the relation between the absolute size of GNP and the changes from year to year. The graph in part B, with a base line at $1,000 billions, can easily give the impression that the growth, relative to the size of GNP, was much greater than it was. When space or other reasons dictate using shortened scales the zero base point should still be used, but with an added break in the scale as shown in part C of Figure 14–2. This will warn the reader that the scale has been reduced.

Another presentation problem concerns the balance of size between vertical and horizontal scales. There is no correct answer to this problem, but the problem can be seen by comparing parts B and C in Figure 14–2. In part C the horizontal scale is twice that in part B. This changes the slope of curve, creating a different perception of growth rate.

A third problem with line diagrams occurs when we try to compare relative and absolute changes among two or more sets of data. Usually we use arithmetic scales where each space unit has identical value. This shows the absolute differences between variables, as in part A of Figure 14–3 which presents the total U.S. population and that of the three Pacific states. This is an arithmetically correct way to present these data, but if we are interested in rates of growth, the visual impressions in part A are not appropriate. If we are

Figure 14-2: U.S. Gross National Product, 1972-1977 ($ billions)

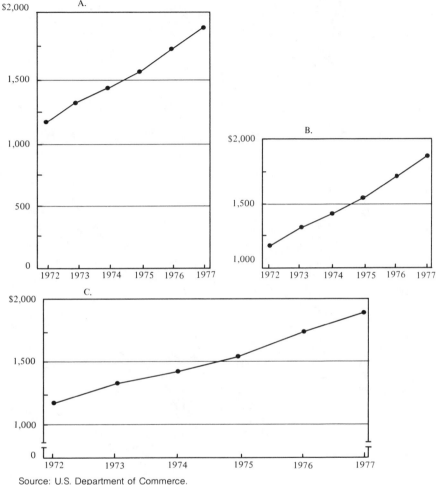

Source: U.S. Department of Commerce.

interested in rates of growth, then a semilogrithmic scale is more useful. A comparison of the line diagrams in parts A and B of Figure 14-3 show how much difference the use of a semilog scale makes. Each is valuable and each is partially misleading. In part A we see clearly that both areas have been growing in population and that the population of the Pacific states is only a small portion of total U.S. population. We can even estimate about what this proportion is. Part B gives us insight into growth rates that are not clear from the arithmetic scale. Part B shows that the Pacific states population has grown at a much faster rate than for the United States in total.

Figure 14–3: Population of the United States and Pacific States Area, 1920–1970 (millions)

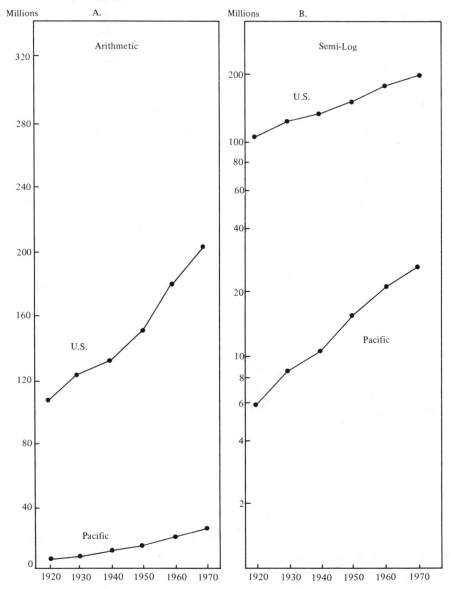

2. *Bar Charts.*   There are a few guidelines and customary practices used in bar chart construction. Vertical bars are normally used for time series and for quantitative classifications (for example, different age groups, income groups). In drafting charts one should generally leave a space between bars equal to one half or more of the width of the bar. An exception to this separation rule is the histogram (a bar chart of a continuous data that have been grouped into a frequency distribution). A second exception is with a multiple variable chart (see part A of Figure 14–4). Scale guidelines on bar charts are also valuable for reader convenience.

Figure 14–4: Examples of Various Types of Bar Charts

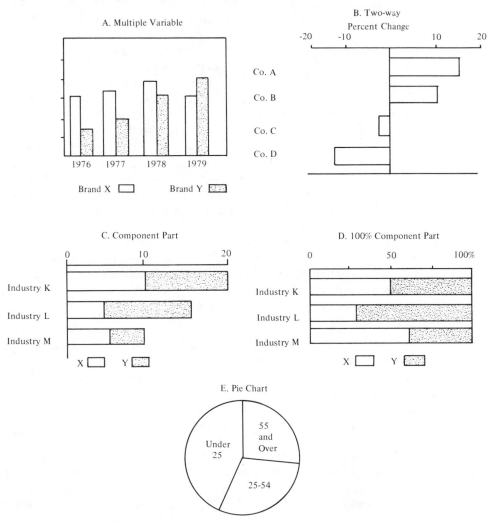

Bar charts come in a variety of patterns. Some widely used designs are illustrated in Figure 14–4. They include (A) multiple variable charts, (B) two direction charts, (C) component part charts, and (D) 100 percent component part charts. The pie chart (a form of area chart) is illustrated in part E of Figure 14–4.

BRIEFING

Nature of Briefings.   Researchers often present their findings orally in a "briefing." These presentations have some unique characteristics that distinguish them from most public speaking. The occasion usually involves only a small group of people. Statistics normally constitute an important portion of topic. The audience members usually are executives with an interest in the topic but with a desire to hear only the critical elements. Speaking time will often be as short as 10 to 20 minutes but may run more than an hour. The presentation is normally followed by questions and discussions.

Preparation.   A successful briefing typically requires a condensation of a lengthy, complex body of information. Since speaking rates should not exceed 100 to 150 words per minute, a 20-minute presentation limits us to about 2,000 to 2,500 words. If we are to communicate effectively under such conditions we must plan carefully. We begin this by asking two questions: First, how long should we plan to talk? Usually there is some indication of the acceptable or planned presentation length. Perhaps it is the custom in an organization for a briefing to take a given allotted time. If the time is severely limited, then the need for topical priorities is obvious. This leads to the second question: What are the purposes of the briefing? Is it to raise concern about certain problems which have been uncovered? Is it to add to the general knowledge of members of the audience? Is it to give them conclusions and recommendations that contribute to their decision making? Questions such as these illustrate the general objectives of the report. After this we should develop a detailed outline of what we are going to say. Such an outline will contain at least the following major parts:

1. Opening.   A brief statement, probably not more than 10 percent of the allotted time, designed to set the stage for the body of the report. The opening should be direct, attention-arresting, and indicate the nature of the discussion to follow. It should explain the nature of the project, how it came about, and what it attempted to do.

2. Findings and Conclusions.   While either logical or psychological formats may be followed in the briefing, it is more common to use the psychological format or a combination logical-psychologic approach. In the latter case the conclusions may be stated immediately after the opening remarks, with each conclusion followed by the findings which support it.

3. Recommendations.   Where appropriate, these are stated as the third stage; each recommendation may be followed by references to the conclusions leading to it. Presented in this manner, they present a natural climax to the report. At the end of the presentation it may be appropriate to call for questions from the audience.

Early in the planning stage we need to make two further decisions. The first concerns the type of audio visuals (A/V) that will be used and the role they will play in the presentation. A/V decisions are important enough that they are often made *before* the briefing outline and text is developed. More will be said about A/V in a later section.

The second important decision concerns the type of speaking aids we expect to use. Will we give a memorized speech, read a paper verbatim, use notes, or what? Most of us will find that memorization is a risky and time-consuming course to follow. Any memory slip during the presentation can be a catastrophe. It is not recommended. Nor is reading a completely written text advised in spite of the fact that this is widely done at professional meetings. Most of us do not read that well, and to try it is to burden the audience with a plodding performance. Notwithstanding this advice, it may be a good idea to write out a complete draft. In this way we can try out lines of argument, experiment with various ways of expressing thoughts, and develop particular phraseology.

It is probably wiser to depend on notes. Audiences accept them and their presence does wonders in allaying speaker fears. Even if we never use them they are there for psychological support. Many prefer to use 5×8 cards for their briefing notes because they hold more information and the fewer cards require less shuffling than do the smaller 3×5 size. Card contents vary widely but some general guides for their design are:

1. Place title and preliminary remarks on the first card.
2. Use each of the remaining cards to carry a major section of presentation, with the amount of detail depending on the needs for statement precision and the speaker's desire for supporting information.
3. Include key phrases, illustrations, statistics, dates, particular turns of phrase, and pronunciation guides for difficult words. Include also quotations and ideas that bear repeating.
4. Along the margin place instructions and cues, such as SLOW, FAST, EMPHASIZE, TRANSPARENCY A, TURN CHART, GO BACK TO CHART 3, and the like.

After the outline and the A/V aids comes the final stage of preparation—the rehearsal. Rehearsal is a prerequisite to effective briefing but *it is a stage too often slighted,* especially by inexperienced speakers. Giving a briefing is an artistic performance, and nothing improves it more than for the speaker to demonstrate mastery of the art. First rehearsal efforts should concentrate on those parts of the presentation that are awkward or poorly developed. After the problem areas have been worked out there should be at least a couple full-scale practices under simulated presentation conditions. At this stage all parts should be timed and edited until the time target is met. Throughout this process a tape recorder is an excellent diagnostic tool.

Delivery. While the content of a report is obviously the chief concern, the speaker's delivery is also an important variable. A polished presentation adds to the receptiveness of the audience, but there is some danger that the presentation may overpower the message. When this occurs listeners may even suspect that an effort is being made to cover deficiencies in research with a "circus" presentation.

Fortunately, the typical research audience knows why it is assembled, has a high level of interest, and does not need to be entertained. Even so, the briefer faces a real challenge in communicating effectively. The delivery should be restrained. Demeanor, posture, dress, and total appearance should be appropriate to the occasion. Speed of speech, clarity of enunciation, pauses, gestures all play their part. Voice pitch, tone quality, and inflections are proper subjects for concern. There is little time for anecdotes and other rapport developing techniques, yet the speaker must get and hold audience attention.

Speaker Problems. Inexperienced speakers have many difficulties in making presentations. They often are nervous at the start of a presentation and may even find breathing difficult. This is natural and should not be of undue concern. It may help in this case to take a deep breath or two, holding each for a brief time before exhaling as fully as possible. This might be done inconspicuously on the way to the podium.

There are a number of other problems which are frequently observed with inexperienced speakers. These may be summarized as follows:

1. Vocal problems
    a. Do you speak so softly that some can not hear you well? It is helpful to have someone in the back of the room who can signal if your voice is not carrying far enough.
    b. Do you speak too rapidly? Remind yourself to slow down. Make deliberate pauses before sentences. Speak words with precision without exaggerating. On the other hand, some people talk too slowly and this tends to make the audience restive.
    c. Do you fail to vary volume, tone quality, change of pace, and rate of speaking? Any or all of these can be used successfully to add interest to the message and engage the audiences' attention. Speakers should not let their words trail off as they complete a sentence.
    d. Do you use overworked pet phrases, repeated "uhs," "you know," and "in other words."
2. Physical problems
    a. Do you rock back and forth on your heels or roll or twist from side to side or lean too much on the lectern?

b.   Do you hitch or tug on clothing, scratch, fiddle with pocket change, keys, pencils, or other devices?

c.   Do you stare into space? This lack of eye contact is particularly bothersome to listeners and is common with inexperienced speakers. Many seem to choose a spot above the heads of the audience and continue to stare at this spot except when looking at notes. *Eye contact is important.* The audience members need to feel that you are looking at them. It may be helpful to pick out about three persons or spots in the audience (left, right, and center) and practice looking at each spot successively as you talk.

d.   Do you misuse visuals by fumbling, putting them on in incorrect order or upside down? Do you turn your back to the audience to read from visuals?

Audio/Visuals.   There is a variety of A/V media which researchers may use with good effect. While there is some use of sound and video players, sound movies, and sound filmstrips, the discussion here is limited to *visual aids* which are relatively simple and inexpensive to make. Six such techniques are:

1.   Chalkboards—This is flexible, inexpensive, and requires little specific preparation. On the other hand, it is not novel, and does not present much of a professional appearance. Furthermore, it reduces speaking time to the extent that it requires the speaker to be writing. If you use the chalkboard be sure to write legibly or print, leave space between lines, and do not talk to the board with your back to the audience.

2.   Handout materials.   These are also inexpensive and can give a professional look if done carefully. Handouts can include pictures and graphic materials which might be difficult to display otherwise. The disadvantages include the time needed to produce them and their distracting impact if not properly used. You may give them out when the audience leaves, but a better use is to refer to them during your talk. If you use them this way, *do not hand them out until you are ready to refer to them.*

3.   Flip charts—You can show color, pictures, and large letters with these. They are easy and inexpensive to make; they can focus listener attention on a specific idea. If not well-made they can be unattractive. Unless they are large they should be restricted to small groups and to types of material which can be summarized in a few words.

4.   Opaque projection—This allows you to project regular printed material on a screen. This is sometimes a great advantage, but the machine is bulky and its magnification is small. It requires more darkness than other methods and is useful only for small groups.

5.   Transparencies—These may be different sizes, but the most common is about the same as an 8 ½ × 11 page. They are easy to make with special colored markers or with a copy machine. They are inexpensive and the

projectors are widely available. You can also show overlays and build-ups. If carelessly made they look very amateurish, but they can look good with careful printing. In using transparencies be sure they are in correct order, and right-side up when you put them on the projector.

6. Slides—Most are 35mm, but larger sizes are sometimes used. They also are relatively inexpensive, can show color, and present a professional looking image if reasonably well done. They are somewhat more difficult to make than the others. When using them be sure the slides are loaded into the projector properly and in sequence.

The choice of speaking aids is largely determined by what you wish them to do, by meeting room conditions, by time and budget constraints, and by available equipment.

Why use them?   Visual aids can serve a number of important functions in a research presentation. The most obvious is to present materials which cannot otherwise by communicated efficiently. For example, statistical relationships are difficult to describe verbally, but a picture or graph communicates the message well. Again, how better to describe some object or material than to show it or picture it?

Visual aids also help the speaker to clarify major points. Through the visual reinforcement of something said verbally, the speaker can stress the importance of certain points. In addition, the use of two channels of communication (hearing and sight) enhances the probability that the listener will understand and remember the message.

A third function of visual aids is to improve the continuity and memorability of the speaker's message. Verbal information is so transient that any slight lapse of listener attention results in losing the information thread. The failure fully to comprehend a given point cannot be remedied by going back to hear again for the speaker has gone on. With a visual aid, however, there is more opportunity to review the point, relate it to an earlier point made by the speaker, and in this way improve retention.

What to Put in Them?   There are differences of opinion as to the proper contents for visual aids. One view is that there should be only a few visuals and they should be largely restricted to pictures and statistics with a minimum of words.[6] Advocates of this position claim that words make visuals dull and uninformative. Too often, this argument goes, visuals are only groups of abstract nouns such as "Objectives, Operations, Preparation, Planning, Productivity, or Progress," and that these are of little communications help.[7] Of course, it is possible to develop dull and uninformative visual aids, but this should not be used as a blanket condemnation of word visuals. The weight of informed opinion seems to be that a well-conceived visual can be made up

---

[6] For this view see Anthony Jay, *Effective Presentation* (London: British Institute of Management, 1970).

[7] Ibid., p. 45.

totally of words. The criterion is "Does it contribute to the effective transmission of a message from speaker to audience?" This requirement can be met with visuals which are all words or all pictures, or a combination; but obviously a set of single abstract nouns does not contribute much.

Some writers on the subject of visual presentations suggest that visuals should be used to present the full outline of a report. One offers the following suggestions as to how a set of visual aids might appear in a briefing on "How to Conduct a Briefing."

	1.	PLAN YOUR BRIEFING[8]
(Transparency 1)	1.1	Decide why you are giving the briefing.
	1.2	Study your expected audience.
	1.3	Anticipate problems, questions, objections.
	1.4	Get facts about time, place, etc.
	2.	DEVELOP YOUR PRESENTATION
(Transparency 2)	2.1	Select your main ideas.
	2.2	Make sure they are vital to the audience.
	2.3	Assemble factual support.
	2.4	Organize your material.
	2.5	Prepare needed visual aids.
	3.	PRACTICE YOUR BRIEFING
(Transparency 3)	3.1	Use your notes for practice.
	3.2	Practice entire briefing at least three times out loud.
	3.3	Cut material to stay within time limit.
	3.4	Rehearse opening and closing especially.
	3.5	Check to see that all material is ready.
	4.	DELIVER YOUR BRIEFING
(Transparency 4)	4.1	Arrive ahead of time.
	4.2	Start on time and end on time.
	4.3	Keep eye contact with audience.
	4.4	Save some time for questions.
	4.5	Summarize main points.
	5.	HOW TO CONDUCT A BRIEFING
(Transparency 5)	5.1	Plan your briefing.
	5.2	Develop your presentation.
	5.3	Practice your briefing.
	5.4	Deliver it.

SUMMARY

The quality of the presentation of research findings can, and often does, have an inordinate effect on a reader's or listener's perceptions of the quality

[8] Reprinted by special permission from Robert Hays, *Practically Speaking—in Business, Industry, and Government* (Reading, Mass.: Addison-Wesley, 1969), pp. 149–53.

of the study. Recognition of this fact should prompt a researcher to make special efforts to communicate skillfully and clearly.

Written reports may be classified as informational or research in nature. The former presents findings with limited analysis, while the latter contains findings, analysis, interpretation, conclusions, and sometimes recommendations. Research reports may follow the short informal format typical of memoranda and letters, or they may be longer and more complex. Long reports are organized in either a logical or psychological sequence. In the former the problem is presented, followed by the findings, conclusions, and recommendations. In the psychological sequence the conclusions and recommendations precede the findings. The logical sequence is more frequently used in reports designed for the scientific or technical reader. The psychological format is common in the report designed for the lay reader or manager.

The writer of research reports should be guided by four questions: (1) What is the purpose of this report? (2) Who will read it? (3) What are the circumstances and limitations under which it is written? and (4) How will the report be used? Reports should also be clearly organized, physically inviting, and easy to read. Writers can achieve these aims if they are careful with mechanical details, writing style, and comprehensibility. There is a special problem with presenting statistical data. While some may be incorporated in the text, most statistics should be placed in tables or graphs. The table or graph form to use depends on the specific data and presentation problem.

Briefings on the findings of a research study are common and should be developed with concern for the communication problems that are unique to oral presentation situations. Briefings are usually under severe time constraints; good briefings require careful organization and preparation. Visual aids are a particularly important aspect of briefings but are too often ignored or treated inadequately.

Whether written or oral, poor presentations do a grave injustice to what might be excellent research. Good presentations, on the other hand, add luster to both the research and the reputation of the researcher.

SUPPLEMENTAL READINGS

1. Berenson, Conrad, and Colton, Raymond. *Research and Report Writing for Business and Economics.* New York: Random House, 1971. Chaps. 8 through 17 cover report writing.

2. Howell, William S., and Borman, Ernest G. *Presentational Speaking for Business and the Professions.* New York: Harper & Row, Publishers, 1971. Thorough treatment of the problems and processes of designing and delivering presentations to business and professional audiences.

3. Lesikar, Raymond V. *How to Write a Report Your Boss Will Read and Remember.* Homewood, Ill.: Dow Jones-Irwin, Inc., 1974. Stresses report writing in a business setting. Appendixes present illustrations of various reports.

4.   Resta, Paul A. *The Research Report.* New York: American Book Company, 1972. A 60-page self-instruction manual on how to organize a scholarly research report.

5.   Spear, Mary Eleanor. *Practical Charting Techniques.* New York: McGraw-Hill Book Company, 1969. A thorough coverage of the principles of graphic presentation.

6.   Strunk, William Jr., and White, E. B. *The Elements of Style.* New York: The Macmillan Company, 1959. A classic on the problems of writing style.

7.   Turabian, Kate L. *A Manual for Writers of Term Papers, Theses, and Dissertations.* 3d. ed. rev. Chicago: University of Chicago Press, 1971. Probably the most widely used manual for academic research writing in social science and business areas.

8.   Welsh, James J. *The Speech Writing Guide.* New York: John Wiley & Sons, Inc., 1968. A short, highly readable guide for business and professional people who need a practical reference tool for writing a presentable speech.

DISCUSSION QUESTIONS

1.   Distinguish:
     a.   Informational and research reports.
     b.   Logical and psychological research report formats.
     c.   Technical and popular reports.
     d.   Topic and sentence outlines.

2.   What should you do about:
     a.   Putting information in a research report concerning the study's limitations?
     b.   The size and complexity of tables in a research report?
     c.   The physical presentation of a report?
     d.   "Pace" in your writing?

3.   What type of report would you suggest be written in each of the following cases:
     a.   The president of the company has asked for a study of the company's pension plan and its comparison to those of other firms in the industry.
     b.   You have been asked to write up a marketing experiment, which you recently completed, for submission to the *Journal of Marketing Research.*
     c.   Your division manager has asked you to prepare a forecast of cash requirements for the division for the next three months.
     d.   The National Institute of Health has given you a grant to study the relation between industrial accidents and departmental employee morale.

4.   Begin on one of the following listed pages with the first complete paragraph and calculate the Fog Index for the text of 100 or more words. Rewrite the material to reduce the index by at least two points.
     a.   Page   69
     b.   Page 167
     c.   Page 271
     d.   Page 377

5. Research reports often contain much statistical materials of great importance, but it is often presented poorly. Suggest five important "shoulds" that a research report writer ought to follow.

6. The typical student research report has many deficiencies in presentation in addition to its limitations in project design and content. Make a list of what you believe to be the major presentation problems with student written research reports. With student oral research reports.

7. What are the major problems that you personally have with writing good reports? What can you do about these problems?

8. Outline a set of visual aids which you might use in an oral briefing on:
   a. How to write a research report.
   b. The outlook for the economy over the next year.
   c. The major analytical article in the latest *Business Week*.

9. There are a number of graphic presentation forms. Which would you suggest using to show each of the following? Why?
   a. A comparison of average annual per capital incomes for the United States and the Soviet Union, 1970 and 1980.
   b. The percentage composition of average family expenditure patterns, by the major types of expenditures, for families whose heads are under 35 years with families whose heads are 55 years or older.
   c. A comparison of the change, between December 31, 1978, and December 31, 1979, of common stock prices of six major electronics firms.

Appendix A

Selected Reference Tools for Students of Business*

INTRODUCTION

The purpose of this guide is to describe the most important bibliographies and other reference works in the field of business. These are some of the tools

---

* Source: Washington University Libraries, revised 1978.

which business students should know before they attempt to write a paper or thesis. They are divided into three main groups:

I. Guides to Reference Materials.
II. Bibliographies.
III. Miscellaneous Reference Works.

I. GUIDES TO REFERENCE MATERIALS

Because this list of reference tools describes only the major works, the student should examine one or more of the guides described below. These guides describe the varied sources of information available in the field of business, tell the purposes for which these sources may be used, and give directions on their use. There are also guides to more specialized topics, such as the guides to statistics listed in the section on that subject.

> *Encyclopedia of Business Information Sources: A Detailed Listing of Primary Subjects of Interest to Managerial Personnel, with a Record of Sourcebooks, Periodicals, Organizations, Directories, Handbooks, Bibliographies, and Other Sources of Information on Each Topic.* 3d ed. Detroit: Gale Research Co., 1976.

The entries are designed to identify the "right place to begin" an information search rather than to answer specific questions. The first volume is arranged alphabetically by general topic; the second, by geographic source.

> Johnson, Herbert Webster. *How to Use the Business Library.* 4th ed. Cincinnati: South-Western Pub. Co., 1972.

This manual serves as a good introduction to the types of materials, such as handbooks, yearbooks, directories, and government publications, which are most useful to business executives.

> Universal Reference System. *Political Science, Government, and Public Policy Series.* Volume 8: *Economic Regulation: Business and Government.* Princeton, N.J.: Princeton Research Publishing Co., 1969.

This multivolume set presents "an annotated and intensively indexed compilation of significant books, pamphlets, and articles, selected and processed by the Universal Reference System—a computerized information retrieval service in the social and behavioral sciences."

> White, Carl Milton. *Sources of Information in the Social Sciences: A Guide to the Literature.* 2d ed. Chicago: American Library Association, 1973.

Chapter 3 is entitled "Economics and Business Administration."

> Sheehy, Eugene, P. *Guide to Reference Books.* 9th ed. Chicago: American Library Association, 1976.

This standard bibliography of reference works includes many titles in business and related fields. This guide will refer to Sheehy occasionally as a source of additional references.

II. BIBLIOGRAPHIES

Briefly defined, a bibliography is a list of books or other printed materials. Most bibliographies are arranged either by author or by subject. The card catalog, one of the most important kinds of bibliographies, lists only books available in a given library, while other bibliographies list books that may not be in the collection. Some bibliographies list only certain types of publications, such as dissertations or government publications. In order to collect all the important references on a subject, it is necessary to know and use a wide variety of bibliographies.

A. The Public Catalog

The catalog is a bibliography of books in a library. Cards for books are filed under author, title, and subject. Subject headings are a frequent cause of difficulties in using the catalog, and the following suggestions may help you save time.

When you are searching for material by subject and are not sure of the correct subject heading, consult the following work:

U.S. Library of Congress.   Subject Cataloging Division. *Library of Congress Subject Headings.* 2 vols. 8th ed. Washington, D.C., 1975.

This list tells what headings are used in the catalog and also provides cross-references from headings that are not used to ones that are. For example, if you should look for the subject Business Arithmetic, this list will tell you that the subject heading used in the catalog is Business Mathematics.

The Library of Congress list also suggests related subjects to consult. For example, under Office Management, you find the related headings Business Records, Credit Managers, Office Procedures, and so forth. Similar cross-references are made on cards filed in the public catalog.

A point to remember is that subject headings are usually specific. When looking for material on "marketing," try that subject first, not the more general subject "business." Cross-references usually will help lead you from the general headings to more specific ones. For example, the cross-references under Business refer to special fields of business, such as Accounting, Advertising, Marketing, and so on. If you do not find enough material under your specific topic, try the next broader topic that includes it.

Subject headings are made only for the three or four most prominent subjects treated in a book; you cannot count on finding subject cards for every topic mentioned. You must use your ingenuity in determining what categories of books could conceivably treat your topic. If you do not find a subject entry for a particular technique used in advertising, try the subject heading Advertising.

You will save time if you learn to recognize the information given on the catalog cards. The following items are included: author; title; publisher; date of publication; number of pages or volumes; series; notes listing the contents;

notes describing special features, such as illustrations, maps, or bibliographies; and a list of subject headings assigned to that book. The description of the book on the catalog card may tell you whether or not it is worth examining.

A library's public catalog does not record every publication received by that library. Among the types of materials often excluded from the catalog are the following:

1. Most U.S. government publications. (See the later sections of this guide which describes government document bibliographies.)
2. Most U.N. publications.
3. Rand Corporation Reports.
4. Reports from companies. (For example, corporation annual reports.)

Another point to keep in mind about a library's public catalog is that it records only the books in that library. If you are engaged in serious research, you cannot afford to limit yourself to the books in one library. Any single collection is limited by the funds available and by the interests of those who influence the book ordering. Instead of depending on the catalog alone, you should turn also to other types of bibliographies.

B. Single Subject Bibliographies

Unfortunately, there is no single comprehensive bibliography of business literature, but there are many bibliographies covering specific areas, such as advertising, marketing, and accounting.

The student might find it advantageous to examine the important bibliographies written on the subject. Books which are primarily bibliographies may be found in the public catalog under the appropriate subject heading, for example, Accounting—Bibliography.

C. General Bibliographies

If you cannot find a bibliography on your subject, or if you feel that the bibliographies you have located are incomplete or out-of-date, you should consult the general bibliographies. This category includes the catalogs of the great national libraries and national and trade bibliographies.

The most important American general bibliographies with a *subject* approach are described below:

A good general reference source for bibliographies in all subject areas is:

Bibliographic Index: A Cumulative Bibliography of Bibliographies. New York: H. W. Wilson, 1937—.

Bibliographies printed in books and periodicals as well as separately published bibliographies are listed by subject.

Association for University Business and Economic Research. *Bibliography of Publications of University Bureaus of Business and Economic Research.* 1950/56— Eugene, Ore.

This is a selective index to reports, bulletins, and monographs published by bureaus of business research affiliated with universities. The supplements also list selected articles appearing in periodicals published by these bureaus. There is an author and subject index.

American Book Publishing Record, BPR. New York: Bowker, 1960—. Vol. 1—. Monthly.

This periodical aims to be a complete record of American books published in the month preceding its date of issue. It is arranged by the Dewey Decimal Classification, with author and title indexes.

Cumulative Book Index: A World List of Books in the English Language. New York: H. W. Wilson, 1928—.

Books published in the English language in the United States, and since 1930, in other parts of the world are recorded by author, title, and subject in this comprehensive bibliography.

Subject Guide to Books in Print. New York: Bowker, 1957—.

Currently available American trade books are listed by subject.

Subject Guide to Forthcoming Books. New York: Bowker, 1967—. Vol. 1—.

This bimonthly publication "aims to list all books expected to be published in the U.S.A. during the next five months."

Most of the general bibliographies are arranged by *author.* If you know the name of an author who has written on your subject, you may use these bibliographies to find out the titles of other books he or she has written. These general bibliographies are also used to verify and complete references when you know the author's name but are not sure of the title, date, or publisher.

Books in Print. New York: Bowker, 1948—.

This is an annual author and title index to the collection of publishers' catalogs known as *Publishers' Trade List Annual.* It can be used as quick identification of a recent American work when only the author or title is known, as well as to determine whether a particular book is available for purchase. For information about books published after this annual appears, use *Forthcoming Books* listed immediately below or the *Cumulative Book Index* and *American Book Publishing Record,* described above.

Forthcoming Books. New York: Bowker, 1966—. Vol. 1—.

This publication is an author-title list, including new books in print.

The National Union Catalog, Pre-1956 Imprints; a Cumulative Author List Representing Library of Congress Printed Cards and Titles Reported by Other American Libraries. London: Mansell, 1968—(in process).

The National Union Catalog: A Cumulative Author List Representing Library of Congress Printed Cards and Titles Reported by Other American Libraries. New York: Roman and Littlefield, Various sets from 1958—.

These companion works and monumental bibliographical tools are especially valuable for providing locations of books in major American libraries.

Libraries with special collections occasionally publish their catalogs in book form, thus expediting the search for hard-to-find material.

Cornell University.   New York State School of Industrial and Labor Relations. Library. *Library Catalog.* 12 vols. & Supplements. Boston: G. K. Hall, 1967–69.

This library is especially strong in labor management relations, human relations in industry, personnel, social insurance and employee welfare, labor economics, labor union organization and administration, labor industry, and international labor conditions and problems.

D.   U.S. Government Publications

Publications issued by the U.S. government contain information of real value to students of business. Some of the bibliographies already described, such as the *National Union Catalogs,* list government publications, as does "PAIS" (described later with the periodical indexes). But in order to be sure of locating all of the relevant materials, you should use the special document bibliographies. The most important ones are listed below. Consult also Sheehy's *Guide to Reference Books.*

Guide to U.S. Government Publications.   McLean, Va.: Documents Index, 1973—.

This invaluable tool provides access to U.S. government serials and periodicals by issuing agency, title, or documents number.

United States. Superintendent of Documents. *Monthly Catalog of United States Government Publications.* Washington, D.C.: U.S. Government Printing Office, 1895—.

Publications issued by all branches of the federal government are listed in this bibliography by the name of the issuing office. There are monthly and annual subject indexes. Starting with January 1963, the index includes some entries for personal authors, and beginning with 1974, there is a title index. Cumulative indexes since 1941 are available.

Remember that the public catalog does not list the majority of government publications. *The Monthly Catalog* serves as a printed catalog to the documents collection because it gives the call numbers (Superintendent of Documents numbers) used to arrange and shelve these publications, just as the public catalog gives Library of Congress numbers.

U.S. Department of Commerce. *Publications; A Catalog and Index.* Washington, D.C.: Government Printing Office. With supplements.

This is a catalog and subject index based on the Commerce Department's biweekly *Business Service Checklist.* Material is included from the Office of Technical Services, the Area Redevelopment Administration, the Business and Defense Services Administration, the Bureau of International Commerce, the National Bureau of Standards, and the Bureau of the Census. The Census Bureau also issues its own catalog along with a basic list which covers publications issued from 1790 to 1972.

U.S. Congress. *Congressional Record.* Washington, D.C.: Government Printing Office, 1873—.

This constitutes "the public proceedings of each House of Congress as reported by the Official Reporters thereof . . . Published each day that one or both Houses are in session, excepting very infrequent instances when two or more unusually small consecutive issues are printed at one time." The weekly index contains many subject headings directly related to business and possibilities of intended or accomplished congressional action, remarks, speeches, and discussion.

E. United Nations Publications

United Nations.   Dag Hammarskjold Library. *UNDEX: United Nations Documents Index.* New York, 1950—.

The UN publishes extensively in the field of international economic problems, for example, finance, natural resources, technical development, and trade. Publications are listed in this Index by issuing body, and indexed by subject. The monthly issues are superseded by an annual cumulation. Be sure to note the four volume cumulative index for the years 1950–1962.

As with U.S. government documents, most UN publications are not listed in the public catalog.

F. Dissertations and Research in Progress

Dissertations are not systematically listed in any of the sources already described. The following specialized bibliographies list completed dissertations and other research projects which are in progress.

January issues of the *Journal of Business* include a list of recently completed doctoral dissertations in the field of business.

American Doctoral Dissertations.   Ann Arbor, Mich.: University Microfilms.

This annual publication provides "a complete listing of all doctoral dissertations accepted by American and Canadian universities. This is published on a school-year basis and is arranged by subject categories and institutions. An author index is an integral part of each publication." Business-related topics may be found under "Business Administration" and "Economics, Commerce — Business."

The title varies, and there are comparable publications covering earlier periods.

Dissertation Abstracts International. Ann Arbor, Mich.: Xerox University Microfilms, 1938—.

Abstracts of doctoral dissertations which are available for purchase in complete form in microfilm or Xerographic reproduction are listed here. The abstracts are arranged by broad subject areas with an author index. Beginning with Volume 27 (1966), *Dissertation Abstracts* was divided into two sections: A: the Humanities and Social Sciences, and B: the Sciences and Engineering. Both sections have indexes which are issued separately. With Volume 30 (1969) Dissertation Abstracts became *Dissertation Abstracts International* to reflect the addition of European universities. The coverage of universities has increased in recent years, and most major institutions are now cooperating, but for the most complete list of dissertations use the *Comprehensive Dissertation Index 1861—1972*, with the annual supplements.

G. Indexes to Periodicals, Newspapers, and Serials

The latest information on most subjects is found in periodicals and newspapers. Some information may never be published in any other form. To locate these articles, it is necessary to use indexes designed for that purpose.

Applied Science and Technology Index (formerly *Industrial Arts Index*). New York: H. W. Wilson, 1913—.

This is a cumulative subject index to English language periodicals which analyzes more than 200 periodicals relevant to the applied sciences. Many of the periodicals indexed have a direct bearing upon business activities and carry business information in the form of reports, articles, news notes, and special issues. Subject headings include "Budget—United States," "Business Management," "Business Charts," "Finance," "Stocks," and so on.

Business Periodicals Index. New York: H. W. Wilson, 1958—.

Approximately 170 business and economics periodicals in the English language are cumulatively indexed by subject. This index is particularly good for the practical aspects of business operations and specific businesses, industries, and trades.

For material before 1958, see the *Industrial Arts Index, 1913–57*.

Index to Legal Periodicals. New York: H. W. Wilson, 1909—.

These monthly indexes, which contain subject headings from many areas of human activity, are published for the American Association of Law Libraries.

New York Times Index. New York: New York Times Co., 1851—.

This most comprehensive newspaper index published is also valuable for establishing dates of articles in other newspapers.

Public Affairs Information Service. *Bulletin.* New York: Public Affairs Information Service, Inc., 1915—.

A large number of English language periodicals from all over the world are selectively indexed and many books, government publications, and pamphlets are listed by subject in this bibliography which covers business, banking, and economics, as well as subjects in the area of public affairs. It is often cited as "PAIS." Note the cumulative indexes for 1915–1974. The *Foreign Language Index* covers materials in French, German, Italian, Portuguese, and Spanish beginning with 1968.

The Rand Corporation. *Selected Rand Abstracts.* Santa Monica, Calif., 1963—. Vol. 1—.

"The Rand Corporation, established in 1948 as an independent, nonprofit organization is engaged in a program of research concerned with the security and public welfare of the United States. This research is financed by the U.S. Air Force, by other government agencies, and by the Corporation." *Selected Rand Abstracts,* a complete guide to current unclassified publications of the Rand Corporation, is published four times each year. The volume is cumulative through the year. Issue Number 4 (December) is the permanent record for the year. Documents issued during the period 1946–62 are listed in the *Index of Selected Publications.*

Social Sciences Citation Index: An International Interdisciplinary Index to the Literature of the Social Sciences. Philadelphia: Institute for Scientific Information, 1969—.

This lists references to publications cited during the period covered as well as original articles. It is especially valuable for tracing a given author's influence in a specific field.

Vertical File Index: A Subject and Title Index to Selected Pamphlet Materials. New York: H. W. Wilson, 1935—. Monthly (except August).

This is a very useful source for locating ephemeral material, much of it free. The *Monthly Catalog* listed above should be consulted for references to pamphlets issued by the U.S. government. Most pamphlets are not cataloged.

The Wall Street Journal Index. Princeton, N.J.: Dow Jones Books, 1957—.

This monthly index is divided into two sections, one for corporate news (arranged by the name of the firm) and one for general news (arranged by subject).

Students whose topic overlaps other fields, such as psychology or sociology, should consult Sheehy's *Guide to Reference Books* for the titles of indexes in those fields.

H.   Lists of Periodicals

Students working with periodicals will occasionally need the kind of information found in the two kinds of periodical lists described below. The first type, represented by the first four directories, indicates what titles are currently being published, and gives their addresses, subscription prices, and similar information. The second type, represented by the last two titles, is primarily intended to inform the user in what libraries the periodicals can be found.

Ayer Directory of Publications. Philadelphia: Ayer Press, 1880—.

This annual list of American newspapers and periodicals is arranged by state and city, and gives detailed information (editor, publisher, address, circulation figures, subscription price) for each title. It has an alphabetical index of the periodical titles and a classified list of trade, technical, and professional journals.

Industrial Marketing. "Guide to Special Issues."

This directory is currently included in each issue. Publications are listed within primary market classifications and are listed for up to three months prior to the advertising closing date. Data include the name of the special issue, date of publication, a brief description of the issue, advertising closing date, and associated services, for example, reader inquiry card.

Standard Periodical Directory. New York: Oxbridge Publishing Company, 1964/65—.

This directory provides a subject arrangement of over 60,000 U.S. and Canadian periodicals, with an alphabetical title index. Entries include such information as publisher, editor, address, frequency, price, circulation, and special features. It covers every type of periodical with the exception of suburban weekly and small daily newspapers.

Ulrich's International Periodicals Directory: A Classified Guide to Current Periodicals, Foreign and Domestic. New York: R. R. Bowker, 1932—.

This bibliography is particularly useful for finding comprehensive lists of periodicals in various subject fields and for determining in what index periodicals are analyzed. It also identifies periodicals containing bibliographies and book reviews.

Union List of Serials in Libraries of the United States and Canada. 3d. ed. 5 vols. New York: H. W. Wilson Company, 1965.

This is the most comprehensive list of periodicals available. It gives a brief bibliographical description of each title and indicates holdings in American libraries. It is a basic tool for identifying periodical titles and for locating specific volumes.

New Serial Titles. Washington, D.C.: Library of Congress, 1950—.

This serves as a supplement to the *Union List of Serials;* it includes much the same type of information and is used for the same purposes.

III. MISCELLANEOUS REFERENCE SOURCES

The emphasis in the preceding sections was bibliographical; that is, most of the works cited are used to find information about published materials. The books described in this section, with few exceptions, are primarily compilations of facts and figures arranged for ease of consultation.

Some of these books will refer you to further, more detailed sources, but all contain explicit answers to many questions. The following are samples of the type of questions answered by these works:

What was the gross national products of the U.S. for the last five years?
What companies manufacture clay pipe?
What is a voucher register?
How many persons are employed in manufacturing in St. Louis, Missouri?

A. Atlases

Atlases are useful to executives in many areas, especially to those con cerned with marketing, exporting and importing, and transportation. No reference is made here to any of the numerous excellent general atlases, descriptions of which can be found in Sheehy's *Guide to Reference Books*. One atlas designed for business use is described below?

Rand McNally and Company. *Commercial Atlas and Marketing Guide.* Chicago: Rand McNally, annual.

This atlas contains reference maps for foreign countries, states of the United States, and Canadian provinces. Special maps cover transportation, communications, population distribution, retail trade and manufacturing, time zones, and airline distances. There are many tables of statistical and factual information useful to executives.

B. Biographical Works

American Assembly of Collegiate Schools of Business. *Faculty Personnel: A Directory of the Instructional Staffs of Member Schools. . . .* St. Louis, Mo.: American Assembly of Collegiate Schools of Business, 1925—.

This directory lists more than 16,100 faculty members from approximately 470 universities and colleges. Included is various background information on full-time faculty with the rank of instructor and above at both accredited and nonaccredited Assembly schools. Faculty members are alphabetically grouped under their current university or college affiliation.

Dun & Bradstreet. Inc. *Dun & Bradstreet Reference Book of Corporate Managements.* New York.

This book lists more than 30,000 officers and directors in the 2,400 companies of greatest investor interest. The entries are arranged alphabetically by the name of the corporation and there is an index to principal officers.

The International Who's Who. London: Europa Publications Ltd., 1935—.

The book contains biographies of people from almost every country in the world and in almost every sphere of human activity."

Standard and Poor's Register of Corporations, Directors, and Executives, United States and Canada. New York: Standard and Poor's Corp., 1928—.

This publication lists the directors and other important executive personnel of over 27,000 industrial corporations. Biographical information for each person includes the following information: business affiliations, business address, home address, fraternal membership, education, and date of birth. This directory also provides the following data for the companies: address of the home office, the principal products, number of employees, and annual sales range. A geographical index lists the corporations by state and city.

Who's Who in Finance and Industry. Chicago: Marquis Who's Who, Inc., 1936—.

This work provides a complete summary of the background of individuals who have distinguished themselves in any area of commercial activity. It includes many more executives than are found in *Who's Who in America* and gives considerably more detail than is given in *Poor's Register*. It lists business affiliations, education, clubs and organizations, and addresses for over 23,000 American and foreign leaders in business administration, production, technology, sales, and business-related professions.

C. Business Services

Because business is a field which changes so rapidly, most reference works soon become out-of-date. The latest factual information on many subjects, such as commodity prices, foreign exchange, securities, and tax regulations, is contained in business service publications, which are kept up-to-date by supplements or loose-leaf revisions.

Directory of Business and Financial Services. New York: Special Libraries Association, 1924—.

This guide describes 1,051 services, including newsletters, bulletins, reports, and other publications, and represents 421 publishers.

Commerce Clearing House.   *Consumerism; New Developments for Business.* Chicago, 1971—.

This publication is a weekly service that briefly explains new developments regarding consumerism in legislation and rulings by government agencies.

Commodity Year Book. New York: Commodity Research Bureau, Inc., 1939—.

This annual volume is "designed to help clarify the great changes taking place in the world of commodities" by means of graphs, charts, tables, and text.

It is updated five times yearly by the *Commodity Year Book Statistical Abstract Service.*

Moody's Industrial Manual. New York: Moody's Investors Service, 1909—.

This annual bound book volume presents the history of the company, a description of the business and its products, a list of principal plants, a list of officers and directors, and financial data, such as the firm's dividend record. It is updated by the semiweekly *Moody's Industrial News Reports,* a loose-leaf service with cumulative indexes.

Other *Moody's Manuals* are devoted to banks, investments, municipalities, public utilities, and transportation firms.

Prentice-Hall. Inc. *Prentice-Hall Federal Taxes.* Englewood Cliffs, N.J., 1921—.

This complete and authoritative service reprints federal tax laws, regulations, rulings, and decisions, along with extensive editorial comment.

Standard & Poor's Corporation. *Standard & Poor's Trade and Securities Statistics* (loose-leaf). New York, 1941—.

This service is issued in three parts: Current Statistics; Business and Finance; and Security Price Index Record.

Two other Standard & Poor's loose-leaf services which can be very valuable to the investor or the researcher into individual companies are:

Standard and Poor's Corporation. *Stock Reports; Over-the-Counter and Regional Exchanges.* 4 vols. New York (loose-leaf, updated regularly).

This contains the Standard N.Y.S.E. Stock Reports, Over-the-Counter and Regional Exchange Reports, Standard A.S.E. Stock Reports, Standard Convertible Securities Reports, and Definitions of Terms.

Daily Stock Price Record: New York Stock Exchange. New York: Standard and Poor's Corporation, 1961—.

This quarterly publication is divided into two parts. Part I, "Major Technical Indicators of the Stock Market," is devoted to market indicators widely followed as technical guides to the stock market. Part II, "Daily and Weekly Stock Action," gives the daily and weekly record of stocks listed either on the NYSE, the ASE, or the OTC Market.

The Value Line Investment Survey. New York: Arnold Bernhard and Co., Inc.

This publication is divided into four parts: These are the (1) Summary and Index; (2) Selection and Opinion; (3) Ratings and Reports; and (4) Miscellaneous. This is a valuable source for regularly updated financial information on hundreds of companies.

University libraries may also have a microfiche file of annual business reports, 10Ks filed with the SEC and prospectuses of companies listed on the American and New York Stock Exchanges. 1970—.

D. Dictionaries and Encyclopedias

For definitions of business terms not found in general dictionaries, consult the following specialized reference works.

Clark, Donald T., and Bert A. Gottfried. *Dictionary of Business and Finance.* New York: Thomas Y. Crowell Company, 1957.

This volume defines terms used in the fields of accounting, advertising, banking, commodities, credit, imports, retailing, the stock market, and other areas of interest to students and executives.

Bogen, Jules Irwin. *Financial Handbook.* 4th ed. New York: The Ronald Press Co., 1968.

This volume is a compendium of information needed by bankers, investors, and financial managers. Topics are presented in brief outline accompanied by many examples and tables.

Heyel, Carl. ed. *The Encyclopedia of Management.* 2d ed. New York: Van Nostrand Reinhold Co., 1973.

This work summarizes the major areas of management and provides references for further reading.

International Encyclopedia of the Social Sciences. 17 vols. New York: Macmillan, 1968.

This basic reference source for the social sciences includes such topics as economics, industrial organization, labor economics, money and banking, public finance, and certain aspects of business management. Bibliographies at the end of each article and a detailed index in the final volume lead to additional sources of information.

Its predecessor, the *Encyclopaedia of the Social Sciences,* New York, Macmillan, 1930, is still valuable for historical and biographical material.

Munn, Glenn G. *Glenn G. Munn's Encyclopedia of Banking and Finance.* 7th ed. Boston, Mass.: Bankers Pub. Co., 1973.

This one-volume encyclopedia includes definitions of words and phrases used in business, as well as encyclopedic articles with bibliographies covering the fields of money, credit, and banking.

Tver, David F. *The Gulf Publishing Company Dictionary of Business and Science.* 3d ed. Houston, Texas: Gulf Publishing Company, 1974.

This dictionary "comprises specialized terminology from such disciplines as medicine, law, psychology, and geology; the rapidly developing jargon of computers, aerospace, and electronics; and such business essentials as labor and personnel, advertising and printing, accounting, finance, business law, and insurance."

E. Directories

Business directories are lists of organizations or companies, systematically arranged, giving addresses, officers, and other data. Many directories dealing with specific industries and trades contain factual and statistical data. Because many of these directories are revised frequently, they are valuable sources of current information.

Klein, Bernard.   *Guide to American Directories: A Guide to the Major Business Directories of the United States, Covering All Industrial, Professional, and Mercantile Categories.* 9th ed. Coral Springs, Fla.: B. Klein Publications, Inc., 1975.

This guide lists directories published by business reference publishers, magazines, trade associations, chambers of commerce, and government agencies.

Thomas Register of American Manufacturers and Thomas Register Catalog File. New York: Thomas Pub. Co., 1905—.

This directory lists approximately 75,000 different products, giving for every product the companies which manufacture it. The main section groups company names by state and city under the product. One volume is an alphabetical list of companies; another contains a brand names index; the final volumes are devoted to catalogs of companies.

Missouri Directory of Manufacturing and Mining. Saint Louis, Mo.: Informative Data Co., 1976.

Manufacturing and mining firms are listed separately in three sections: alphabetically by the name of the establishment; geographically by city; and by product according to the Standard Industrial Classification Number.

Metro St. Louis Directory of Manufacturers. St. Louis, Mo.: St. Louis Regional Commerce and Growth Association, 1976—.

"The *Metro St. Louis Directory of Manufacturers* lists manufacturing establishments (as defined by the Standard Industrial Classification Manual, 1972) located in the following counties of Missouri and Illinois: Missouri—City of St. Louis, Franklin, Jefferson, St. Charles, St. Louis: Illinois—Clinton, Madison, Monroe, St. Clair."

Comparable directories are published for many states and cities of the United States.

Wasserman, Paul.   *Consultants and Consulting Organizations Directory; A Reference Guide to Concerns and Individuals Engaged in Consultation for Business and Industry.* 3d ed., Detroit: Gale Research Co., 1976.

This is a reference guide to concerns and individuals engaged in consultation for business and industry.

———.   *Consumer Sourcebook.* Detroit: Gale Research Co., 1974.

The subtitle of this book provides a thorough description of this book: "A Directory and Guide to Government Organizations; Associations; Centers and Institutes; Media Services; Company and Trademark Information; and Bibliographic Material Relating to Consumer Topics, Sources of Recourse, and Advisory Information." The entries for agencies, organizations and for publications are annotated.

Directories of associations can be very useful in subject approaches to problems.

Gale Research Company. *Encyclopedia of Associations.* Detroit, 1956—.

United States and selected international associations are listed in three volumes:
1. National Organizations of the United States.
2. Geographic and Executive Index.
3. New Associations and Projects.

Brief descriptions of the associations, dates, addresses, officers, meetings, size, and publications are among the details provided.

F. Statistical Works

Guides and Bibliographies. So many publications contain statistics that it is sometimes difficult to find precisely the data you need. Sheehy's *Guide to Reference Books,* the *Business Periodicals Index,* "PAIS," and *The Wall Street Journal* are useful for locating sources for statistics on various subjects. When U.S. government statistics are needed, the relatively new *American Statistics Index* is especially helpful.

American Statistics Index. Washington, D.C.: Congressional Information Service, 1973—.

The cover of this regularly updated service reads, "A comprehensive guide and index to the statistical publications of the U.S. government."

Guide to U.S. Government Statistics. Arlington, Va.: Documents Index, 1956—.

This volume may be used for the quick location of statistical sources by subject and for a description of all of the statistical publications of U.S. government agencies. It is arranged by government agency.

U.S. Office of Management and Budget. Statistical Policy Division, *Statistical Services of the United States Government.* Rev. ed. Washington, D.C.: U.S. Government Printing Office, 1975.

This "is designed to serve as a basic reference document on the statistical programs of the federal government." It is divided into three parts: I. The Statistical System of the Federal Government; II. Principal Social and Economic Statistical Programs; and III. Principal Statistical Publications of Federal Agencies.

Statistics Sources: A Subject Guide to Data on Industrial, Business, Social, Educational, Financial, and Other Topics for the United States and Internationally. 5th ed. Detroit: Gale Research Co., 1977.

U.S. Bureau of the Census. *Directory of Federal Statistics for Local Areas: A Guide to Sources, 1976.* Washington, D.C.: U.S. Department of Commerce, Bureau of the Census, 1978.

This directory provides table-by-table descriptions of statistical reports on areas smaller than states. Only reports issued by federal departments or agencies prior to January 1, 1977, are included. To be included in this directory, a table must provide statistics on a type of local area for the entire United States.

Compilations of Statistics.   The following works are useful compilations of statistics.

U.S. Bureau of the Census. *Statistical Abstract of the United States, 1878—.* Washington, D.C.: U.S. Government Printing Office, 1879—.

This annual compendium of summary statistics on political, social, industrial, and economic organizations of the United States should be the starting point in gathering figures on any topic relating to business subjects. Information is included on federal regions, states, and metropolitan areas. The source notes for the tables and the appended bibliography of sources of statistics lead to more detailed publications of the federal government and of private organizations.

There are three supplements to the *Statistical Abstract.* The *County and City Data Book* provides recent figures for counties, cities, standard metropolitan statistical areas, and urbanized areas. The *Congressional District Data Book* presents a variety of statistical information for districts of the 93d Congress. *Historical Statistics of the United States: Colonial Times to 1970,* 2 vols., has a broad range of data for historical research. This book also provides valuable leads to other sources.

U.S. Office of Business Economics. *Survey of Current Business.* Washington, DC.: U.S. Government Printing Office, 1921—.

Each issue of this periodical contains statistical series on national income, personal income, and expenditures; expenditures for new plants and equipment; production and prices of commodities; and other figures on various aspects of the nation's economy. Historical data for many of the series carried in the monthly issues are available in several supplements, the most important of which is *Business Statistics.* Published in odd-numbered years, this volume is designed to be a handy, comprehensive work. For a list of other supplements to the *Survey of Current Business,* see *Statistical Services of the U.S. Government* or *Guide to U.S. Government Publications.*

Appendix B

Selected Statistical Tables

Table B-1: Proportion of the Area under the Normal Curve with Values as Extreme as the Observed Values of z

z	.00	.01	.02	.03	.04	.05	.06	.07	.08	.09
.0	.5000	.4960	.4920	.4880	.4840	.4801	.4761	.4721	.4681	.4641
.1	.4602	.4562	.4522	.4483	.4443	.4404	.4364	.4325	.4286	.4247
.2	.4207	.4168	.4129	.4090	.4052	.4013	.3974	.3936	.3897	.3859
.3	.3821	.3783	.3745	.3707	.3669	.3632	.3594	.3557	.3520	.3483
.4	.3446	.3409	.3372	.3336	.3300	.3264	.3228	.3192	.3156	.3121
.5	.3085	.3050	.3015	.2981	.2946	.2912	.2877	.2843	.2810	.2776
.6	.2743	.2709	.2676	.2643	.2611	.2578	.2546	.2514	.2483	.2451
.7	.2420	.2389	.2358	.2327	.2296	.2266	.2236	.2206	.2177	.2148
.8	.2119	.2090	.2061	.2033	.2005	.1977	.1949	.1922	.1894	.1867
.9	.1841	.1814	.1788	.1762	.1736	.1711	.1685	.1660	.1635	.1611
1.0	.1587	.1562	.1539	.1515	.1492	.1469	.1446	.1423	.1401	.1379
1.1	.1357	.1335	.1314	.1292	.1271	.1251	.1230	.1210	.1190	.1170
1.2	.1151	.1131	.1112	.1093	.1075	.1056	.1038	.1020	.1003	.0985
1.3	.0968	.0951	.0934	.0918	.0901	.0885	.0869	.0853	.0838	.0823
1.4	.0808	.0793	.0778	.0764	.0749	.0735	.0721	.0708	.0694	.0681
1.5	.0668	.0655	.0643	.0630	.0618	.0606	.0594	.0582	.0571	.0559
1.6	.0548	.0537	.0526	.0516	.0505	.0495	.0485	.0475	.0465	.0455
1.7	.0446	.0436	.0427	.0418	.0409	.0401	.0392	.0384	.0375	.0367
1.8	.0359	.0351	.0344	.0336	.0329	.0322	.0314	.0307	.0301	.0294
1.9	.0287	.0281	.0274	.0268	.0262	.0256	.0250	.0244	.0239	.0233
2.0	.0228	.0222	.0217	.0212	.0207	.0202	.0197	.0192	.0188	.0183
2.1	.0179	.0174	.0170	.0166	.0162	.0158	.0154	.0150	.0146	.0143
2.2	.0139	.0136	.0132	.0129	.0125	.0122	.0119	.0116	.0113	.0110
2.3	.0107	.0104	.0102	.0099	.0096	.0094	.0091	.0089	.0087	.0084
2.4	.0082	.0080	.0078	.0075	.0073	.0071	.0069	.0068	.0066	.0064
2.5	.0062	.0060	.0059	.0057	.0055	.0054	.0052	.0051	.0049	.0048
2.6	.0047	.0045	.0044	.0043	.0041	.0040	.0039	.0038	.0037	.0036
2.7	.0035	.0034	.0033	.0032	.0031	.0030	.0029	.0028	.0027	.0026
2.8	.0026	.0025	.0024	.0023	.0023	.0022	.0021	.0021	.0020	.0019
2.9	.0019	.0018	.0018	.0017	.0016	.0016	.0015	.0015	.0014	.0014
3.0	.0013	.0013	.0013	.0012	.0012	.0011	.0011	.0011	.0010	.0010
3.1	.0010	.0009	.0009	.0009	.0008	.0008	.0008	.0008	.0007	.0007
3.2	.0007									
3.3	.0005									
3.4	.0003									
3.5	.00023									
3.6	.00016									
3.7	.00011									
3.8	.00007									
3.9	.00005									
4.0	.00003									

Table B–2: Table of Critical Values of t

df	Level of Significance for One-Tailed Test					
	.10	.05	.025	.01	.005	.0005
	Level of Significance for Two-Tailed Test					
	.20	.10	.05	.02	.01	.001
1	3.078	6.314	12.706	31.821	63.657	636.619
2	1.886	2.920	4.303	6.965	9.925	31.598
3	1.638	2.353	3.182	4.541	5.841	12.941
4	1.533	2.132	2.776	3.747	4.604	8.610
5	1.476	2.015	2.571	3.365	4.032	6.859
6	1.440	1.943	2.447	3.143	3.707	5.959
7	1.415	1.895	2.365	2.998	3.499	5.405
8	1.397	1.860	2.306	2.896	3.355	5.041
9	1.383	1.833	2.262	2.821	3.250	4.781
10	1.372	1.812	2.228	2.764	3.169	4.587
11	1.363	1.796	2.201	2.718	3.106	4.437
12	1.356	1.782	2.179	2.681	3.055	4.318
13	1.350	1.771	2.160	2.650	3.012	4.221
14	1.345	1.761	2.145	2.624	2.977	4.140
15	1.341	1.753	2.131	2.602	2.947	4.073
16	1.337	1.746	2.120	2.583	2.921	4.015
17	1.333	1.740	2.110	2.567	2.898	3.965
18	1.330	1.734	2.101	2.552	2.878	3.922
19	1.328	1.729	2.093	2.539	2.861	3.883
20	1.325	1.725	2.086	2.528	2.845	3.850
21	1.323	1.721	2.080	2.518	2.831	3.819
22	1.321	1.717	2.074	2.508	2.819	3.792
23	1.319	1.714	2.069	2.500	2.807	3.767
24	1.318	1.711	2.064	2.492	2.797	3.745
25	1.316	1.708	2.060	2.485	2.787	3.725
26	1.315	1.706	2.056	2.479	2.779	3.707
27	1.314	1.703	2.052	2.473	2.771	3.690
28	1.313	1.701	2.048	2.467	2.763	3.674
29	1.311	1.699	2.045	2.462	2.756	3.659
30	1.310	1.697	2.042	2.457	2.750	3.646
40	1.303	1.684	2.021	2.423	2.704	3.551
60	1.296	1.671	2.000	2.390	2.660	3.460
120	1.289	1.658	1.980	2.358	2.617	3.373
∞	1.282	1.645	1.960	2.326	2.576	3.291

Source: Abridged from Table III of Fisher and Yates, *Statistical Tables for Biological, Agricultural and Medical Research,* 6th ed., published by Oliver and Boyd Ltd., Edinburgh, 1963, by permission of the publishers.

Table B–3: Critical Values of Chi Square (χ^2)

df	Probability under H_0 that $\chi^2 \geqq$ Chi Square					
	.99	.98	.95	.90	.80	.70
1	.00016	.00063	.0039	.016	.064	.15
2	.02	.04	.10	.21	.45	.71
3	.12	.18	.35	.58	1.00	1.42
4	.30	.43	.71	1.06	1.65	2.20
5	.55	.75	1.14	1.61	2.34	3.00
6	.87	1.13	1.64	2.20	3.07	3.83
7	1.24	1.56	2.17	2.83	3.82	4.67
8	1.65	2.03	2.73	3.49	4.59	5.53
9	2.09	2.53	3.32	4.17	5.38	6.39
10	2.56	3.06	3.94	4.86	6.18	7.27
11	3.05	3.61	4.58	5.58	6.99	8.15
12	3.57	4.18	5.23	6.30	7.81	9.03
13	4.11	4.76	5.89	7.04	8.63	9.93
14	4.66	5.37	6.57	7.79	9.47	10.82
15	5.23	5.98	7.26	8.55	10.31	11.72
16	5.81	6.61	7.96	9.31	11.15	12.62
17	6.41	7.26	8.67	10.08	12.00	13.53
18	7.02	7.91	9.39	10.86	12.86	14.44
19	7.63	8.57	10.12	11.65	13.72	15.35
20	8.26	9.24	10.85	12.44	14.58	16.27
21	8.90	9.92	11.59	13.24	15.44	17.18
22	9.54	10.60	12.34	14.04	16.31	18.10
23	10.20	11.29	13.09	14.85	17.19	19.02
24	10.86	11.99	13.85	15.66	18.06	19.94
25	11.52	12.70	14.61	16.47	18.94	20.87
26	12.20	13.41	15.38	17.29	19.82	21.79
27	12.88	14.12	16.15	18.11	20.70	22.72
28	13.56	14.85	16.93	18.94	21.59	23.65
29	14.26	15.57	17.71	19.77	22.48	24.58
30	14.95	16.31	18.49	20.60	23.36	25.51

Source: Abridged from Table IV of Fisher and Yates, *Statistics for Biological, Agricultural, and Medical Research,* published by Oliver and Boyd Ltd., Edinburgh, 1963, by permission of the publishers.

Table B–3 (continued)

.50	.30	.20	.10	.05	.02	.01	.001
.46	1.07	1.64	2.71	3.84	5.41	6.64	10.83
1.39	2.41	3.22	4.60	5.99	7.82	9.21	13.82
2.37	3.66	4.64	6.25	7.82	9.84	11.34	16.27
3.36	4.88	5.99	7.78	9.49	11.67	13.28	18.46
4.35	6.06	7.29	9.24	11.07	13.39	15.09	20.52
5.35	7.23	8.56	10.64	12.59	15.03	16.81	22.46
6.35	8.38	9.80	12.02	14.07	16.62	18.48	24.32
7.34	9.52	11.03	13.36	15.51	18.17	20.09	26.12
8.34	10.66	12.24	14.68	16.92	19.68	21.67	27.88
9.34	11.78	13.44	15.99	18.31	21.16	23.21	29.59
10.34	12.90	14.63	17.28	19.68	22.62	24.72	31.26
11.34	14.01	15.81	18.55	21.03	24.05	26.22	32.91
12.34	15.12	16.98	19.81	22.36	25.47	27.69	34.53
13.34	16.22	18.15	21.06	23.68	26.87	29.14	36.12
14.34	17.32	19.31	22.31	25.00	28.26	30.58	37.70
15.34	18.42	20.46	23.54	26.30	29.63	32.00	39.29
16.34	19.51	21.62	24.77	27.59	31.00	33.41	40.75
17.34	20.60	22.76	25.99	28.87	32.35	34.80	42.31
18.34	21.69	23.90	27.20	30.14	33.69	36.19	43.82
19.34	22.78	25.04	28.41	31.41	35.02	37.57	45.32
20.34	23.86	26.17	29.62	32.67	36.34	38.93	46.80
21.24	24.94	27.30	30.81	33.92	37.66	40.29	48.27
22.34	26.02	28.43	32.01	35.17	38.97	41.64	49.73
23.34	27.10	29.55	33.20	36.42	40.27	42.98	51.18
24.34	28.17	30.68	34.38	37.65	41.57	44.31	52.62
25.34	29.25	31.80	35.56	38.88	42.86	45.64	54.05
26.34	30.32	32.91	36.74	40.11	44.14	46.96	55.48
27.34	31.39	34.03	37.92	41.34	45.42	48.28	56.89
28.34	32.46	35.14	39.09	42.56	46.69	49.59	58.30
29.34	33.53	36.25	40.26	43.77	47.96	50.89	59.70

Table B–4: Critical Values of D in the Kolmogorov-Smirnov One-Sample Test

Sample Size N	Level of Significance for $D = $ Maximum $\|F_0(X) - S_N(X)\|$				
	.20	.15	.10	.05	.01
1	.900	.925	.950	.975	.995
2	.684	.726	.776	.842	.929
3	.565	.597	.642	.708	.828
4	.494	.525	.564	.624	.733
5	.446	.474	.510	.565	.669
6	.410	.436	.470	.521	.618
7	.381	.405	.438	.486	.577
8	.358	.381	.411	.457	.543
9	.339	.360	.388	.432	.514
10	.322	.342	.368	.410	.490
11	.307	.326	.352	.391	.468
12	.295	.313	.338	.375	.450
13	.284	.302	.325	.361	.433
14	.274	.292	.314	.349	.418
15	.266	.283	.304	.338	.404
16	.258	.274	.295	.328	.392
17	.250	.266	.286	.318	.381
18	.244	.259	.278	.309	.371
19	.237	.252	.272	.301	.363
20	.231	.246	.264	.294	.356
25	.21	.22	.24	.27	.32
30	.19	.20	.22	.24	.29
35	.18	.19	.21	.23	.27
Over 35	$\dfrac{1.07}{\sqrt{N}}$	$\dfrac{1.14}{\sqrt{N}}$	$\dfrac{1.22}{\sqrt{N}}$	$\dfrac{1.36}{\sqrt{N}}$	$\dfrac{1.63}{\sqrt{N}}$

Source: F. J. Massey, Jr., "The Kolmogorov-Smirnov Test for Goodness of Fit," *Journal of the American Stastical Association*, vol. 46, p. 70. Adapted with the kind permission of the publisher.

Table B–5: Critical Values of *T* in the Wilcoxon Matched-Pairs Test

N	Level of Significance for One-Tailed Test		
	.025	.01	.005
	Level of Significance for Two-Tailed Test		
	.05	.02	.01
6	0	—	—
7	2	0	—
8	4	2	0
9	6	3	2
10	8	5	3
11	11	7	5
12	14	10	7
13	17	13	10
14	21	16	13
15	25	20	16
16	30	24	20
17	35	28	23
18	40	33	28
19	46	38	32
20	52	43	38
21	59	49	43
22	66	56	49
23	73	62	55
24	81	69	61
25	89	77	68

Source: Adapted from Table I of F. Wilcoxon. *Some Rapid Approximate Statistical Procedures* (New York: American Cyanamid Company, 1949), p. 13, with the kind permission of the publisher.

Table B–6: Critical Values of *D* in the Kolmogorov-Smirnov Two-Sample Test (small samples)

N	One-Tailed Test*		Two-Tailed Test†	
	$\alpha = .05$	$\alpha = .01$	$\alpha = .05$	$\alpha = .01$
3	3	—	—	—
4	4	—	4	—
5	4	5	5	5
6	5	6	5	6
7	5	6	6	6
8	5	6	6	7
9	6	7	6	7
10	6	7	7	8
11	6	8	7	8
12	6	8	7	8
13	7	8	7	9
14	7	8	8	9
15	7	9	8	9
16	7	9	8	10
17	8	9	8	10
18	8	10	9	10
19	8	10	9	10
20	8	10	9	11
21	8	10	9	11
22	9	11	9	11
23	9	11	10	11
24	9	11	10	12
25	9	11	10	12
26	9	11	10	12
27	9	12	10	12
28	10	12	11	13
29	10	12	11	13
30	10	12	11	13
35	11	13	12	
40	11	14	13	

* Source: Abridged from I. A. Goodman, "Kolmogorov-Smirnov Tests for Psychological Research," *Psychological Bulletin,* vol. 51, 1951, p. 167, copyright (1951) by the American Psychological Association. Reprinted by permission.

† Source: Derived from Table 1 of F. J. Massey, Jr., "The Distribution of the Maximum Deviation Between Two Sample Cumulative Step Functions," *Annals of Mathematical Statistics,* vol. 23, 1951, pp. 126–27, with the kind permission of the publisher.

Table B–7: Critical Values of D in the Kolmogorov-Smirnov Two-Sample Test for Large Samples (two-tailed test)

Level of Significance	Value of D So Large As To Call for Rejection of H_0 at the Indicated Level of Significance, Where $D = Maximum \left| S_{n_1}(X) - S_2(X) \right|$
.10	$1.22 \sqrt{\dfrac{n_1 + n_2}{n_1 n_2}}$
.05	$1.36 \sqrt{\dfrac{n_1 + n_2}{n_1 n_2}}$
.025	$1.48 \sqrt{\dfrac{n_1 + n_2}{n_1 n_2}}$
.01	$1.63 \sqrt{\dfrac{n_1 + n_2}{n_1 n_2}}$
.005	$1.73 \sqrt{\dfrac{n_1 + n_2}{n_1 n_2}}$
.001	$1.95 \sqrt{\dfrac{n_1 + n_2}{n_1 n_2}}$

* Adapted from N. Smirnov. "Table for Estimating the Goodness of Fit of Empirical Distributions," *Annals of Mathematical Statistics*, vol. 18, 1948, pp. 280–81, with the kind permission of the publisher.

Table B-8: Partial Table of Critical Values of U in the Mann-Whitney Test

Critical Values for One-Tailed Test at $\alpha = .025$ or a Two-Tailed Test at $\alpha = .05$

n_1 \ n_2	9	10	11	12	13	14	15	16	17	18	19	20
1												
2	0	0	0	1	1	1	1	1	2	2	2	2
3	2	3	3	4	4	5	5	6	6	7	7	8
4	4	5	6	7	8	9	10	11	11	12	13	13
5	7	8	9	11	12	13	14	15	17	18	19	20
6	10	11	13	14	16	17	19	21	22	24	25	27
7	12	14	16	18	20	22	24	26	28	30	32	34
8	15	17	19	22	24	26	29	31	34	36	38	41
9	17	20	23	26	28	31	34	37	39	42	45	48
10	20	23	26	29	33	36	39	42	45	48	52	55
11	23	26	30	33	37	40	44	47	51	55	58	62
12	26	29	33	37	41	45	49	53	57	61	66	69
13	28	33	37	41	45	50	54	59	63	67	72	76
14	31	36	40	45	50	55	59	64	67	74	78	83
15	34	39	44	49	54	59	64	70	75	80	85	90
16	37	42	47	53	59	64	70	75	81	86	92	98
17	39	45	51	57	63	67	75	81	87	93	99	105
18	42	48	55	61	67	74	80	86	93	99	106	112
19	45	52	58	65	72	78	85	92	99	106	113	119
20	48	55	62	69	76	83	90	98	105	112	119	127

Critical Values for One-Tailed Test at $\alpha = .05$ or a Two-Tailed Test at $\alpha = .10$

n_2 \ n_1	9	10	11	12	13	14	15	16	17	18	19	20
1											0	0
2	1	1	1	2	2	2	3	3	3	4	4	4
3	3	4	5	5	6	7	7	8	9	9	10	11
4	6	7	8	9	10	11	12	14	15	16	17	18
5	9	11	12	13	15	16	18	19	20	22	23	25
6	12	14	16	17	19	21	23	25	26	28	30	32
7	15	17	19	21	24	26	28	30	33	35	37	39
8	18	20	23	26	28	31	33	36	39	41	44	47
9	21	24	27	30	33	36	39	42	45	48	51	54
10	24	27	31	34	37	41	44	48	51	55	58	62
11	27	31	34	38	42	46	50	54	57	61	65	69
12	30	34	38	42	47	51	55	60	64	68	72	77
13	33	37	42	47	51	56	61	65	70	75	80	84
14	36	41	46	51	56	61	66	71	77	82	87	92
15	39	44	50	55	61	66	72	77	83	88	94	100
16	42	48	54	60	65	71	77	83	89	95	101	107
17	45	51	57	64	70	77	83	89	96	102	109	115
18	48	55	61	68	75	82	88	95	102	109	116	123
19	51	58	65	72	80	87	94	101	109	116	123	130
20	54	62	69	77	84	92	100	107	115	123	130	138

Source: Abridged from D. Auble, "Extended Tables from the Mann-Whitney Statistic," *Bulletin of the Institute of Educational Research* at Indiana University, vol. 1, no. 2, with permission. For tables for other size samples consult this source.

Table B-9: Critical Values of F Distribution for Alpha (α) Equal to 5 Percent

n_1 Degrees of Freedom (Greater Mean Square)

n_2	1	2	3	4	5	6	7	8	9	10	12	15	20	24	30	40	60	120	∞
1	161.4	199.5	215.7	224.6	230.2	234.0	236.8	238.9	240.5	241.9	243.9	245.9	248.0	249.1	250.1	251.1	252.2	253.3	243.3
2	18.51	19.00	19.16	19.25	19.30	19.33	19.35	19.37	19.38	19.40	19.41	19.43	19.45	19.45	19.46	19.47	19.48	19.49	19.50
3	10.13	9.55	9.28	9.12	9.01	8.94	8.89	8.85	8.81	8.79	8.74	8.70	8.66	8.64	8.62	8.59	8.57	8.55	8.53
4	7.71	6.94	6.59	6.39	6.26	6.16	6.09	6.04	6.00	5.96	5.91	5.86	5.80	5.77	5.75	5.72	5.69	5.66	5.63
5	6.61	5.79	5.41	5.19	5.05	4.95	4.88	4.82	4.77	4.74	4.68	4.62	4.56	4.53	4.50	4.46	4.43	4.40	4.36
6	5.99	5.14	4.76	4.53	4.39	4.28	4.21	4.15	4.10	4.06	4.00	3.94	3.87	3.84	3.81	3.77	3.74	3.70	3.67
7	5.59	4.74	4.35	4.12	3.97	3.87	3.79	3.73	3.68	3.64	3.57	3.51	3.44	3.41	3.38	3.34	3.30	3.27	3.23
8	5.32	4.46	4.07	3.84	3.69	3.58	3.50	3.44	3.39	3.35	3.28	3.22	3.15	3.12	3.08	3.04	3.01	2.97	2.93
9	5.12	4.26	3.86	3.63	3.48	3.37	3.29	3.23	3.18	3.14	3.07	3.01	2.94	2.90	2.86	2.83	2.79	2.75	2.71
10	4.96	4.10	3.71	3.48	3.33	3.22	3.14	3.07	3.02	2.98	2.91	2.85	2.77	2.74	2.70	2.66	2.62	2.58	2.54
11	4.84	3.98	3.59	3.36	3.20	3.09	3.01	2.95	2.90	2.85	2.79	2.72	2.65	2.61	2.57	2.53	2.49	2.45	2.40
12	4.75	3.89	3.49	3.26	3.11	3.00	2.91	2.85	2.80	2.75	2.69	2.62	2.54	2.51	2.47	2.43	2.38	2.34	2.30
13	4.67	3.81	3.41	3.18	3.03	2.92	2.83	2.77	2.71	2.67	2.60	2.53	2.46	2.42	2.38	2.34	2.30	2.25	2.21
14	4.60	3.74	3.34	3.11	2.96	2.85	2.76	2.70	2.65	2.60	2.53	2.46	2.39	2.35	2.31	2.27	2.22	2.18	2.13
15	4.54	3.68	3.29	3.06	2.90	2.79	2.71	2.64	2.59	2.54	2.48	2.40	2.33	2.29	2.25	2.20	2.16	2.11	2.07
16	4.49	3.63	3.24	3.01	2.85	2.74	2.66	2.59	2.54	2.49	2.42	2.35	2.28	2.24	2.19	2.15	2.11	2.06	2.01
17	4.45	3.59	3.20	2.96	2.81	2.70	2.61	2.55	2.49	2.45	2.38	2.31	2.23	2.19	2.15	2.10	2.06	2.01	1.96
18	4.41	3.55	3.16	2.93	2.77	2.66	2.58	2.51	2.46	2.41	2.34	2.27	2.19	2.15	2.11	2.06	2.02	1.97	1.92
19	4.38	3.52	3.13	2.90	2.74	2.63	2.54	2.48	2.42	2.38	2.31	2.23	2.16	2.11	2.07	2.03	1.98	1.93	1.88
20	4.35	3.49	3.10	2.87	2.71	2.60	2.51	2.45	2.39	2.35	2.28	2.20	2.12	2.08	2.04	1.99	1.95	1.90	1.84
21	4.32	3.47	3.07	2.84	2.68	2.57	2.49	2.42	2.37	2.32	2.25	2.18	2.10	2.05	2.01	1.96	1.92	1.87	1.81
22	4.30	3.44	3.05	2.82	2.66	2.55	2.46	2.40	2.34	2.30	2.23	2.15	2.07	2.03	1.98	1.94	1.89	1.84	1.78
23	4.28	3.42	3.03	2.80	2.64	2.53	2.44	2.37	2.32	2.27	2.20	2.13	2.05	2.01	1.96	1.91	1.86	1.81	1.76
24	4.26	3.40	3.01	2.78	2.62	2.51	2.42	2.36	2.30	2.25	2.18	2.11	2.03	1.98	1.94	1.89	1.84	1.79	1.73
25	4.24	3.39	2.99	2.76	2.60	2.49	2.40	2.34	2.28	2.24	2.16	2.09	2.01	1.96	1.92	1.87	1.82	1.77	1.71
26	4.23	3.37	2.98	2.74	2.59	2.47	2.39	2.32	2.27	2.22	2.15	2.07	1.99	1.95	1.90	1.85	1.80	1.75	1.69
27	4.21	3.35	2.96	2.73	2.57	2.46	2.37	2.31	2.25	2.20	2.13	2.06	1.97	1.93	1.88	1.84	1.79	1.73	1.67
28	4.20	3.34	2.95	2.71	2.56	2.45	2.36	2.29	2.24	2.19	2.12	2.04	1.96	1.91	1.87	1.82	1.77	1.71	1.65
29	4.18	3.33	2.93	2.70	2.55	2.43	2.35	2.28	2.22	2.18	2.10	2.03	1.94	1.90	1.85	1.81	1.75	1.70	1.64
30	4.17	3.32	2.92	2.69	2.53	2.42	2.33	2.27	2.21	2.16	2.09	2.01	1.93	1.89	1.84	1.79	1.74	1.68	1.62
40	4.08	3.23	2.84	2.61	2.45	2.34	2.25	2.18	2.12	2.08	2.00	1.92	1.84	1.79	1.74	1.69	1.64	1.58	1.51
60	4.00	3.15	2.76	2.53	2.37	2.25	2.17	2.10	2.04	1.99	1.92	1.84	1.75	1.70	1.65	1.59	1.53	1.47	1.39
120	3.92	3.07	2.68	2.45	2.29	2.17	2.09	2.02	1.96	1.91	1.83	1.75	1.66	1.61	1.55	1.50	1.43	1.35	1.25
∞	3.84	3.00	2.60	2.37	2.21	2.10	2.01	1.94	1.88	1.83	1.75	1.67	1.57	1.52	1.46	1.39	1.32	1.22	1.00

Reprinted by permission from *Statistical Methods* by George W. Snedecor and William G. Cochran, sixth edition © 1967 by Iowa State University Press, Ames, Iowa.

Table B-10: Table of Random Digits

97446	30328	05262	77371	13523	62057	44349	85884	94555	23288
15453	75591	60540	77137	09485	27632	05477	99154	78720	10323
69995	77086	55217	53721	85713	27854	41981	88981	90041	20878
69726	58696	27272	38148	52521	73807	29685	49152	20309	58734
23604	31948	16926	26360	76957	99925	86045	11617	32777	38670
13640	17233	58650	47819	24935	28670	33415	77202	92492	40290
90779	09199	51169	94892	34271	22068	13923	53535	56358	50258
71068	19459	32339	10124	13012	79706	07611	52600	83088	26829
55019	79001	34442	16335	06428	52873	65316	01480	72204	39494
20879	50235	17389	25260	34039	99967	48044	05067	69284	53867
00380	11595	49372	95214	98529	46593	77046	27176	39668	20566
68142	40800	20527	79212	14166	84948	11748	69540	84288	37211
42667	89566	20440	57230	35356	01884	79921	94772	29882	24695
07756	78430	45576	86596	56720	65529	44211	18447	53921	92722
45221	31130	44312	63534	47741	02465	50629	94983	05984	88375
20140	77481	61686	82836	41058	41331	04290	61212	60294	95954
54922	25436	33804	51907	73223	66423	68706	36589	45267	35327
48340	30832	72209	07644	52747	40751	06808	85349	18005	52323
23603	84387	20416	88084	33103	41511	59391	71600	35091	52722
12548	01033	22974	59596	92087	02116	63524	00627	41778	24392
15251	87584	12942	03771	91413	75652	19468	83889	98531	91529
65548	59670	57355	18874	63601	55111	07278	32560	40028	36079
48488	76170	46282	76427	41693	04506	80979	26654	62159	83017
02862	15665	62159	15159	69576	20328	68873	28152	66087	39405
67929	06754	45842	66365	80848	15262	55144	37816	08421	30071
73237	07607	31615	04892	50989	87347	14393	21165	68169	70788
13788	20327	07960	95917	75112	01398	26381	41377	33549	19754
43877	66485	40825	45923	74410	69693	76959	70973	26343	63781
14047	08369	56414	78533	76378	44204	71493	68861	31042	81873
88383	46755	51342	13505	55324	52950	22244	28028	73486	98797
29567	16379	41994	65947	58926	50953	09388	00405	29874	44954
20508	60995	41539	26396	99825	25652	28089	57224	35222	58922
64178	76768	75747	32854	32893	61152	58565	33128	33354	16056
26373	51147	90362	93309	13175	66385	57822	31138	12893	68607
10083	47656	59241	73630	99200	94672	59785	95449	99279	25488
11683	14347	04369	98719	75005	43633	24125	30532	54830	95387
56548	76293	50904	88579	24621	94291	56881	35062	48765	22078
35292	47291	82610	27777	43965	31802	98444	88929	54383	93141
51329	87645	51623	08971	50704	82395	33916	95859	99788	97885
51860	19180	39324	68483	78650	74750	64893	58042	82878	20619
23886	01257	07945	71175	31243	87167	42829	44601	08769	26417
80028	82310	43989	09242	15056	48250	04529	96941·	48190	69644
83946	46858	09164	18858	12672	55190	02820	45861	29104	75386
00000	41586	25972	25356	54260	95691	99431	89903	22306	43863
90615	12848	23376	29458	48239	37628	59265	50152	30340	40713
42003	10738	55835	48218	23204	19188	13556	06610	77667	88068
86135	26174	07834	17007	97938	96728	15689	77544	891?6	41252
54436	10828	41212	19836	89476	53685	28085	22878	71868	35048
14545	72034	32131	38783	58588	47499	50945	97045	42357	53536
43925	49879	13339	78773	95626	67119	93023	96832	09757	98545

Source: The Rand Corporation, *A Million Random Digits with 100,000 Normal Deviates*. Glencoe, Ill.: The Free Press, Publishers, 1955, p. 225.

Index

This book has been set VIP, in 10 point and 9 point Souvenir Light, leaded 2 points. Section numbers and titles and chapter numbers and titles are 18 point Helvetica Medium. The size of the type page is 27 by 46 picas.